# Social Policy for Children and Families

## Fourth Edition

Sara Miller McCune founded SAGE Publishing in 1965 to support the dissemination of usable knowledge and educate a global community. SAGE publishes more than 1000 journals and over 600 new books each year, spanning a wide range of subject areas. Our growing selection of library products includes archives, data, case studies and video. SAGE remains majority owned by our founder and after her lifetime will become owned by a charitable trust that secures the company's continued independence.

Los Angeles | London | New Delhi | Singapore | Washington DC | Melbourne

# Social Policy for Children and Families

## A Risk and Resilience Perspective

### Fourth Edition

**Edited by**

**William J. Hall**

*University of North Carolina at Chapel Hill*

**Paul Lanier**

*University of North Carolina at Chapel Hill*

**Jeffrey M. Jenson**

*University of Denver*

**Mark W. Fraser**

*University of North Carolina at Chapel Hill*

Los Angeles | London | New Delhi
Singapore | Washington DC | Melbourne

FOR INFORMATION:

SAGE Publications, Inc.
2455 Teller Road
Thousand Oaks, California 91320
Email: order@sagepub.com

SAGE Publications Ltd.
1 Oliver's Yard
55 City Road
London EC1Y 1SP
United Kingdom

SAGE Publications India Pvt. Ltd.
B 1/I 1 Mohan Cooperative Industrial Area
Mathura Road, New Delhi 110 044
India

SAGE Publications Asia-Pacific Pte. Ltd.
18 Cross Street #10-10/11/12
China Square Central
Singapore 048423

Acquisitions Editor:   Joshua Perigo
Editorial Assistant:   Tiara Beatty
Production Editor:   Megha Negi
Copy Editor:   Erin Livingston
Typesetter:   C&M Digitals (P) Ltd.
Proofreader:   Jeff Bryant
Cover Designer:   Candice Harman
Marketing Manager:   Victoria Velasquez

Library of Congress Cataloging-in-Publication Data

Names: Hall, William James, editor. | Lanier, Paul J., editor. | Jenson, Jeffrey M., editor. | Fraser, Mark W., 1946- editor.

Title: Social policy for children and families : a risk and resilience perspective / [edited by] William James Hall III, Paul J. Lanier, Jeffrey M. Jenson, Mark W. Fraser.

Description: Fourth Edition. | Thousand Oaks: SAGE Publishing, 2021. | Revised edition of Social policy for children and families, [2016]

Identifiers: LCCN 2021004756 | ISBN 9781544371481 (paperback) | ISBN 9781544371467 (epub) | ISBN 9781544371450 (epub) | ISBN 9781544371474 (pdf)

Subjects: LCSH: Children—Government policy—United States. | Child welfare—United States. | Youth—Government policy—United States. | Family policy—United States. | Developmental psychology. | Child development.

Classification: LCC HV741 .S623 2021 | DDC 362.82/5610973—dc23

LC record available at https://lccn.loc.gov/2021004756

This book is printed on acid-free paper.

21 22 23 24 25 10 9 8 7 6 5 4 3 2 1

# CONTENTS

# ACKNOWLEDGMENTS

The ideas expressed in the fourth edition of this volume address many of the most pressing problems confronting children, youth, and families in American society. We thank each of the chapter authors for providing important new information about innovative approaches to social policy in their respective service system domains. Each author's commitment to expanding the application of evidence and principles of risk, protection, and resilience to the design, implementation, and evaluation of social policies for young people and their families is exemplary.

*—William J. Hall*
*—Paul Lanier*
*—Jeffrey M. Jenson*
*—Mark W. Fraser*

## REVIEWER ACKNOWLEDGMENTS

Diana Lang Baltimore, Iowa State University

Gail P. Wise, Southern University at New Orleans

Gail P. Wise, Southern University at New Orleans

Kalani Palmer, Indiana University of Pennsylvania

Lisa Caya, University of Wisconsin -La Crosse

Susan Reid, St. Thomas University

# INTRODUCTION

Nelson Mandela once said, "There can be no keener revelation of a society's soul than the way in which it treats its children" (Nelson Mandela Children's Fund, 2015). Children and youth have fewer rights than adults and depend on parents, caregivers, and other responsible adults for their universal human needs. Indeed, children are among the most vulnerable members of society, navigating formative periods of development in a world constructed and administered by adults. Childhood and adolescence are profound periods of biophysical, psychological, and social development that have long-term implications for health and social well-being into adulthood.

Unfortunately, there is good reason to be concerned about the status and future of American children and youth. They are more likely than any other age group to be poor. Too many children are neglected and subject to abuse and violence. Young people face significant educational, mental, behavioral, and health challenges amid under-resourced and fragmented service systems. Homicide, suicide, and unintentional injury are the leading causes of death for children and adolescents in the United States (National Center for Injury Prevention and Control, 2019). It is the responsibility of all adults in America, especially those in positions of power and influence, to help secure a better society for our young people.

This book aims to inform readers about the policy strategies necessary to tackle the most complex and pressing health and social problems facing American children, youth, and their families. We argue that a person-in-environment and risk and resilience perspective is the best way to approach this work. Begun some 40 years ago, research to trace the causes of social and behavioral health problems facing young people has led to new understandings of the individual, interpersonal, and environmental factors that affect developmental and, indeed, life course outcomes. In the past two decades, attention has been directed to increasing our understanding of the concept of *resilience*, which is the process through which children overcome adverse life circumstances (Fraser et al., 2004). In recent years, knowledge of risk and resilience has been widely used to develop and improve the efficacy of prevention and treatment programs for vulnerable children and families (e.g., Catalano et al., 2012; Jenson & Bender, 2014). Nonetheless, widespread implementation of preventive interventions remains elusive. Even worse is the inadequate application of evidence about risk, protection, and resilience to the design of social policies. National, state, and local policies have the capacity to transform service systems and influence the lives of millions of Americans in ways that promote resilience and well-being. But often, this capacity is unrealized.

The United States has one of the most diverse populations in the world, yet it also has a troubled legacy of racism, economic inequality, and other forms of oppression. Social policies and intervention programs must aim to ameliorate the disparities and inequities that burden marginalized young people and their families and communities.

To neglect such efforts would represent a failure of our core American values of equality, cooperative progress, and liberty, and even worse, it would tacitly represent the support of preventable harm and suffering, the denial of basic human dignity, and the blocking of opportunities for all of our children and youth to fully realize their potentials. We discuss the importance of applying principles of anti-oppression in Chapter 1.

Progress toward improving mental, behavioral, educational, social, and health outcomes for young people can be achieved in the foreseeable future. Through a person-in-environment and risk and resilience perspective, as well as an anti-oppression perspective, we can conceptualize the multiple and interacting factors from all levels of society that shape outcomes and developmental trajectories for young people. By applying principles of anti-oppression and knowledge of risk, protective, and promotive factors to the design of social policy, we can significantly impact the continuum of programs, practices, and services for children, youth, and families. We hope that this book will help students, practitioners, policymakers, and researchers achieve this collective goal to promote child health and social well-being.

## ORGANIZATION OF THE BOOK

The core section of the book is formed by 10 chapters devoted to policies intended to address poverty, child welfare, education, mental health, health, developmental disabilities, substance abuse, immigration, juvenile justice, and gun violence. Chapter authors identify key policies in their respective areas and evaluate the extent to which evidence of risk, protection, and resilience can be used to improve policies, programs, practices, and services. Recommended readings, questions for discussion, and Web-based resources are provided. Authors follow a similar outline in which they

- provide an overview of the purpose or goals of social policy in a substantive area;

- describe the incidence and prevalence of problems affecting children, youth, and families, including disparities and inequities;

- outline prominent risk and protective factors associated with the onset or persistence of the problems identified;

- discuss historical and current policies that have been developed to address these problems;

- evaluate the extent to which policies have been based on evidence about risk, protection, and resilience;

- provide recommendations for improving policies, programs, practices, and services that incorporate research regarding risk, protection, and resilience; and

- discuss ways to integrate programs and services across policy domains or service systems.

Poverty is a foundational problem connected to every substantive problem discussed in this book. In Chapter 2, Trina Williams Shanks, Sandra Danziger, and Patrick Meehan analyze poverty trends and examine contextual risks and protective factors associated with earning a low income at the family and community levels. They critically assess past and current programs and policies intended to reduce and prevent child and family poverty. Recommendations for poverty-alleviating strategies for children, families, and communities are identified.

In Chapter 3, Michelle Johnson-Motoyama, Jill Duerr Berrick, and Andrea Lane Eastman describe American child welfare policies and programs intended to respond to children's need for protection from abuse or harm from their caregivers. In addition to describing the key elements and processes of the child welfare system, the authors also offer suggestions for policies, programs, and practices to prevent child maltreatment and improve services for children and families involved in this key service domain.

In Chapter 4, Andy Frey, Myrna Mandlawitz, Armon Perry, Hill Walker, and Brandon Mitchell focus on school dropout and failure. In addition, they identify risk and protective factors associated with school adjustment and academic achievement. They note that public education policy is closely linked to political ideology and societal values as they outline the development of education policy from its beginning to the current era, which is dominated by the No Child Left Behind Act. They conclude by offering recommendations for education policies and programs based on principles of risk, protection, and resilience.

In Chapter 5, Paul Lanier, Megan Feely, and Mary Fraser review epidemiological research on the scope and burden of child and adolescent mental disorders. They focus on individual, family, and environmental risk and protective factors for behavioral health problems. They describe policies designed to improve access to services for children and youth with mental disorders, including community mental health centers and systems of care.

In Chapter 6, William Hall, Hayden Dawes, Alexandria Forte, Luke Hirst, and Danny Mora trace the development of key public health and health care policies pertaining to infants, children, adolescents, and their parents up to the implementation of the Patient Protection and Affordable Care Act. They discuss prominent and preventable health problems facing young people, including low birth weight, asthma, obesity, sexually transmitted infections, suicide, and COVID-19. Hall and colleagues conclude with a critical appraisal of the American health care system, evidence-informed recommendations to improve the system, and illustrative examples for the integration of health care with other services and resources.

The proportion of children with a developmental disability has increased in recent decades. In Chapter 7, Kiley McLean, Meshan Adams, and Lauren Bishop discuss risk and protective factors for poor outcomes among children with disabilities and their families, including adversities due to systems of oppression. They analyze policies and programs pertaining to education, civil rights, health care, and income for young people with disabilities. Using principles of risk, protection, and resilience, McLean and her colleagues offer policy recommendations for improving services and promoting inclusion, resilience, and quality of life for children and youth with developmental disabilities.

In Chapter 8, Elizabeth Anthony, Jeffrey Jenson, and Matthew Howard review current trends in the prevalence, disparities, etiology, prevention, and treatment of adolescent substance abuse. The authors trace the origins of policies aimed at the prevention and treatment of substance abuse and comment on the relative effectiveness of alternate policy approaches. Anthony and colleagues conclude that principles of risk, protection, and resilience have been influential in improving the efficacy of prevention and treatment programs for young people and reflect on the implications of these findings for substance abuse policy.

The United States was established and transformed by immigrants, yet social policies and public systems often fail to meet the needs and challenges of immigrant groups. In Chapter 9, Megan Finno-Velasquez, Anayeli Lopez, Sophia Sepp, and Marianna Corkill describe present-day immigrant children and families. They provide a comprehensive discussion of federal immigration policy, including pathways to residency and citizenship, and the ways that policies create inequitable access to public assistance, early childhood programs, health care, and mental health services for immigrant children and families.

In Chapter 10, Amy Blank Wilson, Jonathan Phillips, Melissa Villodas, Anna Parisi, and Ehren Dohler trace the evolution of juvenile justice policy from the creation of the first juvenile court to the current era of evidence-based practice. They describe key decision points in the juvenile justice system, strategies to reduce youth contact with the system, and opportunities to address disparities and inequities related to race/ethnicity, gender, and sexual orientation.

In Chapter 11, Chris Rees and Eric Fleegler provide an overview of gun ownership in the United States and describe the epidemiology of firearm homicides and assaults, firearm suicides, unintentional firearm injuries, and school shootings. They also discuss prevention strategies to reduce firearm-related injuries and fatalities.

In the final chapter of the book, we expand on our framework for using principles of risk, resilience, and anti-oppression to develop more fully integrated policies for children, youth, and families. We argue that integration of policy and programs across service domains should be a goal of future policy directives targeting children, youth, and families. Consideration is given consistently to child developmental processes and research in the design of this framework. Recommendations for ways to advance principles of anti-oppression and promote a public health social work framework based on risk, protection, and resilience in policy design, implementation, and evaluation are offered.

## SUMMARY

We hope that the interdisciplinary framework described in this book stimulates innovative ideas about the design of policies for vulnerable children and families. Principles of anti-oppression and of risk and resilience—too often ignored in policy discussions—hold great promise for improving the reach and effectiveness of social policies. We believe that an increased focus on these principles will lead to policies that will improve the health and well-being of all children and families.

# REFERENCES

Catalano, R. F., Fagan, A. A., Gavin, L. E., Greenberg, M. T., Irwin, Jr., C. E., Ross, D. A., & Shek, D. T. (2012). Worldwide application of prevention science in adolescent health. *Lancet, 379,* 1653–1664.

Fraser, M. W., Kirby, L. D., & Smokowski, P. R. (2004). Risk and resilience in childhood. In M. W. Fraser (Ed.), *Risk and resilience in childhood: An ecological perspective* (2nd ed., pp. 13–66). NASW Press.

Jenson, J. M., & Bender, K. A. (2014). *Preventing child and adolescent behavior. Evidence-based strategies in schools, families, and communities.* Oxford University Press.

National Center for Injury Prevention and Control. (2019). *10 leading causes of death by age group, United States—2018.* Centers for Disease Control and Prevention.

Nelson Mandela Children's Fund. (2015). *Nelson Mandela quotes about children.* https://www.nelsonmandelachildrens-fund.com/news/nelson-mandela-quotes-about-children

# 1

# A MULTISYSTEMS RISK AND RESILIENCE APPROACH TO SOCIAL POLICY FOR CHILDREN, YOUTH, AND FAMILIES

William J. Hall, Paul Lanier, Jeffrey M. Jenson, and Mark W. Fraser

Social, political, and economic events of the past several years have had a significant and adverse impact on the lives of young people and their families. While such events have led to a reduction in the provision of family-based programs and policies, they have also afforded a unique opportunity to find new and innovative ways to promote positive outcomes for children, youth, and families. As a result of elections that alter political leadership, events that galvanize public opinion (e.g., pandemics, deadly shootings, and wildfires), and scientific advances that affect our knowledge of social and health problems, we often have opportunities to craft social policies to more proactively and systematically promote the safety, health, and social well-being of young people and their families. As this book describes, significant gains have been made in understanding the individual, family, community, and broader social factors— such as racism and other forms of oppression—that influence child and adolescent developmental outcomes, including high school graduation and, in the long run, labor market participation. Through evaluations, randomized trials, and qualitative studies, we have also learned a great deal about the effectiveness of social policies and programs intended to prevent problems and promote healthy outcomes in children and families. If this knowledge were to be more purposively incorporated in social policy, we would have increased potential to produce healthy development in young people. Yet, current United States (U.S.) social policy and, indeed, policies across the globe are too often characterized by reactive and piecemeal efforts that only shore up under-resourced and fragmented service systems. Today's children and youth face numerous threats—from gun violence to extreme poverty—that are highly preventable through more strategically designed policies, evidence-informed interventions, and efficient, coordinated, and well-resourced service systems. This book aims to inform the current debate about the best way to support children and parents and to provide evidence supporting effective policy approaches that lead to healthy development in young people.

# GROWING UP IN AMERICA: THREATS AND OPPORTUNITIES

Children, youth, and families face enormous challenges in American society. At no time in the country's history have young people and their parents been confronted simultaneously by such a wide array of influences and opportunities. Most children and youth become healthy adults who participate in positive and prosocial activities guided by interests that lead to meaningful and fulfilling lives. However, for some children and youth, the path to adulthood is a journey filled with risk and uncertainty. Because of the adversities these young people face, the prospect of a successful future is often bleak.

If we were to draw a picture depicting the current status of America's children and youth, it would be a portrait of contrasts. Despite being the most economically prosperous country in the world (Organisation for Economic Co-operation and Development, 2020), 16% of children (ages 0–18) in the U.S. live in poverty (Semega et al., 2020). Poverty is related to many health and social problems. Even as society venerates them, children are more likely than all other age groups to be poor. Moreover, young people of color are disproportionately represented in poverty (Children's Defense Fund, 2020). Recent data indicate that 30% of African American, 29% of American Indian, and 24% of Hispanic/Latinx children live in conditions of poverty. Those rates are more than double the poverty rates for Asian (11%) and White (9%) children.

Two thirds of recent high school graduates enroll in colleges or universities (U.S. Bureau of Labor Statistics, 2020a), and the U.S. leads the world in higher education (Quacquarelli Symonds, 2019; Williams & Leahy, 2019). Unfortunately, education as a means to socioeconomic advancement is often blocked for those youth who experience early academic failure or drop out of school. Data show that 2.1 million youth age 16 or older dropped out of school in the 2017–2018 academic year, failing to earn a high school diploma or GED (general equivalency diploma) certificate (Hussar et al., 2020). The overall school dropout rate was 5.1% in 2017–2018; however, American Indian (9.5%), Pacific Islander (8.1%), Hispanic/Latinx (8.0%), and Black (6.4%) youth had higher dropout rates than White (4.2%) and Asian (1.9%) youth.

On a positive note, nearly 30% of high school–age youth volunteer in social causes, a number that has increased significantly in recent decades (Grimm & Dietz, 2018). Other data reveal promising behavioral trends, including a reduction in the prevalence of some problem behaviors. Notably, violent offending among youth rapidly increased between the late 1980s and mid-1990s, but rates of juvenile violent crime have declined significantly since, reaching a historically low level in 2018 (Jenson et al., 2001; Puzzanchera, 2020). Juxtaposed against this promising news are the disturbing accounts of school shootings. There were 66 school shootings with casualties at K–12 schools in 2017–2018 (Wang et al., 2020). School violence is widespread—over 70% of U.S. public schools recorded at least one violent incident in the 2017–2018 school year. The deaths of 20 first-grade children and six educators at Sandy Hook Elementary School in Newtown, Connecticut, in 2012 and the deaths of 14 high school students and three educators at Marjory Stoneman Douglas High School in Parkland, Florida, in 2018 were jolting reminders that students and educators are not always safe in their own schools and communities. Indeed, homicide is the fourth leading cause of death among children and youth ages 1 to 19 in the U.S. (Centers for Disease Control and Prevention [CDC], 2019).

Threats and opportunities for children and youth are not merely social in nature. Approximately one quarter of U.S. land and marine areas are designated as protected or conservation areas (Protected Planet, 2020), and young people and their families have access to thousands of national, state, and local public parks. These spaces provide opportunities for physical activity, social connection, and psychological restoration as well as decrease noise and air pollution. Regrettably, green spaces also face human-caused threats. The U.S. is second only to China in global $CO_2$ emissions (International Energy Agency, 2020), and the U.S. is the biggest generator of waste per capita world-wide (Kaza et al., 2018). Many young people are living in areas with unhealthy ozone or particle pollution and high exposure to toxic chemicals, which threaten their health (American Lung Association, 2020; Landrigan & Goldman, 2011). Fortunately, aware-ness and concern about climate change has risen sharply in the past decade, particu-larly among young people (Reinhart, 2018; Saad, 2019; Scanlon, 2019). Regrettably, policies aimed at climate change have lagged behind levels of public awareness (Mason & Rigg, 2018).

In 2020, children, youth, and families were confronted with a pandemic due to the global outbreak of the novel coronavirus. Although children and youth currently make up a very small proportion of deaths from the coronavirus (CDC, 2020), their lives have been greatly affected by the illness. They have lost family members, friends, and neighbors; and they have experienced the closure of their schools, playgrounds, and other gathering spaces for social, educational, recreational, and cultural activi-ties. Public health experts have raised serious concerns about the cascading effects of the coronavirus on family functioning and on socioemotional development (Family Health in Europe–Research in Nursing Group, 2020; Fegert et al., 2020; Fraenkel & Cho, 2020). The novel coronavirus and the conditions associated with it present new and heightened challenges for shaping social policies aimed at promoting healthy youth development.

## AMERICA'S DIVERSE FAMILIES

While complicating from an intervention standpoint, the diversity of American fam-ilies offers significant strengths in building healthy and resilient youth. The U.S. is perhaps the most diverse nation on Earth—a rich and colorful tapestry of cultures, identities, social groups, and family backgrounds. In its beginning, what is now the U.S. had been a home to hundreds of indigenous cultural groups; it is estimated that as many as 500 languages were spoken by Native Americans prior to 1492 (National Museum of the American Indian, 2007). After centuries of colonization, immigration, and forced displacement, the U.S. population reflects many hundreds of ethnic groups from origins across the globe (U.S. Census Bureau, 2007). The racial diversity of America continues to expand; currently, 60% of the population is classified as White, 18% as Hispanic/Latinx, 13% as Black/African American, 6% as Asian, 3% as multiracial, and 1% as Native American (U.S. Census Bureau, 2019). It is estimated that by 2045, people of color will make up a numerical majority of the population (Vespa et al., 2020). Due to a function of worldwide migration, the U.S. has more immigrants than any other nation; immigrants make up 14% of the U.S. population (Budiman, 2020). The legal status of immigrants varies, with 23% being undocumented, 27% being lawful permanent residents, 5% being temporary residents, and 45% being naturalized citizens.

Despite being the most economically prosperous country, there is significant stratification in socioeconomic status in the U.S., often falling along racial/ethnic lines and immigrant and citizenship status. In 2018, the median household income was approximately $63,000, with the average American household consisting of 2.5 people (Semega et al., 2020). Income-based analyses classify 20% of Americans as lower income, 9% as lower-middle income, 50% as middle income, 12% as upper-middle income, and 9% as high income, with associated median household income ranges for a family of three as follows: ≤ $31,000 (lower income); $31,000–$42,000 (lower-middle income); $42,000–$126,000 (middle income); $126,000–$188,000 (upper-middle income); and ≥ $188,000 (high income; Pew Research Center, 2015b).

The structure and composition of families has shifted in recent decades, expanding from traditional social norms and ideals. Today, less than half of children are raised by two parents in a first marriage (Pew Research Center, 2015a). Increasingly, children are growing up in family arrangements that include single-parent families, unmarried cohabitating parents, and blended families comprised of stepparents, stepsiblings, and/or half-siblings. In addition, traditional gendered arrangements where the father is the breadwinner and the mother is a stay-at-home parent have diminished. Today, the vast majority of children are raised in families in which both parents are employed (U.S. Bureau of Labor Statistics, 2020b). The number of households with multigenerational families living under one roof has also increased (Cohn & Passel, 2018). These families may consist of children, parents, and grandparents living together as well as adult children, their children, and grandparents and great-grandparents living under one roof. The removal of legal barriers to marriage, adoption, and foster care for adults who are lesbian, gay, bisexual, transgender, or queer (LGBTQ) has led to an increase in queer-headed families (i.e., nonheterosexual and/or non-cisgender parents raising children; Goldberg & Allen, 2013; Haden & Applewhite, 2020). In addition, more young people are identifying as LGBTQ and at younger ages today than in past decades (Hall et al., 2020; Newport, 2018). There has also been growing social awareness of people with disabilities and mental impairments, perhaps due to the disability justice and neurodiversity movements. The disability community is a diverse one, with impairments spanning physical, sensory, developmental, learning, medical, and mental issues as well as strengths such as adaptability, perseverance, self-regulation, mutual support, and social collectivism. About 30% of families have at least one family member who has a disability (Wang, 2005). The present-day diverse contexts of families must be considered in the development and implementation of social policies intended to promote child and adolescent well-being.

# CONCEPTUAL FRAMEWORKS TO INFORM SOCIAL POLICY

Multiple conceptual lenses are necessary to think about the many complex issues involved in creating, implementing, and evaluating social policies for children, youth, and families. We present two conceptual frameworks to guide these efforts: (1) a person-in-environment and risk and resilience framework and (2) an intersectional anti-oppression framework. Throughout the book, these frameworks are reflected in the approaches to policies and programs intended to address various social and health problems.

## A Person-in-Environment and Risk and Resilience Framework

An integrated person-in-environment and risk and resilience framework draws on concepts and tenants from a variety of disciplines, including public health, psychology, social work, and sociology. In social work, early pioneer Jane Addams wrote extensively on the impact of social, cultural, and policy environments on the well-being of individuals and families. She called for action and changes in these systems to improve the conditions of children, adults, and families living in poverty and facing distress (Austin, 2001; Germain & Hartman, 1980; Kondrat, 2013). Following the establishment of the National Association of Social Workers in 1955, Harriet Bartlett developed the first conceptualization of the person-in-environment perspective to inform social policy (Bartlett, 1958, 2003). Decades later, Urie Bronfenbrenner (1979) further explicated these concepts in his bioecological systems theory of development, and the ecological perspective has dominated the child development literature for the past several decades.

The person-in-environment and bioecological systems frameworks highly overlap (Bronfenbrenner, 2005; Bronfenbrenner & Morris, 2006; Kondrat, 2013). These frameworks rest on the idea that a young person's life is nested within levels of influence that are characterized by physical and social environments (e.g., home, neighborhood, school, community, parents' workplace, economic system, service systems, governments, built environment, and natural environment); these environments are purported to have both proximal and distal effects on children's lives. For example, a child's home and family context is a proximal system with direct and frequent contact with the child. Systems are also linked with each other, and distal systems can have direct and indirect influences on a child. To illustrate, income support, childcare, and employment policies may influence the ways in which parents interact with their children as well as children's caregiving contexts. This framework also posits that the relationships between children, youth, and families and environmental systems are interactive and bidirectional. Just as the characteristics and resources available to a school influence the quality of the education a child may receive, so too can students and parents influence the school environment through student-led initiatives, cocurricular student groups, and parent–teacher associations or organizations.

Person-in-environment and bioecological systems perspectives evolved to emphasize the importance of history, time, and sociohistorical contexts in understanding child development. For example, historical events like the Great Recession of 2008 or the historical trauma inflicted upon Native Americans have profound effects on the current life experiences of children and families. The timing of life events and interactions also have implications for children. To illustrate, the loss of a job for a single parent may have a more deleterious effect on a child who is age 5 than age 17 because older adolescents are less dependent on their parents; they can seek part-time employment to supplement the family income and they may even have the skills necessary to help their parent find a job. Indeed, there are sensitive and critical periods in childhood and adolescence where events have greater or lesser impacts on overall development. For example, research shows that the first few years of life are critical for language acquisition (Friedmann & Rusou, 2015). And, as our prior discussion of American family diversity illustrates, the importance of the sociohistorical context must be taken into consideration. How can we help immigrant children and families without considering the current social, political, and policy climate they are facing? How can we improve the health care system for children and adolescents without understanding how the system currently functions and is funded? These are among the many vexing questions facing policymakers today.

Fraser and colleagues (Fraser, 2004; Fraser et al., 1999; Fraser et al., 2004; Fraser & Terzian, 2005; Jenson, 2004) integrated ideas and principles from *epidemiology*—the study of the distribution and determinants of diseases and health problems—with key elements of the person-in-environment framework (Kondrat, 2013). They focused on the interplay of factors at the individual and environmental levels that increase the likelihood of health and social problems among young people. Discussed in subsequent chapters, these problems include low birth weight, maltreatment, violence, victimization, school failure, poverty, housing instability, food insecurity, substance abuse, delinquency, sexually transmitted infections (STIs), depression, and anxiety. Fraser and colleagues also emphasized the importance of understanding the factors that protect children and youth and contribute to positive outcomes such as healthy birth weight, positive parent–child relationships, community safety, school success, housing stability, food security, prosocial behavior, and mental health. Key concepts of this integrated model include risk, protective, and promotive factors and the underlying principle of resilience.

## Risk Factors

*Risk factors* are "any event, condition, or experience that increases the probability that a problem will be formed, maintained, or exacerbated" (Fraser & Terzian, 2005, p. 5).

This definition recognizes that the presence of one or more risk factors in a person's life can increase the likelihood that a health or social problem will occur at a later point in time. However, risk factors are not deterministic; the presence of a risk factor does not ensure or guarantee that a specific outcome (e.g., anxiety disorder and school dropout) will inevitably occur. Rather, the presence of a risk factor suggests an increased chance or probability that such a problem might develop.

Risk is temporal, contextual, and often modifiable. Temporally, risk factors precede the development of a deleterious outcome. Contextually, some risk factors depend on or are triggered by the environment. For example, research shows that there are genetic predispositions for many mental health disorders (Cross-Disorder Group of the Psychiatric Genomics Consortium, 2013; Sullivan et al., 2012). Therefore, children with certain genetic traits could be classified as being at higher risk for developing a mental health problem at some point in life. However, the expression of a genetic liability is often epigenetic in the sense that it may require or be based on enabling environmental conditions. In this sense, many risk factors—even genetic ones—are thought to be dependent on the context and, to the extent that the context can be purposively changed, they may be modifiable. The idea that risk factors are malleable through interventions is a key aspect of the risk and resilience perspective. Environmentally, for example, a child may attend a low-resource school where there are overcrowded classrooms, high levels of teacher burnout, few student service professionals (e.g., school counselors and social workers), and limited books and instructional technology—these conditions may increase students' risk for school dropout or not pursuing higher education. But these school risk factors can be modified . . . if we have the collective will to do so.

Because of the context dependence of risk, caution should be taken when ascribing risk to demographic groups. For example, youth who are LGBTQ are at increased risk for experiencing depression (Connolly et al., 2016; Marshal et al., 2011). However, research indicates that it is not these youth's sexual orientation or gender identity itself that causes the risk but rather the negative ways social contexts interact with these youth that increases their risk for depression (Hall, 2018; Hoffman, 2014). From an intervention standpoint, we are interested in both markers of risk and malleable risk factors because children and youth who are more vulnerable to certain problems may need particular interventions to minimize their likelihood for developing a problem. Identifying and targeting modifiable risk conditions is a basis for designing social interventions and public policies.

Although the presence of a single risk factor has the capacity to disrupt healthy development if it is severe or enduring, the presence of cumulative risk is also highly concerning. Risk factors can manifest as bundles, piles, or clusters (e.g., Lanier et al., 2018). For example, a pregnant person may be at increased risk for having a low birth weight baby due to multiple factors present during pregnancy. An expecting parent may live in an impoverished area that is a food desert with limited access to affordable, healthful food. In addition to the expecting parent's risk for poor nutrition, transportation barriers may prevent them from attending recommended prenatal care visits. Risk factors can also function as chains or cascades of risk in which one risk factor leads to others, building over time. For example, a child's parent unexpectedly dies. The remaining parent is stricken with grief and adjusting to the additional stress of being a single parent; consequently, the parent has difficulty helping the child with their grief. The family may move to another part of the country to be closer to extended family; however, the child loses connections with friends, family friends, and caring adults in professional roles. The child develops separation anxiety with depressed mood, which interferes with school and other activities. In this sense, one risk factor chains to another risk factor. Risk accumulates.

From a person-in-environment perspective, risk factors typically occur at individual, family, school, peer, and community levels of influence. It is important to note that common problems in childhood and adolescence, such as aggression, school failure, and substance use, share many of the same risk factors (Jenson & Bender, 2014). This "shared" sense of risk means that effective social policies and programs have the potential to simultaneously affect a number of behaviors and outcomes. Table 1.1 presents common risk factors for childhood and adolescent problems by level of influence. These and other risk factors are discussed in relation to specific problem areas and corresponding policies in ensuing chapters.

## Protective and Promotive Factors

*Protective factors* are characteristics, conditions, and resources that buffer or mitigate the impact of risk, interrupt risk processes, or prevent adverse outcomes altogether (Fraser et al., 1999; Fraser et al., 2004; Fraser & Terzian, 2005). Protective factors can be individual attributes (e.g., emotional self-regulation skills) or environmental characteristics (e.g., positive school climate) that function in three main ways. First, protective factors can cushion against the negative effects of risk factors (e.g., social support from family can buffer the effect of being in a hostile school climate for a student). Second, protective factors can interrupt a risk chain (e.g., coaching for parents whose children exhibit disruptive behavior can promote responsive parenting and prevent child behavior problems from escalating into oppositional defiant disorder, school problems, and child maltreatment). Third, protective factors can prevent the onset of problems (e.g., a baby with a temperament that adapts easily to new situations, accepts regular sleeping and feeding patterns, and usually exhibits a pleasant mood could protect the child from maltreatment ever occurring even if the parent is facing many challenges constraining their capacity for parenting). Table 1.2 shows common protective factors.

Promotive factors for child and adolescent behaviors can be distinguished from protective factors in several ways. As noted above, protective factors serve to reduce or buffer exposure to risk; these are factors in young people's lives that serve to increase positive behavior by offsetting the effects of high levels of risk. In contrast, *promotive factors* represent individual and environmental characteristics that are associated with positive outcomes regardless of underlying levels of risk (Sameroff, 2000). Promotive factors, therefore, promote positive outcomes for all children regardless of risk level whereas protective factors reduce or buffer children who are already at higher risk for adverse outcomes. *Self-efficacy*, the belief that you can successfully perform a set

## Table 1.1 Risk Factors for Childhood and Adolescent Problems by Level of Influence

### Individual Factors

Genetic predisposition

Prenatal or postnatal complications

Chronic illness

Difficult temperament

Poor attachment with parents

Limited capacity for self-regulation

Sedentary behavior and excessive screen time

Low self-worth

Lack of social skills and problem-solving skills

Favorable attitudes toward problematic behaviors

### Family and Household Factors

Family economic hardship

Housing instability

Food insecurity

Parental struggles with mental illness, substance abuse, or criminal activity

Conflict or violence between parents

Harsh or inconsistent parenting practices

Lack of parental warmth and involvement

Child abuse and neglect

Favorable attitudes of parents toward problematic behaviors

### School and Peer Factors

Unsupportive school climate

Low commitment to or engagement in school

Low academic performance

Bullying or rejection by peers

Affiliation with peers who engage in delinquent behavior

Loss of social support

*(Continued)*

**Table 1.1 (Continued)**

**Community and Societal Factors**

High community poverty levels

Presence of toxins, hazards, and health threats

Disadvantaged and disorganized neighborhood

Blocked opportunities for socioeconomic advancement

Discrimination and systemic injustice

Media portrayals of violence and problematic behaviors

Policies and norms favorable to problematic behaviors

*Sources:* Adapted from Fraser et al. (2004); Jenson and Bender (2014); O'Connell et al. (2009); and Rickwood and Thomas (2019).

**Table 1.2 Protective Factors for Childhood and Adolescent Problems by Level of Influence**

**Individual Factors**

Easy temperament

High intelligence

Self-regulation skills, social skills, and problem-solving skills

Positive attitude

Engagement in physical activity

Positive self-concept

Low childhood stress

**Family and Household Factors**

Adequate socioeconomic resources

Authoritative parenting

Supportive and caring relationships among family members

Attachment to parents or caregivers and positive parent–child relationship

Clear expectations for prosocial behavior and values

Support from extended family

Low parental conflict

| School and Peer Factors |
| --- |
| Support for early learning |
| Connectedness and engagement with school |
| Positive teacher expectations |
| Positive student–teacher relationships |
| Effective classroom management |
| School practices and policies against bullying |
| Positive school–family partnership |
| Ability to make friends and get along with others |
| Positive relationships with peers |

| Community and Societal Factors |
| --- |
| Opportunities for education, employment, and other prosocial activities (e.g., athletics, religion/spirituality, culture) |
| Cohesive and supportive neighborhood |
| Supportive relationships with mentors, helping professionals, and other caring adults |
| Positive social norms about behavior |
| Access to green space and recreational space |
| Physical and psychological safety |

*Sources:* Adapted from Fraser et al. (2004); Jenson and Bender (2014); O'Connell et al. (2009); and Rickwood and Thomas (2019).

of tasks and attain a goal (or control outcomes in a certain context), is an example of a promotive factor because it is thought to be beneficial for all children and youth in achieving overall healthy development.

## Resilience

*Resilience* is characterized by successful adaptation in the presence of risk or adversity (Garmezy, 1986; Luthar, 2003; Rutter, 2012; Ungar, 2011; Werner, 1989). This common definition implies that resilience is the outcome of a process involving both risk and protective factors. Unfortunately, when exposure to adversity is very high and protection is low, children and adolescents experience some type of problem or developmental difficulty (e.g., Cicchetti & Rogosch, 1997; Pollard et al., 1999). Yet, most children recover from risk exposure (Boyce, 2017). In vivo, individuals facing a threat often find support and resources in protective factors found in their environments to achieve a more positive outcome than would be expected. Children who experience adverse events such as maltreatment, poverty, and parent mental illness may not develop behavioral health problems because they have supportive friends, family members, and teachers. In addition, some children and youth who experience adversity may not merely cope well, showing adequate adaptation, but may develop new skills, insights, and resources through their resilience or recovery process that enable them to flourish as they move forward in life (Vloet et al., 2017); these outcomes point to the power of resilience in young people's lives. Indeed, there are many expressions and terms to characterize processes leading to resilience (e.g., *overcoming the odds, rebounding, bouncing back, grit, steeling, sustained competence under stress, recovery,* and *post-traumatic growth*).

Figure 1.1 displays the person-in-environment and risk and resilience framework. As seen in this figure, stressors, traumas, and adverse experiences across levels can press down on children, increasing the likelihood of deleterious outcomes. Equally important, protective and promotive factors buffer exposure to risk and support children and families by promoting resilience and general well-being.

We turn next to a discussion of the intersectional anti-oppression framework, our second conceptual model for guiding the development and implementation of social policies for children and families.

## Intersectional Anti-Oppression Framework

*Systems of oppression* are embedded in society in many forms, including racism, nativism, classism, sexism, heterosexism, cisgenderism, and ableism (Garcia & Van Soest, 2019; National Museum of African American History & Culture, 2020; Young, 2018). These systems confer advantages to dominant groups such as White people, native-born citizens, high-income families, men, heterosexuals, cisgender people, and people without disabilities or impairments. At the same time, systems of oppression often disadvantage people of color, immigrants, low-income families, women, queer people, transgender people, and people with disabilities through processes of discrimination, violence, marginalization, exploitation, and disempowerment. Many of the risk factors and processes affecting young people are driven by systems of oppression that pervade U.S. social contexts (e.g., McCrea et al., 2019).

Systems of oppression differentially affect children and youth, depending on an individual's set of identities and social statuses (e.g., racial/ethnic identity and socioeconomic status). The term *intersectionality* was coined by Kimberlé Crenshaw in 1989 to draw attention to the ways in which systems of oppression tend to intersect and influence particular individuals and groups. Forms of intersectionality are often derived from, or lead to, unique experiences of privilege or marginalization that cannot be understood by examining systems of oppression individually or in parallel. For example, a young Black man may face police discrimination that is not entirely due to his race (because force used by police during a stop is often greater for Black men than Black women) and not entirely due to his gender (because force used by police during a stop is often greater for Black men than White men). The discrimination displayed

Figure 1.1 A Person-in-Environment and Risk and Resilience Framework

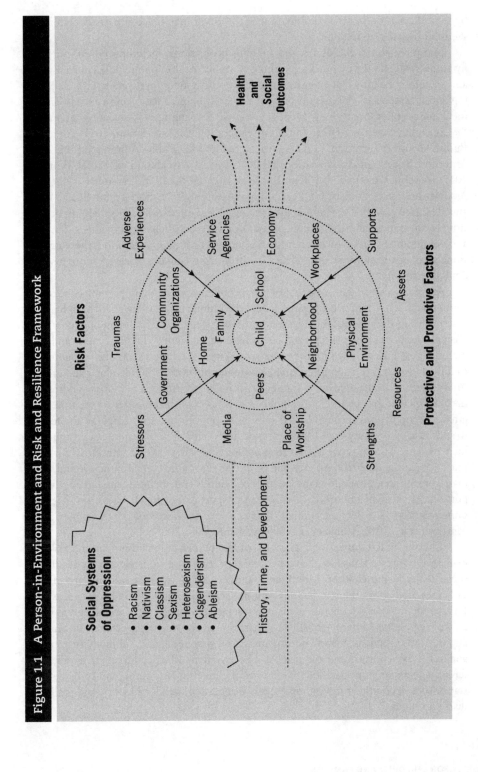

13

by the officer is due to the combination of the Black man's race and gender, an intersection involving oppression.

Many academic disciplines and helping professions, including education, family studies, human development, psychology, public health, public policy, social work, and sociology, acknowledge the importance of understanding diversity and challenging social systems of oppression in their research or practice (American Association for Public Policy Analysis & Management, n. d.; American Association of Family & Consumer Sciences, 2013; American Psychological Association, 2017; American Public Health Association, n. d.; American Society for Public Administration, 2014; American Sociological Association, 2018; National Association of Social Workers, 2017; National Council on Family Relations, 1998, 2018; National Education Association, 2020; Society for Prevention Research, 2020; Society for Social Work and Research, 2020). Through an intersectional anti-oppression lens, helping professionals can understand the unique and multilayered challenges individuals, families, and communities face, which can inform interventions used; in addition, these professionals can advocate for structural and institutional changes to create a more just and equitable society.

An intersectional anti-oppression perspective provides an important context for social policy. This framework acknowledges the unique forms of diversity of individuals and groups in their identities and social statuses. Systems of oppression operate invidiously throughout social contexts and environments, impacting children, youth, and families in different ways. The interconnections of oppressive systems must be accounted for to fully understand the unique experiences of marginalization of individuals and groups. An intersectional anti-oppressive framework can also inform interventions to address the needs of specific groups and inform policies to address problems affecting multiple marginalized populations through linked systems of oppression. An example of the former would be a community-based psychological intervention with Latinx sexual minority men who are HIV positive to improve coping and adherence to antiretroviral treatment (Bogart et al., 2020). An example of the latter would be environmental and waste management policy to address the location of landfills and environmental toxins disproportionately near neighborhoods with high proportions of Black Americans, Mexican immigrants, and low-income families (Bakhtsiyarava & Nawrotzki, 2017; Hunter, 2000; Martuzzi et al., 2010; Mohai et al., 2009; Mohai & Saha, 2007).

The upper left corner of Figure 1.1 of the person-in-environment and risk and resilience framework displays prominent systems of oppression relevant to health and social issues facing children, youth, and families. Although these systems are historically rooted, they continue to be prevalent in U.S. society and in other societies as well. Further, oppression can operate in many ways: intrapersonally (e.g., prejudice and internalized oppression), interpersonally (e.g., harassment and microaggressions), institutionally (e.g., discriminatory laws and organizational practices), and culturally (e.g., ideals and norms benefiting dominant groups). These systems affect children and families differently depending on specific intersections of race/ethnicity, immigrant or citizenship status, socioeconomic standing, sex, sexual orientation, gender identity, and ability or disability status.

# A PUBLIC HEALTH SOCIAL WORK
# INTERVENTION APPROACH

Elements of the person-in-environment and risk and resilience framework and of the intersectional anti-oppression framework provide important principles for developing, implementing, and evaluating interventions aimed at promoting healthy development in young people. These principles—especially reducing risk and promoting resilience—can be maximized in the context of a public health social work intervention approach. In broad terms, *public health* is focused on protecting and improving the health of the entire population. Public health interventions are typically broad in nature and seek to thwart adverse health outcomes among entire communities and population groups. They tend to focus on prevention and health promotion. They include, for example, providing vaccinations for infectious diseases, offering health education to prevent STIs, increasing opportunities for physical activity, conducting communication campaigns about handwashing, and improving access to health care systems. Although *health* is defined holistically as "a state of complete physical, mental, and social well-being and not merely the absence of disease or infirmity" (World Health Organization [WHO], 1948), public health interventions have historically emphasized physical health over mental and social well-being.

A sister profession to public health is social work. *Social work* is focused on helping people meet their basic needs, providing mental health and social services, community organizing, and advocating for social change. Although many social workers work in administration and organizational leadership, policy analysis and advocacy, and community- and systems-level change, the majority of social workers provide direct services to individuals, families, and groups to resolve or prevent psychosocial problems, increase access to social and economic resources, and sustain or enhance strengths and empowerment. By drawing upon both public health and social work approaches, we can comprehensively address the array of often-interconnected health and social problems affecting children, youth, and families.

Understanding social policy is essential not only for policymakers but also for helping professionals whose work is shaped by policy and the systems in which they operate. *Social policies* are sets of standards and rules created by governing bodies or public officials to achieve specific outcomes regarding human welfare by guiding action and decision making. Policies exist in many domains, including housing, labor, child welfare, income assistance, education, health, immigration, law enforcement, and criminal justice. Policies often aim to address particular social problems such as child maltreatment, drug abuse, poverty, and violence. Typically, policies are not intended to remain high-level statements forged by authority figures; rather, they are intended to influence the choices and actions of members of society and professionals at the ground level. McKinlay (1998) described policies as upstream interventions that influence downstream interventions. As shown in Figure 1.2, this stream represents a continuum of interventions with population-level policies on one end and individual-level interventions at another end.

Social policies are crafted to guide and regulate intervention programs, practices, and services. For young people and their families, for example, an anti-bullying policy may be adopted at the state level and implemented at the school level (Hall, 2017). Such a policy may require training all school employees to implement a bullying prevention program, integrating bullying awareness and education into classroom lessons, and providing counseling for students involved in bullying. In this case, by outlining goals and directives, policy lays the groundwork for an array of more specific interventions to be deployed at the local level.

A continuum of interventions, as illustrated in Figure 1.2, can be conceptualized as promoting positive child development, preventing behavior problems that are likely to arise, mitigating the impact of adversity, and remediating problems that have already become manifest (Hawkins et al., 2015; Jenson, 2018, 2020; Jenson & Bender, 2014; Jenson & Hawkins, 2018; Mrazek & Haggerty, 1994; Munoz et al., 1996; National Academies of Sciences, Engineering, and Medicine, 2019a, 2019b; O'Connell et al., 2009). That is, a public health social work approach can provide for health promotion, universal prevention, selective prevention, indicated prevention, and treatment and direct services. The application of principles outlined in the person-in-environment and risk and resilience framework and in the intersectional anti-oppression framework are key to these efforts.

## Applying a Public Health Social Work Intervention Approach

Communities That Care (CTC) is an illustrative example of a public health social work intervention approach. CTC aims to prevent youth problem behaviors such as violence, delinquency, school dropout, and substance abuse (The Center for CTC, 2020). CTC is based on the social development model that centers on a protective mechanism involving several key elements: (1) opportunities for prosocial socialization and behavior for children and youth; (2) child and youth involvement in family, school, community, and peer environments that share values, beliefs, and norms for prosocial behavior; (3) bonding to individuals in these environments in terms of attachment and commitment; (4) rewards for interaction with prosocial groups and communities; and (5) social, cognitive, and emotional skills that enable children and youth to solve problems, to socially interact with others and successfully navigate social situations, and to resist influences and impulses that would violate their norms for behavior (Cambron et al., 2019; Catalano & Hawkins, 1996; Hawkins & Weis, 1985).

CTC is currently being implemented in a variety of cities, towns, neighborhoods, and school catchment areas (The Center for CTC, 2020). Leaders in the CTC communities form a coalition and conduct surveys with youth, parents, and community members to identify risk factors, protective factors, and problem behaviors that are most salient in their local area. Survey results, combined with local administrative data (e.g., school dropout rates), are used to determine which factors and behaviors to target in prevention and intervention efforts; these data also serve as baseline data to evaluate the effectiveness of CTC on targeted outcomes over time. Coalition members then

Figure 1.2   A Public Health Social Work Intervention Approach

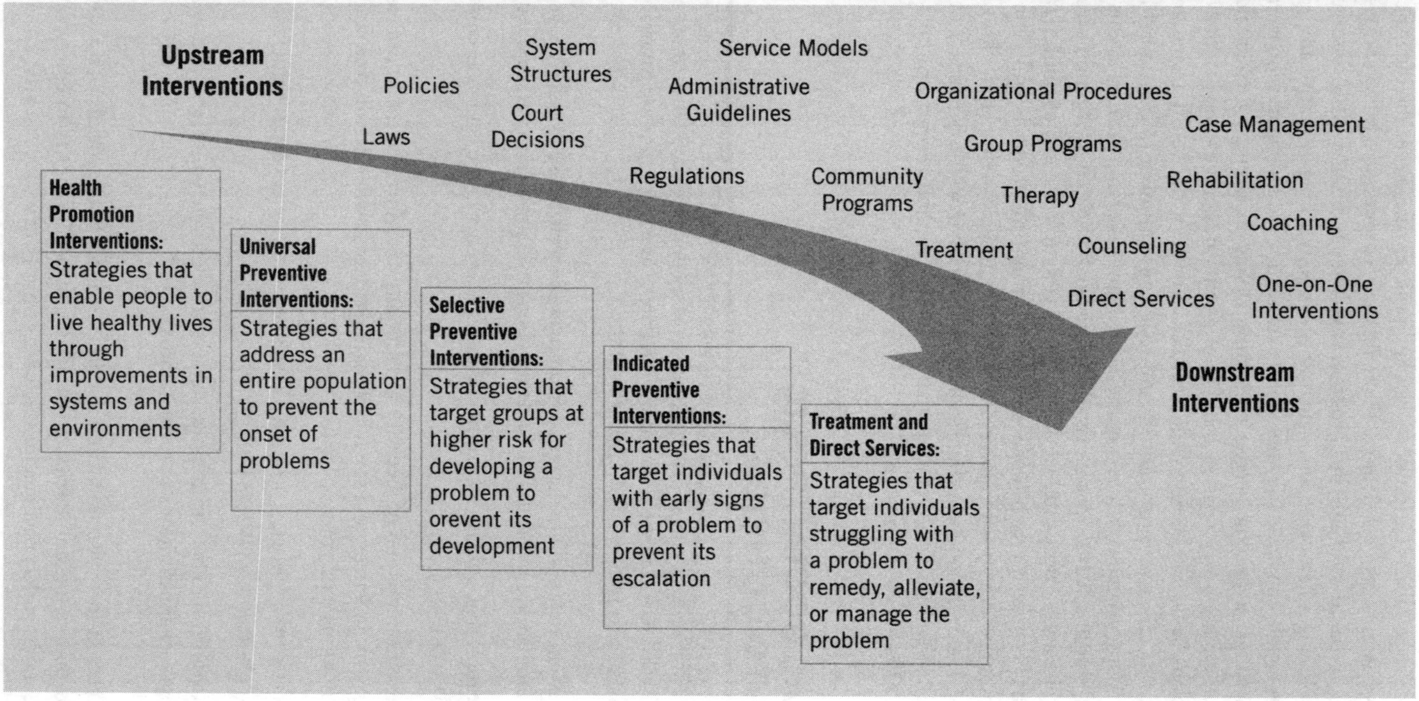

**Upstream Interventions**

Laws
Policies
Court Decisions
System Structures
Administrative Guidelines
Service Models
Regulations
Community Programs
Organizational Procedures
Group Programs
Treatment
Therapy
Counseling
Case Management
Rehabilitation
Direct Services
Coaching
One-on-One Interventions

**Downstream Interventions**

**Health Promotion Interventions:** Strategies that enable people to live healthy lives through improvements in systems and environments

**Universal Preventive Interventions:** Strategies that address an entire population to prevent the onset of problems

**Selective Preventive Interventions:** Strategies that target groups at higher risk for developing a problem to orevent its development

**Indicated Preventive Interventions:** Strategies that target individuals with early signs of a problem to prevent its escalation

**Treatment and Direct Services:** Strategies that target individuals struggling with a problem to remedy, alleviate, or manage the problem

17

select evidence-based intervention programs and policies that target the identified risk and protective factors and implement them in their community. Interventions may include a school-based anti-bullying program involving training staff to intervene in bullying, developing schoolwide anti-bullying policies, teaching empathy and respect to students through classroom lessons, and maintaining adult supervision throughout school settings; a driving license restriction policy to prevent further alcohol-related driving offenses; and a parent training program on family management skills to prevent problem behaviors among children. CTC has been rigorously tested and has been found to be effective in preventing and reducing a number of behavioral health problems in young people (Chilenski et al., 2019; Hawkins et al., 2009; Hawkins et al., 2014; Oesterle et al., 2018). Results from longitudinal research and randomized trials shows significantly lower rates of delinquency; violent behavior; alcohol, cigarette, and marijuana use; severe substance use; suspension from school; and depressive symptoms among youth in CTC intervention communities as compared with control communities. These groundbreaking findings suggest that well-organized and well-implemented community interventions that focus on risk and protection can lead to positive outcomes for young people.

## CRITICAL SOCIAL POLICY ISSUES TO CONSIDER

There are several critical social policy issues to consider as you read the subsequent chapters of this book and move forward in your career as a helping professional, public servant, or social researcher. These issues include

- the extent that policies designed to address the well-being of children, youth, and families are informed by evidence about risk, protection, and resilience;

- the extent that policies recommend, require, or encourage evidence-based interventions;

- the extent that issues of diversity and inequity are addressed in the policies, programs, practices, and services designed to assist America's diverse families and marginalized young people;

- the extent that policies, programs, practices, and services focus sufficiently on prevention and health promotion; and

- opportunities to better integrate services for children, youth, and families across social institutions or system domains.

Using a person-in-environment and risk and resilience framework as well as an intersectional anti-oppression framework in the design of social policy is an emerging challenge. These frameworks provide a means for infusing policy with research knowledge.

Unfortunately, failures litter the policy landscape. For example, school-based sex education policies have historically emphasized abstinence-only sex education (Hall et al., 2019; Sexuality Information and Education Council of the United States, 2019), despite substantial evidence that this approach is ineffective at preventing unwanted adolescent pregnancy and the spread of STIs (Chin et al., 2012; Fox et al., 2019; Kohler et al., 2008; Petrova & Garcia-Retamero, 2015; Underhill et al., 2007). Furthermore, despite the availability of numerous evidence-based comprehensive sex education programs (Goesling et al., 2014; Manlove et al., 2015), federal and state policies continue to recommend and fund abstinence-only programs in schools (Hall et al., 2019; Kaiser Family Foundation, 2018).

Policy often falls short in addressing the inequities and marginalization produced by systems of oppression. For example, bullying in schools continues to be a pervasive and persistent threat to the well-being of youth (Basile et al., 2020), disproportionately affecting youth who are members of minority groups (e.g., LGBTQ youth, immigrant youth, and youth with disabilities; Hall & Chapman, 2018). However, most state anti-bullying policies do not provide specific protections for these vulnerable youth. They fail, on balance, to prohibit bullying based on race, national origin, socioeconomic status, sex, sexual orientation, gender identity, and ability/disability status, despite evidence indicating that such protections may reduce bias-based bullying (Cosgrove & Nickerson, 2017; Hall, 2017; Hall & Dawes, 2019).

As indicated in Figure 1.2 and as suggested by the findings from the CTC studies, greater emphasis must be placed on health promotion and preventive interventions in social policies for children and families. Health promotion resources and activities can be integrated into everyday social settings, especially schools (WHO, 2020). Prevention is particularly relevant to social policies for children and families, as childhood and adolescence represent developmental stages in which young people form patterns of behavior (Jenson, 2020). These patterns, learned in family, school, and other contexts, have important implications far into adulthood (Hall & Rounds, 2013). Rather than health promotion and prevention (e.g., prevention of violence, delinquency, substance abuse, and school dropout), public policies have historically focused on punishment, control, treatment, and rehabilitation (Hawkins et al., 2015; Jenson & Bender, 2014; Jenson et al., 2001). This focus costs the U.S. society hundreds of billions of dollars annually (Miller, 2004; O'Connell et al., 2009). For example, youth perpetration of violence and criminal activity is associated with health care costs for injured victims; property loss or damage; police, legal/court, correctional facility, and probation costs; employment losses; and decreased quality of life for victims and families. The costs of preventing such problems are often a fraction of the cost to address the aftereffects once behavior problems have occurred (Aos et al., 2004; Kuklinski, 2015; WHO, 2014). Prevention research has boomed in recent decades, resulting in dozens of efficacious preventive interventions that are widely available to address mental health problems, school failure, delinquency, substance abuse, risky health behaviors, and violence (Hawkins et al., 2015; Jenson & Bender, 2014; Jenson & Hawkins, 2018).

Finally, public service systems are often fragmented, attempting to address the many needs of children and adolescents in uncoordinated and inefficient ways. Such arrangements are especially deleterious to young people with multiple, high-level needs, such as children and youth with special health care needs. These young people face chronic physical and/or psychological conditions requiring health and other services above what is required for most children and youth (McPherson et al., 1998). These children and their families often depend on an array of services and resources spanning basic needs to specialized medical care that are scattered amongst social service agencies, schools, community-based organizations, and health care systems (Mattson et al., 2019). Indeed, many gaps remain to providing integrated care and services to our most vulnerable children and youth (e.g., An, 2016; Rosen-Reynoso et al., 2016).

## SUMMARY

Knowledge gained from the study of risk, protection, and resilience has improved our understanding of the onset and persistence of many social and health problems. At the same time, the person-in-environment and risk and resilience perspective helps us understand the contextual boundedness of social and health problems. Through the application of an intersectional anti-oppression framework, we may better understand how ideologies and institutionalized practices (often deeply embedded in society) condition opportunity, confer privilege, and promote marginalization. To date, these perspectives and the new knowledge they represent have not been systematically incorporated in the design and implementation of social policies for children and families.

In this chapter, we have outlined a public health social work approach to social policy and intervention. This approach is grounded in frameworks that have emerged from recent research and models that offer enduring perspectives in child development. The incorporation of these frameworks in social policies for children and families is the challenge that we confront as professionals who seek a more just, humane, and enriching society. In subsequent chapters, authors more fully examine this emerging point of view by applying it to a host of policy and practice domains.

## REFERENCES

American Association for Public Policy Analysis & Management. (n. d.). *Code of conduct.* https://www.appam.org/assets/1/7/APPAM_Code_of_Conduct2.pdf

American Association of Family & Consumer Sciences. (2013). *AAFCS code of ethics.* https://higherlogicdownload.s3.amazonaws.com/AAFCS/1c95de14-d78f-40b8-a6ef-a1fb628c68fe/UploadedImages/About/AAFCS_Code_of_Ethics_2013.pdf

American Lung Association. (2020). *State of the air.* Author.

An, R. (2016). Unmet mental health care needs in U.S. children with medical complexity, 2005–2010. *Journal of Psychosomatic Research, 82,* 1–3.

American Psychological Association. (2017). *Ethical principles of psychologists and code of conduct.* https://www.apa.org/ethics/code

American Public Health Association. (n. d.). *Public health code of ethics.* https://www.apha.org/-/media/files/pdf/membergroups/ethics/code_of_ethics.ashx

American Society for Public Administration. (2014). *Code of ethics.* https://www.aspanet.org/ASPA/Code-of-Ethics/Code-of-Ethics.aspx

American Sociological Association. (2018). *Code of ethics.* https://www.asanet.org/sites/default/files/asa_code_of_ethics-june2018a.pdf

An, R. (2016). Unmet mental health care needs in US children with medical complexity, 2005–2010. *Journal of Psychosomatic Research, 82*, 1–3.

Aos, S., Lieb, R., Mayfield, J., Miller, M., & Pennucci, A. (2004). *Benefits and costs of prevention and early intervention programs for youth*. Washington State Institute for Public Policy.

Austin, D. (2001). Guest editor's foreword. *Research on Social Work Practice, 11*(2), 147–151.

Bakhtsiyarava, M., & Nawrotzki, R. J. (2017). Environmental inequality and pollution advantage among immigrants in the United States. *Applied Geography, 81*, 60–69.

Bartlett, H. M. (1958). Toward clarification and improvement of social work practice. *Social Work*, 3–9.

Bartlett, H. M. (2003). Working definition of social work practice. *Research on Social Work Practice, 13*(3), 267–270.

Basile, K. C., Clayton, H. B., DeGue, S., Gilford, J. W., Vagi, K. J., Suarez, N. A., Zwald, M. L., & Lowry, R. (2020). Interpersonal violence victimization among high school students—Youth Risk Behavior Survey, United States, 2019. *Morbidity and Mortality Weekly Report, 69*(1), 28–37.

Bogart, L. M., Barreras, J. L., Gonzalez, A., Klein, D. J., Marsh, T., Agniel, D., & Pantalone, D. W. (2020). Pilot randomized controlled trial of an intervention to improve coping with intersectional stigma and medication adherence among HIV-positive Latinx sexual minority men. *AIDS and Behavior*.

Boyce, W. T. (2017). Epigenomic susceptibility to the social world: Plausible paths to a "newest morbidity." *Academic Pediatrics, 17*(6), 600–606.

Bronfenbrenner, U. (1979). *The ecology of human development: Experiments by nature and design*. Harvard University Press.

Bronfenbrenner, U. (2005). *Making human beings human: Bioecological perspectives on human development*. SAGE.

Bronfenbrenner, U., & Morris, P. A. (2006). The bioecological model of human development. In R. M. Lerner (Ed.), *Handbook of child psychology—Volume 1: Theoretical models of human development* (6th ed., pp. 793–828). Wiley.

Budiman, A. (2020). *Key findings about U.S. immigrants*. Pew Research Center.

Cambron, C., Catalano, R. F., & Hawkins, J. D. (2019). The social development model. In D. P. Farrington, L. Kazemian, & A. R. Piquero (Eds.), *Oxford handbook of developmental and life course criminology* (pp. 224–247). Oxford University Press.

Catalano, R. F., & Hawkins, J. D. (1996). The social development model: A theory of antisocial behavior. In J. D. Hawkins (Ed.), *Delinquency and crime: Current theories* (pp. 149–197). Cambridge University Press.

The Center for Communities That Care (CTC). (2020). *Communities that care*. University of Washington. https://www.communitiesthatcare.net/

Centers for Disease Control and Prevention (CDC). (2019). *Leading causes of death*. https://www.cdc.gov/healthequity/lcod/index.htm

Centers for Disease Control and Prevention (CDC). (2020). *COVID-19 death data and resources*. https://www.cdc.gov/nchs/nvss/vsrr/covid_weekly/index.htm

Children's Defense Fund. (2020). *The state of America's children 2020*. Author.

Chilenski, S. M., Frank, J., Summers, N., & Lew, D. (2019). Public health benefits 16 years after a statewide policy change: Communities That Care in Pennsylvania. *Prevention Science, 20*(6), 947–958.

Chin, H. B., Sipe, T. A., Elder, R., Mercer, S. L., Chattopadhyay, S. K., Jacob, V., Wethington, H. R., Kirby, D., Elliston, D. B., Griffith, M., Chuke, S. O., Briss, S. C., Ericksen, I., Galbraith, J. S., Herbst, J. H., Johnson, R. L., Kraft, J. M., Noar, S. M., Romero, L. M., & Santelli, J. (2012). The effectiveness of group-based comprehensive risk-reduction and abstinence education interventions to prevent or reduce the risk of adolescent pregnancy, human immunodeficiency virus, and sexually transmitted infections: Two systematic reviews for the guide to community preventive services. *American Journal of Preventive Medicine, 42*(3), 272–294.

Cicchetti, D., & Rogosch, F. A. (1997). The role of self-organization in the promotion of resilience in maltreated children. *Development and Psychopathology, 9*, 787–815.

Cohn, D., & Passel, J. (2018). *A record 64 million Americans live in multigenerational households*. Pew Research Center.

Connolly, M. D., Zervos, M. J., Barone, C. J., II, Johnson, C. C., & Joseph, C. L. (2016). The mental health of transgender youth: Advances in understanding. *Journal of Adolescent Health, 59*(5), 489–495.

Cosgrove, H. E., & Nickerson, A. B. (2017). Anti-bullying/harassment legislation and educator perceptions of severity, effectiveness, and school climate: A cross-sectional analysis. *Educational Policy*, *31*(4), 518–545.

Crenshaw, K. (1989). Demarginalizing the intersection of race and sex: A Black feminist critique of antidiscrimination doctrine, feminist theory, and antiracist politics. *University of Chicago Legal Forum*, *1*(8).

Cross-Disorder Group of the Psychiatric Genomics Consortium. (2013). Genetic relationship between five psychiatric disorders estimated from genome-wide SNPs. *Nature Genetics*, *45*(9), 984.

Family Health in Europe–Research in Nursing Group. (2020). The COVID-19 pandemic: A family affair. *Journal of Family Nursing*, *26*(2), 87–89.

Fegert, J. M., Vitiello, B., Plener, P. L., & Clemens, V. (2020). Challenges and burden of the Coronavirus 2019 (COVID-19) pandemic for child and adolescent mental health: A narrative review to highlight clinical and research needs in the acute phase and the long return to normality. *Child and Adolescent Psychiatry and Mental Health*, *14*, 1–11.

Fox, A. M., Himmelstein, G., Khalid, H., & Howell, E. A. (2019). Funding for abstinence-only education and adolescent pregnancy prevention: Does state ideology affect outcomes? *American Journal of Public Health*, *109*(3), 497–504.

Fraenkel, P., & Cho, W. L. (2020). Reaching up, down, in, and around: Couple and family coping during the coronavirus pandemic. *Family Process*.

Fraser, M. W. (2004). The ecology of childhood: A multisystems perspective. In M. W. Fraser (Ed.), *Risk and resilience in childhood* (2nd ed., pp. 1–12). NASW Press.

Fraser, M. W., Kirby, L. D., & Smokowski, P. R. (2004). Risk and resilience in childhood. In M. W. Fraser (Ed.), *Risk and resilience in childhood: An ecological perspective* (2nd ed., pp. 13–66). NASW Press.

Fraser, M. W., Richman, J. M., & Galinsky, M. J. (1999). Risk, protection, and resilience: Towards a conceptual framework for social work practice. *Social Work Research*, *23*, 131–144.

Fraser, M. W., & Terzian, M. A. (2005). Risk and resilience in child development: Practice principles and strategies. In G. P. Mallon & P. McCartt Hess (Eds.), *Handbook of children, youth, and family services: Practice, policies, and programs* (pp. 55–71). Columbia University Press.

Friedmann, N., & Rusou, D. (2015). Critical period for first language: the crucial role of language input during the first year of life. *Current Opinion in Neurobiology*, *35*, 27–34.

Garcia, B., & Van Soest, D. (2019). Oppression. In C. Franklin (Ed.), *Encyclopedia of social work*. National Association of Social Workers Press and Oxford University Press.

Garmezy, N. (1986). On measures, methods, and models. *Journal of the American Academy of Child and Adolescent Psychiatry*, *25*, 727–729.

Germain, C. B., & Hartman, A. (1980). People and ideas in the history of social work. *Social Casework*, *61*(1), 323–331.

Goesling, B., Colman, S., Trenholm, C., Terzian, M., & Moore, K. (2014). Programs to reduce teen pregnancy, sexually transmitted infections, and associated sexual risk behaviors: A systematic review. *Journal of Adolescent Health*, *54*(5), 499–507.

Goldberg, A. E., & Allen, K. R. (2013). *LGBT-parent families*. Springer.

Grimm, R. T., Jr., & Dietz, N. (2018). *Good intentions, gap in action: The challenge of translating youth's high interest in doing good into civic engagement*. Do Good Institute, University of Maryland.

Haden, S. C., & Applewhite, K. (2020). Parents who are lesbian, gay, bisexual, or transgender. In S. Hupp & J. D. Jewell (Eds.), *The encyclopedia of child and adolescent development*. John Wiley & Sons.

Hall, W. J. (2017). The effectiveness of policy interventions for school bullying: A systematic review. *Journal of the Society for Social Work and Research*, *8*(1), 45–69.

Hall, W. J. (2018). Psychosocial risk and protective factors for depression among lesbian, gay, bisexual, and queer youth: A systematic review. *Journal of Homosexuality*, *65*(3), 263–316.

Hall, W. J., & Chapman, M. V. (2018). Fidelity of implementation of a state anti-bullying policy with a focus on protected social classes. *Journal of School Violence*, *17*, 58–73.

Hall, W. J., & Dawes, H. C. (2019). Is fidelity of implementation of an anti-bullying policy related to student bullying and teacher protection of students? *Education Sciences*, *9*, 112.

Hall, W. J., Dawes, H. C., & Plocek, N. (2020). *Sexual orientation identity development milestones among lesbian,* gay, bisexual, and queer people: A systematic review and meta-analysis. [Manuscript submitted for publication]

Hall, W. J., Jones, B. L. H., Witkemper, K. D., Collins, T., & Rodgers, G. K. (2019). State policy on school-based sex education: A content analysis focused on sexual behaviors, relationships, and identities. *American Journal of Health Behavior, 43*, 506–519.

Hall, W. J., & Rounds, K. A. (2013). Adolescent health. In the Public Health Social Work Section of the American Public Health Association, R. H. Keefe, & E. T. Jurkowski (Eds.), *Handbook for public health social work* (pp. 59–80). Springer.

Hawkins, J. D., Jenson, J. M., Catalano, R., Fraser, M. W., Botvin, G. J., Shapiro, V., Hendricks Brown, C., Beardslee, W., Brent, D., Leslie, L. K., Rotheram-Borus, M. J., Shea, P., Shih, A., Anthony, E., Haggerty, K. P., Bender, K., Gorman-Smith, D., Casey, E., & Stone, S. (2015). *Unleashing the power of prevention.* National Academy of Medicine.

Hawkins, J. D., Oesterle, S., Brown, E. C., Abbott, R. D., & Catalano, R. F. (2014). Youth problem behaviors 8 years after implementing the Communities That Care prevention system: A community-randomized trial. *JAMA Pediatrics, 168*(2), 122–129.

Hawkins, J. D., Oesterle, S., Brown, E. C., Arthur, M. W., Abbott, R. D., Fagan, A. A., & Catalano, R. F. (2009). Results of a type 2 translational research trial to prevent adolescent drug use and delinquency: A test of Communities That Care. *Archives of Pediatrics and Adolescent Medicine, 163*(9), 789–798.

Hawkins, J. D., & Weis, J. G. (1985). The social development model: An integrated approach to delinquency prevention. *Journal of Primary Prevention, 6*(2), 73–97.

Hoffman, B. (2014). An overview of depression among transgender women. *Depression Research and Treatment.*

Hunter, L. M. (2000). The spatial association between US immigrant residential concentration and environmental hazards. *International Migration Review, 34*(2), 460–488.

Hussar, B., Zhang, J., Hein, S., Wang, K., Roberts, A., Cui, J., Smith, M., Bullock Mann, F., Barmer, A., & Dilig, R. (2020). *The condition of education 2020. National Center for Education Statistics.* U.S. Department of Education.

International Energy Agency. (2020). $CO_2$ *emissions from fuel combustion.* http://energyatlas.iea.org/#!/tell-map/1378539487

Jenson, J. M. (2004). Risk and protective factors for alcohol and other drug use in childhood and adolescence. In M. W. Fraser (Ed.), *Risk and resilience in childhood: An ecological perspective* (2nd ed., pp. 183–208). NASW Press.

Jenson, J. M. (2018, May 1). *Seven ways to unleash the power of prevention.* Keynote presentation at the Blueprints for Healthy Youth Development Conference in Denver, Colorado, United States.

Jenson, J. M. (2020). Improving behavioral health in young people: It is time for social work to adopt prevention. *Research on Social Work Practice, 30*, 707–711.

Jenson, J. M., & Bender, K. A. (2014). *Preventing child and adolescent behavior. Evidence-based strategies in schools, families, and communities.* Oxford University Press.

Jenson, J. M., & Hawkins, J. D. (2018). Ensuring healthy development for all youth: Unleashing the power of prevention. In R. Fong, J. Lubben, & R. P. Barth (Eds.), *Grand challenges for social work and society: Social progress engineered by science* (pp. 18–35). Oxford University Press.

Jenson, J. M., Potter, C. C., & Howard, M. O. (2001). American juvenile justice: Recent trends and issues in youth offending. *Social Policy and Administration, 35*, 48–68.

Kaiser Family Foundation. (2018). *Abstinence education programs: Definition, funding, and impact on teen sexual behavior.* https://www.kff.org/womens-health-policy/fact-sheet/abstinence-education-programs-definition-funding-and-impact-on-teen-sexual-behavior/

Kaza, S., Yao, L., Bhada-Tata, P., & Van Woerden, F. (2018). *What a waste 2.0: A global snapshot of solid waste management to 2050.* World Bank.

Kohler, P. K., Manhart, L. E., & Lafferty, W. E. (2008). Abstinence-only and comprehensive sex education and the initiation of sexual activity and teen pregnancy. *Journal of Adolescent Health, 42*(4), 344–351.

Kondrat, M. E. (2013). Person-in-environment. In C. Franklin (Ed.), *Oxford research encyclopedia of social work.* National Association of Social Workers Press and Oxford University Press.

Kuklinski, M. R. (2015). Benefit–cost analysis of prevention and intervention programs for youth and young adults: Introduction to the special issue. *Journal of Benefit–Cost Analysis, 6*(3), 455–470.

Landrigan, P. J., & Goldman, L. R. (2011). Children's vulnerability to toxic chemicals: A challenge and opportunity to strengthen health and environmental policy. *Health Affairs, 30*(5), 842–850.

Lanier, P., Maguire-Jack, K., Lombardi, B., Frey, J., & Rose, R. A. (2018). Adverse childhood experiences and child health outcomes: Comparing cumulative risk and latent class approaches. *Maternal and Child Health Journal, 22*(3), 288–297.

Luthar, S. S. (2003). *Resilience and vulnerability: Adaptation in the context of childhood adversities*. Cambridge University Press.

Manlove, J., Fish, H., & Moore, K. A. (2015). Programs to improve adolescent sexual and reproductive health in the US: A review of the evidence. *Adolescent Health, Medicine and Therapeutics, 6*, 47–79.

Marshal, M. P., Dietz, L. J., Friedman, M. S., Stall, R., Smith, H. A., McGinley, J., Thoma, B. C., Murray, P. J., D'Augelli, A. R., & Brent, D. A. (2011). Suicidality and depression disparities between sexual minority and heterosexual youth: A meta-analytic review. *Journal of Adolescent Health, 49*(2), 115–123.

Martuzzi, M., Mitis, F., & Forastiere, F. (2010). Inequalities, inequities, environmental justice in waste management and health. *European Journal of Public Health, 20*(1), 21–26.

Mason, L. R., & Rigg, J. (Eds.). (2018). *People and climate change: Vulnerability, adaptation, and social justice*. Oxford University Press.

Mattson, G., Kuo, D. Z., & Committee on Psychosocial Aspects of Child and Family Health. (2019). Psychosocial factors in children and youth with special health care needs and their families. *Pediatrics, 143*(1).

McCrea, K. T., Richards, M., Quimby, D., Scott, D., Davis, L., Hart, S., Thomas, A., & Hopson, S. (2019). Understanding violence and developing resilience with African American youth in high-poverty, high-crime communities. *Children and Youth Services Review, 99*, 296–307.

McKinlay, J. B. (1998). Paradigmatic obstacles to improving the health of populations: Implications for health policy. *Salud Pública de México, 40*, 369–379.

McPherson, M., Arango, P., Fox, H., Lauver, C., McManus, M., Newacheck, P. W., Perrin, J. M., Shonkoff, J. P., & Strickland, B. (1998). A new definition of children with special health care needs. *Pediatrics, 102*(1), 137–139.

Miller, T. R. (2004). The social costs of adolescent problem behavior. In A. Biglan, P. A. Brennan, S. L. Foster, & H. D. Holder (Eds.), *Helping adolescents at risk: Prevention of multiple problem behaviors* (pp. 31–56). Guilford Press.

Mohai, P., Pellow, D., & Roberts, J. T. (2009). Environmental justice. *Annual Review of Environment and Resources, 34*, 405–430.

Mohai, P., & Saha, R. (2007). Racial inequality in the distribution of hazardous waste: A national-level reassessment. *Social Problems, 54*(3), 343–370.

Mrazek, P. J., & Haggerty, R. J. (Eds.). (1994). *Reducing risks for mental disorders: Frontiers for preventive intervention research*. National Academies Press.

Munoz, R. F., Mrazek, P. J., & Haggerty, R. J. (1996). Institute of Medicine report on prevention of mental disorders: Summary and commentary. *American Psychologist, 51*(11), 1116.

National Academies of Sciences, Engineering, and Medicine. (2019a). *The promise of adolescence: Realizing opportunity for all youth*. The National Academies Press.

National Academies of Sciences, Engineering, and Medicine. (2019b). *Fostering healthy mental, emotional, and behavioral development in children and youth: A national agenda*. The National Academies Press.

National Association of Social Workers. (2017). *Code of ethics*. https://www.socialworkers.org/About/Ethics/Code-of-Ethics/Code-of-Ethics-English

National Council on Family Relations. (1998). *NCFR ethical principles and guidelines for family scientists*. https://www.ncfr.org/board-and-governance/governance/ncfr-ethical-principles-guidelines-family-scientists

National Council on Family Relations. (2018). *Code of professional ethics for certified family life educators*. https://www.ncfr.org/cfle-certification/cfle-code-ethics

National Education Association. (2020). *Code of ethics*. https://www.nea.org/resource-library/code-ethics

National Museum of African American History & Culture. (2020). *Social identities and systems of oppression*. https://nmaahc.si.edu/learn/talking-about-race/topics/social-identities-and-systems-oppression

National Museum of the American Indian. (2007). *Native languages*. Smithsonian Institution.

Newport, F. (2018). *In U.S., estimate of LGBT population rises to 4.5%*. Gallup.

O'Connell, M. E., Boat, T., & Warner, K. E. (Eds.). (2009). *Preventing mental, emotional, and behavioral disorders among young people: Progress and possibilities*. National Research Council and Institute of Medicine; the National Academies Press.

Oesterle, S., Kuklinski, M. R., Hawkins, J. D., Skinner, M. L., Guttmannova, K., & Rhew, I. C. (2018). Long-term effects of the communities that care trial on substance use, antisocial behavior, and violence through age 21 years. *American Journal of Public Health*, 108(5), 659–665.

Organisation for Economic Co-operation and Development. (2020). *National accounts of OECD countries*. OECD Publishing.

Petrova, D., & Garcia-Retamero, R. (2015). Effective evidence-based programs for preventing sexually transmitted infections: A meta-analysis. *Current HIV Research*, 13(5), 432–438.

Pew Research Center. (2015a). *Parenting in America: Outlook, worries, aspirations are strongly linked to financial situation*. Author.

Pew Research Center. (2015b). *The American middle class is losing ground*. Author.

Pollard, J. A., Hawkins, J. D., & Arthur, M. W. (1999). Risk and protection: Are both necessary to understand diverse behavioral outcomes in adolescence? *Social Work Research*, 23, 145–158.

Protected Planet. (2020). *United States of America, North America*. https://www.protectedplanet.net/country/US

Puzzanchera, C. (2020). *Juvenile arrests, 2018*. Office of Juvenile Justice and Delinquency Prevention, U.S. Department of Justice.

Quacquarelli Symonds. (2019). *The strongest higher education systems by country*. https://www.qs.com/the-strongest-higher-education-systems-by-country-overview/

Reinhart, R. J. (2018). *Global warming age gap: Younger Americans most worried*. Gallup.

Rickwood, D. J., & Thomas, K. A. (2019). *Mental wellbeing risk & protective factors*. Sax Institute.

Rosen-Reynoso, M., Porche, M. V., Kwan, N., Bethell, C., Thomas, V., Robertson, J., Hawes, E., Foley, S., & Palfrey, J. (2016). Disparities in access to easy-to-use services for children with special health care needs. *Maternal and Child Health Journal*, 20(5), 1041–1053.

Rutter, M. (2012). Resilience as a dynamic concept. *Development and psychopathology*, 24(2), 335–344.

Saad, L. (2019). *Americans as concerned as ever about global warming*. Gallup.

Sameroff, A. J. (2000). Developmental systems and psychopathology. *Development and Psychopathology*, 12(3), 297–312.

Scanlon, R. (2019). *The generational divide over climate change*. The Chicago Council on Global Affairs.

Semega, J., Kollar, M., Creamer, J., & Mohanty, A. (2020). *Income and poverty in the United States: 2018*. U.S. Census Bureau.

Sexuality Information and Education Council of the United States. (2019). *A history of abstinence-only funding in the U.S.* https://siecus.org/resources/a-history-of-abstinence-only-federal-funding/

Society for Prevention Research. (2020). *Code of conduct: Society for Prevention Research*. https://www.prevention-research.org/about-spr/code-of-conduct-society-for-prevention-research/

Society for Social Work and Research. (2020). *SSWR anti-harassment policy and code of ethics and procedures for review of member conduct*. https://secure.sswr.org/about-sswr/sswr-anti-harassment-policy/

Sullivan, P. F., Daly, M. J., & O'Donovan, M. (2012). Genetic architectures of psychiatric disorders: the emerging picture and its implications. *Nature Reviews Genetics*, 13(8), 537–551.

Underhill, K., Operario, D., & Montgomery, P. (2007). Abstinence-only programs for HIV infection prevention in high-income countries. *Cochrane Database of Systematic Reviews*, 4, 1–143.

Ungar, M. (2011). The social ecology of resilience. Addressing contextual and cultural ambiguity of a nascent construct. *American Journal of Orthopsychiatry*, 81, 1–17.

U.S. Bureau of Labor Statistics. (2020a). *College enrollment and work activity of recent high school and college graduates summary*. https://www.bls.gov/news.release/hsgec.nr0.htm

U.S. Bureau of Labor Statistics. (2020b). *Employment characteristics of families*. Author.

U.S. Census Bureau. (2007). *First, second, and total responses to the ancestry question by detailed ancestry code: 2000.* https://www.census.gov/data/tables/2000/dec/phc-t-43.html

U.S. Census Bureau. (2019). *Population estimates, July 1, 2019.* https://www.census.gov/quickfacts/fact/table/US/PST045219

Vespa, J., Medina, L., & Armstrong, D. M. (2020). *Demographic turning points for the United States: Population projections for 2020 to 2060.* U. S. Census Bureau.

Vloet, T. D., Vloet, A., Bürger, A., & Romanos, M. (2017). Post-traumatic growth in children and adolescents. *Journal of Traumatic Stress Disorders & Treatment, 6*(2), 1–7.

Wang, K., Chen, Y., Zhang, J., & Oudekerk, B. A. (2020). *Indicators of school crime and safety: 2019.* National Center for Education Statistics, U.S. Department of Education, and Bureau of Justice Statistics, Office of Justice Programs, U.S. Department of Justice.

Wang, Q. (2005). *Disability and American families: 2000.* U.S. Census Bureau.

Werner, E. E. (1989). Vulnerability and resiliency: A longitudinal perspective. In M. Brambring, F. Lösel, &

H. Skowronek (Eds.), *Children at risk: Assessment, longitudinal research, and intervention* (pp. 158–172). Walter de Gruyter GmbH.

Williams, R., & Leahy, A. (2019). *Ranking of national higher education systems 2019.* Universitas21.

World Health Organization (WHO). (1948). *Preamble to the Constitution of the World Health Organization as adopted by the International Health Conference, New York,* June 19–22, 1946. Author.

World Health Organization (WHO). (2014). *The case for investing in public health.* https://www.euro.who.int/__data/assets/pdf_file/0009/278073/Case-Investing-Public-Health.pdf

World Health Organization (WHO). (2020). *Health promotion.* https://www.who.int/healthpromotion/healthy-settings/en/

Young, I. M. (2018). Five faces of oppression. In M. Adams, W. J. Blumenfeld, D. C. J. Catalano, K. S. DeJong, H. W. Hackman, L. E. Hopkins, B. J. Love, M. L. Peters, D. Shlasko, & X. Zuniga (Eds.), *Readings for diversity and social justice* (4th ed., pp. 49–58). Routledge.

# 2

# ANTI-POVERTY POLICIES AND PROGRAMS FOR CHILDREN AND FAMILIES

Trina R. Williams Shanks, Sandra K. Danziger, and Patrick J. Meehan

Poverty is a risk factor for many problems experienced by children and youth. Evidence from various disciplines indicates that children growing up in low-income households experience social and health conditions that place them at risk for later academic, employment, and behavioral problems (Conley, 1999; Davis-Kean, 2005; Duncan et al., 2010; Ekono et al., 2016; Guo & Harris, 2000; Hair et al., 2016; Hanson et al., 2013; McLoyd, 1998; Sampson et al., 2002; Williams Shanks & Robinson, 2013; Yoshikawa et al., 2012). Indeed, the detrimental influence of poverty is apparent in all of the substantive policy areas discussed in this book.

Children are poor because they reside in households and/or communities that are poor. Thus, a principal goal of anti-poverty policies is to break the link between poor resources of parents or caregivers and adverse child outcomes. To achieve this goal, some anti-poverty policies and programs provide material support to parents to reduce the pressures they face. Other anti-poverty initiatives offer resources and opportunities directly to children to build their personal capabilities. Evidence suggests that the specific targets of social policy should not be an "either–or" proposition or strategy. That is, studies show that it is important both to support low-income parents and to promote child well-being (Chase-Lansdale & Brooks Gunn, 2014; Haskins et al., 2014; Waldfogel, 2006; Waters Boots et al., 2008).

In this chapter, we examine risk and protective factors associated with childhood and adolescent poverty. Major income-assistance and income-maintenance policies for children and families are reviewed. Trends in anti-poverty policy are noted; particular emphasis is paid to the trends related to the COVID-19 pandemic. We note how poverty in the United States (U.S.) and American social policies aimed at ameliorating childhood poverty compare with approaches in other industrialized countries. Finally, we consider ways to improve on available options in the U.S. by making policies and programs more comprehensive and with greater integration of services to promote better outcomes for all children and families.

Sadly, the year 2020 will forever be remembered for the COVID-19 pandemic. In addition to infecting more than 6 million Americans and killing more than 200,000 in its first eight months, it has wreaked disproportional havoc on the lives of the nation's most vulnerable families. Millions of low-income children saw their lives immeasurably altered through the physical and emotional trauma of contracting COVID-19 themselves, witnessing the illness in a loved one, and loss of family income. As a society, we will be feeling the impacts on their disrupted emotional development and educational attainment for decades. The consequences of the pandemic in both the short and long run are compounded by having further exacerbated preexisting economic disparities.

## PREVALENCE AND TRENDS IN POVERTY

The debate about the best way to measure poverty is long and ongoing (Blank, 2008; Couch & Pirog, 2010). To bring some unity to the study of poverty, the U.S. Census Bureau in the 1960s established income thresholds based on before-tax cash sources to determine whether a household is officially poor. These thresholds are updated annually. As shown in Figure 2.1, child poverty rates reached a low during the late 1960s

**Figure 2.1   Child Poverty Rates in the United States by Race and Ethnicity, 1960–2018**

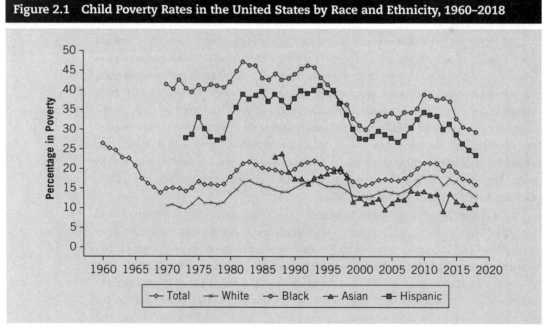

*Source:* U.S. Census Bureau (2020a). https://www.census.gov/data/tables/time-series/demo/income-poverty/historical-poverty-people.html

to early 1970s. Since then, child poverty rates have fluctuated with periodic increases and decreases. Nearly 23% of all children under the age of 18 lived in poverty in 1993; child poverty declined between 1993 and 2002, increased through the Great Recession, then began to decrease again. In 2018, 16.2% of children lived in poverty and, according to the new census report on 2019 (Semega et al., 2020), it decreased again to 14.4% due to lower unemployment rates. But several reports estimate that these gains will have been wiped out by the pandemic in 2020 (see for example, Parolin & Wimer, 2020).

The average poverty rate hides considerable variation by race and ethnicity, as shown in Figure 2.1. Although rates have gone down in the past decade, Black and Hispanic children continue to be twice as likely to be poor compared with Asian and non-Hispanic White children. As shown in Figure 2.2, children residing in female-headed households experience poverty at four times the rate of all other households. These poverty disparities remain high amidst declining child poverty overall.

The 2020 growth of poverty and hardship due to the pandemic has shown steep rises, particularly among families of color. A report by Saenz and Sherman (2020) uses census data to find that from February to May 2020, the number of White children in families with below-poverty earnings rose 17%; for Black children, 27%; and for Hispanic/Latinx children, 29%. Worse yet, the percentage of children living with no earnings rose 30% for Whites, 29% for Blacks, and 58% for Hispanics.

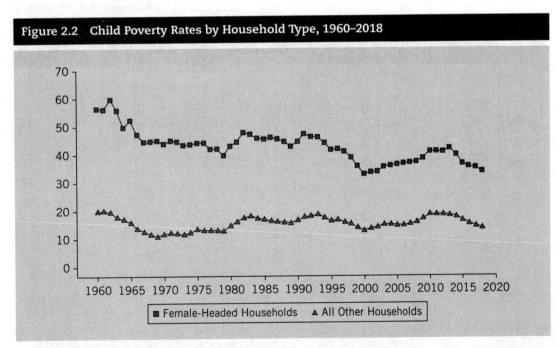

Figure 2.2   Child Poverty Rates by Household Type, 1960–2018

*Source:* U.S. Census Bureau (2020b). https://www.census.gov/data/tables/time-series/demo/income-poverty/historical-poverty-people.html

In spite of the widespread use of the Census Bureau definition and its use of the new Supplemental Poverty measure (Fox, 2018), the measurement of poverty continues to be debated. Critics charge that most surveys that measure income flows into a household miss an important aspect of a household's financial situation because they fail to consider family assets. For example, a family with housing equity, savings, and investments is in a better situation and has more favorable long-term prospects than a family of equal income but no assets. Although there is no official approach to measuring assets, researchers typically calculate assets by using household net worth (Brandolini et al., 2010; Haveman & Wolff, 2004; Shapiro et al., 2009).

Data reflecting household net worth reveal that racial and ethnic disparities in assets are even greater than disparities in income (Lui et al., 2006; Oliver & Shapiro, 1995; Shapiro, 2004; Sullivan et al., 2015). As shown in Figure 2.3, Black and Hispanic/Latinx households at times own about a tenth, respectively, of the median net worth of White households. Although most households faced declines in net worth after the recession of 2007 to 2009, White households have experienced a more rapid increase in net worth since 2013, exacerbating the inequality with Black and Hispanic/Latinx households. Furthermore, as depicted in Figure 2.4, households with children have the lowest levels of net worth. Couples with no children have the most wealth, followed by couples with children, followed by single-parent households with children at a distant third. These households have experienced almost no increase in wealth in the last decade.

The situation is even worse when considering financial net worth, which excludes home equity and the value of vehicles. As many as 63% of families with children are

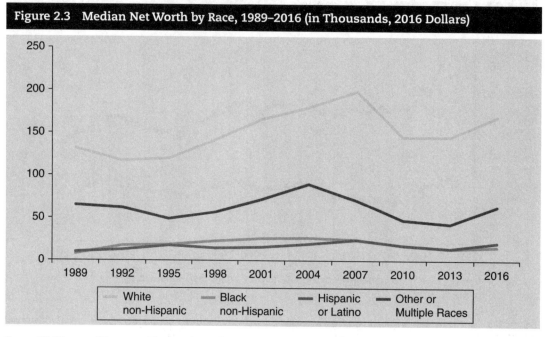

**Figure 2.3  Median Net Worth by Race, 1989–2016 (in Thousands, 2016 Dollars)**

Legend: White non-Hispanic; Black non-Hispanic; Hispanic or Latino; Other or Multiple Races

Source: 2016 Survey of Consumer Finances. https://www.federalreserve.gov/econres/scfindex.htm

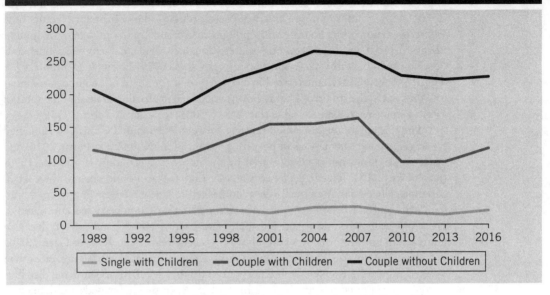

**Figure 2.4  Median Net Worth by Household Types, 1989–2016 (in Thousands, 2016 Dollars)**

— Single with Children    — Couple with Children    — Couple without Children

*Source:* 2016 Survey of Consumer Finances. https://www.federalreserve.gov/econres/scfindex.htm

asset-poor according to this measure, meaning that they lack sufficient financial assets to sustain the household at the poverty line for three months (Rothwell et al., 2019). In fact, female-headed households with children had asset poverty rates as high as 77% in 2007 (Aratini & Chau, 2010).

For a brief moment, it appeared the coronavirus pandemic was reversing these trends. With much of the economy shut down during the spring of 2020, Americans saved money at greater rates than they had in decades (Fitzgerald, 2020). Survey data in the midst of the pandemic suggested a plurality of Americans planned to save more in an emergency fund going forward and to spend less on nonessentials (El Issa, 2020). Of course, much of the saving behavior was in response to job loss or sharply reduced incomes. Many low-income households, but especially those of color, were late with rent or mortgage payments during the pandemic (Ricketts, 2020). Existing inequality exacerbated the extent of the pandemic in the U.S. by making it more difficult for low-income workers to take time off or work from home to avoid exposure (Boushey & Park, 2020).

Another way to think about poverty is at the neighborhood or community level. *Neighborhood poverty* refers to the spatial concentration of poor households in neighborhoods, which are measured by census tracts. Generally, a poor neighborhood is one in which 20% to 40% of residents live below the poverty line. The concentration of the poor in high-poverty census tracts in the U.S. increased dramatically between 1970 and 1990 (Jargowsky, 2013).

In the early period, the growing concentration of poverty resulted from two main macroeconomic changes. First, a decline in manufacturing markets negatively impacted inner cities and resulted in an increase in urban poverty rates. Second, consistent with a systems of oppression perspective (discussed in Chapter 1), factors such as discrimination in the housing and lending markets and rapid suburban development increased racial and socioeconomic segregation such that inner-city neighborhoods became predominantly Black and poor (Jargowsky, 1997; Massey & Denton, 1993). The 1990s were also characterized by an increase in the share of neighborhood poverty that was in the suburbs. That is, poverty declined in all other areas, but the rates of suburban poverty remained stable (Jargowsky, 2003; Kingsley & Pettit, 2016).

The decline in neighborhood poverty between 1990 and 2000 may be explained by neighborhood fluctuations in poverty concentration (Kingsley & Pettit, 2016) and by decreases in overall poverty caused by the improving economy of the late 1990s (Jargowsky, 2003). Recent evidence suggests that the economic decline since 2000 and especially during the Great Recession has led to a new increase in poverty—both nationally and in isolated neighborhood settings. Suburban poverty has continued to grow, especially in western and Sun Belt states, and neighborhood poverty has also increased in midwestern cities and suburbs in recent years (Kneebone & Garr, 2010).

People of color experience community-level poverty at much higher rates than Whites. Figure 2.5 is taken from Kneebone and Holmes (2016) to show the distribution of concentrated poverty by race in the U.S. Such neighborhoods are defined as having a poverty rate of 40% or more. More than one quarter of African Americans

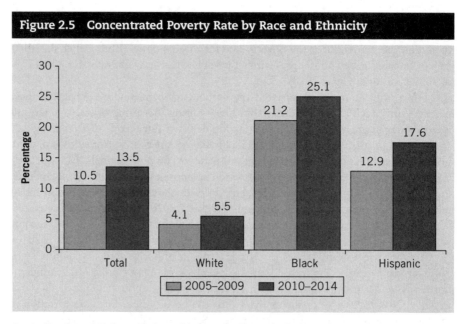

Figure 2.5  Concentrated Poverty Rate by Race and Ethnicity

*Source:* (Kneebone & Holmes, 2016), Brookings Institution analysis of American Community Survey data

live in such neighborhoods. This disparity is even greater among children (Jargowsky, 2003; Sharkey, 2009). Only 1% of White children born between 1955 and 1970 lived in poor neighborhoods, whereas 29% of Black children born during this time lived in poor neighborhoods at some point in their childhood. About 31% of Black children born between 1985 and 2000 experienced neighborhood poverty (Sharkey, 2009). Inequality and poverty in neighborhood contexts for children expose them to serious risks that often compromise normal and healthy development.

## POVERTY, RISK, AND PROTECTION

There are many frameworks theorizing how poverty is related to child outcomes and why low-income youth have worse outcomes than their nonpoor peers. The person-in-environment risk and resilience framework (discussed in Chapter 1) considers the interpersonal and other environmental factors that influence a child in increasingly wider spheres as well as the interactions between the spheres of influence. The communities and institutions that a child interacts with on a regular basis as well as the policies and cultural ideologies that shape them establish the foundation for who the child evolves to become over time.

The mechanisms through which environmental factors associated with poverty and economic inequality influence child outcomes can be complex. Figure 2.6 shares a framework developed by Williams Shanks and Robinson (2013) on how various socio-economic factors interact to influence child-level outcomes. The model begins with the wider cultural and societal context. There are predictable ways that race, ethnicity, gender dynamics, and family formation intersect with structural barriers and institutional norms to expand or limit the likelihood of attaining family-sustaining levels of income, wealth, and education.

Economic resources then shape household-level relationships such as parental involvement and behavior and, even more directly, the degree of economic stress and material hardship experienced within the home. Simultaneously, economic resources influence residential stability and the type of neighborhood in which a child resides. It could be one with high-quality schools and an array of community resources or a situation where the child feels unsafe and experiences multiple traumas. All of these elements combine systematically to influence child outcomes and delimit the likelihood that caring adults are present to mitigate any negative circumstances that arise.

### Interpersonal and Social Risk Factors

Family economic security is a necessary foundation for promoting emotionally responsive parent–child relationships and child well-being. Families living in poverty and struggling to make ends meet will have a more difficult time developing strong bonds with their infants and children because they must also deal with the daily stresses of trying to support basic needs. This includes not only having employment pathways but also economic assets to rely on when times are challenging.

**Figure 2.6 Neighborhood/Community Factors and Systemic Factors**

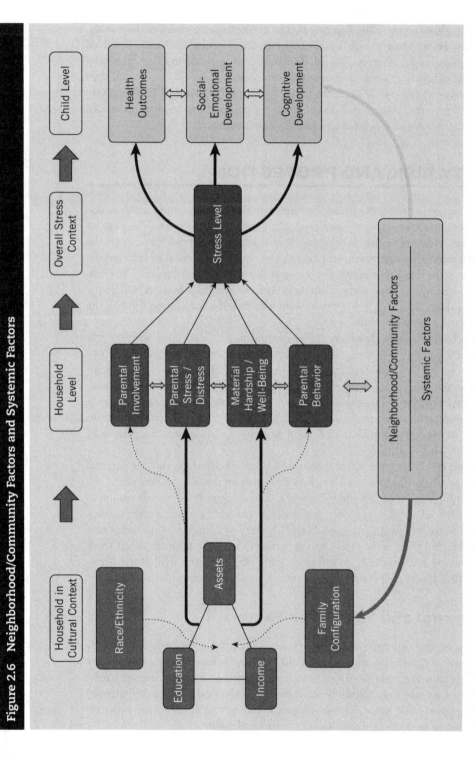

*Source:* Shanks, T. R. & Robinson, C. (2013)2. Assets, economic opportunity and toxic stress: A framework for understanding child and educational outcomes. *Economics of Education Review.*

Although there are many gaps in public programs, states, counties, and other entities often have opportunities to exercise discretion in the implementation of social policies and, as a result, to experiment with new ways to support parent–child relationships among low-income families receiving public assistance. For example, the federal Temporary Assistance for Needy Families (TANF) program gives states the option to exempt single parents from work requirements for up to 12 months if they have a child under the age of 1 (Schott & Pavetti, 2013). Many states have adopted this provision in the TANF program, but wide variability across states exists in the number of months that new parents are provided exemptions. In Michigan, for example, TANF cash assistance recipients are given a two-month exemption period after the birth of a child. In 2018, the variation across states was between 0 and 12 months, according to the Welfare Rules Database (Urban Institute, 2020).

Clearly, the parent–infant bonding period in those first days and months lays the groundwork for a strong parent–child relationship and child development and well-being. Federal TANF policy could improve its support of the parent–infant relationship by mandating that states provide a minimum number of months of work exemption after the birth of a baby. Above and beyond these regulations, federal law could require that states offer an evidenced-informed home-visiting service to families, one that includes infant mental health support for optimal outcomes (Condon, 2019). Similarly, workforce development agencies could consider policies to better support the parent–infant relationship that looks at pairing workforce skill-building opportunities with services that promote the parent–child relationship and child well-being. A 2016 federal report offered guidelines to states for how they might strengthen family support services for TANF families (strengthening TANF outcomes by developing two-generation approaches to building economic security, TANF-ACF-IM-2016-03).

Evidence for the need for such linkages has emerged in recent years. For example, using a nationally representative longitudinal household survey, Shaefer and colleagues (2018) replicated the adverse childhood experiences (ACEs) studies conducted largely with patient records. By linking detailed early family income measures with retrospective reports of early family circumstances and adult well-being, they found that (a) ACE exposure is negatively correlated with childhood income so that higher income in childhood reduces the likelihood of a child experiencing such events as physical abuse, domestic violence, parental depression, and drug violence; (b) exposure to both low income and ACEs exert independent effects on adult socioeconomic and health outcomes; and (c) higher income in childhood may dampen the relationship between exposure to ACEs and some long-term outcomes, including educational attainment, arrest, lung disease, and possibly poverty and smoking. The study concluded that combining early childhood anti-poverty policies together with early intervention family support/infant mental health policies could strengthen long-term human capital and promote overall child well-being.

During the COVID-19 pandemic, low-income children were at greater risk of infection (Goyal et al., 2020), and they were more likely to have had family members die (Drayton, 2020). Cabildo, Graves, Kim, and Russo (2020), for example, found that in Los Angeles, neighborhoods with a higher percentage of residents under 200% of poverty had 3.2 times as many COVID-19 infections as neighborhoods with a lower percentage of residents in poverty. Given that familial death and disease are traumatic experiences, the developmental consequences of the COVID-19 pandemic may be particularly harmful for a generation of low-income children.

## Environmental Risks

In now-classic studies, Wilson (1987, 2009) found that concentrated neighborhood poverty isolates poor residents and limits their exposure to positive role models, employment networks, and community resources. A large body of research has examined the direct and indirect effects of neighborhood poverty on child and adolescent outcomes (Harding, 2003; Hart et al., 2008; Kling et al., 2005; Leventhal & Brooks-Gunn, 2000; Pachter et al., 2006). Many investigators have emphasized the significant and adverse effects of limited local resources and opportunities on children's development. Poor neighborhoods tend to lack quality institutions and social services (Leventhal & Brooks-Gunn, 2000; Sampson et al., 2002). Children growing up in poor neighborhoods witness frequent acts of violence and experience considerable chaos, disorder, and isolation. In such communities, parental stress and a lack of support services negatively affect developmental outcomes in children and youth (Klebanov et al., 1994; Kohen et al., 2008; McLoyd, 1998; Patton et al., 2012; Williams Shanks & Robinson, 2013).

Much research has documented the escalating trend in mass incarceration and its unequal impacts on poor communities and especially on urban communities of color. Loury (2010), for example, noted the "ubiquity" of the impact of criminal justice practices and policies on the incarceration of low-income men, reporting that in some neighborhoods, 1 in 5 adult men may be behind bars on any given day. According to Clear (2009), having so many young men go in and out of jails and prisons is "a central factor determining the social ecology of poor neighborhoods" (p. 10). Research has attempted to disentangle the effects of parental incarceration from the effects of other family and community risk factors in terms of the impact on children (e.g., Wildeman & Turney, 2014; Wildeman & Western, 2010). According to a 2017 National Institute of Justice report, "children whose parents are involved in the criminal justice system, in particular, face a host of challenges and difficulties: psychological strain, antisocial behavior, suspension or expulsion from school, economic hardship, and criminal activity" (Martin, 2017, p. 1). The impacts of disproportionate incarceration are widely felt at the neighborhood, school, and community levels and should be considered when mapping strategies for the implementation of social policies for children, youth, and families.

The causal impact of neighborhood economic quality on long-term child outcomes has been powerfully demonstrated in the recent work of economist Raj Chetty and colleagues (Chetty, n. d.; Chetty et al., 2014; Chetty et al., 2016). By examining the tax records of adults who moved across counties during childhood, they find that the areas in which children grow up affect their prospects for long-term economic mobility, including income, college attendance, and the prospects of teen pregnancy. The characteristics of neighborhoods that have higher rates of upward economic mobility include less segregation by race and income, lower levels of income inequality, better schools, lower rates of crime, and a larger share of two-parent households. Chetty and colleagues (2014) argue for policies to help move families to better neighborhoods and policies to reduce segregation and concentrated poverty.

# ANTI-POVERTY POLICIES AND PROGRAMS

The U.S. has never instituted a comprehensive federal response to child poverty. In fact, no federal role in cash aid to poor children and families existed prior to 1935; only assistance from state, local, and private charities was available. Even today, with an array of federal anti-poverty programs, no policy or program reaches everyone who is eligible, and typically, no priority is given to social development or economic mobility (Williams Shanks, 2014). Although critically important to child well-being, we exclude health insurance, medical care, and educational programs because these topics are covered in other chapters. Table 2.1 provides an overview of some of the major federal programs that offer support for the basic needs of low-income children; participation levels in the major anti-poverty programs between 1960 and 2018 are shown in Figure 2.7.

A helpful way of contextualizing America's commitment to low-income children and families is to understand the difference between federal entitlement programs and those that are at the discretion of state governments. Entitlement programs "require payments to any person . . . that meets the eligibility criteria established by law" (U.S. Senate, n. d.). Moreover, "entitlements constitute a binding obligation on the part of the Federal Government, and eligible recipients have legal recourse if the obligation is not fulfilled." Entitlements thus represent a strong, open-ended commitment to eligible recipients. Who deserves to be an eligible recipient of an open-ended entitlement is contested, and over the decades, there have been many attempts to eliminate or chip away at entitlements in favor of greater devolution and discretion to state governments.

The first federal welfare program, Aid to Dependent Children (ADC), was an open-ended entitlement to low-income mothers with children. Included in the 1935 Social Security Act, the name of the program changed at midcentury to Aid to Families with Dependent Children (AFDC). Participation peaked at 15 million in 1994 amidst backlash toward so-called "welfare queens" and racial stigma directed at beneficiaries. The Personal Responsibility and Work Opportunity Reconciliation Act (PRWORA, Public Law No. 104-93), signed by President Clinton in August 1996, ended AFDC's 60-year history of open-ended entitlement of income support to low-income children and families. Compared with AFDC, the new TANF plays a smaller role as a resource for families.

Several rules restrict participation in TANF, including lifetime time limits for receipt of benefits and, although states are afforded some options for implementation, a mandatory work requirement. States are required to impose sanctions in the form of benefit reduction or case closure to families who do not comply with requirements. States can implement diversion programs to deter or deflect applicants from entering the program (e.g., providing a one-time lump-sum payment to families who agree not to seek cash benefits for a set period of time). TANF disallows parents with a drug felony conviction from receiving benefits, and it requires teenage parents under the age of 18 to live with an adult and attend school as a condition of receiving benefits. New legal immigrants

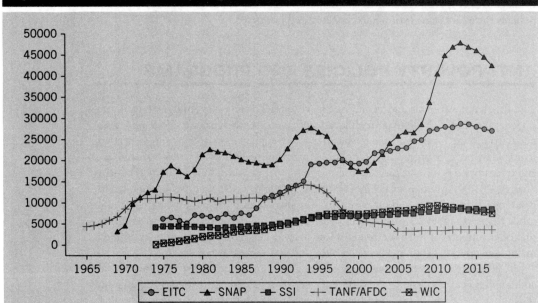

**Figure 2.7   Federal Anti-Poverty Program Participation, 1965 to 2018**

EITC   SNAP   SSI   TANF/AFDC   WIC

*Note:* EITC refers to the Earned Income Tax Credit; SNAP refers to the Supplemental Nutrition Assistance Program; TANF/AFDC refers to Temporary Assistance for Needy Families/Aid to Families with Dependent Children; WIC refers to Women, Infants, and Children.

*Sources:* U.S. Department of Agriculture (2020b). https://www.fns.usda.gov/pd/supplemental-nutrition-assistance-program-snap. U.S. Department of Agriculture (2020a). https://www.fns.usda.gov/pd/wic-program. Internal Revenue Service (2020c). http://www.irs.gov/uac/SOI-Tax-Stats-Historical-Table-1. Internal Revenue Service (2020d). https://www.irs.gov/statistics/soi-tax-stats-individual-statistical-tables-by-size-of-adjusted-gross-income. Social Security Administration (2019a). https://www.ssa.gov/policy/docs/statcomps/supplement/2018/. U.S. Department of Health and Human Services (2019a). https://www.acf.hhs.gov/ofa/resource/tanf-and-afdc-historical-case-data-pre-2012. U.S. Department of Health and Human Services (2019c). https://www.acf.hhs.gov/ofa/resource/tanf-caseload-data-1996-2012.

are not allowed to receive means-tested public benefits, including TANF, for the first five years after entry, according to testimony from Michael Fix of the Migration Policy Institute to the U.S. House Committee on Ways and Means (Fix, 2006).

Neither the critics' dire predictions of increased child poverty nor the proponents' rosy forecasts that children would directly benefit from seeing their mothers take jobs came true in the first decade after the 1996 welfare reform (Danziger, 2010). Studies did not find that welfare leavers had improvements in terms of stress levels and mental health status as they exited the rolls nor did the lives of children improve as a result of welfare reform and increases in the employment of mothers (Danziger, 2010; Edin & Kissane, 2010).

The proportion of families with children in poverty who received benefits fell from 81.6% in 1995 (before the 1996 reform) to 16.8% in 2007 (before the Great Recession;

Congressional Research Service, 2019). As shown in Figure 2.7, the rolls did not rise during or after the recession, despite rising poverty rates. Administrative data from September 2019 indicate that the average number of children in receipt of TANF benefits per month was 1.6 million (Congressional Research Service, 2020). In that year, according to the census poverty report, 10.5 million people aged 18 and under were poor.

In addition, the value of TANF benefits have fallen in inflation-adjusted terms since 1996 (Center on Budget and Policy Priorities, 2020). In 2018, the maximum monthly benefit for a parent with two children ranged from $170 in Mississippi to $1,039 in New Hampshire (Congressional Research Service, 2020). By 2020, in a median state, a family of three received $486 per month (Safawi & Floyd, 2020).

Normatively, AFDC's transition to TANF signaled that low-income families and children were not deserving of an open-ended entitlement to income support. The only other program that offers a cash entitlement to low-income children and families is Supplemental Security Income (SSI). Children under 18 years of age who are blind or have a severe physical or mental impairment are eligible to receive SSI benefits. In 2020, the average monthly benefit for a disabled child was $783 (Social Security Administration, 2020). Recent participation among eligible children has receded from the 2013 high of 1.3 million. Importantly, many children and families experience long delays in the application and review process (U.S. Government Accountability Office, 2009).

The Supplemental Nutrition Assistance Program (SNAP; H.R. 2419, the Food, Conservation, and Energy Act of 2008) is an entitlement of a different sort. SNAP provides food assistance in the form of electronic benefits transfer (EBT) cards, which function as debit cards at retail grocery stores. This in-kind form of support supplements a recipient's income but cannot be converted to cash and can only be used on eligible products. Notably, SNAP does not cover feminine hygiene products or diapers. The average monthly per-person benefit in 2019 was $130 (Food and Nutrition Service, 2020a). The maximum monthly benefit for a family with two adults and three children in 2020 was $768. As shown in Figure 2.7, the rate of participation in SNAP rose dramatically from 2000 to 2013, when it peaked at 47.6 million. However, only 37.9% of low-income (< 185% poverty level) children experiencing food insecurity receive SNAP. In 2020, the monthly number of households receiving SNAP went from 18.8 million in February (before the pandemic) to 22.2 million in April during the height of the first wave of COVID-19 infections (Food and Nutrition Service, 2020b).

The Special Supplemental Nutrition Program for Women, Infants, and Children (WIC) is a federal food-support program for low-income pregnant and postpartum women and their young children (U.S. Department of Agriculture, 2020a). However, states administer WIC and set their own eligibility requirements. Rather than an open-ended entitlement, states provide benefits to individuals through a limited block grant at their discretion. Similar to SNAP, participation in WIC peaked in 2013 at 9.1 million.

An increasingly important addition to anti-poverty efforts is the Earned Income Tax Credit (EITC), a refundable tax credit to low-income workers and their families. In 2019, 25 million families received income support through the federal EITC, down from a recent peak of 28.8 million in 2013. It is estimated that the program lifts 2.5 million children with working parents out of poverty each year (U.S. Department of the Treasury, n. d.-a). For a single person with three or more dependent children, the maximum benefit was $6,660 in 2020 (Internal Revenue Service, 2020a). The maximum allowable income to receive any benefit is $56,844 (married filing jointly with three children or more), which is more than 200% of the federal poverty line. Some states and localities also have tax credits for working low-income families that supplement this program (Purmort, 2010). As Figure 2.7 shows, the number of households receiving the EITC began to exceed TANF participation in the early 1990s, when EITC federal policy expanded. EITC has now outstripped TANF as a source of income support, but it only is available for children with employed parents. Moreover, the 2017 Tax Cuts and Jobs Act changed how the rate of inflation was calculated so that credit increases grow at a slower rate than in previous years (Tax Policy Center, 2020).

The 1996 PRWORA expanded and consolidated federal funding for childcare for employed parents into the Child Care and Development Block Grant (CCDBG). Under this act, states are provided flexibility in determining income and work eligibility, structuring the voucher program, and determining which types and standards of care will be reimbursed at what rates. There is consistent evidence that subsidies facilitate employment of low-income and welfare recipient families (Bainbridge et al., 2003; Blau & Tekin, 2007; Danziger et al., 2004; Meyers et al., 2002; Press et al., 2006). Between 1997 and 2006, public funding for CCDBG more than doubled from $3.7 billion to $9 billion (U.S. House of Representatives, 2018). In 2018, 1.3 million children in 800,000 families received childcare vouchers. This was down from the 2001 peak of 1.8 million children in 1 million families. Although the majority of low-income families rely on childcare that is developmentally inadequate or minimally adequate (Levine Coley et al., 2006; Ryan et al., 2011), this is due in part to the low availability of high-quality care in low-income communities. It is also unclear whether subsidy receipt leads to higher-quality care (Antle et al., 2008; Ryan et al., 2011). Subsidies could be structured to promote use of higher-quality care, but the issue of greatest priority is access, as only 1 in 7 eligible children receive this assistance (Giannarelli et al., 2019). Even worse, since the pandemic caused widespread closure of childcare facilities and schools and high levels of unemployment (that disqualify parents from receiving subsidies), the need for out-of-home early care and education in low-income families is dire.

The federal government also supports the employment of youth and adults through training and education programs designed to ensure that participants are job ready. Although job-training programs were originally designed to assist dislocated workers, they became a part of federal anti-poverty strategies by the 1960s (LaLonde, 1995). Just as PRWORA shifted the focus of welfare toward "work first," the approach of job-training programs has also shifted toward employment. The Workforce Investment Act (WIA) of 1998 was enacted to replace the Job Training Partnership Act (JTPA), with an emphasis on job placement before training or education (Holzer, 2008). With the changes from the JTPA to WIA, substantially fewer low-income youth and adults received training. About 95% of program leavers (i.e., those whom local agencies recorded as having completed or exited the program) reported receiving some form of job training in JTPA compared to 68.4% of exiters from WIA in 2003 (Frank & Minoff, 2005). The Workforce Innovation and Opportunity Act (WIOA) of 2014 replaced WIA, but it did not appropriate funding to maintain training and education at existing levels. Since a peak of $24 billion in the 1970s (in constant 2017 dollars), funding for job training and education has been reduced to $5 billion a year (Cielinski, 2017).

Children and families are not "entitled" to housing in the United States. Eviction and homelessness are common for many low-income families, particularly in urban centers, where rent can often constitute more than half of a household's income (Schuetz, 2020). What federal housing assistance there is comes through the U.S. Department of Housing and Urban Development (HUD). It is administered by local housing authorities, and it takes two main forms: (1) Section 8 housing vouchers for private units and (2) subsidized public housing units. Neither is an entitlement, and both programs serve a small fraction of low-income renters. Both have long waiting lists of families who have applied for assistance. About half of those served in these programs are families with children. Moreover, 5.6 million eligible households with children experience serious housing needs (Turner & Kingsley, 2008). The character of public housing in the U.S. has been changing in the last 20 years as a result of efforts such as Moving to Opportunity (MTO), an initiative to disperse concentrated neighborhood poverty. However, dispersing low-income households has done little to stem the tide of eviction, which has become a way of business in America's urban centers (Desmond, 2017). The COVID-19 pandemic paused evictions for most of the U.S., at least for most of 2020, but most renters' missed payments were not forgiven, leaving them with large debt burdens (Desmond, 2020). And, even before the pandemic, homelessness among families and children has been rising in recent decades (Child Trends, 2019).

Finally, in 1998, the Assets for Independence Act (AFIA) was enacted and funded with $125 million over five years. Annual appropriations for the program from 1999 through 2016 ranged between $10 million and $25 million. The Assets for Independence (AFI) program provided federal funding to support Individual Development Account (IDA) programs at the community level. Paired with local match funding, the program offered incentives for those earning below 200% of the federal poverty line to save for a home, pursue higher education, or capitalize a small business. No funds have been appropriated for the AFI since fiscal year 2017. This is unfortunate, given that it was one of the few sources of federal funding to help low- to moderate-income households build wealth and improve their long-term economic conditions (U.S. Department of Health and Human Services, 2010, 2018; Williams Shanks, 2014).

## American Rescue Plan Act of 2021

The Biden administration's initial signature legislation addresses several of the policy gaps that we have highlighted in this chapter. It also moves toward implementation of many of the recommendations to reduce child poverty in the 2019 National Academy report.

On March 11, 2021, President Joseph R. Biden Jr. signed the American Rescue Plan Act (ARPA) of 2021. This historic legislation greatly expanded the federal safety net for children and families. Among the act's provisions are the following:

- Direct payments of $1,400 for individuals making less than $75,000 a year and for married couples earning under $150,000 (Sprunt, 2021)

- Changes to the Child Tax Credit (Picchi, 2021)
  - The act increases the credit from $2,000 to $3,000 for children between the ages of 6 and 17 and to $3,600 for children under 6 years of age. The credit is for each child in the household.
  - Moreover, the act provides for the credit to be paid out monthly from July to December and the remainder as a tax refund.
  - The act also makes this credit available to households that have no federal tax liability (what is known as a *refundable tax credit*).
- A 15% increase to SNAP benefits and $1.3 billion in additional WIC benefits (Winston & Strawn, 2021)
- Emergency rental assistance, including $5 billion for emergency housing vouchers (Sprunt, 2021)
- $39 billion for childcare benefits (Winston & Strawn, 2021)
- $300 per week of unemployment insurance benefits until September 6, 2021 (Winston & Strawn, 2021)

According to analysis by the Urban Institute (Wheaton et al., 2021), it is anticipated that the act will reduce child poverty by more than half. Importantly, the act will also reduce racial disparities in poverty. Relative to white non-Hispanic individuals, the act will reduce poverty by 42% for Black individuals and 39% for Hispanic individuals, respectively.

The act's passage represents one of the most significant expansions of federal anti-poverty policy since the Great Society of the 1960s. The expanded child tax credit, for example, serves as a form of child allowance, a policy that has been suggested for decades as a way to reduce child poverty (Kuttner, 2021).

Following the COVID-19 pandemic, there appears to be greater willingness to use federal policy to address poverty and historical inequities. This may suggest that the decades of policy retrenchment to state governments has ebbed (Tankersley & DeParle, 2021). The act follows massive federal spending under the Trump administration that may have prevented more severe economic impacts on vulnerable children and families (Casselman, 2021). One caveat is that most of these benefits in the ARPA are temporary. It will be important to monitor whether there is support for making some of the child-focused benefits (such as the monthly Child Tax Credit) permanent.

# COMPARING THE UNITED STATES TO OTHER INDUSTRIALIZED COUNTRIES

Another way to think about the degree to which social policy assists children and families is to compare child poverty in the United States with that in other industrialized countries. The U.S. child poverty rate is higher than all other developed nations. Indeed, it has been four times higher than rates in European countries, such as Norway and Sweden (Lindsey, 2004; Smeeding & Thévenot, 2016). The low child poverty rates in these other nations are achieved through a combination of market earnings and a large proportion of children being lifted from poverty through government policies (Smeeding & Thévenot, 2016). Among peer English-speaking countries, the U.S. falls in the middle when considering family market earnings alone. However, when social insurance benefits and universal benefits such as child allowances as well as other tax credits and transfers are taken into consideration, the U.S. does not lift a similarly high proportion of households out of poverty as Ireland, the United Kingdom, Australia, and Canada—and does an even worse job of lifting children out of deep poverty (National Academies of Sciences, Engineering, and Medicine, 2019).

In sum, a variety of disparate anti-poverty programs in the U.S. provide assistance through cash, food support, tax credits, childcare, workforce development, and housing. Most of these programs are at the discretion of state governments, and low-income children and families are not entitled to housing, childcare, workforce training, or income support. Moreover, many eligible low-income at-risk families are not served, and programs in most states are not integrated with marketplace employment. In some cases, for example, mothers with work requirements may be able to increase earnings through employment. But subsequently, they risk losing eligibility for other forms of assistance, resulting in little aggregate benefit in terms of poverty status (Currie, 2006). There are many gaps in the existing safety net, particularly when viewed from the broader goal of improving outcomes for all children and youth.

## Impacts of Recent Economic Shocks and Policy Responses: The Great Recession to the COVID-19 Pandemic

**BOX 2.1**

### Increased Exposure to Poverty, Unemployment, and Hardship

Before 2020, the Great Recession of 2007 to 2009 was the most severe economic crisis in the United States since the 1930s. Lasting 18 to 24 months, it reduced incomes by an average of 8%, the number of jobs declined by 6%, and unemployment peaked at 10% (Danziger, 2013). Housing and stock prices collapsed, creating widespread residential instability, declining wealth, and wider racial and ethnic disparities

in income. According to the Bureau of Labor Statistics (2020), the percentage of parents with children age 18 or under who were employed (i.e., the employment: population ratio) fell from 79% in 2001 to 74% in 2010; it recovered to only 75% by 2013.

Estimates of extreme poverty among households with children since the Great Recession have been even more alarming. Shaefer and Edin (2013) found a significant increase in families with children living on $2 a day per person

*(Continued)*

(Continued)

or less. The authors reported that by "mid-2011, 1.65 million households with 3.55 million children were living in extreme poverty in a given month . . . constituting 4.3% of all nonelderly households with children" (p. 265). This reflects a 159% increase since 1996, but, when taking into consideration the receipt of public food assistance, housing subsidies, and tax credits, the growth in extreme poverty since 2007 has been 50%. Shaefer and Edin (2013) argued that the disappearance of the cash safety net, slow economic growth during the 2000s, and major job losses of the Great Recession contributed to the growing population of children who experience spells of little to no family income.

Poverty and hardship due to the 2020 COVID-19 pandemic grew steeply, particularly among families of color. The economic fallout across the nation was observed at levels unseen since the Great Depression of the 1930s. Unemployment rates grew from 4.4% in March 2020 to a peak of 14.7% in April and then fell only to 10.2% by July 2020 (Bureau of Labor Statistics, 2020). A report by Saenz and Sherman (2020) used census data and found that from February to May 2020, the number of White children in families with below-poverty earnings rose 17%; for Black children, 27%; and for Hispanic/Latinx children, 29%. Worse yet, the percentage of children living with no earnings rose 30% for Whites, 29% for Blacks, and 58% for Hispanics.

## Family Effects of Economic Crises

Many studies documented effects of the Great Recession on family economic loss, material hardship and stress, and parent and child well-being (e.g., Ananat et al., 2013; Leininger & Kalil, 2014). Sudden and large drops in income, home foreclosures, and housing instability increased debt and spending cutbacks after the Great Recession. Many indicators of child well-being, from health to child behavior to cognitive skills, were adversely affected by these economic shocks. Furthermore, parents with severe economic loss and instability tend to live in poor and jobless communities characterized by low-quality early childhood education and inadequate public schools. The combination of low income, difficult living conditions, and poor-quality education significantly increases risk for adverse outcomes during childhood and adolescence.

Family effects of the pandemic, particularly for low-income families, were well documented. For example, Ananat and Gassman-Pines (2020) monitored hourly service workers with a young child in a large U.S. city. By the end of March 2020, work hours fell precipitously, as did income. For over one third of the families, income fell by more than half and 41% of the workers lost their jobs. The mental health of the parents and children deteriorated quickly. Few of the families had access to resources such as unemployment insurance, emergency food, or childcare services. They were worried about paying rent and buying groceries in the next few months.

Studies have noted that economic hardship and shocks are especially harmful during infancy. Johnson and Schoeni (2011) used national longitudinal survey data to analyze the impact of early life experiences on later behavior. They found that poor health at birth *and* limited parental resources (including low income, lack of health insurance, and unwanted pregnancy) interfered with cognitive development and health outcomes in childhood, led to reduced educational attainment during adolescence, and led to worse labor market and health outcomes in adulthood.

Studies of the Great Recession have also raised long-term warning signs. Ananat and colleagues (2013) found that variation in a state's job losses among adults were related to the state's average student math scores. This relationship was strong even when the findings for students whose parents lost jobs were compared with those for students whose parents remained employed. The authors showed that the Great Recession affected all students in impoverished geographic areas, not only those whose parents had lost jobs. Children were also affected by job losses among family friends and neighbors and by resulting changes to their communities and classrooms.

## Stimulus Policies, Economic Safety Nets, and Impacts for Families

Research also illustrates the positive impacts of having economic safety nets before and/or during economic crises. For example, Short (2013) found that 18% of children who were 18 years of age or younger were poor in 2010. She estimated that this rate would have increased by four percentage points had the EITC not been in place at the time. Short also suggested that food assistance through SNAP, housing subsidies, and school lunch participation reduced poverty by several percentage points. She concluded that poverty would decline if more people had access to anti-poverty programs.

Analysts from the Center on Budget and Policy Priorities examined the effects of the expansion of safety net programs (e.g., child tax credit, EITC, food stamps, and unemployment) that were included in the American Recovery and Reinvestment Act of 2009 (ARRA; Sherman, 2011). They found that in 2011, 9 million poor children were lifted out of poverty when these benefits were considered. However, while the official child poverty rate increased from 18% to 22% during the Great Recession, evidence suggests that income from these programs helped keep this increase from being even higher. This finding suggests that the increase in child

poverty was partially offset by supports found in the ARRA. Unfortunately, these supports expired at the end of the Great Recession.

In response to COVID-19, the Coronavirus Aid, Relief, and Economic Security (CARES) Act passed in March 2020 provided for one-time economic impact payments to American households of up to $1,200 per adult for individuals whose income was less than $99,000 (or $198,000 for joint filers) and $500 per child under 17 years old—or up to $3,400 for a family of four (U.S. Department of the Treasury, n. d.-b). In addition, the CARES Act provided substantial resources for small businesses and expanded unemployment benefits in several ways. These included expansions of who was eligible for benefits and increases both in weekly benefit levels for four months (through July 2020) and in the number of weeks of jobless benefits that someone could receive (Parrott et al., 2020).

Although the one-time payment and expanded unemployment had the potential to prevent or reduce poverty, this was true only for those who qualified for and received the full set of benefits over the period when the assistance was available. This left out many families who were ineligible and many more who received partial support. It left them with months of hardship as long as unemployment remained high and the virus continued unabated (Parolin et al., 2020).

Further, as we write, the coronavirus has continued to spread across the United States, and the government has failed to pass an additional relief package that would extend unemployment benefits and family supports designed to prevent hunger, help with rent and evictions, and stave off further joblessness (Parrott et al., 2020). The impacts of COVID-19 are compellingly clear, and the situation is dire. The Center on Budget and Policy Priorities has been tracking the COVID-19 recession's effects on hardships in the Census Bureau's Household Pulse Survey.

*(Continued)*

(Continued)

As of late July 2020, the data suggested that 8 million children were living in a household that was behind on rent, and between 9 and 17 million children were living in households where children did not eat enough because they could not afford it (Stone, 2020).

According to a recent National Bureau of Economic Research report, the COVID-19 recession has been deeper and came on more rapidly than other economic crises (Bitler et al., 2020). The set of benefit expansions legislated in its first few months improved the responsiveness of the safety net and reduced suffering. However, food insecurity rates tripled and food pantry use spiked, and this increase in need was particularly high for families with children. Bitler and colleagues concluded that this extraordinarily high need was due to the relief coming too late; the relief was too modest relative to need and its coverage gaps excluded too many groups.

Many analysts have raised concerns about the sufficiency of safety net programs during difficult economic conditions. They have argued against policies that result in budget cuts to programs for families affected by economic hardships. Beyond poverty reduction, many government programs have long-term beneficial outcomes for high-risk children. For example, Almond, Hoynes, and Schanzenbach (2011) found positive long-term impacts on adult health and economic well-being for high-risk infants born in U.S. counties where the early food stamp program had begun compared with children born in areas where the federal program had not yet started. Using national longitudinal panel survey data and administrative data, Almond and colleagues found that exposure to the program before the age of 5 led to greater long-term economic self-sufficiency and lower risk for diabetes and heart disease. Findings such as these have an important implication for the provision of emergency relief in times of crisis: Cuts in safety net programs may have long-term adverse consequences for children. Moreover, expansions of emergency anti-poverty programs produce both short- and long-term positive effects on developmental outcomes for high-risk children.

# USING KNOWLEDGE OF RISK, PROTECTION, AND RESILIENCE TO ACHIEVE SERVICE INTEGRATION: POLICY INITIATIVES TO REDUCE CHILDHOOD POVERTY

Targeted income support programs for the most economically needy families have typically not been designed to focus on long-term child outcomes or to address the toxic stress of living in poverty. In this chapter, we advocate for the reform and development of poverty-alleviating strategies that include family relationship supports, address the needs of parents to balance work and family demands, and consider environmental and community disparities.

Several generations of researchers, practitioners, advocates, and policy analysts have documented the deleterious impacts of economic insecurity and poverty on child well-being. Today, we know even more now about how income deficits ripple through families and create toxic stressors or ACEs. Yet, in the U.S., our provisions of basic needs assistance are limited in the numbers of eligible people they reach and how they serve families that qualify. Benefit systems vary—across and even within states—and they rarely work in concert with one another or address the collateral consequences of poverty on children. What if we developed new social policies for basic assistance that aimed to coordinate the distribution of assistance for food, income, housing, or employment in a way that acknowledges the additional burdens and stresses on these families?

Aside from the eligibility calculations, we do very little intake, outreach, or referral designed to assess and address the risk factors affecting parents and children. Current policies provide child-related exemptions from certain work requirements and family leave guarantee requirements of certain employers, but most impoverished parents face terrible choices in applying for and participating in anti-poverty programs. These circumstances beg the question: Do U.S. social welfare policies put children's care and support first, or do they present obstacles to keep the financial help from reaching children and families most in need?

A further issue confronting many programs is that they do not reach all of those they are intended to serve. Due to funding limitations and design features (such as broad state discretion in implementation), housing, TANF, and childcare assistance reach a minority of the poor while SNAP and the EITC are utilized by many (as shown in Table 2.1). Even health care coverage, which has increased since the Affordable Care Act and State Child Health Insurance and Medicaid expansions, fails to reach many low-income children across the states.

A groundbreaking report by the National Academies of Sciences, Engineering, and Medicine Produced (2019) synthesized the effects of income on child well-being and examined several of the longstanding policy levers designed to reduce child poverty. It empirically tested a series of combined sets of policy initiatives that would reduce poverty and cost less than the long-term costs of child poverty. The recommendations included expanding the EITC, increasing the minimum wage, and expanding the housing voucher program. The report further proposed innovations to restore eligibility for SNAP, TANF, and SSI for legal immigrants and to create a child allowance and a child support assurance program. A combination of work-oriented programs and income-support programs would incentivize employment and reduce child poverty—putting the U.S. in line with other high-income countries.

Although the combination of packages with the intention of reducing child poverty is novel, many of the individual policies in the National Academies report are not new. Indeed, they have been tried in other countries and in a few specific geographic locales in the U.S. One approach that exists in at least 14 industrialized democratic countries is a universal child benefit (or allowance). The definition of a full universal child benefit (UCB) is "a cash payment or tax transfer made on a regular basis to children, independently of their socioeconomic or other characteristics"

**Table 2.1   Characteristics of Current Federal Anti-Poverty Programs**

| Program | When Began | Participation | Percentage of Eligible Served | Eligibility | Purpose (and Site for Further Information) | Discretionary/ Entitlement |
|---|---|---|---|---|---|---|
| Subsidized Housing | 1937 | 1.9 million[a] | 21%[b] | Very low-income families; income limits vary based on housing authority area | Subsidized housing units are located in buildings that are publicly managed (i.e., public housing) or privately owned and managed under government contracts https://www.hud.gov/sites/dfiles/Main/documents/HUDPrograms2018.pdf | Discretionary |
| Supplemental Nutrition Assistance Program (SNAP) | 1964 | 35.7 million people[c] | 84%[d] | Gross monthly income < 130% federal poverty level (FPL); net monthly income <100% FPL | Provides poor families with assistance in purchasing food they need http://www.fns.usda.gov/snap | Entitlement |
| Women, Infants, and Children (WIC) | 1972 | 6.4 million[e] | 51.1%[f] | States set income eligibility (between 185% and 100% FPL) and nutrition risk eligibility | Provides food, health-care referrals, and nutrition education for low-income pregnant and postpartum women and to infants and children up to age 5 http://www.fns.usda.gov/wic | Discretionary |
| Supplemental Security Income (SSI) | 1974 | 3.4 million[g] | 2.4%[h] | Age 65 or older, blind, or disabled and have limited income and resources | Income assistance for aged, blind, and disabled people who have little or no income http://www.socialsecurity.gov/ssi | Entitlement |

| Program | When Began | Participation | Percentage of Eligible Served | Eligibility | Purpose (and Site for Further Information) | Discretionary/ Entitlement |
|---|---|---|---|---|---|---|
| Section 8 | 1974 | 2.1 million[a] | 21%[b] | Household income up to 80% of the area median | A housing voucher program that allows participants to rent privately owned residences from participating owners. Renters pay 30% of family income toward housing costs http://hud.gov/topics/ housing_choice_voucher_ program_section_8 | Discretionary |
| Earned Income Tax Credit (EITC) | 1975 | 25 million[i] | 78%[j] | Income limits based on family size | A refundable tax credit to low-income workers (especially targeted at those with qualifying, dependent children) http://www.eitc.irs.gov | Entitlement |
| Child Care and Development Block Grant (CCDBG) | 1996 | 1.3 million in 0.8 million families[k] | 16%[l] | States determine income and work status eligibility | Childcare vouchers are provided to families who choose the type of care (including formal centers, family care homes, relative care, and care by nonrelatives) http://acf.hhs.gov/occ/fact-sheet | Discretionary |
| Temporary Assistance to Needy Families (TANF) | 1996 | 2 million[m] | 22%[n] | States determine eligibility of families with children | Cash assistance with a work requirement; five-year limited term of lifetime federal assistance http://benefits.gov/ benefit/613 | Discretionary |

(Continued)

| Table 2.1 | (Continued) | | | | | |
|---|---|---|---|---|---|---|
| Program | When Began | Participation | Percentage of Eligible Served | Eligibility | Purpose (and Site for Further Information) | Discretionary/ Entitlement |
| Workforce Innovation and Opportunity (WIOA) | 1998 | 1.3 million exiters[o] | Not available | Adults, dislocated workers, and youth aged 16 to 24 who face employment challenges and are primarily low income | Job search and placement assistance and labor market information ("core" services) then career counseling and assessment ("intensive" services) before job training or education http://www.doleta.gov/programs | Discretionary |

*Sources:*

[a]U.S. Department of Housing and Urban Development (n. d.).

[b]Kingsley (2017).

[c]U.S. Department of Agriculture (2020b).

[d]U.S. Department of Agriculture (2019).

[e]U.S. Department of Agriculture (2020a).

[f]U.S. Department of Agriculture (2019).

[g]Social Security Administration (2019b).

[h]Social Security Administration (2019c).

[i]Internal Revenue Service (2020e).

[j]Internal Revenue Service (2020b).

[k]U.S. Department of Health and Human Services (2019b).

[l]U.S. House of Representatives (2018)

[m]U.S. Department of Health and Human Services (2020b).

[n]Meyer & Floyd (2020).

[o]U.S. Department of Labor (2020).

(UNICEF, 2020, p. 12). Some countries have age restrictions and residency or citizenship requirements for UCBs, but the basic premise is a universal, unconditional cash transfer given for all children. In the U.S., the Alaska Permanent Fund Dividend can be considered a variant of such an approach. Data suggest that child allowances are a substantive contributor to overall reductions in child poverty. Analyses of the costs and benefits of such a policy in the U.S. indicate that it is likely to improve outcomes for children (National Academies of Sciences, Engineering, and Medicine, 2019; Shaefer et al., 2017).

## Child Development Accounts

Another promising approach involves investing in the long-term growth and development of children. Building upon the human capabilities frame of Sen (1993, 1999), Sherraden (1991) has argued that although income-support policies provide an important safety net, they are insufficient. He suggests that helping low-income households build tangible financial assets leads to positive changes in self-efficacy and civic participation, which in turn contribute to improvements in child well-being (Sherraden, 2005). This "assets" perspective has been receiving greater attention and is shaping policy innovations (Cramer & Williams Shanks, 2014).

Building on the work of Sherraden (2005) and others, child development accounts (CDAs) have been launched in multiple countries and throughout the U.S. CDAs are intended to reduce poverty and promote child development (Elliott & Lewis, 2018; Huang et al., 2020; Prosperity Now, n. d.; Williams Shanks et al., 2010). The vision is that every child receives from birth a subsidized savings or investment account. CDAs are universal, progressive (with subsidies going to the poor), and lifelong. Deposits are intended to provide a foundation for family financial capability. A primary use of the account, thus far, has been to save for college or postsecondary education. However, fund administrators could agree to release money for other approved purposes (e.g., home purchase, business start-up, or transportation). The intent of CDA programs is to provide young people with resources to support whatever choices might help them build personal capabilities and get started in life, regardless of their parents' financial situation. Globally, CDAs exist in Canada, Israel, Singapore, South Korea, Taiwan, and the United Kingdom. In the U.S., universal statewide CDA programs have been approved in California, Illinois, Maine, Nebraska, Nevada, Pennsylvania, and Rhode Island. With the goal of reducing racial wealth disparities, Hamilton and Darity (2010) proposed a more generous version of CDAs called "baby bonds." A version of this idea was introduced in a bill by Senator Cory Booker (Kijakazi & Carther, 2020) and as a policy platform in the state of New Jersey (Tully, 2020).

## Neighborhood-Based Comprehensive Community Building

Another approach is to systematically integrate programs and services on the ground in neighborhoods and schools. One local cross-system policy and program is the Harlem Children's Zone (HCZ) in New York City (McCarthy & Jean-Louis, 2016). The HCZ has had visionary leadership in Geoffrey Canada and colleagues, generous funding, and committed staff. Over time and through trial and error, HCZ developed what is called a "cradle-to-career intervention" with an array of community programs and educational innovations in a 97-block area of Harlem (HCZ, n. d.; McCarthy & Jean-Louis, 2016). Specific interventions include parenting classes in *The Baby College*; prekindergarten instruction in *Harlem Gems*; two charter schools; and an array of afterschool, health, college-preparatory, employment-training, and substance-abuse programs and services. Initial evidence shows that children who are enrolled in the HCZ schools have better attendance, more time in classroom instruction, and better achievement scores in math and English than those who are not enrolled—and these low-income students of color reduce achievement gaps and do as well as their more well-off peers (McCarthy & Jean-Louis, 2016; Tough, 2008).

In 2010, the federal government launched a Promise Neighborhood initiative based on the HCZ model. In 2012, Promise Neighborhood planning and implementation grants were given to communities in 20 states and the District of Columbia. Between 2016 and 2018, another round of Promise Neighborhood implementation grants were awarded. HCZ continues to consult with these sites and any location that wants to replicate its model (HCZ, n. d.; U.S. Department of Education, 2018). Like any program with strong community connections, HCZ staff and volunteers can also be responsive to the COVID-19 pandemic and address the emerging needs of local youth and families as they arise.

Such neighborhood-based comprehensive community-building strategies are expensive and require time to develop. The Annie E. Casey Foundation funded a series of neighborhood-change initiatives aimed at childhood poverty, including the Rebuilding Communities and Making Connections programs (Annie E. Casey Foundation, 2010). The Skillman Foundation launched comprehensive community-building initiatives in six neighborhoods in Detroit through its Good Neighborhoods Initiative (Allen-Meares et al., 2017; Skillman Foundation, n. d.). Efforts to assess and evaluate these long-term comprehensive change projects face major research challenges (Kubisch et al., 2002; Stone, 1996; Taylor et al., 2018). Although much has been learned, no clear blueprint exists today to transform low-income communities into safe and healthy places for children. But the work is ongoing.

## CONCLUSION

Although there are decades of data on the impact of poverty on children, the novel coronavirus has had devastating consequences that are not yet fully realized and understood. Rather than returning to the preexisting inequities that put low-income children and their families at a severe disadvantage, it would be much better for children if we were, as a society, to forge ahead to develop and implement a package of policies and programs along the lines of what has been proposed by the National Academies of Sciences. With policies intentionally designed to reduce poverty and support all children, the consequences of growing up poor might be less severe. For poor children, multiple levels of influence must be targeted concomitantly. The earlier interventions become available to families, the more effective they will be in reducing problems for low-income children.

# REFERENCES

Allen-Meares, P. G., Shanks, T. R., Gant, L. M., Hollingsworth, L., & Miller, P. L. (2017). *A twenty-first century approach to community change: Partnering to improve life outcomes for youth and families in under-served neighborhoods.* Oxford University Press.

Almond, D., Hoynes, H., & Schanzenbach, D. W. (2011). Inside the war on poverty: The impact of the food stamp program on birth outcomes. *Review of Economics and Statistics, 93*(2), 387–403.

Ananat, E. O., & Gassman-Pines, A. (2020). Work schedule unpredictability: Daily occurrence and effects on working parents' well-being. *Journal of Marriage and Family,* jomf.12696.

Ananat, E. O., Gassman-Pines, A., Francis, D., & Gibson-Davis, C. (2013). *Children left behind: The effects of statewide job loss on student achievement* (Working Paper). National Bureau of Economic Research.

Annie E. Casey Foundation. (2010). *The East Baltimore revitalization initiative.* https://www.aecf.org/resources/the-east-baltimore-revitalization-initiative-1/

Antle, B., Frey, A., Barbee, A., Frey, S., Grisham-Brown, J., & Cox, M. (2008). Child care subsidy and program quality revisited. *Early Education and Development, 19,* 560–573.

Aratini, Y., & Chau, M. (2010). Asset poverty and debt among families with children. National Center for Children in Poverty. https://www.nccp.org/publication/asset-poverty-and-debt-among-families-with-children/

Bainbridge, J., Meyers, M. K., & Waldfogel, J. (2003). Child care policy reform and the employment of single mothers. *Social Science Quarterly, 84,* 771–791.

Bitler, M., Hoynes, H. W., & Schanzenbach, D. W. (2020). *The social safety net in the wake of COVID-19* (Working Paper). National Bureau of Economic Research. https://www.nber.org/papers/w27796?mc_cid=78ecfd7d49&mc_eid=835dce3faf

Blank, R. M. (2008). Presidential address: How to improve poverty measurement in the United States. *Journal of Policy Analysis and Management, 27,* 233–254.

Blau, D., & Tekin, E. (2007). The determinants and consequences of child care subsidies for single mothers in the USA. *Journal of Population Economics, 20,* 719–741.

Board of Governors of the Federal Reserve System. (2020). *Survey of consumer finances.* Author. https://www.federalreserve.gov/econres/scfindex.htm

Boushey, H., & Park, S. (2020). The coronavirus recession and economic inequality: A roadmap to recovery and long-term structural change. *Washington Center for Equitable Growth.* https://equitablegrowth.org/the-coronavirus-recession-and-economic-inequality-a-roadmap-to-recovery-and-long-term-structural-change/

Brandolini, A., Magri, S., & Smeeding, T. M. (2010). Asset-based measurement of poverty. *Journal of Policy Analysis and Management, 29*(2), 267–284.

Bureau of Labor Statistics. (2020). *The employment situation—July 2020 (Economic News Release USDL-20-1503).* https://www.bls.gov/news.release/archives/empsit_08072020.htm

Cabildo, M., Graves, E. M., Kim, J., & Russo, M. (2020). How race, class, and place fuel a pandemic [Report]. *Race Counts.* https://www.racecounts.org/covid/

Casselman, B. (2021). How the U.S. got it (mostly) right in the economy's rescue. *The New York Times*. https://www.nytimes.com/2021/03/15/business/economy/coronavirus-economic-policy.html

Center on Budget and Policy Priorities. (2020). *Chart book: Temporary assistance for needy families*. https://www.cbpp.org/research/family-income-support/chart-book-temporary-assistance-for-needy-families

Chase-Lansdale, P. L., & Brooks-Gunn, J. (2014). Two-generation programs in the twenty-first century. *The Future of Children, 24*(1), 13–39.

Chetty, R. (n. d.). *Raj Chetty*. http://www.rajchetty.com/

Chetty, R., Hendren, N., & Katz, L. F. (2016). The effects of exposure to better neighborhoods on children: New evidence from the moving to opportunity experiment. *American Economic Review, 106*(4), 855–902.

Chetty, R., Hendren, N., Kline, P., & Saez, E. (2014). Where is the land of opportunity? The geography of intergenerational mobility in the United States. *The Quarterly Journal of Economics, 129*(4), 1553–1623.

Child Trends. (2019). *Children and youth experiencing homelessness*. https://www.childtrends.org/indicators/homeless-children-and-youth

Cielinski, A. (2017). Federal investment in employment and job training services has declined over the last 40 years [Fact Sheet]. *Center for Law and Social Policy*. https://www.clasp.org/publications/fact-sheet/federal-investment-employment-and-job-training-services-has-declined-over

Clear, T. R. (2009). *Imprisoning communities: How mass incarceration makes disadvantaged neighborhoods worse*. Oxford University Press.

Condon, E. (2019). Maternal infant and early childhood home visiting: A call for paradigm shift in state approaches to funding. *Policy Politics and Nursing Practice, 20*(1), 28–40.

Congressional Research Service. (2019). *Poverty in the United States in 2018: In brief*. https://fas.org/sgp/crs/misc/R46000.pdf

Congressional Research Service. (2020). *The temporary assistance for needy families (TANF) block grant: Responses to frequently asked questions*. https://fas.org/sgp/crs/misc/RL32760.pdf

Conley, D. (1999). *Being Black, living in the red: Race, wealth, and social policy in America*. University of California Press.

Couch, K. A., & Pirog, M. A. (2010). Poverty measurement in the U.S., Europe, and developing countries. *Journal of Policy Analysis and Management, 29*(2), 217–226.

Cramer, R., & Williams Shanks, T. R. (2014). *The assets perspective the rise of asset building and its impact on social policy*. Palgrave Macmillan.

Currie, J. M. (2006). *The invisible safety net: Protecting the nation's poor children and families*. Princeton University Press.

Danziger, S. (2013). Evaluating the effects of the great recession. *The ANNALS of the American Academy of Political and Social Science, 650*(1), 6–24.

Danziger, S. K. (2010). The decline of cash welfare and implications for social policy and poverty. *Annual Review of Sociology, 36*, 523–545.

Danziger, S. K., Ananat, E., & Browning, K. (2004). Child care subsidies and the transition from welfare to work. *Family Relations, 53*, 219–228.

Davis-Kean, P. E. (2005). The influence of parent education and family income on child achievement: The indirect role of parent expectations and the home environment. *Journal of Family Psychology, 19*(2), 294–304.

Desmond, M. (2017). *Evicted: Poverty and profit in the American city*. Thorndike Press.

Desmond, M. (2020, August 29). The rent eats first, even during a pandemic. *The New York Times*. https://www.nytimes.com/2020/08/29/opinion/sunday/coronavirus-evictions-superspreader.html

Drayton, T. (2020, August 26). 1 in 3 Black Americans knows someone who died of Covid-19. These stories capture the toll taken by the disease. *Vox*. https://www.vox.com/first-person/2020/8/26/21400035/coronavirus-covid-19-mortality-black-americans

Duncan, G. J., Ziol-Guest, K. M., & Kalil, A. (2010). Early childhood poverty and adult attainment, behavior, and health. *Child Development, 81*(1), 306–325.

Edin, K., & Kissane, R. J. (2010). Poverty and the American family: A decade in review. *Journal of Marriage and Family, 72*, 460–479.

Ekono, M., Jiang, Y., & Smith, S. (2016). *Young children in deep poverty [Fact Sheet]*. https://www.nccp.org/publication/young-children-in-deep-poverty/

El Issa, E. (2020, June 11). Survey: How the pandemic alters Americans' financial habits. *NerdWallet*. https://www.nerdwallet.com/article/finance/covid-19-study

Elliott, W., & Lewis, M. (2018). *Making education work for the poor: The potential of children's savings accounts.* Oxford University Press.

Fitzgerald, M. (2020, May 29). U.S. savings rate hits record 33% as coronavirus causes Americans to stockpile cash, curb spending. *CNBC.* https://www.cnbc.com/2020/05/29/us-savings-rate-hits-record-33percent-as-coronavirus-causes-americans-to-stockpile-cash-curb-spending.html

Fix, M. (2006). *Immigrants' costs and contributions: The effects of reform.* https://www.migrationpolicy.org/sites/default/files/publications/FixTestimony072606.pdf

Food and Nutrition Service. (2020a). National level annual summary. *SNAP Data Tables.* https://fns-prod.azureedge.net/sites/default/files/resource-files/SNAPsummary-7.pdf

Food and Nutrition Service. (2020b). *Supplemental nutrition assistance program.* https://fns-prod.azureedge.net/sites/default/files/resource-files/SNAPsummary-7.pdf

Fox, L. (2018). *The supplemental poverty measure: 2017.* The United States Census Bureau. https://www.census.gov/library/publications/2018/demo/p60-265.html

Frank, A., & Minoff, E. (2005). *Declining share of adults receiving training under WIA are low-income or disadvantaged.* Center for Law and Social Policy. https://www.clasp.org/publications/report/brief/declining-share-adults-receiving-training-under-wia-are-low-income-or

Giannarelli, L., Adams, G., Minton, S., & Dwyer, K. (2019, May 23). What if we expanded child care subsidies? *Urban Institute.* https://www.urban.org/research/publication/what-if-we-expanded-child-care-subsidies

Goyal, M. K., Simpson, J. N., Boyle, M. D., Badolato, G. M., Delaney, M., McCarter, R., & Cora-Bramble, D. (2020). Racial/ethnic and socioeconomic disparities of SARS-CoV-2 infection. *Pediatrics.* https://pediatrics.aappublications.org/content/146/4/e2020009951

Guo, G., & Harris, K. M. (2000). The mechanisms mediating the effects of poverty on children's intellectual development. *Demography, 37*(4), 431–447.

Hair, N. L., Hanson, J. L., Wolfe, B. L., & Pollak, S. D. (2016). Association between child poverty and academic achievement—In reply. *Journal of the American Medical Association Pediatrics, 170*(2), 180.

Hamilton, D., & Darity, W. (2010). Can "baby bonds" eliminate the racial wealth gap in putative post-racial America? *The Review of Black Political Economy, 37*(3–4), 207–216.

Hanson, J. L., Hair, N., Shen, D. G., Shi, F., Gilmore, J. H., Wolfe, B. L., & Pollak, S. D. (2013). Family poverty affects the rate of human infant brain growth. *PLoS ONE, 8*(12), e80954.

Harding, D. J. (2003). Counterfactual models of neighborhood effects: The effect of neighborhood poverty on dropping out and teenage pregnancy. *American Journal of Sociology, 109*(3), 676–719.

Harlem Children's Zone (HCZ). (n. d.). *Harlem children's zone.* https://hcz.org/

Hart, D., Atkins, R., & Matsuba, M. K. (2008). The association of neighborhood poverty with personality change in childhood. *Journal of Personality and Social Psychology, 94*(6), 1048–1061.

Haskins, R., Garfinkel, I., & McLanahan, S. (2014). Introduction: Two-generation mechanisms of child development. *The Future of Children, 24*(1), 3–12.

Haveman, R. H., & Wolff, E. N. (2004). The concept and measurement of asset poverty: Levels, trends, and composition for the U.S., 1983–2001. *Journal of Economic Inequality, 2*, 145–169.

Holzer, H. (2008). Workforce development and the disadvantaged: New directions for 2009 and beyond. *Urban Institute.* https://www.urban.org/research/publication/workforce-development-and-disadvantaged

Huang, J., Zou, L., & Sherraden, M. (Eds.). (2020). *Inclusive child development accounts: Toward universality and progressivity.* Routledge.

Internal Revenue Service. (2020a). *Earned income tax credit income limits and maximum credit amounts.* https://www.irs.gov/credits-deductions/individuals/earned-income-tax-credit/earned-income-tax-credit-income-limits-and-maximum-credit-amounts

Internal Revenue Service. (2020b). EITC participation rate by states. *Earned Income Tax Credit & Other Refundable Credits.* https://www.eitc.irs.gov/eitc-central/participation-rate/eitc-participation-rate-by-states

Internal Revenue Service. (2020c). *SOI tax stats—Historical table 1.* https://www.irs.gov/statistics/soi-tax-stats-historical-table-1

Internal Revenue Service. (2020d). *SOI tax stats—Individual statistical tables by size of adjusted gross income*. https://www.irs.gov/statistics/soi-tax-stats-individual-statistical-tables-by-size-of-adjusted-gross-income

Internal Revenue Service. (2020e). Statistics for tax returns with EITC. *Earned Income Tax Credit & Other Refundable Credits*. https://www.eitc.irs.gov/eitc-central/statistics-for-tax-returns-with-eitc/statistics-for-tax-returns-with-eitc

Jargowsky, P. A. (1997). *Poverty and place: Ghettos, barrios, and the American city*. Russell Sage Foundation.

Jargowsky, P. A. (2003). Stunning progress, hidden problems: The dramatic decline of concentrated poverty in the 1990s. *Brookings*. https://www.brookings.edu/research/stunning-progress-hidden-problems-the-dramatic-decline-of-concentrated-poverty-in-the-1990s/

Jargowsky, P. A. (2013, December 18). Concentration of poverty in the new millennium. *The Century Foundation*. https://tcf.org/content/report/concentration-of-poverty-in-the-new-millennium/

Johnson, R. C., & Schoeni, R. F. (2011). The influence of early-life events on human capital, health status, and labor market outcomes over the life course. *The B.E. Journal of Economic Analysis & Policy*, *11*(3). http://www.degruyter.com/view/j/bejeap.2011.11.issue-3/bejeap.2011.11.3.2521/bejeap.2011.11.3.2521.xml

Kijakazi, K., & Carther, A. (2020, January 23). How baby bonds could help Americans start adulthood strong and narrow the racial wealth gap. *Urban Institute*. https://www.urban.org/urban-wire/how-baby-bonds-could-help-americans-start-adulthood-strong-and-narrow-racial-wealth-gap

Kingsley, G. T. (2017). Trends in housing problems and federal housing assistance. *Urban Institute*. https://www.urban.org/sites/default/files/publication/94146/trends-in-housing-problems-and-federal-housing-assistance.pdf

Kingsley, G. T., & Pettit, K. L. S. (2016, June 4). Concentrated poverty. *Urban Institute*. https://www.urban.org/research/publication/concentrated-poverty

Klebanov, P. K., Brooks-Gunn, J., & Duncan, G. J. (1994). Does neighborhood poverty and family poverty affect mothers' parenting, mental health, and social support? *Journal of Marriage and Family*, *56*(2), 441–455.

Kling, J. R., Ludwig, J., & Katz, L. F. (2005). Neighborhood effects on crime for female and male youth: Evidence from a randomized housing voucher experiment. *Quarterly Journal of Economics*, *120*, 87–130.

Kneebone, E., & Garr, E. (2010). The suburbanization of poverty: Trends in metropolitan America, 2000 to 2008 (Metropolitan Policy Program). *Brookings Institute*. https://www.brookings.edu/research/the-suburbanization-of-poverty-trends-in-metropolitan-america-2000-to-2008/

Kneebone, E., & Holmes, N. (2016). U.S. concentrated poverty in the wake of the Great Recession. *Brookings Institute*. https://www.brookings.edu/research/u-s-concentrated-poverty-in-the-wake-of-the-great-recession/

Kohen, D. E., Leventhal, T., Dahinten, V. S., & McIntosh, C. N. (2008). Neighborhood disadvantage: Pathways of effects for young children. *Child Development*, *79*(1), 156–169.

Kubisch, A. C., Auspos, P., Brown, P., Chaskin, R., Fulbright-Anderson, K., & Hamilton, R. (2002). *Voices from the field II: Reflections on comprehensive community change*. Aspen Institute.

Kuttner, R. (2021). Biden's child tax credit as universal basic income. *The American Prospect*. https://prospect.org/economy/bidens-child-tax-credit-as-universal-basic-income/

LaLonde, R. J. (1995). The promise of public sector-sponsored training programs. *The Journal of Economic Perspectives*, *9*(2), 149–168.

Leininger, L. J., & Kalil, A. (2014). Economic strain and children's behavior in the aftermath of the Great Recession. *Journal of Marriage and Family*, *76*(5), 998–1010.

Leventhal, T., & Brooks-Gunn, J. (2000). The neighborhoods they live in: The effects of neighborhood residence on child and adolescent outcomes. *Psychological Bulletin*, *126*(2), 309–337.

Levine Coley, R., Li-Grining, C. P., & Chase-Lansdale, P. L. (2006). *Low-income families' child care experiences: Meeting the needs of children and families*. Lawrence Erlbaum.

Lindsey, D. (2004). *The welfare of children*. Oxford University Press.

Loury, G. C. (2010). Crime, inequality, and social justice. *Daedalus*, *139*(3), 134–146.

Lui, M., Robles, B., Leondar-Wright, B., Brewer, R., & Adamson, R. (2006). *The color of wealth: The story behind the U.S. racial wealth divide*. New Press.

Martin, E. (2017). Hidden consequences: The impact of incarceration on dependent children. *National Institute of Justice*. https://www.ncjrs.gov/pdffiles1/nij/250349.pdf

Massey, D. S., & Denton, N. A. (1993). *American apartheid: Segregation and the making of the underclass*. Harvard University Press.

McCarthy, K., & Jean-Louis, B. (2016). Harlem children's zone. *Center for the Study of Social Policy*. https://cssp.org/wp-content/uploads/2018/08/Harlem-Childrens-Zone.pdf

McLoyd, V. C. (1998). Socioeconomic disadvantage and child development. *American Psychologist, 53*, 185–204.

Meyer, L., & Floyd, I. (2020). Cash assistance should reach millions more families to lessen hardship. *Center on Budget and Policy Priorities*. https://www.cbpp.org/research/family-income-support/cash-assistance-should-reach-millions-more-families

Meyers, M. K., Heintze, T., & Wolfe, D. A. (2002). Child care subsidies and the employment of welfare recipients. *Demography, 39*, 165–179.

National Academies of Sciences, Engineering, and Medicine. (2019). *A roadmap to reducing child poverty*. The National Academies Press.

Oliver, M. L., & Shapiro, T. M. (1995). *Black wealth/White wealth: A new perspective on racial inequality*. Routledge.

Pachter, L. M., Auinger, P., Palmer, R., & Weitzman, M. (2006). Do parenting and the home environment, maternal depression, neighborhood, and chronic poverty affect child behavioral problems differently in different racial-ethnic groups? *Pediatrics, 117*, 1329–1338.

Parolin, Z., Curran, M., & Wimer, C. (2020). The CARES Act and poverty in the COVID-19 crisis: Promises and pitfalls of the recovery rebates and expanded unemployment benefits. *Policy & Social Policy Brief, 4*(8). https://static1.squarespace.com/static/5743308460b5e922a25a6dc7/t/5eefa3463153d0544b7f08b4/1592763209062/Forecasting-Poverty-Estimates-COVID19-CARES-Act-CPSP-2020.pdf

Parolin, Z., & Wimer, C. (2020). Forecasting estimates of poverty during the COVID-19 crisis. *Poverty & Social Policy Brief, 4*(6). https://static1.squarespace.com/static/5743308460b5e922a25a6dc7/t/5e9786f17c4b4e20ca02d16b/1586988788821/Forecasting-Poverty-Estimates-COVID19-CPSP-2020.pdf

Parrott, S., Sherman, A., Llobrera, J., Mazzara, A., Beltran, J., & Leachman, M. (2020). More relief needed to alleviate hardship. *Center on Budget and Policy Priorities*. https://www.cbpp.org/research/poverty-and-inequality/more-relief-needed-to-alleviate-hardship

Patton, D. U., Woolley, M. E., & Hong, J. S. (2012). Exposure to violence, student fear, and low academic achievement: African American males in the critical transition to high school. *Children and Youth Services Review, 34*(2), 388–395.

Picchi, A. (2021). Child tax credit: Millions of parents could soon get up to $3,600 per child. *CBS News*. https://www.cbsnews.com/news/child-tax-credit-stimulus-covid-relief-bill-2021-03-16/

Press, J. E., Fagan, J., & Laughlin, L. (2006). Taking pressure off families: Child-care subsidies lessen mothers' work-hour problems. *Journal of Marriage and Family, 68*(1), 155–171.

Prosperity Now. (n. d.). *Find a children's savings account program* [Map]. https://prosperitynow.org/map/childrens-savings

Purmort, J. (2010). Making work supports work: A picture of low wage workers in America (Making Work Supports Work). *National Center for Children in Poverty*. https://www.nccp.org/publication/making-work-supports-work-tools-for-policy-analysis/

Ricketts, L. (2020). Housing distress in the time of COVID-19. *Federal Reserve Bank of St. Louis: On the economy blog*. https://www.stlouisfed.org/on-the-economy/2020/august/housing-distress-time-covid19

Rothwell, D. W., Ottusch, T., & Finders, J. K. (2019). Asset poverty among children: A cross-national study of poverty risk. *Children and Youth Services Review, 96*(C), 409–419.

Ryan, R. M., Johnson, A., Rigby, E., & Brooks-Gunn, J. (2011). The impact of child care subsidy use on child care quality. *Early Childhood Research Quarterly, 26*(3), 320–331.

Saenz, M., & Sherman, A. (2020). Research note: Number of people in families with below-poverty earnings has soared, especially among Black and Latino individuals (poverty and inequality). *Center on budget and policy priorities*. https://www.cbpp.org/research/poverty-and-inequality/research-note-number-of-people-in-families-with-below-poverty

Safawi, A., & Floyd, I. (2020). TANF benefits still too low to help families, especially Black families, avoid increased

hardship. *Center on Budget and Policy Priorities*. https://www
.cbpp.org/research/family-income-support/tanf-benefits-
still-too-low-to-help-families-especially-black

Sampson, R. J., Morenoff, J. D., & Gannon-Rowley, T.
(2002). Assessing "neighborhood effects": Social processes
and new directions in research. *Annual Review of Sociology*,
*28*(1), 443–478.

Schott, L., & Pavetti, L. (2013). Changes in TANF work
requirements could make them more effective in promoting employment. *Center on Budget and Policy Priorities*.
https://www.cbpp.org/sites/default/files/atoms/files/2-26-
13tanf.pdf

Schuetz, J. (2020). Exclusive communities deepen inequality in every metro area (up front). *Brookings Institute*.
https://www.brookings.edu/blog/up-front/2020/07/16/
exclusive-communities-deepen-inequality-in-every-met
ro-area/

Semega, J., Kollar, M., Shrider, E. A., & Creamer, J. (2020).
Income and poverty in the United States: 2019 (No. P60-
270). *U.S. Census Bureau*. https://www.census.gov/library/
publications/2020/demo/p60-270.html

Sen, A. (1993). Capability and well-being. In M. Nussbaum
& A. Sen (Eds.), *The quality of life* (pp. 30–53). Clarendon
Press.

Sen, A. (1999). *Development as freedom*. Knopf.

Shaefer, H. L., & Edin, K. (2013). Rising extreme poverty
in the United States and the response of federal means-
tested transfer programs. *Social Service Review*, *87*(2), 250–
268.

Shaefer, H. L., Garfinkel, I., Harris, D., Waldfogel, J.,
Wimer, C., &Wu , P. (2017, March). Convert the child
tax credit into a universal child allowance. *Grand Challenges for Social Work*. https://aaswsw.org/wp-content/
uploads/2017/03/PAS.10.1-002.pdf

Shaefer, H. L., Lapidos, A., Wilson, R., & Danziger, S.
(2018). Association of income and adversity in childhood
with adult health and well-being. *Social Service Review*,
*92*(1), 69–92.

Shapiro, T. M. (2004). *The hidden cost of being African American: How wealth perpetuates inequality*. Oxford University
Press.

Shapiro, T. M., Oliver, M. L., & Meschede, T. (2009). *The
asset security and opportunity index*. Brandeis University.

Sharkey, P. (2009). Neighborhoods and the Black–White
mobility gap (economic mobility project). *Pew Charitable
Trusts*. https://www.pewtrusts.org/en/research-and-anal
ysis/reports/0001/01/01/neighborhoods-and-the-black
white-mobility-gap

Sherman, A. (2011). Poverty and financial stress would
have been substantially worse in 2010 without government
action, new census data show. *Center on Budget and Policy
Priorities*. https://www.cbpp.org/research/poverty-and-fin
ancial-distress-would-have-been-substantially-worse-in-
2010-without

Sherraden, M. W. (1991). *Assets and the poor: A new American welfare policy*. M.E. Sharpe.

Sherraden, N. (2005). Assets and public policy. In M. Sherraden (Ed.), *Inclusion in the American dream: Assets, poverty,
and public policy* (pp. 3–19). Oxford University Press.

Short, K. (2013). The research supplemental poverty measure: 2012 (No. P60-257). *U.S. Census Bureau*. https://www
.census.gov/library/publications/2013/demo/p60-247.html

Skillman Foundation. (n. d.). *Who we are*. https://www
.skillman.org/who-we-are/

Smeeding, T., & Thévenot, C. (2016). Addressing child
poverty: How does the United States compare with other
nations? *Academic Pediatrics*, *16*(3), S67–S75.

Social Security Administration. (2019a). *Annual statistical
supplement 2018 (annual statistical supplement)*. https://www
.ssa.gov/policy/docs/statcomps/supplement/2018/

Social Security Administration. (2019b). *SSI annual statistical report, 2018* (SSA Publication No. 13-11827).
https://www.ssa.gov/policy/docs/statcomps/ssi_asr/2018/
ssi_asr18.pdf

Social Security Administration. (2019c). Table IV.B7.—
Federal SSI prevalence rates, as of December, 1975–2043.
*2019 Annual Report of the SSI Program*. https://www.ssa
.gov/OACT/ssir/SSI19/IV_B_Recipients.html#935854

Social Security Administration. (2020). *Understanding Supplemental Security Income SSI benefits—2020 edition*. https://
www.ssa.gov/ssi/text-benefits-ussi.htm

Sprunt, B. (2021). Here's what's in the American Rescue Plan.
*NPR*. https://www.npr.org/sections/coronavirus-live-up-
dates/2021/03/09/974841565/heres-whats-in-the-ameri
can-rescue-plan-as-it-heads-toward-final-passage

Stone, C. (2020). 6 signs that the labor market remains in deep trouble. *Center on Budget and Policy Priorities*. https://www.cbpp.org/blog/6-signs-that-the-labor-market-remains-in-deep-trouble

Stone, R. (1996). *Core issues in comprehensive community-building initiatives*. Chapin Hall Center for Children at the University of Chicago.

Sullivan, L., Meschede, T., Dietrich, L., Shapiro, T., Traub, A., Ruetschlin, C., & Draut, T. (2015). The racial wealth gap: Why policy matters (racial wealth audit). *Institute for Assets and Social Policy at Brandeis University and DEMOS*. http://racialwealthaudit.org/the-racial-wealth-gap-why-policy-matters/

Tankersley, J., & DeParle, J. (2021). Two decades after the "End of Welfare," Democrats are changing direction. *The New York Times*. https://www.nytimes.com/2021/03/13/business/economy/child-poverty-stimulus.html?-searchResultPosition=43

Tax Policy Center. (2020). Briefing book. What is the earned income tax credit? *Tax Policy Center*. https://www.taxpolicycenter.org/briefing-book/what-earned-income-tax-credit#:~:text=As%20a%20result%20of%20legislation,couples%20than%20for%20single%20individuals.&text=The%20Tax%20Cuts%20and%20Jobs%20Act%2C%20enacted%20in%202017%2C%20adopted,tax%20system%20beginning%20in%202018

Taylor, C., Schorr, L. B., Wilkins, N., & Smith, L. S. (2018). Systemic approach for injury and violence prevention: What we can learn from the Harlem Children's Zone and Promise Neighborhoods. *Injury Prevention, 24*(Suppl 1), i32–i37.

Tough, P. (2008). *Whatever it takes: Geoffrey Canada's quest to change Harlem and America*. Houghton Mifflin.

Tully, T. (2020, August 25). $1,000 'baby bond' proposed in N. J. in bid to narrow the wealth gap. *The New York Times*. https://www.nytimes.com/2020/08/25/nyregion/baby-bond-nj.html

Turner, M. G., & Kingsley, G. T. (2008). Federal programs for addressing low-income housing needs. *Urban Institute*. https://www.urban.org/research/publication/federal-programs-addressing-low-income-housing-needs

UNICEF. (2020). *Universal child benefits*. https://www.unicef.org/sites/default/files/2020-07/UCB-ODI-UNICEF-Report-2020.pdf

Urban Institute. (2020). Table L6: Work-related exemption when caring for a child under X months. *TANF Policy Tables*. https://wrd.urban.org/wrd/tables.cfm

U.S. Census Bureau. (2020a). Table 3. Poverty status of people by age, race, and Hispanic origin. *Historical Poverty Tables: People and Families—1959 to 2019*. https://www.census.gov/data/tables/time-series/demo/income-poverty/historical-poverty-people.html

U.S. Census Bureau. (2020b). Table 4. Poverty status of families by type of family, presence of related children, race, and Hispanic origin. *Historical Poverty Tables: People and Families—1959 to 2019*. https://www.census.gov/data/tables/time-series/demo/income-poverty/historical-poverty-people.html

U.S. Department of Agriculture. (2019a). *National- and state-level estimates of WIC eligibility and WIC program reach in 2017*. https://fns-prod.azureedge.net/sites/default/files/resource-files/WICEligibles2017-Volume1.pdf

U.S. Department of Agriculture. (2019b). *Trends in supplemental nutrition assistance program participation rates: Fiscal year 2010 to fiscal year 2017 (summary)*. https://fns-prod.azureedge.net/sites/default/files/resource-files/Trends2010-2017-Summary.pdf

U.S. Department of Agriculture. (2020a). *Special supplemental nutrition assistance program for women, infants, and children (WIC)*. http://www.fns.usda.gov/wic/

U.S. Department of Agriculture. (2020b). *Supplemental nutrition assistance program (SNAP)*. https://www.fns.usda.gov/snap/supplemental-nutrition-assistance-program

U.S. Department of Education. (2018). *Promise Neighborhoods*. https://promiseneighborhoods.ed.gov/

U.S. Department of Health and Human Services. (2010). Assets for independence program: Status at the conclusion of the tenth year. *Administration of Children and Families, Office of Community Services*. https://www.acf.hhs.gov/sites/default/files/ocs/exec_summary_afi_tenth_report_to_congress_0.pdf

U.S. Department of Health and Human Services. (2018). AFI fact sheet. *Administration for Children and Families, Office of Family Support*. https://www.acf.hhs.gov/ocs/resource/afi-fact-sheet

U.S. Department of Health and Human Services. (2019a). AFDC caseload data 1960–1995. *Administration for Children and Families, Office of Family Assistance*.

https://www.acf.hhs.gov/ofa/resource/tanf-and-afdc-his torical-case-data-pre-2012

U.S. Department of Health and Human Services. (2019b). FY 2018 preliminary data table 1—Average monthly adjusted number of families and children served. *Administration for Children and Families, Office of Child Care*. https://www.acf.hhs.gov/occ/resource/fy-2018-preliminary-data-table-1

U.S. Department of Health and Human Services. (2019c). TANF caseload data 1996–2015. *Administration for Children and Families, Office of Family Assistance*. https://www.acf.hhs.gov/ofa/resource/tanf-caseload-data-1996-2012

U.S. Department of Health and Human Services. (2020). *TANF: Total number of recipients*. https://www.acf.hhs.gov/sites/default/files/ofa/fy2019_tanf_caseload_trec.pdf

U.S. Department of Housing and Urban Development. (n.d.). *Picture of subsidized housing*. Assisted Housing: National and Local; Office of Policy Development and Research. https://www.huduser.gov/portal/datasets/assthsg.html

U.S. Department of Labor. (2020). PY 2018 WIOA national performance summary (annual report). *Employment and Training Administration*. https://www.doleta.gov/Performance/Results/AnnualReports/PY2018/PY-2018-WIOA-National-Performance-Summary-3.27.2020.pdf

U.S. Department of the Treasury. (n. d.-a). Earned income tax credit & other refundable credits. *Internal Revenue Service*. https://www.eitc.irs.gov/

U.S. Department of the Treasury. (n. d.-b). *The CARES Act works for all Americans*. https://home.treasury.gov/policy-issues/cares

U.S. Government Accountability Office. (2009). *Social Security Administration: Further actions needed to address disability claims and service delivery challenges* (GAO-09-511T). https://www.gao.gov/products/GAO-09-511T

U.S. House of Representatives. (2018). *2018 Green Book*. https://greenbook-waysandmeans.house.gov/2018-greenbook

U.S. Senate. (n. d.). *Glossary term: Entitlement*. https://www.senate.gov/reference/glossary_term/entitlement.htm

Waldfogel, J. (2006). *What children need*. Harvard University Press.

Waters Boots, S., Macomber, J., & Danziger, A. (2008). Family security: Supporting parents' employment and children's development (Paper No. 3; New Safety Net). *Urban Institute*. https://www.urban.org/sites/default/files/publication/33056/411718-Family-Security-Supporting-Parents-Employment-and-Children-s-Development.PDF

Wheaton, L., Minton, S., Giannarelli, L., & Dwyer, K. (2021). 2021 poverty projections: Assessing four American Rescue Plan policies. *Urban Institute*. https://www.urban.org/research/publication/2021-poverty-projections-assessing-four-american-rescue-plan-policies

Wildeman, C., & Western, B. (2010). Incarceration in fragile families. *The Future of Children, 20*(2), 157–177.

Wildeman, C., & Turney, K. (2014). Positive, negative, or null? The effects of maternal incarceration on children's behavioral problems. *Demography, 51*(3), 1041–1068.

Williams Shanks, T. R., Kim, Y., Loke, V., & Destin, M. (2010). Assets and child well-being in developed countries. *Children and Youth Services Review, 32*(11), 1488–1496.

Williams Shanks, T. R. (2014). *The evolution of anti-poverty policies and programs*. Palgrave Macmillan.

Williams Shanks, T. R., & Robinson, C. (2013). Assets, economic opportunity and toxic stress: A framework for understanding child and educational outcomes. *Economics of Education Review, 33*, 154–170.

Wilson, W. J. (1987). *The truly disadvantaged: The inner city, the underclass, and public policy*. The University of Chicago Press.

Wilson, W. J. (2009). *More than just race: Being Black and poor in the inner city*. W.W. Norton.

Winston & Strawn, LLP. (2021). *United States: Principal components of the American Rescue Plan Act of 2021 Relating to COVID-19 relief and stimulus*. https://www.mondaq.com/unitedstates/operational-impacts-and-strategy/1047226/principal-components-of-the-american-rescue-plan-act-of-2021-relating-to-covid-19-relief-and-stimulus-

Yoshikawa, H., Aber, J. L., & Beardslee, W. R. (2012). The effects of poverty on the mental, emotional, and behavioral health of children and youth: Implications for prevention. *American Psychologist, 67*(4), 272.

## ADDITIONAL READING

Bane, M. J., Zenteno, R. M., & David Rockefeller Center for Latin American Studies (Eds.). (2009). *Poverty and poverty alleviation strategies in North America*. Harvard University Press.

Berger, L. M., Cancian, M., & Magnuson, K. (2018). Anti-poverty policy innovations: New proposals for addressing poverty in the united states. *RSF: The Russell Sage Foundation Journal of the Social Sciences, 4*(3), 1.

Cramer, R., & Williams Shanks, T. R. (2014). *The assets perspective the rise of asset building and its impact on social policy*. Palgrave Macmillan.

Desmond, M. (2015). Severe deprivation in America: An introduction. *RSF: The Russell Sage Foundation Journal of the Social Sciences, 1*(2), 1.

Desmond, M. (2017). *Evicted: Poverty and profit in the American city*. Thorndike Press.

Edin, K., & Shaefer, H. L. (2015). *$2.00 a day: Living on almost nothing in America*. Houghton Mifflin Harcourt.

Seefeldt, K. S. (2017). *Abandoned families: Social isolation in the twenty-first century*. Russell Sage Foundation.

## WEB-BASED RESOURCES

Center for Social Development, Washington University in St. Louis: https://csd.wustl.edu/

Center on Poverty and Social Policy: https://www.povertycenter.columbia.edu

Center on the Developing Child at Harvard University: https://developingchild.harvard.edu/

Institute for Research on Poverty, University of Wisconsin–Madison: https://www.irp.wisc.edu/

National Academies of Sciences, Engineering, and Medicine. https://www.nap.edu/catalog/25246/a-roadmap-to-reducing-child-poverty

National Center for Children in Poverty: https://www.nccp.org/

The Opportunity Atlas: https://opportunityatlas.org/

Poverty Solutions: https://poverty.umich.edu/

Spent: http://playspent.org/flash/Share.php

Stanford Center on Poverty and Inequality: https://inequality.stanford.edu/

# 3

# CHILD WELFARE POLICY

## Michelle Johnson-Motoyama, Jill Duerr Berrick, and Andrea Lane Eastman

Parents, guardians, or other caregivers assume a fundamental role in caring for children. Under some circumstances, however, parents may be unable to provide the protective care that children need. This might be due to death, abandonment, or an extended disabling condition. In other situations, parents may be unable or unwilling to provide the protective care that children require. All nations have enacted laws to respond to children's need for protection from absence or harm from their caregivers (Berrick et al., in press), and the U.N. Convention on the Rights of the Child (UNCRC), the most widely adopted human rights international convention ever enacted (UNICEF, 2005, as cited in Waldock, 2016), specifies all governments' obligations to protect children from abuse, neglect, and exploitation (Article 19, UNCRC).

Though all countries have policies designed to protect children, the differences in policy approaches between countries are great. The United States (U.S.) child welfare system, in comparison to other western, industrialized nations, has been characterized as a "child protection system," with a relatively high threshold for government involvement, a focus on harm or risk of harm, a targeted approach that is more treatment oriented than prevention focused, and a time-limited approach to services. This is in contrast to other countries that are characterized as "family support systems," offering extended, universal, comprehensive services to address a wide range of child and family needs (Gilbert et al., 2011). Trends in contemporary child welfare policy in the U.S. suggest that a gradual shift is underway. With aspirations toward building policy structures that can support and preserve families, international policy approaches are converging.

The laws structuring child welfare in the U.S. are shaped by an overarching federal policy context. These policies are the focus of this chapter. It is important to note, however, that within that larger frame, child welfare policy varies significantly across the 50 states, the U.S. territories, and tribal nations. For example, definitions of child maltreatment vary, types of mandated reporters are not uniform, family assessment strategies are diverse, and preferences about children's out-of-home care settings are notably different. Similarly, state funding to support programs defined by policy are markedly dissimilar (Berrick & Heimpel, 2020). Where possible, we offer examples of these state policy approaches to showcase this national variability.

The number of federal policies shaping child welfare and the historical antecedents of these policies are too numerous to be fully captured in a single chapter; we instead attempt to offer the broad outlines of the U.S. policy context from child maltreatment prevention to early intervention, targeted response, and permanency. Undergirding these various laws, child safety serves as a unifying principle of the field.

---

## EARLY FOUNDATIONS OF TODAY'S CHILD WELFARE SYSTEM

Prior to the emergence of today's child protection system, the fates of abused, neglected, and abandoned children largely depended on extended family members, private charitable organizations, and the kindness, malice, or indifference of strangers. In time, a doctrine of *parens patriae* ("ultimate parent or parent of the country" in Latin) granted states the authority to intervene in the protection of children. In the late 1800s and early 1900s, reformers established specialized juvenile courts across the country, and judges were given broad *parens patriae* authority to make abuse and neglect determinations and decisions about children's custodial arrangements on behalf of the state (Sankaran, 2009). In the context of growing acceptance and institutionalization of the *parens patriae* doctrine, the U.S. Congress established a broad role for the federal government in the welfare of children with the creation of the U.S. Children's Bureau in 1912. However, several years would pass before the introduction of a formal governmental response to child maltreatment. In the wake of the Great Depression, the Social Security Act of 1935 furthered the government's role in ensuring children's welfare by creating the Aid to Dependent Children (ADC) cash assistance program and expanding the role of the Children's Bureau in its implementation through cooperation with state public welfare agencies. Public assistance in the form of ADC (and, later, Aid to Families with Dependent Children [AFDC] in 1962) continued as the single federal response to child and family need (Berrick & Heimpel, 2020). However, a series of developments in the 1960s brought new perspectives to bear on harm to children. In 1962, C. Henry Kempe and his colleagues published the "Battered Child Syndrome," which presented new clinical evidence regarding non-accidental injuries in children who were often very young, chronically neglected, and malnourished (Kempe et al., 1962). That same year, the 1962 Social Security Amendments created a new funding stream, AFDC-Foster Care, to implement the "Flemming Rule," a legal response stemming from denials of public assistance to largely single, Black mothers whose homes were deemed "unsuitable" because of children born outside of marriage. Under the Amendments, AFDC-Foster Care provided public welfare offices with federal matching funds to protect children by removing them from homes considered unfit (Berrick & Heimpel, 2020). Public demands for a governmental response to protect children ultimately resulted in laws defining child maltreatment and requiring the mandated reporting of child abuse and neglect to public social service agencies in every state and the District of Columbia. Congress passed the 1974 Child Abuse Prevention and Treatment Act (CAPTA; Public Law [P.L.] 93-247), which further formalized the role of the federal government in family life and placed it squarely within a federal response that continues to rely on public surveillance of harm to children. Today, the Children's Bureau provides guidance to states in response to federal legislative mandates and disburses federal funding for state and tribal child welfare programs to offer a continuum of services in response to reports of child maltreatment from investigations and targeted services to out-of-home placements, permanency, and independent living services.

# DEFINING CHILD MALTREATMENT

The CAPTA sets forth minimum standards of caregiving that are used by child welfare professionals, law enforcement, the courts, and others to determine whether state intervention into family life is necessary or warranted to protect children. Last reauthorized in December 2010 by P.L. 111-320 and recently amended by the Victims of Child Abuse Reauthorization Act of 2018 (P.L. 115-424), CAPTA defines child abuse and neglect as "any recent act or failure to act on the part of a parent or caretaker which results in death, serious physical or emotional harm, sexual abuse or exploitation" or "an act or failure to act which presents an imminent risk of serious harm." The Justice for Victims of Trafficking Act of 2015 (P.L. 114-22) further defines child victims of sex trafficking as victims of child abuse and neglect and of sexual abuse. State laws and regulations typically go beyond CAPTA's minimum standards by defining specific abusive and neglectful behaviors, specifying individuals that may be reported as suspected perpetrators, and setting standards to guide reporting to child protective services (CPS) agencies (Child Welfare Information Gateway, 2019).

States may also exempt certain behaviors or conditions from definitions of maltreatment, such as physical discipline without injury, the inability to care for a child solely for financial reasons, and the forgoing of medical treatment due to religious beliefs. Most states include definitions of physical abuse, neglect, sexual abuse, and emotional abuse, though the composite behaviors indicative of each type of maltreatment vary from state to state. States may define child maltreatment in both civil and criminal statutes. In most states, individuals with a relationship to a child or those deemed responsible for a child's care may be reported to CPS under civil statutes. Typically, allegations of harm to children by strangers or individuals not involved in a child's care are processed under a state's criminal statutes. However, in at least 16 states, child protection agencies accept reports concerning any individual regardless of the individual's relationship to the child when the report alleges that the child is the victim of human or sex trafficking. Typically, a report must be made when an individual knows or has reasonable cause to believe or suspect that a child has been subjected to maltreatment (Child Welfare Information Gateway, 2019). Notably, child maltreatment definitions vary considerably from state to state and frequently change in response to federal requirements and local circumstances.

## MANDATED REPORTING: WHO IS REQUIRED TO REPORT CHILD MALTREATMENT?

In addition to defining child maltreatment, CAPTA requires each state to specify the individuals who are required to report known or suspected child abuse and neglect to CPS agencies. Approximately 18 states and Puerto Rico require universal mandated reporting, where any person who suspects child abuse and neglect is legally required to report it (Child Welfare Information Gateway, 2019). However, most states and territories mandate members of specific professions that serve or are in frequent contact with children to report, such as teachers, childcare providers, physicians and health care professionals, social workers, law enforcement personnel, and others. Most states require mandatory reporters to report the facts and circumstances that led them to suspect child maltreatment and impose penalties on mandated reporters who fail to report but typically do not place the burden of proof on the reporter. States vary with regard to inclusion of the reporters' name in the report, disclosure of the reporter's identity, and privileged communications. States may also require specific reporting procedures when child maltreatment is the suspected cause of a child's death. As with definitions of child abuse and neglect, mandated reporting laws vary from jurisdiction to jurisdiction and change over time.

## THE CHILD PROTECTIVE SERVICES RESPONSE: SCREENING, INVESTIGATIONS, AND ASSESSMENTS

Once a report of alleged child maltreatment is made to a child protection hotline, a series of events, authorized by state, tribal, and agency policies and funded through a combination of CAPTA Title I and local funding, is set into motion with the overarching goal of assuring child safety. The timing of events may vary in day-to-day practice by jurisdiction but typically follow a common trajectory. After a child protection agency receives a report of possible child maltreatment by phone and, in some states, through the internet, the report is screened by a CPS worker to determine whether it meets statutory definitions of child maltreatment and other criteria for acceptance. Most states have turned to safety assessment instruments to assist with screening decisions and the prioritization of response times. The increased use of safety assessments and other predictive tools has been driven by dramatic increases in reports over time, historically insufficient resources to investigate every report received, and the need to minimize the "false positives" that result in needless encroachments into family life and the "false negatives" that may have dire consequences for children when maltreatment is overlooked (Damman et al., 2020). In 2018 alone, an estimated 4.3 million reports involving approximately 7.8 million children were received by CPS agencies nationally. Of those referrals received, an average of 56% of reports or 32.5 per 1,000 children in the national child population were screened in for investigation or further assessment, with the proportion of referrals screened in ranging from 14% to 98% across jurisdictions (U.S. Department of Health and Human Services [USDHHS], 2020).

If a report is assigned for investigation or further assessment, most states require investigations to commence within 72 hours or in less time if a child is suspected to be in imminent danger (Child Welfare Information Gateway, 2017). Investigations of child maltreatment reports serve at least four purposes: to determine if a child has been harmed or is at risk of harm, to identify the person responsible for the maltreatment, to reduce risk and increase the child's safety, and to determine the need for services to support the family. Investigations may be conducted by the CPS agency, a law enforcement agency, by both agencies in cooperation, or by teams of professionals. States often require CPS workers to use decision-making tools to assess immediate risk and safety and to formulate a plan of care. When an investigation yields evidence to suggest maltreatment has occurred, investigated reports are often classified as *substantiated* or *indicated* and children are considered victims. States may classify reports as *unsubstantiated* or *not indicated* when an investigation is unable to confirm the occurrence of maltreatment; children in such cases are considered non-victims (Child Welfare Information Gateway, 2017). Notably, the level of evidence required for such determinations varies from state to state. In 2018, approximately 678,000 children were found to be victims of child maltreatment, a rate of 9.2 victims per 1,000 children in the national child population (USDHHS et al., 2020).

Over time, child welfare services reforms at the local levels have shaped practice as well as the federal policies that guide screening and investigation. In the 1970s and 1980s, reports of maltreatment to child protection agencies began to soar in the context of growing recognition of complex social conditions involving poverty and drug and HIV epidemics, along with an expanded role for CPS in child sexual abuse cases. In 1985, the National Children's Advocacy Center created a multidisciplinary team approach involving professionals from multiple agencies to minimize the trauma to children resulting from multiple interviews in sexual abuse investigations. The approach now serves as a model for more than 1,000 Children's Advocacy Centers operating across U.S. states and abroad (National Children's Advocacy Center, 2020). The Victims of Child Abuse Act of 1990, most recently reauthorized in 2019 (P.L. 115-424), was passed to provide funding to assist local communities in coordinating multidisciplinary team investigations, prosecutions, and intervention services for child sexual abuse victims.

The practice reform of alternative or differential response (DR) also emerged in the 1990s in response to calls for family-centered approaches to child protection (Waldfogel, 1998). DR programs seek to promote family engagement and allow agencies to assign reports to two or more discrete child protective response pathways based on level of risk and other critical factors (Child Welfare Information Gateway, 2014). In child protection systems using DR, families may receive an assessment and voluntary services in a non-investigative pathway without a formal determination of child maltreatment or entry of the name of the alleged perpetrator into a central child abuse and neglect registry. Statutory amendments made to the CAPTA Reauthorization Act of 2010 (P.L. 111-320) have promoted DR and other preventive approaches. In 2011, Congress passed the Child and Family Services Improvement and Innovation Act (P.L. 112-34) to provide states with funding waivers to conduct demonstration projects that often included DR–based child welfare system reforms. By 2018, jurisdictions in 25 states had some type of DR program in place (USDHHS et al., 2020). Thus, while child protection agencies follow a common trajectory in response to alleged reports of maltreatment, considerable variation exists in screening and investigation/assessment practices across jurisdictions with implications for who goes on to receive targeted services.

## TARGETED SERVICES: FAMILY SUPPORT AND FAMILY PRESERVATION

States and local agencies offer an array of services to children and families as part of the CPS response with the goals of promoting child safety, permanency, and child well-being. The services that children and caregivers receive are often minimal with one or two brief visits or referrals to other social service agencies. In some cases, services are more extensive or longer term to include case management or intensive family-centered services. Research suggests that most children and families who are reported to child protection agencies could benefit from targeted services (see Jonson-Reid et al., 2017). However, in 2018, less than two thirds (57.7%) of children with substantiated reports and one third (33.7%) of children with unsubstantiated reports (including children served through DR) received such services (USDHHS et al., 2020).

State and local agencies rely on a patchwork of funding available through federal, state, and local financing streams to provide an array of services. Title XX of the Social Security Act (Social Services Block Grant; P.L. 93-647) was passed in 1974 to allow states to use federal funds to prevent or remedy neglect, abuse, or exploitation. However, Social Services Block Grant allocations have historically been insufficient to address the growing needs and expanding mandates of child protection. With an uptick in family separation in the 1970s and 1980s that mirrored the rise in child maltreatment reports, hundreds of thousands of children were placed in out-of-home care with few services or supports to decrease family risk or enhance family resilience. In 1990, the U.S. Advisory Board on Child Abuse and Neglect sounded an alarm regarding the nation's child protection crisis with the first in a series of influential reports (U.S. Advisory Board on Child Abuse and Neglect, 1990). A few years later, the Family Preservation and Support Services Act (P.L. 103-66) of 1993 was passed to strengthen efforts to prevent entry into out-of-home care through an infusion of funding under Title IV-B of the Social Security Act. The program provided funding for states to create a continuum of services to promote family strengths, enhance parental functioning, and preserve families in crisis. Subsequently, the Child Welfare Waiver Demonstration Program was authorized as part of the Social Security Amendments of 1994 (P.L. 103-432). The waiver demonstration program provided a limited number of states with the flexible use of federal funding to test approaches to prevent foster care entry, such as services for caregivers with substance use disorders and intensive family preservation programs. The program also allowed states to experiment with new approaches to promote permanency.

As the 1990s wore on, outcry concerning child fatalities, research indicating the limits of certain family preservation programs, and growing concerns about children lingering in out-of-home care contributed to calls to strengthen efforts to protect children and to promote permanency (U.S. Advisory Board on Child Abuse and Neglect, 1991, 1992, 1993). The 1997 Adoption and Safe Families Act (ASFA) reauthorized the Family Preservation and Support Services Act and renamed it the Promoting Safe and Stable Families program (P.L. 107-133, Title IV-B Subpart 2). ASFA also extended and expanded the Child Welfare Waiver Demonstration Program until 2006. In 2011, the Child and Family Services Improvement and Innovation Act (P.L. 112-34) reinstated the waiver program with an emphasis on developing the research base for strategies to prevent out-of-home care and facilitate permanency. Evidence from several states suggests that the flexible use of funding was used to increase the availability of new or expanded services to prevent out-of-home placement. Some waiver programs also demonstrated preliminary successes in improving child safety, permanency, and well-being outcomes for children and families (James Bell Associates, 2019).

The benefits reaped from waiver programs, which ended in 2019, paved the way for the Family First Prevention Services Act of 2018 (FFPSA; P.L. 115-123). FFPSA represented a marked change in child welfare financing by expanding the use of federal Title IV-E program funding beyond foster care expenses to include evidence-based services intended to prevent out-of-home care. Eligible children include those determined by state and tribal agencies to be at imminent risk of removal into foster care but can remain safely in the home of a parent or relative with a set of Title IV-E prevention services, including mental health treatment, substance abuse treatment, and in-home parent training. While FFPSA represents a historic milestone in the story of child protection, several concerns remain, including its exclusive focus on children who have already experienced child maltreatment or face imminent risk of foster care placement, the time-limited nature of services, a narrow financing of clinical services with limited evidence of effectiveness with diverse populations and lack of availability in certain geographic areas, and failure to address the dire economic circumstances that continue to plague the vast majority of families who come to the attention of CPS. Such shortcomings may have the unintended result of exacerbating disparities that currently exist within the child welfare system based on factors such as race, ethnicity, socioeconomic status, and geography.

## PROMOTING CHILD SAFETY AND WELL-BEING IN OUT-OF-HOME CARE

Although the architecture of the child welfare system—in principle—is designed to remediate the need for out-of-home care, some family circumstances pose significant risks to children's safety such that separation of children from their parents is necessary. About a quarter million children enter out-of-home care in the U.S. each year (USDHHS et al., 2019), though for most, their stay is temporary.

Prior to 1980, or 1978 for Native American/Alaska Native children (see Box 3.1), there were no federal standards for foster care. State and local practices varied dramatically. Moreover, evidence indicated that children's experiences in care were highly varied. Standards for removal decisions were extremely broad and imprecise, accountability mechanisms to track children's trajectories in care were uneven and children were sometimes lost in the system, quality of care varied dramatically, large numbers of children were served in institutional settings, placement instability was rampant, children's stay in care could be indefinite, parents were infrequently afforded due process, and efforts to return children to their birth families were highly irregular (Fanshel & Shinn, 1978; Maas & Engler, 1964; Wald, 1976).

In 1980, Congress passed the Adoption Assistance and Child Welfare Act (AACWA; P.L.96-272), setting the parameters for children's out-of-home stay. The law established few absolute requirements for states, though it set conditions for federal funds, thus offering substantial financial incentives for state participation (Berrick & Heimpel, 2020). States were required to offer "reasonable efforts" to prevent placement and to support family reunification. States were also required to establish written documents (i.e., case plans) to describe standards for services and care and goals for permanency. The law specified that child welfare agencies should prioritize reunification for children placed in out-of-home care, offering services to support parents in reaching that goal. For parents unable to reunify, adoption was accorded significant weight as a second-best permanency option for children, and adoption subsidies were established to help families take on the financial responsibilities associated with a new family member.[1] Legal guardianship was also an approved permanency measure, and long-term foster care was reserved only for children who could not otherwise secure a permanent family. In order to establish checks and balances, children's entry to care required a judicial determination (except in the case of short-term voluntary placements), and periodic case reviews were required in order to track each family's progress. Congress established preferences for children's care arrangement during their separation from family. Child welfare agencies were to strive to utilize "placement settings in the least restrictive (most family like) setting available and in close proximity to the parent's home, consistent with the best interest of the child" (AACWA, 1980, Definition 5a). Many of the provisions of AACWA have been retained and most subsequent federal policy builds on or adjusts to these fundamental standards.

Although the national caseload initially fell, most states saw sharp increases in their out-of-home care caseload relatively soon after AACWA's implementation. In the early 1980s, about 4.2 children per 1,000 were in out-of-home care; this increased to almost 7 children per 1,000 a decade later (Tatara, 1994). To absorb the rapidly rising foster care caseload, many states turned to extended relatives as children's foster care providers. Enthusiasm for kinship care came about, in part, following a U.S. Supreme Court ruling (*Miller v. Youakim*, 1979) allowing federal funds to pay for kinship foster parent subsidies. But the transition also reflected shifting views in the field at large, to appreciate family and embrace family strengths. As described previously, these sentiments to privilege family preservation were given substance in 1993 when Congress passed the Family Preservation and Family Support provisions of P.L. 103-66, which provided funding for support services to families as a means of stemming new entrants to care.

Entries to care, however, were largely unaffected. The foster care caseload continued to rise, and by the mid-1990s, Congress again addressed a number of issues in foster care through federal policy. The laws developed in the late 1990s focused largely on the back end of the child welfare system (opportunities for exits from care) in contrast to the 1993 Family Preservation provisions, which are emblematic of a front-end approach to curb children's entry to care. Specifically, in 1994, Congress passed the Multi-Ethnic Placement Act (P.L. 103-382), followed by the 1996 Interethnic Adoption Provisions (P.L. 104-188) to facilitate adoption for children of color. Prior to these policies, child welfare agencies in the 1970s and 1980s emphasized same-race foster and adoptive placements as culturally responsive practice (Crumbley, 1999). But research evidence suggested that length of stay for children of color—particularly Black children—was longer and that opportunities for adoption were fewer (Barth, 1997). Some argued that these practices, though well intentioned, had the effect of creating unequal access to permanency for children of color and therefore contributed to unequal treatment (Bartholet, 1999). The result was a policy that prohibited states from delaying or denying a child's foster care or adoptive placement based on the child's or the potential caregiver's race, color, or national origin. The law also required states to make diligent efforts to recruit foster and adoptive parents who reflect the racial or ethnic diversity of the children needing care.

Not long after, Congress again turned its attention to the back end of foster care, instituting the ASFA. Designed as a corrective to some of the perceived flaws of the 1980 law, ASFA shortened the amount of time available to parents to change the circumstances that brought their child to care. Specifically, whereas AACWA allowed a parent 18 months of services to support reunification, ASFA shortened the period of reunification to 12 months. Thereafter, all children in care were required to have a *permanency plan* that specified the expected lasting home. Further, the law specified that if a child remained in care for 15 of 22 months (barring some exceptions), the state is obliged to make efforts to terminate parental rights and seek an alternative permanency arrangement for the child, with preference given to adoption. States were offered significant incentives to increase the number of adoptions performed and, notably, adoptions rose. From 1997 to 2002, the number of U.S. adoptions from foster care increased by 62% (Swensen, 2004). The policy also clarified the role of relatives as priority placements for children in need of out-of-home care. The most recent federal data suggest that 32% of children live with relative foster parents in out-of-home care, almost half (46%) live with nonrelative foster parents, and about one in ten lives in a group home or institutional care setting (USDHHS et al., 2019).

Finally, given concerns that some states had interpreted the "reasonable efforts" provision of AACWA too liberally (Kim, 1999), ASFA clarified a series of aggravated circumstances that could disqualify a parent from receiving any reunification services; in these instances, opportunities for reunification would be bypassed, and children could become available for adoption almost immediately.

ASFA provided an important, clarifying frame for the field of child welfare. It made clear that the fundamental goal of the field is to protect and promote children's safety. This focal orientation allowed for a narrowing of eligibility and an opportunity to make more uniform the criteria used across states and jurisdictions to determine state involvement in family life. A secondary goal was to promote permanency for children—including a legal and affective lifelong relationship with an adult caregiver. And finally, the law promoted the goal of child well-being, though funding and policy guidance to implement the third goal was never established.

Though most federal child welfare policy has been universally implemented for all groups, some policies have focused specifically on a target issue, population, or age group. Federal policy in support of children's relatives, for example, has evolved over time. The ASFA specified a preference for relative placements. As a result, child welfare professionals now routinely privilege kin in selecting children's care arrangement. As mentioned, the most recent federal data shows that almost one third of children (32%) in out-of-home care are living in kinship foster care (USDHHS et al., 2019). Kin were again the subject of legislative interest when, in 2008, Congress passed the Fostering Connections to Success and Increasing Adoptions Act (P.L. 110-351). The policy created a funding stream for relatives to assume legal guardianship. The law was based on research showing that transitioning children in kinship foster care to funded permanency opportunities such as kin adoption or kin guardianship could ensure stability for children and cost-savings to the state (Testa, 2002). Although adoption had always been available to kin, significant evidence suggested that many kin were reticent to pursue adoption because of concerns about the implications of terminating a relative's parental rights (Burnette, 1997). Legal guardianship, on the other hand, was seen as a more family-responsive permanency option, as it allows for a legal custodial relationship with the child without the finality of terminating parental rights. The most recent federal data—including information about kin and nonkin caregivers—indicates that about 11% of children exit out-of-home care to legal guardianship (USDHHS et al., 2019).

The federal emphasis on family-based or family-like care was reaffirmed in 2018 when Congress passed the FFPSA. In addition to the prevention-oriented components of this law (described previously), FFPSA encouraged states to place children in family-based settings whenever possible. More important, the law discouraged placement in group or congregate care settings, limiting federal funding for these settings to only two weeks.

Other policies that target a specific group of children have been focused on older youth in care (Box 3.4), Native American/Alaska Native children (Box 3.3), and children who are experiencing commercial sexual exploitation (Box 3.5).

# CHILD MALTREATMENT IN THE UNITED STATES TODAY

Unfortunately, child maltreatment is not an uncommon experience in the U.S. today. State CPS agencies are required to report annual data related to child abuse and neglect to the Children's Bureau of the USDHHS Administration for Children and Families (USDHHS et al., 2020). A national snapshot of data shows that in 2018, an estimated 3,534,000 children and adolescents were investigated by CPS due to alleged abuse or neglect—nearly 5 out of every 100 children in the U.S. Each year, one out of every 100 children had a substantiated report. About 85% of these children and adolescents had one allegation type in 2018: 60% were neglected, 11% were physically abused, and 7% were sexually abused. Fifteen percent had two or more maltreatment types documented. In 2018, an estimated 1,770 children died of abuse and neglect.

Importantly, yearly estimates show that the number of children who receive a CPS investigation or alternative response is increasing, particularly among racial and ethnic minorities (U.S. Census Bureau, 2019; USDHHS et al., 2019). CPS investigation rates for Black and Hispanic children have increased steadily since 2014. Fifteen per 1,000 American Indian or Alaska Native children and 14 per 1,000 Black children were substantiated as victims in 2018, compared to a rate of 8 per 1,000 White children (USDHHS et al., 2020). These data show that Black children are almost four times as likely as White children to be investigated for maltreatment annually.

Historically, the burdens of child abuse and neglect have been assessed using an annual snapshot of data. However, one year of data cannot describe the risk of child maltreatment across the life course, particularly for at-risk subgroups. When children and adolescents are followed longitudinally, from birth to age 18, more than a third of U.S. children experience a substantiated report to CPS for abuse or neglect by the age of 18 (Kim et al., 2017). The lifetime estimate is much higher than the number of children whose maltreatment is substantiated yearly (USDHHS et al., 2020). Longitudinal data show that the risk for a substantiated maltreatment report is highest in the first few years of life (Wildeman et al., 2014). Disparities are notable among children who are Black (53%) and Hispanic (32%) in comparison to children who are White (23%) or Asian/Pacific Islander (10%; Kim et al., 2017).[2] The disparities of race/ethnicity persist beyond substantiated child maltreatment reports. Black children in the U.S. make up only 14% of the country's child population but nearly a quarter of those in foster care (U.S. Census Bureau, 2019; USDHHS et al., 2019).

Other subgroups of children and youth are also at increased risk for CPS involvement and are disproportionally engaged with the child welfare system, including children with disabilities and youth who identify as lesbian, gay, bisexual, transgender, or queer/questioning (LGBTQ).

Children with disabilities are more likely to be maltreated, to experience multiple forms of maltreatment, and to experience multiple episodes of maltreatment in comparison to peers without disabilities (Sullivan & Knutson, 2000). The type of disability tends to be related to the timing and severity of maltreatment (Leeb et al., 2012).

Some youth who identify as LGBTQ face verbal and physical harassment or rejection when they disclose their sexual identity to family members, which sometimes results in out-of-home placement or homelessness (Baams et al., 2019). As a result, LGBTQ youth are overrepresented in the child welfare system (Mallon et al., 2006; McCormick et al., 2017; Wilson et al., 2014). For example, a study of youth in Los Angeles (ages 12–21) found that 19% of youth in foster care identified as LGBTQ, which means that LGBTQ youth are in foster care at a rate 1.5 to 2 times greater than their representation in the general population (Wilson et al., 2014). LGBTQ youth also encounter challenges in the child welfare system more than youth in care who do not identify as LGBTQ (Mallon et al., 2006; McCormick et al., 2017). LGBTQ youth in foster care have more placement instability and more mental health–related hospitalizations, and they experience higher rates of homelessness after they exit care in comparison to youth in care who do not identify as LGBTQ (Wilson et al., 2014). Permanency and placement options are limited for many LGBTQ youth, which means these youth are more likely to be placed in congregate settings and age out of foster care (Mallon et al., 2006).

Knowledge on risk factors can improve insight about the cause of child maltreatment and policy and practice aimed at prevention (Mulder et al., 2018), and ample research has focused on risk and protective factors for child abuse and neglect. Risk factors associated with child maltreatment and CPS involvement include parent and family, health, and financial indicators. Parent factors such as substance abuse (see Box 3.2), high stress, aggressive behaviors, low self-esteem, experience of maltreatment as a child, and intimate partner violence relate to a child's risk for maltreatment (Assink et al., 2019; Freisthler et al., 2017; Stith et al., 2009; van IJzendoorn et al., 2020; Yampolskaya & Banks, 2006). Family factors can also be protective for children, such as having two legal parents established at birth, having non-teen parents, having parents with a high school degree, and having parents with an employment history (Culhane et al., 2003; Foust et al., 2020; Slack et al., 2011). Child health indicators, such as birth at a healthy weight without abnormalities or disabilities, and a mother's access to and receipt of timely prenatal care can also guard against maltreatment (Assink et al., 2019; Foust et al., 2020; Sullivan & Knutson, 2000). Conversely, low socioeconomic status places children at increased risk for CPS involvement (van IJzendoorn et al., 2020).

Risk factors vary across maltreatment types. Child neglect is the most common form of maltreatment and is related to parental factors such as substance abuse, history of criminal offense, psychiatric diagnoses, and a low educational level (Mulder et al., 2018; Yampolskaya & Banks, 2006). Sexual abuse is associated with the maltreatment of siblings, parenting problems (e.g., poor parent–child relationships), a nonnuclear family structure (e.g., the presence of a stepfather or a stepfather-like figure), and family problems (e.g., social isolation; Assink et al., 2019). Importantly, all forms of maltreatment are related to a parent's history of maltreatment in childhood (Assink et al., 2019; van IJzendoorn et al., 2020). Clinicians often work to address child factors, but parent-related factors may be key to preventing maltreatment because they are more closely tied to child risk.

## EVALUATING THE NATION'S CHILD PROTECTION POLICY RESPONSE

Today's child protection response operates in the context of three principles that were codified through the ASFA: safety, permanency, and well-being. How effective is the U.S. strategy of protecting vulnerable children in light of these principles? This question is partly addressed through the federal government's periodic monitoring of state performance on the Child and Family Services Reviews (CFSRs). The CFSR process builds on efforts to review child and family services programs that began in the 1990s and was established in 2000 to evaluate the states' substantial conformity on seven specific outcomes and seven system indicators (Children's Bureau, 2020a). The CFSR safety outcomes prioritize the protection of children from abuse and neglect and the safe maintenance of children in their homes whenever appropriate and possible. The permanency outcomes focus on the permanence and stability of children's living situations and the continuity of family relationships. Family and child well-being outcomes center on building enhanced capacity to provide for children's needs, providing appropriate services to children to meet their educational needs, and providing adequate services to meet the physical and mental health needs of children.

The overarching purpose of the CFSR process is to help states improve outcomes for children who receive services through the child welfare system. Thus, the Children's Bureau intentionally sets a high bar for achieving substantial conformity—95% of reviewed cases are expected to meet the government's standards. In the latest round of reviews, which concluded in 2018, state performance varied widely and only two indicators were met by a small number of states. Four states achieved substantial conformity in protecting children from abuse and neglect. Six states achieved substantial conformity in ensuring that children in contact with the child welfare system received appropriate services to meet their educational needs (Children's Bureau, 2020a). Consequently, program improvement plans were developed to support jurisdictions in achieving substantial conformity in all areas in future reviews. While many states have made strides in implementing the principles of safety, permanency, and well-being, findings from the CFSR process suggest that public policies designed to protect children are missing their mark in responding to and addressing the ongoing public health crisis of child maltreatment.

As mentioned earlier, as many as 37% of U.S. children will have a report to CPS accepted for investigation at least once over the course of childhood (Kim et al., 2017). Notably, the Children's Bureau's safety standards only apply to children who meet criteria for an investigative response, with few resources dedicated to prevention (see Box 3.1). Part of the criteria used to determine whether a child protection agency will initiate a response is the state's definition of child maltreatment. However, little is known about the effects of decades of changes in federal and state definitions, standards for reporting, and mandated reporting laws on child protection caseload dynamics or the safety of children (National Research Council, 2014).

Today, when children are reported to child protection agencies, approximately 40% do not receive an investigative response or assessment and are screened out, despite evidence to suggest that a call to a child protection hotline is the best predictor of a later child maltreatment fatality (U.S. Commission to Eliminate Child Abuse and Neglect Fatalities, 2016). Notably, screening decisions are informed by a broad array of case, worker, and organizational factors such as resource constraints (Damman et al., 2020). Such decisions are made using risk assessment instruments and predictive approaches with varying levels of validity or reliability (Van der Put et al., 2017). Little is known about the trajectories of children in screened-out reports because individual information is typically not collected or recorded systematically in child protection data systems for these children. However, studies suggest that between 25% to 31% of children who are screened out are likely to return to child protection agencies again (Conley & Berrick, 2010; Dumas et al., 2015; Loman et al., 2009). When reports are accepted for investigation, a substantial number of children are subsequently re-reported, suggesting that for many children, the experience of maltreatment is a recurring one. Recent data suggest that nearly 14% of children reported to child protection agencies within the first 12 years of life are likely to experience two subsequent reports; 2% of children may experience as many as six subsequent reports (Kim & Drake, 2019).

When reports are assigned for a response, public policy prioritizes child safety. The investigatory or assessment response initiated by child protection agencies, which is typically required to occur within 72 hours, happens in a timely way in less than a handful of states (Children's Bureau, 2020a), raising questions about the capacity of CPS to perform this critical function. The investigatory process typically combines a forensic fact-finding process to confirm whether child maltreatment has occurred with assessments of child safety and risk to inform case planning. Reports may be *confirmed*, *indicated*, or *substantiated* using standards of evidence that vary from state to state. Concerns have been raised about the meaning, value, and use of substantiation or related determinations in practice and policy making (Drake, 1996; Kohl et al., 2009). In theory, the substantiation decision typically requires a high level of harm and a high level of evidence to confirm the report (Drake, 1996). However, high levels of harm or risk of harm may exist in investigated cases without sufficient evidence to confirm maltreatment. Indeed, little variation typically exists regarding risk factors, recidivism, or the long-term health consequences of children in substantiated and unsubstantiated reports (e.g., Hussey et al., 2006; Kohl et al., 2009; Kugler et al., 2019). Yet, the substantiation decision often serves as the gateway to the receipt of services, to court involvement, and to the inclusion of individuals in central child abuse and neglect registries. Many states also base their decisions to expunge reports of abuse and neglect from central registries based on report substantiation with long-term implications for parents that can impact employment and therefore the economic stability of their families well after presenting conditions have been resolved (Henry et al., 2020).

The value of family integrity is expressed in public child protection policy through the financing of services through Title IV-B of the Social Security Act, the Social Services Block Grant, and other federal, state, and local funding streams (Rosinsky & Williams, 2018). The effectiveness of the child protection response largely hinges on the notion that an array of time-limited services, coupled with safety monitoring and the threat of a child's removal, are sufficient to ameliorate the conditions that bring children to the attention of child protection agencies. Therefore, child protection agencies are evaluated in their provision of services to protect children in their homes, to prevent removal, and to enhance the capacity of families to provide for their children's needs. However, results from the CFSRs suggest that the provision of services to children and families is highly uneven across jurisdictions. In 2018, the Children's Bureau found concerted efforts to provide services in only 45% of cases, with delays in providing services and a lack of effort to engage parents in services cited as practice concerns. Only 36% of families had enhanced capacity to provide for their children's needs after their involvement with child protection agencies. The CFSR process also assesses whether agencies make concerted efforts to assess and address safety concerns for the vast majority of children (80%) who remain in their own homes following an investigation. Agencies conducted ongoing assessments that accurately assessed all risk and safety concerns in 62% of applicable cases, suggesting the safety concerns of more than a third of children went overlooked (Children's Bureau, 2020a).

Very little is known about the effectiveness of services when they are provided by child protection agencies due to historically limited investments in data and research (Jonson-Reid et al., 2017). Some studies suggest that receipt of child protection services can contribute to short-run gains for certain children and families, while other studies find no effect of services on maltreatment recurrence (Russell et al., 2018). Services appear to be effective when they are matched to families' needs; however, many families under the supervision of child protection services do not receive services that are matched to their needs or they receive unneeded services (Simon, 2020). However, with few exceptions, studies of child protection services have lacked comparison groups, thereby limiting the ability to make causal inferences about the effects of CPS. Today's child protection response is also intended to embrace a systems of care perspective drawn from wraparound services in the children's mental health field to meet families' needs (see Chapter 5 on Child Mental Health Policy). The integrative approach is based on principles of interagency collaboration and community-based services, practices tailored to family needs that draw upon family strengths, authentic participation and partnerships with families and children, cultural competence, and systems accountability (Perry & Fusco, 2013). However, the extent to which child protection agencies have been successful in implementing the system of care guidance, and to what end, also remains unclear.

Despite these limitations, significant strides have been made in the past 20 years to develop, implement, test, and disseminate evidence-based programs for preventing recurring child abuse and neglect. Though the effects of such programs on direct measures of child maltreatment are generally modest (Euser et al. 2015), evidence suggests that outcomes for families served through the child protection response can be improved through the integration of developmentally appropriate, evidence-based interventions into existing service arrays. However, to date, these programs have had limited uptake in the child welfare system (Saul et al., 2008; Toth & Manly, 2011). The promise of evidence-based services was most recently reflected in the FFPSA, which builds on the Title IV-E waiver program by formalizing financial inducements for child protection agencies to use funds previously limited to foster care expenditures for specific evidence-based services to prevent foster care entry. The extent to which the promise of evidence-based services is realized remains to be seen.

Experimentation with practice reforms such as DR, which seeks to enhance family engagement and expand access to voluntary preventive services in lieu of court-mandated services, has yielded findings to suggest that some children and families can be served safely through a voluntary service model (Fluke et al., 2019; Fuller & Zhang, 2017). While many questions about DR remain, national data suggest that states using DR programs experience fewer victims and foster care entries over time when compared to states without the program (Johnson-Motoyama et al., 2020), suggesting the program may play an important role in secondary prevention.

As we consider the back end of the system, there is much that we know and a good deal still to discover. We know, for example, that when children are removed to out-of-home care, federal policy strongly favors placement with extended relatives. Although this policy approach aligns with our principles regarding family continuity, the evidence in support of a policy preference for kinship care is somewhat equivocal. On the one hand, there is some evidence to suggest that outcomes for children placed with kin are positive. A review of a number of studies based largely on caregiver reports of children's behavior and based on placement stability patterns suggests the benefits of kinship care (Winokur et al., 2018). Other research, however, shows strong selection effects into kinship care (i.e., kinship caregivers are less likely to accept children with more challenging conditions; Koh & Testa, 2011), shifting one's interpretation of these and other studies.

When research takes into account the children who are more likely to be placed in kinship care, some studies find important negative effects associated with adolescent pregnancy, substance use, delinquency, health, and mental health outcomes (Andersen & Fallesen, 2015; Fechter-Leggett & O'Brien, 2010; Font, 2014; Ryan et al., 2010; Sakai et al., 2011). Research evidence would suggest that principles of family continuity, if combined with theory and evidence about child development and positive parenting, can offer children important protective experiences in out-of-home care, but blind reliance on the principle of family continuity may not serve the best interests of children.

Just as kinship care is a heterogeneous phenomenon, with benefits for some children and hazards for others, the evidence on group care is also mixed, in spite of the fact that substantial policy directives guard against its use. *Group care* is a vague term that captures a wide range of placement settings; comparing research findings across studies, therefore, is challenging. In general, developmental theory indicates that group care is contraindicated for young children (see, for example, Berrick et al., 1998; Dozier et al., 2014). For older youth, studies generally suggest that outcomes are comparable to specialized foster care (Barth et al., 2007; James et al., 2012), though the availability of an ample supply of foster parents may limit this placement opportunity for some children.

Following placement into care, public policy prioritizes reunification for children and their parents (except under extraordinary circumstances). Policymakers have embraced this outcome because it aligns with our principles regarding family integrity. Reunification is a frequent outcome for children taken in to care; about one half of children who are removed to care are returned to their families (USDHHS et al., 2019). The research evidence in support of reunification on children's beneficial outcomes, however, is weak. Children who are reunified have relatively high rates of instability and many are returned to care. Depending on the circumstances of the child and family, between 3% and almost 30% of children reenter out-of-home care (Children's Bureau, 2020b). Given that entries to care are predicated on new incidents of maltreatment (Biehal, 2007; Connell et al., 2009), these findings are of concern. In addition to instability, many families experience considerable vulnerability. As a result, outcomes associated with reunification can be troubling. One study comparing older youth who aged out of care to youth who were reunified indicated that reunification provided a buffering effect against the risk of homelessness (Fowler et al., 2017). But in other areas, reunification effects are more sobering. Methodologically rigorous studies generally find that behavioral and academic outcomes associated with reunification are worse than remaining in care (Bellamy, 2008; Sinclair et al., 2005; Taussig et al., 2001) and that reunified children are exposed to more adverse life events in childhood (Lau et al., 2003). These findings do not suggest that reunification should not be pursued. Outcomes for reunified families might be better if parents were offered post-reunification services and general supports. Unlike policies in support of adoptive parents or kin guardians, however, federal policy provides neither monthly subsidies nor services to parents following reunification. Research is sorely needed to identify evidence-based strategies that help families reunify and that allow children to safely remain at home. Despite our policy goals to reunify children with their families, we have almost no evidence to suggest which services are most effective in helping families achieve this goal.

For children who are unable to reunify, public policy supports adoption as a next best alternative. The evidence suggests that adoption confers a number of benefits to children, including increased stability (Rolock, 2015; Smith et al., 2006), a sense of belonging (Brodzinsky et al., 1998), and generally positive long-term outcomes (Triseliotis, 2002). These relative advantages may be based, in part, on selection effects; children adopted from care are younger, on average, and they have therefore been exposed to a shorter duration of maltreatment (Snowden et al., 2008).

Typically, they also have fewer health- or mental health–related problems compared to children who are not adopted out of care (Snowden et al., 2008). The U.S. is widely acknowledged as an *adoption nation* (Pertman, 2011); the rate of adoption out of foster care is much higher in the U.S. than in any other western industrialized country (Skivenes et al., in press). The combination of public acceptance and policy enthusiasm with positive research findings suggest that adoption from care is unlikely to abate in the near term.

Some children neither go home nor are adopted. For these children who are placed with kin, federal policy promotes legal guardianship by offering a monthly long-term subsidy. As indicated previously, recent legislation in support of legal guardianship was, in part, based on research evidence showing the relational and financial benefits relative to long-term foster care (Testa, 2002).

Finally, some children remain in foster care long-term, though public policy largely shuns this outcome. In general, we have few studies that accurately estimate the proportion of children who remain in care long-term. Federal data indicate that the current foster care caseload includes 27% of children who have been in care for two years or longer (USDHHS et al., 2019), though point-in-time estimates typically overestimate the proportion of children with longer durations in care. Two recent studies examined the likelihood that an infant placed in care would experience a continuous placement until age 18. In both studies, significantly fewer than 1% of children grew up in care (Magruder & Berrick, in review; Wulczyn, 2020). This is a substantial improvement from the circumstances of children in the 1950s and 1960s where one study indicated that the majority of children taken into care remained there long-term (Maas & Engler, 1959). The limited evidence available to test the effects of long-term foster care suggest a permanency alternative that should be avoided. In addition to the significant likelihood of placement instability as children's duration in care extends (Rubin et al., 2007), some evidence suggests that children's developmental outcomes are worse compared to a return home or adoption (Lloyd & Barth, 2011).

But among the children and youth who remain in care, some will eventually age out. Federal law allows states to extend foster care benefits beyond age 18 to support positive young adult outcomes. There is, indeed, some evidence to suggest that remaining in care beyond age 18 offers short-term benefits; youth are comparatively less likely to experience homelessness, unemployment, or joblessness (Courtney et al., 2016). These findings, of course, are driven by the conditions of the policy, as youth are not eligible for a foster care extension unless they are engaged in school or work; the monthly subsidy is designed for board and care (Child Welfare Information Gateway, 2017). In terms of the risk of homelessness over time, it appears that beneficial outcomes are short-lived (Dworsky & Courtney, 2010), and effects associated with educational achievement are modest at best (Okpych et al., 2019).

In general, there is a stirring debate about the merits of out-of-home care as a policy strategy for protecting children whose safety is seriously compromised. Some argue that foster care is deployed too often, that there are too many children in care, that the care is harmful to children, and that foster care as an institution is destructive to communities of color—particularly Black and Native American communities (Roberts, 2002; for a thoughtful review of these issues, see Font & Gershoff, 2020). Although the principles of federal child welfare policy eschew foster care, the limited funding and services available to support families and protect children are often insufficient to prevent placement into care. Foster care is typically a relatively short-term experience; about one quarter of children leave care within six months following entry (USDHHS et al., 2019). As such, it can be difficult for research to disentangle the effects of foster care from the effects of the vulnerabilities that placed children at risk prior to and after a foster care episode. Whether out-of-home care confers net advantages that are greater than remaining in an abusive home is a critical question for the field.

Developmental theory and compelling evidence (Doyle, 2007) suggest that placement into care when circumstances do not seriously warrant this intrusive measure is inappropriate, results in negative outcomes for children, and should be avoided. Federal policy largely speaks to this issue by requiring reasonable efforts to prevent placement, whenever possible. On balance, the evidence on the effects of foster care generally find no effect or marginally positive effects in the areas of academic achievement (Bald et al., 2019; Berger et al., 2015; Horwitz et al., 2001; Zajac et al., 2019). Other studies show protective effects against adolescent parenting (Font et al., 2019), marginally positive effects relating to mental health (Conn et al., 2015), and no effect (positive or negative) on behavior problems (Berger et al., 2009).

# RECOMMENDATIONS FOR CHILD WELFARE POLICY

Unlike many other developed countries, U.S. public child protection policies, with few exceptions, focus on addressing maltreatment after it occurs, a policy paradigm that can best be described as "too little, too late." Past research generally suggests that any report to child protection is an important "signal of child risk" (Putnam-Hornstein, 2011). Public investments in child protection approximate $30 billion per year across federal, state, and local funding sources; however, this figure amounts to less than 1% of total federal spending (Rosinsky & Williams, 2018). As a result, most agencies have limited capacity to respond to the considerable influx of reports of alleged maltreatment. Large numbers of children and families are turned away, only to return to the door of child protection as maltreatment recurs or intensifies. When children and families do receive a response, access to services is uneven, services may be ill-matched to concerns, safety monitoring is irregular, and the services provided to treat or prevent the recurrence of maltreatment are often ineffective or of unknown effectiveness (Children's Bureau, 2020a; Jonson-Reid et al., 2017; Russell et al., 2018). Yet, child maltreatment is a major, preventable public health problem related to a host of negative health outcomes throughout the life course (Gilbert et al., 2009; Wildeman & Emanuel, 2014). Child abuse and neglect can cause death or serious injury. Chronic maltreatment can have long lasting effects such as mental health issues, drug and alcohol problems, risky sexual behavior, obesity, and criminal behavior (Gilbert et al., 2009). The consequences of child abuse and neglect are not restricted to individuals but also impact neighborhoods, communities, and society. Economic estimates suggest child maltreatment may cost the U.S. billions of dollars annually given increased expenditures for specialized treatment, health care needs, child welfare expenses, juvenile justice involvement, special education, and lost productivity (Fang et al., 2012).

The U.S. public policy paradigm situates child protection agencies at the base of a figurative waterfall of child abuse and neglect concerns. These concerns are shaped by individual and relationship factors as well as broad societal dynamics including poverty, racism, gender-based violence, and community violence (Fortson et al., 2016). For example, studies of racial and ethnic disparities in CPS suggest that poverty often explains the greater involvement of Black, Hispanic, and Native American children in the child welfare system (e.g., Drake et al., 2009; Maguire-Jack et al., 2015; Putnam-Hornstein et al., 2013). Structural racism provides a framework for understanding how social forces and ideologies inform the policies and institutional dynamics that produce and maintain inequalities among racial and ethnic groups across multiple domains of risk and protection for child maltreatment (Gee & Ford, 2011). For example, the disproportional impacts of the COVID-19 pandemic in the U.S. have amplified stark differences in opportunity, access to resources, and health status along socioeconomic and racial and ethnic lines. While the pandemic's effects on child maltreatment have not yet been determined, the crisis crystallizes the need for public policies that address the "upstream" factors that disproportionally impact the children and families who are disproportionally served "downstream" in the nation's hospitals and other first-responder systems. The important public policy opportunity for the field of child welfare is similar. Public policies to protect children and strengthen families must also look "upstream" by addressing the conditions that give rise to disproportionate maltreatment risk while simultaneously pursuing prevention strategies that build resilience and nurturing relationships well before children reach beleaguered child protection agencies at the bottom of the waterfall.

Policies that address conditions through primary prevention have the potential to reach broad segments of the U.S. population with sustainable impacts on reducing child maltreatment (Klevens et al., 2015). A growing body of research on the relationship between income support and child maltreatment suggests that even small amounts of income matter for prevention. Policies that facilitate greater access to concrete supports such as Temporary Aid to Needy Families, the Supplemental Nutrition Assistance Program, child care subsidies, and the Earned Income Tax Credit (Ginther & Johnson-Motoyama, 2017; Maguire-Jack et al., in press) are related to reductions in child maltreatment. Increases in the minimum wage (Raissian & Bullinger, 2017), supportive housing (Farrell et al., 2018), state expansions in Medicaid (Brown et al., 2019), and child support pass-throughs (Cancian et al., 2013) have also been associated with reductions in child maltreatment.

Public policies must also prioritize developmentally informed systems of violence prevention that promote healthy, nurturing relationships across the life course from infancy through adulthood. A critical body of research suggests that those who experience violence at one point in life have an increased likelihood of experiencing multiple forms of violence at other points in life. Similarly, those who commit violence in one context are likely to commit violence again in other contexts (Turner et al., 2010). Notably, multiple forms of violence share common consequences and common risk and protective factors over the life course (Wilkins et al., 2014). Therefore, policies that promote coordinated, comprehensive violence prevention strategies across the life course are likely to be more effective than policies that pursue specific forms of violence in isolation. This approach requires next-level policies that cross academic disciplines, funding streams, and service sectors to build systems of prevention that truly embody principles of child safety, permanency, and well-being—through societal investments in healthy relationships and the contexts that support them.

**BOX 3.1**

## Child Maltreatment Prevention

Although the prevention of child maltreatment calls for a broad range of policies and practices, limited federal governmental funding and leadership have been devoted to preventing child maltreatment before it occurs. In its early years, the Child Abuse Prevention and Treatment Act (CAPTA) mandated funding for self-help prevention programs founded by parent advocates, authorized research into child abuse prevention and treatment, and created the National Center on Child Abuse and Neglect (now the Office on Child Abuse and Neglect) within the Children's Bureau to carry out a broad range of activities. However, primary prevention would not become a major focus for at least two more decades, given CAPTA's immediate priority of responding to existing or ongoing child maltreatment.

In the early 1990s, the U.S. Advisory Board on Child Abuse and Neglect, a Blue-Ribbon expert panel, ushered in a series of influential reports that culminated in the major federal prevention policies and programs in place today by sounding an alarm about the nation's child protection crisis (U.S. Advisory Board on Child Abuse and Neglect, 1990, 1991, 1992, 1993). The advisory board made several recommendations, including steps to replace the existing child

protection system with a national, child-centered, neighborhood-based child protection strategy. Though this vision was never realized, efforts were made to expand funding for the primary prevention of child maltreatment with the Human Service Amendments of 1994, establishing a new Title II of CAPTA that was most recently reauthorized as the Community-Based Child Abuse Prevention (CBCAP) grants under the Keeping Families Safe Act of 2003 (P.L. 108-36). CBCAP is funded through a small formula grant (approximately $53.6 million in FY 2020) to state lead agencies to support family strengthening and support services, interagency collaboration and the development of prevention networks, and technical assistance with a strong emphasis on parent leadership in planning, implementation, and evaluation (FRIENDS National Center for Community-Based Child Abuse Prevention, 2020).

With the turn of the 21st century, scientific breakthroughs in early childhood brain development and the long-term consequences of early exposure to adverse childhood experiences (ACEs; Felitti et al., 1998) drove renewed interest in prevention and efforts to increase coordination across early childhood and early intervention systems. In the context of rising governmental accountability in the late 1990s, increasing emphasis was placed on advancing interdisciplinary research to inform the development and testing of evidence-based interventions. CAPTA research investments in nurse home visiting for at-risk expectant women and parents with young children proved fruitful in advance of major federal investments in the Maternal, Infant, and Early Childhood Home Visiting (MIECHV) program through the Patient Protection and Affordable Care Act of 2010. Administered through the Health Resources and Services Administration, MIECHV receives $400 million per year to implement evidence-based home visiting programs, with investments reaching 36% of all urban and 22% of all rural U.S. counties in FY 2018 (Administration for Children and Families, 2020). Despite CAPTA's financial opportunities for states to develop child abuse and neglect prevention programs, its narrow approach fails to address the depth and complexity of concerns facing families with low income, leading to calls for a public health approach to child maltreatment prevention (Lonne et al., 2019) that address ACEs as well as the adverse community experiences that heighten risk for child maltreatment (Jones Harden et al., 2020).

BOX 3.2

## Substance Abuse and Child Welfare Policy

Over the past three decades, child protection policy has sought to respond to the damaging effects of caregiver substance abuse on children and families. The Abandoned Infants Assistance Act of 1988 (AIA; P.L. 100-505) was passed in response to the rising number of infants and young children abandoned in hospitals during the 1980s "crack epidemic." The AIA emphasized services for infants prenatally exposed to drugs and for children with AIDS.

The nation's opioid epidemic has occurred in roughly three waves that began in the late 1990s with prescription opioid abuse. Today's widespread manufacture and use of methamphetamine also began in the 1990s, with important implications for child protection. The calls for timely permanency planning that were codified in the Adoption and Safe Families Act (ASFA) of 1997 (P.L. 105-89) highlighted the need for timely treatment services for families with substance abuse concerns (Green et al., 2006). ASFA also required the USDHHS to report on the scope of the problem of substance use among families served through child protection agencies and the outcomes of provided services.

In 2003, the Keeping Children and Families Safe Act (P.L. 108-36) created new requirements for states to develop policies and procedures (known as "plans of safe care") to address the needs of an exponentially increasing number of infants affected by prenatal drug exposure. In 2006, the Child and Family Services Improvement Act (P.L. 109-288) created the Regional Partnership Grant program to address the safety, permanency, and well-being of children affected by methamphetamine and other substances through a range of activities and interventions. By the 2000s, reauthorizations of the AIA had extended services from infants to children and adolescents, and several states had made changes to their definitions of child

*(Continued)*

(Continued)

maltreatment to include prenatal substance exposure (Child Welfare Information Gateway, 2019).

The second wave of the opioid epidemic began in 2007 with a rapid increase in heroin-related mortalities as prescription opioids became harder to obtain. Sharp increases in deaths related to synthetic opioids such as fentanyl marked the beginning of the epidemic's third wave in 2013 (Ciccarone, 2019). Over the course of the epidemic, the prevalence of parental alcohol or other drug use among children removed into out-of-home care rose from 18.5% in 2000 to 35.3% in 2016 (National Center on Substance Use and Child Welfare, 2020). The ongoing role of addiction in rising foster care caseloads contributed to the passage of the Comprehensive Addiction and Recovery Act of 2016 (CARA; P.L. 114-198), which extended CAPTA's "plans of

safe care" to new populations: infants exposed prenatally to any substance, infants affected by withdrawal symptoms, and infants affected by fetal alcohol spectrum disorder. CARA also created new opportunities for states to address the health and substance use treatment needs of affected family members or caregivers.

On the heels of CARA, the Family First Prevention Services Act of 2018 (FFPSA; P.L. 115-123) made profound changes to Title IV-E by financing time limited, evidence-based substance abuse treatment, mental health, and in-home skill-based services for children at risk of foster care entry. FFPSA also amended Title IV-E to authorize financing for eligible children to be placed with their parent in a residential, family-based substance use treatment facility. The success of these promising efforts to reduce or prevent foster care entry remains to be seen.

BOX 3.3

## Indian Child Welfare Act (ICWA)

The history of U.S. policies toward tribal communities is a sordid and sobering litany of injustices. Child welfare practices were complicit in enforcing laws designed to disrupt families, communities, and tribal sovereignty. For example, in the 1950s and 1960s, the federal government spearheaded the Indian Adoption Project in collaboration with the Child Welfare League of America (Balcom, 2007). The goal was to place tribal children into White adoptive homes in the hopes that they would assimilate, discard their native identity, and blend with the dominant culture, thus contributing to a solution to the "Indian problem" in America. Race-mismatched

placements were typical in foster care as well (Unger, 1977). Some estimates indicate that over 80% of tribal children in foster or adoptive placements in the 1960s were living in non-tribal families. Removals to foster care were also astonishingly high. Estimates from the mid-1970s suggest that upward of one quarter of all tribal children had been separated from their parents and moved to foster care (MacEachron et al., 1996).

In response to these troubling findings, Congress passed the Indian Child Welfare Act (ICWA) in 1978 (P.L. 95-608), specifying new federal policy regarding child welfare practice for tribal children. The overriding goals of ICWA were to give tribal governments jurisdiction over tribal children in matters concerning child welfare, to encourage the development of tribal services for tribal families, and to keep tribal children within their family or tribe if removed to foster care. Although the law has faced numerous court challenges (most recently, *Brackeen v. Zinke*, 2018 and *Brackeen v. Bernhardt*, 2019; cases that center on the primary issues of tribal rights vs. parents' rights), the policy still guides practice for Native American and Alaska Native children who belong to federally recognized tribes.

Regarding foster care placements, the ICWA specified a hierarchy of placement settings to meet the needs of tribal children. Kinship caregivers are privileged, followed by foster parents from the same tribe as the child, followed by foster parents from other tribes. Foster care with nonrelative non-tribal members can only be considered if other placement preferences have been exhausted. During a child's stay in out-of-home care, child welfare professionals must make "active efforts" (in contrast to "reasonable efforts" specified in Adoption Assistance and Child Welfare Act [AACWA] for non-tribal children) to reunify. And due to the very high rates of adoption for tribal children, ICWA set standards for adoption very high. The courts must find native parents unfit "beyond a reasonable doubt" whereas courts deciding non-tribal cases (under AACWA jurisdiction) must make findings based on "clear and convincing evidence." Overall, the law aims to privilege tribal rights over individual or family rights, thereby reinforcing the importance of tribal sovereignty and continuity.

## Transition Age Youth

A number of federal laws have attempted to be responsive to the needs of older youth exiting out-of-home care, commonly referred to as *transition-age youth* (TAY). TAY are at increased risk of exiting foster care without achieving permanency (in the form of adoption, a legal guardianship, or relative care; Jones, 2019). The Foster Care Independence Act of 1999 (P.L. 106-169) established a specialized Independent Living Skills program for older youth in care to help them prepare for the transition to adulthood. The 2003 Adoption Incentive Act (P.L. 108-145) offers states financial incentives to boost the rate of adoption for children ages nine or older. And the Preventing Sex Trafficking and Strengthening Families Act of 2014 (P.L. 113-183) and Justice of Victims of Trafficking Act of 2015

(P.L. 114-22) focus resources and renewed attention to youth who may be victims of commercial sexual exploitation (see Box 3.5 for additional information).

The most profound policy change to affect the lives of older youth in out-of-home care is the 2008 Fostering Connections to Success and Increasing Adoptions Act (FCSA). This law allowed states to extend foster care services to youth older than age 18. Prior to the FCSA, youth typically exited care at the legal age of adulthood (age 18), a process known as *aging out* or *emancipating*. The FCSA was written in response to well-documented adverse outcomes for TAY aging out of foster care in the United States, such as low educational attainment, high rates of unemployment and poverty, homelessness,

*(Continued)*

BOX 3.4

(Continued)

mental health issues, incarceration, and premature death (Culhane et al., 2011; Liles et al., 2016). Youth who remained in care until age 21 and who were simultaneously required to engage in education or employment generally saw improved outcomes (Courtney et al., 2007). Depending on state regulations, youth currently age out between ages 18 and 21 and are no longer eligible for services or adoption. As of 2019, 28 states had extended care available to youth beyond age 18, typically on the condition that the youth participate in school or work (Rosenberg & Abbott, 2019).

Effectively serving TAY is essential, given higher-than-average rates of homelessness, incarceration, and early parenting (Dworsky et al., 2013), experiences that have long-term implications. The Midwest Evaluation of the Adult Functioning of Former Foster Youth, a longitudinal study, found that TAY aging out of foster care are at high risk for becoming homeless during the transition to adulthood. An estimated 36% of former foster youth who participated in the survey had been homeless at least once by age 26. Homelessness in young adulthood was associated with running away while in foster care, greater placement instability, being male, a history of physical abuse, delinquent behaviors, and mental health disorders.

Nationally, the teen pregnancy rate has dropped significantly in the United States; however, TAY in foster care are at increased risk of early parenthood (Hamilton & Mathews, 2016). Among all 17-year-old girls in foster care in California, 19% had given birth at least once before age 19 and 35% had given birth before age 21 (Putnam-Hornstein et al., 2016). As a result, many youths in foster care are becoming parents when they age out of care, placing stress on both the mother and child. Importantly, two-generation child protective services

(CPS) involvement is common (Eastman & Putnam-Hornstein, 2019). Estimates of children born to mothers in foster care experiencing CPS involvement in early childhood range between 39% and 53% (Dworsky, 2015; Eastman & Putnam-Hornstein, 2019). Factors that were associated with a lower risk of two-generation CPS involvement included being older at the time of birth and having established paternity. Risk factors included a documented maternal mental illness and a history of running away from care. The analysis in California was conducted before and after the implementation of the FCSA and showed that the proportion of children reported to CPS for maltreatment declined over time from 63% of children born to mothers in foster care in 2009 to 46% in 2012. While two-generation rates of CPS involvement decreased, the proportion of mothers remaining in care at older ages increased. These data, though only correlational, may suggest that recent policies aimed at supporting parents in care (such as the FCSA) may be related to the shrinking proportion of child maltreatment reports over time among children born to mothers in foster care.

Older youth in foster care are also at increased risk of juvenile justice system involvement (Cutuli et al., 2016; Herz et al., 2010). Black males, children who live in congregate foster care settings, and those with placement instability have the greatest risk of juvenile justice involvement. Youth who interact with both CPS and the juvenile justice systems are called *dual system youth* and have greater and more complex needs than those involved with only one system (Herz et al., 2010; Herz et al., 2012). The majority of these youth experience mental health problems and/or substance abuse issues. However, dual system youth may be less likely to receive comprehensive, coordinated care because these systems are not necessarily designed to work collaboratively, and because child welfare and juvenile justice information systems are rarely integrated. Most agencies do not capture information about a youth's contact with other systems and, as a result, these youth go undetected by service providers. If systems coordinate with data sharing and the development of case plans, services may better address the effects of childhood trauma (Herz et al., 2012).

Independent living services aim to prepare TAY in foster care to be self-sufficient after exiting foster care and hope to prevent homelessness, early pregnancy, and incarceration. The Chafee Foster Care Independence Program (P.L. 106-169) was launched in 2000 and grants federal funds to provide foster youth with independent living services (Collins, 2004; Collins et al., 2010). States that draw down federal dollars to implement independent living services for TAY are also required to collect data for the National Youth in Transition Database, a repository for tracking youth and services offered so the effects of these programs can be examined (Dworsky & Crayton, 2009).

Independent living services target several domains, including secondary and postsecondary education, vocational training and employment, budgeting and financial management, health education, housing, and youth development (Collins, 2004). Specifically, programs include the Independent Living Aftercare Program, which provides former foster youth with life skills training (Courtney et al., 2018). A national survey of TAY foster youth found that about half of youth received at least one type of independent living service (Okpych, 2015). By age 21, between a quarter and a third of TAY surveyed had received independent living services related to education, employment, and health education (Courtney et al., 2007). Recent policy developments provide an opportunity to improve outcomes for TAY, but challenges still exist (Courtney, 2009). Policy and program development must be informed by research and evaluation to determine program effectiveness and improve coordination among service providers.

## Sex Trafficking and Child Pornography

Commercial sexual exploitation (CSE) of children is a type of abuse that includes minor-victim sex trafficking and pornography (Victims of Trafficking and Violence Protection Act H.R. 3422 106d., 2000). Minor-victim sex trafficking is a commercial sex act where the person induced to perform the act is younger than 18 years old. Given the nature of sex trafficking, there are no accurate estimates of how many youths are affected (Gibbs et al., 2018; Office of Juvenile Justice and Delinquency Prevention, 2014). Trafficked children and youth suffer from physical health injuries, unplanned pregnancies, reproductive health problems (sexually transmitted infections), mental health problems (i.e., post-traumatic stress disorder, depression, suicidality), and substance abuse issues (Clawson & Grace, 2007; Gibbs et al., 2018).

*(Continued)*

**BOX 3.5**

(Continued)

There are known subgroups of children and adolescents who are at increased risk for commercial exploitation—specifically, racial minority youth and lesbian, gay, bisexual, transgender, and queer/questioning (LGBTQ) youth and young females (Liles et al., 2016). Experiencing trauma and running away are the two factors most related to risk of trafficking, experiences that are common among those who have contact with child welfare agencies (Choi, 2015; Courtney et al., 2004)

Research validates that children in the child welfare system are at increased risk of CSE. Preliminary analyses suggest the large majority of children and youth who experience CSE have a history of child protective services (CPS) involvement, including placement in foster care (Feldman, 2007). Extensive childhood sexual abuse often precedes CSE (Farley, 2006). Given that CPS has contact with youth at risk of CSE, there is an opportunity to implement prevention and early intervention services that, if effective, may dramatically reduce the CSE of children.

Despite historically being victims of statutory rape and child abuse, children and youth who experience CSE have been charged with crimes through the delinquency system (i.e., prostitution; Sewell, 2012). Thankfully, a wave of legislation has focused on supporting child victims of exploitation. Federal laws and state policies have altered the child welfare system's role with respect to children and youth who experience CSE.

First, the 2000 federal Trafficking Victims Protection Act (TVPA; P. L. 106-386) specified that any child under age 18 who is exploited for sexual acts (prostitution) is considered a commercially sexually exploited child and a victim of human trafficking (Liles et al., 2016; Victims of Trafficking and Violence Protection Act H.R. 3422 106d., 2000). This reframing signified a significant reform in the way victims of CSE are viewed and, as a result, supported with services.

Second, the 2014 Preventing Sex Trafficking and Strengthening Families Act (P.L. 113-183) mandated state child welfare agencies to screen, identify, document, and serve the children under their supervision who were identified as victims of sex trafficking or at risk for sex trafficking (Gibbs et al., 2018). The law enhanced data collection requirements; agencies must report child victims of sex trafficking to law enforcement and annually report data on the number of victims to the federal government through the Adoption and Foster Care Analysis and Reporting System. The law requires child welfare agencies to develop and implement policies for children who go missing from foster care placements (i.e., runaway) to assess if sexual exploitation occurred while they were absent from supervision.

Third, the 2015 Justice for Victims of Trafficking Act (JVTA; P.L. 114-22) requires state child welfare agencies to consider any child victim of sex trafficking as a victim of child abuse (Gibbs et al., 2018). This change required states to revise policies; revise definitions of child maltreatment to be inclusive of CSE; and implement new training, prevention, and screening services. In alignment with policies to support TAY, the JVTA also allows states to extend these services to exploited youth between ages 18 and 23.

State adoption of these federal policies varies. The large majority of states have passed Safe Harbor Laws (Gibbs et al., 2018; Williams, 2017). Safe Harbor Laws refer to policies that divert children and adolescents who have experienced sexual exploitation to the child welfare system for services rather than through the justice system to be arrested and/or prosecuted (Gibbs et al., 2018; Liles et al., 2016). States differ in terms of which offenses are covered under immunity, requirements for diversion (from juvenile justice to child welfare), and the ages protected by the laws (which range from 16 to 24 years; Gibbs et al., 2018). Some states have implemented these policies, but the effects of these laws are limited if there are no funds for victim-centered services (Geist, 2012; Gibbs et al., 2018; Shared Hope International, 2012). Therefore, even victims of CSE who live in Safe Harbor states may have few shelter or placement options and little access to health, mental health, legal, and social services (Gibbs et al., 2018; Smith et al., 2009). Child welfare agencies are developing more specialized services to identify CSE victims, provide safe placements and services, and coordinate among systems to ensure safety and stability (Walker, 2013). Currently no uniform process exists nationally.

CSE can be addressed by identifying children and youth who may be at risk using screening tools, providing specialized services and supports for children and their families or caregivers, and establishing safe and secure emergency and transitional placements (Walker, 2013). The large majority of states have implemented training programs for child welfare workers, first responders, law enforcement, and others who are likely to come into contact with CSE victims, which aids with identification and service provision (Gibbs et al., 2018; Walker, 2013; Williams, 2017). A number of states also offer specialized group and residential care for child trafficking victims, focused on addressing the needs of youth who have contact with traffickers, are at risk for runaway behavior or sexual acting out, or are LGBTQ youth (Gibbs et al., 2018). As this field of policy and practice develops, it will be important to coordinate, collect, and share data across systems to better understand the scope of the problem, the level of interaction with multiple systems, and the specific needs of CSE victims (Walker, 2013).Oltu compestiae conscibus

## NOTES

1. Adoption subsidies were initially provided only for "hard to place" children, including large sibling groups, children with disabling conditions, or children from racial/ethnic minority groups. Later federal policy (ASFA) expanded eligibility for adoption subsidies.

2. The data show that 23% of Native American children were reported; however, this is likely a substantial undercount due to (1) inconsistencies in Native American racial self-identification in census data and (2) issues related to communication between tribal and state child protection agencies.

## REFERENCES

Administration for Children and Families. (2020). *The maternal, infant, and early childhood home visiting program.* https://mchb.hrsa.gov/sites/default/files/mchb/Maternal-ChildHealthInitiatives/HomeVisiting/pdf/programbrief.pdf

Andersen, S. H., & Fallesen, P. (2015). Family matters? The effect of kinship care on foster care disruption rates. *Child Abuse and Neglect, 48*, 68–79.

Assink, M., van der Put, C. E., Meeuwsen, M. W. C. M., de Jong, N. M., Oort, F. J., Stams, G. J. J. M., & Hoeve, M. (2019). Risk factors for child sexual abuse victimization: A meta-analytic review. *Psychological Bulletin, 145*(5), 459–489.

Baams, L., Wilson, B. D., & Russell, S. T. (2019). LGBTQ youth in unstable housing and foster care. *Pediatrics, 143*(3), e20174211.

Balcom, K. (2007). The logic of exchange: The Child Welfare League of America, the Adoption Resource Exchange movement, and the Indian Adoption Project. *Adoption and Culture, 1*(1), 5–67.

Bald, A., Chyn, E., Hastings, J. S., & Machelett, M. (2019). *The causal impact of removing children from abusive and neglectful homes*. National Bureau of Economic Research.

Barth, R. P. (1997). Effects of age and race on the odds of adoption versus remaining in long-term foster care. *Child Welfare, 76*(2), 285.

Barth, R. P., Greeson, J. K., Guo, S., Green, R. L., & Hurley, S. (2007). Outcomes for youth receiving intensive in-home therapy or residential care: A comparison using propensity scores. *American Journal of Orthopsychiatry, 77*(4), 497–505.

Bartholet, E. (1999). *Nobody's children: Abuse and neglect, foster drift, and the adoption alternative*. Beacon Press.

Bellamy, J. (2008). Behavioral problems following reunification of children in long-term foster care. *Children and Youth Services Review, 30*(2), 216–228.

Berger, L., Bruch, S. K., Johnson, E. I., James, S., & Rubin, D. (2009). Estimating the "impact" of out-of-home placement on child well-being: Approaching the problem of selection bias. *Child Development, 80*(6), 1856–1876.

Berger, L., Cancian, M., Han, E., Noyes, J., & Rios-Salas, V. (2015). Children's academic achievement and foster care. *Pediatrics, 135*(1), 109–116.

Berrick, J. D., Barth, R. P., Needell, B., & Jonson-Reid, M. (1998). *The tender years: Toward developmentally sensitive child welfare services for very young children*. Oxford University Press.

Berrick, J. D., Gilbert, N., & Skivenes, M. (in press). *International handbook of child protection systems*. Oxford University Press.

Berrick, J. D., & Heimpel, D. (2020). How federal laws relating to foster care financing shape child welfare services. In J. Dwyer (Ed.), *Oxford handbook of children and the law*. Oxford University Press.

Biehal, N. (2007). Reuniting children with their families: Reconsidering the evidence on timing, contact and outcomes. *The British Journal of Social Work, 37*(5), 807–823.

Brackeen v. Bernhardt, No. 18–11479 (U.S. Court of Appeals for the Fifth Circuit, August 9, 2019).

Brackeen v. Zinke, 4:17-cv-00868-O, United States District Court, N.D. Texas, Fort Worth Division (October 4, 2018).

Brodzinsky, D. M., Smith, D. W., & Brodzinsky, A. B. (1998). *Children's adjustment to adoption: Developmental and clinical issues*. SAGE.

Brown, E. C., Garrison, M. M., Bao, H., Qu, P., Jenny, C., & Rowhani-Rahbar, A. (2019). Assessment of rates of child maltreatment in states with Medicaid expansion vs states without Medicaid expansion. *JAMA Network Open, 2*(6), e195529–e195529.

Burnette, D. (1997). Grandparents raising grandchildren in the inner city. *Families in Society, 78*(5), 489–501.

Cancian, M., Yang, M. Y., & Slack, K. S. (2013). The effect of additional child support income on the risk of child maltreatment. *Social Service Review, 87*(3), 417–437.

Child Welfare Information Gateway. (2014). *Differential response to reports of child abuse and neglect*. U.S. Department of Health and Human Services, Children's Bureau.

Child Welfare Information Gateway. (2017). *Making and screening reports of child abuse and neglect*. U.S. Department of Health and Human Services, Children's Bureau.

Child Welfare Information Gateway. (2019). *Definitions of child abuse and neglect*. U.S. Department of Health and Human Services, Children's Bureau.

Children's Bureau. (2020a). *Child and family services reviews aggregate report: Round 3: Fiscal years 2015–2018*. JBS International, Inc.

Children's Bureau. (2020b). *Child welfare outcomes report data*. Administration for Children and Families. https://cwoutcomes.acf.hhs.gov/cwodatasite/fourTwo/index

Choi, K. (2015). Risk factors for domestic minor sex trafficking in the United States: A literature review. *Journal of Forensic Nursing, 11*(2), 66–76.

Ciccarone, D. (2019). The triple wave epidemic: Supply and demand drivers of the US opioid overdose crisis. *International Journal of Drug Policy, 71*, 183–188.

Clawson, H., & Grace, L. (2007). *Finding a path to recovery: Residential facilities for minor victims of domestic sex trafficking.* Office of the Assistant Secretary for Planning and Evaluation (ASPE), U.S. Department of Health and Human Services. https://aspe.hhs.gov/system/files/pdf/75186/ib.pdf

Collins, M. E. (2004). Enhancing services to youths leaving foster care: Analysis of recent legislation and its potential impact. *Children and Youth Services Review, 26*(11), 1051–1065.

Collins, M. E., Spencer, R., & Ward, R. (2010). Supporting youth in the transition from foster care: Formal and informal connections. *Child Welfare, 89*(1), 125–143.

Conley, A., & Berrick, J. (2010). Community-based child abuse prevention: Outcomes associated with a differential response program in California. *Child Maltreatment, 15*(4), 282–292.

Conn, A. M., Szilagyi, M. A., Jee, S. H., Blumkin, A. K., & Szilagyi, P. G. (2015). Mental health outcomes among child welfare investigated children: In-home versus out-of-home care. *Children and Youth Services Review, 57*, 106–111.

Connell, C. M., Vanderploeg, J. J., Katz, K. H., Caron, C., Saunders, L., & Tebes, J. K. (2009). Maltreatment following reunification: Predictors of subsequent child protective services contact after children return home. *Child Abuse and Neglect, 33*(4), 1–20.

Courtney, M. (2009). The difficult transition to adulthood for foster youth in the US: Implications for the state as corporate parent. *Social Policy Report/Society for Research in Child Development, 23*, 3–18.

Courtney, M., Dworsky, A., Cusick, G. R., Havlicek, J., Perez, A., & Keller, T. (2007). *Midwest evaluation of adult functioning of former foster youth: Outcomes at age 21.* Chapin Hall Center for Children at the University of Chicago. https://www.chapinhall.org/wp-content/uploads/Midwest-Eval-Outcomes-at-Age-21.pdf

Courtney, M., Okpych, N. J., Charles, P., Mikell, D., Stevenson, B., Kindle, B., & Feng, H. (2016). *Findings from the California youth transitions to adulthood study (CalYOUTH): Conditions of youth at age 19.* Chapin Hall Center for Children at the University of Chicago. https://www.chapinhall.org/wp-content/uploads/CY_YT_RE0516_4-1.pdf

Courtney, M., Okpych, N. J., Park, K., Harty, J., Feng, H., Torres-García, A., & Sayed, S. (2018). *Findings from the California youth transitions to adulthood study (CalYOUTH): Conditions of youth at age 21.* Chapin Hall at the University of Chicago. https://www.chapinhall.org/wp-content/uploads/CY_YT_RE0518_1.pdf

Courtney, M., Terao, S., & Bost, N. (2004). *Midwest evaluation of the adult functioning of former foster youth: Conditions of youth preparing to leave state care.* Chapin Hall Center for Children at the University of Chicago. http://citeseerx.ist.psu.edu/viewdoc/download?doi=10.1.1.599.150&rep=rep1&type=pdf

Crumbley, J. (1999). *Transracial adoption and foster care: Practice issues for professionals.* Child Welfare League of America.

Culhane, D., Byrne, T., Metraux, S., Moreno, M., Toros, H., & Stevens, M. (2011). *Young adult outcomes of youth exiting dependent or delinquent care in Los Angeles county.* Conrad N. Hilton Foundation. https://www.hiltonfoundation.org/wp-content/uploads/2019/10/Hilton_Foundation_Report_Final-3.pdf

Culhane, J. F., Webb, D., Grim, S., & Metraux, S. (2003). Prevalence of child welfare services involvement among homeless and low-income mothers: A five-year birth cohort study. *Journal of Sociology and Social Welfare, 30*, 79–96.

Cutuli, J. J., Goerge, R. M., Coulton, C., Schretzman, M., Crampton, D., Charvat, B. J., Lalich, N., Raithel, Jessica, A., Gacitua, C., & Lee, E. L. (2016). From foster care to juvenile justice: Exploring characteristics of youth in three cities. *Children and Youth Services Review, 67*, 84–94.

Damman, J. L., Johnson-Motoyama, M., Wells, S. J., & Harrington, K. (2020). Factors associated with the decision to investigate child protective services referrals: A systematic review. *Child & Family Social Work.*

Doyle, J. J. (2007). Child protection and child outcomes: Measuring the effects of foster care. *American Economic Review, 97*(5), 1583–1610.

Dozier, M., Kaufman, J., Kobak, R., O'Connor, T. G., Sagi-Schwartz, A., Scott, S., Shauffer, C., Smetana, J., van IJzendoorn, M. H., & Zeanah, H. (2014). Consensus statement on group care for children and adolescents: A statement of policy of the American Orthopsychiatric Association. *American Journal of Orthopsychiatry, 84*(3), 219–225.

Drake, B. (1996). Unraveling "unsubstantiated." *Child Maltreatment, 1*(3), 261–271.

Drake, B., Lee, S. M., & Jonson-Reid, M. (2009). Race and child maltreatment reporting: Are Blacks overrepresented? *Children and Youth Services Review, 31*(3), 309–316.

Dumas, A., Elzinga-Marshall, G., Monahan, B., van Buren, M., & Will, M. (2015). *Child welfare screening in Wisconsin: An analysis of families screened out of child protective services and subsequently screened in.* http://www.lafollette.wisc.edu/images/publications/workshops/2015-dcf.pdf.

Dworsky, A. (2015). Child welfare services involvement among the children of young parents in foster care. *Child Abuse & Neglect, 45,* 68–79.

Dworsky, A., & Courtney, M. E. (2010). *Extended foster care delays but does not prevent homelessness.* Chapin Hall Center for Children at the University of Chicago. https://www.chapinhall.org/research/extended-foster-care-delays-but-does-not-prevent-homelessness/#:~:text=Extended%20Foster%20Care%20Delays%20but%20Does%20Not%20Prevent%20Homelessness,-2010&text=Results%20from%20our%20analysis%20of,but%20does%20not%20prevent%20it.

Dworsky, A., & Crayton, C. (2009). *National youth in transition database: Instructional guidebook and architectural blueprint.* American Public Human Services Association, Chapin Hall at the University of Chicago, and Center for State Foster Care and Adoption Data.

Dworsky, A., Napolitano, L., & Courtney, M. (2013). Homelessness during the transition from foster care to adulthood. *American Journal of Public Health, 103*(Suppl 2), S318–S323.

Eastman, A. L., & Putnam-Hornstein, E. (2019). An examination of child protective service involvement among children born to mothers in foster care. *Child Abuse & Neglect, 88,* 317–325.

Euser, S., Alink, L. R., Stoltenborgh, M., Bakermans-Kranenburg, M. J., & van IJzendoorn, M. H. (2015). A gloomy picture: A meta-analysis of randomized controlled trials reveals disappointing effectiveness of programs aiming at preventing child maltreatment. *BMC Public Health, 15*(1), 1068.

Fang, X., Brown, D. S., Florence, C. S., & Mercy, J. A. (2012). The economic burden of child maltreatment in the United States and implications for prevention. *Child Abuse & Neglect, 36*(2), 156–165.

Fanshel, D., & Shinn, E. (1978). *Children in foster care.* Columbia University Press.

Farley, M. A. (2006). Prostitution, trafficking, and cultural amnesia: What we must not know in order to keep the business of sexual exploitation running smoothly. *Yale Journal of Law & Feminism, 18*(1).

Farrell, A. F., Britner, P. A., Kull, M. A., Struzinski, D. L., Somaroo-Rodriguez, K., Parr, K., Westberg, L., Cronin, B., & Humphrey, C. (2018). *Connecticut's intensive supportive housing for families program.* Chapin Hall at the University of Chicago.

Fechter-Leggett, M. O., & O'Brien, K. (2010). The effects of kinship care on adult mental health outcomes of alumni of foster care. *Children and Youth Services Review, 32,* 206–213.

Feldman, C. (2007). Report finds 2,000 of state's children are sexually exploited, many in New York City. *The New York Times.* https://www.nytimes.com/2007/04/24/nyregion/24child.html

Felitti, V. J., Anda, R. F., Nordenberg, D., Williamson, D. F., Spitz, A. M., Edwards, V., & Marks, J. S. (1998). Relationship of childhood abuse and household dysfunction to many of the leading causes of death in adults: The Adverse Childhood Experiences (ACE) study. *American Journal of Preventive Medicine, 14*(4), 245–258.

Fluke, J. D., Harlaar, N., Brown, B., Heisler, K., Merkel-Holguin, L., & Darnell, A. (2019). Differential response and children re-reported to child protective services: County data from the national child abuse and neglect data system (NCANDS). *Child Maltreatment, 24*(2), 127–136.

Font, S. A. (2014). Kinship and nonrelative foster care: The effect of placement type on child well-being. *Child Development, 85*(5), 2074–2090.

Font, S. A., Cancian, M., & Berger, L. (2019). Prevalence and risk factors for early motherhood among low-income, maltreated, and foster youth. *Demography, 56,* 261–284.

Font, S. A., & Gershoff, E. T. (2020). *Foster care and best interests of the child: Integrating research, policy, and practice.* Springer.

Fortson, B. L., Klevens, J., Merrick, M. T., Gilbert, L. K., & Alexander, S. P. (2016). *Preventing child abuse and neglect: A technical package for policy, norm, and programmatic activities.* Centers for Disease Control and Prevention.

Foust, R., Prindle, J., Eastman, A. L., Dawson, W. C., Mitchell, M., Nghiem, H. T., & Putnam-Hornstein, E. (2020). *California strong start index documentation.* Children's Data Network. https://www.datanetwork.org/wp-content/uploads/CASSi-FINAL-1-14-2020.pdf

Fowler, P. J., Marcal, K. E., Zhang, J., Day, O., & Landsverk, J. (2017). Homelessness and aging out of foster care: A national comparison of child welfare-involved adolescents. *Children and Youth Services Review, 77,* 27–33.

Freisthler, B., Wolf, J. P., Wiegmann, W., & Kepple, N. J. (2017). Drug use, the drug environment, and child physical abuse and neglect. *Child Maltreatment, 22*(3), 245–255.

FRIENDS National Center for Community-Based Child Abuse Prevention. (2020). *Current CBCAP program instruction.* https://friendsnrc.org/cbcap/current-cbcap-program-instruction/

Fuller, T., & Zhang, S. (2017). The impact of family engagement and child welfare services on maltreatment re-reports and substantiated re-reports. *Child Maltreatment, 22*(3), 183–193.

Gee, G. C., & Ford, C. L. (2011). Structural racism and health inequities: Old issues, new directions. *Du Bois Review: Social Science Research on Race, 8*(1), 115–132

Geist, D. (2012). Finding safe harbor: Protection, prosecution, and state strategies to address prostituted minors. *Legislation and Policy Brief, 4*(2), 66–127.

Gibbs, D. A., Feinberg, R. K., Dolan, M., Latzman, N. E., Misra, S., & Domanico, R. (2018). *Report to congress: The child welfare system response to sex trafficking of children.* U.S. Department of Health and Human Services, Administration for Children and Families. https://www.cwla.org/wp-content/uploads/2019/08/Child-Welfare-System-Response-to-Sex-Trafficking-of-Children-Aug2019.pdf

Gilbert, R., Widom, C. S., Browne, K., Fergusson, D., Webb, E., & Janson, S. (2009). Burden and consequences of child maltreatment in high-income countries. *The Lancet, 373*(9657), 68–81.

Gilbert, N., Parton, N., & Skivenes, M. (Eds.). (2011). *Child protection systems: International trends and orientations.* Oxford University Press.

Ginther, D., & Johnson-Motoyama, M. (2017, November 2–4). *Do TANF policies affect child abuse and neglect?* [Conference presentation]. APPAM 39th Annual Fall Research Conference, Chicago, IL, United States.

Green, B. L., Rockhill, A., & Furrer, C. (2006). Understanding patterns of substance abuse treatment for women involved with child welfare: The influence of the Adoption and Safe Families Act (ASFA). *The American Journal of Drug and Alcohol Abuse, 32*(2), 149–176.

Hamilton, B. E., & Mathews, T. J. (2016). *Continued declines in teen births in the United States, 2015 (NCHS data brief, 259).* National Center for Health Statistics. https://www.cdc.gov/nchs/data/databriefs/db259.pdf

Henry, C., Sonterblum, L., & Lens, V. (2019). The collateral consequences of state central registries: Child protection and barriers to employment for low-income women and women of color. *Social Work, 64*(4), 373–375.

Herz, D., Lee, P., Lutz, L., Stewart, M., Tuell, J., Wiig, J., Bilchik, S., & Kelley, E. (2012). *Addressing the needs of multi-system youth: strengthening the connection between child welfare and juvenile justice.* Center for Juvenile Justice Reform & Robert F. Kennedy Children's Action Corps.

Herz, D. C., Ryan, J. P., & Bilchik, S. (2010). Challenges facing crossover youth: An examination of juvenile-justice decision making and recidivism. *Family Court Review, 48*(2), 305–321.

Horwitz, S. M., Balestracci, K. M., & Simms, M. D. (2001). Foster care placement improves children's functioning. *Archives of Pediatrics & Adolescent Medicine, 155*(11), 1255–1260.

Hussey, J. M., Chang, J. J., & Kotch, J. B. (2006). Child maltreatment in the United States: Prevalence, risk factors, and adolescent health consequences. *Pediatrics, 118*(3), 933–942.

James, S., Roesch, S., & Zhang, J. (2012). Characteristics and behavioral outcomes for youth in group care and family-based care: A propensity score matching approach using national data. *Journal of Emotional and Behavioral Disorders, 20*(3), 144–156.

James Bell Associates. (2019). *Summary of the Title IV-E child welfare waiver demonstrations.* Children's Bureau.

Johnson-Motoyama, M., Ginther, D., Fluke, J., & Phillips, R. (2020). *Did differential response systems reduce child neglect and foster care entries in the U.S.? Results from a national study* [Conference Presentation]. Society for Social Work & Research 24th Annual Conference, Washington, DC, United States.

Jones Harden, B., Simons, C., Johnson-Motoyama, M., & Barth, R. (2020). The child maltreatment prevention landscape: Where are we now, and where should we go? *The Annals of the American Academy of Political and Social Science, 692*(1), 97–118.

Jones, L. (2019). Remaining in foster care after age 18 and youth outcomes at the transition to adulthood: A review. *Families in Society, 100*(3), 260–281.

Jonson-Reid, M., Drake, B., Kohl, P., Guo, S., Brown, D., McBride, T., Kim, H., & Lewis, E. (2017). What do we really know about usual care child protective services? *Children and Youth Services Review, 82,* 222–229.

Kempe, C. H., Silverman, F. N., Steele, B. F., Droegemueller, W., & Silver, H. K. (1962). The battered-child syndrome. *Jama, 181*(1), 17–24.

Kim, C. (1999). Putting reason back into the reasonable efforts requirements in child abuse and neglect cases. *University of Illinois Law Review, 1999*(1), 287–326.

Kim, H., & Drake, B. (2019). Cumulative prevalence of onset and recurrence of child maltreatment reports. *Journal of the American Academy of Child & Adolescent Psychiatry, 58*(12), 1175–1183.

Kim, H., Wildeman, C., Jonson-Reid, M., & Drake, B. (2017). Lifetime prevalence of investigating child maltreatment among US children. *American Journal of Public Health, 107*(2), 274–280.

Klevens, J., Barnett, S. B. L., Florence, C., & Moore, D. (2015). Exploring policies for the reduction of child physical abuse and neglect. *Child Abuse & Neglect, 40,* 1–11.

Koh, E., & Testa, M. (2011). Children discharged from kin and non-kin foster homes: Do the risks of foster care re-entry differ? *Children and Youth Services Review, 33,* 1497–1505.

Kohl, P. L., Jonson-Reid, M., & Drake, B. (2009). Time to leave substantiation behind: Findings from a national probability study. *Child Maltreatment, 14*(1), 17–26.

Kugler, K. C., Guastaferro, K., Shenk, C. E., Beal, S. J., Zadzora, K. M., & Noll, J. G. (2019). The effect of substantiated and unsubstantiated investigations of child maltreatment and subsequent adolescent health. *Child Abuse & Neglect, 87,* 112–119.

Lau, A. S., Litrownik, A. J., Newton, R. R., & Landsverk, J. (2003). Going home: The complex effects of reunification on internalizing problems among children in foster care. *Journal of Abnormal Child Psychology, 31*(4), 345–359.

Leeb, R. T., Bitsko, R. H., Merrick, M. T., & Armour, B. S. (2012). Does childhood disability increase risk for child abuse and neglect? *Journal of Mental Health Research in Intellectual Disabilities, 5*(1), 4–31.

Liles, B. D., Blacker, D. M., Landini, J. L., & Urquiza, A. J. (2016). A California multidisciplinary juvenile court: Serving sexually exploited and at-risk youth: Specialized court for sexually exploited youth. *Behavioral Sciences & the Law, 34*(1), 234–245.

Lloyd, E. C., & Barth, R. P. (2011). Developmental outcomes after five years for foster children returned home, remaining in care, or adopted. *Children and Youth Services Review, 33,* 1383–1391.

Loman, L. A., Shannon, C., Sapokaite, L., & Siegel, G. (2009). *Minnesota parent support outreach program evaluation: Final report.* Institute of Applied Research.

Lonne, B., Scott, D., Higgins, D., & Herrenkohl, T. I. (Eds.). (2019). *Re-visioning public health approaches for protecting children* (Vol. 9). Springer.

Maas, H., & Engler, R. (1959). *Children in need of parents.* Columbia University Press.

Maas, H., & Engler, R. (1964). *Children in need of parents.* Columbia University Press.

MacEachron, A. E., Gustavsson, N. S., Cross, S., & Lewis, A. (1996). The effectiveness of the Indian Child Welfare Act of 1978. *Social Service Review, 70*(3), 451–463.

Magruder, J., & Berrick, J. D. (in review). *A longitudinal investigation of infants and out-of-home care.*

Maguire-Jack, K., Johnson-Motoyama, M., & Parmenter, S. (in press). Economic supports for working parents: The relationship of TANF, child care subsidy, SNAP, and EITC to child maltreatment prevention. *Aggression and Violent Behavior, Special Issue on Family Violence and Public Policy: Existing Trends and Emerging Needs.*

Maguire-Jack, K., Lanier, P., Johnson-Motoyama, M., Welch, H., & Dineen, M. (2015). Geographic variation in racial disparities in child maltreatment: The influence of county poverty and population density. *Child Abuse & Neglect, 47,* 1–13.

Mallon, G. P., Lakin, D., & Lyons, N. (2006). Facilitating permanency for youth. In L. Frey, G. Cushing, M. Freundlich, & E. Brenner (Eds.), *Achieving permanency for adolescents in foster care: A guide for legal professionals* (pp. 45–62). American Bar Association. https://www.americanbar.org/content/dam/aba/administrative/child_law/PermanencyforAdolescents.pdf

McCormick, A., Schmidt, K., & Terrazas, S. (2017). LGBTQ youth in the child welfare system: An overview of research, practice, and policy. *Journal of Public Child Welfare*, *11*(1), 27–39.

Miller v. Youakim, 440 U.S. 125 (1979). https://scholar.google.com/scholar_case?case=7210856946147879173&hl=en&as_sdt=6&as_vis=1&oi=scholarr

Mulder, T. M., Kuiper, K. C., van der Put, C. E., Stams, G.-J. J. M., & Assink, M. (2018). Risk factors for child neglect: A meta-analytic review. *Child Abuse & Neglect*, 77, 198–210.

National Center on Substance Use and Child Welfare (2020). *Child welfare and alcohol and drug use statistics*. https://ncsacw.samhsa.gov/research/child-welfare-and-treatment-statistics.aspx

National Children's Advocacy Center. (2020). *National Children's Advocacy Center history*. https://www.nationalcac.org/history/

National Research Council. (2014). *New directions in child abuse and neglect research*. National Academies Press.

Office of Juvenile Justice and Delinquency Prevention. (2014). *Commercial sexual exploitation of children sex trafficking literature review*. Author. https://www.ojjdp.gov/mpg/litreviews/CSECSexTrafficking.pdf

Okpych, N. J. (2015). Receipt of independent living services among older youth in foster care: An analysis of national data from the U.S. *Children and Youth Services Review*, *51*, 74–86.

Okpych, N. J., Park, S. E., & Courtney, M. E. (2019). *California foster youth in extended care have better postsecondary education outcomes*. Chapin Hall Center for Children at the University of Chicago. https://www.chapinhall.org/research/california-foster-youth-in-extended-care-have-better-postsecondary-education-outcomes/

Perry, M. A., & Fusco, R. A. (2013). Child welfare practice in a systems of care framework. In *Contemporary issues in child welfare practice* (pp. 1–15). Springer.

Pertman, A. (2011). *Adoption nation: How the adoption revolution is transforming our families and America*. Harvard Common Press.

Putnam-Hornstein, E. (2011). Report of maltreatment as a risk factor for injury death: A prospective birth cohort study. *Child Maltreatment*, *16*(3), 163–174.

Putnam-Hornstein, E., Hammond, I., Eastman, A. L., McCroskey, J., & Webster, D. (2016). Extended foster care for transition-age youth: An opportunity for pregnancy prevention and parenting support. *The Journal of Adolescent Health: Official Publication of the Society for Adolescent Medicine*, *58*(4), 485–487.

Putnam-Hornstein, E., Needell, B., King, B., & Johnson-Motoyama, M. (2013). Racial and ethnic disparities: A population-based examination of risk factors for involvement with child protective services. *Child Abuse & Neglect*, *37*(1), 33–46.

Raissian, K. M., & Bullinger, L. R. (2017). Money matters: Does the minimum wage affect child maltreatment rates? *Children and Youth Services Review*, *72*, 60–70.

Roberts, D. (2002). *Shattered bonds: The color of child welfare*. Civitas Books.

Rolock, N. (2015). Post-permanency continuity: What happens after adoption and guardianship from foster care? *Journal of Public Child Welfare*, *9*, 153–173.

Rosenberg, R., & Abbott, S. (2019). *Supporting Older Youth Beyond Age 18: Examining Data and Trends in Extended Foster Care*. Child Trends. https://www.childtrends.org/publications/supporting-older-youth-beyond-age-18-examining-data-and-trends-in-extended-foster-care

Rosinsky, K., & Williams, S. C. (2018). *Child welfare financing SFY 2016: A survey of federal, state, and local expenditures*. Child Trends.

Rubin, D. M., O'Reilly, A. L., Luan, X., & Localio, A. R. (2007). The impact of placement stability on behavioral well-being for children in foster care. *Pediatrics*, *119*(2), 336–344.

Russell, J. R., Kerwin, C., & Halverson, J. L. (2018). Is child protective services effective? *Children and Youth Services Review*, *84*, 185–192.

Ryan, J. P., Hong, J. S., Herz, D., & Hernandez, P. M. (2010). Kinship foster care and the risk of juvenile delinquency. *Children and Youth Services Review*, *32*, 1823–1830.

Sakai, C., Lin, H., & Flores, G. (2011). Health outcomes and family services in kinship care: Analysis of a national sample of children in the child welfare system. *Archives of Pediatrics and Adolescent Medicine*, *165*(2), 159–165.

Sankaran, V. S. (2009). Parens patriae run amuck: The child welfare system's disregard for the constitutional rights of nonoffending parents. *Temple Law Review*, *82*(1), 55–88.

Saul, J., Duffy, J., Noonan, R., Lubell, K., Wandersman, A., Flaspohler, P., Stillman, L., Blachman, M., & Dunville, R. (2008). Bridging science and practice in violence prevention: Addressing ten key challenges. *American Journal of Community Psychology*, *41*(3), 197–205.

Sewell, A. (2012). Most L.A. county youths held for prostitution come from foster care. *Los Angeles Times*. https://www.latimes.com/archives/la-xpm-2012-nov-27-la-me-1128-sex-trafficking-20121128-story.html

Shared Hope International. (2012). *Protected innocence challenge: State report cards on the legal framework of protection for the nation's children*. Author. http://sharedhope.org/wp-content/uploads/2012/09/ProtectedInnocenceChallenge_FINAL_2012_web2.pdf

Simon, J. D. (2020). An examination of needs, matched services, and child protective services re-report among families with complex needs. *Journal of the Society for Social Work and Research*, *11*(2).

Sinclair, I., Baker, C., Wilson, K., & Gibbs, I. (2005). *Foster children: Where they go and how they get on*. Jessica Kingsley.

Skivenes, M., Thoburn, J., & Poso, T. (Eds.). (in press). *Adoption from care: International perspectives on children's rights, family preservation, and state intervention*. Policy Press.

Slack, K. S., Berger, L. M., Dumont, K., Yang, M.-Y., Kim, B., Ehrhard-Dietzel, S., & Holl, J. L. (2011). Risk and protective factors for child neglect during early childhood: A cross-study comparison. *Children and Youth Services Review*, *33*(8), 1354–1363.

Smith, L., Vardaman, S., & Snow, M. (2009). *Domestic minor sex trafficking: America's prostituted children*. Shared Hope International. https://sharedhope.org/wp-content/uploads/2012/09/SHI_National_Report_on_DMST_2009.pdf

Smith, S. L., Howard, J. A., Garnier, P. C., & Ryan, C. (2006). Where are we now? *Adoption Quarterly*, *9*(4), 19–44.

Snowden, J., Scott, L., & Sieracki, J. (2008). Predictors of children in foster care being adopted: A classification tree analysis. *Children and Youth Services Review*, *30*(11), 1318–1327.

Stith, S. M., Liu, T., Davies, L. C., Boykin, E. L., Alder, M. C., Harris, J. M., Som, A., McPherson, M., & Dees, J. E. M. E. G. (2009). Risk factors in child maltreatment: A meta-analytic review of the literature. *Aggression and Violent Behavior*, *14*(1), 13–29.

Sullivan, P. M., & Knutson, J. F. (2000). Maltreatment and disabilities: A population-based epidemiological study. *Child Abuse & Neglect*, *24*(10), 1257–1273.

Swensen, K. (2004). *The adoption incentives program*. Congressional Research Service. http://congressionalresearch.com/RL32296/document.php?study=Child+Welfare+The+-Adoption+Incentives+Program

Tatara, T. (1994). Some additional explanations for the recent rise in the U.S. child substitute care population: An analysis of national child substitute care flow data and future research questions. In R. P. Barth, J. D. Berrick, & N. Gilbert (Eds.), *Child welfare research review* (Vol. 1, pp. 126–145). Columbia University Press.

Taussig, H. N., Clyman, R. B., & Landsverk, J. (2001). Children who return home from foster care: A 6-year prospective study of behavioral health outcomes in adolescence. *Pediatrics*, *108*(1), 1–7.

Testa, M. (2002). Subsidized guardianship: Testing an idea whose time has finally come. *Social Work Research*, *26*(3), 145–158.

Toth, S. L., & Manly, J. T. (2011). Bridging research and practice: Challenges and successes in implementing evidence-based preventive intervention strategies for child maltreatment. *Child Abuse & Neglect*, *35*(8), 633–636.

Triseliotis, J. (2002). Long-term foster care or adoption? The evidence examined. *Child & Family Social Work*, 7, 23–33.

Turner, H. A., Finkelhor, D., & Ormrod, R. (2010). Poly-victimization in a national sample of children and youth. *American Journal of Preventive Medicine*, *38*(3), 323–330.

Unger, S. (1977). *The destruction of American Indian families*. Association on American Indian Affairs.

U.S. Advisory Board on Child Abuse and Neglect. (1990). *Child abuse and neglect: Critical first steps in response to a national emergency*. Author.

U.S. Advisory Board on Child Abuse and Neglect. (1991). *Creating caring communities: Blueprint for an effective federal policy on child abuse and neglect*. U.S. Government Printing Office.

U.S. Advisory Board on Child Abuse and Neglect. (1992). *The continuing child protection emergency: A challenge to the nation*. U.S. Government Printing Office.

U.S. Advisory Board on Child Abuse and Neglect. (1993). *Neighbors helping neighbors: A new national strategy for the protection of children*. U.S. Government Printing Office.

U.S. Census Bureau. (2019). *Race data tables*. Author. https://www.census.gov/topics/population/race/data/tables.html

U.S. Commission to Eliminate Child Abuse and Neglect Fatalities. (2016). *Within our reach: A national strategy to eliminate child abuse and neglect fatalities*. U.S. Government Printing Office.

U.S. Department of Health and Human Services (USDHHS), Administration for Children and Families, & Children's Bureau. (2020). *Child maltreatment 2018*. Author. https://www.acf.hhs.gov/sites/default/files/cb/cm2018.pdf

U.S. Department of Health and Human Services (USDHHS), Administration for Children and Families, Administration on Children, Youth and Families, & Children's Bureau. (2019). *The AFCARS report #26*. Author. https://www.acf.hhs.gov/sites/default/files/cb/afcarsreport26.pdf

van der Put, C. E., Assink, M., & van Solinge, N. F. B. (2017). Predicting child maltreatment: A meta-analysis of the predictive validity of risk assessment instruments. *Child Abuse & Neglect, 73*, 71–88.

van IJzendoorn, M. H., Bakermans-Kranenburg, M. J., Coughlan, B., & Reijman, S. (2020). Annual research review: Umbrella synthesis of meta-analyses on child maltreatment antecedents and interventions: Differential susceptibility perspective on risk and resilience. *Journal of Child Psychology and Psychiatry, 61*(3), 272–290.

Victims of Trafficking and Violence Protection Act H.R. 3422 106d., no. P.L. 106-386, Congress (2000).

Wald, M. S. (1976). State intervention on behalf of neglected children: Standards for removal of children from their homes, monitoring the status of children in foster care, and termination of parental rights. *Stanford Law Review, 28*(4), 623–706.

Waldfogel, J. (1998). *The future of child protection: How to break the cycle of abuse and neglect*. Harvard University Press.

Waldock, T. (2016). Theorising children's rights and child welfare paradigms. *International Journal of Children's Rights, 24*, 304–329.

Walker, K. (2013). *Ending the commercial sexual exploitation of children: A call for multi-system collaboration in California*. California Child Welfare Council. https://youthlaw.org/wp-content/uploads/2015/01/Ending-CSEC-A-Call-for-Multi-System_Collaboration-in-CA.pdf

Wildeman, C., Emanuel, N., Leventhal, J. M., Putnam-Hornstein, E., Waldfogel, J., & Lee, H. (2014). The prevalence of confirmed maltreatment among US children, 2004 to 2011. *JAMA Pediatrics, 168*(8), 706–713.

Wilkins, N., Tsao, B., Hertz, M. F., Davis, R., & Klevens, J. (2014). *Connecting the dots: An overview of the links among multiple forms of violence*. Centers for Disease Control and Prevention.

Williams, R. (2017). Safe harbor: State efforts to combat child trafficking. *National Conference of State Legislatures*. https://www.ncsl.org/Portals/1/Documents/cj/SafeHarbor_v06.pdf

Wilson, B., Cooper, K., Kastanis, A., & Nezhad, S. (2014). Sexual and gender minority youth in foster care: Assessing disproportionality and disparities in Los Angeles. *Williams Institute*.https://williamsinstitute.law.ucla.edu/wp-content/uploads/SGM-Youth-in-Foster-Care-Aug-2014.pdf

Winokur, M. A., Holtan, A., & Batchelder, K. E. (2018). Systematic review of kinship care: Effects on safety, permanency, and well-being outcomes. *Research on Social Work Practice, 28*(1), 19–32.

Wulczyn, F. (2020). Foster care in a life course perspective. *Annals of the American Academy of Political and Social Sciences, 692*(1), 227–252.

Yampolskaya, S., & Banks, S. M. (2006). An assessment of the extent of child maltreatment using administrative databases. *Assessment, 13*(3), 342–355.

Zajac, L., Raby, K. L., & Dozier, M. (2019). Receptive vocabulary development of children placed in foster care and children who remained with birth parents after involvement with child protective services. *Child Maltreatment, 24*(1), 107–112.

# 4

# EDUCATION POLICY FOR CHILDREN, YOUTH, AND FAMILIES

Andy J. Frey, Myrna R. Mandlawitz, Armon R. Perry, Hill M. Walker, and Brandon D. Mitchell

Public education in the United States (U.S.) occurs in the context of a complex and often contentious system composed of diverse interest groups. Several competing viewpoints about the primary purpose of education lie at the heart of debates on education policy. These competing interests include preparing students for the workforce, teaching basic academic skills, developing social and cognitive skills, and preparing youth to be productive future citizens (Fuhrman & Lazerson, 2005). The purpose of this chapter is to identify and describe significant education policies of the past century in the context of a risk, protection, and resilience framework. Herein, we discuss the prevalence and trends for school dropout and failure; identify and describe the primary risk and protective factors associated with school adjustment and academic achievement; summarize past and present education policies; and consider and discuss ways in which principles of risk, protection, and resilience might be used to develop or enhance education policy.

## TRENDS IN SCHOOL FAILURE AND ACADEMIC ACHIEVEMENT

Public education is often referred to as "the great equalizer." This label suggests that access to education plays a prominent role in the acquisition of economic and social benefits associated with gainful employment and, more generally, positive life course outcomes. Unfortunately, evidence from years of research indicates that access to quality public education is far from equal, as noted in student-level risk factors, differential dropout rates and achievement gaps, and systemic racism.

Studies have shown that student-specific factors are associated with dropout and academic failure (Fall & Roberts, 2012; Wang & Fredricks, 2014). These student-specific risk factors include truancy (Zhang et al., 2010), low academic achievement, student misbehavior, suspensions and expulsions (Noltemeyer et al., 2015), negative narrative comments in school records, frequent referrals for in- and out-of-school problems (Arcia, 2006; Finn et al., 2008), the number of elementary schools attended, and early involvement in the juvenile justice system (Sweeten, 2006).

In 2017, the dropout rate for African American (5.7%) and Hispanic students (9.5%) was higher than the dropout rate for their White counterparts (4.6%; U.S. Department of Commerce, 2018). Historically, marginalized groups have faced severe challenges and discrimination in their attempts to take advantage of educational opportunities. Despite progress on many fronts, recent reports have indicated that the American education system is still struggling to reach all students effectively. Although it is widely known that a lack of educational attainment has a deleterious impact on future economic status, many children begin school without the necessary readiness skills, and these children experience a pattern of failure that leads to dropout and poor prospects for employment. Additionally, achievement gaps in reading and math between Black/White students and White/Latinx students can be detected from early childhood onward, have been tracked since the 1970s by analysis of the National Assessment of Educational Progress, and have persisted (Musu-Gillette et al., 2017). Further, McFarland and colleagues (2018) note that by the end of fourth grade, Latinx and Black children are two years behind their White peers and that this gap expands up to four years by the end of high school. These gaps have fluctuated over the years and have been declining since the 1990s (Center for Education Policy Analysis, 2019) yet remain disconcerting.

As noted in a recent article by Crutchfield, Phillip, and Frey (2020), structural racism in schools and its effects on students' educational experiences are increasingly becoming a priority focus of local and national significance. Crutchfield and colleagues (2020) note that referrals to lower and remedial academic tracks represent another manifestation of structural racism in school settings. With regard to referrals, Black and Latinx students are three times as likely to be referred to special education as are White students (U.S. Department of Education [USDOE], 2016; Zhang et al., 2014) and are more likely to be put on track for an alternative to a high school diploma (Felton, 2017). Further, Black and Latinx students are under-screened and under-selected for gifted programs when compared to their White and Asian peers (McFarland et al., 2018; Scialabba, 2017).

In addition to these individual risk factors, larger environmental influences also affect school failure and dropout rates. The notion of school engagement is central to the influence of environmental factors. Students perform better and achieve at higher levels when they feel a sense of attachment to school, which is characterized by bonding or connection that occurs through a process of school engagement (Fredricks, 2011). Conversely, students who are unable to establish a connection to school and thus cannot fully engage in the schooling process are at increased risk for dropout (Kemp, 2006). Lack of engagement may occur among students whose families move frequently (South et al., 2007) and those who have negative interactions with school personnel or who are minimally involved in extracurricular activities (Kemp, 2006).

For other students, particularly for youth of color, school structure and culture are often quite different from those in the home. This disparity often alienates students and contributes to disengagement and subsequent dropout (Patterson et al., 2007).

Youth of color are at greatest risk for school adjustment problems during the elementary grades, and they are more likely than other students to become school dropouts (Patterson et al., 2007; Substance Abuse and Mental Health Services Administration, 2008). This pattern also contributes to higher dropout rates in urban areas that are heavily populated by racial and ethnic minorities (Patterson et al., 2007). As shown in Table 4.1, overall graduation rates increased slightly from the 2014–2015 to the 2017–2018 academic year. However, graduation rates were higher for White students than for both African American and Hispanic/Latinx students. Carpenter and Ramirez (2007) examined reasons for school dropout and found that being retained in a grade (or held back) predicted school dropout for all races, whereas family composition and time spent on homework were factors related to school dropout only for White and Hispanic/Latinx students. Among African American students, the number of suspensions and level of parental involvement in school predicted school dropout (Carpenter & Ramirez, 2007). Most important, these findings suggest that many racial and ethnic differences in academic achievement and dropout rates may stem from key differences in risk status at the family, school, and neighborhood levels. These outcomes, however, are at least in part the consequence of differential treatment in the educational setting or implicit bias.

Implicit bias represents subconscious beliefs regarding inferiority, criminality, and other pathologizing perspectives toward students of color (Neal-Jackson, 2020). Biases are perpetuated by both individual and structural factors, including school policies, code of conduct, behavioral and social norms (Dixson et al., 2006). The school system has a long history of being socialized around White customs, norms, and ideology (Donnor, 2013). Because of this, Black students are increasingly being subjected to extreme levels of school surveillance (Kupchik, 2016). For instance, Morris (2016) cites two instances of Black females of only six years of age, one arrested and the other handcuffed, both due to classroom tantrums. Rising rates of school surveillance

**Table 4.1  Public High School Four-Year Adjusted Cohort Graduation Rates**

|  | 2014–2015 | 2017–2018 |
|---|---|---|
|  | % | % |
| **Race/Ethnicity** | | |
| White | 87 | 89 |
| Black/African American | 75 | 79 |
| Hispanic/Latinx | 78 | 81 |
| Total | 83 | 85 |

*Source:* National Center for Education Statistics (2020, p. 3).

is evidenced by the influx of school resource officers, metal detectors, and security cameras, all of which subtly frame the students as criminals needing to be monitored within a system increasingly mirroring that of a prison (Kupchik, 2016). Finally, the incongruence between teacher and student demographics appear to exacerbate school tensions, propelling biases in a way that often goes unnoticed (Neal-Jackson, 2020). Howard (2019) reports that White teachers operate in over 80% of classrooms, and over 40% of schools do not employ a single teacher of color. Furthermore, the largely White, middle class, and female teaching demographics may be inhibitive to fostering relationships between teachers and students, leading to cultural inconsistencies, biases, and pathologizing perspectives toward students of color (Abacioglu et al., 2019).

# RISK AND PROTECTIVE FACTORS FOR SCHOOL ADJUSTMENT AND ACHIEVEMENT PROBLEMS

The term *risk factor* was defined by Fraser and Terzian (2005) as "any event, condition, or experience that increases the probability that a problem will be formed, maintained, or exacerbated" (p. 5). Risk factors for school-related problems may be either specific or general in nature. Within the context of education, nonspecific risk factors such as poverty are not directly related to school adjustment and achievement problems. Nevertheless, such factors have the potential to create maladaptive emotional and behavioral contexts and outcomes, which in turn can have an adverse effect on academic performance (Greenberg et al., 1999). Nonspecific risk factors may set into motion what Fraser and colleagues have called a "chain of risk" (Fraser et al., 2004), which can culminate in negative outcomes such as academic failure.

Other risk factors directly affect the likelihood of school adjustment and academic failure. For example, factors such as neighborhood disorganization and violence (Nettles et al., 2008) and low commitment to schooling contribute to truancy, poor grades, and poor overall academic performance (Carnahan, 1994). As shown in Table 4.2, risk factors occur at the individual, family, school, and neighborhood levels of influence.

*Protective factors* are characteristics or traits that buffer and moderate exposure to risk. In high-risk situations, protective factors such as attachment to teachers or other adults at school have the potential to reduce risk and decrease the likelihood of school-related problems. In the absence of risk, protective factors have a neutral effect. The concept of promotion is closely related to protection. *Promotive factors* are defined as forces that exert positive influences on behavior, irrespective of the presence or absence of risk (Sameroff & Gutman, 2004; Zimmerman et al., 2013). Examples of promotive factors include high intelligence and strong social skills, which can promote positive behavioral outcomes regardless of risk exposure. Table 4.3 summarizes protective and promotive factors that affect academic performance.

## Table 4.2  Risk Factors for Academic Failure by Level of Influence

| Level of Influence | Risk Factors |
| --- | --- |
| Individual | • Lack of learning-related social skills (e.g., listening, participating in groups, staying on task, organizational skills)<br>• Substance use<br>• Pregnancy<br>• Challenging behavior<br>• Limited intelligence<br>• Presence of a disability<br>• Minority status<br>• Special education status<br>• Inability to read by the fourth grade |
| Family | • Residential mobility<br>• Early exposure to familial antisocial behavior<br>• Parent–child conflict<br>• Lack of connectedness with peers, family, school, and community |
| School | • Large school size<br>• Limited school resources<br>• High staff turnover<br>• Inconsistent classroom-management practices<br>• High percentage of low socioeconomic status students<br>• Negative school and classroom climate<br>• School violence<br>• Overcrowding<br>• High student-to-teacher ratios<br>• Insufficient curricular and course relevance<br>• Weak, inconsistent adult leadership<br>• Poor building design<br>• Overreliance on physical security measures |
| Neighborhood | • Poverty<br>• Violence (including gang violence)<br>• Disorganization and low social cohesion<br>• Low percentage of affluent neighbors |

| Table 4.3 | Promotive and Protective Factors for Academic Failure by Level of Influence | |
|---|---|---|
| **Level of Influence** | **Promotive Factors** | **Protective Factors** |
| Individual | • Cognitive skills (e.g., intelligence, ability to work collaboratively with others, and capacity to focus in the face of distraction)<br>• High socioemotional functioning<br>• Ability to adapt to changes in school or work schedule<br>• Effective and efficient communication skills<br>• Ability to use humor to de-escalate negative situations<br>• Social skills<br>• Understanding and accepting capabilities and limitations<br>• Maintaining a positive outlook<br>• Involvement in extracurricular activities | |
| School | • Positive and safe environment<br>• Setting high academic and social expectations<br>• Positive relationships with teachers<br>• School bonding<br>• Positive and inclusive school climate<br>• Positive ratings for overall educational performance | • Positive school climate<br>• Classroom-management strategies that reduce classroom disruption and increase learning<br>• School bonding<br>• Consistent and firm rules for students |
| Peer | | • Acceptance by prosocial peers<br>• Involvement in positive peer groups |

# EDUCATION POLICY: PAST AND PRESENT

American educational policies and practices are profoundly influenced by political ideology, which is most frequently viewed in terms of a conservative or liberal perspective. Historically, a conservative view of education has promoted the idea that individual students have the capacity to earn—or fail to earn—their place among the academic elite. Policy approaches based on conservative views tend to emphasize knowledge-centered education, traditional forms of learning and curricula, respect for authority and discipline, and the adoption of rigorous academic standards. In contrast, educational approaches based on liberal perspectives have tended to support curricula that are responsive to the individual as well as to social and environmental contexts (Apollonia & Abrami, 1997). A chronology of important educational policies and programs of the past 100 years are reviewed and summarized in Table 4.4. The impact of policies that have been subjected to evaluation is also discussed.

## Early Public Policy

From its inception, public education was thought of as a social vehicle for minimizing the importance of class and wealth and for determining who might excel economically. Social policy in the late 19th and early 20th centuries was based on the liberal ideas of Horace Mann and John Dewey. In the mid-19th century, Mann proclaimed that education, more than any other process, was the great equalizer of people from various walks of life (Cremin, 1957). Similarly, Dewey's (1916) philosophy of education held the role of education as the "leveler" of the socially advantaged and disadvantaged. Education policy also stemmed from the conservative notion that mass education was necessary to ensure that the citizenry could obey the law, vote knowledgeably, pay taxes, serve competently on juries, and participate in the armed forces (Derezinski, 2004).

Schooling gradually became compulsory. The Massachusetts Compulsory School Attendance Act of 1852 required public school attendance for all able-bodied children unless a child's parent could establish that the child was obtaining equivalent instruction outside the public schools. By 1918, 48 states had adopted similar school attendance policies (Derezinski, 2004). This change resulted in state-level educational systems based on the idea that all children must attend school and graduate. But schools were segregated by race under the separate-but-equal clause in *Plessy v. Ferguson* (1896), which initially supported separate transportation systems for African American and White people and, later, separate public school systems for African American and White people.

## Education Policy From 1930 to 1970

In the post–World War I era, education policy was dominated by debates about the academic and social goals of education and by discussions about whether all

**Table 4.4    Major American Education Policies, Court Cases, and Public Reports, 1852–2017**

| Policy, Court Case, or Public Report | Date | Summary | Influence on Education |
|---|---|---|---|
| Compulsory School Attendance Act | 1852 | Required public school attendance for all able-bodied children of a certain age, unless the parent of the child could establish that the child was obtaining equivalent instruction outside of the public schools | Resulted in programs designed to have all children attend school and graduate. Existing programs would need to change to accommodate a very different student population that had not previously attended school. |
| *Plessy v. Ferguson* | 1896 | Commonly referred to as "separate but equal," this decision supported separate transportation systems for Blacks and Whites. | Validated the belief that separate schools for Blacks and Whites was a constitutionally sound practice |
| National School Lunch Act | 1946 | The purpose of the act was to provide for the health and well-being of the nation's children by assisting states in providing a school lunch program. | Recognized that external factors, such as hunger and inadequate nutrition, played a part in children's ability to attend and learn in school |
| *Brown v. Board of Education* | 1954 | The U.S. Supreme Court ruled that laws assigning students to schools based on race were unconstitutional. The court ruled unanimously that such laws violated the 14th Amendment's guarantee that the rights of all Americans deserved equal protection. The rationale for the verdict was that being separated from White students could result in feelings of inferiority in students of color and compromise their futures. | Desegregation gained momentum and competed for attention in the national spotlight and attempted to force school districts to desegregate. |
| Numerous Public Reports | Late 1960s and early 1970s | Highlighted the structural inequalities in the educational system (particularly for African American children and those from disadvantaged backgrounds) and the relationship between socioeconomic status and unequal educational outcomes | Justified busing students between schools and between school districts, suggesting that reassigning poor students to schools with middle-class students would improve poor students' academic achievement |

| Policy, Court Case, or Public Report | Date | Summary | Influence on Education |
|---|---|---|---|
| Head Start Act | 1965 | Head Start was designed to address a host of factors that affect poor children and their families, with the ultimate goal of increasing early school readiness by providing health, educational, nutritional, family support, social, and other services for 3- and 4-year-old children from low-income households. | As the first primary prevention program of its kind, Head Start was designed to prepare disadvantaged children on a universal level for kindergarten. |
| Elementary and Secondary Education Act (ESEA) | 1965 | The ESEA of 1965 provided funds for compensatory education in schools that had high percentages of disadvantaged students (Title I). | Title I has had the greatest impact on high-risk youth and has been the largest source of federal funding for poor children in schools, serving 10 million children in more than 50,000 schools. |
| *Milliken v. Bradley* | 1974 | The courts declared that if segregation was the result of an individual's choice, school districts could not be forced to remedy the situation. | Released a district from desegregation orders after it demonstrated it had done everything possible to desegregate schools. This ruling set a precedent for similar rulings that resulted in an end to racially balanced schools in many American cities. |
| Education of All Handicapped Children Act (Public Law [P.L.] 94-142) | 1975 | Provided screening and identification for children with a wide range of disabilities and required schools to provide a variety of services for children based on an individualized education program developed by school district personnel, including teachers, parents, and the child, as appropriate | Altered the education of those with disabilities for many years to come |
| A Nation at Risk | 1983 | Cited high rates of adult illiteracy and low achievement test scores as indicators of declining literacy and educational standards. The report | Federal, state, and local policy switched to the improvement of curriculum, school-based management, |

*(Continued)*

Table 4.4 (Continued)

| Policy, Court Case, or Public Report | Date | Summary | Influence on Education |
|---|---|---|---|
| | | recommended that educational policies strive to improve education for all students and develop more rigorous and measurable standards to assess academic performance. It highlighted the failure of education to ameliorate social problems and blamed these policies for producing mass mediocrity in education that resulted in the decline of authority and standards in schools. | the tightening of standards, the importance of discipline, and the establishment of academic goals and assessment. |
| Individuals with Disabilities Education Act (reauthorization of P.L. 94-142) | 1990 | The Education for All Handicapped Act was renamed the Individuals with Disabilities Education Act. This new iteration of P.L. 94-142 added social work services to the list of "related services." The act also required transition planning for students moving to post-school training and/or employment. In addition, the categories of autism and traumatic brain injury were added to the list of disabilities qualifying children for services. | Marked a broader look at disability and the services that might be necessary for children to be successful in school and beyond |
| America 2000 | 1992 | President George H. Bush called for voluntary testing in Grades 4, 8, and 12 and proposed six goals for education, called America 2000. | Began what would become a major movement toward standards- and accountability-based education policy |
| Goals 2000 | 1994 | President Bill Clinton proposed this initiative, which enacted the six national education goals proposed by President George H. Bush. | Continued the trend toward standards and accountability testing |
| Improving America's Schools Act (IASA; reauthorization of ESEA) | 1994 | IASA was much more comprehensive than the previous version of ESEA, promoting alignment of curriculum and instruction, professional development, school leadership, accountability, and school improvement to help students meet challenging state standards. | IASA codified much of the earlier discussion about school improvement and continued a focus on what conditions are important for students to be able to learn. |

| Policy, Court Case, or Public Report | Date | Summary | Influence on Education |
|---|---|---|---|
| | | IASA included several new programs: (a) the Safe and Drug-Free Schools and Communities Act to encourage safe learning environments; (b) the Gun-Free Schools Act, conditioning states' receipt of ESEA funds on having in place zero-tolerance policies for students bringing weapons to school; and (c) provisions promoting gender equity in education. | |
| Individuals with Disabilities Education Act (reauthorization of P.L. 94-142) | 1997 | Recommended that behavior intervention plans based on a functional behavior assessment should be developed for children suspected of having a severe emotional disturbance Behavior intervention plans were mandated for children with disabilities who had been suspended for 10 days or more before a change of placement could be initiated. For the first time, the law mentioned having, at parents' or school districts' discretion, participation of specialized instructional support personnel, including school social workers, as team members. | Marked the beginning of a trend in educational policy to promote positive, proactive strategies for children with challenging behavior |
| No Child Left Behind (NCLB; reauthorization of ESEA) | 2001 | NCLB was designed to create a stronger, more accountable education system; to change the culture of education; and to use evidence-based strategies found to be effective through rigorous research.<br><br>NCLB holds students accountable to high educational outcomes and standards. NCLB requires each state to set clear and high standards and to put an assessment system in place to measure student progress toward those standards. | Initiated a focus on evidence-based strategies in regular education and provided a much stronger emphasis on accountability testing than previous policies had |

*(Continued)*

**Table 4.4 (Continued)**

| Policy, Court Case, or Public Report | Date | Summary | Influence on Education |
|---|---|---|---|
| Individuals with Disabilities Education Improvement Act (reauthorization of P.L. 94-142) | 2004 | Mandated the use of interventions known to be effective and placed a premium on primary prevention by substantially altering the screening and identification procedures for children with learning disabilities; it also added "early intervening services" for struggling students not yet identified as needing special education services | Continued the trend to promote positive, proactive interventions and to adopt interventions supported by the scientific literature |
| *Parents Involved in Community Schools v. Seattle School District No. 1* | 2007 | The U.S. Supreme Court struck down voluntary student assignment plans in Louisville, Kentucky, and Seattle, Washington, thereby continuing and extending the trend toward resegregation in the public schools. | Extended the trend toward resegregation in public schools and illustrated the deep divisions between the liberal and conservative factions of the newly configured Supreme Court. The ruling applied pressure on school districts that rely on race-conscious criteria to assign students to schools to revisit their plan so it fits within the context of this precedent. |
| American Recovery and Reinvestment Act | 2009 | This large economic stimulation package included emergency funds for education programs, including the creation of several new programs, to offset the effects of the country's economic recession. | Several states received significant funds from competitive grant programs, including Race to the Top and Investing in Innovation, and large one-time investments were made in key formula grant programs, including Title I of the ESEA and the IDEA state grant program. Also, the State Fiscal Stabilization Fund provided funds to states to save over 300,000 education jobs, including school social workers. |

| Policy, Court Case, or Public Report | Date | Summary | Influence on Education |
|---|---|---|---|
| Every Student Succeeds Act (ESSA; reauthorization of ESEA) | 2015 | ESSA is the most recent reauthorization of the ESEA. The law retained key elements of NCLB, such as the requirement for states to work to turn around the lowest 5% of schools. ESSA also continued standards, testing, and accountability requirements but gave states much greater flexibility in designing these systems and reduced federal influence in these areas. | ESSA shifted much of NCLB's federal focus, decision making, and responsibility for closing achievement gaps back to the states and local school districts. |
| *Endrew F. v. Douglas County School District RE-1* (U.S. S.Ct., 2017) | 2017 | *Endrew F.* was a reexamination of the "free appropriate public education" (FAPE) standard in the Individuals with Disabilities Education Act. In the seminal 1982 *Rowley* case interpreting FAPE, the Supreme Court had held that FAPE meant an education "reasonably calculated to enable the child to receive benefit." The *Endrew F.* holding stated that FAPE means an education "reasonably calculated to enable a child to make progress appropriate in light of the child's circumstances." | There is a difference of opinion about the impact of *Endrew F.* Some disability advocates believe the court handed down a more rigorous FAPE standard, whereas many school districts asserted they had already been providing more than "de minimis" services. Thus far, special education hearing officers have used basically the same reasoning as under *Rowley* in deciding special education due process complaints. |

children should receive the same quality of education. Although a focus on curriculum and teaching methods was ever present, a values-based debate ensued that was associated with the issues of equity and excellence. By 1930, the direction of education policy shifted toward equality in education. During the 1930s, the National Association for the Advancement of Colored People initiated a campaign to overthrow the *Plessy v. Ferguson* (1896) decision, with school desegregation as a major goal. As the achievement gap between advantaged and disadvantaged students became increasingly evident, efforts at desegregation in public education gained momentum and competed for policy attention in the national spotlight.

The achievement gap between White and African American students as well as the achievement gap between economically advantaged and disadvantaged children became the most important educational issues of the century in the 1940s. The debate that ensued served as a catalyst for efforts to close the achievement gap and to maximize educational opportunities for people of color. The integration movement scored a significant victory in 1954, when the U.S. Supreme Court ruling in *Brown v. Board of Education of Topeka* (1954) established that laws assigning students to schools based on race were unconstitutional. The Supreme Court ruled unanimously that such laws violated the 14th Amendment's guarantee that the rights of all Americans deserved equal protection. Chief Justice Warren delivered the courts uniramous decision stating,

> To separate them from others of similar age and qualifications solely because of their race generates a feeling of inferiority as to their status in the community that may affect their hearts and minds in a way unlikely ever to be undone.

It took nearly two decades for all states to comply with the court's order to desegregate schools, and many of the initial advancements achieved by integration have since given way.

During this same period, conservatives attacked progressive directions in education, suggesting that the American education system was sacrificing intellectual goals for social ends. The discussion between the progressives, who saw the educational arena as the most legitimate vehicle for leveling the playing field, and the critics, who demanded more academic rigor in education, became known as "The Great Debate" (Ravitch, 1983). This debate was fueled by the launching of the Soviet space satellite, Sputnik—an event that suggested that the U.S. was no longer the world's leader in scientific research and development. From the mid-1950s to the mid-1960s, the pursuit of excellence, standards-based education, curriculum reform, assessment, and accountability gained momentum. However, standards-based education would not take center stage in education policy until the 1980s.

The 1960s witnessed great divisiveness in education policy as illustrated by the tension evident in the eventual move toward a more liberal reform orientation. This change mirrored larger societal issues, predominantly the emphasis on equity issues raised by the civil rights movement. In the 1960s and early 1970s, several influential books highlighted the structural inequalities in the educational system, particularly for African American children and children from disadvantaged backgrounds (Clark, 1965; Kohl, 1967; Kozol, 1967; Rosenfeld, 1971). These books, along with a report by Coleman (1966) titled *Equality of Educational Opportunity*, highlighted the relationship between socioeconomic status and disparity in educational outcomes. The Coleman report suggested that the composition of the student body within schools was highly correlated with student achievement (Sadovnik et al., 2001). The implications of the report were shocking, primarily because Coleman set out to demonstrate that the achievement gap between African American and White students could be attributed to the organizational structure of American schools. The Coleman report justified busing students between schools and between school districts, suggesting that reassigning poor students to schools with middle-class students would equalize educational opportunities. Many researchers, who questioned the premise, method, and findings, challenged the report.

Other progressive policies also emerged in the 1960s. In 1965, the Head Start Act funded an innovative preschool program for disadvantaged children. Head Start was designed to address a host of factors that affected poor children and their families, specifically school readiness. The goal of the program was to increase early school readiness by providing health, educational, nutritional, family support, social, and other services to preschool children from low-income households.

Congress also passed the Elementary and Secondary Education Act (ESEA) in 1965. Similar to the Head Start Act, the ESEA was passed on the assumption that inequities in educational opportunities were largely responsible for the achievement gap between advantaged and disadvantaged children. ESEA provided funds for schools that had high percentages of disadvantaged students to compensate for many years of unequal education under segregation. ESEA has been revised and reauthorized several times since 1965. Provisions of the act are currently responsible for funding bilingual education; education for homeless, migrant, and neglected children; drug education; and teacher training (Nelson et al., 2004).

Title I of ESEA has had the greatest impact on vulnerable and high-risk youth. Title I has been the largest source of federal funding for poor children in schools for 40 years (Cook, 2005), serving more than 33.4 million students in more than 66,000 schools in the 2011–2012 school year alone (Institute of Education Sciences, 2014). In addition, the Safe and Drug-Free Schools and Communities (SDFSC) program provides early screening; remedial academic support; and prevention programming that addresses issues of violence, substance abuse, sexual abuse, and teenage pregnancy. Funds support transition programs for youth coming to public schools from residential and juvenile justice settings as well.

## Education Policy From 1970 to 2000

The 1970s brought new attempts to integrate schools through complex busing plans and magnet schools designed to attract White students to neighborhood schools that they would not ordinarily attend (Cecelski, 1994). However, desegregation became increasingly difficult to maintain as a host of court cases gradually began to undo the *Brown* mandate. In the 1974 case of *Milliken v. Bradley*, the U.S. Supreme Court declared that if segregation was the result of an individual's choice, school districts could not be forced to remedy the situation. Put simply, once a district had done all it could to desegregate its schools, the district was released from further desegregation orders. Similar rulings led to renewed efforts to achieve a racial balance in schools in many American cities (Nelson et al., 2004).

In 1975, Congress passed the Education of All Handicapped Children Act (EHA; P.L. 94-142), which altered educational patterns for students with disabilities. EHA provided screening and identification services for children with a wide range of disabilities and required schools to offer a variety of services for them based on an individualized education program developed by a school district representative, teachers, parents, and the student, as appropriate. The EHA was designed to ensure (a) screening and identification of children with disabilities; (b) provision of a free appropriate public education (FAPE) for children with disabilities, including special education and related services; (c) inclusion of students in the least restrictive environment with nondisabled students to the greatest extent possible; and (d) procedural safeguards to ensure that students' right to a FAPE was protected.

In the late 1970s, many proponents of conservative policies argued that the mission and reach of schools had become too broad. Challenging the authority of schools to address social and behavioral problems, some spoke critically of the way in which EHA interfered with individual freedoms. Many experts argued that progressive reforms had not only failed to narrow the achievement gap between advantaged and disadvantaged children but also had exacerbated problems in the schools related to discipline and other behavioral issues. Anyon (1997) suggested that this belief was fueled by the publication of *A Nation at Risk*, a report on the state of U.S. education issued by the National Commission on Excellence (1983). The report was issued in 1983 under Terrel Bell, President Ronald Reagan's secretary of education; it discussed the ongoing problems of declining literacy and education standards, leading to high rates of adult illiteracy and low achievement test scores. The report recommended that educational policies should strive to improve educational experiences for all students and to develop more rigorous and measurable standards to assess academic performance. *A Nation at Risk* paved the way for educational reform efforts focused on excellence for all students rather than concentrating on subgroups of children such as high-risk youth or children with disabilities. The report highlighted the failure of education to ameliorate social problems and blamed past policies for producing mass mediocrity in education, which—according to the report's authors—resulted in the decline of authority and standards in schools.

Subsequently, the focus of most federal, state, and local policy switched to the improvement of curriculum, school-based management, tightening of standards and discipline, and the establishment of academic goals and assessments. School-based management emphasized a structural shift away from bureaucratic boards of education to local forms of control. New policies were developed to engage parents, teachers, and administrators in decision-making processes. Teacher empowerment, a concept closely related to school-based management, was emphasized as a way to give teachers more decision-making responsibilities within schools. In addition, school choice options, such as vouchers, charter schools, and magnet schools, were created to provide parents with alternatives to the traditional public-school offerings.

The EHA was renamed the Individuals with Disabilities in Education Act (IDEA) in 1990, and *social work services* were added for the first time in the list of possible related services. The ESEA was reauthorized again in 1994 as the Improving America's Schools Act. That reauthorization included the SDFSC Act to promote safe and drug-free learning environments. The act also supported linguistically diverse children and promoted the inclusion and participation of women in all aspects of education. These funds were used for whole school reform, compensatory education, remediation for the country's most disadvantaged children, and free and reduced-price lunches for children in need. Partially because the discipline provisions in IDEA made expelling a student with a severe emotional disturbance nearly impossible, the Gun-Free Schools Act of 1994 was passed, which allowed ESEA funds to be given only to those states that adopted zero-tolerance policies for weapons on school grounds. Public and political concern over discipline-related policies also heightened in the mid-1990s with the outbreak of mass shootings in schools (Jenson & Howard, 1999). This heightened awareness of the safety risk in the school environment resulted in the expansion of zero-tolerance policies for less severe infractions. Alternative schools and increased school security strategies were also implemented to address school safety issues. However, a substantial body of evidence suggests that exclusionary discipline measures such as office referrals, suspension and expulsion, additional security, and other punitive alternatives exacerbate the very problems they are intended to address (Skiba, 2002). Furthermore, the evidence suggests that children of color, particularly African Americans, are disproportionately represented among the students receiving such discipline, which is also evidence of institutional biases inherent in the use of exclusionary discipline (Skiba et al., 2000). The overreliance on punishment and exclusionary practices in the presence of convincing evidence to suggest the practices are ineffective has resulted in the development of policies during the past decade that mandate the use of evidence-based, or empirically supported, practices.

Head Start, which has served as a laboratory for a variety of prevention and early intervention projects since its inception in 1965, was expanded in 1995 (Love et al., 2006). Specifically, Early Head Start was launched to expand Head Start services to pregnant women and to children during the birth- to 3-year period, thereby providing earlier opportunities for preventive interventions. Federal appropriations for Head Start tripled during the 1990s, both to increase the number of children served and to improve the quality of programs, but funding has remained level since the early 2000s. In program year 2017–2018, the Head Start and Early Head Start programs served 1.05 million children and pregnant mothers. In fiscal year (FY) 2019, 947,000 families cumulatively were served throughout the program year (Administration for Children and Families, 2020).

Finally, in 1997, IDEA was again reauthorized, focusing on ensuring that children with disabilities were exposed to positive, proactive interventions. Specifically, IDEA recommended certain measures for any student whose behavior challenges impeded their ability to learn. The first step was for qualified professionals to conduct a functional behavioral assessment of the student and then construct a behavior intervention plan based on that assessment. In addition, a new or revised behavior plan was mandated after a child with a disability had been suspended for more than 10 days or before a change of placement to a more restrictive setting (i.e., alternative classroom or school). IDEA was also noteworthy for mandating the inclusion of parents in the planning process for their child.

## Education Policy From 2001 to 2010

The momentum of educational reforms in the 1990s culminated in the passage of the 2001 No Child Left Behind Act (NCLB). NCLB was the most sweeping federal reform in education since ESEA was passed in 1965. Technically, NCLB was the most recent reauthorization of ESEA. However, NCLB added many new initiatives. For example, NCLB was designed to create a stronger, more accountable education system; to change the culture of education; and to use evidence-based strategies that have been determined effective through rigorous research. Rather than providing specific resources for at-risk youth, NCLB proposed assisting children and youth by holding them accountable to high educational outcomes and standards. NCLB required each state to set clear and high standards and to put an assessment system in place to measure student progress toward those standards (Paige, 2002). Specifically, NCLB required states to test all students annually in Grades 3 through 8 and once in Grades 10 through 12 in reading and math. NCLB also required that scores reported by states be disaggregated by poverty, race and ethnicity, disability, and English-language proficiency so that potential achievement gaps could be identified. Schools that failed to make adequate yearly progress toward goals were identified for improvement and subject to corrective action. NCLB mandated that teachers use strategies that have been shown to be effective. In addition to its emphasis on early reading programs, NCLB is noteworthy for its attention to the critical role that parents play in children's educational experiences. NCLB dramatically affected educational practices, which now place a premium on students meeting standards of learning and assessment and on school-based management, teacher empowerment, and school choice (e.g., vouchers, magnet schools, charter schools, and privatization options).

The Individuals with Disabilities Education Improvement Act of 2004, a reauthorization of P.L. 94-142, continued the trend of promoting the adoption of effective interventions and placed a premium on primary prevention by substantially altering the screening and identification procedures for children with learning disabilities. Specifically, the act permits school districts to use a process that determines if the child responds to scientific, research-based intervention as a part of the evaluation procedures used to assess functional capacity. This response-focused method can replace assessment using the discrepancy between ability and achievement to identify students with learning difficulties, but data from this process must be only one component of a comprehensive evaluation. This approach, referred to as Response to Intervention, has been applied to academic and behavioral supports in special and routine education. Batsche and colleagues (2005) defined Response to Intervention as the practice of (a) providing effective instruction and interventions based on students' needs and (b) regularly monitoring students' progress to guide decisions about changes in instruction or goals. The model suggests that more intensive interventions should be considered for individual students based on their response (or lack thereof) to less-intensive, high-quality interventions.

In 2007, the U.S. Supreme Court struck down voluntary student assignment plans in Louisville, Kentucky, and Seattle, Washington, thereby continuing and extending the trend toward resegregation in public schools. In the 2007 case, *Parents Involved in Community Schools v. Seattle School District No. 1*, the petitioners contended that assigning students to schools solely to achieve racial balance in the schools was a violation of individuals' rights guaranteed under the 14th Amendment (e.g., Equal Protection

Clause) as well as the Civil Rights Act of 1964. The Louisville and Seattle districts argued unsuccessfully that educational and social benefits such as socialization and good citizenship are derived from an educationally diverse learning environment and that because racial diversity was their primary interest, promoting that interest using race-conscious criteria alone was necessary and justified. Although the justices were sharply divided in a 5–4 vote, the court's opinion allows districts to use race-conscious measures so long as such measures do not use race to treat individual students differently "solely on the basis of a systematic individual typing by race" (*Parents Involved in Community Schools v. Seattle School District No. 1*, 2007, p. 7). Even though the decision appears likely to result in increased educational resegregation, it does not overtly forbid school districts that are seeking diversity to pursue that goal by using race-conscious means.

## Education Policy From 2011 to 2017

In the early 21st century, all federal policy—including education policy—was affected by the deepening divide between conservative and progressive philosophies about the role of the federal government. The advent and influence of the Tea Party and other populist movements within the Republican ranks further fueled an already highly charged political climate.

Conservatives, mostly Republicans, supported leaving education decisions to states and local school districts, including choices about how federal dollars would be spent. They asserted that local communities and school administrators were in the best position to know the demographics and needs of their students and thus fewer federal mandates should be attached to how funds are used. On the other hand, progressives (largely Democrats) supported greater oversight by the federal government, citing inequities in access to quality education and disparities in outcomes across student populations. They highlighted a strong federal presence, including investment in education, as critical to ensuring success for all students.

Those differences in philosophy pervaded discussions on a number of key education issues. Policy themes focused on early childhood education, school choice, college- and career-readiness, and standards and high-stakes assessments. The importance of evidence-based practice, professional preparation and evaluation, and school improvement and reform were at the forefront in many of these discussions. Finally, after an extended delay, Congress acted to reauthorize the ESEA, then known as NCLB, and passed the Every Student Succeeds Act (ESSA; P.L. 114-95, 129 Stat. 1802 [Dec. 10, 2015]). The passage of ESSA came with the acknowledgment that the goal of closing the achievement gaps for the four subgroups specifically named in the law (disadvantaged students, racial and ethnic minorities, students with disabilities, and English language learners) had still not been met.

*Early Childhood Education.* With a strong push from the Obama administration, Congress took a much closer look at the impact of early education. The politics of the debate centered on whether existing programs were adequate and, in some instances, duplicative or whether a more expansive approach and investment in early childhood education was necessary. President Obama proposed the Preschool for All program in every budget from FY 2013 to FY 2017. The proposal each of those years was for mandatory funding of $75 billion over 10 years to support state efforts to provide access to high-quality preschool for all four-year-olds from low- and moderate-income families. Under the proposal, states were required to hire only preschool teachers with at least a bachelor's degree; provide ongoing professional development; have low staff–child ratios and class sizes; provide a full-day program; and offer developmentally appropriate, evidence-based instructional programs as well as comprehensive support services for children. Although the full proposal was never enacted into law, one aspect—Preschool Development Grants—was funded in FY 2014 and FY 2015. Subsequently, when the ESEA was reauthorized, the law included a new version of the Preschool Development Grants, jointly administered by the U.S. Departments of Education and Health and Human Services. These competitive one-year grants to states were designed to enhance and better coordinate early childhood education programs in order to improve quality, access, and transition to elementary school, targeting resources to low-income families.

*State versus Federal Control of Education.* The philosophical divide between progressives and conservatives was particularly evident in the ESEA debate, and consensus on how to reconcile differing views of state versus federal role in education proved elusive. The House, under Republican leadership, passed the Student Success Act in July 2013, which block granted a number of ESEA programs and expanded use of funds for private school options. Requirements for state standards and high-stakes tests, including public reporting, were continued in the bill, while any requirements related to highly qualified teachers were eliminated. In October 2013, the Senate health, education, labor and pensions committee under Democratic leadership passed its bill, Strengthening America's Schools Act, although the full Senate never acted on the legislation. While also requiring adoption of academic standards and continuation of testing, the bill was a more comprehensive federal approach to education. The Senate committee bill maintained much more of the then-current law than the House version and did not use the block grant approach. The legislation required states to identify certain categories of schools for interventions, while the House did not define a system of school improvement or intervention. The debate on reauthorization of the ESEA continued into the next session of Congress.

*College and Career Readiness.* The USDOE acknowledged that NCLB needed changes to meet the goals of the law. With Congress still debating possible amendments to the law, the department granted states ESEA "flexibility" (waivers) from certain provisions of the law. To receive those waivers, states were required to adopt college- and career-ready standards in at least mathematics and reading/language arts and high-stakes assessments to measure student growth for Grades 3–8 and at least once in high school. In addition, rather than the federally imposed accountability provisions of the law, states had to develop their own "differentiated recognition, accountability, and support" for all their school districts and for all Title I schools within those districts. Receipt of a waiver also required adoption of new teacher and principal evaluation systems, allowing states to adopt one system to be used in all its districts or flexibility for school districts to adopt their own evaluation plans. Waivers continued to be granted through the life of NCLB.

*Activism in Education.* Under the Obama administration and led by Secretary of Education Arne Duncan, the USDOE took an activist role in education policy, drawing criticism at times from both sides of the political aisle. In addition to the ESEA waivers, the administration established several competitive grant programs first funded under the American Recovery and Reinvestment Act in FY 2009, including Race to the Top (RTTT) and Investing in Innovation (i3). Several states received significant federal funding under RTTT, for which they promised to adopt rigorous academic standards and use results on aligned high-stakes tests in evaluating teacher and principal performance. States also agreed to allow expansion of charter schools and use of alternative certification for teachers. The administration proposed different foci for RTTT grants in subsequent fiscal years, including a school district rather than state competition for funds and another iteration targeting early childhood programs. The program was last funded in FY 2013. Some critics of the program said states had not been able to deliver on their promises, with little improvement in student outcomes, while others said investing these funds in foundational programs such as ESEA and the IDEA would provide every state more resources to bolster achievement.

*Standards and High-Stakes Assessments.* For Grades K–12, the education debate centered on Common Core State Standards (CCSS). It is important to note that CCSS was a bottom-up effort rather than a federal program, initiated by the Council of Chief State School Officers representing state superintendents of education and the National Governors Association. Federal involvement in CCSS arose when the Department of Education tied RTTT funding to adoption of rigorous state standards, which many people viewed as an endorsement of CCSS. However, CCSS remained a state-driven process with 40+ states voluntarily adopting standards, despite critics who labeled CCSS as national standards or a national curriculum. While some states eventually rescinded adoption of CCSS, those same states have new state standards with a strong resemblance but different name to the politically charged CCSS.

*Guidance and Regulations.* In addition to congressional action, policy can be affected through the regulatory process and the use of agency guidance. The Department of Education used both during the Obama administration. In 2014, the Departments of Education and Justice jointly established the Supportive School Discipline Initiative, with guidance to school districts on how to reduce the disparate impact of school discipline policies on students of color. The Department of Education issued guidance in 2016 to address implementation of Title IX (Education Amendments of 1972) prohibiting sex discrimination in educational programs and activities by recipients of federal aid, with a focus on discrimination based on gender identity and transgender youth specifically. Two regulations were also promulgated in 2016. The first was designed to address significantly disproportionate representation of students of color in special education and the disproportionately higher numbers of those students receiving harsher discipline or placement in more restrictive settings. The second set of regulations linked evaluation of and federal funding for teacher preparation programs to the success of their graduates.

*Reauthorization of the Elementary and Secondary Education Act.* Major federal education laws generally require reauthorization by Congress after five years, but that time frame is rarely met. After several attempts to reauthorize the ESEA, last passed by Congress in 2001 and known as NCLB, Congress succeeded in revamping the law in 2015. The newest iteration—ESSA—retained key elements of NCLB, such as requiring states to work to turn around the lowest 5% of schools, but also eliminated other provisions including tying teacher evaluations to student outcomes. A significant change was the imposition of restrictions on the Secretary of Education's authority, as some in Congress felt Secretary Duncan had overreached and had turned the Department of Education into a "federal school board." ESSA also continued standards, testing, and accountability requirements but gave states much greater flexibility in designing these systems and reduced federal influence in these areas.

## Education Policy From 2017 to 2020

The election of Donald Trump as president in 2016 caught many people in Washington off guard, and plans to continue the education policies of the Obama administration were quickly upended by the new administration. The confirmation of Betsy DeVos as U.S. Secretary of Education brought to the education policy discussion a strong voice for private schools, including federal funding of private schools through vouchers and other financial mechanisms. The Trump administration also sought to significantly reduce the federal role in education while concomitantly increasing state and local control. The mechanisms to achieve that goal were mainly through deregulation and elimination of guidance from previous administrations and by decreasing the federal investment in education and making the use of funds a more flexible local decision. School safety also continued as a serious policy discussion, including conversations on school mental health services, gun restrictions, and hardening of school campuses. This issue was heightened by the deadliest school shooting in U.S. history on February 14, 2017; Nikolas Cruz, a 19-year-old former student, entered Marjory Stoneman High School in Parkland, Florida, and opened fire with a semiautomatic rifle. Cruz fled the scene by blending in with other students and was apprehended later the same day. In all, 17 students and staff were killed and another 17 were injured.

*Deregulation and Rollback of Previous Department of Education Guidance.* Employing the rarely used Congressional Review Act (CRA), the Trump administration rescinded a number of Obama-era regulations and guidance. The CRA allows Congress to issue a joint resolution of disapproval within 60 days of the effective date of a regulation; in effect, overturning the agency's rule. Congress reversed regulations related to teacher preparation programs and ESSA accountability. In addition, the Department of Education rolled back guidance under Title IX of the Education Amendments of 1972 related to discrimination based on gender identity, specifically the use of school bathrooms and locker rooms by transgender students. The department also rolled back guidance on the disparate impact of school discipline of students of color, a recommendation of the president's Federal School Safety Commission. An attempt to delay implementation of regulations related to significant disproportionality of students of color in special education resulted in a legal challenge by special education advocates. The U.S. District Court for the District of Columbia ordered the regulation to go into effect, and the Department of Justice subsequently dismissed the department's appeal of the ruling (*COPAA v. DeVos et.al.*, 2019).

*Privatization and School Vouchers.* In President Trump's plan for his first 100 days in office, he announced a $20 billion federal voucher plan for children in poverty. The intention was to redirect most, if not all, of the $14 billion from the Title I compensatory education program under the ESEA, which is directed to low-income students. Known as *portability*, this "voucherization" of the Title I program had been a standard of the Republican party's education platform for a number of years. In theory, families would receive a cash payment and could use that money for tuition at any public or private school. A coalition of education, civil rights, disability, and religious organizations in Washington worked tirelessly against voucher mechanisms. In fact, some religious and secular private schools stated they would not accept vouchers because their missions would be inhibited by subjecting them to a host of federal laws under which they were currently exempt. Notwithstanding, the Department of Education budget in each of the years of the Trump administration included a voucher proposal. The most recent proposal for FY 2021, known as "Education Freedom Scholarships," would come with a price tag of $50 billion over 10 years. Thus far, Congress has declined to enact any of these proposals.

*Education Budgets and Block Grants.* Although both Democratic and Republican administrations since the 1960s have used block grants (i.e., consolidating programs into one larger vehicle), in the Reagan presidency, block grants became synonymous with decreased funding. With the Trump administration's interest in privatization and local control of education, new proposals for FY 2021 expand the Reagan concept. Twenty-nine K–12 federal education programs would be consolidated into a block grant, with a cut in funding of 20% below the total funding for those programs in FY 2020. In addition, the administration proposed to consolidate several higher education programs targeted at first-generation college attendees, again cutting the overall funding below the current level. The department's rationale for the K–12 block grant is to allow states and local school districts broad discretion over the use of those funds, supporting local control and allowing a significant reduction in federal department staff currently administering the 29 programs proposed for consolidation. This would further reduce the federal footprint in education.

*School Safety.* In the aftermath of school shootings (e.g., the tragedy at Marjory Stoneman Douglas High School), the president appointed the Federal School Safety Commission charged with developing recommendations to address school safety. Even before the commission wrote its report, critics of Obama-era school discipline policies said the rules limited schools' ability to discipline students. The commission responded by recommending rescission of the Obama administration's school discipline guidance, which was focused on disparate impact on students of color. Among other recommendations were arming school personnel, installing upgraded security hardware, hiring additional school resource officers, and working more closely with law enforcement. While the report also called for increased mental health supports and services, the commission recommended that states, rather than the federal government, provide more funding for schools to create a positive school climate so students would feel more connected to the school community.

*Next Steps.* The Trump Administration, through the USDOE, has championed privatization and local control. Passage of the Coronavirus Aid, Relief, and Economic Security Act (CARES; P.L. No. 116-136, 134 Stat. 281; March 27, 2020) to address economic relief during the COVID-19 pandemic provided another vehicle for the department to enhance support to private schools. The department's interpretation of how CARES Act funds should be distributed under the ESSA Title I "equitable services" provision to private schools created a great deal of controversy, as the department's interpretation would have increased some states' distribution to private schools by close to 300%. Despite concerns from both Democrats and Republicans, the department proceeded to issue an Interim Final Rule—in effect, an emergency regulation—to implement its interpretation. Subsequently, four lawsuits were filed to stop implementation of the rule, which was ultimately vacated in a decision by the U.S. District Court of the District of Columbia in September 2020 (*NAACP v. DeVos*, 2020). The U.S. Supreme Court also accepted review of a private school aid question in its 2019–2020 term. In June 2020, the court ruled in *Espinoza v. Montana Dept. of Revenue* (2020) that Montana's voucher program must fund private religious schools if it funds secular private schools, opening the door for new and expanded publicly funded private school voucher programs. Whether these trends of local control and privatization continue as national education policy will likely be an ongoing conversation now and into future administrations.

## International Education Policy

International education policy is shaped by cultural, societal, and economic influences (Oplatka, 2018). Trends in globalization influence education policies in both the developed and less economically developed countries and have deep ties to neoliberalism—as evidenced by a growing push for a one-size-fits-all model of education (Gibton, 2013). Currently, the primary mechanism influencing policies and dictating a globalized educational system is the Organization for Economic Cooperation and Development's (OECD, 2019) subsidiary, the Programme for International Student Assessment (PISA, 2019).

The PISA, now in nearly 80 countries, conducts assessments on 15-year-olds every three years. These assessments focus on the themes of mathematics, reading, and science, with the hope of assessing whether students can transfer knowledge learned in school to real-world situations (PISA, 2019). The World Bank supplies aid to countries contingent on participation in PISA (Auld et al., 2019). An increasing amount of educational data represents an important technological shift that may help improve student outcomes; however, there is no accountability regarding the incompatible curricula across nations and schools. Moreover, PISA assessments focus on skills that are not necessarily taught in any school system (Labaree, 2014); PISA assesses critical thinking skills that requires students to draw on real-world problem-solving skills rather than memorization of facts. Meanwhile, PISA's testing and evaluation serve as a platform for global educational comparison, driving policies, and influencing education in both the developed and least developed countries (Hargreaves & Shirley, 2012). Although widespread, PISA as global education policy has many limitations. It promotes comparisons across countries that have hugely different characteristics and it is not based on evidence.

With regard to evidence, a landmark study found no association between increases in human capital and enhanced educational attainment (Pritchett, 1999). In 2014, a research group consisting of over 80 individuals, including academic scholars, principals, and teachers, petitioned the head of PISA, Dr. Andreas Schleicher, urging him to consider reform efforts before moving forward with subsequent rounds of assessment. Their letter cited an array of issues associated with the assessment, including the sensationalization of results, lack of external oversight, high cost to nations, and lack of transparency regarding the role of for-profit enterprises (Strauss, 2014). PISA's impact on policy has been so dubious that the phrase "PISA shock" was used after Germany and Denmark went through vigorous policy reform to address their less-than-ideal performance on PISA's first round of testing in 2000 (Breakspear, 2012).

PISA has resulted in international comparisons that are inappropriate. For example, there were significant reports claiming Shanghai's results did not represent an accurate sample of the population and were thus misleading or altogether inaccurate (Dews, 2016). Similarly, Loveless (2019) argued that PISA scores in China are not truly representative because the majority of the country live in non-tested, rural regions. Meanwhile in Finland, people are ethnically and economically homogenous, with low rates in crime and poverty (Hargreaves & Shirley, 2012). Finland's educational system reflects their values in equality with 99% of students completing basic school—among the lowest dropout rates in the world (Chung, 2019). Taken as a whole, vast differences in the sociodemographic characteristics of countries render uncontrolled comparisons spurious. Global educational policies, such as PISA, that promote international benchmarking standards produce simplistic findings that are prone to misinterpretation.

In conclusion, international education policy is trending toward the standardization of teaching and learning. It has focused on test-based accountability and student productivity similar to the U.S. As a result, privatization is proliferating through all facets of education; meanwhile, the importance of developing innovative and creative skills is often overlooked (Hargreaves & Shirley, 2012). PISA has expanded to engulf 80% of the world's economies, and it promotes a testing culture (Mundy et al., 2016). Skeptics argue that it is not clear that PISA-related academic skills are highly correlated with life course outcomes in developing countries (Chung, 2019; Labaree, 2014).

While international policy bares little to no indication that it is informed by a risk and resilience perspective, Li, Martin, and Yeung (2017) analyzed several papers looking at academic risk and resilience in the Asian context. They found factors that reinforced Western-based findings on risk and resilience while adding some factors they call "uniquely Asian," including increased self-reliance and a stronger emphasis on persistence than for Western children. Their findings emphasize the importance of considering culture and context when evaluating academic resilience. From a risk and resilience framework, it may be prudent to promote systems that emphasize healthy teacher–student relationships while underscoring the importance of developing the whole child in cultural context. Ultimately, the best protective factors are those that envelop educational attainment within efforts to promote human development and growth. As the expansion of PISA benchmarking continues, global educational policies risk failing to measure a child's worth, well-being, and emotional development.

## SUMMARY OF FEDERAL POLICY

Public education in the U.S. has witnessed a number of reform movements in the past century. From the end of World War I until the mid-1940s, education policy focused on equity and attempted to narrow or eliminate the achievement gap between advantaged and disadvantaged youth. From the 1950s to the 1970s, issues of equity dominated federal education policy. However, policies favoring equity in education were not without criticism during these years; many critics of equity policies believed intellectual and academic goals were being sacrificed for social ends. These attacks created fertile ground for alternative strategies to spring forth, such as the adoption of standards, curriculum reform, and accountability systems. Since the mid-1970s, most education policies and programs have been more closely aligned with the standards-based education movement, which has focused more heavily on the use of standardized assessment as a measure of improvement, possibly to the detriment of addressing nonacademic barriers to learning. More recently, the debates over federal versus state and local control of education and the use of public funds to support private education have played significant roles in formation of education policy.

## PRINCIPLES OF RISK, PROTECTION, AND RESILIENCE IN EDUCATION POLICY

Evidence exists to both support and criticize the effectiveness of the policies and programs discussed in the prior section. Next, we briefly evaluate the extent to which historic and current educational policies and programs have been based on principles of risk and resilience. We begin with those that are clearly within this framework.

Several policies illustrate the relationship between risk, protection, and educational approaches to change and reform. For example, Head Start, IDEA, and NCLB/ESSA emphasize principles that are consistent with the models of risk and resilience discussed earlier in this chapter. Head Start targets youth who are at highest risk for academic failure because of low socioeconomic status. The program attempts to bolster school readiness skills, and this approach is consistent with evidence suggesting that the preschool years represent a critical developmental phase for prevention and early intervention services (Reid, 1993). Although IDEA permits intervention with children before they enter school and targets children at risk of developing disabilities and school failure, most IDEA funding is intended for children who are already identified as having a disability. In addition, ESSA attempts to raise awareness of the achievement gap and encourages school districts to address the gap by requiring states to report standardized test scores disaggregated by poverty, race/ethnicity, disability, and English-language proficiency. The recent ESSA emphasis on standards-based education sets high academic expectations for all students, and such expectations are an identified protective factor against school failure and dropout (Furlong & Morrison, 2000).

The emphasis on evidence-based prevention efforts highlighted in IDEA is compatible with risk and protective factors. This emphasis should result in improvements to the learning environment, such as school connectedness, school climate, teacher expectations, family involvement, and community services to support students and families. Many of these improved environmental conditions have been highlighted previously as key protective influences for children (Daily et al., 2020; Haberman, 2000; Hawkins et al., 1999).

Other policies appear to ignore principles of risk and resilience at best and to undermine or contradict such principles at worst. Specifically, zero-tolerance policies, particularly those that apply to minor infractions, have been shown to increase the risk of poor outcomes among high-risk children in general and among youth of color specifically (Okilwa & Robert, 2017; Skiba & Peterson, 1999).

In sum, the application of risk and protective factors to the design of educational policy is inconsistent. Some policies (e.g., the Compulsory School Attendance Act, the Head Start Act, EHA, and IDEA), court cases (e.g., *Brown v. Board of Education*), and programs (e.g., Head Start and special education) are intended to help students prevail over adversity, a key idea in the concept of resilience. Other policies (e.g., ESSA and Gun-Free Schools Act) and court cases (e.g., *Plessy v. Ferguson* and *Milliken v. Bradley*) ignore or may even reject the constructs of risk and resilience. New and sustained efforts are needed to implement a risk and resilience framework in education policy.

# USING PRINCIPLES OF RISK, PROTECTION, AND RESILIENCE TO ACHIEVE INTEGRATED EDUCATION POLICY

Principles of risk, protection, and resilience can be applied to education policy in two fundamental ways. One option requires policymakers to focus efforts on youth who are most likely to experience school adjustment and achievement problems. Such a strategy tends to concentrate program and policy efforts on youth from disadvantaged backgrounds because socioeconomic status is a key risk factor for school failure (Brooks-Gunn & Duncan, 1997). A second approach uses knowledge of risk, protection, and resilience to design promotive educational policies and programs that are beneficial for all children, regardless of risk exposure. We begin our discussion with policy recommendations for programs that promote healthy outcomes for all children and youth.

## Promotive Interventions and Strategies

We recommend educational policies and programs that promote social competence, develop caring relationships, and create high expectations for all students. Policies that promote participation in positive academic and social groups, enhance school bonding or connectedness, and create positive and safe learning environments should receive priority in national policy and program debates. Simply adopting effective promotion interventions and strategies is not sufficient to produce sustainable change. Specific promotion strategies include the following:

- Establishing positive behavioral and rigorous academic expectations for all students

- Making positive environmental arrangements (e.g., lighting, noise, traffic patterns, crowd size) and providing active supervision of students

- Applying consequences to encourage desired behavior and discourage undesirable behavior

- Developing school and community linkages

- Developing school and home linkages

- Using Office of Civil Rights data (publicly available at https://ocrdata.ed.gov/DistrictSchoolSearch), or state or local district level data, to explore and demonstrate existing disproportionality in school practices such as academic placement and disciplinary actions (Crutchfield et al., 2020)

Other programs designed to positively affect school culture, such as restorative practices (e.g., restorative circles, mindfulness, collaborative agreements, problem solving), trauma-informed practices, conflict resolution, peer mediation, and anti-bullying strategies, illustrate the growing emphasis on changing peer and institutional culture and are likely to have protective value. Recent research has demonstrated that many strategies and programs work for a short time but that effects quickly fade; thus, there is a need to learn more about the specific conditions and settings in which intervention effects can be sustained over time (Duncan, 2009). A report by the Center for Mental Health in Schools (2002) indicated that school-based reform efforts have been unsuccessful because projects and services designed to remove barriers to learning are usually viewed as supplementary services. The result may be seen in the fragmentation of services, marginalization of professionals, and overall inadequacies in policy reform. Specialized instructional support personnel (SISP)—including school social workers, school psychologists, speech language pathologists, school nurses, and school counselors—must be trained to support the primary mission of schools. Furthermore, policies are needed to enhance standards while promoting reasonable professional–student ratios for all schools and students.

A critically important element in affecting positive change in schools is the process of *enculturation*, or "the manner in which a school embeds a systems change process into its own unique culture, assumes 'ownership' of the process, and has the process become a part of business as usual at the school" (Sailor et al., 2009, p. 664). Policies and programs should be designed so as to increase service cohesion by addressing the need for multiple interventions within schools in an integrated fashion. Walker and colleagues (1996) suggested that prevention efforts have generally lacked coordination and integration because no comprehensive strategic plan for coordinating and linking behavioral supports existed at the school or district level. Evidence from efficacious school-based practices also supports the need to attend to interactions among key individual and environmental factors (Shinn & Walker, 2010). Over the past several decades, our knowledge of "what works" in school-based prevention programs has increased dramatically (Jenson & Bender, 2014). For example, it is widely believed that interventions are more effective if they are integrated and coordinated with other interventions along a continuum of support representing primary, secondary, and tertiary levels of intervention (Dunlap et al., 2009). Primary prevention practices focus on supporting academic success and desirable behavior and preventing initial occurrences of academic failure or problem behavior. Secondary prevention, which is more intense and applied with fewer students, seeks to prevent repeated academic failure and the reoccurrence of problem behavior. Finally, tertiary-level interventions focus on students who have serious academic or behavioral problems that constitute a chronic condition. Within this continuum, the promise of primary prevention is increasingly emphasized because it not only is efficient and effective but also increases the likelihood that the needs of students with elevated risk status will be targeted for intervention. We believe that targeted educational policies and programs should focus on schools that have high percentages of students living in poverty and that identification of and intervention with high-risk students should occur as early as possible. Examples of targeted policies and programs are reviewed next.

# THE ROLE OF TARGETED INTERVENTIONS AND STRATEGIES

## Redistribution of Tax Dollars to Support Schools in Low-Income Neighborhoods

The most obvious recommendation for using principles of risk and protection in targeted educational policy may involve school financing. Nearly 50% of school funding comes from local property taxes (Nelson et al., 2004). Therefore, adequately funding schools in low-income neighborhoods is an ongoing challenge to equity in education. To address this problem, a larger percentage of school financing may need to come from state and federal taxes rather than from local tax bases. Equalizing the funding base between advantaged and disadvantaged communities would likely not be sufficient to produce equal educational outcomes, given variations in individual, family, neighborhood, and community risk factors across schools and communities. Furthermore, providing more money to disadvantaged schools would require people in wealthy districts to partially fund lower-resource districts. Redistributing tax resources on the basis of need/risk factors is routinely done at the national, state, county, and school district levels. But the magnitude of redistribution that would be required to address the disadvantage faced by many schools would likely engender heated debate. However, such a strategy may well be entirely necessary to create positive change and promote effective policies based on principles of risk and protection.

## Early Identification and Intervention at the Point of School Entry

Between 10% and 14% of children up to 5 years old experience social or emotional problems that adversely affect their functioning and development (e.g., school readiness skills), with children living in poverty being more likely to experience these problems (Brauner & Stephens, 2006; Duncan et al., 1994). Whether in preschool or early elementary school, the importance of early screening for risk factors that lead to poor educational outcomes cannot be overstated. Given the proper tools, it requires minimal effort for educators to predict—with great accuracy—which children will require extensive academic or behavioral supports (Dever et al., 2018). Systemwide screening, particularly for emotional and behavioral indicators leading to school failure, may be a cost-effective strategy to improve educational outcomes. We believe that school readiness skills should be the primary focus of policy reforms and recommend increased funding for intervention programs that target these skills.

As noted, several federal programs, such as those promoted through Title IV and Title V funds, provide nonspecific funding to address a wide range of educational issues. Title I is consistent with the risk and protection framework because the primary criteria to access these funds are linked to students' socioeconomic status. However, there is no mandate requiring that interventions created with these funds address risk and protective factors. In addition, there are no mandates requiring that the funds, or a portion of the funds, be used for evidence-based interventions. Policymakers should address these gaps in funding mandates to ensure that funds are used for effective early intervention programs that have sustained effects. For example, early intervention programs that focus on family risk factors are particularly promising; Duncan and Brooks-Gunn (2000) reported that interventions targeting parenting practices can mediate up to half of the impact of poverty on child development.

The quality of the language environment to which a child is exposed in the first years of life is a harbinger of their school success years later as they begin the schooling process. One of the most powerful things that can be done to enhance a child's potential school success is to improve their language skills. Vocabulary, as reflected in the diversity and number of words a child knows, is a key to better understanding and using language which, in turn, increases reading readiness and academic performance. We know that there is a very strong association between socioeconomic status and reading achievement such that children who come from low-income households often suffer in their academic performance due to family poverty and its effects on development (Wood et al., 2021).

In a now-classic study, Hart and Risley (1995) conducted a remarkable study of this topic. They selected three types of families to systematically observe and recorded family–child language interactions within their home environments. These were welfare families, average working-class families, and professional families (Hart & Risley, 2003). On average, children from welfare families were exposed to only 616 words per hour in contrast to hourly rates for average working families (1,251 words) and professional families (2,153). By age 3, this disparity results in children of professional families hearing, on average, 4 million more words than their less affluent peers. Given current preschool and school practices, these children can never catch up and close this gap. The seminal work of Hart and Risley has been confirmed and expanded by additional studies from other researchers such as Fernald et al. (2013) and Snow (2013).

Children who struggle with reading mastery by the end of Grade 3, when reading is used as a tool for learning, often come from this language background. We have the ability to accurately identify these children in kindergarten and first grade through brief, highly accurate literacy assessments. A widely used assessment for this purpose is the Diagnostic Indicators of Basic Emerging Literacy Skills (DIBELS, 8th edition; Center on Teaching and Learning, College of Education, University of Oregon, Eugene, OR 97403). Given the brevity and accuracy of this assessment, it could easily be used as a mandated universal screening procedure to identify potentially challenged readers as early as possible. Some recommended vocabulary and language development strategies for use by parents and within preschool settings are listed below:

- Introduce and use new, interesting words in natural conversations.

- Use gestures and facial expressions to help the child make sense of the new words.

- Use songs and rhymes to help introduce new words.

- Talk daily with the child and prompt them to talk with siblings and peers.

- Read to the child daily, have the child look at the book, and explain graphics and illustrations.

- Develop a love of reading in the child.

- Help the child practice using new words in daily conversations.

- Ask your child questions that require more than one-word answers.

The presence of high-quality primary prevention programs is increasingly being recognized as a necessary prerequisite for more intensive interventions (Greenberg, 2004; Scott et al., 2009). In sum, a series of policy and system reforms is needed to improve the condition of the country's schools. Principles of risk, protection, and resilience promotion offer a framework for thinking more systematically about a continuum of education policy defined by levels of service. Moreover, integration of policy and programs across other systems of care should be a part of such a continuum.

## Targeted and Intensive Strategies to Integrate Education Policy

It is both important and challenging to envision integrating educational policies and programs across service domains such as child welfare, substance abuse, mental health, juvenile justice, developmental disabilities, and health. In many respects, the compartmentalized approach used to channel federal and state funding as well as the isolated educational training of school personnel with alternative professional schools (e.g., education, psychology, and social work) runs counter to the vision of cohesive, integrated services. Given the number of children involved in the educational system, the number of hours children spend in school, and the number of families and communities that can be linked by mobilized schools, we believe that the education system is an ideal context in which to identify children in need of services across many domains. The following case study (Box 4.1) demonstrates how services can lack integration and coordination.

---

**BOX 4.1**

### A Case for Integrated Service Delivery

Jeremy is a 14-year-old male who was physically and sexually abused as a young child. His mother was incarcerated when he was 6 years old, and her parental rights were terminated when Jeremy was 8 years old. He experienced six out-of-home placements before age 10, when he was finally placed in a stable foster care home with loving and supportive parents.

Jeremy has struggled socially and emotionally in school since kindergarten, but he was not identified for special education services under the severe emotional disturbance (SED) category until his current foster parents advocated for an evaluation when he was 11 years of age. He

has done well in some settings, but he was suspended 13 times during his first year of middle school. Jeremy has been convicted twice for misdemeanor charges and is currently on probation.

He receives a variety of support services from a learning specialist and a school social worker at his middle school, a counselor at the local mental health agency, and a child protection caseworker. Jeremy reports to a probation officer regularly and sees a psychiatrist yearly for medication monitoring. These individuals have not met together, and many of the services provided to Jeremy are duplicated across settings.

Jeremy's circumstances are made worse by the lack of collaboration and coordination across his various service providers. Cross-system funding for education, health, and social services may be one means for achieving integrated practice. Cross-system funds could be used to

- provide early screening to identify children most at risk;

- promote school readiness skills for high-risk youth;

- deliver comprehensive services and case management to children who display signs of adjustment problems before the second grade;

- provide seamless access to and provision of educational, health, and social services through support service providers and family resource or youth service centers; and

- implement primary prevention programs at key developmental stages.

An integrated approach to service delivery would be very beneficial to youth such as Jeremy and his foster parents. First, if the services provided by his teacher, learning specialist, school social worker, counselor, caseworker, probation officer, and psychiatrist were monitored and coordinated, each provider would know what other services Jeremy was receiving and how he was functioning in other aspects of his life. Such an approach could reduce redundancy in service provision and would likely be more cost-effective. Second, an integrated service-delivery system would facilitate communication between professionals and allow each provider access to the information the other providers possess. Third, an integrated approach would also produce one set of goals, one treatment plan, and one system to evaluate progress. In addition, an integrated strategy would likely make it easier for his foster parents to attend the requisite meetings associated with each service. Last, it is exciting to imagine the range and quality of services that could be put in place if the departments of education, juvenile justice, and child welfare shared costs, problem ownership, and approaches for all the services directed toward complex cases such as Jeremy's. Most important, if an integrated approach—perhaps provided through a primary health care agency—had been in place to offer assessment and service delivery early in Jeremy's life, it is possible his early antisocial behavior and poor school readiness would have raised warning flags that might have altered Jeremy's path to later destructive outcomes (for more on integrated primary care, see Fraser et al., 2018).

## CONCLUDING REMARKS

Education policy in the past century has vacillated among progressive and conservative ideologies, which has led to inconsistent and constantly changing priorities and practices in schools. According to Anyon (1997), education policy continues to revolve "around the tensions between equity and excellence, between the social and intellectual functions of schooling, and over such questions as, 'Education for whom and support for whose interests?'" (p. 87). Policy directed at the nation's schools has lacked a guiding set of consistent values and principles. Principles of risk, protection, and resilience offer promise as a framework for designing and enhancing education policy and programs. Policy makers at all levels would do well to incorporate these principles into the nation's struggling educational system.

## QUESTIONS FOR DISCUSSION

1. What are the major risk factors for school failure? Which of these risk factors should receive the most attention in educational policy and why?

2. What educational policies and programs over the past 100 years have best served the concept of risk and resilience? Why?

3. What have been the major trends in policy and practice reform since 2000?

4. What factors inhibit the integration of policies and programs across problem domains?

5. What are some possible solutions to the barriers to the integration of policies and programs across problem domains?

## REFERENCES

Abacioglu, C. S., Zee, M., Hanna, F., Soeterik, I. M., Fischer, A. H., & Volman, M. (2019). Practice what you preach: The moderating role of teacher attitudes on the relationship between prejudice reduction and student engagement. *Teaching and Teacher Education, 86*, 102887.

Administration for Children and Families. (2020). *Head Start fact sheet*. U.S. Department of Health and Human Services. https://eclkc.ohs.acf.hhs.gov/sites/default/files/pdf/no-search/hs-program-fact-sheet-2019.pdf

Anyon, J. (1997). *Ghetto schooling: A political economy of urban reform*. Teachers College Press.

Apollonia, S., & Abrami, P. C. (1997). Student ratings: The validity of use. *American Psychologist, 52*, 1199–1208.

Arcia, E. (2006). Achievement and enrollment status of suspended students: Outcomes in a large, multicultural school district. *Education & Urban Society, 38*, 359–369.

Auld, E., Rappleye, J., & Morris, P. (2019). PISA for Development: How the OECD and World Bank shaped education governance post-2015. *Comparative Education, 55*, 197–219.

Batsche, G. M., Elliott, J., Graden, J. L., Grimes, J., Kovaleski, J. F., & Prasse, D. (2005). *Response to intervention: Policy considerations and implementation*. National Association of State Directors of Special Education.

Brauner, C. B., & Stephens, B. C (2006). Estimating the prevalence of early childhood serious emotional/behavioral disorder: Challenges and recommendations. *Public Health Reports, 121*, 303–310.

Breakspear, S. (2012). *The policy impact of PISA: An exploration of the normative effects of international benchmarking in school system performance*. OECD Education Working Papers, No. 71. OECD Publishing (NJ1).

Brooks-Gunn, J., & Duncan, G. J. (1997). The effects of poverty on children. *Future of Children, 7*, 55–71.

Brown v. Board of Education of Topeka, 347 U.S. 483 (1954).

Carnahan, S. (1994). Preventing school failure and dropout. In R. J. Simeonsson (Ed.), *Risk, resilience, and prevention: Promoting the well-being of all children* (pp. 103–124). Paul H. Brooks.

Carpenter, D. M., & Ramirez, A. (2007). More than one gap: Dropout rate gaps between and among Black, Hispanic, and White students. *Journal of Advanced Academics, 19*, 32–64.

Cecelski, D. (1994). *Along freedom road*. University of North Carolina Press.

Center for Education Policy Analysis. (2019). *Racial and ethnic achievement gaps*. https://cepa.stanford.edu/edu cational-opportunity-monitoring-project/achievement-gaps/race/#second

Center for Mental Health in Schools. (2002). *An introductory packet: About mental health in schools* (ERIC Document No. 463509). University of California at Los Angeles. http://www.eric.ed.gov/ERICDocs/data/ericdocs2sql/content_storage_01/0000019b/80/19/f2/3a.pdf

Chung, J. (2019). *PISA and global education policy: Understanding Finland's success and influence*. BRILL.

Clark, K. (1965). *Dark ghetto: Dilemmas of social power*. Harper & Row.

Coleman, J. S. (1966). *Equality of educational opportunity* (No. OE-38001). National Center for Education Statistics.

Cook, G. (2005). Title I at 40. *American School Board Journal, 192*, 24–26.

COPAA v. DeVos et.al., 365 F.Supp.3d 28 (D.D.C. 2019).

Cremin, L. A. (1957). *The republic and the school: Horace Mann on the education of free men*. Teachers College Press.

Crutchfield, J., Phillipo, K., & Frey, A. J. (2020). Structural racism in schools: A view through the lens of the National School Social Work Practice Model. *Children & Schools*. Advance online publication. https://doi.org/10.1093/cs/cdaa015

Daily, S. M., Mann, M., Lilly, C., Dyer, A., Smith, M. L., & Kristjansson, A. (2020). School climate as an intervention to reduce academic failure and educate the whole child: A longitudinal study. *Journal of School Health, 90*, 182–193.

Derezinski, T. (2004). School attendance. In P. Allen-Meares (Ed.), *Social work services in schools* (4th ed., pp. 95–118). Allyn & Bacon.

Dever, B. V., Dowdy, E., DiStefano, C, & Kilgus, S.P. (2018). Examining the stability, accuracy, and predictive validity of behavioral–emotional screening scores across time to inform repeated screening procedures. *School Psychology Review, 47*, 360–371.

Dewey, J. (1916). *Democracy and education*. Macmillan.

Dews, F. (2016). Tom Loveless: Shanghai PISA test scores almost meaningless; Hukou a factor. *Brookings Institute*. https://www.brookings.edu/blog/brookings-now/2013/12/03/tom-loveless-shanghai-pisa-test-scores-al most-meaningless-hukou-a-factor/

Dixson, A. D., Rousseau, C. K., Anderson, C. R., & Donnor, J. K. (Eds.). (2006). *Critical race theory in education: All God's children got a song*. Taylor & Francis.

Donnor, J. K. (2013). Education as the property of whites: African Americans continued quest for good schools. In M. Lynn & A. D. Dixson (Eds.), *Handbook of critical race theory in education* (pp. 195–203). Routledge.

Duncan, A. (2009). *Secretary Duncan's plenary address* [Paper presentation]. Annual Institute of Education Sciences conference, Washington, DC, United States.

Duncan, G. J., & Brooks-Gunn, J. (2000). Family poverty, welfare reform, and child development. *Child Development, 71*, 188–161.

Duncan, G. J., Brooks-Gunn, J., & Klebanov, P. K. (1994). Economic deprivation and early childhood development. *Child Development, 65*, 296–318.

Dunlap, G., Sailor, W., Horner, H. F., & Sugai, G. (2009). Overview and history of positive behavior support. In W. Sailor, G. Dunlap, G. Sugai, & H. F. Horner (Eds.), *Handbook of positive behavior support: Issues in clinical child psychology* (pp. 3–16). Springer.

Espinoza v. Montana Dept. of Revenue, 591 U.S. (2020).

Fall, A., & Roberts, G. (2012). High school dropouts: Interactions between social context, self-perceptions, school engagement, and student dropout. *Journal of Adolescence, 35*, 787–798.

Felton, E. (2017). Special education's hidden racial gap. *The Hechinger Report*. https://hechingerreport.org/spe cial-educations-hidden-racial-gap/

Fernald, A., Marchman, V. A., & Weisleder, A. (2013). SES differences in language processing skill are evident at 18 months. *Developmental Science, 16*, 234–248.

Finn, J. D., Fish, R. M., & Scott, L. A. (2008). Educational sequelae of high school misbehavior. *Journal of Educational Research, 101*, 259–274.

Fraser, M. W., Kirby, L. D., & Smokowski, P. R. (2004). Risk and resilience in childhood. In M. W. Fraser (Ed.),

*Risk and resiliency in childhood: An ecological perspective* (2nd ed, pp. 13–66). NASW Press.

Fraser, M. W., Lombardi, B. M., Wu, S., Zerden, L. D. S., Richman, E. L., & Frayer, E. P. (2018). Integrated primary care and social work: A systematic review. *Journal of the Society for Social Work and Research, 9*, 175–215.

Fraser, M. W., & Terzian, M. A. (2005). Risk and resilience in child development: Practice principles and strategies. In G. P. Mallon & P. M. Hess (Eds.), *Handbook of children, youth, and family services: Practices, policies, and programs* (pp. 55–71). Columbia University Press.

Fredricks, J. (2011). Engagement in school and out of school contexts: A multidimensional view of engagement. *Theory into Practice, 50*, 327–335.

Fuhrman, S., & Lazerson, M. (2005). *The public schools.* Oxford University Press.

Furlong, M., & Morrison, G. (2000). The school in school violence. *Journal of Emotional & Behavioral Disorders, 8,* 71–82.

Gibton, D. (2013). *Law, education, politics, fairness England's extreme legislation for education reform.* Institute of Education Press.

Greenberg, M. T. (2004). Current and future challenges in school-based prevention: The researcher perspective. *Prevention Science, 5*, 5–13.

Greenberg, M. T., Domitrovich, C., & Bumbarger, B. (1999). *Preventing mental disorders in school-age children: A review of the effectiveness of prevention programs.* Pennsylvania State University, Prevention Research Center for the Promotion of Human Development.

Haberman, M. (2000). Urban schools: Day camps or custodial centers? *Phi Delta Kappan, 82,* 203–208.

Hargreaves, A., & Shirley, D. L. (2012). *The global fourth way: The quest for educational excellence.* Corwin Press.

Hart, B., & Risley, T. R. (1995). *Meaningful differences in the everyday lives of young American children.* Brookes.

Hart, B., & Risley, T. R. (2003). The early catastrophe: The 30-million-word gap by age 3. *American Educator, 27,* 4–9.

Hawkins, J. D., Catalano, R. F., Kosterman, R., Abbott, R. D., & Hill, K. G. (1999). Preventing adolescent health-risk behaviors by strengthening protection during childhood. *Archives of Pediatrics & Adolescent Medicine, 153,* 226–234.

Howard, T. C. (2019). *Why race and culture matter in schools: Closing the achievement gap in America's classrooms.* Teachers College Press.

Institute of Education Sciences. (2014). *Common core of data.* National Center for Education Statistics. http://nces.ed.gov/ccd/

Jenson, J. M., & Bender, K. A. (2014). *Preventing child and adolescent problem behavior: Evidence-based strategies in schools, families, and communities.* Oxford University Press.

Jenson, J. M., & Howard, M. O. (1999). *Youth violence: Current research and recent practice innovations.* NASW Press.

Kemp, S. (2006). Dropout policies and trends for students with and without disabilities. *Adolescence, 41,* 235–250.

Kohl, H. (1967). *36 children.* New American Library.

Kozol, J. (1967). *Death at an early age: The deconstruction of the hearts and minds of Negro children in the Boston public schools.* Houghton Mifflin.

Kupchik, A. (2016). *The real school safety problem: The long-term consequences of harsh school punishment.* University of California Press.

Labaree, D. F. (2014). Let's measure what no one teaches: PISA, NCLB, and the shrinking aims of education. *Teachers College Record, 116,* 1–14.

Li, H., Martin, A. J., & Yeung, W. J. J. (2017). Academic risk and resilience for children and young people in Asia. *Educational Psychology, 37,* 921–929.

Love, J. M., Tarullo, L. B., Raikes, H., & Chazen-Cohen, R. (2006). Head Start: What do we know about its effectiveness? What do we need to know? In K. McCartney & D. Phillips (Eds.), *Blackwell handbook on early childhood development* (pp. 550–575). Blackwell.

Loveless, T. (2019, December 19). The children PISA ignores in China. *Brookings Institute.* https://www.brookings.edu/blog/brown-center-chalkboard/2019/12/19/the-children-pisa-ignores-in-china/.

McFarland, J., Hussar, B., Wang, X., Zhang, J., Wang, K., Rathbun, A., Barmer, A., Forrest Cataldi, E., & Bullock Mann, F. (2018). *The condition of education 2018 (NCES 2018-144).* U.S. Department of Education. National Center for Education Statistics. https://nces.ed.gov/pubsearch/pubsinfo.Asp?pubid=2018144.

Milliken v. Bradley, 418 U.S. 717 (1974).

Morris, M. (2016). *Pushout: The criminalization of Black girls in schools*. The New Press.

Mundy, K., Green, A., Lingard, B., & Verger, A. (Eds.). (2016). *Handbook of global education policy*. Wiley-Blackwell.

Musu-Gillette, L., de Brey, C., McFarland, J., Hussar, W., Sonnenberg, W., & Wilkinson-Flicker, S. (2017). *Status and trends in the education of racial and ethnic groups 2017 (NCES 2017-051)*. U.S. Department of Education, National Center for Education Statistics. http://nces.ed.gov/pubsearch

NAACP v. DeVos, No. 20-cv-1996-DLF, D.D.C. (2020).

National Center for Education Statistics. (2020). *Public high school graduation rates*. Author. https://nces.ed.gov/programs/coe/indicator_coi.asp

National Commission on Excellence. (1983). *A nation at risk. The imperative for educational reform*. Author. http://www2.ed.gov/pubs/NatAtRisk/index.html

Neal-Jackson, A. (2020). Muting Black girls: How office referral forms mask dehumanising disciplinary interactions. *Journal of Educational Administration and History, 52*, 295–308.

Nelson, J. L., Palonsky, S. B., & McCarthy, M. R. (2004). *Critical issues in education: Dialogues and dialectics* (5th ed.). McGraw-Hill.

Nettles, S., Caughy, M., O'Campo, P. (2008). School adjustment in the early grades: Toward an integrated model of neighborhood, parental, and child processes. *Review of Educational Research, 78*, 3–32.

Noltemeyer, A. L., Ward, R. M., & Mcloughlin, C. (2015). Relationship between school suspension and student outcomes: A meta-analysis. *School Psychology Review, 44*, 224–240.

Okilwa, N., & Robert, C. (2017). School discipline disparity: Converging efforts for better student outcomes. *Urban Review, 49*, 239–262.

Oplatka, I. (2018). *Reforming education in developing countries: From neoliberalism to communitarianism*. Routledge.

Organization for Economic Cooperation and Development (OECD). (2019). *Who pays for PISA for development?* https://www.oecd.org/pisa/pisa-for-development/20-Who-pays-for-PISA-D.pdf.

Paige, R. (2002). An overview of America's education agenda. *Phi Delta Kappan, 83*, 708–713.

Parents Involved in Community Schools v. Seattle School District No. 1, 127 U.S. 2738 (2007).

Patterson, J. A., Hale, D., & Stessman, M. (2007). Cultural contradictions and school leaving: A case study of an urban high school. *High School Journal, 91*, 1–15.

Plessy v. Ferguson, 163 U.S. 537 (1896).

Programme for International Student Assessment (PISA). (2019). *About PISA*. https://www.oecd.org/pisa/aboutpisa/.

Pritchett, L. (1999). *Where has all the education gone?* The World Bank.

Ravitch, D. (1983). *The troubled crusade: An American education, 1945–1980*. Basic Books.

Reid, J. B. (1993). Prevention of conduct disorder before and after school entry: Relating interventions to developmental findings. *Development and Psychopathology, 5*, 243–262.

Rosenfeld, G. (1971). *"Shut those thick lips!" A study of slum school failure*. Holt, Rinehart, & Winston.

Sadovnik, A. R., Cookson, P. W., & Semel, S. F. (2001). *Exploring education: Introduction to the foundations to education*. Allyn & Bacon.

Sailor, W., Wolf, N., Choi, H., & Roger, B. (2009). Sustaining positive behavior support in a context of comprehensive school reform. In W. Sailor, G. Dunlap, G. Sugai, & R. Horner (Eds.), *Handbook of positive behavior support: Issues in clinical child psychology* (pp. 633–670). Springer.

Sameroff, A. J., & Gutman, L. M. (2004). Contributions of risk research to the design of successful interventions. In P. Allen-Meares & M. W. Fraser (Eds.), *Intervention with children and adolescents: An interdisciplinary perspective* (pp. 9–26). Allyn & Bacon.

Scialabba, N. (2017). *How implicit bias impacts our children in education*. American Bar Association.

Scott, T. M., Anderson, C. M., Mancil, R., & Alter, P. (2009). Function-based supports for individual students in school settings. In W. Sailor, G. Dunlap, G. Sugai, & H. F. Horner (Eds.), *Handbook of positive behavior support: Issues in clinical child psychology* (pp. 421–441). Springer.

Shinn, M. R., & Walker, H. M. (2010). *Interventions for achievement and behavior problems in a three-tier model including RTI*. National Association for School Psychologists.

Skiba, R. (2002). Special education and school discipline: A precarious balance. *Behavioral Disorders, 27*, 81–97.

Skiba, R., Michael, R. S., Nardo, A.C., & Peterson, R. (2000). *The color of discipline: Sources of racial and gender disproportionality in school punishment.* http://www.indiana.edu/~safeschl/cod.pdf

Skiba, R., & Peterson, R. (1999). The dark side of zero tolerance: Can punishment lead to safe schools? (ERIC Document No.ED 456 546). *Phi Delta Kappan, 80*, 381–382.

Snow, K. (2013, October). *New research on early disparities: Focus on vocabulary and language processing.* (NAEYC) [Blog]. http://www.naeyc.org

South, S. J., Haynie, D. L., & Bose, S. (2007). Student mobility and school dropout. *Social Science Research, 36*, 68–94.

Strauss, V. (2014, May 13). Academics call for pause in PISA tests. *Washington Post.* https://www.washingtonpost.com/news/answer-sheet/wp/2014/05/13/academics-call-for-pause-in-pisa-tests/?arc404=true.

Substance Abuse and Mental Health Services Administration. (2008). *National household survey on drug abuse: Main findings.* U.S. Department of Health and Human Services.

Sweeten, G. (2006). Who will graduate? Disruption of high school education by arrest and court involvement. *Justice Quarterly, 23*, 462–480.

U.S. Department of Commerce. (2018). *Percentage of high school dropouts among persons 16 to 24 years old (status dropout rate), by sex and race/ethnicity: Selected years, 1960 through 2017.* https://nces.ed.gov/programs/digest/d18/tables/dt18_219.70.asp

U.S. Department of Education (USDOE). (2016). *Racial and ethnic disparities in special education: A multi-year disproportionality analysis by state, analysis category, and race/ethnicity.* National Center for Education Statistics. https://www2.ed.gov/programs/osepidea/618-data/LEA-racial-ethnic-disparities-tables/disproportionality-analysis-by-state-analysis-category.pdf

Walker, H., Horner, R. H., Sugai, G., Bullis, M., Sprague, J. R., Bricker, D., & Kaufman, M. J. (1996). Integrated approaches to preventing antisocial behavior patterns among school-age children and youth. *Journal of Emotional & Behavioral Disorders, 4*, 193–256.

Wang, M., & Fredricks, J. (2014). The reciprocal links between school engagement, youth problem behaviors, and school dropout during adolescence. *Child Development, 85*, 722–737.

Wood, C. L., Schatschneider, C, Veldnick, A. (2021). The relation between academic word use and reading comprehension for students from diverse backgrounds. *Language, Speech & Hearing Services in Schools, 52*, 273–287.

Zhang, D., Katsiyannis, A., Ju, S., & Roberts, E. (2014). Minority representation in special education: 5-year trends. *Journal of Child and Family Studies, 23*, 118–127.

Zhang, D., Willson, V., Katsiyannis, A., Barrett, D., Ju, S., & Wu, J. Y. (2010). Truancy offenders in the juvenile justice system: A multicohort study. *Behavioral Disorders, 35*, 229–242.

Zimmerman, M. A., Stoddard, S. A., Eisman, A. B., Caldwell, C. H., Aiyer, S. M., & Miller, A. (2013). Adolescent resilience: Promotive factors that inform prevention. *Child Development perspectives, 7*, 215–220.

# ADDITIONAL READING

Sailor, W., Dunlap, G., Sugai, G., & Horner, R. (2009). *Handbook of positive behavior support.* Springer.

Sprague, J. R., & Walker, H. (2000). Early identification and intervention for youth with antisocial and violent behavior. *Exceptional Children, 66*, 367–379.

Walker, H., & Shinn, M. K. (2010). *Interventions for achievement and behavior problems: Preventive and remedial approaches* (Vol. 3). National Association of School Psychologists.

Zaff, J. F., & Malone, T. (2020). Moving beyond academics: The role off adult capacity in keeping young people in school. *Youth and Society, 52*, 55–77.

## WEB-BASED RESOURCES

Center on Education Policy: http://www.cep-dc.org/

Education Commission of the States: http://www.ecs.org/

Education Policy and Leadership Center: http://www.eplc.org/about_description.html

Education Policy Institute: http://www.educationalpolicy.org/

# 5

# CHILD MENTAL HEALTH POLICY

## Paul Lanier, Megan Feely, and Mary E. Fraser

The individual, family, and public health burden of mental illness begins in childhood. Like health care policy more broadly, the primary goal of child mental health policy is to ensure that children and their families can access and afford effective care when it is needed. Further, child mental health policy seeks to create conditions that prevent or reduce the risk of children ever developing a severe mental health disorder. Although recent decades have shown a substantial increase in the availability of evidence-based prevention and treatment options, families today continue to face the same barriers to high-quality mental health care and social conditions that increase risk for disorders. One out of every five children and adolescents in the United States (U.S.) has a diagnosed mental, emotional, or behavioral disorder that increases their risk for poor outcomes such as school failure, alcohol or other drug use, violent conduct, or suicide (Burns et al., 1995; Costello et al., 2003). The prevalence and impact of mental, emotional, and behavioral disorders makes children's mental health a major public health concern in this country (Perou et al., 2013). However, studies continue to find that only about 20% of children in need of services received mental health care, with the highest unmet need among low-income and other vulnerable families (Hodgkinson et al., 2017; Kataoka et al., 2002).

Without comprehensive policies and interventions that diminish risk and strengthen protection for youth with mental health disorders, the outcomes for at-risk youth can be expected to be poor. This forecast is supported by a body of literature on risk factors associated with emotional and behavioral problems in childhood as well as a growing body of evidence on protective factors that mitigate the effects of these problems. Because children with mental health disorders are found in all public child-serving agencies, public policies are needed that promote cross-agency, integrated approaches to providing effective risk and protection systems and services.

In this chapter, we will review the advances in public policy that have improved access to and quality of care and outline the strategies policymakers can take to continue closing the service gap. First, we will review the epidemiological research to understand the scope and burden of children's mental disorders. Next, we will examine the literature on risk and protective factors for mental health disorders in children and adolescents and summarize the complex evolution of child mental health policy in the U.S. Then shifting to policy, case examples of state policies designed to improve access to services for youth with mental disorders are described. Finally, suggestions are made for future policies to ensure that all children have access to the mental health care they need.

## EPIDEMIOLOGY OF CHILDREN'S MENTAL HEALTH DISORDERS

The Centers for Disease Control and Prevention (CDC) defines *childhood mental disorders* as serious changes in the way children typically learn, behave, or handle their emotions, which cause distress and problems getting through the day (CDC, 2020). Symptoms and types of mental disorders in children vary greatly, just as they do among adults. Many common mental health problems, such as anxiety and depression, begin in childhood but are not always recognized or diagnosed.

A defining feature of the mental health field is the use of a system of classification that relies on diagnostic categories linked to service strategies, both psychosocial and pharmacological. The primary classification source used in the U.S. is the *Diagnostic and Statistical Manual of Mental Disorders* (*DSM*), published by the American Psychiatric Association (APA) and currently in its fifth edition (*DSM-5*; APA, 2013). In general, diagnosing and classifying emerging mental health disorders in childhood can be challenging. The *Diagnostic Classification of Mental Health and Developmental Disorders of Infancy and Early Childhood (DC: 0-5)* manual is similar to the *DSM-5* but is published by ZERO TO THREE (2016) and focuses on disorders in early childhood (Zeanah et al., 2017). These classification systems are typically used in studies attempting to quantify the prevalence of mental health disorders in children.

Public health surveillance of mental disorders among children has improved in recent years, providing valuable updates to previous general population prevalence estimates. However, published estimates still vary depending on the exact definition, the measure used to identify the disorder, and the population. Table 5.1 displays the most common *DSM-5* diagnoses found in children and youth. The first column shows the diagnostic prevalence rates for each disorder within the subgroup of youth based on findings from the National Adolescent and Child Treatment Study. The second column includes lifetime prevalence estimates of disorders for children aged 3 to 17 years from the National Survey of Children's Health (NSCH) from 2017 and 2018. The third column includes lifetime prevalence estimates for adolescents aged 13 to 18 years from another nationally representative survey using a diagnostic interview, the National Comorbidity Study-Adolescent Supplement (NCS-A; Merikangas et al., 2010).

Children's mental disorders vary in severity as well as type. The federal government's criteria for identifying severe mental health disorders in childhood, known as *severe emotional disturbance* (SED), requires a diagnosable disorder that results in limited functioning in family, social, and academic activities (Center for Behavioral

Health Statistics and Quality, 2016). According to the Surgeon General's (1999) report on mental health, at least 1 in 10 young people, or as many as 6 million youth, meet the criteria for SED. Prior prevalence estimates have ranged from 9% to 26% (Brauner & Stephens, 2006); the most recent research indicates a 22% lifetime prevalence of SED among adolescents (Merikangas et al., 2010) and a 6% prevalence in school populations (Li et al., 2010). Although many youths with SED have multiple social and health problems that lead to referral or involvement in the mental health, special education, child welfare, and juvenile justice systems (Brauner & Stephens, 2006; Brendenberg et al., 1990), only 59% of children with SED receive any type of formal mental health care (Commonwealth Fund, 2006).

Studies indicate that the prevalence of SED is higher among certain groups of children. Children suffering from SED are more likely to be male, low-income, and from a racial or ethnic minority group (Mark & Buck, 2006; Wagner et al., 2005). Among special education students, those identified as having an emotional disturbance have poorer social skills, communication skills, and cognitive and academic functioning and are more likely to change schools and be suspended or expelled (Wagner et al., 2005). Children and adolescents with SED have symptoms that substantially disrupt their social, academic, and emotional functioning. Many children are in out-of-home placements or are at risk for such placement, highlighting the need for cross-system service coordination.

The next section will review the most common mental disorders in childhood. A detailed description of the diagnostic criteria that distinguishes one disorder from another is beyond the scope of this chapter. However, understanding how disorders are categorized and the symptoms associated with a childhood mental disorder is important when designing policies to improve access to care. Further, diagnostic categories and criteria are constantly changing as new research and discoveries in the field are made. For example, the *DSM-5* added two new disorders (social communication disorder and disruptive mood dysregulation disorder), added new subtypes, and changed the diagnostic criteria for other disorders (Substance Abuse and Mental Health Services Administration [SAMHSA], 2016). We encourage the reader to dive deeper into the etiology (causes of a disorder) and epidemiology (identifying and quantifying a disorder) before analyzing or developing policy related to any given mental health disorder.

Anxiety disorders are the most common mental health problem found in childhood and adolescence (Merikangas et al., 2010). Anxiety disorders manifests in a variety of forms, including phobias, separation anxiety disorders, and generalized anxiety disorders. Phobias are fears that are out of proportion to the actual danger posed by the object or situation. One of the most common phobias among children and adolescents is social anxiety disorder, which is characterized by an unremitting fear of embarrassment in social and performance situations that sometimes leads to full-blown panic attacks. Children and adolescents with this disorder tend to avoid social situations and try to avoid going to school. Separation anxiety disorder occurs in about 8% of adolescents and is characterized by irrational fears that parents will be killed or taken away, which may lead to clinging behavior, difficulty falling asleep at night, and an inability to participate in school and social events away from home. The disorder can last for many years and can be a precursor to panic disorder and agoraphobia that

**Table 5.1  Diagnostic Prevalence Rates for Children**

| Diagnosis | SED Population (8 to 18 Years)[a] | General Child Population (3 to 17 Years)[b] | General Adolescent Population (13 to 18 Years)[c] |
|---|---|---|---|
| Anxiety<br><br>Phobias, separation anxiety disorder, generalized anxiety disorder, obsessive-compulsive disorder, post-traumatic stress disorder | 41.0% | 8.8% | 31.9% |
| Depression<br><br>Major depressive disorder, dysthymia | 18.5% | 4.7% | 11.7% |
| Behavioral or conduct disorder | | 8.5% | |
| Conduct disorder | 66.9% | | 6.8% |
| Oppositional defiant disorder | | | 12.6% |
| Attention deficit hyperactivity disorder (ADHD) | 11.7% | 9.7% | 8.7% |
| Other mental health condition | | 4.4% | |
| Childhood schizophrenia | 4.7% | | |
| Feeding and eating disorders | | | 2.7% |

*Source:*

[a]Greenbaum et al. (1996).

[b] National Survey of Children's Health (2017–2018).

[c] Merikangas et al. (2010).

may be experienced as an adult. Generalized anxiety disorder is characterized by excessive and persistent worry. Children and adolescents with this anxiety disorder tend to be perfectionists and insecure.

Obsessive-compulsive disorder was previously classified as an anxiety disorder in the *DSM-IV* and is now given its own classification in the *DSM-5*. Obsessive-compulsive disorder is characterized by recurrent, time-consuming, obsessive, or compulsive thoughts or behaviors that cause distress or impairment. The obsessions may be intrusive images, thoughts, or impulses. Compulsive behaviors, such as hand washing and other cleaning rituals, are considered to be attempts to displace obsessive thoughts. Prevalence estimates range from 1% to 2% for children and adolescents (APA, 2000; Perou et al. 2013).

Post-traumatic stress disorder (PTSD) is a prolonged, pathologic anxiety that occurs in both adults and adolescents following a severe trauma. Listed as an anxiety disorder in *DSM-IV*, PTSD was also reclassified in the *DSM-5* into trauma- and stressor-related disorders. The onset of PTSD in adolescence is common and may impair the acquisition of life skills needed for independent, self-sufficient living. PTSD is common among youth who have been victims of physical or sexual abuse and who have witnessed violence in their homes or neighborhoods. An estimated 5% of adolescents suffer from PTSD in their lifetime (Merikangas et al., 2010).

Depression in children and adolescents usually presents in two different forms. A diagnosis of a depressive disorder requires either a depressed, irritable mood or a diminished interest or pleasure in activities. Accompanying symptoms must include some combination of significant weight change, either gain or loss; sleep disturbance; loss of energy or feelings of extreme fatigue; psychomotor agitation or retardation; feelings of worthlessness or inappropriate guilt; diminished ability to think or concentrate; and recurrent thoughts of death. These symptoms must be present for at least two weeks and produce significant functional impairment.

Disruptive behavior disorders, such as conduct disorder or oppositional defiant disorder (ODD), are based on a repetitive and persistent pattern of behavior in which the basic rights of others or the major age-appropriate social norms or rules are violated. Characteristic behaviors of conduct disorder include aggression toward persons or animals, destruction of property, deceitfulness, and theft. Girls with a conduct disorder are prone to early sexual activity and homelessness. Those with an early onset of conduct disorder have a worse prognosis and are at higher risk for adult disorders. Conduct disorder frequently co-occurs with attention deficit hyperactivity disorder (ADHD). ODD is typically characterized by problem behaviors such as persistent arguing, habitual fighting, and frequent loss of temper. Children and adolescents with this disorder frequently test limits, deliberately refuse to comply with adult requests, and intentionally annoy others. These behaviors lead to difficulties with family members, peers, and teachers. ODD is sometimes a precursor of conduct disorder.

As implied by the name, ADHD is made up of two distinct sets of symptoms. Although these two problems often co-occur, one set of symptoms can be present without the other. Children with attention deficit disorder have difficulty paying attention and are easily distracted. These children are often disorganized, and they have difficulty following through with tasks. The symptoms of hyperactivity include a compulsion to move that may be expressed as fidgeting, squirming, or wriggling around when seated or getting up and moving around the room. Children with ADHD often perform poorly at school and have difficulties with peer relationships. Hyperactive behavior is often associated with the development of conduct disorder and ODDs.

Eating disorders (now classified as *feeding and eating disorders* in *DSM-5*) such as anorexia nervosa and bulimia nervosa, are the most fatal mental disorders, with 10% of cases ending in death (Arcelus et al., 2011; Steiner & Lock, 1998). The prevalence of eating disorders is a particular concern because these disorders are among the most common chronic illnesses of adolescent girls, following obesity and asthma (Lucas et al., 1991; Stice & Agras, 1998). Anorexia nervosa is characterized by a distorted body image that triggers an intense fear of gaining weight. The symptoms of bulimia nervosa include recurrent episodes of binge eating and purging.

Although rare, childhood onset schizophrenia is a serious form of psychotic disorder that is challenging to diagnose and treat. Children with schizophrenia may experience auditory and visual hallucinations and delusions and feel detached from the real world. It is sometimes difficult to distinguish between childhood schizophrenia and autism. Onset of adult schizophrenia usually occurs between puberty and young adulthood. Children with an earlier onset of schizophrenia generally experience symptoms that are longer lasting and more severe (APA, 2000).

In this chapter, the term *SED* is used to refer to a diagnosed mental health problem that results in significant functional impairment. However, readers should note that simply having a diagnosis of a mental health disorder does not mean that a child is seriously emotionally disturbed or impaired. Also, the symptoms children experience over time may fluctuate in severity due to environmental stressors or in response to treatment. Moreover, it is important to recognize that the different diagnostic categories relate to different risks and intervention strategies. For example, the needs of children with feeding and eating disorders differ markedly from those with conduct disorders. Thus, child mental health policies must address a wide range of behaviors and conditions that are differentially categorized by diagnostic labels and terms such as SED. Also, note that the term *behavioral health* or *behavioral disorder* is often used to encompass mental health as well as substance use disorders. We limit our discussion in this chapter to mental health disorders; please refer to Chapter 8 for a detailed discussion regarding substance use policy. Next, we describe risk and protective factors for mental health disorders in childhood.

# A RISK, PROTECTION, AND RESILIENCE PERSPECTIVE ON MENTAL HEALTH DISORDERS

Policy strategies designed to prevent or treat child mental health disorders should reflect the intended public health goal and target population. The mental health intervention spectrum (shown below in Figure 5.1) displays the range of intervention goals from mental health promotion through prevention, treatment, and maintenance (Institute of Medicine, 1994; National Research Council and Institute of Medicine, 2009). Mental health promotion strategies focus on promotive factors to improve well-being rather than preventing or treating a disorder. Universal prevention strategies also target the general public or whole population but are intended to reduce the risk for developing mental health disorders. Selective and indicated interventions strengthen protective factors to reduce known risks among subgroups who are at higher risk or who have already shown signs of a mental health disorder. Prevention strategies all focus on reducing risk prior to a formal diagnosis. Once a child is diagnosed, treatment and maintenance strategies are provided. We apply these definitions to the discussion that follows.

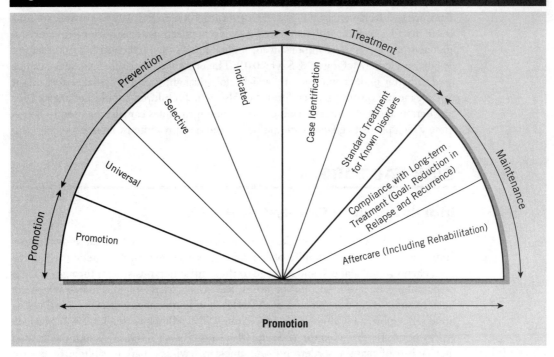

Allen-Meares and Fraser (2004) outlined a set of empirically supported principles to describe the concepts of risk, protection, and resilience. These principles inform our discussion of mental health disorders and child mental health policy. Allen-Meares and Fraser argued that (a) identifiable risk and protective factors exist for social and mental health problems in childhood, (b) cumulative risk is generally more predictive of developmental outcomes than any single risk factor, (c) some risk factors are more responsive than others to change strategies, (d) reduction of risk can produce improved outcomes, and (e) more salutary outcomes occur when risk factors are reduced and protective factors are increased. In addition, Allen-Meares and Fraser noted important differences between protective and promotive factors. Protective factors reduce, suppress, and buffer risk but are neutral (i.e., have no effect) in the absence of risk. In contrast, promotive factors, which are the opposite of risk factors, operate actively to promote positive developmental outcomes for all youths.

Most serious childhood emotional disorders are considered to be biosocial in nature. Although children endure many negative life experiences, most children are naturally resilient. That is, when faced with adversity, children tend to make self-righting adaptations. However, such adaptations do not happen in isolation. Resilience results from the nexus of genetic, individual, social, and environmental conditions that facilitate coping and adaptive functioning following adversity (Ioannidis et al., 2020). The scientific community has generally concluded that mental health problems emerge in children and adolescents when there is a biological vulnerability combined with exposure to adverse environmental factors (Surgeon General, 1999). Further, we now know that the combined dynamic relationship between gene activation (epigenetics) and environment is more important for mental health than the contribution of nature or nurture alone (McGowan & Szyf, 2010). The principles of risk and resilience can be used to better understand not only which biological and environmental factors might predict mental disorders in children but also which children should be targeted for prevention and early intervention efforts. These principles can also be used to determine which protective factors should be bolstered to promote resilience.

# RISK FACTORS

## Individual- and Family-Level Risk

Shown in Table 5.2, biological risk factors can occur at either the individual or family level. Common examples of biological risk factors include genetic predisposition, chemical imbalances, and damage to the central nervous system through trauma or prenatal exposure to alcohol or drugs. Researchers have established clear genetic links to some conditions, including ADHD, mood and anxiety disorders, and childhood schizophrenia (Goodman & Stevenson, 1989; Jellinek & Synder, 1998; Maziade & Raymond, 1995; McGowan & Szyf, 2010; Rutter et al., 1999). Although the genetic mechanism of many disorders remains unclear, having a parent, sibling, or even a grandparent with a mental health problem increases a person's odds for developing a mental disorder.

Gender is correlated with a higher risk of diagnosis of certain emotional and behavioral disorders. For instance, girls are at greater risk than boys for internalizing mental health problems such as depression, anxiety, and suicide (Spirito et al., 1993). Adolescent girls are about twice as likely as boys to be diagnosed with mood, anxiety, and eating disorders, whereas boys are twice as likely as girls to be diagnosed with conduct disorder and ADHD (Merikangas et al., 2010; Nolen-Hoeksema & Girgus, 1994; Perou et al., 2013; Piquero & Chung, 2001; Robins, 1991; Rogers et al., 1997; Ross & Ross, 1982).

Once a child is diagnosed with one disorder, the risk of having additional mental health problems, referred to as *comorbidity*, is increased. Also, individuals with mental health disorders are more likely to develop a substance use disorder, referred to as a co-occurring disorder. Children and youth with a history of psychiatric disorder have been found to be three times more likely to have a subsequent diagnosis of psychiatric disorder. It is not unusual to see a progression from one diagnosis to another, such as from a diagnosis of depression to a diagnosis of anxiety and from a diagnosis of anxiety back to a diagnosis of depression. Similarly, a common diagnosis pattern might start with ADHD and move to ODD or start with a diagnosis of anxiety and conduct disorder and expand to include a diagnosis of substance abuse. Sequential diagnosis may be more common among girls (Costello et al., 2003).

Some risk factors can be detected in early childhood indicating a genetic mechanism and, likely, a function of maternal health during pregnancy. For example, a difficult early temperament is related to emotional and behavioral problems later in life. Agitated and tearful infants have been found to show symptoms of anxiety by the age of 4 years (Kagan et al., 1998). Connections between difficult infant temperaments and conduct disorder have also been observed (Olds et al., 1998).

Family-level risk factors typically include those involving the child's parents or caregivers, siblings, and close family group. For example, mental health disorders are more likely to develop among children who witnessed or experienced violence in the home. Witnessing violent acts can have long-term deleterious effects on children (Jenkins & Bell, 1997). The Children's Defense Fund (1995) has estimated that each year, between 3 million and 10 million children are witnesses to domestic violence. Results from a nationally representative survey suggest 20% of children witness family assaults in their lifetime (Finkelhor et al., 2009).

Exposure to substantial incidents of violence can impair a child's capacity for emotional regulation (Gerrity & Folcarelli, 2008). In turn, a child's problems with controlling his or her anger and regulating mood can seriously complicate the child's ability to perform in school and to develop healthy peer relations (Fairbank et al., 2007). Child abuse and neglect can negatively affect both neurological and psychosocial development, including the formation of personal morals and values, the capacity for relationships, the development of respect for social institutions and mores, and the ability to comply with rules of social conduct (Putnam, 2006). Although the risk process is not well understood, the experience of physical and sexual abuse increases a child's risk for major depressive and anxiety disorders (Dykman et al., 1997; Flisher et al., 1997; Silverman et al., 1996), conduct disorders (Livingston et al., 1993), ADHD (Wolfe et al., 1994), and eating disorders (Douzinas et al., 1994).

Dysfunctional parenting—rejection, neglect, maltreatment, and inability to provide appropriate structure and supervision—is associated with increased risk of emotional and behavioral disorders in children and adolescents (Johnson et al., 2001; Resnick & Burt, 1996). In one review, Loeber and Stouthamer-Loeber (1996) noted that poor parental supervision and lack of parental involvement were among the strongest correlates of conduct disorder in children. Other research has linked harsh, abusive, and inconsistent discipline patterns to serious conduct problems in children (Lahey et al., 1995; Robins, 1991; Shaw et al., 2003). In stressed or large families, parental attention can be in short supply and may be unduly focused on negative behaviors. Because such behaviors garner much-desired parental attention, the negative and aggressive behaviors are reinforced, which may lead to patterns of antisocial behaviors (Surgeon General, 1999).

In a review of the mental health research literature, a report by the U.S. Surgeon General noted that exposure to emotional abuse and physical violence disrupted the normal development of children and adolescents and had profound effects on mental, physical, and emotional health. The review found that children's exposure to abuse and violence was associated with characteristics such as insecure attachment; impaired social functioning with peers; and psychiatric disorders such as PTSD, ADHD, conduct disorder, and depression (Surgeon General, 1999).

In addition, a number of studies have linked poor family management and emotional climate to depression in children. As compared with families raising children who are not depressed, families of children with depression tend to be less emotionally expressive, more hostile, more critical, and less accepting. Families with depressed children also have family structures that are less cohesive, more disorganized, and more conflictual in nature than families without depressed children (Gilbert, 2004).

Parents who are depressed themselves find it hard to provide consistent discipline, supervision, and emotionally positive interactions with their children (Wilson & Durbin, 2010). Children and adolescents of parents with depression have been found to be at increased risk for internalizing and externalizing disorders (Goodman et al., 2011; Wickramaratne & Weissman, 1998). Not surprisingly, parental mental illness itself is associated with poor parenting ability (Oyserman et al., 2000).

**Table 5.2  Risk and Protective Factors for Child and Adolescent Mental Health Disorders**

| | Individual | Familial | Extrafamilial |
|---|---|---|---|
| **Risk** | • Genetic vulnerability to a mental health disorder<br>• Low self-esteem<br>• Difficult temperament<br>• Victim of physical/sexual abuse<br>• Chronic childhood illness or developmental delay<br>• Previous diagnosis of a mental health disorder<br>• Social isolation<br>• Rejection by peers | • Insufficient income for family economic stability<br>• Parental substance abuse<br>• Parental mental illness<br>• Multiple moves<br>• Poor maternal bonding and attachment<br>• Four or more siblings | • Structural racism (e.g., poorly performing schools, mass incarceration)<br>• Interpersonal racism<br>• Limited pathways for academic or professional success<br>• Frequent community violence<br>• Stressful environments in school or community<br>• Toxic physical environment |
| **Protective & Promotive** | • Good social skills<br>• Academic achievement<br>• Easygoing temperament | • Stable economic situation<br>• Good communication<br>• Cohesive family<br>• Secure attachment, strong maternal bond | • Presence of nurturing/caring adults<br>• Positive social/emotional environment in childcare or school<br>• Opportunities and support for achievement |

## Community, Social, and Environmental Risk

A child's social and physical environment is an equally important determinant of later mental health problems as individual factors (Sameroff & Gutman, 2004). Again, it is most likely the interaction of genes and the social environment that drives risk and protection for mental health disorders. Bronfenbrenner's (1979) ecological model of child and adolescent development stressed the importance of contextual factors, including families, communities, and social institutions. Children and youth at high risk for SED are more likely to be raised in environments that heighten the effects of biological vulnerability (Caspi et al., 2000; Resnick & Burt, 1996). In addition to poverty, some of the more common environmental risks that exacerbate vulnerability include exposure to familial and community violence, toxin exposure, and parental psychopathology or criminality.

A physical environment contaminated with air pollution, tobacco smoke, and chemical exposures effects the ways our genes are expressed, which can contribute to the development of numerous health and mental health problems (Martin & Fry, 2018). In particular, lead exposure has an established connection with impaired infant brain development and later academic performance, juvenile delinquency, and a host of mental health disorders (Marshall et al., 2020; Rauh & Margolis, 2016). Exposure to natural disasters is also a source of traumatic experiences. For example, children who experienced Hurricane Katrina demonstrated high levels of trauma symptoms, and one study found that half of these children met the criteria for referral for mental health services (Osofsky et al., 2009).

Exposure to experiences in childhood that can be traumatic is widespread; however, the prevalence estimates vary depending on which experiences are included and how many of these adverse experiences are identified as possibilities. Although not all adverse experiences would be considered traumatic, findings from studies of adverse childhood experiences (ACEs) indicate a high prevalence of potentially traumatic adverse experiences during childhood. A recent study examining state-level data from the Behavioral Risk Factor Surveillance System found that 62% of adults reported at least one ACE in childhood, and 25% reported three or more ACEs (Merrick et al., 2018). Based on parent or caregiver self-report of their own child from the NSCH (2017–2018), over 40% of children under 18 years of age have experienced at least one ACE and 20% have experienced two or more ACEs. Indeed, it is estimated that nearly half of children entering kindergarten have had at least one adverse experience (Zill & West, 2001). Moreover, increased exposure to ACEs in childhood is related to a greater likelihood of developing a variety of behavioral, health, and mental health problems, including smoking, multiple sexual partners, heart disease, cancer, lung disease, liver disease, sexually transmitted diseases, substance abuse, depression, and suicide attempts (Lu et al., 2008). Research has also identified a dose–response wherein the more ACEs one experiences, the greater the risk of health problems. Compared with peers who did not experience adverse events in childhood, adults who experienced four or more categories of childhood adverse events (e.g., having witnessed violence, having a parent who abused alcohol or drugs, or having lived in poverty) had a fourfold to 12-fold increased risk for alcoholism, drug abuse, depression, and suicide attempts (Felitti et al., 1998).

One limitation of the ACEs research is the lack of a consistent definition of what particular experiences should be included as adverse and what is a traumatic experience (i.e., results in symptoms of trauma). Research using a broader definition of individual adverse experiences have found quite a high prevalence of trauma symptoms among children exposed to adverse experiences. For example, a longitudinal study of children living in a primarily rural area found that by age 16, more than 67% of the children reported exposure to at least one adverse event (Copeland et al., 2007). Those events included child maltreatment or domestic violence, a major medical trauma, a traffic injury, a traumatic loss of a significant other, or sexual assault. Negative life events have also been associated with poor emotional and behavioral outcomes in children and adolescents (Gerrity & Folcarelli, 2008; Goodyer, 1990; Kessler, 1997; Tiet et al., 2001). Examples of negative life events include multiple moves; loss of a parent through death, divorce, or out-of-home placement; physical assault; exposure to violent acts; and injury. A longitudinal study found that suicidal ideation in 16-year-olds was strongly predicted by early adversities such as childhood maltreatment, residential instability, and community violence (Thompson et al., 2012). Although the role that exposure to adverse experiences plays in the development of various disorders is emerging, experiencing adverse events appears to affect emotional regulation and the processing of social information. New research continues to identify epigenetic changes in biological stress response systems associated with trauma exposure (Jiang et al., 2019). Regardless of the exact definitions of adverse experiences and mental health problems, the association between these two factors is consistent.

The effects of negative life events also appear to differ by gender. For example, depression is associated with loss and grief, particularly in girls (Breier et al., 1988; Goodyer, 2001; Moore et al., 1999). The earlier a child experiences the loss of a parent or caretaker, the more severe the outcome. Being a victim of a crime, a violent act, or an assault is strongly associated with PTSD and conduct disorder in both girls and boys (Famularo et al., 1992); however, the association between being a victim of crime, violence, or assault and the occurrence of ODD is particularly strong among girls (Tiet et al., 2001). Among boys, a parent being arrested and jailed is strongly associated with conduct disorder and dysthymia, whereas among girls, parental arrest is more often associated with conduct disorder and overanxious disorder.

In sum, a number of risk factors are associated with mental health disorders in children and adolescents. These risk factors can be grouped at the individual, family, and environmental levels. In summary, individual risk appears to be related to the number of risk factors a child has in various domains (Fergusson et al., 1994; Rutter, 1979). Although cumulative risk appears to be more important than any single risk factor, the combination of specific risk factors is likely to be associated with differing health outcomes, although there is substantial variation in the outcomes across individuals (Lanier et al., 2018; Sameroff & Gutman, 2004).

We conclude this section on risk factors by addressing two risk factors for mental health problems that likely have the greatest implications for social policy: racism and poverty. Biological and family risk factors are difficult or even impossible to modify directly through state or federal legislation. However, both racism and poverty are generated from public policy and therefore can be directly reduced through changes in policy.

For persons of color, racism is a significant and constant stressor and is more severe for individuals who are Black/African American or Indigenous (Gaylord-Harden & Cunningham, 2009). Racism influences an individual's experience through a combination of interpersonal racist interactions and structural racism (Bailey et al., 2017; Harrell, 2000). *Structural racism* is defined as "the totality of ways in which societies foster racial discrimination through mutually reinforcing systems," (Bailey et al., 2017, p. 1453) including housing, education, and health care. The constant and interacting stressors of interpersonal interactions and a discriminatory environment have detrimental impacts on the health and mental health of persons of color. For example, after controlling for other factors, experiences of racial discrimination increase the chances of depression and anxiety in African American adolescents (Bailey et al., 2017; Cooper et al., 2013). The mediators between racism and adverse outcomes include but are not limited to economic injustice, psychosocial trauma, and political exclusion (Bailey et al., 2017). As a result of structural racism, the percentage of people of color living in poverty is much higher than the percentage of people who are White. For many children, this means that the risks of racism and poverty are compounded and much more prevalent in communities where many people of color live. Public policies can either perpetuate structural racism or try to dismantle the racist structures. Policies that directly address structural racism across systems are most likely to effectively address racial mental health inequity (Bailey et al., 2017; Reskin, 2012).

Poverty is associated with a higher prevalence of mental health problems in children and with most of the other risk factors for mental health problems. Children with SED have been found to be overrepresented in low-income families (Mark & Buck, 2006). Early childhood poverty in particular has been shown to have an association with depression, antisocial behavior, adolescent anxiety, and adolescent hyperactivity (McLeod & Shanahan, 1996; Pagani et al., 1997). The ways that poverty is associated with mental health problems is uncertain and many other factors are likely intermediaries. At the familial level, poverty is associated with increased violence and parental substance abuse (Rutter, 1985; Spearly & Lauderdale, 1983). Werner and Smith (1992) found that low parental income was the single greatest predictor of emotional disturbances in youth under 18 years of age. Poverty is also associated with living in an area with increased toxins such as lead in the physical environment (Taylor, 2014).

Similarly, poor social and economic conditions have been correlated with family pathology, child abuse, and poor parental supervision. However, the causal pathway is uncertain. Instead, living in poverty may produce poor child mental health outcomes because the parental experience of financial strain and economic loss diminishes some parents' capacity to provide involved and supportive parenting (Linver et al., 2004; Oyserman, 2004). Another environmental pathway of poverty may be related to nutrition. Even after controlling for poverty status, food insecurity has been found to increase the risk for adolescent mental health disorder (McLaughlin et al., 2012).

# PROTECTIVE AND PROMOTIVE FACTORS

Protective factors reduce or buffer risk while promotive factors enhance positive outcomes for all youth regardless of the presence of risk. It should be clear to the reader when comparing the length of the sections in this chapter on risk and protection that much more is known about risk for mental health disorders than the factors that promote mental health or buffer against risk. Protective and promotive factors are relevant in the development of mental health problems and in minimizing the adverse outcomes for children who develop a mental health disorder. Indeed, the impact of risk factors on children's outcomes can be moderated by protective factors. For example, if there are many protective and promotive factors present in a family, a child may experience fewer mental health problems when one or more adverse events occur. Furthermore, just as a greater number of risk factors are associated with increased risk, mental health resilience can be a function of the number of protective and promotive factors present in a child or adolescent's life (Sameroff et al., 1999). Garmezy (1993) identified three broad sets of variables that have potential to operate as protective factors. Many of these are also promotive factors and include (a) child characteristics, such as easy temperament, cognitive skills, and social skills; (b) family characteristics, such as families that are marked by warmth, cohesion, and structure; and (c) the social characteristic of having a support system available.

For children and youth who have a SED, according to findings from the National Adolescent and Child Treatment Study, a longitudinal study of youth with SED, negative outcomes can be mitigated with adaptive social behavior, such as interpersonal relationship skills or coping skills (Armstrong et al., 2003). Good communication skills have also been found to be protective against hospital readmissions among children with SED (Greenbaum et al., 1996). Life history reports of adolescents treated for mental health problems indicate that young people who had positive life outcomes tended to have had more stable living situations, better family relationships, and more positive relationships with peers. Findings from studies sponsored by the World Health Organization have suggested that adversities such as the long-term disability associated with childhood schizophrenia can be minimized through supportive relationships with family or community members (Hopper & Wanderling, 2000). Thus, just as poor parenting practices are risk factors for many antisocial behaviors (Loeber et al., 1998), warm, supportive family relationships and parental monitoring appear to function as protective and promotive factors for both boys and girls (Fraser, 2004; Green, 1995; Santilli & Beilenson, 1992).

To balance the focus on ACEs with a focus on protection and mental health promotion, researchers have forwarded a complementary framework known as the Health Outcomes of Positive Experience (HOPE) model (Sege et al., 2017). The report from the HOPE authors identified five recommendations: (1) advance a positive construct of health and HOPE; (2) invest in science-aligned interventions; (3) specify, develop, and deploy a common set of positive experiences; (4) establish policies to generate opportunities; and (5) enable innovation and implementation of best practices. Regarding policies, the authors argue that policies such as universal paid parental leave is one policy strategy to build a foundation of healthy development. Policies that reduce families' financial stress and increase the time that parents can spend caring for children facilitate the conditions for the promotive factors listed above.

## MENTAL HEALTH RISK, PROTECTION, AND RESILIENCE IN THE ERA OF COVID-19

At the time of the writing of this new book edition, the world is gripped by an unrelenting global pandemic from a novel coronavirus (COVID-19). Although evidence is still emerging, survey research from around the world indicates that parents and caregivers are experiencing tremendous stress due to the pandemic, economic downturn, and associated social distancing policies, such as school and childcare closure (Brown et al., 2020; Chung et al., 2020; Jiao et al., 2020; Lee & Ward, 2020). Further, it appears this increased stress has the potential to dramatically impact caregiver health and child health and well-being. In April of 2020, the U.S. had an unemployment rate of 14.7%, the highest unemployment rate since the Second World War (U.S. Bureau of Labor Statistics, 2020). In addition to massive job losses, many children experienced the death or severe illness of a parent or other family member; this occurred disproportionately in Black and Hispanic/Latino communities (Fortuna et al., 2020). The pandemic magnified underlying inequities in the societal structure, exacerbated many of the risks for mental health problems for children, and undermined the promotive and protective factors that many families had been able to provide before the pandemic.

In addition to these changes, the delivery of mental health care was disrupted. When it was possible for the clinician, patient, and family, some of these services shifted to telemental health services through various internet platforms or, in some cases, phone calls. However, not all families had the technology or capacity to facilitate this type of interaction, and telemental health for children and adolescents is not a well-developed field. Additionally, children who were receiving mental health services through schools may have experienced a disruption or loss of these services. Other types of natural disasters, such as Hurricane Katrina, have resulted in an increase in the percentage of children and youth experiencing mental health problems (Osofsky et al., 2009). Consequently, experts are anticipating an increase in trauma-related symptoms from the pandemic even though the consequences will take years to be fully understood.

## HISTORY OF FEDERAL CHILD MENTAL HEALTH POLICY IN THE UNITED STATES

Whereas risk and protection are relatively new concepts, the concept of childhood mental illness has a history dating to the late 19th century. The first discussion in a textbook of psychological problems in children was Maudsley's chapter on "The Insanity of Early Life" in 1867 (Hergenhahn, 2001; Parry-Jones, 1989). However, the prevailing thought was that people could not "go mad" until they had reached adulthood. Children and adolescents who exhibited serious emotional or behavioral symptoms were hospitalized or imprisoned alongside adults. A public system devoted solely to child mental health did not emerge for another 100 years.

The federalist system of the U.S. limits the authority of the federal government and gives considerable power to each state to determine how that state is run. This leads to significant variation across states in the number, type, and quality of mental health services. The federal government has three main policy levers to influence services at the state level: (1) creating specific funding opportunities such as incentivizing new systems of care, (2) the establishment of national standards, and (3) and determining what mental services public insurance (i.e., Medicaid) will pay for. Most federal policies focus on the structure in which care is delivered to increase the coordination, accessibility, and availability of mental health services.

Medicaid is the federal health care program for low-income individuals (and some other groups) and pays for about 50% of all mental health services provided to poor children and adolescents (Kenny et al., 2002). Thus, policies flowing from federal and state Medicaid offices are as influential on state child mental health delivery systems as the federal policy initiatives that come through the National Institute of Mental Health (NIMH), the SAMHSA, or the Center for Mental Health Services. Because they are funded through a combination of state and federal dollars, Medicaid programs vary dramatically across states. For allowable expenses, state Medicaid dollars are matched by federal dollars using a formula based on the average state income (Artiga et al., 2017). States with lower average incomes have a higher match rate and states with higher incomes have a lower match rate. By federal statute, the lowest match is 1:1, meaning that every state receives at least $1 in federal Medicaid spending for every $1 in state Medicaid spending. States with lower average incomes receive more federal dollars for each dollar they spend, such as $2 in federal Medicaid spending for every $1 in state Medicaid spending. While this should incentivize spending, it also magnifies the effect of state-level cuts in lower-income states because for every dollar of state spending that is cut from Medicaid, three dollars of services are lost ($1 from the state and $2 from the federal program). The Affordable Care Act, discussed in more detail later in the chapter, allowed states to expand Medicaid coverage and receive the federal match for persons previously ineligible for the federal matching funds, such as single adults without children making up to 138% of the federal poverty level. Services that Medicaid covers and changes in that coverage over time significantly influence the type and availability of state mental services (Frank et al., 2003).

## Precursors of Mental Health Policy

### Early 1900s

The earliest public mental health efforts on behalf of children were a result of changes in the justice system that came about at the turn of the 20th century in approaches to handling "wayward" youth. Public policy in juvenile justice was changing from an approach that focused on punitive measures to an approach that sought corrective measures. The nation's first juvenile court was established in Chicago in 1899. In 1909, several members of the Hull House Association board became impressed with the new juvenile courts and created the Juvenile Psychopathic Institute to study the problems of juvenile offenders. The institute's first director, William Healy, MD, was a pioneer in the field and applied emerging psychiatric theory related to children and adolescents to individualize treatment of juvenile offenders. Growing from Healy's influence, juvenile court clinics developed across the country, providing the first publicly funded community mental health services to troubled youth. Even though mental health theory and practice provided a foundation for much of the evolving juvenile justice and child welfare policies, no formal child mental health policy had yet been developed (Jones, 1999).

## 1920s

During the 1920s, juvenile court clinics began serving more than children with antisocial problems, and they became attached to a variety of new structures such as charities, universities, and teaching hospitals. Referred to as *child guidance clinics*, their major areas of concentration became school and home problems. Child guidance clinics primarily served children and adolescents with internalizing problems, and the clinicians used Freudian and Ericksonian developmental theories in addressing those problems.

## 1930s

The federal government first became involved in child mental health policy in the 1930s through the advocacy of the federal Children's Bureau, which supported the development of a child mental health field and advocated for the expansion of child guidance clinics. Child guidance clinics became the major source of mental health care for children and youth until the 1970s.

## 1940s

World War II brought an unexpected focus to the mental health needs of children. Because of the huge military draft, life histories were available for hundreds of thousands of young soldiers from varied backgrounds and socioeconomic levels. By the end of the war, it was apparent that soldiers who had behavior problems as children were much more likely to be prematurely discharged, disciplined, wounded, or killed (Schowalter, 2003). Studies from military records provided evidence that mental illness is blind to both race/ethnicity and income and that the outcomes of mental health problems are costly to both individuals and society.

# The Introduction of Community Mental Health Centers

## 1960s–1970s

In 1963, President John F. Kennedy signed the Mental Retardation Facilities and Community Mental Health Center Act, which changed the face of mental health care nationally. The law focused primarily on adults with mental illness and established funding for community mental health centers. These centers were designed to provide mental health services in the community rather than in hospital settings. Similar to the child guidance movement that had preceded it, the Community Mental Health Center Act provided mental health services to only a small percentage of children with SED. The act did not mandate that affordable mental health services be provided to all children in need (Lourie & Hernandez, 2003) and little, if any attention was afforded to prevention or early intervention.

However, advocacy efforts on behalf of children and youth with emotional problems continued to grow, which eventually led Congress to establish the Joint Commission on the Mental Health of Children. In its 1969 report, the commission found that millions of children and youth were not receiving the mental health services they needed. Moreover, many of those receiving care were served in inappropriately restrictive settings, such as state psychiatric hospitals. In 1975, Congress acted to require community mental health centers to serve children and adolescents.

Despite the congressional mandate to provide mental health services to children and adolescents, community mental health centers were slow to respond. A report issued by the President's Commission on Mental Health (1978) strongly criticized community mental health centers for their failure to address the needs of children and youth with serious emotional and behavioral problems. President Jimmy Carter's Mental Health Commission also noted that few communities were providing either the number or the continuum of services needed. Therefore, the commission recommended that a community-based network of integrated services be developed to meet the needs of seriously emotionally disturbed children and adolescents.

## 1980s

Although similar recommendations had been voiced throughout the 1970s, it was not until the 1982 publication of Jane Knitzer's widely read book, *Unclaimed Children*, that Congress mobilized to take action. Knitzer boldly stated that of 3 million children and adolescents with SED in the U.S., 2 million did not receive the services they needed. Furthermore, Knitzer reported that at least 40% of hospital placements for children were in inappropriately restrictive settings, including facilities for people with mental retardation and adult psychiatric hospital wards. She observed that most states had no specific policies for children with SED and noted that millions of "unclaimed" children were adrift in the public health, mental health, education, juvenile justice, and child welfare systems; these children were not receiving appropriate mental health services (Knitzer, 1982).

## The Era of Systems of Care

Knitzer (1982) documented a lack of services; poor coordination among service agencies; overuse of residential and institutional care; and failure of the federal, state, and local governments to respond to the crisis. In suggesting ways to improve these conditions, she coined the term *system of care* to describe a new approach to addressing children's mental health needs. In 1984, Congress appropriated funds to the NIMH to establish a national agenda to deal with the problems outlined by Knitzer. In response, NIMH created the Child and Adolescent Service System Program (CASSP).

Following the example of the innovative Community Support Program for adults with serious and persistent mental illness, CASSP focused on the needs of children with SED by providing financial incentives to states to develop systems of care to serve these children. The CASSP initiative was the first federal mental health program to clearly identify youth with SED as its target population. CASSP created a movement and momentum for change. It became the vehicle for the development and articulation of federal and state child mental health policy.

The CASSP program was based on the following four assumptions:

1. Children and adolescents with SED are found in all of the nation's public health, mental health, education, juvenile justice, and child welfare systems.

2. Most children and adolescents with serious problems are served in more than one of these agencies at the same time.

3. Regardless of the agencies with which children are affiliated, the mental health needs of children have been overlooked and have not been addressed appropriately.

4. Few states have planning mechanisms to identify children and adolescents who are served across multiple systems.

The policy imperative in the CASSP initiative was to develop a multiagency approach to the delivery of mental health services.

In a widely circulated monograph, Stroul and Friedman (1986) defined Knitzer's concept of a system of care (SOC) as "a comprehensive spectrum of mental health and other necessary services, which are organized into a coordinated network to meet the multiple and changing needs of children and adolescents with severe emotional disturbances and their families" (p. iv). These authors stated that an SOC should be a community-based, child-centered, family-focused, and culturally competent approach to integrating services. The multiple needs of each child and family should be met by providing a full range of services, including mental health, substance abuse, health, social, educational, and vocational services, with case management providing the mechanism to guide the family toward the appropriate mix and timing of services. Figure 5.2 illustrates a model SOC for mental health service delivery.

The ideal SOC includes enough flexibility to allow services to be tailored to the specific needs of the child and family involved, regardless of which agency has overall responsibility for the child or which system provided the services. For example, a child or adolescent with a SED might have psychological needs that require intervention by a mental health center, special education needs filled by the school system, and residential needs for a structured living environment provided by a social services agency.

**1980s–early 1990s**

Stroul and Friedman's (1986) outline of an SOC was used as the blueprint by the CASSP program for organizing child mental health services across the country. To receive federal funding, states were expected to create a protocol for interagency cooperation that would effectively coordinate all child-serving agencies and services. Coordination and cooperative development were to start at the state level and then be replicated at the local (usually county) level. States were urged to develop strategies and methods for pooling financial resources among agencies so that all needed services could be provided, regardless of the child's service eligibility or insurance coverage. By the fall of 1990, all 50 states and the District of Columbia had received CASSP grants. By 1995, all states had at least one state-level, full-time child mental health specialist working to develop a statewide SOC (Davis, Yelton, Katz-Leavy, & Lourie, 1995).

# SYSTEMS OF CARE AND MENTAL HEALTH POLICY

The policy of creating SOCs to serve the mental health needs of the nation's youth was formally endorsed in 1992 when Congress passed the Children's and Community Mental Health Services Improvement Act, also referred to as the Children's Mental Health Initiative (CMHI). (See Table 5.3 for a listing of federal mental health policy initiatives.) This act created a program called the Comprehensive Community Mental Health Services for Children and Their Families. Administered by the Center for Mental Health Services in the SAMHSA, this program provided grants to states to expand the SOC concept. To date, this program is the largest federal initiative supporting the development of children's mental health services.

By the close of the 20th century, at least half of the states had enacted laws requiring some sort of SOC (Davis, Yelton, & Katz-Leavy, 1995). The Children's and Community Mental Health Services Improvement Act provided nearly $460 million in federal funding to 67 local SOCs that served more than 40,000 children across the country (Center for Mental Health Services, 1999). Now, many years after their initial authorization, SOCs continue to be the primary policy approach to governing public mental health systems. Experts in this area now propose that "some elements of the system of care philosophy and approach can be found in nearly all communities across the nation" (Stroul & Friedman, 2011, p. 2). Congress continues to provide annual funding through a competitive grant structure to states wishing to enhance their SOCs. The CMHI has invested over $1.6 billion in grants to all 50 states and many territories and American Indian/Alaska Native communities to develop sustainable SOCs. The major principles underlying this approach remain intact.

The ongoing issues related to the implementation of SOCs are particularly apparent when one looks at *where* children receive mental health services. The SOC approach demands that services be family-driven, child-centered, and delivered in a least-restrictive community-based setting. However, some children have symptoms that

## Figure 5.2  A System of Care Framework for Children and Adolescents

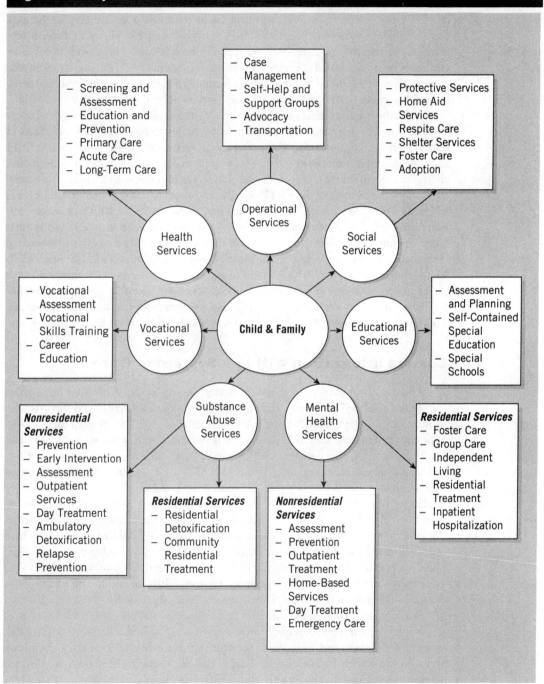

- Screening and
  Assessment
- Education and
  Prevention
- Primary Care
- Acute Care
- Long-Term Care

- Case
  Management
- Self-Help and
  Support Groups
- Advocacy
- Transportation

- Protective Services
- Home Aid
  Services
- Respite Care
- Shelter Services
- Foster Care
- Adoption

Health
Services

Operational
Services

Social
Services

- Vocational
  Assessment
- Vocational
  Skills Training
- Career
  Education

Vocational
Services

**Child & Family**

Educational
Services

- Assessment
  and Planning
- Self-Contained
  Special
  Education
- Special
  Schools

Substance
Abuse
Services

Mental
Health
Services

*Nonresidential
Services*
- Prevention
- Early Intervention
- Assessment
- Outpatient
  Services
- Day Treatment
- Ambulatory
  Detoxification
- Relapse
  Prevention

*Residential Services*
- Residential
  Detoxification
- Community
  Residential
  Treatment

*Nonresidential
Services*
- Assessment
- Prevention
- Outpatient
  Treatment
- Home-Based
  Services
- Day Treatment
- Emergency Care

*Residential Services*
- Foster Care
- Group Care
- Independent
  Living
- Residential
  Treatment
- Inpatient
  Hospitalization

require a higher level of care and need longer-term services at facilities in which they can receive constant professional supervision. Children with SED may require placement in a psychiatric residential treatment facility (PRTF); a facility may be the only way for children to access the combination of needed services. However, these placements are restrictive to the patients and are an extremely costly way to deliver services; advocates have questioned the legal and ethical acceptability of their use. There is also concern that the Medicaid reimbursement formula and lack of community-based mental health services is driving the use of these services more than child need.

Given the major expense of PRTFs to the Medicaid system, the federal government initiated a waiver demonstration program in ten states to serve children with SED in their homes and communities. The evaluation of this program was completed in 2013 and concluded that children in the waiver program maintained and often improved their clinical functional status (Urdapilleta et al., 2013). On average, state Medicaid costs were never more than a third of the PRTF costs, saving about $40,000 per child. While there will likely always be children with SED that may require care in a PRTF or other institutional setting, this evaluation demonstrated that most children can be served in their home or community. Receiving services in their community also has the advantage of maintaining natural supports with the child's family, peers, and school. The major challenge is ensuring that services are available and accessible in every community. From a policy and cost-effectiveness standpoint, it makes sense to invest in developing community-based program infrastructure, adequately reimbursing providers, and supporting workforce development to avoid these more expensive and restrictive care settings.

## Service Integration Within a System of Care

There is no single system of mental health care for youth. A growing body of literature has described the overall characteristics of children with SED and their families (Epstein et al., 1995; Quinn & Epstein, 1998; Wagner et al., 2005). Most of these studies indicated that children with SED have a number of common risk factors, including inadequate social skills, poor academic performance, family violence, alcohol and drug use, and mental illness. However, more youth with SED are found in other service systems than are treated within the child mental health system, and many youths with less-severe challenges also receive their mental health services in other systems. For example, up to 80% of all children entering the juvenile justice system have mental health disorders (President's New Freedom Commission on Mental Health, 2003), and researchers have estimated that 20% of incarcerated youth have SED, which is double the rate of SED found in the general population (Mears & Aron, 2003). Nearly 20% of children with SED are involved in the child welfare system; a staggering 70% of youth with SED receive mental health services from local school systems (Ali et al., 2019; Sanchez et al., 2018).

Because child welfare and juvenile justice systems serve a significant number of youth with SED and public schools provide many mental health services, policies that determine the types and qualities of services in these other systems are a significant factor in the mental health care landscape. Policies requiring that trauma-informed services be provided in schools or to child welfare–involved children have reshaped the services that are available. More recently, requirements for evidence-based practices in

## Table 5.3 Major Federal Mental Health Policy Initiatives

| Policy | Date | Impact |
|---|---|---|
| Mental Retardation Facilities and Community Mental Health Center Construction Act (P.L. 88-164) | 1963 | Established funding to build and staff community mental health centers |
| Community Mental Health Center Act Amendments of 1965 (P.L. 91-211) | 1965 | Grants were provided to support the development of mental health services in low-income areas; included a new program of grants to support further development of children's services<br><br>Extended grant eligibility to centers serving those with alcohol and substance abuse problems |
| Social Security Amendments of 1965 | 1965 | Provided funding for medically necessary services to low-income families, pregnant women, and persons who are aged, blind, and disabled; coverage of most mental health services was optional to states |
| Education of All Handicapped Children Act (P.L. 94-162) | 1974 | Required that schools provide mental health services to children with serious emotional disturbances (SEDs) as part of their Individualized Education Program (IEP) |
| Community Mental Health Center Act Amendment (P.L. 94-63) | 1975 | Required community mental health centers to provide mental health services to children and adolescents |
| Mental Health Systems Act (P.L. 96-398) | 1980 | Based on recommendations of the President's Commission on Mental Health and designed to improve services for people with severe, persistent mental disorders |
| Omnibus Budget Reconciliation Act (OBRA; P.L. 97-35) | 1981 | Repealed the Mental Health Systems Act and consolidated social services funding into a single block grant that allows each state to determine the spending of its funds; act required that 10% of mental health block grant funds be spent on children and adolescents.<br><br>Federal role became providing technical assistance to improve state and local providers of mental health services |
| Alcohol, Drug, and Mental Health Administration (ADAMHA) Appropriations Act | 1984 | Directed the National Institute of Mental Health (NIMH) to provide incentive grants to states to develop state and local-level child mental health structures to coordinate care to children with SED and their families; NIMH created the Child and Adolescent Service System Program (CASSP) |

*(Continued)*

CHAPTER 5 • CHILD MENTAL HEALTH POLICY

Table 5.3   (Continued)

| Policy | Date | Impact |
|---|---|---|
| Children's and Community Mental Health Services Improvement Act | 1992 | Created the Comprehensive Community Mental Health Services for Children and Their Families Program within the Center for Mental Health Services, which provided funding to states to develop systems of care for children with SED |
| Surgeon General's Reports | 2000 | Called for increased research on and use of evidence-based mental health practices |
| President's New Freedom Commission Report on Mental Health and the Federal Action Agenda | 2003–2005 | Called for a transformation of the mental health system, recommending a public health approach that emphasizes mental health promotion, early identification, and treatment |
| The Home- and Community-Based Alternatives to Psychiatric Residential Treatment Facilities Medicaid Demonstration Waiver (Deficit Reduction Act of 2005, P.L. 109-171) | 2005 | Allowed ten state grantees to use Medicaid reimbursement to serve children/youth with SED in their homes and communities versus care in psychiatric residential treatment facilities |
| Project LAUNCH (Linking Actions for Unmet Needs in Children's Health; Substance Abuse and Mental Health Services Administration) | 2008 | Provided grants to states to address unmet mental health needs for children 0 to 8 years of age by funding community-based strategies to integrate and enhance services |
| Maternal, Infant, and Early Childhood Home Visiting (MIECHV) | 2010 | Provided funding for states to expand the evidence-based home visiting program for low-income families |
| Patient Protection and Affordable Care Act (ACA; P.L. 111-148) | 2010–2014 | Reformed the U.S. health care system

Several aspects of the ACA will impact children's mental health, including coverage of mental health conditions as part of the essential benefits package, funding for prevention, expansion of Medicaid/ Children's Health Insurance Program (CHIP), improved care coordination, and no coverage denial for preexisting mental health conditions |
| Child and Family Services Improvement and Innovation Act* | 2011 | For children in foster care, required states to have protocols for the appropriate use and monitoring of psychotropic medications of children and to monitor or treat emotional trauma associated with the maltreatment or removal |

| Policy | Date | Impact |
|--------|------|--------|
| Cures Act | 2016 | Grant programs for early identification and intervention, integration of pediatric mental and primary health care, and federal funding for comprehensive community mental health services for children |
| Every Student Succeeds Act (ESSA) | 2015 | Block grant funding, some of which had to be used to improve student mental and behavioral health |
| Family First Prevention Services Act (FFPSA)* | 2018 | Increased federal reimbursement of mental health and substance use prevention services for children and families who are "candidates" for foster care<br><br>Limited reimbursement for use of residential treatment facilities in foster care and added requirements that improve the quality of care in residential treatment programs, such as using a trauma-informed model and integrating family members into the treatment program |

*Child welfare law provisions only apply to children involved with the child welfare system.

child welfare through the 2018 Family First Legislation are expected to have significant repercussions for service availability and provision. Limits on the use of psychotropics in child welfare–involved populations are changing the mix of services that are available to child welfare agencies in treating youth with mental health or behavioral concerns. In addition to federal policies that set the direction for mental health services, policies focused on other child-serving systems drive the type and availability of mental health services in those systems (e.g., trauma-informed schools, child welfare psychotropics, residential services, etc.).

Children interacting with these separate systems need appropriate mental health care that is tailored to meet their individual needs. Over the past 20 years, mental health leaders, policymakers, and service providers have been struggling with how to best integrate mental health services into these systems. The most common state-level integration approaches involve coordinating mental health, child welfare, and juvenile justice services using one of the following three structures:

1. Separate agencies are maintained as individual departments. In this model, coordination of services is accomplished through formal interagency planning structures.

2. A part or all of the three agencies (mental health, child welfare, and juvenile justice) are housed within a single umbrella department, such as a department of human services. Each division maintains its own staff, policy development process, and budget. Coordination is facilitated because each agency reports to a single department director, and departmental rules and procedures that might inhibit service integration can be changed without legislative intervention.

3. The three agencies are combined into a single departmental agency, with a single agency budget and policy-making body.

Each of these options has advantages and disadvantages, but much of the effectiveness of the option depends on how it is implemented at the state level. The first option requires ongoing coordination of services, but each agency maintains a specific focus. The second option may improve service coordination, but it still requires a high degree of coordination and communication across systems. The third system has the fewest barriers to coordinated services; however, combining all three can create a very large agency, making management time-consuming, cumbersome, and often inefficient. Turf issues remain problematic. In addition, many child advocates object to the fact that the allocation of funds across different child populations would occur within a single budget process that might not be open to the public for review and comment.

States have found that restructuring alone does not overcome turf issues, policy conflicts, leadership challenges, and inadequate or disproportionate funding. Arguably, the most important elements of successful service integration are agreeing on a common target population and blending funding streams so that an appropriate set of individually tailored services can be provided. Which agency provides the actual services may not be as important as having an arrangement in place so that services are provided to children who need them, regardless of the child's custody status or the family's financial ability to pay for services.

## Systems of Care Implementation Evaluations

SOCs are evaluated on their processes and outcomes. Early evaluation studies of SOCs in the 1990s found improvements in processes but no clinically significant improvements in outcomes compared to the previous services (Bickman et al., 1996). The lack of efficacy of the services that were delivered in the SOC was identified as the reason for these lackluster results and the varying outcomes (e.g., hospitalizations vs. behavioral measures vs. satisfaction) made the evaluation challenging (Bickman, 1996). More recent evaluations have found better results, but the studies have generally lacked a comparison group. The Comprehensive Community Mental Health Services for Children and Their Families program is evaluated annually by SAMHSA. Findings from these evaluations have been detailed in annual reports to Congress reports, available on the SAMHSA website (2020). These evaluations have used parent and teacher reports of youth behavior as well as youth self-reports from model SOCs. The findings have indicated that youth served in these SOCs demonstrate positive benefits as compared with their preenrollment behavior, including fewer emotional and behavioral problems, improved school performance, and a lower likelihood of engaging in harmful behaviors.

The Center for Mental Health Services conducted reviews of SOC implementation in 1995 and 2002. Researchers from both reviews found that substantial changes had occurred in each funded site. Indeed, changes in policies and procedures had been made that facilitated cross-agency training, programming, and co-location of services. The researchers also found changes that enhanced interagency communication and collaboration. Even so, no site had implemented all the aspects required of a comprehensive SOC model (Stroul, 2006; Vinson et al., 2001).

Despite the positive outcomes of model SOCs, and notwithstanding the federal support allocated to states, SOCs have proven difficult to implement and sustain. The model requires many systems-level alterations, including developing links among child-serving agencies, creating a continuum of community-based services, blending funding streams, developing interagency policy, and organizing treatment teams to coordinate care.

Interagency coordination issues emerged as significant barriers in the SOC approach. Some of the challenges may be referred to as "turf problems"; these issues revolved around poor interagency collaboration, which was attributable to factors such as a lack of trust, a sense of competition, a fear of sharing resources, and a lack of understanding regarding the partner agencies' mandates and capacities. A second set of logistical challenges has also emerged, including the difficulty of integrating data across agencies, barriers to information sharing (such as HIPPA requirements), awareness and accessibility of community services, eligibility requirements, and limits on availability of specialized services within the continuum of care, such as infant mental health or expertise in working with adolescents. In addition to these turf and logistical problems, the greatest barrier to full-scale change was likely the sheer amount of time required to develop meaningful collaborations (Behar, 2003).

The federal approach to SOCs provides an example of the tension between federal care recommendations and available funding. Federal grant funding for SOCs allowed for different types of services to be provided, but many of these services are not reimbursable under Medicaid. Consequently, many states have struggled to sustain and expand their SOC approach after the federal funding period (Stroul & Manteuffel, 2007). The most recent federal report of the CMHI grants for SOCs found that by the end of the four-year grant period, only 60% of services were determined to be sustainable (SAMHSA, 2020). Few states are able to support child mental health services with state dollars that are not also attached to federal Medicaid funds, which limits the types of services that can be offered and restricts access for children not covered by Medicaid.

Unfortunately, state spending limits for Medicaid and expansion initiatives for mental health services are frequently in conflict. Although federal Medicaid policies have become more flexible over the past years, most state policies on Medicaid spending have become increasingly restrictive. Because Medicaid spending has been the highest growth factor in most states' budgets, state-level Medicaid policies are frequently focused on cost containment, especially in times of economic downturn or recession. In turn, the state mental health departments try to stretch their limited funds by matching state appropriations to federal Medicaid funds in categories of allowable expenses to maximize the federal match and the federal dollars. Unfortunately, the current Medicaid program has inherent limitations and barriers related to supporting SOC structures.

# THE FORT BRAGG STUDY

During the early 1990s, the Department of Defense and NIMH funded a major research study to test the impact of developing comprehensive and coordinated continuums of care for youth with SED at Fort Bragg, North Carolina. The demonstration program sought to fill the service gap between outpatient therapy and inpatient hospitalization by providing non-clinic–based services such as in-home crisis stabilization, afterschool group treatment, therapeutic foster care, and crisis management.

The Fort Bragg study demonstrated substantial system improvements, including increased service capacity, enhanced collaboration among service agencies, and reduced use of hospitals and residential treatment facilities. However, as described earlier in this chapter, the demonstration program did not produce significant clinical outcomes with regard to alleviation of symptoms, increased functioning, or reduction of impairments (Bickman et al., 1995). The findings of the Fort Bragg project were in line with the evaluation results of the Robert Wood Johnson Foundation Mental Health Services Program for Youth, which examined the development of SOCs in eight communities over a 10-year period (Cross & Saxe, 1997; Johnsen et al., 1996).

These disappointing findings initiated an ongoing debate in the child mental health field. Some researchers have advocated for a change in policy emphasis from system development to service effectiveness (Salzer & Bickman, 1997), whereas others continued to support large systems reforms (Hernandez & Hodges, 2003). Recent policy discourse has suggested requiring simultaneous system reform and the delivery of evidence-based interventions (Burns, 2001; Rosenblatt & Woodbridge, 2003). Although the risk and resilience framework for targeting interventions is not yet widely used within the mental health field, many policy leaders and advocates are focusing attention on identifying and using evidence-based practices that will provide cost-effective client-level improvements.

## THE RISK, PROTECTION, AND RESILIENCE FRAMEWORK AND MENTAL HEALTH POLICY

The risk, protection, and resilience perspective provides a promising new framework in which to develop new mental health policies as it offers a valuable cross-problem, multidisciplinary approach for individually tailored interventions within an integrated SOC. Although it is not yet used widely within the mental health field, there are several good examples of its potential benefit. The Ventura County System of Care (Box 5.2) and the Willie M. Program (Box 5.1) will be described here as case examples. The Willie M. Program, which grew out of a class action lawsuit, provides a good example of using the risk and resilience framework to individualize care. The Ventura County System of Care was enacted by state statute and required its county agencies to work together. Ventura County's success in providing integrated services to SED youth led to statewide legislation supporting SOCs and has opened the door for multiagency prevention and early intervention approaches targeted at children and youth at risk for mental health problems.

## Program and Case Example

### The Willie M. Program

BOX 5.1

The Willie M. Program grew out of a class action lawsuit (*Willie M. et al. v. James B. Hunt Jr. et al.*, 1980) filed against the State of North Carolina on behalf of children with severe emotional disturbances (SEDs) and aggressive behavior who were institutionalized because of inadequate community-based care. Seeing the negotiations to settle the lawsuit as an opportunity to improve the service structure, administrators in the North Carolina Division of Mental Health, Developmental Disabilities, and Substance Abuse Services (MH/DD/SAS) created a comprehensive continuum of community-based care for high-risk and hard-to-manage children and adolescents with SED.

To be represented and served under the class action suit, youths had to meet criteria as a class member: be younger than 18 years old; have a serious emotional, mental, or neurological disorder; have a history of violent or chronically aggressive behavior; have been placed in public custody, such as institutions, or be at risk of such placement; or have been denied access to needed treatment or educational services. Although many youths met the criteria, four youths were ultimately named as plaintiffs in the litigation. Willie M., the first of four plaintiffs, was an 11-year-old boy diagnosed as emotionally disturbed with unsocialized aggression.

The North Carolina Department of Human Services avoided a trial by agreeing to the court's complaints and demands. Each member of the class was guaranteed individualized treatment in the least restrictive setting possible. The treatment was to be based on the child's needs rather than the availability of service providers to provide a service or set of services. If needed services did not exist, such services were to be created.

Leaders within the Division of MH/DD/SAS welcomed the challenge and advocated for the development of local systems of care (SOCs) within which they could create and provide services to class members. The Willie M. Program became among the first model SOCs in the country, serving as many as 1,500 severely aggressive youth with SED a year; two thirds of them lived in specialized foster care or group homes. The SOC required cooperative arrangements among the multiple agencies serving these youth. Court officers monitored the interagency relationships, making sure that public education, child welfare, and juvenile justice personnel worked in concert with the division of MH/DD/SAS on behalf of these children. Comprehensive case management, also called *wraparound case management*, was the primary tool used to tailor services to the individual needs of members of the class action lawsuit. Each class member was required to have an individual habilitation plan. Beginning in 1995, the individual habilitation plan was based on an assessment process that reviewed both risk and protective factors.

An Assessment and Outcomes Instrument (AOI) was created to assess and to measure the progress of children in the Willie M. Program. The instrument used a risk and protective factor perspective and measured both fixed characteristics (i.e., factors that could not be changed through intervention, such as the loss of a parent) and dynamic characteristics (i.e., factors that were malleable in treatment, such as school performance). Risk factors included family-level characteristics (e.g., living in poverty, parental loss, parental mental health and substance abuse problems, parental criminality, and large family size) and individual-level

*(Continued)*

(Continued)

characteristics (e.g., fetal substance exposure, neurologic or developmental disorders, poor mother–infant attachment, difficult or shy early temperament, witness to violent acts, history of physical and sexual abuse, school failure, and delinquent behavior). Of the possible 30 risk factors assessed by the AOI, each of the *Willie M.* class members had experienced an average of 13 risk factors—a number that far exceeds most definitions of a high-risk youth (e.g., Rutter, 1979). Consistent with the literature on risk and conduct disorders, most *Willie M.* class members with poor behavioral outcomes had histories of negative parent–child interactions and poor academic performance. Better behavioral outcomes were predicted by protective factors such as having good skills in areas such as problem solving, interpersonal relationships, and reading; having social support networks available, including involvement with family members and prosocial peers; and having a parent who was consistently employed (Vance et al., 2002).

Each member's individual rehabilitation plan specified interventions that were likely to result in positive behavioral changes. Because most risk factors associated with *Willie M.* class members were fixed historical experiences and family features that were not amenable to change, few options were available that would reduce the impact of those risk factors on current behaviors. However, evaluations of the Willie M. Program found that strengthening protective factors was directly associated with improved behavioral outcomes (Bowen & Flora,

2002; Vance et al., 2002). Depending on individual needs, protective factors such as reading skills, relationships with adults, social skills, positive beliefs and attitudes, and involvement in community activities were strengthened through a variety of targeted interventions. In addition, parental and caretaker positive discipline skills were strengthened. The protective factors that were found to be strongly associated with behavioral improvement included increased levels of home and school social skills. Interventions targeting these factors included teaching skills in anger management, empathy development, and making and keeping friends (Bowen & Flora, 2002). Because of these positive behavioral changes, youth served in the Willie M. Program attended school more often and had fewer arrests. Class member and family satisfaction with services was high. As an individualized SOC was successfully developed, the *Willie M.* class action lawsuit was resolved in 2000.

The Willie M. Program in North Carolina was both successful and expensive. The court demanded the provision of needed services, regardless of cost. Many state legislators resented this open-checkbook approach. As costs went up for class members' services, appropriations to other parts of the mental health system declined or were not increased accordingly. Once the class action lawsuit was resolved and its mandates removed, funding for the Willie M. Program was reduced and realigned within the division of MH/DD/SAS.

## BOX 5.2

## Ventura County System of Care

In 1985, the California State Legislature passed a landmark bill (Assembly Bill [AB] 3920)

authorizing a demonstration program to integrate mental health services across a core group of service systems, including child welfare, public education, and juvenile justice. The legislation provided for creation of a comprehensive, coordinated system of care (SOC) and facilitated interagency cooperation by integrating numerous federal and state statutes that addressed public mental health services for children and by amending various statutes and regulations. Ventura County was selected as one of three demonstration sites under AB 3920. As part of the demonstration program, all child-serving agencies in Ventura County were required to engage in interagency planning and to develop interagency protocols and agreements that emphasized providing services to children in their homes or in the least restrictive setting.

The Ventura County System of Care had five interdependent components as outlined in the enabling legislation: (a) a clearly defined target population, (b) a systemwide goal to preserve family unity and locally based treatment, (c) a commitment to developing collaborative programs of services and standards tailored to individual needs of children and their families, (d) a continuum of service options and settings that cross agency boundaries, and (e) a mechanism for system evaluation.

Client outcomes for the Ventura County System of Care reflected a cross-agency perspective. The overarching goal was for children with serious emotional disturbances to remain or to be reunified with their families, to attend and progress in public schools, and—as appropriate—to desist from problem behavior such as delinquency and drug use. A cross-agency target population experiencing serious emotional disturbance (SED) was identified, including populations within each agency that had been mandated for services. The target population included emotionally or behaviorally disordered youth, such as (a) court dependents whose histories included neglect, physical or sexual abuse, multiple foster home placements,

residential treatment, and psychiatric hospitalization; (b) court wards for whom the public sector had legal responsibility because of delinquent behavior and who were at risk of out-of-home placement; (c) special education pupils who required mental health services to benefit from their Individualized Education Program; and (d) children who were not part of a formal agency other than mental health and who were at risk of out-of-home placement to state hospitals or residential treatment.

Mental health treatment was integrated into the service systems of the other major child-serving public agencies. The county mental health department was given responsibility for serving the mental health needs of the targeted children involved in the public school, child welfare, and juvenile justice systems. Mental health staff located their services in places where targeted children lived and went to school, a step that required reorganization of the department of mental health. Most of the mental health staff was deployed to agency and school settings to provide or supervise mental health services in those settings. Depending on the needs of the agency, mental health staff provided consultation, assessments, case management, counseling, day treatment, special day classes, in-home care, family therapy, enriched foster-home care services, or crisis intervention.

The state legislation that created the demonstration project also facilitated the blending of categorical funds so that each agency domain was enabled to determine the array of mental health services it needed. Specific roles and relationships between agencies were delineated in interagency agreements and facilitated by a number of interagency coordinating mechanisms. An interagency juvenile justice council became the policy-making body of the county system. This policy-making body was created to serve as a vehicle for identifying problems, developing interagency solutions, and working through agency conflicts.

*(Continued)*

(Continued)

The council's permanent members included the county counselor, the public defender, the district attorney, the sheriff, the chief administrative officer of the juvenile court, the director of probation, a member of the board of supervisors, the superintendent of schools, the director of the department of child welfare, and the director of the department of mental health. Still in operation today, the council reviews all agency budgets and looks for ways to mingle and coordinate funding streams.

The Ventura County demonstration project met the system-level performance outcomes required by the statute. By integrating mental health services into each system, more children were served—especially children from ethnic minority backgrounds—and fewer youth required placement in restrictive and costly state hospitals or residential treatment centers. The project netted a substantial savings to the state. The demonstration program was expanded to more counties in 1989. In 1992, the California State Legislature enacted the Children's Mental Health Services Act, which expanded the SOC model to all counties. In 2001, the legislature enacted a law requiring an agency-integrated SOC statewide (Stortz, 2003).

California can be a beacon for other states. Its formal adoption of SOC principles and policies in statutes has provided fiscal incentives for many local county collaborations. The state's shift to the rehabilitative option for federal Medicaid billing has allowed clinical staff to work outside of their offices and support field-based, in-home, and wraparound service delivery models. A state match to the federal Early and Periodic Screening, Diagnostic, and Treatment (EPSDT) program has provided an important fiscal engine to expand and sustain services and supports to children and youth 0 to 21 years old. Most recently, the California Mental Health Services Act (Proposition 63), enacted in 2007, has provided additional and ongoing state funds to further transform the mental health system in California with increased funding for mental health promotion, prevention, and early intervention services to children and adolescents statewide (Hodges et al., 2007).

## Criticisms of Child Mental Health Policies

Child mental health policies in the U.S. have been widely criticized over the past 50 years. The mental health services and programs resulting from these policies have been described as fragmented, spotty, nontargeted, and generally ineffective (Joint Commission on the Mental Health of Children, 1969; Knitzer, 1982; Lourie & Hernandez, 2003; President's Commission on Mental Health, 1978). In response to this criticism, Congress supported the creation of SOCs to coordinate and enhance mental health care to youth with SED. Private funding sources, such as the Robert Wood Johnson and Annie E. Casey foundations, also contributed millions of dollars to develop model SOCs across the country. Unfortunately, the evaluations of many of these model programs have produced only mixed results.

Although supportive of the SOC concept, child mental health advocacy groups such as the Federation of Families for Children's Mental Health and the Child and

Adolescent Network (a branch of the National Alliance for the Mentally Ill) remain frustrated by and critical of the slow process of implementation. These advocacy groups have not seen policy rhetoric translated into significant changes at the child or family level. Their criticisms were echoed in both the Surgeon General's (2000) national action agenda and the report of the President's New Freedom Commission on Mental Health (2003). The Surgeon General (2000) stated that despite the existence of mental health programs in many communities, the nation lacked a basic infrastructure for adequate mental health care and that "unmet need for services remains as high today as it was 20 years ago" (p. 13).

Two years after the Surgeon General's report, President Bush signed Executive Order 13263 establishing the President's New Freedom Commission on Mental Health. The executive order charged the commission with the responsibility of conducting a comprehensive study of the problems and gaps in the nation's mental health service system. In his cover letter to the President's New Freedom Commission on Mental Health (2003) final report, Michael Hogan, chair of the commission, wrote,

> Today's mental health care system is a patchwork relic—the result of
> disjointed reforms and policies. Instead of ready access to quality care,
> the system presents barriers that all too often add to the burden of mental
> illnesses for individuals, their families, and our communities. (p. 1)

# TRANSFORMATION OF THE MENTAL HEALTH SYSTEM

As a way to address these gaps and fundamentally transform how mental health care is delivered in America, the New Freedom Commission on Mental Health's report recommended a public health model of mental health care that would support mental health promotion and early intervention efforts as well as direct treatment services that have demonstrated efficacy. SAMHSA followed up on the commission's report by creating a Federal Mental Health Action Agenda and inviting key federal agencies to help propose a set of action steps to address the commission's vision and to move its agenda forward (SAMHSA, 2005). The key federal agencies contributing to this agenda of action steps included the departments of Education, Housing and Urban Development, Justice, Labor, and Veterans' Affairs, all the divisions within the Department of Health and Human Services, and the Social Security Administration. Transforming payment models is a critical step in reforming the SOC to prevent these new reforms from experiencing the same problems as the SOCs have had with sustaining services.

Regardless of how smoothly a SOC functions, if the interventions that are being applied are ineffective, then children and youth will not experience improvements in functioning. An increased focus on quality and efficacy of care has led to increased attention on evidence-based programs (EBPs). These are programs or specified practices that have been assessed through rigorous research processes to determine if they result in significant improvements to patients. The determination of an EBP is usually made by a clearinghouse that has the capacity to assess the research methods that were used and to categorize the programs into evidentiary categories to facilitate comparisons across programs. The evaluation criteria and the names of EBP categories (i.e., evidence-based, evidence-informed, promising) vary across clearinghouses. Some commonly used clearinghouses are the California Evidence-Based Clearinghouse for Child Welfare (CEBC) and the Results First Clearinghouse Database housed by The Pew Charitable Trust. The Title IV-E Prevention Services Clearinghouse is recent as of the writing of this chapter, but because it identifies programs that are eligible for reimbursement under the 2018 Family First Prevention Services Act, it is likely to become influential in future service delivery.

## Transforming Mental Health in Early Childhood

An increased focus on prevention is a key part of a functioning mental health system and utilizes the public health approach to mental health. Because a child's early experience lays the foundation for lifelong mental health, there has been more focus on the experiences children have in early childhood. A key element of the current mental health system has been an increased focus on promoting mental health starting in early childhood. This focus is supported by research on attachment, which identifies secure early attachment as a positive foundation for later social-emotional development and brain development. In particular, the plasticity and vulnerability of children's brains makes early childhood an important time for promotive and positive interventions. Additionally, improving the parent–child relationship is amenable to evidence-based interventions. Many of these interventions will also support children's later social-emotional development. There are several examples of ways to develop and expand federal policy based on compelling evidence from rigorous longitudinal research.

Home visiting has been used successfully as a public health strategy for over a century to help pregnant women and new parents in their roles as caregivers and families with young children to cope with the challenges of early childhood. Many countries have universal home visiting programs in which every family receives at least one visit in the home environment to check in, answer questions, and provide referrals. Although the U.S. does not offer universal home visiting, the most rigorous research demonstrating the impact of home visiting on a broad range of outcomes, including child development, was generated from programs implemented in the U.S. Although services for home visiting are expanding, one national estimate suggests that 23 million children could potentially benefit from home visiting and only about 300,000 currently receive evidence-based home visiting services (National Home Visiting Resource Center, 2019).

Building on research findings from specific models (e.g., Dozier et al., 2008; Olds, 2013), comprehensive evidence reviews (e.g., Mathematica, 2020), and the growing literature demonstrating the need for primary prevention strategies beginning at birth, advocates successfully pushed for a federal investment in home visiting. Since 2010, the MIECHV program authorized by the Patient Protection and Affordable Care Act has been providing funding to serve families through state grants for home visiting services. To ensure that tested programs are implemented, there are specific requirements for the evidence required for a home visiting model to be approved for use in the MIECHV program. The MIECHV program was reauthorized in 2018 for funding through 2022.

Notwithstanding, home visiting alone is not sufficient to promote healthy child development. A comprehensive set of services and support for all parents is needed. The challenge of the early childhood system will be to develop strategies to ensure that the right program reaches the right family at the right time and to create communities that are more supportive of children and families, thus reducing the number of children who need services. The CDC developed a strategy known as Essentials for Childhood. The program provides a roadmap for states and communities to cultivate "safe, stable, and nurturing relationships and environments" for children. While a major focus is on the prevention of child abuse and neglect, both of which are risk factors for child mental health disorders, promoting positive relationships and environments is a shared strategy for enhancing protective factors for child mental health. The Essentials for Childhood strategies focus on changing social norms and public policies to reflect the importance of healthy child development using the best available information.

Early childhood systems could also benefit from improved integration across agencies to remove service silos. For example, the child welfare system is mandated by law to ensure the well-being of children in care. However, despite being heavy users of mental health services, outcomes for children in foster care consistently fall well behind those of other children, particularly in areas of mental health. This issue has recently received attention from policymakers and has sparked an explicit focus on promoting child socioemotional well-being for child welfare systems. Recent policies for child welfare–involved children have included provisions requiring certain services to be trauma-informed and limiting the use of psychotropic medication for children and youth in foster care. These are positive steps toward a higher quality of care for these children and youth.

The childcare setting is another sector of early childhood policy that can have an impact on children's emotional development. Some of the strongest research demonstrating the return on investment for early childhood comes from enhanced childcare programs such as the Chicago Child–Parent Centers and the Perry Preschool Project (Temple & Reynolds, 2007). While childcare programs focus primarily on school readiness, research is demonstrating that socioemotional skill development, and not only the traditional academic focus on building intellectual knowledge, may be the key to improving later outcomes for disadvantaged populations. Federal childcare settings such as those provided by Head Start are critical to the development of the social skills and emotional regulation needed to succeed in school.

## Transforming Mental Health Care Through the Affordable Care Act

Now a decade into implementation, transformation of the mental health system at the national level has been driven largely by the implementation of the ACA. States have a great deal of discretion in reforming their health care systems, so there has been significant variation in how the law is interpreted. However, we highlight three themes that have improved the accessibility and quality of services for children: the parity of physical and mental health, the focus on prevention and early intervention, and the integration of physical and behavioral health care. *Behavioral health care* includes a range of prevention and treatment services related to mental health and substance abuse.

Under the ACA, all benchmark insurance plans must provide a set of "essential health benefits." Pediatric care and behavioral health services are examples of this class of services that must be covered in all plans. Furthermore, the ACA mandates full parity for mental health and substance abuse services with physical health services. Building on the progress of the Mental Health Parity and Addiction Equity Act of 2008, the ACA expanded mental health parity to individual health insurance coverage. *Parity* means that mental health services cannot have higher costs (i.e., copays) or different coverage limits compared with physical health services in the same plan. This aspect of the law attempts to lower barriers to mental health services related to out-of-pocket costs or limitations in certain insurance plans. Advocates have been fighting for mental health parity for years, and prior successes laid the groundwork for guaranteeing its inclusion in the ACA.

An overarching theme of the ACA is prevention. Although much of the focus is targeted at costly preventable physical health outcomes, there is also a clear emphasis on early detection of mental health problems in children and expansion of evidence-based preventive interventions. Mental and emotional well-being is listed as one of seven priority areas in the first National Prevention Strategy. The first recommendation in this priority area is to "promote positive early childhood development, including positive parenting and violence-free homes." Also outlined in the ACA are appropriations for mental health screening that have been directed to support the expansion of behavioral health services in federally qualified health centers. Screening for child depression in primary care centers is one of a fairly short list of federally endorsed preventive services. Many preventive services that will now be offered to parents may also have an indirect impact on preventing child mental health problems by targeting the risk factors discussed earlier. For example, women's preventive services, including domestic violence screening, are provided with no copay.

The details of how service-integration strategies will be implemented are still evolving. However, the basic idea is that the delivery system for health services, including mental health services, should be easier for patients to access, with less duplication and complexity in the system. This benefits patients but also should make the health care system more efficient and reduce unnecessary cost. One strategy will be to shift the financing structure away from a fee-for-service, volume-driven algorithm to an outcomes-driven algorithm. Providers delivering different types of services to the same pool of patients will have an incentive to work together through some arrangement such as an accountable care organization or health home. It makes sense to have clinical social workers, pediatricians, school nurses, and others on the same page regarding the care plans of children and, administratively, to have a shared incentive to produce better child-centered outcomes.

Integration of behavioral health into primary care is also a core strategy of another major federal program. Project LAUNCH (Linking Actions for Unmet Needs in Children's Health), funded by SAMHSA, focuses on children (up to 8 years of age) and provides five-year grants to communities to improve service delivery for children's mental health. There are many exciting and innovative examples of communities bringing child mental health into the primary care office. This program also supports mental health consultation in childcare settings and enhanced home visiting services that target child socioemotional development. Service coordination for child mental health has been attempted in prior SOC efforts with mixed success. It remains to be seen how integration with primary-care systems will affect access to high-quality mental health care and service coordination for all children.

## SUMMARY

In 2008, the National Center for Children in Poverty published a study as a 25-year follow-up to Jane Knitzer's (1982) heralded report, *Unclaimed Children: The Failure of Public Responsibility to Children in Need of Mental Health Services*. In the intervening years, although there has been an explosion of knowledge about the biological and social determinants of mental disorders in childhood and about the provision of preventive and treatment services, the report found that state policies and the SOCs in place for most troubled children and youth appear all too similar to those criticized 25 years earlier (Cooper et al., 2008).

This is not to say that there has been no change. The vast majority of states were found to have taken tangible steps to improve their mental health delivery systems for children. However, a closer analysis revealed that those changes, while promising, were often limited in scope and depth. Although all 50 states reported that they had incorporated SOC values and principles into their delivery systems, only 18 states had taken steps to sustain these efforts through legislation and regulation, practice standards, and strategic planning. Too few resources were expended for states to develop a workable, comprehensive policy framework for addressing the needs of children and youth with serious mental health conditions. Even fewer resources had been committed by states to implement service systems and/or integrate approaches grounded in the public health framework of mental health prevention, promotion, and early intervention (Cooper et al., 2008).

Much can be learned, however, from the Ventura County System of Care and the Willie M. Program case examples provided in this chapter. In addition, lessons about the effectiveness of mental health policies and programs can be derived from many other state and local efforts on behalf of children and adolescents with mental health problems. Based on these examples and a growing base of evidence-supported program, at least four core strategies for policy reform in child mental health should be considered:

1. Structures should be developed to integrate mental health services into key child-serving agencies, such as public education, child welfare, and juvenile justice.

2. Systematic assessment should identify malleable risk and protective and promotive factors.

3. Evidence-based interventions should be selected and provided to reduce risk and strengthen protective and promotive factors.

4. Services should be developmentally and culturally appropriate and sequenced sufficiently early in childhood to disrupt negative developmental trajectories.

The developmental timing of identifying and treating mental health disorders is critical and efforts are increasingly focused on moving these services to younger ages. Mental health disorders can often be identified in young children and adolescents (Kenny et al., 2002). Yet these disorders are often diagnosed and treated when youth are older, resulting in state legislatures spending millions of dollars annually treating older youth with serious emotional and behavioral disorders. Too often, these funds are expended in the juvenile justice and child welfare systems, which begs the question, "Are these efforts too little, too late?" Increasingly, many experts think this is the case.

In many communities, mental health services are now being integrated into public schools through programs such as school-based health clinics. These clinics improve access to primary health care and provide a less-stigmatized entry into mental health services for many youth (Wu et al., 2010). School-based health clinics provide preventive and early intervention screenings for many health conditions that inhibit learning. Regular screenings for emotional and behavioral problems can also be incorporated into clinic services.

For these reasons, schools may be the best public setting in which to identify troubled children and to link them with appropriate services. More than 50 million youth attend U.S. public schools (U.S. Department of Education, 2020). The integration of mental health and public school policies has the potential to save public money and private heartache by positioning resources to detect and treat mental

health problems before they become florid disorders. School-based health centers (SBHCs) continue to gain resonance with policymakers as a prevention-, promotion-, and treatment-oriented mental health initiative. The 2016–2017 count of SBHCs identified over 2,500 SBHCs in 48 of 50 states; Washington, DC; and Puerto Rico, doubling the number of SBHCs 20 years ago (Love et al., 2019).

SBHCs became a federally authorized program in the ACA, including $11 billion in federal funding; it was a historic victory to recognize them as part of the federally supported health care system. This historic health reform legislation allows eligible SBHCs to receive funds supporting management and operation of programs, salaries for health care professionals and other personnel, purchase or lease of equipment, construction projects, and training. However, the SBHC authorization will be a hollow victory unless it is followed by appropriations. Currently, only $200 million in capital improvements have been funded, with no federal financial support for the actual provision of mental health services in SBHCs. The bulk of funding to operate SBCHs come from state government budgets, estimated at $91 million in 2016–2017 (Love et al., 2019). Until funds are appropriated, only limited federal support exists for SBHC operations, leaving little hope for a substantial expansion of these services (Love et al., 2019; Sebelius, 2010).

Although there is still much work to do, this is an exciting time for child mental health policy. The coming years could yield an improvement in the availability of mental health services as federal policies and programs such as Project LAUNCH are implemented in states. The focus on prevention, screening, and early detection coupled with the broad dissemination of evidence-based interventions holds promise for a dramatic impact on the course of mental illness and the public health burden at a population level. As with any policy, the details of how these policies are implemented and the strategies for continued sustainability when federal funding and oversight are removed are critical to maintaining any progress. Ensuring adequate funding and the availability of a well-trained workforce are key challenges to overcome at the federal and state policy levels.

We now know a great deal about risk and protective factors for childhood mental health disorders. Arguably, the two most important findings are (1) that identifying, diagnosing, and treating high-risk children early may interrupt developmental trajectories that lead to poor outcomes in adolescence and adulthood and (2) that there are many extrafamilial factors that may be the most significant risks for causing mental disorders and are best addressed by broader policies. Policymakers and leaders across mental health, child welfare, public education, and juvenile justice systems should focus on coordinating efforts to prevent the development of mental health problems and to deliver effectives services to minimize poor outcomes.

## QUESTIONS FOR DISCUSSION

1. What child mental health policies and practices have inhibited the integration of mental health services into other child-serving systems such as juvenile justice and child welfare?

2. Are there reasons to keep child-serving agencies organizationally separate at the state level? What about at the local level?

3. Given what we know about risk factors for a variety of emotional and behavioral disorders, how can we combine mental health and public education resources to support prevention and early intervention strategies?

## REFERENCES

Ali, M. M., West, K., Teich, J. L., Lynch, S., Mutter, R., & Dubenitz, J. (2019). Utilization of mental health services in educational setting by adolescents in the United States. *Journal of School Health*, *89*(5), 393–401. https://doi.org/10.1111/josh.12753

Allen-Meares, P., & Fraser, M. W. (2004). *Intervention with children and adolescents: An interdisciplinary perspective*. Allyn & Bacon.

American Psychiatric Association (APA). (2000). *Diagnostic and statistical manual of mental disorders* (4th ed., text revision). Author.

American Psychiatric Association (APA). (2013). *Diagnostic and statistical manual of mental disorders* (5th ed.). Author.

Arcelus, J., Mitchell, A. J., Wales, J., & Nielsen, S. (2011). Mortality rates in patients with anorexia nervosa and other eating disorders: A meta-analysis of 36 studies. *Archives of General Psychiatry*, *68*(7), 724–731. https://doi.org/10.1001/archgenpsychiatry.2011.74

Armstrong, K. H., Dedrick, R. F., & Greenbaum, P. E. (2003). Factors associated with community adjustment in young adults with serious emotional disturbance: A longitudinal analysis. *Journal of Emotional and Behavioral Disorders*, *1*, 66–76. https://doi:10.1177/106342660301100201

Artiga, S., Hinton, E., Rudowitz, R., & Musumeci, M. (2017). Current flexibility in Medicaid: An overview of federal standards and state options. *San Francisco: Henry J. Kaiser Family Foundation*. https://www.kff.org/medicaid/issue-brief/current-flexibility-in-medicaid-an-overview-of-federal-standards-and-state-options/

Bailey, Z. D., Krieger, N., Agénor, M., Graves, J., Linos, N., & Bassett, M. T. (2017). Structural racism and health inequities in the USA: Evidence and interventions. *The Lancet*, 389(10077), 1453–1463. https://doi.org/10.1016/S0140-6736(17)30569-X

Behar, L. B. (2003). Mental health management environments: Children's mental health services—The challenge of changing policy and practice. In W. R. Reid & S. B. Silver (Eds.), *Handbook of mental health administration and management* (pp. 149–162). Brunner-Routledge.

Bickman, L. (1996). Implications for evaluators from the Fort Bragg evaluation. *Evaluation Practice*, 17(1), 57–74. https://doi.org/10.1016/S0886-1633(96)90039-2

Bickman, L., Guthrie, P. R., Foster, E. M., Lamber, E. W., Summerfelt, W. T., Breda, C. S., & Heflinger, C. A. (1995). *Evaluating managed mental health services: The Fort Bragg experiment*. Plenum.

Bickman, L., Heflinger, C. A., Lambert, E. W., & Summerfelt, W. T. (1996). The Fort Bragg managed care experiment: Short term impact on psychopathology. *Journal of Child and Family Studies*, 5(2), 137–160. https://doi.org/10.1007/BF02237936

Bowen, N. K., & Flora, D. B. (2002). When is it appropriate to focus on protection in interventions for adolescents? *American Journal of Orthopsychiatry*, 72, 526–538. https://doi:10.1037/0002-9432.72.4.526

Brauner, C. B., & Stephens, C. B. (2006). Estimating the prevalence of early childhood serious emotional/behavioral disorders: Challenges and recommendations. *Public Health Reports*, 121(3), 303–310. https://dx.doi.org/10.1177%2F003335490612100314

Breier, A., Kelsoe, J. R., Kirwin, P. D., Bellar, S. A., Wolkowitz, O. M., & Pickar, D. (1988). Early parental loss and development of adult psychopathology. *Archives of General Psychiatry*, 45, 987–993. https://doi.org/10.1001/archpsyc.1988.01800350021003

Brendenberg, N., Freidman, R., & Silver, S. (1990). The epidemiology of childhood psychiatric disorders: Prevalence findings from recent studies. *Journal of the American Academy of Child and Adolescent Psychiatry*, 29, 76–83. https://doi.org/10.1097/00004583-199001000-00013

Bronfenbrenner, U. (1979). *The ecology of human development: Experiments by nature and design*. Harvard University Press.

Brown, S. M., Doom, J. R., Lechuga-Peña, S., Watamura, S. E., & Koppels, T. (2020). Stress and parenting during the global COVID-19 pandemic. *Child Abuse & Neglect*, 104699. https://dx.doi.org/10.1016%2Fj.chiabu.2020.104699

Burns, B. J. (2001). Commentary on the special issue on the national evaluation of the Comprehensive Community Mental Health Services for Children and Their Families program. *Journal of Emotional and Behavioral Disorders*, 9, 71–76. https://doi:10.1177/106342660100900108

Burns, B. J., Costello, E. J., Angold, A., Tweed, D., Stangl, D., Farmer, E. M., & Erkanli, A. (1995). Children's mental health service use across service sectors. *Health Affairs*, 14, 147–159. https://doi:10.1377/hlthaff.14.3.147

Caspi, A., Taylor, A., Moffitt, T. E., & Plomin, R. (2000). Neighborhood deprivation affects children's mental health: Environmental risks identified in a genetic design. *Psychological Science*, 11(4), 338–342. https://doi.org/10.1111%2F1467-9280.00267

Center for Behavioral Health Statistics and Quality. (2016). *2014 National survey on drug use and health: DSM-5 Changes: Implications for child serious emotional disturbance* [unpublished internal documentation]. Substance Abuse and Mental Health Services Administration, Rockville, MD.

Center for Mental Health Services. (1999). *Annual report to Congress on the evaluation of the Comprehensive Community Mental Health Services for Children and Their Families Program*. ORC Macro.

Centers for Disease Control and Prevention (CDC). (2020, August). *What are childhood mental disorders?* https://www.cdc.gov/childrensmentalhealth/basics.html

Children's Defense Fund. (1995). *The state of America's children yearbook: 1995*. Author.

Chung, G., Chan, X., Lanier, P., & Ju, P. W. Y. (2020, June 25). *Associations between work-family balance, parenting stress, and marital conflicts during COVID-19 pandemic in Singapore*. https://doi.org/10.31219/osf.io/nz9s8

Commonwealth Fund, Commission on a High Performance Health System. (2006). *Why not the best? Results from a national scorecard on U.S. health system performance*. Author. http://www.commonwealthfund.org/Content/Publications/Fund-Reports/2006/Sep/Why-Not-the-Best-Results-from-a-National-Scorecard-on-U-S-Health-System-Performance.aspx

Cooper, J. L., Aratani, Y., Knitzer, J., Douglas-Hall A., Masi, R., Banghard, P., & Dababnah, S. (2008). *Unclaimed children revisited: The status of children's mental health policy in the United States*. The National Center for Children in Poverty.

Cooper, S. M., Brown, C., Metzger, I., Clinton, Y., & Guthrie, B. (2013). Racial discrimination and African American adolescents' adjustment: Gender variation in family and community social support, promotive and protective factors. *Journal of Child and Family Studies, 22*(1), 15–29. https://psycnet.apa.org/doi/10.1007/s10826-012-9608-y

Copeland, W. E., Keeler, G., Angold, A., & Costello, E. J. (2007). Traumatic events and posttraumatic stress in childhood. *Archives of General Psychiatry, 64*, 577–584. https://doi:10.1001/archpsyc.64.5.577

Costello, E. J., Mustillo, S., Erkanli, A., Keeler, G., & Angold, A. (2003). Prevalence and development of psychiatric disorders in childhood and adolescence. *Archives of General Psychiatry, 60*, 837–844. https://doi:10.1001/archpsyc.60.8.837

Cross, T. P., & Saxe, L. (1997). Many hands make mental health systems a reality: Lessons from the mental health services program for youth. In C. T. Nixon & D. A. Northrup (Eds.), *Children's mental health services: Research, policy, and evaluation* (pp. 45–72). SAGE.

Davis, M., Yelton, S., & Katz-Leavy, J. (1995). *State child and adolescent mental health: Administration, policies, and laws*. University of South Florida, Florida Mental Health Institute.

Davis, M., Yelton, S., Katz-Leavy, J., & Lourie, I. (1995). Unclaimed children revisited. *Journal of Mental Health Administration, 22*, 142–166. https://doi.org/10.7916/D8BR91XN

Douzinas, N., Fornari, V., Goodman, B., Sitnick, T., & Packman, L. (1994). Eating disorders and abuse. *Child Psychiatric Clinics of North America, 3*, 777–796. https://doi.org/10.1016/S1056-4993(18)30470-X

Dozier, M., Peloso, E., Lewis, E., Laurenceau, J. P., & Levine, S. (2008). Effects of an attachment-based intervention on the cortisol production of infants and toddlers in foster care. *Development and Psychopathology, 20*(3), 845–859. https://doi.org/10.1017/s0954579408000400

Dykman, R. A., McPherson, B., Ackerman, P. T., Newton, J. E., Mooney, D. M., Wherry, J., & Chaffin, M. (1997). Internalizing and externalizing characteristics of sexually and/or physically abused children. *Integrative Physiological & Behavioral Science, 32*, 62–74. https://doi:10.1007/BF02688614

Epstein, M. H., Cullinan, D., Quinn, K. P., & Cumblad, C. (1995). Personal, family, and service use characteristics of young people served by an interagency community-based system of care. *Journal of Emotional and Behavioral Disorders, 3*, 55–64. https://doi:10.1177/106342669500300107

Fairbank, J. A., Putnam, F. W., & Harris, W. W. (2007). The prevalence and impact of child traumatic stress. In M. J. Friedman, T. M Keane, & P. A. Resick (Eds.), *A handbook of PTSD: Science and practice* (pp. 229–251). Guilford Press.

Famularo, R., Kinscherff, R., & Fenton, T. (1992). Psychiatric diagnoses of maltreated children: Preliminary findings. *Journal of American Academy of Child and Adolescent Psychiatry, 31*, 863–867. https://doi.org/10.1097/00004583-199209000-00013

Felitti, V. J., Anda, R. F., Nordenberg, D., Williamson, D. F., Spitz, A. M., Edwards, V., Koss, M., & Marks, J. S. (1998). Relationship of childhood abuse and household dysfunction to many of the leading causes of death in adults: The Adverse Childhood Experiences (ACE) study. *American Journal of Preventive Medicine, 14*, 245–258. https://doi:10.1016/S0749-3797(98)00017-8

Fergusson, D. M., Horwood, L. J., & Lynsky, M. T. (1994). The childhoods of multiple problem adolescents: A 15-year longitudinal study. *Journal of Child Psychology and Psychiatry, 35*, 1123–1140. https://doi:10.1111/j.1469-7610.1994.tb01813.x

Finkelhor, D., Turner, H., Ormrod, R., & Hamby, S. L. (2009). Violence, abuse, and crime exposure in a national sample of children and youth. *Pediatrics, 124*(5), 1411–1423. https://doi.org/10.1542/peds.2009-0467

Flisher, A. J., Kramer, R. A., Hoven, C. W., Greenwald, S., Alegria, M., Bird, H. R., Canino, G., Connell, R., & Moore, R. E. (1997). Psychosocial characteristics of physically abused children and adolescents. *Journal of the American Academy of Child and Adolescent Psychiatry, 36*, 123–131. https://doi:10.1097/00004583-199701000-00026

Fortuna, L. R., Tolou-Shams, M., Robles-Ramamurthy, B., & Porche, M. V. (2020). Inequity and the disproportionate impact of COVID-19 on communities of color in the United States: The need for a trauma-informed social justice response. *Psychological Trauma: Theory, Research, Practice, and Policy, 12*(5), 443–445. https://doi.org/10.1037/tra0000889

Frank, R. G., Goldman, H. H., & Hogan, M. (2003). Medicaid and mental health: Be careful what you ask for.

*Health Affairs, 22*(1), 101–113. https://doi.org/10.1377/hlthaff.22.1.101

Fraser, M. W. (Ed.). (2004). *Risk and resilience in childhood: An ecological perspective* (2nd ed.). NASW Press.

Garmezy, N. (1993). Children in poverty: Resilience despite risk. *Psychiatry, 56,* 127–136. https://doi.org/10.1080/00332747.1993.11024627

Gaylord-Harden, N. K., & Cunningham, J. A. (2009). The impact of racial discrimination and coping strategies on internalizing symptoms in African American youth. *Journal of Youth and Adolescence, 38*(4), 532–543. https://doi.org/10.1007/s10964-008-9377-5

Gerrity, E., & Folcarelli, C. (2008). *Child traumatic stress: What every policymaker should know.* National Center for Child Trauma Stress.

Gilbert, C. (2004). Childhood depression: A risk factor perspective. In M. W. Fraser (Ed.), *Risk and resilience in childhood: An ecological perspective* (2nd ed., pp. 315–346). NASW Press.

Goodman, R., & Stevenson, J. (1989). A twin study of hyperactivity—II. The etiological role of genes, family relationships and perinatal adversity. *Journal of Child Psychology and Psychiatry, 30,* 691–709. https://doi:10.1111/j.1469-7610.1989.tb00782.x

Goodman, S. H., Rouse, M. H., Connell, A. M., Broth, M. R., Hall, C. M., & Heyward, D. (2011). Maternal depression and child psychopathology: A meta-analytic review. *Clinical Child and Family Psychology Review, 14*(1), 1–27. https://doi.org/10.1007/s10567-010-0080-1

Goodyer, I. (1990). *Life experiences, development, and childhood psychiatry.* John Wiley.

Goodyer, I. (2001). Life events: Their nature and effects. In I. M. Goodyer (Ed.), *The depressed child and adolescent* (2nd ed., pp. 204–232). Cambridge University Press.

Green, W. (1995). Family, peer, and self factors as predictors of male and female adolescent substance abuse at 9th and 12th grade. *Dissertation Abstracts International: Section B: Sciences and Engineering, 55,* 2771.

Greenbaum, P. E., Dedrick, R. F., Friedman, R., Kutash, K., Brown, E., Lardieri, S., & Pugh, A. (1996). National adolescent and child treatment study (NACTS): Outcomes for individuals with serious emotional and behavioral disturbance. *Journal of Emotional and Behavioral Disorders, 4,* 130–146. https://doi:10.1177/106342669600400301

Harrell, S. P. (2000). A multidimensional conceptualization of racism-related stress: Implications for the well-being of people of color. *American Journal of Orthopsychiatry, 70*(1), 42–57. https://doi.org/10.1037/h0087722

Hergenhahn, B. R. (2001). *An introduction to the history of psychology* (4th ed.). Wadsworth.

Hernandez, M., & Hodges, S. (2003). Building upon the theory of change for systems of care. *Journal of Emotional and Behavioral Disorders, 11,* 19–26. https://doi:10.1177/106342660301100104

Hodges, S., Ferreira, K., Israel, N., & Mazza, J. (2007). *Strategies for system of care development: Locally identified factors for system implementation* (Supplement to issue brief 2, Lessons from successful systems: Critical factors in system of care implementation). University of South Florida, Louis de la Parte Florida Mental Health Institute, Research and Training Center for Children's Mental Health.

Hodgkinson, S., Godoy, L., Beers, L. S., & Lewin, A. (2017). Improving mental health access for low-income children and families in the primary care setting. *Pediatrics, 139*(1), e20151175. https://doi.org/10.1542/peds.2015-1175

Hopper, K., & Wanderling, J. (2000). Revisiting the developed versus developing country distinction in course and outcome in schizophrenia: Results from IsoS, the WHO collaborative follow-up project. International study of schizophrenia. *Schizophrenia Bulletin, 26,* 835–846. https://doi.org/10.1093/oxfordjournals.schbul.a033498

Ioannidis, K., Askelund, A. D., Kievit, R. A., & Van Harmelen, A. L. (2020). The complex neurobiology of resilient functioning after childhood maltreatment. *BMC Medicine, 18*(1), 1–16. https://doi.org/10.1186/s12916-020-01657-z

Institute of Medicine. (1994). *Reducing risks for mental disorders: Frontiers for preventive intervention research.* In P. J. Mrazek & R. J. Haggerty (Eds.), *Committee on Prevention of Mental Disorders, Division of Biobehavorial Sciences and Mental Disorders.* National Academy Press.

Jellinek, M., & Synder, J. (1998). Depression and suicide in children and adolescents. *Pediatrics in Review, 19,* 255–265. https://doi.org/10.1542/pir.36-7-299

Jenkins, E., & Bell, C. (1997). Exposure and response to community violence among children and adolescents. In J. Osofsky (Ed.), *Children in a violent society* (pp. 9–31). Guilford Press.

Jiang, S., Postovit, L., Cattaneo, A., Binder, E. B., & Aitchison, K. J. (2019). Epigenetic modifications in stress response genes associated with childhood trauma. *Frontiers in Psychiatry*, *10*, 808. https://dx.doi.org/10.3389%2Ffpsyt.2019.00808

Jiao, W. Y., Wang, L. N., Liu, J., Fang, S. F., Jiao, F. Y., Pettoello-Mantovani, M., & Somekh, E. (2020). Behavioral and emotional disorders in children during the COVID-19 epidemic. *The Journal of Pediatrics*, *221*, 264. https://doi.org/10.1016/j.jpeds.2020.03.013

Johnsen, M. C., Morrissey, J. P., & Calloway, M. O. (1996). Structure and change in child mental health service delivery networks. *Journal of Community Psychology*, *24*, 275–289. https://doi.org/10.1002/(SICI)1520-6629(199607)24:3%3C275::AID-JCOP7%3E3.0.CO;2-W

Johnson, J. G., Cohen, P., Kasen, S., Smailes, E., & Brook, J. S. (2001). Association of maladaptive parental behavior with psychiatric disorder among parents and their offspring. *Archives of General Psychiatry*, *58*, 453–460. https://doi:10.1001/archpsyc.58.5.453

Joint Commission on the Mental Health of Children. (1969). *Crisis in child mental health: Challenges for the 1970s*. Harper & Row.

Jones, K. (1999). *Taming the troublesome child: American families, child guidance, and the limits of psychiatric authority*. Harvard University Press.

Kagan, J., Snidman, N., & Arcus, D. (1998). Childhood derivatives of high and low reactivity in infancy. *Child Development*, *69*, 1483–1493. https://psycnet.apa.org/doi/10.2307/1132126

Kataoka, S. H., Zhang, L., & Wells, K. B. (2002). Unmet need for mental health care among US children: Variation by ethnicity and insurance status. *American Journal of Psychiatry*, *159*(9), 1548–1555. https://doi.org/10.1176/appi.ajp.159.9.1548

Kenny, H., Oliver, L., & Poppe, J. (2002). *Mental health services for children: An overview*. National Conference of State Legislatures.

Kessler, R. C. (1997). The effects of stressful life events on depression. *Annual Review of Psychology*, *48*, 191–214. https://10.1146/annurev.psych.48.1.191

Knitzer, J. (1982). *Unclaimed children*. Children's Defense Fund.

Lahey, B. B., Loeber, R., Hart, E. L., Frick, P. J., Applegate, B., Zhang, Q., Green, S. M., & Russo, M. F. (1995). Four-year longitudinal study of conduct disorder in boys: Patterns and predictors of persistence. *Journal of Abnormal Psychology*, *104*, 83–93. http://10.1037/0021–843X.104.1.83

Lanier, P., Maguire-Jack, K., Lombardi, B., Frey, J., & Rose, R. A. (2018). Adverse childhood experiences and child health outcomes: Comparing cumulative risk and latent class approaches. *Maternal and Child Health Journal*, *22*(3), 288–297. https://doi.org/10.1007/s10995-017-2365-1

Lee, S., & Ward, K. P. (2020). *Mental health, relationships, and coping during the coronavirus pandemic* (Research brief). Parenting in Context Research Lab, University of Michigan. https://www.parentingincontext.org/

Li, F., Green, J. G., Kessler, R. C., & Zaslavsky, A. M. (2010). Estimating prevalence of serious emotional disturbance in schools using a brief screening scale. *International Journal of Methods in Psychiatric Research*, *19*(S1), 88–98. https://doi.org/10.1002/mpr.315

Linver, M., Fuligni, A., Hernandez, M., & Brooks-Gunn, J. (2004). Poverty and child development: Promising interventions. In P. Allen-Meares & M. W. Fraser (Eds.), *Intervention with children and adolescents: An interdisciplinary perspective* (pp. 106–129). Allyn & Bacon.

Livingston, R., Lawson, L., & Jones, J. G. (1993). Predictors of self-reported psychopathology in children abused repeatedly by a parent. *Journal of the American Academy of Child and Adolescent Psychiatry*, *32*, 948–953. https://10.1097/00004583–199309000–00009

Loeber, R., Farrington, D. P., Stouthamer-Loeber, M., & Van Kammen, W. B. (1998). Multiple risk factors for multi-problem boys: Co-occurrence of delinquency, substance use, attention deficit, conduct problems, physical aggression, covert behavior, depressed mood, and shy/withdrawn behavior. In R. Jessor (Ed.), *New perspectives on adolescent risk behavior* (pp. 90–149). Cambridge University Press.

Loeber, R., & Stouthamer-Loeber, M. (1996). The development of offending. *Criminal Justice and Behaviour*, *23*, 12–24. http://10.1177/0093854896023001003

Lourie, I. S., & Hernandez, M. (2003). A historical perspective on national child mental health policy. *Journal of Emotional and Behavioral Disorders*, *2*, 5–9. http://10.1177/106342660301100102

Love, H. E., Schlitt, J., Soleimanpour, S., Panchal, N., & Behr, C. (2019). Twenty years of school-based health care growth and expansion. *Health Affairs*, *38*(5), 755–764. https://doi.org/10.1377/hlthaff.2018.05472

Lu, W., Mueser, K. T., Rosenberg, S. D., & Jankowski, M. K. (2008). Correlates of adverse childhood experiences among adults with severe mood disorders. *Psychiatric Services*, *59*, 1018–1026. https://10.1176/appi.ps.59.9.1018

Lucas, A. R., Beard, C. M., O'Fallon, W. M., & Kurland, L. T. (1991). 50-year trends in the incidence of anorexia nervosa in Rochester, MN: A population-based study. *American Journal of Psychiatry*, *148*, 917–922. https://doi .org/10.1176/ajp.148.7.917

Mark, T. L., & Buck, J. A. (2006). Characteristic of U.S. youth with serious mental disturbances: Data from the National Health Interview Study. *Psychiatric Services*, *57*, 1573–1578. https://10.1176/appi.ps.57.11.1573

Marshall, A. T., Betts, S., Kan, E. C., McConnell, R., Lanphear, B. P., & Sowell, E. R. (2020). Association of lead-exposure risk and family income with childhood brain outcomes. *Nature Medicine*, *26*(1), 91–97. https://doi .org/10.1038/s41591-019-0713-y

Martin, E. M., & Fry, R. C. (2018). Environmental influences on the epigenome: Exposure-associated DNA methylation in human populations. *Annual Review of Public Health*, *39*, 309–333. https://doi.org/10.1146/annurev-publhealth-040617-014629

Mathematica. (2020). *OPRE Report #2019-93: Home visiting evidence of effectiveness review.* https://homvee.acf.hhs .gov/publications/HomVEE-Summary

Maziade, M., & Raymond, V. (1995). The new genetics of schizophrenia. In C. L. Shriqui & H. A. Nasrallah (Eds.), *Contemporary issues in the treatment of schizophrenia* (pp. 61–79). American Psychiatric Press.

McGowan, P. O., & Szyf, M. (2010). The epigenetics of social adversity in early life: Implications for mental health outcomes. *Neurobiology of Disease*, *39*(1), 66–72. https://doi .org/10.1016/j.nbd.2009.12.026

McLaughlin, K. A., Green, J. G., Alegría, M., Jane Costello, E., Gruber, M. J., Sampson, N. A., & Kessler, R. C. (2012). Food insecurity and mental disorders in a national sample of US adolescents. *Journal of the American Academy of Child & Adolescent Psychiatry*, *51*(12), 1293–1303. https://doi .org/10.1016/j.jaac.2012.09.009

McLeod, J. D., & Shanahan, M. J. (1996). Poverty, parenting and children's mental health. *American Sociological Review*, *58*, 351–366. https://10.2307/2095905

Mears, D. P., & Aron, L. Y. (2003). Addressing the needs of youth with disabilities in the juvenile justice system: The current state of knowledge. *The Urban Institute.* http:// www.urban.org/UploadedPDF/410885_youth_with_ disabilities.pdf

Merikangas, K. R., He, J., Burstein, M., Swanson, S. A., Avenevoli, S., Cui, L., Benjet, C., Georgiades, K., & Swendsen, J. (2010). Lifetime prevalence of mental disorders in US adolescents: Results from the National Comorbidity Study-Adolescent Supplement (NCS-A). *Journal of the American Academy of Child and Adolescent Psychiatry*, *49*(10), 980–989. https://dx.doi.org/10.1016%2Fj .jaac.2010.05.017

Merrick, M. T., Ford, D. C., Ports, K. A., & Guinn, A. S. (2018). Prevalence of adverse childhood experiences from the 2011–2014 Behavioral Risk Factor Surveillance System in 23 states. *JAMA Pediatrics*, *172*(11), 1038–1044. https://10.1001/jamapediatrics.2018.2537

Moore, S. M., Rohde, P. L., Seeley, J. R., & Lewinsohn, P. M. (1999). Life events and depression in adolescence: Relationship loss as a prospective risk factor for first onset of major depressive disorder. *Journal of Abnormal Psychology*, *108*, 606–614. https://10.1037/0021–843X.108.4.606

National Home Visiting Resource Center. (2019). *2019 home visiting yearbook.* James Bell Associates and the Urban Institute.

National Research Council and Institute of Medicine. (2009). *Preventing mental, emotional, and behavioral disorders among young people: Progress and possibilities.* The National Academies Press.

National Survey of Children's Health (NSCH). (2017–2018). *National Survey of Children's Health 2017–2018 survey.* Data Resource Center for Child and Adolescent Health supported by the U.S. Department of Health and Human Services, Health Resources and Services Administration (HRSA), Maternal and Child Health Bureau (MCHB). http://www.childhealthdata.org/browse/survey

Nolen-Hoeksema, S., & Girgus, J. S. (1994). The emergence of gender differences in depression during adolescence. *Psychological Bulletin*, *115*, 424–443. https://10.1037/0033–2909.115.3.424

Olds, D. (2013). Moving toward evidence-based preventive interventions for children and families. In *C. Henry Kempe: A 50 year legacy to the field of child abuse and neglect* (pp. 165–173). Springer Netherlands.

Olds, D., Henderson, C. R., Jr., Cole, R., Eckenrode, J., Kitzman, H., Luckey, D., Pettitt, L., Sidora, K., Morris, P., & Powers, J. (1998). Long-term effects of nurse home visitation on children's criminal and antisocial behavior. *Journal of the American Medical Association, 280*, 1238–1244. https://10.1001/jama.280.14.1238

Osofsky, H. J., Osofsky, J. D., Kronenberg, M., Brennan, A., & Hansel, T. C. (2009). Posttraumatic stress symptoms in children after Hurricane Katrina: Predicting the need for mental health services. *American Journal of Orthopsychiatry, 79*(2), 212–220. https://doi.org/10.1037/a0016179

Oyserman, D. (2004). Depression during the school-aged years. In P. Allen-Meares & M. W. Fraser (Eds.), *Intervention with children and adolescents: An interdisciplinary perspective* (pp. 264–281). Allyn & Bacon.

Oyserman, D., Mowbray, C. T., Allen-Meares, P. A., & Firminger, K. B. (2000). Parenting among mothers with a serious mental illness. *American Journal of Orthopsychiatry, 70*, 296–315. https://10.1037/h0087733

Pagani, L., Boulerice, B., Tremblay, R. E., & Vitaro, F. (1997). Behavioral development in children of divorce and remarriage. *Journal of Child Psychology and Psychiatry, 38*, 769–781. https://10.1111/j.1469–7610.1997.tb01595.x

Parry-Jones, W. L. (1989). Annotation: The history of child and adolescent psychiatry: Its present day relevance. *Journal of Child Psychology and Psychiatry, 30*, 3–11. https://10.1111/j.1469–7610.1989.tb00766.x

Perou, R., Bitsko, R. H., Blumberg, S. J., Pastor, P., Ghandour, R. M., Gfroerer, J. C., Hedden, S. L., Crosby, A. E., Visser, S. N., Schieve, L. A., Parks, S. E., Hall, J. E., Brody, D., Simile, C. M., Thompson, W. W., Baio, J., Avenevoli, S., Kogan, M. D., & Huang, L. N. (2013). Mental health surveillance among children—United States, 2005–2011. *Morbidity and Mortality Weekly Report, 62*(02), 1–35.

Piquero, A. R., & Chung, H. L. (2001). On the relationships between gender, early onset, and the seriousness of offending. *Journal of Criminal Justice, 29*, 189–206. https://10.1016/S0047–2352(01)00084–8

President's Commission on Mental Health. (1978). *Report of the sub-task panel on infants, children and adolescents*. Government Printing Office.

President's New Freedom Commission on Mental Health. (2003). *Achieving the promise: Transforming mental health care in America* (Final report, DHHS Pub. No. SMA-03–3832). U.S. Department of Health and Human Services.

Putnam, F. W. (2006). The impact of trauma on child development. *Juvenile and Family Court Journal, 57*(1), 1–11. https://10.1111/j.1755–6988.2006.tb00110.x

Quinn, K. P., & Epstein, M. H. (1998). Characteristics of children, youth, and families serviced by local interagency systems of care. In M. H. Epstein, K. Kutash, & A. Duchowski (Eds.), *Outcomes for children and youth with emotional and behavioral disorders and their families: Programs and evaluation best practices* (pp. 81–114). PRO-ED.

Rauh, V. A., & Margolis, A. E. (2016). Research review: Environmental exposures, neurodevelopment, and child mental health—new paradigms for the study of brain and behavioral effects. *Journal of Child Psychology and Psychiatry, 57*(7), 775–793. https://doi.org/10.1111/jcpp.12537

Reskin, B. (2012). The race discrimination system. *Annual Review of Sociology, 38*, 17–35. https://doi.org/10.1146/annurev-soc-071811-145508

Resnick, G., & Burt, M. R. (1996). Youth at risk: Definitions and implications for service delivery. *American Journal of Orthopsychiatry, 66*, 172–188. https://10.1037/h0080169

Robins, L. N. (1991). Conduct disorder. *Journal of Child Psychology and Psychiatry and Allied Disciplines, 32*, 193–212. https://10.1111/j.1469–7610.1991.tb00008.x

Rogers, L., Resnick, M. D., Mitchel, J. E., & Blum, R. W. (1997). The relationship between socioeconomic status and eating disorders in a community sample of adolescent girls. *International Journal of Eating Disorders, 22*, 15–23. https://10.1002/(SICI)1098–108X(199707)22:1<15::AID-EAT2>3.0.CO;2–5

Rosenblatt, A., & Woodbridge, M. W. (2003). Deconstructing research on systems of care for youth with EBD: Frameworks for policy research. *Journal of Emotional and Behavior Disorders, 11*, 27–37. https://10.1177/106342660301100105

Ross, D. M., & Ross, S. A. (1982). *Hyperactivity: Current issues, research, and theory*. John Wiley.

Rutter, M. (1979). Protective factors in children's responses to stress and disadvantage. In M. W. Kent & J. E. Rolf (Eds.), *Primary prevention of psychopathology: Vol. 3. Social competence in children* (pp. 49–74). University Press of New England.

Rutter, M. (1985). Resilience in the face of adversity: Protective factors and resistance to psychiatric disorders. *British Journal of Psychiatry, 147,* 598–611. https://10.1192/bjp.147.6.598

Rutter, M., Silberg, J., O'Conner, T., & Simonoff, E. (1999). Genetics and child psychiatry: I. Advances in quantitative and molecular genetics. *Journal of Child Psychology and Psychiatry and Allied Disciplines, 40,* 3–18. https://10.1111/1469–7610.00422

Salzer, M., & Bickman, L. (1997). Delivering effective children's services in the community: Reconsidering the benefits of system interventions. *Applied & Preventive Psychology, 6,* 1–13. https://10.1016/S0962–1849(05)80062–9

Sameroff, A. J., Bartko, W. T., Baldwin, A., Baldwin, C., & Seifer, R. (1999). Family and social influences on the development of child competence. In M. Lewis & C. Feiring (Eds.), *Families, risk, and competence* (pp. 167–185). Lawrence Erlbaum.

Sameroff, A. J., & Gutman, L. M. (2004). Contributions of risk research to the design of successful interventions. In P. Allen-Meares & M. W. Fraser (Eds.), *Intervention with children and adolescents: An interdisciplinary perspective* (pp. 9–26). Allyn & Bacon.

Sanchez, A. L., Cornacchio, D., Poznanski, B., Golik, A. M., Chou, T., & Comer, J. S. (2018). The effectiveness of school-based mental health services for elementary-aged children: A meta-analysis. *Journal of the American Academy of Child & Adolescent Psychiatry, 57*(3), 153–165. https://doi.org/10.1016/j.jaac.2017.11.022

Santilli, J. S., & Beilenson, P. (1992). Risk factors for adolescent sexual behavior, fertility and sexually transmitted diseases. *Journal of School Health, 62,* 271–279. https://10.1111/j.1746–1561.1992.tb01243.x

Schowalter, J. E. (2003, September 1). A history of child and adolescent psychiatry in the United States. *Psychiatric Times, 20*(9). http://www.psychiatrictimes.com/display/article/10168/48051?pageNumber=1

Sebelius K. (2010, April 7). *Opening plenary remarks.* Presented at Coalition for Community Schools National Forum, Philadelphia, Pennsylvania, United States.

Sege, R., Bethell, C., Linkenbach, J., Jones, J., Klika, B., & Pecora, P. J. (2017). *Balancing adverse childhood experiences with HOPE: New insights into the role of positive experience on child and family development.* The Medical Foundation. http://www.cssp.org

Shaw, D. S., Gillion, M., Ingoldsby, E. M., & Nagin, D. (2003). Trajectories learning to school-age conduct problems. *Developmental Psychology, 39,* 189–200. https://10.1037/0012–1649.39.2.189

Silverman, A. B., Reinherz, H. Z., & Giaconia, R. M. (1996). The long-term sequelae of child and adolescent abuse: A longitudinal community study. *Child Abuse and Neglect, 20,* 709–723. https://10.1016/0145–2134(96)00059–2

Spearly, J., & Lauderdale, M. (1983). Community characteristics and ethnicity in the prediction of child maltreatment rates. *Child Abuse and Neglect, 7,* 91–105. https://10.1016/0145–2134(83)90036–4

Spirito, A., Bond. A., Kurkjian, J., Devost, L., Bosworth, T., & Brown, L. K. (1993). Gender differences among adolescent suicide attempters. *Crisis, 14,* 178–184.

Steiner, H., & Lock, L. (1998). Anorexia nervosa and bulimia nervosa in children and adolescents: A review of the past 10 years. *Journal of the American Academy of Child and Adolescent Psychiatry, 37,* 352–359. https://doi.org/10.1097/00004583-199804000-00011

Stice, E., & Agras, W. S. (1998). Predicting onset and cessation of bulimic behaviors during adolescence: A longitudinal grouping analysis. *Behavior Therapy, 29,* 257–276. https://10.1016/S0005–7894(98)80006–3

Stortz, M. (2003). *The tale of two settings: Institutional and community-based mental health services in California since realignment in 1991.* California Protection and Advocacy. http://www.disabilityrightsca.org/pubs/540301.pdf

Stroul B. A. (2006). *The sustainability of systems of care: Lessons learned. A report on the special study on the sustainability of systems of care.* ORC Macro.

Stroul, B. A., & Friedman, R. M. (1986). *A system of care for severely emotionally disturbed children and youth.* Georgetown University Center for Child and Human Development.

Stroul, B. A., & Friedman, R. M. (2011). *Issue brief: Strategies for expanding the system of care approach.* Technical Assistance Partnership for Child and Family Mental Health.

Stroul, B. A., & Manteuffel, B. A. (2007). The sustainability of systems of care for children's mental health: Lessons learned. *Journal of Behavioral Health Services and Research, 34,* 237–259. https://10.1007/s11414–007–9065–3

Substance Abuse and Mental Health Services Administration (SAMHSA). (2005). *Transforming mental health care in America: The federal action agenda: First steps*. Author.

Substance Abuse and Mental Health Services Administration (SAMHSA). (2020). *The comprehensive community mental health services for children with serious emotional disturbances program: 2017 report to congress*. Author. https://store.samhsa.gov/sites/default/files/d7/priv/cmhi-2017rtc.pdf

Substance Abuse and Mental Health Services Administration (SAMHSA). (2016). *DSM-5 changes: Implications for child serious emotional disturbance*. Author. https://www.ncbi.nlm.nih.gov/books/NBK519712/

Surgeon General. (1999). *Mental health: A report from the Surgeon General*. Department of Health and Human Services.

Surgeon General. (2000). *Report of the surgeon general's conference on children's mental health: A national action agenda*. Department of Health and Human Services.

Taylor, D. (2014). *Toxic communities: Environmental racism, industrial pollution, and residential mobility*. NYU Press.

Temple, J. A., & Reynolds, A. J. (2007). Benefits and costs of investments in preschool education: Evidence from the Child–Parent Centers and related programs. *Economics of Education Review, 26*(1), 126–144. https://doi.org/10.1016/j.econedurev.2005.11.004

Thompson, R., Litrownik, A. J., Isbell, P., Everson, M. D., English, D. J., Dubowitz, H., Proctor, L. J., & Flaherty, E. G. (2012). Adverse experiences and suicidal ideation in adolescence: Exploring the link using the LONGSCAN samples. *Psychology of Violence, 2*(2), 211. https://dx.doi.org/10.1037%2Fa0027107

Tiet, Q. Q., Bird, H. R., Hoven, C. W., Moore, R., Wu, P., Wicks, J., Jensen P., Goodman S., & Cohen, P. (2001). Relationship between specific adverse life events and psychiatric disorders. *Journal of Abnormal Child Psychology, 29*, 153–164. https://10.1023/A:1005288130494

Urdapilleta, O., Kim, G., Wang, Y., Howard, J., Varghese, R., Waterman, G., Busam, S., & Palmisano, C. (2013). *National evaluation of the Medicaid demonstration waiver home- and community-based alternatives to psychiatric residential treatment facilities: Final report*. IMPAQ International.

U.S. Bureau of Labor Statistics. (2020, September 8). Unemployment Rate (UNRATE). *FRED, Federal Reserve Bank of St. Louis*. https://fred.stlouisfed.org/series/UNRATE

U.S. Department of Education, National Center for Education Statistics. (2020). *Back to school statistics*. https://nces.ed.gov/fastfacts/

Vance, J. E., Bowen, N. K., Fernandez, G., & Thompson, S. (2002). Risk and protective factors as predictors of outcome in adolescents with psychiatric disorder and aggression. *Journal of the American Academy of Child & Adolescent Psychiatry, 41*, 36–43. https://10.1097/00004583-200201000-00009

Vinson, N. B., Brannan, A. M., Baughman, L. N., Wilce, M., & Gawron, T. (2001). The system-of-care model: Implementation in twenty-seven communities. *Journal of Emotional and Behavioral Disorders, 9*, 30–42. https://10.1177/106342660100900104

Wagner, M., Kutash, K., Duchnowski, A. J., Epstein, M. H., & Sumi, W. C. (2005). The children and youth we serve: A national picture of the characteristics of students with emotional disturbances receiving special education. *Journal of Emotional and Behavioral Disorders, 13*, 79–96. https://10.1177/10634266050130020201

Werner, E. E., & Smith, R. S. (1992). *Overcoming the odds: High risk children from birth to adulthood*. Cornell University Press.

Wickramaratne, P. J., & Weissman, M. M. (1998). Onset of psychopathology in offspring by developmental phase and parental depression. *Journal of the American Academy of Child and Adolescent Psychiatry, 37*, 933–942. https://10.1097/00004583-199809000-00013

Willie M. et al. v. James B. Hunt Jr. et al., Civil No. C-C-79-294-M (W.D. N.C. 1980).

Wilson, S., & Durbin, C. E. (2010). Effects of paternal depression on fathers' parenting behaviors: A meta-analytic review. *Clinical Psychology Review, 30*(2), 167–180. https://doi.org/10.1016/j.cpr.2009.10.007

Wolfe, D. A., Sas, L., & Wekerle, C. (1994). Factors associated with the development of posttraumatic stress disorder among child victims of sexual abuse. *Child Abuse and Neglect, 18*, 37–50. https://10.1016/0145-2134(94)90094-9

Wu, P., Katic, B. J., Liu, X., Fan, B., & Fuller, C. J. (2010). Mental health service use among suicidal adolescents: Findings from a U.S. national community survey. *Psychiatric Services, 61*, 17–24. https://10.1176/appi.ps.61.1.17

Zeanah, C. H., Carter, A. S., Cohen, J., Egger, H., Gleason, M. M., Keren, M., Lieberman, A., Mulrooney, K., & Oser, C. (2017). Introducing a new classification of early childhood disorders: DC: 0-5™. *ZERO TO THREE, 37*(3), 11–17.

ZERO TO THREE. (2016). *DC: 0-5: Diagnostic classification of mental health and developmental disorders of infancy and early childhood.* Author.

Zill, N., & West, J. (2001). *Entering kindergarten: A portrait of American children when they begin school: Findings from the Condition of Education 2000* (NCES 2001–035). Department of Education, Government Printing Office. http://files.eric.ed.gov/fulltext/ED448899.pdf

## ADDITIONAL READING

Burns, B. J., Phillips, S. D., Wagner, H. R., Barth, R. P., Kolko, D. J., Campbell, Y., & Landsverk, J. (2004). Mental health need and access to mental health services by youths involved with child welfare: A national survey. *Journal of the American Academy of Child & Adolescent Psychiatry, 43*(8), 960–970. https://doi.org/10.1097/01.chi.0000127590.95585.65

Costello, E. J., Angold, A., Burns, B. J., Stangl, D. K., Tweed, D. L., Erkanli, A., & Worthman, C. M. (1996). The Great Smoky Mountains Study of youth: Goals, design, methods, and the prevalence of *DSM-III-R* disorders. *Archives of General Psychiatry, 53*, 1129–1136. https://doi.org/10.1001/archpsyc.1996.01830120067012

National Alliance for the Mentally Ill. (2001). *Families on the brink: The impact of ignoring children with serious mental illness.* Author.

## WEB-BASED RESOURCES (GENERAL)

Bazelon Center for Mental Health Law: http://www.bazelon.org/

Mental Health America: http://www.nmha.org/

National Alliance on Mental Illness: http://www.nami.org/

National Federation of Families: http://www.ffcmh.org

National Institute of Mental Health: http://www.nimh.nih.gov/

Substance Abuse and Mental Health Services Administration: https://www.samhsa.gov/#

## WEB-BASED RESOURCES (EVIDENCE-BASED PRACTICES)

Association for Cognitive and Behavioral Therapies & Society of Clinical Child and Adolescent Psychology: https://effectivechildtherapy.org/

National Child Traumatic Stress Network: https://www.nctsn.org/

# 6

# HEALTH POLICIES AND PROGRAMS FOR CHILDREN AND YOUTH

William J. Hall, Hayden C. Dawes, Alexandria B. Forte, Luke E. Hirst, and Danny Mora

## PURPOSE AND GOALS OF HEALTH POLICIES FOR CHILDREN AND YOUTH

The World Health Organization (WHO) defines *health policies* as "decisions, plans, and actions that are undertaken to achieve specific health care goals within a society" (2020c). In the United States, the U.S. Department of Health and Human Services (HHS) is tasked with the goal of advancing the health of all Americans. Currently, the main goals of HHS (2018) regarding health care are to

- promote affordable health care;

- expand safe, high-quality health care options;

- improve access to health care and expand choices for care and services;

- strengthen and expand the health care workforce (e.g., physicians, nurses, dentists, pharmacists, psychologists, social workers);

- empower people to make informed choices for healthier living;

- prevent, treat, and control communicable diseases and chronic conditions;

- reduce the impact of mental and substance use disorders through prevention, early intervention, treatment, and recovery support; and

- prepare for and respond to public health emergencies.

Every 10 years, HHS develops measurable objectives for various health outcomes through the Healthy People initiative (HHS, 2020). The Healthy People objectives are developed to clearly communicate priority areas for health improvement to stakeholders at the national, state, and local levels. The objectives also allow for the monitoring of our nation's progress in reaching health goals. Although efforts to improve the health of Americans have historically focused on the health care system, more recently, there is increased attention on social determinants of health. The WHO (2020e) defines *social determinants of health* as "the conditions in which people are born, grow, work, live, and age, and the wider set of forces and systems shaping the conditions of daily life." Research increasingly shows that social factors (e.g., one's socioeconomic status, literacy level, housing stability, neighborhood safety, access to healthful food, social support systems, and exposure to stress) significantly influence individuals' health status, life expectancy, and quality of life (Braveman et al., 2011; Marmot & Wilkinson, 2005). Indeed, although the health care system plays a significant role in advancing population health, social determinants play a much larger role (Artiga & Hinton, 2018; Braveman & Gottlieb, 2014). Therefore, although this chapter primarily focuses on the health care system and health policies, we want to emphasize the importance of social determinants of health, including the social issues (e.g., poverty, education, violence, and child welfare) described in other chapters of this book.

Health policy is a complex policy domain that focuses on many issues, including medical treatment and preventive services, health insurance, health care financing, health education, provider cultural competency, and health equity. In this chapter, we will address many of these issues. We will present a historical overview of U.S. health policy pertaining to children, adolescents, and families; describe prominent health problems facing children and adolescents; discuss key health care system problems; recommend evidence-informed system changes to promote health for children, youth, and families; and provide illustrative examples of the integration of health care and other services for children and adolescents.

## HISTORICAL OVERVIEW OF CHILD HEALTH POLICY

Health policy for children and adolescents has developed in a piecemeal way, with policy initiatives often having been episodic responses to the failure of the private marketplace (Barr et al., 2003). Although the federal government was involved to some extent in responding to children's health needs through the establishment of the Children's Bureau in 1912 and then later through the establishment of the Maternal and Child Health service system, it did not become heavily involved in financing health care for children and youth until the establishment of the Medicaid program in 1965. Table 6.1 provides a chronological listing of major policy initiatives and their primary purposes.

At the turn of the 20th century, living conditions were so poor for many American families that the average state infant mortality rate was 150 per 1,000. In some industrial cities, it was as high as 180 per 1,000 (Margolis & Kotch, 2013). In response to this high infant mortality rate, social workers joined forces with public health workers and advocates from the fields of education, medicine, and labor to lobby for the passage of legislation to establish the Children's Bureau in 1912. The Children's Bureau was initially created with a mandate to study the problem of infant mortality and address the problem by disseminating information on promising interventions to the states. Based on the success of the Children's Bureau, Congress passed the Sheppard-Towner

Table 6.1 **Chronology of Key Child Health Policy Legislation, 1900 to 2020**

| Year | Legislation | Purpose |
|------|-------------|---------|
| 1912 | Children's Bureau established | Studied and began to address the high rates of infant mortality |
| 1921 | Sheppard-Towner Maternity and Infancy Act | Established the first national Maternal and Child Health program; provided grants-in-aid to states to develop local and state maternal and child health infrastructures |
| 1935 | Social Security Act, including Title V Maternal and Child Health program | Title V created a coordinated Maternal and Child Health service system based on a federal–state partnership |
| 1965 | Title XIX amendment to the Social Security Act | Established the Medicaid program to provide health insurance to children and families in poverty |
| 1981 | Omnibus Budget Reconciliation Act of 1981 (OBRA '81) Maternal and Child Health services block grant amendments to Title V | Shifted program planning, control, and accountability for Maternal and Child Health programs from federal to state and local governments |
| 1989 | Omnibus Budget Reconciliation Act (OBRA '89) | Established stricter reporting requirements for Title V and supported development of systems of care for children with special health care needs (CSHCN); expanded the Early and Periodic Screening, Diagnostic, and Treatment (EPSDT) program; mandated Medicaid coverage of children younger than 6 years with family income up to 133% of federal poverty level (FPL) |
| 1996 | Personal Responsibility and Work Opportunity Reconciliation Act (PRWORA) | Unlinked Medicaid eligibility and public assistance |
| 1997 | Title XXI, State Children's Health Insurance Program (SCHIP) established | Expanded the health insurance safety net to cover more low-income children who were not eligible for Medicaid and whose families could not afford private insurance |
| 2003 | Jobs and Growth Tax Relief Reconciliation Act | Raised all state Medicaid matching rates by 2.95 percentage points for the period of April 2003 through June 2004 as a temporary federal fiscal relief for the states due to the downturn of the economy, provided that the state maintains its Medicaid eligibility levels |
| 2006 | Deficit Reduction Act (DRA) of 2005 | Allowed states to impose cost-sharing for most services on children eligible for Medicaid on an "optional" basis (generally those with family incomes above 100% of the FPL); required all children and parents who apply for Medicaid and who claim to be U.S. citizens to document |

*(Continued)*

**Table 6.1** (Continued)

| Year | Legislation | Purpose |
|------|-------------|---------|
| | | their citizenship and identity (Medicare beneficiaries and most individuals with disabilities were exempted from this requirement); allowed states to offer disabled children under 19 with family incomes below 300% of FPL to purchase Medicaid coverage by paying income-related premiums |
| 2009 | Children's Health Insurance Program Reauthorization Act (CHIRPA) | Expanded Children's Health Insurance Program (CHIP) to an additional 4 million children; gave states the option to eliminate a five-year waiting period for legal immigrant children and pregnant women to be eligible for Medicaid and CHIP; rescinded the August 17 directive, which had restricted states' ability to cover children in families with income above 250% of the FPL |
| 2009 | American Recovery and Reinvestment Act (ARRA) | Provided enhanced Medicaid matching funds to states from October 1, 2008, through December 31, 2010, to help states maintain Medicaid eligibility levels and enrollment |
| 2010 | Patient Protection and Affordable Care Act (ACA) | Expanded health insurance coverage to 32 million people by 2019; prevented states from reducing income eligibility threshold for CHIP and maintained current income eligibility for children's Medicaid until 2019; regulated insurance companies to prevent insurers from dropping individuals when they become sick and denying coverage for preexisting conditions |
| 2015 | Medicare Access and CHIP Reauthorization Act | Reauthorized funding for CHIP through 2017 |
| 2017 | Tax Cuts and Jobs Act | Repealed the ACA individual mandate requiring Americans under 65 to have health insurance or pay a penalty |
| 2018 | Helping Ensure Access for Little Ones, Toddlers, and Hopeful Youth by Keeping Insurance Delivery Stable (HEALTHY KIDS) Act | Reauthorized funding for CHIP through 2023 |
| 2018 | Advancing Chronic Care, Extenders, and Social Services (ACCESS) Act | Extended funding for CHIP through 2027 and funding for the Maternal, Infant, and Early Childhood Home Visiting Program through 2022; renamed the Abstinence Education program and appropriated funding for it |
| 2020 | Consolidated Appropriations Act | Repealed taxes on high-cost employer-sponsored health coverage (i.e., "Cadillac" plans), excise taxes on medical devices and taxes applying to most health insurance companies |

Maternity and Infancy Act in 1921, creating the first national maternal and child health program that provided grants-in-aid to states. The Sheppard-Towner Act represented the first federal effort to establish a maternal and child health infrastructure within the states, and it laid the groundwork for future collaboration between state and federal governments to address maternal and child health (Kessel et al., 2003; Margolis & Kotch, 2013). During the eight years for which the act was in effect, the number of permanent maternal and child health centers and state child hygiene and welfare programs increased.

The Sheppard-Towner Act was not renewed in 1929, and the Great Depression had a major impact on the ability of states to provide maternal and child health services. These events contributed to an increase in infant mortality across the nation. In response to rising infant mortality rates and the widespread poverty among women and children, Title V of the Social Security Act was passed in 1935. Title V had three parts that were administered under the Children's Bureau: (1) maternal and child health (MCH) services enabled states to expand services that had been provided by the Sheppard-Towner Act; (2) the Services for Crippled Children's Program enabled states to locate and provide medical and other services for children who had "crippling conditions"; and (3) Child Welfare Services enabled states to provide services to homeless, dependent, and neglected children (Kessel et al., 2003). Title V funding through the Services for Crippled Children's Program was the only source of federal funding for CSHCN (the majority of whom needed orthopedic treatment as a result of the polio epidemic) until 1965, when the Medicaid program was established.

Title V has been amended numerous times over the past decades. The Omnibus Budget Reconciliation Act (OBRA '81) of 1981, Public Law (P.L.) 97-35, consolidated seven Title V categorical programs into a block grant program. The Omnibus Budget Reconciliation Act of 1989 (OBRA '89; P.L. 101-239), introduced stricter requirements for state planning and reporting regarding use of Title V funds. OBRA '89 gave authority to the MCH Bureau to help develop systems of care for CSHCN and their families and expanded the mission of related programs to promote the development of community-based systems of services (McPherson et al., 1998). State health departments administer the Title V MCH Services Block Grant Program (Maternal and Child Health Bureau, n. d.). The federal government requires states to conduct a statewide needs assessment every five years and to submit a plan for meeting those needs. Title V block grant funds are used primarily for service system development to reduce infant mortality and the incidence of disabilities and to provide and ensure access to health care for women of reproductive age; access to preventive and primary care services for children; and access to family-centered, community-based, coordinated care for CSHCN.

The Medicaid program was enacted in 1965 as a joint state and federally funded health insurance program for women who were on public assistance and their children and other persons who were older, blind, or disabled. Each state administers its own Medicaid program according to federal guidelines. The federal government provides matching funds for some of the state Medicaid costs (on average about 57% of costs are matched). In 1967, the Early and Periodic Screening, Diagnostic, and Treatment (EPSDT) program was created as a unique prevention component of the Medicaid program to ensure that children receiving Medicaid would receive preventive health services in addition to acute and chronic medical care (Sardell & Johnson, 1998). The EPSDT program requires states to offer age-appropriate screenings and immunizations, follow-up diagnostic services, and medical treatment. Because many states never fully implemented their EPSDT program, and to increase the number of children receiving preventive care, Congress included provisions in OBRA '89 that expanded the EPSDT program. The expanded provisions required states to conduct aggressive outreach and case-finding efforts as well as to provide enabling services such as case management, transportation, and translation services (Rosenbach & Gavin, 1998).

During the 1980s and 1990s, the rates of children and youth covered by private health insurance substantially declined. This decline was the result of several factors, including the loss of manufacturing jobs, which often offered employees and their families affordable health insurance, and the concomitant rise in lower-paying service jobs, which often did not offer employees health insurance. The proportion of workers who were hired to fill contract or part-time positions, which typically do not carry health insurance benefits for the workers or their families, also increased. In addition, during this period, the cost of health insurance for employers rose significantly, and many employers changed policies to cover only the employee and not the family (Moniz & Gorin, 2014).

To deal with the loss of private health insurance coverage and the resulting increase in uninsured children and youth, Congress passed a series of Medicaid expansions beginning in the mid-1980s. For example, the Omnibus Budget Reconciliation Act of 1989 (OBRA '89) required states to cover pregnant women and children up to the age of 6 years with family incomes that were up to 133% of federal poverty guidelines. The early expansions focused solely on infants and young children. Later, the Omnibus Budget Reconciliation Act of 1990 (OBRA '90) mandated coverage of adolescents up to 16 years of age with family incomes of as much as 100% of the federal poverty guidelines (Newacheck et al., 1999).

These Medicaid expansions began the "unlinking" of Medicaid and public assistance status. This unlinking process was finally completed in 1996 with the passage of the Personal Responsibility and Work Opportunity Reconciliation Act (PRWORA; Moniz & Gorin, 2014). PRWORA separated the determination of eligibility for Medicaid from receipt of public assistance, which was called Temporary Assistance for Needy Families (TANF). The federal government required states to provide Medicaid coverage for children up to the age of 5 years in families with incomes of as much as 133% of the poverty guidelines and to cover children from the ages of 6 to 19 years old in families with incomes at or below the federal poverty level (FPL).

The Balanced Budget Act of 1997 created the State Children's Health Insurance Program (SCHIP) to address the large number of uninsured children of low-income working families who were not eligible for Medicaid because their family income exceeded the eligibility criteria. Unlike Medicaid, SCHIP is not an entitlement program. Under federal legislation, states have been given tremendous flexibility to use SCHIP allocations to create separate SCHIP programs, expand their Medicaid programs, or develop a combination of both. States are also allowed to determine SCHIP eligibility; among the states, eligibility ranges from less than 200% to 400% of the federal poverty guidelines. State dollars are matched by federal dollars. States with lower per capita income receive a higher federal match rate. States are also allowed to require monthly premiums or copayments for participation in their SCHIP programs. In 2009, premiums were required by 35 states, with some premiums as high as $100 or more per month (Henry J. Kaiser Family Foundation, 2009). The success of SCHIP has been highly variable and largely dependent on each state conducting aggressive and effective outreach, enrollment, and renewal efforts. Because of barriers to enrollment and renewal, many eligible children are currently not enrolled. In addition, because of constraints on state budgets, outreach efforts have been reduced in many states, and some states have enacted measures to restrict coverage in their SCHIP programs. In 2009, Congress passed the Children's Health Insurance Program Reauthorization Act (CHIPRA) and increased the funding by $33 billion with the expectation that 4.1 million additional children would be covered by 2013 (Moniz & Gorin, 2014). Through a series of legislative acts signed by Presidents Obama and Trump, the Children's Health Insurance Program (CHIP) has been funded through 2027 (Orris & Boozang, 2018).

The landmark health care reform legislation, the Patient Protection and Affordable Care Act (ACA), was signed into law by President Barack Obama in March 2010. The overall goals of the ACA are to (1) expand health insurance coverage, (2) increase focus on prevention, and (3) improve health care efficiency and reduce costs (Hellerstedt, 2013). Key provisions of the act that affect children and youth include (1) eliminating lifetime caps on insurance coverage; (2) preventing states from reducing the income eligibility threshold for CHIP, extending CHIP funding, and providing funding for increased outreach efforts to enroll eligible children; (3) requiring insurers to cover comprehensive screenings and preventative care at no cost to the patient; (4) mandating Medicaid coverage for children aging out of the foster care system up to the age of 26 years; (5) barring insurance companies from denying coverage for preexisting conditions; (6) allowing families to purchase child-only insurance packages; (7) allowing young adults to remain on their parents' insurance until they reach 26 years of age; (8) establishing a $200 million federal authorization program to expand school-based health centers (SBHCs); and (9) including $1.5 billion for the Home Visitation Grant Program to implement evidence-based maternal, infant, and early childhood visitation models (First Focus, 2012). Under the ACA, individuals were required to have minimal health insurance coverage or pay a penalty; federal subsidies or tax credits may be used to help offset costs for low- and middle-income people who must purchase individual plans.

Since the enactment of the ACA, efforts have been made to repeal the law in whole and in part, and numerous lawsuits have been filed against specific provisions of the ACA. In 2012, the U.S. Supreme Court upheld the constitutionality of the ACA but ruled that the ACA-mandated expansion of Medicaid coverage would not be required for states. This expansion would have covered adults under the age of 65 years, including many low-income parents with incomes up to 133% of the FPL. The Tax Cuts and Jobs Act of 2017 eliminated the fine for violating the individual mandate starting in 2019, and the Consolidated Appropriations Act of 2020 repealed three taxes designed to financially support the ACA (i.e., the "Cadillac" tax on health insurance benefits, the excise tax on medical devices, and the Health Insurance Tax). The absence of an individual mandate raised the question of the constitutionality of the ACA again, and in 2020, the Supreme Court agreed to review the ACA, likely issuing a ruling on its validity in 2021 (Jost, 2020).

# HEALTH PROBLEMS FOR CHILDREN AND ADOLESCENTS

Infants, children, and adolescents in the United States (U.S.) experience a range of health problems, with some of the most frequent being low birth weight (LBW), asthma, obesity, sexually transmitted infections (STIs), and suicide. We will describe the prevalence of these health problems; health disparities associated with race/ethnicity, socioeconomic status, sex, sexual orientation, and gender identity; and multilevel risk and protective factors for these problems.

## Low Birth Weight

Infants with low birth weight (LBW) are defined as those weighing less than 2,500 grams (about 5.5 pounds). The rate of LBW in the U.S. was highest in 2006 at 8.26%. In 2018, the rate of LBW was 8.3%, which was an increase from 2012 when the rate was 8.0%. The rate of infants born in 2018 with very low birth weight (VLBW)—that is, weighing less than 1,500 grams—has been stable at 1.4% (Martin et al., 2019). LBW and VLBW are a serious public health concern because they can lead to adverse health outcomes throughout life. Infants born with a LBW and a VLBW are at an increased risk for a host of health and developmental problems, including neonatal mortality, neurodevelopmental disorders, respiratory distress syndrome, cardiac problems, and delayed cognitive functioning (Arpino et al., 2010; Bhutta et al., 2002; Reuner et al., 2009). Compared with infants of normal birth weight, LBW infants face a greater than fivefold increase in risk of death during their first year and VLBW infants incur a tenfold increase for risk of death in their first year (Martin et al., 2019).

Racial/ethnic disparities have been found in the prevalence of LBW and VLBW infants. In 2018, the rate of LBW for children with African American mothers (13.3%) was almost two times the rate reported for those with either White mothers (7.0%) or Hispanic/Latina mothers (7.5%; Martin et al., 2019). Research indicates the impact of maternal stress, particularly stress caused by racism (Kim & Saada, 2013; Lu et al., 2010), and the role of living in hyper-segregated residential areas (Mehra et al., 2017) as primary risk factors for having LBW babies. A variety of other risk factors, including genetics, lifestyle, and environmental conditions, can affect birth weight. Maternal risk factors for LBW include smoking or drug use during pregnancy, limited or late prenatal care, and the number of previous pregnancies (Khan et al., 2016). Although 54% of women cease smoking during pregnancy, 11% of women smoked during their pregnancy (Tong et al., 2013).

Early childbearing (i.e., maternal age 15 years or younger) has also been noted as a significant risk factor for LBW (Gibbs et al., 2012). Most likely, biological as well as social factors contribute to this relationship. Although early childbearing occurs across the socioeconomic spectrum, researchers investigating maternal age trends have argued that the incidence of early childbearing is disproportionately high among women of color and women in poverty (Chen et al., 2008). These researchers also found that the poverty faced by many young women contributes to their delayed entry into prenatal care, inadequate weight gain during pregnancy, and increased incidence of perinatal medical complications. The nutritional demands of normal physiological development during adolescence may be one factor contributing to the increased prevalence of LBW among newborns of adolescent mothers because these demands create a maternal–fetal competition for nutrients (Kramer & Lancaster, 2010). This competition may be exacerbated in low-income families, which often experience food insecurity because they cannot afford food and they live in communities where nutritious foods may be less available or cost prohibitive.

In the past two decades, a significant increase in the rate of multiple gestations has been seen in the U.S., mostly because of delayed childbearing and increased use of fertility drugs and procedures (Balasch & Gratacós, 2011). These increases in multiple births, particularly twin births, had a significant impact on the increased incidence of LBW, preterm delivery, and prenatal mortality in the U.S. (Brown et al., 2020).

## Asthma

*Asthma* is a chronic respiratory disease that causes swollen airways, making it harder to move air in and out of the body. Asthma is characterized by recurrent periods of inflammation in the respiratory tract, shortness of breath, coughing, and wheezing. It is the most common chronic illness and the most prevalent cause of disability among children in the U.S. (Williams et al., 2009; Wu et al., 2008). Indeed, the prevalence of childhood asthma has more than doubled since 1980 (Akinbami et al., 2009). Being the third most common cause of pediatric hospitalization, it has been diagnosed in about 6 million U.S. children and adolescents, representing 8% of the U.S. population younger than age 18 (Centers for Disease Control and Prevention [CDC], 2018a). Over half of children with asthma reported at least one asthma attack in the past year (CDC, 2014a). Asthma is the second most costly health problem among children in the U.S. (Soni, 2014).

Racial/ethnic disparities exist for childhood asthma. Black (14%) and Hispanic/Latinx (8%) children have higher rates of asthma compared with White children (6%; CDC, 2018a). And the asthma mortality rate per million is significantly higher in Black children (21.8) compared to White children (9.5).

While the exact causes of asthma are not fully understood, an array of risk factors increases children's risk of developing asthma; many of these risk factors are related to poverty. Low socioeconomic status and family income are associated with both previous asthma diagnosis and incidence of asthma attacks (Williams et al., 2009). Children living below the FPL are more likely to have been diagnosed with asthma (19%) than those living between 100% and 200% of federal poverty guidelines (14%) and those living at or above 200% of the FPL (12%; CDC, 2013). Children receiving Medicaid are more likely to have been diagnosed with asthma (18%) at some point in their lives than children with private insurance (12%). Research suggests that poverty at the individual, household, and community levels is directly associated with both increased risk of developing asthma and increased risk of experiencing greater severity of asthma attacks (Midodzi et al., 2010; Subbarao et al., 2009; Thakur et al., 2013; Williams et al., 2009).

Biosocial and environmental factors are associated with increased risk for the development of asthma. Exposure to tobacco smoke, most commonly from parental smoking in the household, increases the likelihood of developing childhood asthma as well as exacerbating existing asthma (Baena-Cagnani et al., 2009; Gerald et al., 2009; Lawson et al., 2014). Research also indicates that prenatal exposure to tobacco smoke increases the risk that a child will develop asthma (Baena-Cagnani et al., 2009; Midodzi et al., 2010). Other environmental risks include dust mite, cat, and cockroach allergens (Subbarao et al., 2009; Wang et al., 2009). One study showed that exposure to cockroaches at some point in childhood significantly increased the risk for developing asthma, and exposure to cockroach allergens during infancy was associated with a twofold increase in the risk of developing asthma (Salam et al., 2004).

Other health-related issues also affect children's risk of asthma. There is evidence of an association between LBW and childhood asthma (Ahmad et al., 2009; Midodzi et al., 2010). In addition, overweight and obese children and adolescents not only are more likely to develop asthma but also are more likely to develop severe asthma, which is associated with more frequent hospital and clinic visits for asthma-related issues (Black et al., 2013; Liu et al., 2013).

Asthma accounts for more than 13.8 million missed school days (CDC, 2015). However, only 14 states have guidelines allowing for schools to have a quick-relief medication (i.e., inhaler) available for students with asthma. In states without these guidelines, school districts can put in place a protective policy to provide immediate access to such medications. Currently, there are two major programs available for schools to offer proper asthma education and management to their students. The most widely recognized management program is Open Airways for Schools, which targets children 8–11 years old to help them to improve asthma self-management skills to decrease emergencies and increase awareness (American Lung Association, 2020b). Another highly successful program is Kickin' Asthma, which focuses on helping children and adolescents identify asthma triggers and the proper use of medication (American Lung Association, 2020a).

## Obesity

In the U.S., the prevalence of young people experiencing obesity continues to rise (Hales et al., 2018). *Overweight* and *obese* are terms that refer to ranges of body weight that exceed what is considered healthy for a given height. *Overweight* is defined as a body mass index (BMI) at or above the 85th percentile and lower than the 95th percentile, and *obesity* is defined as a BMI at or above the 95th percentile for youth of same age and sex. *Severe obesity* is defined as a BMI at or above 120% of the 95th percentile (Ogden & Flegal, 2010). Although BMI is used as an indicator of health, it has received just criticism in recent years due to the inaccurate measurement of fat in overall body composition, yet it remains the most widely used measure of body composition by health researchers and professionals (Freedman & Sherry, 2009). Nonetheless, there may be some utility in using BMI with additional measures to inform a comprehensive assessment of an individual's health (Burkhauser & Cawley, 2008).

Over 40% of children and adolescents in the U.S. age 2–19 experience being overweight, obese, or severely obese (16.6%, 18.5%, and 5.6%, respectively; Hales et al., 2018). Prevalence rates of obesity increase with age: 14% of children between the ages of 2 and 5 years are obese, 18% of children between the ages of 6 and 11 years are obese, and 21% of adolescents between ages of 12 and 19 years are obese. Rates of obesity do not differ markedly by gender. On the other hand, there are significant differences by race/ethnicity. Rates of being overweight and obese are highest among Hispanic/Latinx (26%) and Black (22%) children, with White (14%) and Asian (11%) children experiencing lower prevalence rates (Hales et al., 2017).

Childhood and adolescent obesity is associated with a number of health problems, including high blood pressure, high cholesterol, impaired glucose tolerance, insulin resistance and Type 2 diabetes, sleep apnea, asthma, bone and joint problems, fatty liver disease, gallstones, heartburn, and low self-esteem (Güngör, 2014; Han et al., 2010; Kelly et al., 2013; Reilly & Kelly, 2011; Sahoo et al., 2015; Visness et al., 2010). Youth who are obese have a higher likelihood of experiencing weight bias, or prejudicial and negative attitudes toward those with excess weight (Pearl, 2018). Studies have shown that weight bias impacts the quality of health care received by patients with health care providers engaging in less rapport building and displaying less respect for patients with obesity (Phelan et al., 2015; Puhl et al., 2016). Additionally, experiencing weight bias is a risk factor associated with disordered eating (Puhl & Suh, 2015). Therefore, experiencing obesity is an indicator of risk for future health problems.

Various risk factors predispose children and adolescents to become overweight and obese. Emerging research suggests that maternal obesity during pregnancy may be associated with childhood obesity (Clausen et al., 2008; Dabelea & Crume, 2011; Heerwagen et al., 2010; Yu et al., 2013). Conversely, breastfeeding has been found to be protective against youth experiencing obesity (Metzger & McDade, 2010). Children's dietary behaviors also influence their weight. Growing evidence supports the relationship between the consumption of sugar-sweetened beverages and childhood obesity (Keller & Bucher Della Torre, 2015). Other dietary risk factors for child obesity include buying lunch at school, eating dinner without parental supervision, missing breakfast, and consuming fewer calories at breakfast and more at dinner (Antonogeorgos et al., 2012; Gleason & Dodd, 2009; Liu et al., 2012).

Children's food and beverage intake is highly dependent on what is available at home, which is dependent on the availability and cost of foods and beverages in local food outlets (Sharifi et al., 2016). Living in a food-insecure home may increase the prevalence of obesity for children (Eisenmann et al., 2011). Lower-income children and adolescents are more likely to be obese than their higher-income peers (Ogden et al., 2018). Researchers found that higher prices for fresh fruits and vegetables in neighborhood food outlets were significantly associated with higher BMIs among children (Sharifi et al., 2016). Indeed, the food environment around a child's home can impact the likelihood of children experiencing obesity by limiting the ability of parents to obtain healthful foods for their children (Forte et al., 2020). When discussing childhood obesity, understanding environmental factors such as poverty, food deserts, food swamps, and lack of transportation are important to consider (Lamichhane et al., 2012).

In addition to the home and neighborhood context, the school environment can also shape factors related to obesity. In terms of health education for children and adolescents, 25% of U.S. school districts do not require that elementary, middle, and high schools teach students about nutrition and dietary behavior. In addition, only 61% of U.S. school districts require that elementary, middle, and high schools teach students about physical activity and fitness (CDC, 2016). Low levels of physical activity are associated with childhood obesity (Miguel-Berges et al., 2018). Approximately 40% of U.S. school districts do not require that elementary schools provide students with regularly scheduled recess. In addition, 11% of districts do not have a policy requiring physical education for middle and high school students (CDC, 2016). Engagement in sedentary activities, such as watching television, playing video games, using a computer, and using the telephone, is associated with child obesity (Fang et al., 2019).

There is a dearth of literature on protective factors against obesity for youth. Nonetheless, participation in a sports team has been found to be protective for youth experiencing obesity (Vos & Welsh, 2010). Involvement in extracurricular activities and afterschool programs decrease the likelihood of youth experiencing obesity. Obesity is a result of a multitude of factors, including the home environment. Financial stability in the home increases the likelihood of youths consuming healthful foods regularly (Lappan et al., 2020). Parents who model healthy behaviors with food for children and have positive interactions with food may protect against obesity (Schwartz et al., 2011).

## Sexually Transmitted Infections

*Sexually transmitted infections (STIs)* are infections or diseases that are passed from one person to another during unprotected sex or genital contact (e.g., human papilloma virus, herpes, chlamydia, gonorrhea, HIV/AIDS, syphilis). STIs are a significant health problem facing U.S. adolescents. Compared with adults, adolescents and emerging adults are at increased risk for acquiring STIs (CDC, 2018b). Although those between the ages of 15 and 24 years represent only 25% of the sexually experienced population in the U.S., this age group accounts for almost half of the estimated 20 million new STI cases each year.

Although there has been a decline from the percentage of high school students who report having had sex from 48% in 2007 to 40% in 2017 in addition to a decline in those who had four or more partners (15% in 2007 to 10% in 2017), there remains concerning patterns regarding the sexual health of youth. Namely, there was a decline in reported condom use from 62% to 54%. This is important given that correct condom use is known as a key to prevent the transmission of STIs (CDC, 2018b).

Unprotected sexual intercourse can lead not only to STIs but also to unwanted pregnancy; therefore, teen pregnancy rates are considered to be an indicator of rates of high-risk sexual behavior. The most recent data show that 43 out of 1,000 women (nearly 5%) between the ages of 15 and 19 years became pregnant in 2013 (Kost et al., 2017). This rate represents a 30-year low in the teen pregnancy rate due to significant drops between 2008 and 2013. Nonetheless, 77% of teen pregnancies are unplanned (CDC, 2012). The connection between unintended teen pregnancies and STI risk is crucial because risky sexual behaviors that may result in pregnancy also place adolescents at high risk for STIs.

It is difficult to estimate national STI rates because states have different reporting requirements. Currently, chancroid, chlamydia, gonorrhea, syphilis, HIV, and hepatitis B are the only STIs reported by every state to the CDC (Workowski & Berman, 2010). The accurate collection of incidence and prevalence data is profoundly inhibited by the wide variation in the quality of surveillance data at local and state levels as well as the lack of standardized state reporting mechanisms for many common STIs, including genital herpes (herpes simplex viruses Type 1 and Type 2) and human papillomavirus. Disparities in reporting between public and private health care providers further challenge accurate STI data collection, resulting in the potential underestimation of STIs diagnosed in the private health sector (Rounds, 2004). In addition, many STIs can be asymptomatic and remain undetected, which further contributes to the underestimation of STI rates among adolescents. Lack of access to health care—a significant issue among many adolescents—may also add to the underestimation of STI rates.

Chlamydia and gonorrhea are the most prevalent among the STIs that states are required to report to the CDC, and each can cause serious health consequences if undetected or left untreated, particularly in young women (CDC, 2018b). In 2018, nearly 62% of all reported chlamydia infections (for which data on age were available) were among young people between the ages of 15 and 24 years. Among women, the highest age-specific reported prevalence rates of chlamydia were among those age 15 to 19 years and those between the ages of 20 and 24 years, with 3,307 and 4,065 cases per 100,000 females, respectively. These rates were significantly higher than those among men in the same age groups.

Although compared with many other STIs, syphilis is relatively rare among U.S. adolescents and young adults. From 2017 to 2018, reported cases increased by 15% among persons 15 to 19 years old and 10% among persons 20 to 24 years old. The prevalence rates of syphilis are 8 reported cases per 100,000 persons 15 to 19 years old and 28 reported cases per 100,000 persons 20 to 24 years old (CDC, 2018b).

Approximately 62% of gonorrhea infections reported in 2018 were among those 15 to 24 years old (CDC, 2018b). The rates of gonorrhea were highest among women between the ages of 15 and 24 years old and among men between 20 and 24 years old. For young women (age 15 to 19), there were 548 cases of gonorrhea per 100,000. Among young men (age 15 to 19), the gonorrhea incidence rate was significantly lower, at 320 cases per 100,000.

As previously noted, states are not required to report cases of herpes simplex virus and human papillomavirus to the CDC (Workowski & Berman, 2010). Both of these viral infections can be asymptomatic and therefore are frequently transmitted to others by those unaware of their infection. There is little precise information about the prevalence of either STI among adolescents in the U.S., although both are widely prevalent among young people. The prevalence of these STIs is an important public health concern because prior exposure to STIs has been linked to predisposition for contracting the HIV virus (CDC, 2014b).

Human immunodeficiency virus (HIV), the virus that leads to acquired immunodeficiency syndrome (AIDS), disproportionately affects adolescents in the U.S. In 2018, 21% of all new HIV infections in the U.S. occurred among young people 13 to 24 years old, the majority of whom acquired the virus through sexual transmission (CDC, 2018b). Within this age group, gay, bisexual, and other men who have sex with men are particularly affected by HIV/AIDS. The large majority of new HIV/AIDS cases among male adolescents 13 to 19 years old were attributed to male-to-male sexual contact. In addition, there is a racial disparity in the HIV/AIDS epidemic in the U.S., with African American adolescents disproportionately affected. The link between HIV and other STIs is important because the presence of a STI places an individual at greater risk for contracting HIV when exposed to the virus through sexual contact. Adolescents are shown to be the least likely to be aware of their infection compared to any other age group. Adolescents, compared to all people with HIV, have the lowest level of viral suppression. This is concerning as those who are infected and are taking the appropriate course of medication can have an undetectable viral load, essentially being at no risk of transmitting HIV to HIV-negative sex partners.

There are key health disparities within adolescents along the lines of race, sexual orientation, and gender. As compared with young men, the higher rates of STIs among young women appear to be based in both behavior and physiology. Behaviorally, young women have a greater likelihood of choosing older, experienced sexual partners, which increases their potential exposure to STIs (Manlove et al., 2006). The higher rates of STIs among young women are also accounted for, in part, by anatomy, which makes females physiologically more susceptible to many STIs than males. Research shows that compared to their heterosexual counterparts, lesbian, gay, bisexual, transgender, or queer (LGBTQ) youth are at higher risk of contracting STIs (Everett, 2013; Reisner, Vetters et al., 2015). LGBTQ youth are more likely to engage in risky sexual behaviors (e.g., early age of sexual debut, having multiple partners, substance use before sex, and not using condoms or contraception), which puts them at increased risk of contracting STIs (Everett et al., 2014; Kann et al., 2016). African Americans are also at an elevated HIV/STI contraction risk; research suggests this is possibly due to structural contextual factors such as socioeconomic status, residential segregation, and incarceration rates (Banks et al., 2020). Latinx and Indigenous (e.g., American Indian and Alaska Native) communities also face similar structural factors that possibly lead to elevated risk. In 2010, there were almost three times as many Hispanic/Latinx adolescents (ages 13–19) that were diagnosed with HIV as compared to White youth (American Psychological Association, 2014). American Indian/Alaska Native youth reportedly experience STI contractions (i.e., gonorrhea, chlamydia, syphilis) that are over and above that of White youth (CDC, 2018b). As compared with adults, many biological, developmental, and social factors place adolescents at higher risk for contracting STIs. Table 6.2 presents a summary of risk and protective factors associated with adolescent STIs.

## Table 6.2  Risk and Protective Factors for Adolescent Sexually Transmitted Infection

### Risk Factors

| Individual Factors | Interpersonal Factors | Social Environmental Factors |
|---|---|---|
| • Early puberty<br>• Early initiation of sexual activity<br>• Lack of knowledge about sexuality and safer sex practices<br>• Inability to use condoms properly<br>• Low self-efficacy about safer sex<br>• Negative attitudes, beliefs, and intentions about safer sex practices<br>• Lack of communication skills to negotiate sexual activity with a partner<br>• Inaccurate perception of risk and having a sense of invulnerability<br>• A history of sexual abuse or violence victimization<br>• Engagement in sex work<br>• Psychological distress, including depressive symptoms<br>• Substance use/abuse (tobacco, alcohol, and illicit drugs) | • Poor parent–adolescent relationship and communication<br>• Lack of parental monitoring<br>• Family norms that accept early initiation of sexual intercourse and multiple partners<br>• Parents being unemployed<br>• Family homelessness or youth living away from their family<br>• Peer norms supporting early initiation of sex and multiple partners<br>• Affiliation with a gang<br>• Involvement in delinquent behavior<br>• Lack of partner support for using condoms<br>• Partner with a STI<br>• Unprotected intercourse with multiple sexual partners | • Lack of universal access to health care<br>• Poor access to STI prevention, screening, medical care, and counseling<br>• Limited sex education<br>• Lack of access to condoms<br>• Media that sexualize vulnerable populations and promote risky sexual practices<br>• Lack of economic and educational opportunities for adolescents |

### Protective Factors

| Individual Factors | Interpersonal Factors | Social Environmental Factors |
|---|---|---|
| • Motivation to avoid STIs<br>• Belief that condoms are effective<br>• Prior use of condoms<br>• Regular use of contraception | • Positive parental monitoring<br>• Parent–child communication about STI prevention<br>• Positive peer norms and support for condom use<br>• Participation in sports or exercise activities<br>• Having a monogamous sexual relationship<br>• Partner supports condom use | • Presence of caring adults in the community<br>• Access to comprehensive sex education |

*Sources:* Kirby & Lepore (2007); Rounds (2004).

Given the risk and protective factors in Table 6.2, the importance of access to sex education, especially for high-risk populations (e.g., LGBTQ), is clear. Policies on sex education can mandate that essential content be taught to adolescents in school, including in-depth information about contraceptive and barrier methods, communication about sexual consent, empowered sexual decision making, healthy relationships, sexual violence, and diversity in sexual orientation and gender (Hall et al., 2019). The National Sex Education Standards provide a comprehensive framework for K–12 curriculum content (Future of Sex Education Initiative, 2020).

## Suicide

Suicide is the second leading cause of death among adolescents age 10 to 19 (Curtin & Heron, 2019). After reaching a historic low in 2007, the adolescent suicide rate has been rising steadily, with the current rate (12 deaths per 100,000) approximately double the 2007 rate. These rates are likely underestimates of the problem (Rockett et al., 2011). For instance, certain suicide methods that may be more ambiguous than others (e.g., self-poisoning vs. jumping off a bridge) lead to the misclassification of some suicide deaths. Suicide is precipitated by *suicidal ideation* (i.e., seriously thinking about ending one's own life), *suicide plans* (i.e., making plans for how to end one's life), and/or *suicide attempts* (i.e., trying to end one's life but resulting in survival). Recent data from high school age youth show that 17% seriously considered suicide, 14% made a plan for suicide, and 7% attempted suicide (Ivey-Stephenson et al., 2020).

Certain groups are at higher risk for suicidality. Although young women report higher rates of suicidal ideation and behavior, young men are more likely to die from suicide (CDC, 2019; Ivey-Stephenson et al., 2020). Youth who are LGBTQ have higher rates of suicidality compared to their cisgender heterosexual peers (Johns et al., 2019, 2020). Although White and Asian (17%) youth are slightly more likely to think about suicide than Black (15%) and Hispanic/Latinx (16%) youth, Black (10%) and Hispanic/Latinx (8%) youth are more likely to attempt suicide than White and Asian (6%) youth (Ivey-Stephenson et al., 2020).

A number of psychosocial risk and protective factors for suicidality have been documented (Table 6.3). These factors suggest multiple avenues for preventive interventions. Universal screening of youth for signs and risks for suicidality in schools and other settings (e.g., primary care) could identify youth at increased risk for suicide and more targeted interventions could be employed. Training for *gatekeepers* (i.e., individuals who have regular or everyday contact with youth and can recognize and refer someone at risk of suicide), such as teachers, school staff, classmates, coaches, pediatricians, and social workers, have shown evidence of effectiveness (Isaac et al., 2009). Once youth at risk for suicide have been identified, they can be referred to mental health services and interventions to improve family, peer, school, and community connections and relationships.

## Table 6.3 Risk and Protective Factors for Youth Suicidality

### Risk Factors

| Individual Psychological Factors | Family, Peer, and Other Interpersonal Factors | Social Circumstances |
|---|---|---|
| • Mental illness, particularly depression<br>• Substance abuse, particularly alcohol<br>• Impulsive aggression<br>• Lack of problem-solving skills<br>• Lack of emotional self-regulation skills<br>• Hopelessness<br>• Low self-esteem and negative self-concept<br>• Neuroticism<br>• Anhedonia<br>• Previous suicidal ideation or behavior<br>• Use of maladaptive coping strategies (e.g., rumination and suppression) | • Family history of mental illness, substance abuse, or suicidality<br>• Parental conflict or family violence<br>• Physical, sexual, or emotional abuse<br>• Poor family communication<br>• Interpersonal losses (e.g., relationship breakup, death of a friend, loss of a parent)<br>• Peer rejection and bullying victimization<br>• Poor peer relationships<br>• Loneliness and social isolation | • Exposure to suicidal behavior that could be imitated<br>• Information on and availability of means for suicide<br>• Legal or disciplinary problems<br>• Poor school performance and disengagement with school |

### Protective Factors

| Individual Psychological Factors | Family, Peer, and Other Interpersonal Factors | Social Circumstances |
|---|---|---|
| • Reasons for living<br>• Academic achievement | • Family cohesion<br>• Positive parent–child relationships<br>• High parental expectations for education and behavior<br>• Contact with helpful and responsible adults<br>• Connectedness with school | • Restriction of lethal means<br>• Availability and quality of mental health services |

*Sources:* Bilsen (2018); Bridge et al. (2006); Carballo et al. (2020); Cha et al. (2018); King & Merchant (2008); Macgowan, (2004).

## Coronavirus Disease 2019 (COVID-19)

The novel coronavirus identified at the end of 2019 led to the global pandemic of COVID-19, an infectious respiratory disease that has killed over 500,000 Americans at the end of February 2021 (CDC, 2021a). Although children and adolescents make up very few of these deaths compared to adults and older adults in particular, COVID-19 has ravaged families and severely disrupted the American economy and social life. The virus mainly spreads from person to person through respiratory droplets produced when an infected person coughs, sneezes, or talks. Transmission of the virus can occur by some-one inhaling these droplets, droplets landing on someone's mouth or nose, or touching surfaces containing droplets and then touching one's nose, mouth, or eyes. A person infected with the virus may not display any symptoms but can still spread the virus.

Several effective vaccines for the virus have been developed yet only 7.5% of Americans have been fully vaccinated as of March 1, 2021 (CDC, 2021b). Efforts to curb the spread of the coronavirus have focused on human behavior, including handwashing, mask wearing, physical distancing, limiting the size of gatherings, and imposing shutdowns and stay-at-home orders. Despite evidence of the effectiveness of wearing face masks (Anfinrud et al., 2020; Chu et al., 2020; Leffler et al., 2020; Leung et al., 2020; Lyu & Wehby, 2020; MacIntyre & Chughtai, 2020), neither Congress nor the Trump or Biden administrations have attempted a national mask mandate. And only 35 states have mandated mask wearing in public (Markowitz, 2021). In California, residents are required to wear a mask in public spaces, both indoor and outdoor. Conversely, a statewide mask requirement has not been issued in Florida, but about one third of Florida counties have mask mandates. This patchwork of policies raises concerns about the nation's capacity to contain the spread of the virus.

U.S. government action also fell short in coronavirus testing early in the pandemic under the Trump administration, although as of February 22, 2021, the U.S. ranks third in the world in testing (Statista, 2021). The CDC (2020) recommends that peo-ple with symptoms of COVID-19 (i.e., fever, cough, fatigue, headache, muscle ache, sore throat, nasal congestion, difficulty breathing, nausea, and diarrhea) get tested as well as people who have had close contact with someone who is infected. Hopefully, the nation's testing capacity will continue to expand, which includes the proportion of people tested and rapid results. Genetic tests via nasal swab or saliva, as well as antigen tests, will be key to these efforts. New confirmed cases of the virus must be isolated for at least two weeks and their contacts should be traced (WHO, 2020a, 2020b, 2020d).

With the rollout of vaccines for the coronavirus currently underway, the issue of vaccine policy is salient. Given that these vaccines are safe and highly effective in pre-venting COVID-19 (CDC, 2021c), widespread distribution and uptake of the vaccines will be essential to prevent further escalation of infections and deaths from COVID-19 (DeRoo et al., 2020). However, public polls suggest that many Americans are hesitant or resistant to getting vaccinated for COVID-19 (Agiesta, 2021; Brenan, 2021; Hamel et al., 2021). Undoubtedly, a strong public health education campaign is needed to provide accurate and scientific information about vaccination.

Since the 1790s, with the creation of the first vaccine, vaccination has been one of the greatest preventive interventions for global public health. Once deadly or debilitating diseases such as smallpox, polio, measles, mumps, rubella, whooping cough, and diphtheria have been nearly eradicated in the U.S. thanks to vaccination. Given the benefits of vaccination, all 50 states require children to have received certain vaccinations before entering public school or daycare (CDC, 2017). Five states grant exemptions to children for medical reasons only, and 45 states grant exemptions for medical reasons and objections based on religion or personal beliefs (National Conference of State Legislatures, 2020). However, some states' laws note that exemptions might not be recognized during an outbreak or epidemic (CDC, 2017). In the U.S., parent refusal of all vaccines is very rare, with a refusal rate of about 1% (Dempsey et al., 2011; Hill et al., 2018). However, even this small minority of refusals has led to outbreaks of measles and pertussis or whooping cough (Phadke et al., 2016).

The COVID-19 crisis raises several vaccination policy issues. The fundamental conflict is between people's rights to safety, protection, and life and individuals' rights to bodily integrity (i.e., an individual's body should not be violated and they should have autonomy and self-determination regarding their body) as well as parents' rights (i.e., parents should raise their children as they see fit). These conflicts raise difficult questions in light of the COVID-19 pandemic and vaccination: Should parents be allowed to refuse a safe and effective vaccine for COVID-19 for their children based on religious or personal beliefs? Should unvaccinated children be allowed to attend daycare or public school? Should conditions for unvaccinated children to attend daycare or public school be required, such as wearing face masks or being tested for COVID-19 regularly? At what age could adolescents consent to vaccination without parental approval? Indeed, these are difficult questions that must be addressed by policymakers in this new COVID-19 era. Nonetheless, people's right to safety and life as well as the government's duty to protect American lives from a deadly pandemic supersede certain individual rights.

# HEALTH CARE SYSTEM PROBLEMS FOR CHILDREN, ADOLESCENTS, AND FAMILIES

## Access to Health Care

The primary function of the health care system is to provide people with medical and preventive care. Substantial evidence shows that health insurance is the key facilitator of children, youth, and families accessing health care services, and lack of health insurance coverage is a significant barrier to accessing care (Bailey et al., 2016; Choi et al., 2011; DeVoe et al., 2010; DeVoe et al., 2012; Howell & Kenney, 2012; Tumin et al., 2019). Children who lack insurance coverage or who experience insurance instability (i.e., disruptions in coverage) are significantly more likely to lack a usual source of care, delay care, or have unmet medical needs than children with insurance (Cassedy et al., 2008). Access to services can reduce the negative effects of a health problem. For example, ongoing treatment, management, and education regarding asthma could reduce the likelihood that a child with asthma would experience an acute episode requiring emergency treatment. Access to health care can also interrupt an escalating risk chain. For example, early detection, treatment, and counseling and education for a STI could reduce the likelihood that an adolescent would develop serious sexual and reproductive health problems. Health care access can even prevent the onset of health problems. For example, an expecting parent receiving recommended prenatal care could prevent birth complications. Indeed, having health insurance and accessing care are protective and promotive factors for positive health outcomes, and not having insurance is a risk factor.

With the expansions of Medicaid and CHIP as well as the ACA marketplaces and subsidies, the rate of uninsured children dropped significantly in recent years, reaching an all-time low of 4.7% in 2016 (Figure 6.1; Berchick et al., 2019). However, the uninsured rate has been increasing since that time. This is likely due to efforts to nullify pieces of the ACA (e.g., eliminating the individual mandate, cutting funding for enrollment assistance, and shortening enrollment periods) and the Trump administration approving waivers that allow states to impose barriers to accessing Medicaid coverage (e.g., work requirements for parents, coverage lockout penalties, eliminating retroactive coverage, and imposing premiums; Alker & Roygardner, 2019; Flowers & Accius, 2019). Currently, just over half of children have private health insurance (e.g., parents' employer-sponsored plans and market plans), about 40% of children are covered by Medicaid or CHIP, and about 5% of children are uninsured (Berchick et al., 2019). The uninsured rate is highest among children from Native American, Hispanic/Latinx, immigrant, low-income, and Southern families (Child Trends, 2018; Seiber, 2014).

**Figure 6.1  Percentage of Uninsured U.S. Children and Adolescents (Ages 0–18)**

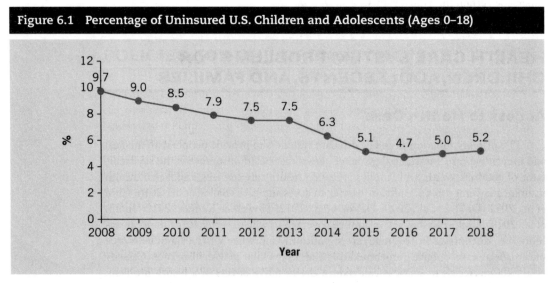

*Source:* Berchick et al., 2019.

Unfortunately, although having health insurance facilitates access to care, it does not guarantee that children will receive the care they need. Other barriers exist; for example, many pediatricians do not accept Medicaid because of lower payment rates. On average, Medicaid pays two thirds of what Medicare pays for primary care services (Zuckerman et al., 2017). In addition, regardless of the type of insurance, families are facing high out-of-pocket costs for health care services, which make care especially cost-prohibitive for lower-income families (Kirzinger et al., 2019; Ortegren, 2019). Ironically, the U.S. spends more on health care than any other country, yet a large segment of the population does not have health coverage, and access to health care providers and resources (e.g., hospital beds) is more limited compared to other industrialized nations (Anderson et al., 2019; Papanicolas et al., 2018). The U.S. is the only high-income industrialized nation without universal health coverage (Boerma et al., 2014).

## Quality of Health Care

The U.S. lags behind many other peer nations in a variety of health quality indicators: infant mortality; LBW; childhood vaccination for diphtheria, tetanus, pertussis, and measles; teen pregnancy; child and adolescent obesity; and youth asthma mortality (Global Asthma Network, 2018; Organisation for Economic Co-operation and Development, 2019). These indicators raise concerns about the quality of the U.S. health system, especially regarding its capacity for prevention. Indeed, the U.S. health care system has been criticized because it overwhelmingly focuses on medical treatment—one study reported that only 5% of U.S. spending on health care went to population-wide health promotion and prevention (Marvasti & Stafford, 2012; McGinnis et al., 2002). Investment in prevention, early intervention, and public health promotion can advance healthy development among children and adolescents as well as prevent the onset or escalation of diseases and disorders that have long-term implications for health into adulthood.

A barrier to improving the quality of health care may be the structure of financial incentives. Currently, the health care system is based on a *fee-for-service* model wherein health care providers receive a payment for each service provided (e.g., office visit, test, and procedure). This model raises a potential conflict of interest between providers' financial self-interests and the interests of patients because fee-for-service rewards production volume instead of better health outcomes. Concerns with fee-for-service models have led to new initiatives, including *pay-for-performance* programs or *value-based reimbursement* wherein providers receive financial incentives for meeting performance measures (James, 2012). Performance measures encompass multiple dimensions of quality, including safety, clinical care, efficiency and cost reduction, and patient and caregiver satisfaction.

Another aspect of quality in the health care system relates to lower quality of care provided to minoritized patient groups. Mounting research has evidenced that many health care providers have negative or biased attitudes toward certain patients (e.g., people of color, LGBTQ people, and immigrants) that can affect the quality of care provided (Berdahl et al., 2010; Calvo & Hawkins, 2015; Chapman et al., 2018;

Coker et al., 2010; Hall et al., 2013; Hall et al., 2015; Lopez et al., 2018; Sabin et al., 2015). For example, people of color reported difficulty in getting appointments, being given less time and attention than White patients or being made to wait while White patients were prioritized, providers and staff acting disrespectfully or applying negative stereotypes, and receiving substandard care (Cochran et al., 2007; Greer, 2010; Ross et al., 2012; Salm Ward et al., 2013; Sanchez-Birkhead et al., 2011; Tandon et al., 2005). LGBTQ people, particularly transgender people, have reported negative health care experiences, such as being denied equal treatment or services as well as providers and staff being disrespectful, expressing discomfort or disapproval about their sexual or gender identity, applying stereotypes about LGBTQ people, and perpetrating verbal and physical harassment (Dawes et al., 2021; Kcomt, 2019; Rossman et al., 2017; Shires & Jaffee, 2015). Immigrants have reported difficulty in making health care appointments, a lack of adequate interpretive services, feeling ignored and stereotyped by providers, and receiving substandard care (Cristancho et al., 2008; Gurman & Becker, 2008). Indeed, much work is needed to ensure access to quality health care for all Americans.

## Fragmentation in Health Care

The Agency for Healthcare Research and Quality (AHRQ) defines *coordinated health care* as "deliberately organizing patient care activities and sharing information among all of the participants concerned with a patient's care to achieve safer and more effective care" (2018). Research shows that coordination of health care leads to better health outcomes for children and adolescents, especially those with special health care needs (Antonelli et al., 2009; Lipkin et al., 2005). Unfortunately, many U.S. children, youth, and families navigate fragmented care systems. For example, a child with multiple health care needs (e.g., typical pediatric needs, moderate separation anxiety, and recurrent ear infections with hearing impairment and speech delays) may seek care from an array of providers scattered across the U.S. health care system (e.g., a pediatrician who operates in a small solo practice; a psychologist working at a group practice focused on mental health; an audiologist and an ear, nose, and throat physician located at a large hospital system; and a speech-language pathologist working at the child's school). Such an arrangement can lead to obstacles in providers sharing information and tracking a patient's care activities, treatment progress, and current condition as well as obstacles for parents who have to coordinate appointments, transport the child, navigate different payment arrangements, and share information between providers.

Fragmentation of providers across various locations and systems is often exacerbated by the fragmentation of patient health/medical records. Although the collection, storage, and use of electronic health records has increased in recent decades, numerous issues need to be addressed for their full potential to be realized. For example, there are dozens of different electronic health record software systems, which does not facilitate the availability and exchange of patient information. Further, some electronic health record systems are highly complex and take time for providers to learn and use easily (Boonstra et al., 2014).

A final fragmentation issue concerns payers. There are over 900 health insurance companies in the U.S. offering different insurance plans with varying benefits and cost sharing arrangements (National Association of Insurance Commissioners, 2019). Additionally, numerous government-sponsored health coverage programs exist: CHIP, Federal Employees Health Benefits Program, Indian Health Service, Medicaid, Medicare, Military Health System and Tricare, and the Veteran Health Administration. Given this dizzying and excessive array of health coverage providers and plans, Americans spend nearly $1 trillion annually on billing and insurance-related costs, which include overhead costs for the health insurance industry and providers' costs for claims submission, claims reconciliation, and payment processing (Gee & Spiro, 2019).

# IMPROVING THE HEALTH CARE SYSTEM TO PROMOTE CHILD, ADOLESCENT, AND FAMILY HEALTH AND RESILIENCE

To promote the health of children, adolescents, and families and to prevent the deleterious health problems discussed previously (e.g., LBW), the U.S. should transition to a health care system with universal coverage. This could be accomplished through a single-payer model (present in the United Kingdom, Italy, Spain, and Canada) or a public choice model (present in Germany, France, and Japan). Either model would be a substantial improvement from the current U.S. health care system.

## Single-Payer Model

A *single-payer model* would be a publicly run, government-sponsored health insurance program for all Americans, and health care providers and hospital systems would remain in the private sector (Crowley et al., 2020; Fox & Poirier, 2018; Liu & Brook, 2017). The need for private health insurance would be eliminated or only ancillary. This model would provide a uniform and comprehensive set of benefits, involve minimal or no cost-sharing, and allow patients to choose providers. The current multi-payer system financed by employers, consumers, and taxpayers would be simplified, with coverage financed by taxation. Cost regulation would be imperative to control excessive health care costs; negotiate prescription drug prices; compensate providers fairly; curtail reimbursement for low-value and ineffective services; and base reimbursement on services that are clinically effective, cost-effective, and valued by patients. A major strength of a single-payer model is that administrative complexity, costs, and burdens would be greatly reduced because benefits and reimbursements would be standard. Another strength of this model is portability—your insurance remains the same whether you change jobs, lose your job, or move, and all providers would be in-network. Although a single-payer model has many advantages, transitioning to such a system may be infeasible in the near future due to limited political support, public skepticism, opposition from the health insurance industry, and high up-front costs. Transitioning to a public choice model is more feasible because it would build upon employer-sponsored coverage, which most Americans are satisfied with (Collins & Gunja, 2019).

## Public Choice Model

A *public choice model* (also called a *social health insurance model*) would rely on employer-sponsored health insurance and a public insurance plan administered by the government (Carrin & James, 2004; Crowley et al., 2020). The public insurance plan would provide a comprehensive set of benefits, and minimum benefit standards would be set for employer-sponsored plans. Employees could choose the public plan instead of their employer's plan, and in this case, employers would need to contribute to the public plan. Employers could also choose to finance the enrollment of their employees in the public plan rather than offering their own private plan. Cost regulations similar to the single-payer model would also be needed in the public plan; however, certain cost reductions would be more difficult to achieve without the monopsony power inherent in the single-payer model. Although individuals with the public plan would have portability, private insurance plans could still form limited provider networks, which may restrict patient access to some providers. Premiums and cost-sharing in the public plan should be income-adjusted to protect low-income families and those with disabilities or serious health problems. Low-income individuals and families as well as those with special health care needs, chronic diseases, or catastrophic illnesses would benefit from no cost-sharing for needed care and services. Annual and lifetime out-of-pocket cost limits would also be needed. Medical problems have been the most common reason for declaring bankruptcy in America (Himmelstein et al., 2009). A major disadvantage of the public choice model compared to the single-payer model is that administrative costs and burdens would remain.

## System Needs Regardless of Model

Regardless of whether the U.S. transitions toward a single-payer or public choice model, certain issues are key. First, all insurance plans should be required to cover essential benefits, such as the 10 service categories specified in the ACA (i.e., primary care, preventive services, hospitalizations, emergency services, pregnancy- and new-born-related care, pediatric care, rehabilitation, mental and behavioral health services, laboratory services, and prescription drugs); however, dental health care, vision services, and hearing aids could also be added to the list of essential benefits. Second, there must be greater investment in primary care, preventive interventions, early screening and intervention, and mental and behavioral health care. Certain services can be provided at no or minimal cost to patients. These actions can facilitate early detection and intervention as well as prevent health problems from escalating and leading to greater burdens in morbidity and mortality as well as high costs in the long term. A child's early years are important not only for preventive care (e.g., well-baby checkups and immunizations) but also for screenings to detect developmental and health problems. Among young people, adolescents are a particularly vulnerable group because they have a high likelihood of engaging in high-risk behaviors (e.g., unprotected sex and substance use) that have long-term consequences (Hall & Rounds, 2013). Third, provider shortages must be addressed. In the coming years, shortages of primary care providers and pediatric subspecialists are projected, especially in the South, impoverished areas, rural areas, and large urban areas (IHS Markit, 2020). To address these shortages, training programs should increase enrollment, the federal government can offer student loan forgiveness programs, and reimbursement rates for primary care and other value-based services should reflect the importance of these services. A final issue is to promote *patient-centered medical homes* (also referred to as *primary care medical homes* [PCMH]) for everyone—young and old, especially those with special health care needs. PCMHs are a model of care in which the core functions of primary care are delivered under one roof (AHRQ, n. d.). A medical home should be accessible, family-centered, continuous, comprehensive, coordinated, compassionate, and culturally effective (American Academy of Pediatrics, n. d.).

# INTEGRATION OF SERVICES FOR CHILDREN AND YOUTH

Meeting the health and social needs of children and adolescents requires approaches that promote integration and collaboration among service systems. School-based health centers (SBHCs) are a prime example of effective service integration to address the array of needs for children and adolescents. In addition to SBHCs that serve the general population of children and adolescents, we also want to highlight transgender care centers in which health care services are integrated with other services and resources for a specific population group.

## School-Based Health Centers

In the U.S., the first school-based health initiative began in New York City in 1894 to assess and contain children with contagious diseases, such as measles, scarlet fever, whooping cough, and tuberculosis (Keeton et al., 2012). In 1902, the first school nurse began providing treatment and care to students and making home visits to provide health education to families regarding hygiene and other methods of disease control. The first SBHCs were opened in the late 1960s and early 1970s in Cambridge, Massachusetts; Dallas, Texas; and Saint Paul, Minnesota, to provide accessible and affordable health care to poor children. In 1978, the Robert Wood Johnson Foundation sponsored the expansion of SBHCs throughout the U.S. in an effort to increase access to community-based health care for children and adolescents in underserved communities. Through these efforts, policymakers became more aware of SBHCs and their value. In 1995, the Health Resource and Service Administration began providing grant funding for SBHCs (Gustafson, 2005). Since the 1990s, the number of SBHCs has increased with the help of multiple funding streams. As part of the ACA, $200 million was appropriated to SBHCs between 2010 and 2013 to improve and expand services to an estimated 875,000 youth per year, a 50% increase compared with youth served in 2009 (HHS, 2011). A national SBHC advocacy organization, the School-Based Health Alliance, noted in a position statement that the SBHC model has the components of a PCMH as outlined in the ACA and that SBHCs across the country should strive to meet PCMH goals and standards (School-Based Health Alliance, n. d.).

There are over 2,500 SBHCs located on elementary, middle, and high school campuses across the country (Love et al., 2019). These centers provide a range of services, including primary medical care, mental and behavioral health care, reproductive health services, dental/oral health care, and health education and promotion. Once primarily located in inner cities, SBHCs have expanded to rural, suburban, and urban areas (Lofink et al., 2013; Love et al., 2019). SBHCs typically operate via a partnership between a school district and a local health organization such as a community health center, hospital, or health department. Most SBHCs are open five days a week before, during, and after school. SBHC staff include a mix of professionals: physicians, nurse practitioners, physician assistants, nurses, dieticians, dental hygienists, psychologists, counselors, social workers, and health educators (Brown & Bolen, 2012; Love et al., 2019).

SBHCs rely on various funding and billing sources. Over 80% of SBHCs bill a state Medicaid agency, 71% bill Medicaid managed care organizations, 64% bill private insurance, and 40% bill Tri-Care (i.e., the health insurance program for military families; Lofink et al., 2013). In addition to billing, SBHCs receive funds from state governments (75%), the federal government (53%), private foundations (40%), school districts (33%), hospitals (33%), local governments (32%), private health insurance organizations (27%), businesses (18%), and professional associations (7%).

## Primary Care

SBHCs provide a range of primary care services, including physical exams, immunizations, treatment for acute illnesses and injuries, treatment for common chronic diseases (e.g., asthma and diabetes), and routine health screening (Brown & Bolen, 2012). Researchers found significantly higher overall completion rates for immunization series among adolescents at SBHCs compared to those at community health centers despite serving an adolescent population with lower health insurance coverage (Federico et al., 2010). In a study of children with asthma, those with SBHCs showed less activity restriction due to asthma and fewer emergency department visits compared with the non-SBHC group (Mansour et al., 2008).

## Mental and Behavioral Health Care

In order to meet both the physical and mental health needs of youth, 78% of SBHCs provide some form of mental/behavioral health care (Lofink et al., 2013). These services include crisis intervention (78%), individual psychosocial assessment and treatment (73%), case management (69%), classroom behavior support (62%), substance abuse counseling (53%), assessment and treatment of learning problems

(50%), peer mediation (43%), and prescription and management of psychoactive medication (39%). A longitudinal study showed that adolescents who were enrolled in a school with a SBHC were more likely to access mental health services (Guo et al., 2008). The authors of another study concluded that "on-site mental health services and their immediate availability for crisis intervention allow teenagers to engage in individual, family, and group treatment before problems become so severe that they interfere with their education" (Pastore & Techow, 2004, p. 194). A study in Oregon found that students in schools with access to mental health services through SBHCs showed lower rates of depression and suicide risk than students without access to SBHCs (Bains et al., 2017).

## Health Education and Prevention

Most SBHCs are also involved in health education and prevention activities in the areas of violence, substance use, nutrition, and physical activity. SBHC engagement in prevention activities varies by the type of preventive intervention (i.e., individual, small group, classroom, and schoolwide interventions). Depending on the intervention format, 35% to 83% of SBHCs were involved in bullying and violence prevention, 30% to 76% were involved in school safety planning, 20% to 76% were involved in sexual assault and rape prevention and counseling, and 23% to 76% were involved in intimate partner and dating violence prevention and counseling (Lofink et al., 2013). In terms of substance use, 36% to 82% of SBHCs were involved in some form of tobacco preventive intervention, 34% to 78% were involved in alcohol preventive interventions, and 33% to 78% were involved in drug preventive interventions. Finally, 37% to 90% of SBHCs were involved in health promotion activities regarding healthy eating, active living, and weight management.

## Sexual and Reproductive Health Care

Many SBHCs in middle and high schools provide sexual/reproductive health services in the form of abstinence counseling (82%), pregnancy testing (81%), STI diagnosis and treatment (69%), testicular examinations (69%), contraceptive counseling (65%), and gynecological examinations (59%; Lofink et al., 2013). Half of SBHCs were prohibited from dispensing contraceptives, most often due to school, district, and state policies. In centers that were allowed to provide contraceptive services, SBHCs were more likely to provide condoms as opposed to other methods of birth control, such as the pill (Fothergill & Feijoo, 2000). Although prenatal care is not available in most SBHCs, a study comparing adolescents showed that those receiving prenatal care in SBHCs had babies with higher birth weight compared with those receiving prenatal care in hospitals (Barnet et al., 2003). Further, studies show that receiving prenatal care in SBHCs is associated with lower rates of absenteeism and dropout (Barnet et al., 2003; Barnet et al., 2004).

## Oral and Dental Health Care

Dental and oral health services are becoming more available at SBHCs and are provided on-site and through mobile units. Over 70% of SBHCs reported conducting dental screenings, which may be conducted by a dental/oral health or primary care provider (Lofink et al., 2013). In addition, almost 40% of SBHCs provide dental examinations by either a dentist or dental hygienist and over 30% of SBHCs provide dental cleanings. Barriers to providing these services include cost, equipment needs, provider availability, space, and reimbursement.

## Evaluations of School-Based Health Centers: Acceptability and Accessibility

Evaluation findings of the acceptability of SBHCs among students have been promising. One study found that 86% of students rated the quality of care from their SBHC as satisfactory to excellent and 79% rated privacy in their SBHC as satisfactory to excellent (Santelli et al., 1996). Similarly, another study found that 92% of students were satisfied with the services received at their SBHC, 79% felt comfortable receiving care at their SBHC, and 74% felt that their visits were confidential (Pastore et al., 1998).

SBHCs provide developmentally appropriate and comprehensive care to children and adolescents in a familiar and accessible setting. The SBHC model links schools, communities, and health systems to provide an array of primary and preventive health care services. SBHCs were designed to address barriers in access to care and help meet the needs of underserved children. The convenient location allows youth to access care in a timely manner, which might otherwise be delayed. Parents do not have to take time off from work to take their child to a provider, which may be particularly challenging for low-income and single-parent families. Furthermore, children do not have to miss school to receive care (Gustafson, 2005). In addition, despite recent improvements to expand health insurance coverage among children, millions of children remain uninsured or underinsured. Low-income and racial/ethnic minority children are less likely to have a regular source of health care and therefore may benefit from the SBHC model (Brown & Bolen, 2012). In some rural areas, SBHCs are the only source of primary care for children and youth (Hossain et al., 2014). SBHCs are also beneficial for youth with multiple health needs as well as high-risk youth, who benefit from immediate access to care (Jepson et al., 1998). Youth are more likely to use health care services on a "spontaneous basis" (Pastore & Techow, 2004, p. 195); therefore, SBHCs offer location, convenience, confidentiality, and trust—all factors associated with the utilization of health and psychosocial services by youth (Brindis et al., 2003).

## Transgender Care Centers

### The Need for Gender-Affirming Care

Transgender and gender-diverse youth experience many health disparities when compared to the larger population; they are at a higher risk for depression, anxiety, eating disorders, self-harm, suicide, substance abuse, homelessness, physical violence, high-risk sexual behaviors, and HIV infection (Dowshen et al., 2016; Rafferty et al., 2018). In addition to facing interpersonal and institutional discrimination (e.g., alienation from families of origin and inequitable policies), transgender individuals also frequently contend with a lack of access to quality health care (Rafferty et al., 2018). Barriers can include a lack of providers familiar with transgender health issues, stigma and discrimination from providers, inability to pay for service, denial of insurance coverage for gender-related care, and inability to access legal documents that reflect their gender identity (Dowshen et al., 2016; Gridley et al., 2016; Lerner & Robles, 2017; Reisner et al., 2016; Stroumsa, 2014). These barriers lead to low rates of health care utilization by transgender people, which in turn can lead to further health complications and to individuals seeking medical treatment (such as hormones for gender transition) from potentially unsafe sources (Dowshen et al., 2016; Reisner et al., 2016).

All of these barriers must be managed at the same time as dealing with other potential stressors that often accompany being transgender, such as managing family and peer responses, navigating school and other systems in a new gender presentation, and addressing mental health challenges (Tishelman et al., 2015). We know that the health of transgender people intersects strongly with their biological, psychological, and social outcomes (Hughes et al., 2017; Lerner & Robles, 2017). Thus, there is a critical need for the provision of more gender-affirming care to counter these barriers, and integrated care is one promising way to do so (Reisner et al., 2016).

## The Roles of Integrated Gender Care Centers

Gender-related care frequently requires continuity of care to provide necessary follow-up for treatments with long-term effects. Communication between physical and mental health providers can be critical in determining the appropriate care related to gender transition. For example, research shows that psychiatric symptoms in transgender individuals often improve upon medical intervention for their gender dysphoria, suggesting that it might be the underlying cause (Spack et al., 2012). For these reasons, providing the various types of services needed under one roof can greatly diminish the stress faced by patients and can improve continuity and coordination of care.

In a 2018 policy statement, the American Academy of Pediatrics put forth that the best provision of gender-affirmative care models for youth is through integration of medical, mental health, and social services. Such services and resources include primary care, mental health care, endocrinology, other medical specialists as appropriate, assistance in accessing legal services and resources, advocacy, and support services for the whole family (Dowshen et al., 2016; Rafferty et al., 2018). Additional wraparound services provided at some institutions include voice therapy, STI prevention and treatment, reproductive health services, support groups, pharmacy services, and advocacy around school-based interactions.

## Creating Gender-Affirming Organizations

A few examples of integrated care programs featuring a special focus on gender-diverse youth are the Gender Multispecialty Service (GeMS) program at Boston Children's Hospital, Howard Brown Health in Chicago, and the Mazzoni

Center in Philadelphia. GeMS was the first multidisciplinary medical and mental health program housed in a pediatric academic center in North America to explicitly serve gender-variant youth (Tishelman et al., 2015). Some of the youth-specific services provided at these centers include family support, drop-in clinics, social events, and assistance in navigating school systems. Other organizations providing integrated transgender care, often as part of a broader focus on health care for LGBTQ people or other underserved populations, include Callen-Lorde Community Health Center in New York City; Fenway Health in Boston; Health Brigade in Richmond, Virginia; Lyon Martin Health Services and Women's Community Clinic in San Francisco; Tom Waddell Urban Health Clinic in San Francisco; the Transgender Care Navigation Program at the University of California–San Francisco; and Whitman-Walker Health in Washington, DC.

A common thread among health care centers focusing on the transgender population is a strengths-based view of human gender diversity, recognizing gender affirmation as an important part of routine treatment rather than the pathologization of being transgender as a disorder (Reisner, Bradford et al., 2015; Reisner et al., 2016). Creating a gender-affirming organization requires integration of gender-affirming practices at every level. In addition to the medical providers themselves being knowledgeable about relevant treatment options, it is essential for all staff across the agency to be culturally competent to work with gender-diverse populations, including those in administrative offices, clinical research, and community engagement programs. In addition, electronic health records, billing systems, and insurance plans need to be able to capture appropriate information, such as a client's preferred name and gender pronouns (Dowshen et al., 2016; Rafferty et al., 2018; Reisner, Bradford et al., 2015).

## Evaluation of Transgender Care Centers

Little research has been conducted to evaluate outcomes at transgender care centers, but there is evidence that retention rates of transgender patients improve when they have multidisciplinary service provider teams (Harris et al., 2003, as cited by Hughes et al., 2017). It is also clear that access to gender-affirming medical treatment can significantly improve not only physical health but also mental health and quality of life (Dowshen et al., 2016; Rafferty et al., 2018; Reisner et al., 2016). The centers discussed above have reported a high demand for their services, which was often not apparent before opening, indicating that providers outside of these agencies may not yet be aware of the needs that exist in their communities (Spack et al., 2012; Tishelman et al., 2015; Vance et al., 2014). For example, at Fenway Health in Boston, after implementing a modified informed consent model for cross-sex hormone therapy, the Transgender Health Program saw an increase from 90 active patients in 2006 to over 1,200 active patients in 2014 (Reisner, Bradford et al., 2015)—a 1,333% increase in eight years. Indeed, transgender care centers are a prime example of the pressing need to integrate services for young people in order to promote health and well-being.

# CONCLUSION

U.S. health policy for children, adolescents, and parents has developed in a piecemeal way, often in response to failures of the complex multi-payer private marketplace system. Failure to provide all children and youth with health coverage demonstrates that health care is not held as a fundamental human right in the U.S., the wealthiest nation in the world. Without universal access to high-quality treatment and preventive care, our most vulnerable and marginalized young people and their families may suffer. The shortcomings and failures of the U.S. health care system threaten the health and well-being of children and youth, who face numerous challenges to healthy development (e.g., LBW, asthma, obesity, STIs, and suicide), which can be addressed with preventive services. We have outlined multiple recommendations for improving U.S. health policy and illustrative examples of service integration. The time for policymakers to act is now, for the health of American children, youth, and families.

# REFERENCES

Agency for Healthcare Research and Quality (AHRQ). (n. d.). *Defining the PCMH*. https://pcmh.ahrq.gov/page/defining-pcmh

Agency for Healthcare Research and Quality (AHRQ). (2018). *Care coordination*. https://www.ahrq.gov/ncepcr/care/coordination.html

Agiesta, J. (2021). *CNN poll: Americans' willingness to get the coronavirus vaccine is on the rise*. https://www.cnn.com/2021/01/21/politics/cnn-poll-coronavirus-vaccine/index.html

Ahmad, N., Biswas, S., Bae, S., Meador, K. E., Huang, R., & Singh, K. P. (2009). Association between obesity and asthma in US children and adolescents. *Journal of Asthma, 46*, 642–646.

Akinbami, L. J., Moorman, J. E., Garbe, P. L., & Sondik, E. J. (2009). Status of childhood asthma in the United States, 1980–2007. *Pediatrics, 123*, S131–S145.

Alker, J., & Roygardner, L. (2019). *The number of uninsured children is on the rise*. Georgetown University Health Policy Institute.

American Academy of Pediatrics. (n. d.). *What is a medical home?* https://medicalhomeinfo.aap.org/overview/Pages/Whatisthemedicalhome.aspx

American Lung Association. (2020a). *Kickin' asthma*. https://www.lung.org/lung-health-diseases/lung-disease-lookup/asthma/asthma-education-advocacy/kickin-asthma

American Lung Association. (2020b). *Open airways for schools*. https://www.lung.org/lung-health-diseases/lung-disease-lookup/asthma/asthma-education-advocacy/open-airways-for-schools

American Psychological Association. (2014). *Youth at disproportionate risk*. https://www.apa.org/pi/lgbt/programs/safe-supportive/disproportionate-risk

Anderson, G. F., Hussey, P., & Petrosyan, V. (2019). It's still the prices, stupid: Why the US spends so much on health care, and a tribute to Uwe Reinhardt. *Health Affairs, 38*(1), 87–95.

Anfinrud, P., Stadnytskyi, V., Bax, C. E., & Bax, A. (2020). Visualizing speech-generated oral fluid droplets with laser light scattering. *New England Journal of Medicine, 382*, 2061–2063.

Antonelli, R. C., McAllister, J. W., & Popp, J. (2009). *Making care coordination a critical component of the pediatric health system: A multidisciplinary framework*. The Commonwealth Fund.

Antonogeorgos, G., Panagiotakos, D. B., Papadimitriou, A., Priftis, K. N., Anthracopoulos, M., & Nicolaidou, P. (2012). Breakfast consumption and meal frequency interaction with childhood obesity. *Pediatric Obesity, 7*(1), 65–72.

Arpino, C., Compagnone, E., Montanaro, M. L., Cacciatore, D., De Luca, A., Cerulli, A., Di Girolamo, S., & Curatolo, P. (2010). Preterm birth and neurodevelopmental outcome: A review. *Child's Nervous System, 26*(9), 1139–1149.

Artiga, S., & Hinton, E. (2018). *Beyond health care: The role of social determinants in promoting health and health equity.* Kaiser Family Foundation.

Baena-Cagnani, C. E., Gomez, R. M., Baena-Cagnani, R., & Canonica, G. W. (2009). Impact of environmental tobacco smoke and active tobacco smoking on the development and outcomes of asthma and rhinitis. *Current Opinion in Allergy and Clinical Immunology, 9*, 136–140.

Bailey, S. R., Marino, M., Hoopes, M., Heintzman, J., Gold, R., Angier, H., O'Malley, J. P., & DeVoe, J. E. (2016). Healthcare utilization after a children's health insurance program expansion in Oregon. *Maternal and Child Health Journal, 20*(5), 946–954.

Bains, R. M., Cusson, R., White-Frese, J., & Walsh, S. (2017). Utilization of mental health services in school-based health centers. *Journal of School Health, 87*(8), 584–592.

Balasch, J., & Gratacós, E. (2011). Delayed childbearing: Effects on fertility and the outcome of pregnancy. *Fetal Diagnosis and Therapy, 29*(4), 263–273.

Banks, D. E., Hensel, D. J., & Zapolski, T. C. (2020). Integrating individual and contextual factors to explain disparities in HIV/STI among heterosexual African American youth: A contemporary literature review and social ecological model. *Archives of Sexual Behavior.*

Barnet, B., Arroyo, C., Devoe, M., & Duggan, A. K. (2004). Reduced school dropout rates among adolescent mothers receiving school-based prenatal care. *Archives of Pediatrics & Adolescent Medicine, 158*, 262–268.

Barnet, B., Duggan, A. K., & Devoe, M. (2003). Reduced low birth weight for teenagers receiving prenatal care at a school-based health center: Effect of access and comprehensive care. *Journal of Adolescent Health, 33*, 349–358.

Barr, D. A., Lee, P. R., & Benjamin, A. E. (2003). Health care and health care policy in a changing world. In H. M. Wallace, G. Green, & K. Jaros (Eds.), *Health and welfare for families in the 21st century* (2nd ed., pp. 262–42). Jones & Bartlett.

Berchick, E. R., Barnett, J. C., & Upton, R. D. (2019). *Health insurance coverage in the United States: 2018.* U.S. Census Bureau.

Berdahl, T., Owens, P. L., Dougherty, D., McCormick, M. C., Pylypchuk, Y., & Simpson, L. A. (2010). Annual report on health care for children and youth in the United States: Racial/ethnic and socioeconomic disparities in children's health care quality. *Academic Pediatrics, 10*(2), 95–118.

Bhutta, A. T., Cleves, M. A., Casey, P. H., Cradock, M. M., & Anand, K. J. (2002). Cognitive and behavioral outcomes of school-aged children who were born preterm: A meta-analysis. *Jama, 288*(6), 728–737.

Bilsen, J. (2018). Suicide and youth: Risk factors. *Frontiers in Psychiatry, 9*, 540.

Black, M. H., Zhou, H., Takayanagi, M., Jacobsen, S. J., & Koebnick, C. (2013). Increased asthma risk and asthma-related health care complications associated with childhood obesity. *American Journal of Epidemiology, 178*, 1120–1128.

Boerma, T., Eozenou, P., Evans, D., Evans, T., Kieny, M. P., & Wagstaff, A. (2014). Monitoring progress towards universal health coverage at country and global levels. *PLOS Medicine, 11*(9), e1001731.

Boonstra, A., Versluis, A., & Vos, J. F. (2014). Implementing electronic health records in hospitals: A systematic literature review. *BMC Health Services Research, 14*(1), 370.

Braveman, P., Egerter, S., & Williams, D. R. (2011). The social determinants of health: Coming of age. *Annual Review of Public Health, 32*, 381–398.

Braveman, P., & Gottlieb, L. (2014). The social determinants of health: It's time to consider the causes of the causes. *Public Health Reports, 129*(Sup 2), 19–31.

Brenan, M. (2021). *Two-thirds of Americans not satisfied with vaccine rollout.* Gallup. https://news.gallup.com/poll/329552/two-thirds-americans-not-satisfied-vaccine-rollout.aspx

Bridge, J. A., Goldstein, T. R., & Brent, D. A. (2006). Adolescent suicide and suicidal behavior. *Journal of Child Psychology and Psychiatry, 47*(3–4), 372–394.

Brindis, C. D., Klein, J., Schlitt, J., Santelli, J., Juszcak, L., & Nystrom, R. (2003). School-based health centers: Accessibility and accountability. *Journal of Adolescent Health, 32S*, 98–107.

Brown, C. C., Moore, J. E., Felix, H. C., Stewart, M. K., & Tilford, J. M. (2020). County-level variation in low birth-weight and preterm birth: An evaluation of state Medicaid expansion under the Affordable Care Act. *Medical Care, 58*(6), 497–503.

Brown, M. B., & Bolen, L. M. (2012). School-based health centers. In *Encyclopedia of adolescence* (pp. 2506–2511). Springer.

Burkhauser, R. V., & Cawley, J. (2008). Beyond BMI: The value of more accurate measures of fatness and obesity in social science research. *Journal of Health Economics, 27*(2), 519–529.

Calvo, R., & Hawkins, S. S. (2015). Disparities in quality of healthcare of children from immigrant families in the US. *Maternal and Child Health Journal, 19*(10), 2223–2232.

Carballo, J. J., Llorente, C., Kehrmann, L., Flamarique, I., Zuddas, A., Purper-Ouakil, D., Hoekstra, P. J., Coghill, D., Schulze, U. M. E., Dittman, R. W., Buitelaar, Castro-Fornleles, J., Lievesley, K., Santosh, P., & Arango, C. (2020). Psychosocial risk factors for suicidality in children and adolescents. *European Child & Adolescent Psychiatry*, 1–18.

Carrin, G., & James, C. (2004). *Reaching universal coverage via social health insurance: Key design features in the transition period.* World Health Organization.

Cassedy, A., Fairbrother, G., & Newacheck, P. W. (2008). The impact of insurance instability on children's access, utilization, and satisfaction with health care. *Ambulatory Pediatrics. 8*(5), 321–328.

Centers for Disease Control and Prevention (CDC). (2012). *Sexually transmitted diseases surveillance 2011.* U.S. Department of Health and Human Services.

Centers for Disease Control and Prevention (CDC). (2013). *Summary health statistics for U.S. children: National Health Interview Survey, 2012.* http://www.cdc.gov/nchs/data/series/sr_10/sr10_258.pdf

Centers for Disease Control and Prevention (CDC). (2014a). *2012 National Health Interview Survey (NHIS) data.* http://www.cdc.gov/Asthma/nhis/2012/data.htm

Centers for Disease Control and Prevention (CDC). (2014b). *HIV among youth.* http://www.cdc.gov/hiv/pdf/risk_youth_fact_sheet_final.pdf

Centers for Disease Control and Prevention (CDC). (2015). *Asthma-related missed school days among children aged 5–17 years.* https://www.cdc.gov/asthma/asthma_stats/missing_days.htm

Centers for Disease Control and Prevention (CDC). (2016). *Results from the school health policies and practices study 2016.* https://www.cdc.gov/healthyyouth/data/shpps/pdf/shpps-results_2016.pdf

Centers for Disease Control and Prevention (CDC). (2017). *State school immunization requirements and vaccine exemption laws.* The Centers for Disease Control and Prevention's Public Health Law Program.

Centers for Disease Control and Prevention (CDC). (2018a). *Asthma in children.* https://www.cdc.gov/vitalsigns/childhood-asthma/index.html

Centers for Disease Control and Prevention (CDC). (2018b). *Sexually transmitted disease surveillance 2018.* https://www.cdc.gov/std/stats18/default.htm

Centers for Disease Control and Prevention (CDC). (2019). *Leading causes of death.* https://www.cdc.gov/healthequity/lcod/index.htm

Centers for Disease Control and Prevention. (2020). *COVID-19 testing overview.* https://www.cdc.gov/coronavirus/2019-ncov/symptoms-testing/testing.html

Centers for Disease Control and Prevention (CDC). (2021a). *COVID-19 death data and resources.* https://www.cdc.gov/nchs/nvss/vsrr/covid19/index.htm

Centers for Disease Control and Prevention (CDC). (2021b). *COVID-19 vaccinations in the United States.* https://covid.cdc.gov/covid-data-tracker/#vaccinations

Centers for Disease Control and Prevention (CDC). (2021c). *Benefits of getting a COVID-19 vaccine.* https://www.cdc.gov/coronavirus/2019-ncov/vaccines/vaccine-benefits.html

Cha, C. B., Franz, P. J., Guzmán, E. M., Glenn, C. R., Kleiman, E. M., & Nock, M. K. (2018). Annual research review: Suicide among youth–epidemiology, (potential) etiology, and treatment. *Journal of Child Psychology and Psychiatry, 59*(4), 460–482.

Chapman, M. V., Hall, W. J., Lee, K., Colby, R., Coyne-Beasley, T., Day, S., Eng, E., Lightfoot, A. F, McGowan, J., Merino, Y., Siman, F. M., Thatcher, K. J., Thomas, T., & Payne, B. K. (2018). Making a difference in medical trainees' attitudes toward Latino patients: A pilot study of an intervention to modify implicit and explicit attitudes. *Social Science & Medicine, 199*, 202–208.

Chen, X. K., Wen, S. W., Fleming, N., Yang, Q., & Walker, M. C. (2008). Increased risks of neonatal and post-neonatal mortality associated with teenage pregnancy had different explanations. *Journal of Clinical Epidemiology, 61*, 688–694.

Child Trends. (2018). *Health care coverage for children*. https://www.childtrends.org/indicators/health-care-coverage

Choi, M., Sommers, B. D., & McWilliams, J. M. (2011). Children's health insurance and access to care during and after the CHIP expansion period. *Journal of Health Care for the Poor and Underserved, 22*(2), 576–589.

Chu, D. K., Akl, E. A., Duda, S., Solo, K., Yaacoub, S., Schünemann, H. J., El-harakeh, A., Bognanni, A., Lotfi, T., Loeb, M., Hajizadeh, A., Bak, A., Izcovich, A., Cuello-Garcia, C. A., Chen, C., Harris, D. J., Borowiack, E., Chamseddine, F., Schünemann, F., . . . & Reinap, M. (2020). Physical distancing, face masks, and eye protection to prevent person-to-person transmission of SARS-CoV-2 and COVID-19: A systematic review and meta-analysis. *The Lancet.*

Clausen, T. D., Mathiesen, E. R., Hansen, T., Pedersen, O., Jensen, D. M., Lauenborg, J., & Damm, P. (2008). High prevalence of Type 2 diabetes and pre-diabetes in adult offspring of women with gestational diabetes mellitus or Type 1 diabetes: The role of intrauterine hyperglycemia. *Diabetes Care, 31*(2), 340–346.

Cochran, B. N., Peavy, K. M., & Cauce, A. M. (2007). Substance abuse treatment providers' explicit and implicit attitudes regarding sexual minorities. *Journal of Homosexuality, 53*(3), 181–207.

Coker, T. R., Austin, S. B., & Schuster, M. A. (2010). The health and health care of lesbian, gay, and bisexual adolescents. *Annual Review of Public Health, 31*, 457–477.

Collins, S. R., & Gunja, M. Z. (2019). What do Americans think about their health coverage ahead of the 2020 election? *Commonwealth fund.* https://www.commonwealthfund.org/publications/issue-briefs/2019/sep/what-do-americans-think-health-coverage-2020-election

Cristancho, S., Garces, D. M., Peters, K. E., & Mueller, B. C. (2008). Listening to rural Hispanic immigrants in the Midwest: A community-based participatory assessment of major barriers to health care access and use. *Qualitative Health Research, 18*(5), 633–646.

Crowley, R., Daniel, H., Cooney, T. G., & Engel, L. S. (2020). Envisioning a better US health care system for all: Coverage and cost of care. *Annals of Internal Medicine, 172*(Suppl. 2), S7–S32.

Curtin, S. C., & Heron, M. (2019). *Death rates due to suicide and homicide among persons aged 10–24: United States, 2000–2017*. National Center for Health Statistics, Centers for Disease Control and Prevention, U.S. Department of Health and Human Services.

Dabelea, D., & Crume, T. (2011). Maternal environment and the transgenerational cycle of obesity and diabetes. *Diabetes, 60*(7), 1849–1855.

Dawes, H. C., Klein, L. B., Hirst, L. E., Forte, A. B., Gibbs, D. J., & Hall, W. J. (2021). *Experiences of LGBTQ people of color in mental health services and substance abuse services: A systematic review* [manuscript submitted for publication].

Dempsey, A. F., Schaffer, S., Singer, D., Butchart, A., Davis, M., & Freed, G. L. (2011). Alternative vaccination schedule preferences among parents of young children. *Pediatrics, 128*(5), 848–856.

DeRoo, S. S., Pudalov, N. J., & Fu, L. Y. (2020). Planning for a COVID-19 vaccination program. *JAMA, 323*(24), 2458–2459.

DeVoe, J. E., Ray, M., Krois, L., & Carlson, M. J. (2010). Uncertain health insurance coverage and unmet children's health care needs. *Family Medicine, 42*(2), 121–132.

DeVoe, J. E., Tillotson, C. J., Wallace, L. S., Lesko, S. E., & Pandhi, N. (2012). Is health insurance enough? A usual source of care may be more important to ensure a child receives preventive health counseling. *Maternal and Child Health Journal, 16*(2), 306–315.

Dowshen, N., Meadows, R., Byrnes, M., Hawkins, L., Eder, J., & Noonan, K. (2016). Policy perspective: Ensuring comprehensive care and support for gender nonconforming children and adolescents. *Transgender Health, 1*(1), 75–85.

Eisenmann, J. C., Gundersen, C., Lohman, B. J., Garasky, S., & Stewart, S. D. (2011). Is food insecurity related to overweight and obesity in children and adolescents? A summary of studies, 1995–2009. *Obesity Reviews, 12*(5), e73–e83.

Everett, B. G. (2013). Sexual orientation disparities in sexually transmitted infections: Examining the intersection between sexual identity and sexual behavior. *Archives of Sexual Behavior, 42*(2), 225–236.

Everett, B. G., Schnarrs, P. W., Rosario, M., Garofalo, R., & Mustanski, B. (2014). Sexual orientation disparities in sexually transmitted infection risk behaviors and risk determinants among sexually active adolescent males: Results from a school-based sample. *American Journal of Public Health, 104*(6), 1107–1112.

Fang, K., Mu, M., Liu, K., & He, Y. (2019). Screen time and childhood overweight/obesity: A systematic review and meta-analysis. *Child Care, Health and Development, 45*(5), 744–753.

Federico, S. G., Abrams, L., Everhart, R. M., Melinkovich, P., & Hambidge, S. J. (2010). Addressing adolescent immunization disparities: A retrospective analysis of school-based health center immunization delivery. *American Journal of Public Health, 100*, 1630–1634.

First Focus. (2012). *Top 10 Affordable Care Act wins for kids*. http://www.firstfocus.net/top-10-affordable-care-act-wins-for-kids-0%20

Flowers, L., & Accius, J. (2019). *The new Medicaid waivers: Coverage losses for beneficiaries, higher costs for states*. AARP Public Policy Institute.

Forte, A., Mcbride, M., Gibbs, D., Johnson, T., Masa, R., & Zerden, L. (2020). *Exploring the relationship between the built food environment and obesity among African Americans: A systematic review* [manuscript submitted for publication].

Fothergill, K., & Feijoo, A. (2000). Family planning services at school-based health centers: Findings from a national survey. *Journal of Adolescent Health, 27*, 166–169.

Fox, A., & Poirier, R. (2018). How single-payer stacks up: Evaluating different models of universal health coverage on cost, access, and quality. *International Journal of Health Services, 48*(3), 568–585.

Freedman, D. S., & Sherry, B. (2009). The validity of BMI as an indicator of body fatness and risk among children. *Pediatrics, 124*(Supplement 1), S23–S34.

Future of Sex Education Initiative. (2020). *National sex education standards: Core content and skills, K–12* (2nd ed.). https://advocatesforyouth.org/wp-content/uploads/2020/03/NSES-2020-web.pdf

Gee, E., & Spiro, T. (2019). *Excess administrative costs burden the U.S. health care system*. Center for American Progress.

Gerald, L. B., Gerald, J. K., Gibson, L., Patel, K., Zhang, S., & McClure, L. A. (2009). Changes in environmental tobacco smoke exposure and asthma morbidity among urban school children. *Chest, 135*, 911–916.

Gibbs, C. M., Wendt, A., Peters, S., & Hogue, C. J. (2012). The impact of early age at first child birth on maternal and infant health. *Paediatric & Perinatal Epidemiology, 26*, S259–S284.

Gleason, P. M., & Dodd, A. H. (2009). School breakfast program but not school lunch program participation is associated with lower body mass index. *Journal of the American Dietetic Association, 109*(2), S118–S128.

Global Asthma Network. (2018). *The global asthma report 2018*. Author.

Greer, T. M. (2010). Perceived racial discrimination in clinical encounters among African American hypertensive patients. *Journal of Health Care for the Poor and Underserved, 21*(1), 251–263.

Gridley, S. J., Crouch, J. M., Evans, Y., Eng, W., Antoon, E., Lyapustina, M., Schimmel-Bristow, A., Woodward, J., Dundon, K., Schaff, R., McCarty, C., Ahrens, K., & Breland, D. J. (2016). Youth and caregiver perspectives on barriers to gender-affirming health care for transgender youth. *The Journal of Adolescent Health: Official Publication of the Society for Adolescent Medicine, 59*(3), 254–261.

Güngör, N. K. (2014). Overweight and obesity in children and adolescents. *Journal of Clinical Research in Pediatric Endocrinology, 6*(3), 129.

Guo, J. J., Wade, T. J., & Keller, K. N. (2008). Impact of school-based health centers on students with mental health problems. *Public Health Reports, 123*, 768–780.

Gurman, T. A., & Becker, D. (2008). Factors affecting Latina immigrants' perceptions of maternal health care: Findings from a qualitative study. *Health Care for Women International, 29*(5), 507–526.

Gustafson, E. M. (2005). History and overview of school-based health centers in the US. *Nursing Clinics of North America, 40*, 595–606.

Hales, C. M., Carroll, M. D., Fryar, C. D., & Ogden, C. L. (2017). *Prevalence of obesity among adults and youth: United States, 2015–2016*. National Center for Health Statistics.

Hales, C. M., Fryar, C. D., Carroll, M. D., Freedman, D. S., & Ogden, C. L. (2018). Trends in obesity and severe obesity prevalence in US youth and adults by sex and age, 2007–2008 to 2015–2016. *JAMA, 319*(16), 1723–1725.

Hall, W. J., Chapman, M. V., Lee, K. M., Merino, Y. M., Thomas, T. W., Payne, B. K., Eng, E., Day, S. H., & Coyne-Beasley, T. (2015). Implicit racial/ethnic bias among health care professionals and its influence on health care outcomes: A systematic review. *American Journal of Public Health, 105*(12), e60–e76.

Hall, W. J., Jones, B. L. H., Witkemper, K. D., Collins, T., & Rodgers, G. K. (2019). State policy on school-based sex education: A content analysis focused on sexual behaviors, relationships, and identities. *American Journal of Health Behavior*, *43*, 506–519.

Hall, W. J., Kresica, A. M., & McDougald, A. M. (2013). School counselors' education and training, competency, and supportive behaviors concerning gay, lesbian, and bisexual students. *Professional School Counseling*, *17*, 130–141.

Hall, W. J., & Rounds, K. A. (2013). Adolescent health. In the Public Health Social Work Section of the American Public Health Association, R. H. Keefe, & E. T. Jurkowski (Eds.), *Handbook for public health social work* (pp. 59–80). Springer.

Hamel, L., Kirzinger, A., Lopes, L., Kearney, A., Sparks, G., & Brodie, M. (2021). KFF COVID-19 vaccine monitor: January 2021. *Kaiser Family Foundation*. https://www.kff.org/report-section/kff-covid-19-vaccine-monitor-january-2021-vaccine-hesitancy/

Han, J. C., Lawlor, D. A., & Kimm, S. Y. (2010). Childhood obesity. *Lancet*, *375*, 1737–1748.

Harris, S. K., Samples, C. L., Keenan, P. M., Fox, D. J., Melchiono, M. W., Woods, E. R., & Boston HAPPENS Program. (2003). Outreach, mental health, and case management services: Can they help to retain HIV-positive and at-risk youth and young adults in care? *Maternal and Child Health Journal*, *7*, 205–218.

Heerwagen, M. J., Miller, M. R., Barbour, L. A., & Friedman, J. E. (2010). Maternal obesity and fetal metabolic programming: A fertile epigenetic soil. *American Journal of Physiology-Regulatory, Integrative and Comparative Physiology*, *299*(3), R711–R722.

Hellerstedt, W. L. (2013). The Affordable Care Act: What are its goals and do we need it? *Healthy Generations, 2013*. University of Minnesota, Center for Leadership Education in Maternal and Child Public Health. http://www.epi.umn.edu/mch

Henry J. Kaiser Family Foundation. (2009). *Enrolling uninsured low-income children in Medicaid and SCHIP*. http://www.kff.org/medicaid/upload/2177_06.pdf

Howell, E. M., & Kenney, G. M. (2012). The impact of the Medicaid/CHIP expansions on children: A synthesis of the evidence. *Medical Care Research and Review*, *69*(4), 372–396.

Hill, H. A., Elam-Evans, L. D., Yankey, D., Singleton, J. A., & Kang, Y. (2018). Vaccination coverage among children aged 19–35 months—United States, 2017. *Morbidity and Mortality Weekly Report*, *67*(40), 1123.

Himmelstein, D. U., Thorne, D., Warren, E., & Woolhandler, S. (2009). Medical bankruptcy in the United States, 2007: Results of a national study. *The American Journal of Medicine*, *122*(8), 741–746.

Hossain, M., Coughlin, R., & Zickafoose, J. (2014). CHIPRA quality demonstration: States help school-based health centers strengthen their medical home features. *Agency for Healthcare Research and Quality*. https://www.ahrq.gov/policymakers/chipra/demoeval/what-we-learned/highlight08.html

Hughes, R. L., Damin, C., & Heiden-Rootes, K. (2017). Where's the LGBT in integrated care research? A systematic review. *Families, Systems, & Health*, *35*(3), 308–319.

IHS Markit. (2020). *The complexities of physician supply and demand: Projections from 2018 to 2033*. Association of American Medical Colleges.

Isaac, M., Elias, B., Katz, L. Y., Belik, S.-L., Deane, F. P., Enns, M. W., Sareen, J., & The Swampy Cree Suicide Prevention Team. (2009). Gatekeeper training as a preventative intervention for suicide: A systematic review. *The Canadian Journal of Psychiatry*, *54*(4), 260–268.

Ivey-Stephenson, A. Z., Demissie, Z., Crosby, A. E., Stone, D. M., Gaylor, E., Wilkins, N., Lowry, R., & Brown, M. (2020). Suicidal ideation and behaviors among high school students—Youth Risk Behavior Survey, United States, 2019. *Morbidity and Mortality Weekly Report*, *69*(Suppl. 1), 47–55.

James, J. (2012). Pay-for-performance. *Health Affairs*, *34*(8), 1–6.

Jepson, L., Juszczak, L., & Fisher, M. (1998). Mental health care in a high school based health service. *Adolescence*, *33*, 1–15.

Johns, M. M., Lowry, R., Andrzejewski, J., Barrios, L. C., Demissie, Z., McManus, T., Rasberry, C. N., Robin, L., & Underwood, J. M. (2019). Transgender identity and experiences of violence victimization, substance use, suicide risk, and sexual risk behaviors among high school students—19 states and large urban school districts, 2017. *Morbidity and Mortality Weekly Report*, *68*(3), 67.

Johns, M. M., Lowry, R., Haderxhanaj, L. T., Rasberry, C. N., Robin, L., Scales, L., Stone, D., & Suarez, N. A. (2020). Trends in violence victimization and suicide risk by sexual identity among high school students—Youth Risk Behavior Survey, United States, 2015–2019. *Morbidity and Mortality Weekly Report, 69*(Suppl. 1), 19–27.

Jost, T. (2020). The supreme court will decide the fate of the Affordable Care Act—again. *The Commonwealth Fund.* https://www.commonwealthfund.org/blog/2020/supreme-court-will-decide-fate-affordable-care-act-again

Kann, L., Olsen, E. O., McManus, T., Harris, W. A., Shanklin, S. L., Flint, K. H., Queen, B., Lowry, R., Chyen, D., Whittle, L., Thornton, J., Lim, C., Yamakawa, Y., Brener, N., & Zaza, S. (2016). Sexual identity, sex of sexual contacts, and health-related behaviors among students in Grades 9–12—United States and selected sites, 2015. *Morbidity and Mortality Weekly Report: Surveillance Summaries, 65*(9), 1–202.

Kcomt, L. (2019). Profound health-care discrimination experienced by transgender people: Rapid systematic review. *Social Work in Health Care, 58*(2), 201–219.

Keeton, V., Soleimanpour, S., & Brindis, C. D. (2012). School-based health centers in an era of health care reform: Building on history. *Current Problems in Pediatric and Adolescent Health Care, 42*, 132–158.

Keller, A., & Bucher Della Torre, S. (2015). Sugar-sweetened beverages and obesity among children and adolescents: A review of systematic literature reviews. *Childhood Obesity, 11*(4), 338–346.

Kelly, A. S., Barlow, S. E., Rao, G., Inge, T. H., Hayman, L. L., Steinberger, J., Urbina, E. M., Ewing, L. J., & Daniels, S. R. (2013). Severe obesity in children and adolescents: Identification, associated health risks, and treatment approaches: A scientific statement from the American Heart Association. *Circulation, 128*(15), 1689–1712.

Kessel, W., Jaros, K., & Harker, P. T. (2003). The Social Security Act and maternal and child health services: Securing a bright future. In H. M. Wallace, G. Green, & K. Jaros (Eds.), *Health and welfare for families in the 21st century* (2nd ed., pp. 164–170). Jones & Bartlett.

Khan, A., Nasrullah, F. D., & Jaleel, R. (2016). Frequency and risk factors of low birth weight in term pregnancy. *Pakistan Journal of Medical Sciences, 32*(1), 138.

Kim, D., & Saada, A. (2013). The social determinants of infant mortality and birth outcomes in Western developed nations: A cross-country systematic review. *International Journal of Environmental Research and Public Health, 10*(6), 2296–2335.

King, C. A., & Merchant, C. R. (2008). Social and interpersonal factors relating to adolescent suicidality: A review of the literature. *Archives of Suicide Research, 12*(3), 181–196.

Kirby, D., & Lepore, G. (2007). *A matrix of risk and protective factors affecting teen sexual behavior, pregnancy, childbearing, and sexually transmitted disease.* The National Campaign to Prevent Teen Pregnancy.

Kirzinger, A., Muñana, C., Wu, B., & Brodie, M. (2019). *Americans' challenges with healthcare costs.* Kaiser Family Foundation.

Kost, K., Maddow-Zimet, I., & Arpaia, A. (2017). *Pregnancies, births and abortions among adolescents and young women in the United States, 2013: National and state trends by age, race and ethnicity.* Guttmacher Institute.

Kramer, K. L., & Lancaster, J. B. (2010). Teen motherhood in cross cultural perspective. *Annals of Human Biology, 37*, 613–628.

Lamichhane, A. P., Puett, R., Porter, D. E., Bottai, M., Mayer-Davis, E. J., & Liese, A. D. (2012). Associations of built food environment with body mass index and waist circumference among youth with diabetes. *International Journal of Behavioral Nutrition and Physical Activity, 9*(1), 1–11.

Lappan, S. N., Parra-Cardona, J. R., Carolan, M., & Weatherspoon, L. (2020). Risk and protective factors associated with childhood obesity in a sample of low-income, single female, parent/guardian households: Implications for family therapists. *Family Process, 59*(2), 597–617.

Lawson, J. A., Janssen, I., Bruner, M. W., Hossain, A., & Pickett, W. (2014). Asthma incidence and risk factors in a national longitudinal sample of adolescent Canadians: A prospective cohort study. *BMC Pulmonary Medicine, 14*, 51.

Leffler, C. T., Ing, E. B., Lykins, J. D., Hogan, M. C., McKeown, C. A., & Grzybowski, A. (2020). Association of country-wide coronavirus mortality with demographics, testing, lockdowns, and public wearing of masks. *medRxiv.* https://www.medrxiv.org/content/10.1101/2020.05.22.20109231v5

Lerner, J. E., & Robles, G. (2017). Perceived barriers and facilitators to health care utilization in the United States for transgender people: A review of recent literature. *Journal of Health Care for the Poor and Underserved, 28*(1), 127–152.

Leung, N. H., Chu, D. K., Shiu, E. Y., Chan, K.-H., McDevitt, J. J., Hau, B. J., Yen, H.-L., Li, Y., Ip, D. K., Peiris, J. S., Seto, W. H., Leung, G. M., Milton, D. K., & Cowling, B. J. (2020). Respiratory virus shedding in exhaled breath and efficacy of face masks. *Nature Medicine, 26*(5), 676–680.

Lipkin, P. H., Alexander, J., Cartwright, J. D., Desch, L. W., Duby, J. C., Edwards, D. R., Elias, E. R., Johnson, C. P., Levey, E. B., Murphy, N. A., Myers, S., Henderson Tilton, A., Crider, B., Lollar, D., Macias, M. M., McPherson, M., & Skipper, S. M. (2005). Care coordination in the medical home: Integrating health and related systems of care for children with special health care needs. *Pediatrics, 116*(5), 1238–1244.

Liu, J. H., Jones, S. J., Sun, H., Probst, J. C., Merchant, A. T., & Cavicchia, P. (2012). Diet, physical activity, and sedentary behaviors as risk factors for childhood obesity: An urban and rural comparison. *Childhood Obesity, 8*(5), 440–448.

Liu, J. L., & Brook, R. H. (2017). What is single-payer health care? A review of definitions and proposals in the US. *Journal of General Internal Medicine, 32*(7), 822–831.

Liu, P. C., Kieckhefer, G. M., & Gau, B. S. (2013). A systematic review of the association between obesity and asthma in children. *Journal of Advanced Nursing, 69*, 1446–1465.

Lofink, H., Kuebler, J., Juszczak, L., Schlitt, J., Even, M., Rosenberg, J., & White, I. (2013). *2010–2011 School-based health alliance census report.* School-Based Health Alliance.

Lopez, M. A., Faro, E. Z., Oyeku, S. O., & Raphael, J. L. (2018). *Disparities in child health: A solutions-based approach.* Springer.

Love, H. E., Schlitt, J., Soleimanpour, S., Panchal, N., & Behr, C. (2019). Twenty years of school-based health care growth and expansion. *Health Affairs, 38*(5), 755–764.

Lu, M. C., Kotelchuck, M., Hogan, V., Jones, L., Wright, K., & Halfon, N. (2010). Closing the Black–White gap in birth outcomes: A life-course approach. *Ethnicity & Disease, 20*(Suppl. 2), 62–76.

Lyu, W., & Wehby, G. L. (2020). Community use of face masks and COVID-19: Evidence from a natural experiment of state mandates in the US: Study examines impact on COVID-19 growth rates associated with state government mandates requiring face mask use in public. *Health Affairs, 39*(8), 1419–1425.

Macgowan, M. J. (2004). Suicidality among youths. In M. W. Fraser (Ed.), *Risk and resilience in childhood: An ecological perspective* (2nd ed., pp. 347–383). NASW Press.

MacIntyre, C. R., & Chughtai, A. A. (2020). A rapid systematic review of the efficacy of face masks and respirators against coronaviruses and other respiratory transmissible viruses for the community, healthcare workers and sick patients. *International Journal of Nursing Studies,* 103629.

Manlove, J., Terry-Humen, E., & Ikramullah, E. (2006). Young teenagers and older sexual partners: Correlates and consequences for males and females. *Perspectives on Sexual and Reproductive Health, 38,* 197–207.

Mansour, M. E., Rose, B., Toole, K., Luzader, C. P., & Atherton, H. D. (2008). Pursuing perfection: An asthma quality improvement initiative in school-based health centers with community partners. *Public Health Reports, 123,* 717–730.

Margolis, L. H., & Kotch, J. B. (2013). Tracing the historical foundations of maternal and child health to contemporary times. In J. B. Kotch (Ed.), *Maternal and child health: Programs, problems, and policy in public health* (3rd ed., pp. 11–34). Jones & Bartlett Learning.

Markowitz, A. (2021). State-by-state guide to face mask requirements. *AARP.* https://www.aarp.org/health/healthy-living/info-2020/states-mask-mandates-coronavirus.html

Marmot, M., & Wilkinson, R. G. (Eds.). (2005). *Social determinants of health.* Oxford University Press.

Martin, J. A., Hamilton, B. E., Osterman, M. J., & Driscoll, A. K. (2019). Births: Final data for 2018. *National Vital Statistics Reports, 68*(13).

Marvasti, F. F., & Stafford, R. S. (2012). From "sick care" to health care: Reengineering prevention into the US system. *The New England Journal of Medicine, 367*(10), 889–891.

Maternal and Child Health (MCH) Bureau. (n. d.). *Programs: Title V block grant to states.* http://mchb.hrsa.gov/programs/

McGinnis, J. M., Williams-Russo, P., & Knickman, J. R. (2002). The case for more active policy attention to health promotion. *Health Affairs, 21*(2), 78–93.

McPherson, M., Arango, P., Fox, H., Lauver, C., McManus, M., Newacheck, P. W., Perrin, J. M., Shonkoff, J. P, & Strickland, B. (1998). A new definition of children with special health care needs. *Pediatrics, 102,* 137–140.

Mehra, R., Boyd, L. M., & Ickovics, J. R. (2017). Racial residential segregation and adverse birth outcomes: A systematic review and meta-analysis. *Social Science & Medicine, 191*, 237–250.

Metzger, M. W., & McDade, T. W. (2010). Breastfeeding as obesity prevention in the United States: A sibling difference model. *American Journal of Human Biology, 22*(3), 291–296.

Midodzi, W. K., Rowe, B. H., Majaesic, C. M., Saunders, L. D., & Senthilselvan, A. (2010). Early life factors associated with incidence of physician-diagnosed asthma in preschool children: Results from the Canadian Early Childhood Development cohort study. *Journal of Asthma, 47*, 7–13.

Miguel-Berges, M. L., Reilly, J. J., Aznar, L. A. M., & Jiménez-Pavón, D. (2018). Associations between pedometer-determined physical activity and adiposity in children and adolescents: Systematic review. *Clinical Journal of Sport Medicine, 28*(1), 64–75.

Moniz, C., & Gorin, S. (2014). *Health care policy and practice: A biopsychosocial perspective.* (4th ed.). Routledge.

National Association of Insurance Commissioners. (2019). *Statistical compilation of annual statement information for health insurance companies in 2018.* Author.

National Conference of State Legislatures. (2020). *States with religious and philosophical exemptions from school immunization requirements.* https://www.ncsl.org/research/health/school-immunization-exemption-state-laws.aspx

Newacheck, P. W., Brindis, C. D., Cart, C. U., Marchi, K., & Irwin, C. E., Jr. (1999). Adolescent health insurance coverage: Recent changes and access to care. *Pediatrics, 104*, 195–202.

Ogden, C. L., Carroll, M. D., Fakhouri, T. H., Hales, C. M., Fryar, C. D., Li, X., & Freedman, D. S. (2018). Prevalence of obesity among youths by household income and education level of head of household—United States 2011–2014. *Morbidity and Mortality Weekly Report, 67*(6), 186.

Ogden, C. L., & Flegal, K. M. (2010). Changes in terminology for childhood overweight and obesity. *Age, 12*(12).

Organisation for Economic Co-operation and Development. (2019). *Health at a glance 2019: OECD indicators.* Author.

Orris, A., & Boozang, P. (2018). Children's Health Insurance Program extended through fiscal year 2027.

*State Health & Value Strategies.* https://www.shvs.org/childrens-health-insurance-program-extended-through-fiscal-year-2027/

Ortegren, F. (2019). *How U.S. health policy changes have affected healthcare costs over time.* The Clever Data Center.

Papanicolas, I., Woskie, L. R., & Jha, A. K. (2018). Health care spending in the United States and other high-income countries. *JAMA, 319*(10), 1024–1039.

Pastore, D. R., Juszczak, L., Fisher, M. M., & Friedman, S. B. (1998). School-based health center utilization: A survey of users and nonusers. *Archives of Pediatrics & Adolescent Medicine, 152*, 763–767.

Pastore, D. R., & Techow, B. (2004). Adolescent school-based health care: A description of two sites in their 20th year of service. *Mount Sinai Journal of Medicine, 71*, 191–196.

Pearl, R. L. (2018). Weight bias and stigma: Public health implications and structural solutions. *Social Issues and Policy Review, 12*(1), 146–182.

Phadke, V. K., Bednarczyk, R. A., Salmon, D. A., & Omer, S. B. (2016). Association between vaccine refusal and vaccine-preventable diseases in the United States: A review of measles and pertussis. *JAMA, 315*(11), 1149–1158.

Phelan, S. M., Burgess, D. J., Yeazel, M. W., Hellerstedt, W. L., Griffin, J. M., & van Ryn, M. (2015). Impact of weight bias and stigma on quality of care and outcomes for patients with obesity. *Obesity Reviews, 16*, 319–326.

Puhl, R., Phelan, S., Nadglowski, J., & Kyle, T. (2016). Overcoming weight bias in the management of patients with diabetes and obesity. *Clinical Diabetes, 34*(1), 44–50.

Puhl, R., & Suh, Y. (2015). Stigma and eating and weight disorders. *Current Psychiatry Reports, 17*(3), 1–10.

Rafferty, J., American Academy of Pediatrics Committee on Psychosocial Aspects of Child and Family Health, American Academy of Pediatrics Committee on Adolescence, & American Academy of Pediatrics Section on Lesbian, Gay, Bisexual, and Transgender Health and Wellness. (2018). Ensuring comprehensive care and support for transgender and gender-diverse children and adolescents. *Pediatrics, 142*(4).

Reilly, J. J., & Kelly, J. (2011). Long-term impact of overweight and obesity in childhood and adolescence on morbidity and premature mortality in adulthood: Systematic review. *International Journal of Obesity, 35*(7), 891–898.

Reisner, S. L., Bradford, J., Hopwood, R., Gonzalez, A., Makadon, H., Todisco, D., Cavanaugh, T., VanDerwarker, R., Grasso, C., Zaslow, S., Boswell, S. L., & Mayer, K. (2015). Comprehensive transgender healthcare: The gender affirming clinical and public health model of Fenway Health. *Journal of Urban Health: Bulletin of the New York Academy of Medicine, 92*(3), 584–592.

Reisner, S. L., Radix, A., Deutsch, M. B. (2016). Integrated and gender-affirming transgender clinical care and research. *Journal of Acquired Immune Deficiency Syndromes, 72*(3), S235–S242.

Reisner, S. L., Vetters, R., White, J. M., Cohen, E. L., LeClerc, M., Zaslow, S., Wolfrum, S., & Mimiaga, M. J. (2015). Laboratory-confirmed HIV and sexually transmitted infection seropositivity and risk behavior among sexually active transgender patients at an adolescent and young adult urban community health center. *AIDS Care, 27*(8), 1031–1036.

Reuner, G., Hassenpflug, A., Pietz, J., & Philippi, H. (2009). Long-term development of low-risk low birth weight preterm born infants: Neurodevelopmental aspects from childhood to late adolescence. *Early Human Development, 85*, 409–413.

Rockett, I. R., Kapusta, N. D., & Bhandari, R. (2011). Suicide misclassification in an international context: Revisitation and update. *Suicidology Online, 2*, 48–61.

Rosenbach, M. L., & Gavin, N. I. (1998). Early and periodic screening, diagnosis, and treatment and managed care. *Annual Review of Public Health, 19*, 507–525.

Ross, P. T., Lypson, M. L., & Kumagai, A. K. (2012). Using illness narratives to explore African American perspectives of racial discrimination in health care. *Journal of Black Studies, 43*(5), 520–544.

Rossman, K., Salamanca, P., & Macapagal, K. (2017). "The doctor said I didn't look gay": Young adults' experiences of disclosure and non-disclosure of LGBTQ identity to healthcare providers. *Journal of Homosexuality, 64*(10), 1390.

Rounds, K. A. (2004). Preventing sexually transmitted infections among adolescents. In M. W. Fraser (Ed.), *Risk and resilience in childhood: An ecological perspective* (2nd ed., pp. 251–280). NASW Press.

Sabin, J. A., Riskind, R. G., & Nosek, B. A. (2015). Health care providers' implicit and explicit attitudes toward lesbian women and gay men. *American Journal of Public Health, 105*(9), 1831–1841.

Sahoo, K., Sahoo, B., Choudhury, A. K., Sofi, N. Y., Kumar, R., & Bhadoria, A. S. (2015). Childhood obesity: Causes and consequences. *Journal of Family Medicine and Primary Care, 4*(2), 187–192.

Salam, M. T., Li, Y. F., Langholz, B., & Gilliland, F. D. (2004). Early-life environmental risk factors for asthma: Findings from the children's health study. *Environmental Health Perspectives, 112*, 760–765.

Salm Ward, T. C., Mazul, M., Ngui, E. M., Bridgewater, F. D., & Harley, A. E. (2013). "You learn to go last": Perceptions of prenatal care experiences among African-American women with limited incomes. *Maternal and Child Health Journal, 17*(10), 1753–1759.

Sanchez-Birkhead, A. C., Kennedy, H. P., Callister, L. C., & Miyamoto, T. P. (2011). Navigating a new health culture: Experiences of immigrant Hispanic women. *Journal of Immigrant and Minority Health, 13*(6), 1168–1174.

Santelli, J., Kouzis, A., & Newcomer, S. (1996). School-based health centers and adolescent use of primary care and hospital care. *Journal of Adolescent Health, 19*, 267–275.

Sardell, A., & Johnson, K. (1998). The politics of EPSDT policy in the 1990s: Policy entrepreneurs, political streams, and children's health benefits. *Milbank Quarterly, 76*, 175–205.

School-Based Health Alliance. (n. d.). *Position statement: School-based health centers and the patient-centered medical home.* http://www.sbh4all.org/site/c.ckLQK-bOVLkK6E/b.8943407/k.C6F6/PatientCentered_Medical_Home.htm

Schwartz, C., Scholtens, P. A., Lalanne, A., Weenen, H., & Nicklaus, S. (2011). Development of healthy eating habits early in life: Review of recent evidence and selected guidelines. *Appetite, 57*, 796–807.

Seiber, E. E. (2014). Covering the remaining uninsured children–almost half of uninsured children live in immigrant families. *Medical Care, 52*(3), 202.

Sharifi, M., Sequist, T. D., Rifas-Shiman, S. L., Melly, S. J., Duncan, D. T., Horan, C. M., Smith, R. S., Marshall, R., & Taveras, E. M. (2016). The role of neighborhood characteristics and the built environment in understanding racial/ethnic disparities in childhood obesity. *Preventive Medicine, 91*, 103–109.

Shires, D. A., & Jaffee, K. (2015). Factors associated with health care discrimination experiences among a national sample of female-to-male transgender individuals. *Health & Social Work*, 40(2), 134–141.

Soni, A. (2014). *The five most costly children's conditions, 2011: Estimates for the U.S. civilian noninstitutionalized children, ages 0–17.* http://meps.ahrq.gov/mepsweb/data_files/publications/st434/stat434.shtml

Spack, N. P., Edwards-Leeper, L., Feldman, H. A., Leibowitz, S., Mandel, F., Diamond, D. A., & Vance, S. R. (2012). Children and adolescents with gender identity disorder referred to a pediatric medical center. *Pediatrics*, 129(3), 418–425.

Statista. (2021). *Rate of coronavirus (COVID-19) tests performed in the most impacted countries worldwide.* https://www.statista.com/statistics/1104645/covid19-testing-rate-select-countries-worldwide/

Stroumsa, D. (2014). The state of transgender health care: Policy, law, and medical frameworks. *American Journal of Public Health*, 104(3), e31–e38.

Subbarao, P., Mandhane, P. J., & Sears, M. R. (2009). Asthma: Epidemiology, etiology and risk factors. *Canadian Medical Association Journal*, 181, E181–E190.

Tandon, S. D., Parillo, K. M., & Keefer, M. (2005). Hispanic women's perceptions of patient centeredness during prenatal care: A mixed-method study. *Birth*, 32(4), 312–317.

Thakur, N., Oh, S. S., Nguyen, E. A., Martin, M., Roth, L. A., Galanter, J., Gignoux, C. R., Eng, C., Davis, A., Meade, K., LeNoir, M. A., Avila, P. C., Farber, H. J., Serebrisky, D., Brigino-Buenaventura, E., Rodriguez-Cintron, W., Kumar, R., Williams, L. K., Bibbins-Domingo, K., . . . & Burchard, E. G. (2013). Socioeconomic status and childhood asthma in urban minority youths. The GALA II and SAGE II Studies. *American Journal of Respiratory and Critical Care Medicine*, 188, 1202–1209.

Tishelman, A. C., Kaufman, R., Edwards-Leeper, L., Mandel, F. H., Shumer, D. E., & Spack, N. P. (2015). Serving transgender youth: Challenges, dilemmas and clinical examples. *Professional Psychology, Research and Practice*, 46(1), 37–45.

Tong, V. T., Dietz, P. M., Morrow, B., D'Angelo, D. V., Farr, S. L., Rockhill, K. M., & England, L. J. (2013). Trends in smoking before, during, and after pregnancy—Pregnancy risk assessment monitoring system, United States, 40 sites, 2000–2010. *Morbidity and Mortality Weekly Report: Surveillance Summaries*, 62(6), 1–19.

Tumin, D., Miller, R., Raman, V. T., Uffman, J. C., & Tobias, J. D. (2019). Patterns of health insurance discontinuity and children's access to health care. *Maternal and Child Health Journal*, 23(5), 667–677.

U.S. Department of Health and Human Services (HHS). (2011). *The Affordable Care Act and the school-based health center capital program.* http://www.hhs.gov/healthcare/facts/factsheets/2011/12/sbhc.html

U.S. Department of Health and Human Services (HHS). (2018). *Strategic plan FY 2018–2022.* https://www.hhs.gov/about/strategic-plan/index.html

U.S. Department of Health and Human Services (HHS). (2020). *Healthy people 2030 framework.* https://www.healthypeople.gov/2020/About-Healthy-People/Development-Healthy-People-2030/Framework

Vance, S. R., Ehrensaft, D., & Rosenthal, S. M. (2014). Psychological and medical care of gender nonconforming youth. *Pediatrics*, 134(6), 1184–1192.

Visness, C. M., London, S. J., Daniels, J. L., Kaufman, J. S., Yeatts, K. B., Siega-Riz, A. M., Calatroni, A., & Zeldin, D. C. (2010). Association of childhood obesity with atopic and nonatopic asthma: Results from the National Health and Nutrition Examination Survey 1999–2006. *Journal of Asthma*, 47(7), 822–829.

Vos, M. B., & Welsh, J. (2010). Childhood obesity: Update on predisposing factors and prevention strategies. *Current Gastroenterology Reports*, 12(4), 280–287.

Wang, J., Visness, C. M., Calatroni, A., Gergen, P. J., Mitchell, H. E., & Sampson, H. A. (2009). Effect of environmental allergen sensitization on asthma morbidity in inner-city asthmatic children. *Clinical and Experimental Allergy*, 39, 1381–1389.

Williams, D. R., Sternthal, M., & Wright, R. J. (2009). Social determinants: Taking the social context of asthma seriously. *Pediatrics*, 123, S174–S184.

Workowski, K., & Berman, S. (2010). STD treatment guidelines, 2010. *Morbidity and Mortality Weekly Reports*, 59 (RR12), 1–110. http://www.cdc.gov/mmwr/preview/mmwrhtml/rr5912a1.htm

World Health Organization (WHO). (2020a). *Considerations for quarantine of contacts of COVID-19 cases: Interim guidance.* https://www.who.int/publications/i/item/considerations-for-quarantine-of-individuals-in-the-context-of-containment-for-coronavirus-disease-(covid-19)

World Health Organization (WHO). (2020b). *Contact tracing in the context of COVID-19.* https://www.who.int/publications/i/item/contact-tracing-in-the-context-of-covid-19

World Health Organization (WHO). (2020c). *Health policy.* https://www.who.int/topics/health_policy/en/

World Health Organization (WHO). (2020d). *Public health surveillance for COVID-19: Interim guidance.* https://www.who.int/publications/i/item/who-2019-nCoV-surveillanceguidance-2020.7

World Health Organization (WHO). (2020e). *Social determinants of health.* https://www.who.int/social_determinants/en/

Wu, A. C., Smith, L., Bokhour, B., Hohman, K. H., & Lieu, T. A. (2008). Racial/ethnic variation in parent perceptions of asthma. *Ambulatory Pediatrics, 8*(2), 89–97.

Yu, Z., Han, S., Zhu, J., Sun, X., Ji, C., & Guo, X. (2013). Pre-pregnancy body mass index in relation to infant birth weight and offspring overweight/obesity: A systematic review and meta-analysis. *PLOS ONE, 8*(4), e61627.

Zuckerman, S., Skopec, L., & Epstein, M. (2017). *Medicaid physician fees after the ACA primary care fee bump.* Urban Institute.

# 7

# POLICIES AND PROGRAMS FOR CHILDREN AND YOUTH WITH DISABILITIES

Kiley J. McLean, Meshan R. Adams, and Lauren Bishop

About one in six or 17% of children have a diagnosed developmental disability and this percentage has increased significantly over the past 20 years (Centers for Disease Control and Prevention [CDC], 2019a). Due to advances in early identification and diagnosis, many children under the age of 3 have developmental delays that vary in severity. The increase in prevalence of childhood disability is well-documented (Zablotsky et al., 2019), but the full reasons for this increase are yet to be completely understood. Developmental disabilities are lifelong, and people with disabilities are living longer than ever before as a result of social and medical progress (World Health Organization & World Bank, 2011). Disability knows no geographical, ethnic, or socio-economic boundaries, though disparities exist in disability prevalence and access to services and supports. Racial and socioeconomic disparities contribute to both onset and poor outcomes for children with disabilities.

This chapter will discuss the increasing prevalence of childhood disability as well as the risk and protective factors regarding the onset of disability and life outcomes for these children. Policies and programs pertaining to education, civil rights, health care, and income that have enhanced the lives of children with disabilities and their families will be discussed and evaluated in terms of risk and protective factors. Recommendations and conclusions based on these policies will be provided with the goal of promoting and building inclusion, resilience, and overall better quality of life for this growing population.

## TERMINOLOGY: INTELLECTUAL AND DEVELOPMENTAL DISABILITIES

*Intellectual and developmental disabilities* are lifelong disabilities that typically present at birth and can negatively affect the trajectory of a child's physical, intellectual, and/or emotional development (CDC, 2019b). These disabilities affect multiple body parts and systems, including the nervous system, sensory system, and metabolism (National Dissemination Center for Children with Disabilities, 2011). Like all children, children with disabilities develop at different paces and have strengths and challenges that are as unique as they are. However, because intellectual and developmental disabilities often describe "deficits" in functioning, many children with these diagnoses experience challenges across different domains. Children with intellectual and developmental disabilities may experience challenges expressing their wants and needs or taking care of themselves independently. They may have difficulty in school with language, reading, reasoning, or memory. Children with intellectual and developmental disabilities may have difficulty socially with empathy, communication skills, or friendships. They may also have difficulty independently practicing personal care, meeting job responsibilities, or managing money as they enter into adulthood and become more independent. With this in mind, policies related to education, health care, and income must adapt to accommodate their specific needs.

The term *intellectual disability*, formerly known as *mental retardation*, refers to limitations in the ability to learn and problem solve as well as function in daily life at the expected level for someone's age (CDC, 2019b). *Developmental disabilities* is an umbrella term that includes intellectual disability as well as other lifelong disabilities that present at birth or during childhood. Developmental disabilities include impairments in physical behavior, learning, language, or other behavioral areas. Common developmental disabilities include autism spectrum disorder, Down syndrome, cerebral palsy, fragile X syndrome, attention deficit hyperactivity disorder, fetal alcohol spectrum disorders, hearing loss, vision impairment, muscular dystrophy, and other developmental delays. The incidence and prevalence of these disabilities has increased significantly in the past decade. Thus, policies must continue to expand to support the success of children diagnosed with intellectual and developmental disabilities.

## INCREASING PREVALENCE OF INTELLECTUAL AND DEVELOPMENTAL DISABILITIES

The most recent estimates in the United States (U.S.) indicate that about 17% of children age 3 to 17 years have one or more developmental disabilities (Zablotsky et al., 2019). This national prevalence study of developmental disabilities used National Health Interview Survey data from 2009 to 2017 to explore changes and trends over time associated with demographic and socioeconomic characteristics. During this time period, they found significant increases in the overall rate of developmental disability, largely because of increases in attention deficit hyperactivity disorder, autism spectrum disorder, and intellectual disability.

This increase in the prevalence of diagnosed attention deficit hyperactivity disorder among U.S. children could be driven by the better identification of children who meet criteria for attention deficit hyperactivity disorder as well as the increased availability of treatment. The sizable increase in autism spectrum disorder is similarly explained by improved identification as well as rising parental awareness and changing provider practices, including universal developmental screening by 18 to 24 months of age (Zablotsky et al., 2019). Health care professionals, such as pediatricians, typically diagnose developmental delays through developmental screenings provided during a well-child visit.

There are also changes in the prevalence of developmental disabilities by demographic and socioeconomic groups. Boys are more likely than girls to be diagnosed with any developmental disability. Children with low birth weight at less than 2500 g (5.5 lbs.), non-Hispanic White children, children with public insurance, children with mothers with less than a college education, and children living in a household less than 200% of the federal poverty line also had higher rates of developmental disability. Interestingly, children who had any form of public health insurance were more likely to be diagnosed with any and each of the individual developmental disabilities when compared with children with only private health insurance. Finally, a higher prevalence of identified disabilities was found among children living in rural areas (Zablotsky et al., 2019). These complex risk and protective factors, along with accessibility of services and interventions, may be contributing to these changes in disability prevalence by demographic and socioeconomic groups as well as outcomes overtime.

## RISK FACTORS IN THE ONSET OF DISABILITY

Developmental disabilities occur among all racial, ethnic, and socioeconomic groups, and most developmental disabilities are thought to be caused by a complex mix of factors including (but not limited to) genetics, parental health and behaviors during pregnancy, complications during pregnancy or birth, infections the mother might have had during pregnancy or the child might have had during early life, childhood injuries, and exposure of the mother to high levels of environmental toxins, such as lead (CDC, 2019a). For some developmental disabilities, such as fetal alcohol syndrome, which is caused by large consumptions of alcohol during pregnancy, the cause of disability is clearer. Most developmental disabilities are associated with either the presence of an extra copy of a chromosome (e.g., Down syndrome, in which there are three copies of chromosome 21) or mutations to genes that result in an expansion, duplication, or deletion of one or many DNA sequences (Miles, 2011). Gene mutations can be inherited mutations or new (*de novo*) mutations. However, the current scientific consensus is that most intellectual and developmental disabilities do not have a single genetic cause, even though the specific genetic etiology of many intellectual and developmental disabilities is currently unknown. Relative to genetic factors, environmental or social factors play a relatively minor role in the risk of onset for intellectual and developmental disabilities. It is crucial to ensure that policies do not rely on misinformation of causes of disability, such as vaccine-associated disability or poor parenting.

Social determinants of health, apart from biological or genetic risk factors, may contribute to the prevalence of developmental disability in different groups of children. In the National Health Interview Survey project, service accessibility and availability were inversely associated with the prevalence of developmental disabilities (Zablotsky et al., 2019). For example, the higher prevalence of developmental disabilities among children living in rural areas may be related to risk factors in rural areas, including greater financial difficulties, lack of transportation, and less access to services and treatments.

Poverty is a risk factor for childhood disability. The onset and severity of childhood disability is strongly associated with poverty and socioeconomic status (SES). Children living in poverty have higher rates of disability associated with mental health challenges than other children (National Academies of Sciences, Engineering, and Medicine [NASEM], 2015). Poverty is associated with other social risk factors as well, including belonging to a cultural, ethnic, or racial minority group; single parenthood; and low education, which have a cumulative effect on overall child health and disability. Children born in low-income households are more likely to be born preterm, to have worse birth outcomes, and to demonstrate higher proportions of developmental disadvantage—all of which can precede developmental disability diagnosis. Overall, research suggests that the accumulation of social disadvantage—in terms of income, race, ethnicity, or other social factors—is strongly related to poorer child health and increased childhood disability.

Furthermore, late diagnoses or misdiagnoses several years after the onset of symptoms has been evident, particularly among children from marginalized groups. Disparities in age of diagnosis can be particularly problematic for developmental disabilities such as autism spectrum disorder, where early diagnosis can trigger early intervention, which then leads to better long-term outcomes (Bishop-Fitzpatrick & Eisenbaum, 2016). Diagnostic disparities are exacerbated for children of color and children from low-socioeconomic backgrounds. For example, autism spectrum disorder can be diagnosed in children as early as 12 months of age. Recent studies have shown that Black and Hispanic/Latinx children who meet the diagnostic criteria for autism are less likely than White children to be identified with autism in their health and education records (Mandell et al., 2009). Furthermore, compared to White children, Black children are more than twice as likely to receive a misdiagnosis of conduct disorder and five times more likely to receive a misdiagnosis of adjustment disorder before an autism spectrum disorder diagnosis, suggesting that clinicians are attributing symptoms of autism to behavioral and emotional problems in Black children (Mandell et al., 2007). The Institute of Medicine's report, *Unequal Treatment*, has suggested that racial differences in diagnostic patterns such as these may be attributable to systemic inequities in access to care, general prejudices held by clinicians, and stereotyping about health-related behaviors (Institute of Medicine, 2003).

## RISK FACTORS IN POOR OUTCOMES FOR CHILDREN WITH DISABILITIES

People with disabilities are among one of the most marginalized populations in society. People with disabilities are at risk for worse health outcomes, lower educational achievements, less economic participation, higher rates of unemployment, and higher rates of poverty than those without disabilities (World Health Organization & World Bank, 2011). These disparities are not inherent to having a diagnosis of a disability because outcomes vary significantly from one person with a disability to another and can be attributed to many societal, environmental, and systemic factors (Institute of Medicine, 2007). Societal, environmental, and systemic risk factors that can marginalize people with disabilities include ableism, poverty, social isolation, child maltreatment, racism, homophobia, and discrimination (Table 7.1). A better understanding of these risk factors can assist in shaping effective and inclusive policies and programs to address inequities and promote positive outcomes for the disability community.

## Ableism

Disability itself is not necessarily a risk factor for poor outcomes experienced by those that belong to this community; ableism, however, is a significant risk factor.

*Ableism* is the discrimination of and social prejudice against people with disabilities based on the belief that typical abilities are superior. At its heart, ableism is rooted in the assumption that disabled people require 'fixing' and defines people by their disability. Like racism and sexism, ableism classifies entire groups of people as 'less than,' and includes harmful stereotypes, misconceptions, and generalizations of people with disabilities. (Access Living, 2020, p. 1)

These negative cultural attitudes toward disability and those with disabilities can undermine opportunities for students to participate fully and be successful in school and

| Table 7.1 | Risk and Protective Factors for Children With Disabilities and Their Families | |
|---|---|
| **Risk Factors** | **Protective Factors** |
| Ableism | Social and emotional well-being of caregivers |
| Poverty | Community inclusion and social support |
| Lack of access to services and supports | Early diagnosis and intervention |
| Child maltreatment | Adequate and inclusive medical, financial, and educational resources |
| Social isolation | Self-determination and empowerment |
| Racism and cultural insensitivity | |
| Homophobia and heterosexist discrimination | |

everyday life. Internalized ableism has led many children with disabilities to view their disability as negative, tragic, and a condition to be "overcome" (Ferguson & Asch, 1989; Rousso, 1984). In early education, ableism harmfully prevails when services provided to children focus on their disability at the exclusion of all else—a focus on fixing and finding a cure rather than supporting and adapting settings to the child's unique needs. Pervasive ableism in education of children with disabilities not only reinforces prejudice but also contributes to low levels of educational attainment (Hehir, 2009).

## Poverty

Not only is poverty a risk factor for disability, but disability is a risk factor for family poverty. A review of literature that examined the impact of poverty on the quality of life in families of children with disabilities found that 28% of children with disabilities, ages 3 to 21, are living in families whose total income is less than the income threshold set by the U.S. Census Bureau (Park et al., 2002). They found that poverty in these families affected overall health, productivity, home and neighborhood environment, emotional well-being, and family interactions. These families had limited health care access, fewer opportunities for leisure activities, unsafe surrounding neighborhoods and unclean homes, increased levels of stress, and marital conflict. This is largely due to the substantial financial burden of raising a child with a disability in a largely unaccommodating society.

Despite having policies in place to offset some of these costs, most families are providing significant out-of-pocket payments to support their children. Children with developmental disabilities may require extensive therapies, home adaptations, specific diets, assistive technology, or equipment to ensure their success. This can be particularly burdensome on low-income families, who might also benefit from but cannot afford caregiver support and respite care. This financial burden falls even heavier on marginalized communities. Roughly 19% of children live in poverty, with higher rates for children among racial and ethnic minority groups. The percentages of children living in poverty are highest in Black and American Indian/Alaska Native children and lowest in White and Asian children (de Brey, 2019).

The adverse effects of childhood poverty are well-documented. They encompass adverse psychosocial and environmental effects including child maltreatment, inadequate housing, limited access to developmentally appropriate and high-quality educational experiences, and suboptimal nutrition (Pascoe et al., 2016). Policies that aim to raise family incomes for those with children with disabilities would contribute to improved family well-being and quality of life and begin to confront systemic and long-term inequities, particularly those faced by families of color.

## Social Isolation

The historical oppression, cultural devaluation, social marginalization, and bullying of people with disabilities is disgraceful and many people with disabilities continue to feel devalued and disempowered in contemporary U.S. society. This presents serious risks for the emotional well-being of this population. Social isolation in the general population is strongly linked to poorer outcomes (Krahn et al., 2015). There is limited research on the long-term effects of social isolation in children and youth with disabilities, but adults with disabilities have been shown to have worse functional, social, health, and employment outcomes.

Many children with developmental disabilities have difficulty socially with empathy, communication skills, or friendships. Because of this, children with developmental disabilities are at increased risk of socioemotional and behavioral challenges including social isolation, bullying, peer rejection, and loneliness (Al-Yagon & Mikulincer, 2004). Children with disabilities are more likely to be bullied. In one study of 8- to 17-year-olds, researchers found that children with autism spectrum disorder were more than three times as likely to be bullied than their peers without autism (Twyman et al., 2010). Children with medical conditions that affect their appearance, such as cerebral palsy, muscular dystrophy, and spina bifida, frequently report being called names related to their disability (Dawkins, 1996). Among adults with speech impairments as children, 83% said that they were teased or bullied, and 71% of those who had been bullied said that it happened at least once a week (Hugh-Jones & Smith, 1999). This is a very serious issue for children with disabilities, and policies must specifically engage schools and the wider society on anti-bullying initiatives.

Parents of children with disabilities are at higher risk of poor emotional well-being as well. These parents are more likely to experience stress, psychological distress, and depression than parents of children without disabilities (King et al., 1999). Child behavior problems, social isolation from other families, and lack of social support predict poor parental emotional well-being. With that in mind, family-centered policies that seek to improve and protect both financial and emotional well-being are key to improving overall outcomes.

## Child Maltreatment

Children with developmental disabilities are at heightened risk for child maltreatment (McDonnell et al., 2019). Children with disabilities are three times more likely to experience abuse or neglect than their peers without disabilities (Jones et al., 2012). The isolation; discrimination; and lack of financial, medical, and social support can contribute to the high risk of abuse or neglect seen in this population. Children with disabilities are already vulnerable, and they may have difficulty protecting themselves, understanding what maltreatment or inappropriate behavior is, or expressing or reporting when an abusive situation has occurred. Thus, policies must include child maltreatment protections for this particularly vulnerable population.

## Racism and Cultural Insensitivity

Cultural differences in the acceptance of disability are also factors in how some children of color utilize and receive disability services. Intolerance and rejection experienced by people of color can influence whether or not they pursue services and support for their disability. Research with African American students with disabilities found that these students were predisposed to barriers of fear, alienation, and negative self-concept. They reported many concerns, such as not wanting to self-disclose their disability to service providers, fear of losing control over their futures, concern about additional alienation, and being perceived as failures in their community (Ball-Brown & Frank, 1993). African American students already face discrimination because of systemic and institutional racism. The additional classification of a disability unfortunately puts them at risk for another form of discrimination and oppression in the form of ableism.

Additionally, research in the African American community found that there is a tendency to hide or minimize disability. Some Asian cultures view disability as a symptom of spiritual weakness. Religious beliefs have played a role in disability decisions in some portions of the Hispanic/Latinx populations (Ball-Brown & Frank, 1993). Furthermore, language barriers and differences in communication styles can complicate the relationship among families and service providers, a relationship that is already fraught with distrust due to historically discriminatory events and practices in health care.

A recent study on parents' reports of children's autism spectrum disorder symptoms found racial differences in parental reports of concern about their children's development to their health care providers (Donohue et al., 2019). Parents of lower SES reported fewer autism concerns than parents of higher SES, and Black parents reported fewer autism concerns than White parents. Compared to Black parents, White parents were twice as likely to report concerns about their children's social skills and four times more likely to report a concern about the presence of restricted or repetitive behaviors. This reduced reporting may further contribute to delayed service access or misdiagnoses of children with autism spectrum disorder among families with low SES and families of color. Policies need to ensure that systems of care are linguistically and culturally appropriate to all families of those with disabilities.

## Homophobia and Heterosexist Discrimination

Disabled people who identify as part of the lesbian, gay, bisexual, transgender, queer, intersex, or asexual (LGBTQIA) communities also experience unique challenges. There is limited research and resources on this community due to stigma and misconceptions of people with developmental disabilities as asexual or hypersexual (Noonan & Gomez, 2011). Because of this, accessing affordable and inclusive health care and community services is more challenging for LGBTQIA people with disabilities. LGBTQIA youth with disabilities report higher rates of harassment, bullying, and exclusion and experience more comorbid mental health issues as a result (Movement Advancement Project, 2019). Policies intended to support people with disabilities must ensure accessibility in education, housing, and health care to those with intersectional identities.

# PROTECTIVE FACTORS THAT ENHANCE OUTCOMES FOR CHILDREN WITH DISABILITIES

Unfortunately, less is known about the factors that can protect and improve outcomes for children with developmental disabilities. Of course, exposure to risk can increase the likelihood of a negative outcome, and in turn, protection from those risks can decrease its likelihood. Children with disabilities born to higher-income families are more likely to have better health and educational outcomes. That being said, children and youth are resilient, and the majority have positive outcomes despite vulnerability and heightened risk.

## Social and Emotional Well-Being of Caregivers

Some studies have found that for young children with learning disabilities, secure attachment with their mother could serve as a protective factor in decreasing social and emotional difficulties for both child and mother (Al-Yagon & Mikulincer, 2004). Others have begun to investigate the positive effect of social support provided to caregivers on their accessibility to professional counseling and resources to promote their own and their child's emotional well-being. The physical and mental health of caregivers is important because it affects their capacity to provide the care their child needs.

## Community Inclusion and Social Support

Other protective factors associated with childhood disability include positively involving extended family as well as having a broader peer network and inclusive community (Ha et al., 2011). Supportive schools, faith-based organizations, and disability and advocacy organizations have been shown to improve quality of life for families and children. Community inclusion enriches the lives of all family members, addressing their needs for human interaction. It can also help children with disabilities develop skills for potential employment and daily living.

## Early Diagnosis and Intervention

Access to early and accurate diagnosis and early intervention improve outcomes for children with disabilities and their families. Quality early intervention can enhance development of infants and toddlers with disabilities, reduce educational costs, maximize independence, and enhance the capacity of families to meet their children's needs (Goode et al., 2011). Following early diagnosis and intervention, access to adequate and inclusive medical, financial, and educational resources throughout the lifespan are key to better outcomes for both children and families.

## Self-Determination and Empowerment

Self-determination has garnered quite a bit of attention in the disability community over the past decade, with a strong research base suggesting that children and youth with disabilities who harness skills of self-determination may experience better outcomes during childhood and into adulthood. Wehmeyer (2005) defined *self-determined behavior* as "volitional actions that enable one to act as the primary causal agent in one's life and to maintain or improve one's quality of life" (p. 117). *Self-determined behavior* refers to actions based on four essential characteristics: (a) the person acts autonomously, (b) the behavior(s) are self-regulated, (c) the person initiates and responds to the event(s) in a psychologically empowered manner, and (d) the person acts in a self-realizing manner (Wehmeyer et al., 2003).

Research has shown that children with disabilities can develop self-determination skills when provided with appropriate supports in school or at home (Palmer et al., 2012). These skills result in more positive school and community outcomes as well as better quality of life. Studies found that children with intellectual and developmental disabilities left school with more self-determination and achieved greater independence, higher employment rates, and greater inclusive living in the community (Sowers & Powers, 1995; Wehmeyer & Schwartz, 1997). Self-determination and empowerment of those with disabilities can serve as a protective factor, and programs and policies should include access to supports that establish these skills at a young age.

In summary, the development and trajectories of children with disabilities are shaped by biological, social, and environmental risk and protective factors that emerge within the family, community, and larger society (Table 7.1). Responsive public policies that can serve as protective factors and promote resilience will be discussed next.

# RISK, RESILIENCE, AND PROTECTION IN POLICIES FOR CHILDREN WITH DISABILITIES

Over the past century, broad and extraordinary changes have been made to the policies that support children with disabilities and their families. Not too long ago, it was believed that people with disabilities were incapable of organized, concerted political action and advocacy. In the mid-1900s, most people with disabilities were segregated into institutions as parents were told by professionals that this was the only opportunity their child would have once they received a diagnosis (Pfeiffer, 1993). Children with disabilities and their families did not have access to the appropriate education, health care, and income supports needed for their success.

Over the past few decades, parents of children with disabilities led effective and assertive advocacy to close most institutions and develop educational systems that are more inclusive, individually tailored, and protective. These advocacy efforts have had a lasting impact on the educational system. In the 1980s and 1990s, self-advocates with disabilities forged the Disability Rights Movement, which catalyzed the Americans with Disabilities Act (ADA) of 1990 prohibiting discrimination on the basis of disability. With medical, diagnostic, and technological advances, attitudes toward the capability of persons with disabilities shifted, and the federal government responded in support. Medicaid advances in long-term services and supports allowed more children with disabilities to live at home and participate in their communities. Supplemental Security Income of the Social Security Act of 1935 recognized the extra costs of raising a child with a disability and began monthly income supports to families in need. Deficit perspectives toward people with disabilities have begun to be replaced by civil and human rights perspectives, which is evident in the drastic transformation of policy and practice over the past century.

The extent to which knowledge of risk and protective factors have contributed to the development of these policies is unknown, though they have certainly improved related outcomes. Despite this, gaps in current disability policy still exist. Disparities in student success, related to race, ethnicity, and SES, are evident in the special education system. The limited funding provided by Supplemental Security Income (SSI) often falls short of the significant costs parents take on for their children. Institutions are still open in many states as cuts to Medicaid continue to be proposed. The following section will provide an overview and history of policies intended to support children with disabilities and their families. We will also critique the current effectiveness of these policies based on the aforementioned risk and protective factors as well as provide recommendations to advocates and providers for improvement in policies and practices.

## Education

### A Brief History of Special Education in the United States

Before the passage of the Individuals with Disabilities Education Improvement Act (IDEIA) of 2004, "the fate of many individuals with disabilities was likely to be dim" (U.S. Department of Education, 2007). The only opportunities for accommodations for children with disabilities were in state-run institutions. Public schools could deny an education to any child deemed "uneducable" (Martin et al., 1996). Over 200,000 children with unique needs and no options were brought to restrictive institutions to face a life of minimal food, clothing, or shelter.

By the 1960s, the number of children living in institutions was high, with a staff to student ratio of 50 to 1. President Kennedy was closely tied to the lives of those with disabilities because of his sister, Rosemary Kennedy, and formed the President's Panel on Mental Retardation in 1962. Three years later, Senator Robert Kennedy famously toured the Willowbrook State School in New York. As many Americans closely followed on television, the Senator compared the conditions he viewed in the institution to that of a "snake pit." The next year, hidden cameras in Willowbrook exposed the neglect and daily abuse faced behind its closed doors. "There is a hell on earth, and in America there is a special inferno—the institution" (Spaulding & Pratt, 2015, p. 102). A resident, Bernard Carabello, described the institutional mistreatment:

> I got beaten with sticks, belt buckles. I got my head kicked into the wall by staff. . . .
> Most of the kids sat in the day room naked, with no clothes on. There was a lot
> of sexual abuse going on from staff to residents, also. (Holburn, 1997, p. 381)

## Table 7.2  Major U.S. Policies for Children With Disabilities and Their Families

| Policy Domain | Policies | Funding Source | Core Features |
|---|---|---|---|
| Education | Section 504 of the Rehabilitation Act of 1953; Education for all Handicapped Children Act of 1975, replaced by Individuals with Disabilities Education Improvement Act (IDEIA) | Local and state (limited federal funding) | Children with disabilities are entitled to a free and appropriate public education in the least restricted environment; Individualized Education Program (IEPs) and 504 plans |
| Early Intervention | Part C of IDEIA | Local and state (limited federal funding) | Children birth to 3 with disabilities or possible developmental delays are eligible for individualized services to promote their development. |
| Civil Rights | Americans with Disabilities Act of 1990 | | Prohibits discrimination against children with disabilities in all areas of public life, including childcare, schools, hospitals, and transportation. |
| Health Care | Medicaid and Children's Health Insurance Program (CHIP); home and community-based waivers | Jointly by the state and federal government | Varies by state; provides health insurance to children with special health care needs as well as services and supports to be integrated into schools and communities |
| Income | Supplemental Security Income (SSI) and Social Security Disability Insurance (SSDI) through the Social Security Act | Federal funding | SSDI requires work history; SSI provides monthly cash assistance to low-income children with disabilities, regardless of work history. |

In 1971, 13 parents of children with disabilities in Pennsylvania had had enough. They sued the state of Pennsylvania, its agencies, and the school district for failure to provide their children and many others with a publicly supported education. In *PARC v. Commonwealth of Pennsylvania* (1972), these parents argued on the grounds that the state was violating the equal protection clause of the 14th Amendment (Yell et al., 1998). The court ordered the state to provide education to all developmentally disabled children, including those living in institutions, within one year. Galvanized by the momentum, another dedicated group of parents expanded this decision to include all handicapped children in the landmark case *Mills v. the Board of Education of District of Columbia* (1972).

In 1973, Section 504 of the Rehabilitation Act, the first civil rights law for persons with disabilities, was passed. It required schools not to discriminate against people with disabilities and to provide them with "reasonable accommodations" (Turnbull et al., 2010). With this foundation and a steadfast community of parents and self-advocates across the country, Public Law 94-142: The Education for all Handicapped Children Act of 1975, was enacted. This civil rights law, which resulted from years of advocacy, guaranteed a free and appropriate public education in the least restricted environment to each child with a disability in every state and locality across the country (U.S. Department of Education, 2019). In 1997, this law was renamed the Individuals with Disabilities Education Act (IDEA) and it articulated several main purposes to improve access to education for children with disabilities: to improve how children with disabilities are identified and educated, to evaluate the success of these efforts, and to provide due process protections for children and families (U.S. Department of Education, 2007). In the years that followed, IDEA was expanded to include early intervention programming, transitions services from high school to adult living, and employment and community living services. IDEA was reauthorized in 2004 under the IDEIA. Currently, IDEIA is still colloquially referred to as *IDEA* by families, people with disabilities, and professionals and is thus referred to as *IDEA* in this chapter.

Finally, and most recently, parents took another case surrounding IDEA to the Supreme Court in the *Endrew F. v. the Douglas County School District* (2017) case (Yell & Bateman, 2017). Endrew's parents believed they needed reimbursement from the U.S. Department of Education when they transferred their son to a private special education school and he immediately made more progress than in his prior public school placement. Up until this point, the Supreme Court ruled that the free and appropriate education guaranteed in the IDEA only needed to provide students with "some educational benefit." His parents argued that states should be required to provide children with disabilities with educational opportunities that are substantially equal to the opportunities afforded to children without disabilities—"meaningful educational benefit." The Supreme Court ruled in favor of Endrew F. on March 22, 2017, re-standardizing what "appropriate progress" a child with disabilities will make in a classroom.

## The Principles of the IDEA

There are six principles that guide IDEA:

1.  Zero reject: This prohibits schools from excluding any student with a disability from a free and appropriate public education. This applies to children and students ages 3–21, no matter how severe their disability may seem. This applies to all school districts and private schools (if the public system places a student in a private school) as well as state-operated programs, such as psychiatric hospitals or institutions. Through this, all students are educable.

2.  Nondiscriminatory evaluation: This requires educators to evaluate students fairly in determining if they have a disability, and if so, what kind and how extensive. This evaluation must be carried out in a culturally responsive and linguistically appropriate way. This portion of IDEA puts procedural safeguards in place to ensure that students are evaluated correctly in initial evaluations and receive necessary services and supports as a result.

3.  Appropriate education: This requires schools to provide individually tailored instruction for each student in their special education system. Educators individualize learning by developing and formalizing an Individualized Education Program (IEP) for students ages 3–21. Plans for early intervention for children birth through age 2 and their families are known as Individualized Family Service Plans (IFSPs).

4.  Least restrictive environment: This requires schools to educate children with disabilities alongside children without disabilities "to the maximum extent possible." IDEA re-emphasized this principle, advocating that students with disabilities should only be placed in separate classes when the nature or severity of their disability is to an extent in which they will not receive an appropriate education in a general education classroom with additional services. The least restrictive environment is the typical education classroom with in-class supports and the most restrictive environment is a separate special education school with a residential placement on site. Regardless of final placement, the IEP must still identify opportunities for the child with a disability to interact with peers without disabilities.

5.  Procedural due process: This provides safeguards for children and their families to ensure that best educational practices are taking place. This includes the right to mediation, request for complaint investigation, and/or a due process hearing. This also gives parents the right to appeal to a federal district court if they are unhappy with their child's placement or progress and, if they prevail, the right to receive attorneys' fees.

6.  Parental and student participation: This gives parents the right to access their child's educational records and to participate in the decision-making process for their child's IEP. This ensures that schools collaborate with parents and

students with disabilities in designing their special education services. Once a child turns 18, these rights transfer to the child with a disability (Alquraini, 2013; Lipkin & Okamoto, 2015; Turnbull et al., 2010).

## 504 Plans and IEPs

Section 504 and IDEA have overlapping requirements, such as providing students with disabilities with accommodations at no cost to the parents; however, Section 504 is not special education legislation but rather civil rights legislation. Section 504 of the Rehabilitation Act of 1973 intended to eliminate discrimination on the basis of disability in any program receiving federal financial assistance; therefore, this law has direct application to students with disabilities in K–12 public education. Section 504 accommodations are typically provided to students with disabilities who are not eligible for or do not receive special education under IDEA (Madaus & Shaw, 2008). Section 504 is used for students who are learning in a general education classroom and require a support or change to the learning environment in order to be successful. A child can have any type of disability and this disability must interfere with the child's ability to learn in the general education classroom in order to receive such an accommodation. That being said, the definition of a disability under Section 504 is much broader than that under IDEA (Rosenfeld, 1996). For example, children with allergies, asthma, or a temporary disability may qualify for an accommodation through Section 504 but not qualify for services under IDEA. Examples of the reasonable accommodations that can be provided to a child with a disability at school include preferential seating, extended time on tests, regular nurse visits for medications, modified textbooks, or behavior management support (U.S. Department of Education, 2019).

IEPs are much more formal, truly individualized documents that have stringent eligibility requirements. An IEP is developed for each student in special education and it features the goals and objectives of their special education programming, their placement, and evaluation criteria for measuring progress (Yell et al., 1998). IEP team members include the parents, general education teachers, special education teachers, a school system representative, a transition service agency representative, a person who can interpret evaluation results (such as a school psychologist), the student (when appropriate), and anyone else with insight into or special expertise about the child (U.S. Department of Education, 2018). This team must review the child's IEP once a year in order to determine if the child is meeting their annual goals and, if not, what can be added or changed to ensure their success.

When a child is initially referred for special education services, they must receive a formal evaluation prior to initiation of the IEP process. Many parents pay for a private evaluation to speed up this process; however, that can be a very substantial out-of-pocket expense. School districts will evaluate the child free of cost and must respond to a request for evaluation from parents in a "reasonable period of time" (Rosenfeld, 1996). For school districts with limited trained personnel (e.g., school psychologists), this may take quite a few weeks. Parents do have the right to take their child for an independent educational evaluation and can ask the school system to pay for it (U.S. Department of Education, n. d.).

There are 13 qualifying categories for disability that a child must be evaluated for to receive an IEP: autism, deaf-blindness, deafness, emotional disturbance, hearing impairment, intellectual disability, multiple disabilities, orthopedic impairment, other health impairment, specific learning disability, speech or language impairment, traumatic brain injury, or visual impairment (including blindness; U.S. Department of Education, 2018). Services that can be provided to a child through an IEP include (but are not limited to) speech-language pathology, physical and occupational therapy, counseling, psychological services, assistive technology, or specialized transportation services to and from school. These are all covered under Part C of IDEA: services for school-aged children.

## Part C of IDEIA: Early Intervention

Part C of IDEA is intended "to enhance the development of infants and toddlers with disabilities, to minimize their potential for developmental delay, and to recognize the significant brain development that occurs during a child's first 3 years of life" (U.S. Department of Education, 2018). It seeks to reduce potentially escalating educational costs for districts and families through early intervention and to maximize the potential of a child with disabilities. Part C can play a critical role in a family and child's future by providing proactive, relationship-based, individualized, and accessible early intervention services (Adams et al., 2013). Services provided include family training and home visits, occupational and physical therapy, early identification, screening, assessment for developmental delays, vision and hearing services, and social work services. Early intervention services are available in every state and territory and are offered at free or reduced costs. Health care providers can refer a family for early intervention services or parents can call their state early intervention program themselves.

## Disparities in Special Education

Parents or caregivers—who most often serve as the main advocates for their child—have great difficulty navigating our complex special education system and securing the appropriate educational services that their family needs. Research suggests a strong positive correlation between parental or caregiver involvement in the educational process and student success (Dickenson et al., 2017), although this is potentially confounded by the fact that parents or caregivers who are less privileged are often limitedly able to participate in the educational process because of a combination of factors, including nonstandard work schedules, lack of comfort interfacing with school personnel, and discrimination and structural inequalities. IDEA emphasizes the importance of parental and caregiver involvement; however, parents' capacity to participate in and contribute to the special education process varies by race, ethnicity, SES, and parental education. Most parents lack formal knowledge of, feel intimidated toward, and have difficulty understanding specific jargon about the special education process (Trainor, 2010). Participating in the highly regulated process of writing an IEP, for example, often relies on parents' social and cultural capital. Access to capital as well as the time, effort, and money required in securing special education services is not equitable across groups.

One study found that European American parents across socioeconomic groups described a sense of relief in finding an educational diagnosis for their child's "problem," allowing them to call on their network of professionals outside the school district to attend to their child's needs and provide appropriate services (Trainor, 2010). Compared to parents with less social and cultural capital, these parents often articulated a sophisticated understanding of their child's label and the implications it would have for their child's educational opportunities. These parents were more likely to be college educated and wealthy, drawing on their cultural and economic capital to find informational resources and private specialists.

Parents of children of color, especially those involved in the special education system, face the most structural and systemic barriers to parental involvement in schools. Studies show that teachers are less likely to respond favorably to parents who do not share the same cultural capital as the White, middle-class culture of most schools (Trainor, 2010). This finding has strong implications for parents of color trying to advocate for their children with disabilities or argue for a change in their IEPs. Lower-income parents of color typically do not have the same social capital or networks to draw on as White middle-class parents (Goss, 2019). Even wealthy parents of color are often excluded from parent networks that could provide the personal support to navigate the special education system.

With this in mind, there is a long-standing critique of special education that children of color are overrepresented in special education programs (Ferri & Connor, 2005). The U.S. Office of Civil Rights has reported a consistent problem of overrepresentation of minority children in certain disability categories since the 1970s. Evaluation instruments used in special education for labeling and placement decisions are often not culturally, socially, or linguistically sensitive, reflecting stereotypic beliefs about White intellectual superiority. Many children of color are misdiagnosed for years. All of this has contributed to worse post-school outcomes for children of color. The persistent achievement gap between White students and Black, Latinx, and immigrant students as well as the consistent diagnostic disparities among non-White children and those from low socioeconomic families in special education provides overwhelming evidence that the American special education system continues to fall short in supporting students of color and their families.

## Recommendations for Education Policy

IDEA presumes that all parents know how to effectively advocate for their children in the special education system. Schools should inform parents of the Federally Funded Parent Training and Information Centers that exist in each state to empower historically underserved communities, including families who are culturally and linguistically diverse. There is one center in each state and they help parents understand IDEA, the IEP process, 504 plans, and what a child's disability label means (U.S. Department of Education, 2018). These centers can prepare parents to effectively communicate and advocate to school personnel and other providers. Very few parents know that this resource is available to them. Schools need to treat all parents, regardless of race, ethnicity, education, or SES as valuable partners on the special education or IEP team. Schools should offer to hold IEP meetings outside of typical school hours to accommodate parents in jobs without flexible schedules and provide interpreters when needed.

Teacher education programs and school districts must prioritize professional development and training related to student diversity. Special educators need to be more prepared to teach in a diverse classroom. Additionally, educators making special education referrals must recognize how their own cultural backgrounds and biases may be affecting their decision. When determining IDEA eligibility, educators should use assessment tools validated in the population to which the student belongs. Finally, community outreach to improve access to early intervention to low-income marginalized communities can promote equity in educational outcomes moving forward.

At a macro-level, IDEA is the most important catalyst for the progress we have witnessed over the past 40 years in special education. However, there are still issues to be addressed. As of 2009, over 32,000 individuals with disabilities still resided in institutions. In 2014, 151 institutions for individuals with intellectual and developmental disabilities remained open. IDEA is based on the assumption that the cost of educating children with disabilities is more than twice the average cost (measured as the national average per pupil expenditure) of educating typically developing children (O'Hara et al., 2016). Congress determined that the federal government would pay up to 40% of this "excess" cost, which is referred to as *full funding*. Since 1981 (the first year that full funding was specified as 40% of average per pupil expenditure), the federal share has consistently remained at less than half of this commitment.

In 2015, the National Education Association's Education Policy and Practice Department released data showing the funding gap and cost shift for each state. In that fiscal year, the federal appropriation was $17.2 billion less than full funding, shifting that cost to states and districts (National Education Association, n. d.). Because IDEA funding has remained stagnant at less than half of its federal promise, a determination cannot be made about the potential effects of fully funding the IDEA and outcomes of school dropout, unemployment, and poverty. However, research has consistently shown that those with less than a high school diploma have a substantially higher rate of poverty and considerably lower earnings. Research has also evidenced that the quality of education determines high school graduation rates. And with that in mind, about 1 in 5 people with a disability have less than a high school diploma compared to 1 in 10 people with no disability (U.S. Bureau of Labor Statistics, 2015). Those who drop out of high school are unlikely to have the minimum skills to be successful in the labor force.

## Civil Rights

### A Brief History of the Disability Rights Movement

Perhaps the most widely known and celebrated disability rights law in the U.S. is the ADA. Though introduced in 1988 and signed into law in 1990, its history dates back to when people with disabilities (self-advocates), alongside parents of children with disabilities, challenged the segregation and societal barriers faced in their communities and began the disability rights movement (Baird, 2009). Local groups organized and began to advocate for the rights of people with disabilities, and the independent living movement was established to fight against institutionalization. After decades of campaigning, advocating, and lobbying, the disability rights movement achieved the ADA, which prohibits discrimination on the basis of disability and mandates equal treatment and equal access for people with disabilities.

The disability rights movement, organized primarily by people with disabilities themselves, began to take shape in the 1960s alongside the African American civil rights movement (Heyer, 2015). The disability rights movement, though often less widely known, emerged through the leadership of disability advocates such as Ed Roberts, Judy Heumann, Evan Kamp Jr., Fred Fay, Wade Blank, and Justin Dart Jr. It involved organizing, protesting, drafting legislation, testifying, lobbying, and filing lawsuits (Baird, 2009). It involved challenging stereotypes and rallying for institutional change. Previously, many Americans assumed that "problems" experienced by those with disabilities in education or employment were inevitable consequences of physical or mental impairment rather than a result of societal barriers, prejudices, and ableism.

Though the Rehabilitation Act of 1973 and the Education for All Handicapped Children Act of 1975 had been enacted, disability rights activists lobbied for broad and consolidated anti-discrimination policy, similar to the 1964 Civil Rights Act. The Civil Rights Act of 1964 prohibited discrimination on the basis of race, color, religion, national origin, and sex, with no reference to persons with disabilities (ADA National Network, n. d.) In March 1990, the ADA was gaining Congressional support, and disability activists descended to the Capitol to urge its passage. During that month, activists staged the infamous "Capitol Crawl" organized by a national grassroots community, ADAPT, in which protestors left their wheelchairs and crawled up the Capitol steps to demonstrate the inaccessibility they face on a daily basis (Kamalipour & Carilli, 1998). Many other such demonstrations and advocacy efforts took place before the ADA was finally signed into law in July by President George H.W. Bush.

## The Americans with Disabilities Act

The ADA is divided into five titles (or sections) that relate to different aspects of daily life:

- *Title I Employment*. This assists people with disabilities in accessing the same employment opportunities and benefits as those without disabilities. Employers with 15 or more employees must provide a reasonable accommodation to an employee with a disability that qualifies.

- *Title II Public Services*: State and Local Government. This ensures accessibility to people with disabilities in public entities, including state and local government agencies, courts, school districts, universities, community colleges, and public transportation.

- *Title III Public Accommodations and Services Operated by Private Entities*. This prohibits places of public accommodation from discriminating against individuals with disabilities. Public accommodations include privately owned, leased, or operated facilities such as hotels, restaurants, doctor's offices, private schools, banks, day care centers, health clubs, sports stadiums, movie theaters, and so on.

- *Title IV Telecommunications.* This requires telephone and internet companies to provide a system that allows individuals with hearing- or speech-related disabilities to be able to communicate over the phone.

- *Title V Miscellaneous Provisions.* This covers insurance issues and defines explicit restrictions against retaliation or coercion against someone with a disability who exerts their civil rights.

The ADA is crucial to the inclusion of children with disabilities and their families. It requires childcare providers, through Title III, to not discriminate on the basis of disability and to provide equal opportunity to participate in a childcare center's programs and services. It also provides accessibility to hospitals and public transportation. It allows children with disabilities to participate and engage in their community by providing access to sports stadiums, libraries, movie theatres, and restaurants. Furthermore, the ADA is a crucial disability rights law that will ensure accommodations for children as they grow older and continue on in education and employment.

### Recommendations for Civil Rights Policy

Despite the significant gains that the ADA and the disability rights movement have made, gaps still remain. Discrimination and ableism still exist. Poor enforcement of the law is evident in the number of businesses and agencies that are unaware of or that choose to ignore the civil rights of people with disabilities (Shapiro, 1994). There are many businesses that remain inaccessible to people with disabilities because by law, they are only required to make "reasonable accommodations" to ensure accessibility, and the definition of "reasonable" is often at the discretion of businesses (ADA National Network, n. d.). People with disabilities still remain employed in isolated, sheltered workshops and are paid far less than minimum wage. Many disability advocates have called for paratransit reform due to late arrivals and lack of proper equipment. The ADA sets many reasonable minimal requirements; however, additional measures are needed to ensure the inclusion of the disability community in American society.

## Health Care and Community-Based Services

### Medicaid, Children's Health Insurance Program, and Home and Community-Based Services

Medicaid provides health care coverage to more than 40 million people in the U.S. (Bruen & Holahan, 2001). Medicaid recipients include low-income adults, children, pregnant women, elderly adults, and individuals of all ages with disabilities. According to The Medicaid and Children's Health Insurance Program (CHIP) Payment and

Access Commission 2018 report to Congress, over 10 million people qualify for Medicaid on the basis of disability alone. CHIP and Medicaid are administered by states according to federal guidelines and are funded jointly by states and the federal government through a matching grant. Because of this, these programs can look different from state to state. However, Congress created an "enhanced" federal matching rate for CHIP that is generally 15 percentage points higher than the Medicaid rate. For example, if a state has a 50% match rate for Medicaid, they may have a 65% match rate for CHIP (Centers for Medicaid and Medicare Services [CMS], n. d.). This is intended to incentivize states to provide robust programming to children with special health care needs so that they receive early detection and care.

As of 2017, Medicaid and CHIP covered about half (47%) of children with special health care needs (Musumeci, 2018), which include physical disabilities, intellectual and developmental disabilities, and serious behavioral disorders or mental illnesses (CMS, n. d.). According to the U.S. Department of Health and Human Services, these children "have or are at increased risk for chronic physical, developmental, behavioral, or emotional conditions and also require health and related services of a type or amount beyond that required by children generally" (Health Resources and Services Administration, 2019). Medicaid provides a broad range of medical and long-term care services to these children, many of which are not covered at all or have coverage that is only available in limited amounts through private insurance. Medicaid and CHIP make coverage affordable and available to many children with disabilities and their families.

Children can qualify for Medicaid/CHIP through multiple pathways. They can qualify based solely on their family's income: As of January 2017, the median financial eligibility level for Medicaid and CHIP children nationally is 255% FPL ($52,989/year for a family of four in 2018) (Musumeci, 2018). They can also qualify through a disability-related pathway: States must provide Medicaid benefits for children who qualify for SSI. Because Medicaid provides services that private insurance does not for children with disabilities, higher-income families can also elect to buy-in to Medicaid. This allows Medicaid to fill in coverage gaps for higher-income families. Additionally, all states have opted to cover children with significant disabilities living at home through a "Katie Beckett" pathway, which disregards parental income and assets in determining a child's eligibility. Pathways to Medicaid/CHIP eligibility are complex and vary greatly by state; however, it is imperative that families know there are multiple avenues to qualifying for coverage.

CHIP provides the Medicaid benefit for children known as Early and Periodic Screening, Diagnostic, and Treatment (EPSDT) services (CMS, n. d.). EPSDT services provide a comprehensive selection of preventive, dental, vision, hearing, mental health, developmental, and other specialty services to children under age 21. Based on federal guidelines, screening services include physical exams, immunizations, laboratory tests, health education, and comprehensive health and developmental histories.

Medicaid is also intended to provide a broad range of medical and long-term care services to people with intellectual and developmental disabilities to support them in living in their homes and communities rather than in institutions. Private insurance does not sufficiently cover long-term care services needed by those with disabilities. These services are also known as home and community-based services

(HCBS). Medicaid HCBS waivers are the largest–and often the only—provider of long-term services and supports for children with intellectual and developmental disabilities in the U.S. They waive the cost of essential services and supports for children with disabilities. Medicaid HCBS waivers are designed to help children and adults with disabilities get the care they need in their communities rather than in institutions. Again, because Medicaid is funded jointly by states and the federal government, these HCBS waivers vary greatly from state to state. States choose to target their waivers where the need is greatest. Although the services and supports provided by Medicaid HCBS vary by state, a few of the common services and supports that Medicaid HCBS can provide to a child with disabilities include the following:

- Therapy and supplemental services through special education in school
- Assistive technology
- In-home nursing
- Transportation
- Home and vehicle modifications
- Art, music, and play therapies
- Prevocational services
- Respite care and family support services

## Demographics of Medicaid/CHIP Children With Special Health Care Needs

Because of the eligibility requirements, most of the children with special health care needs who received Medicaid/CHIP are part of low- to middle-income families (Musumeci, 2018). Forty-five percent of Medicaid/CHIP children reside in a household below the federal poverty level (FPL) and over three quarters (79%) of Medicaid/CHIP children live in families with incomes below 200% FPL (which equates to less than $43,440 for a family of three in 2020; Health Resources and Services Administration, 2019). Medicaid and CHIP are particularly crucial protective health care policies for children of color, who are disproportionately represented among beneficiaries because they are more likely to be economically disadvantaged. Thirty-seven percent of CHIP/Medicaid beneficiaries are Hispanic, 33% are White, 20% are African American, 6% are another race/ethnicity, and 3% are Asian (Georgetown University Center for Children and Families, 2017). Medicaid and CHIP address disparities in health care access for children and families of color, especially those with disabilities.

## Recommendations for Health Care and Community-Based Services Policy

There are both racial and disability equity implications of proposals to restrict Medicaid and CHIP. Proposals are routinely considered that would restructure the financing of these health programs. Under the current matched grant funding structure, the federal government has a commitment to help states cover costs of Medicaid services and supports. Essentially, when a state spends money on providing an eligible beneficiary with services, the state is guaranteed reimbursement from the federal Medicaid program at the state match rate (which is typically around 60%; Rudowitz et al., 2018). If a state increases its Medicaid spending, federal funding will increase as well. Through this funding structure, states have considerable flexibility in how they administer their programs and what additional services and supports they will provide, such as HCBS services to children with disabilities.

Proposals for block grants or per capita caps would cut state flexibility and alter this partnership. Under a block grant funding structure, states would have a preset amount of funding based on how much a state spent in a previous year. It would also set the total amount of federal reimbursement and states would be responsible for covering the costs beyond their federal allotment (Rudowitz et al., 2018). Under a block grant, if a program cost exceeded the federal spending cap due to a variety of reasons (such as increased enrollment), states would have to spend more or reduce services. This has the possibility of forcing states to reduce eligibility or limit their services and supports to children with disabilities to save money. Under a per capita cap, the federal government would set a limit on state reimbursement per enrollee (Cassidy, 2013). Children with disabilities who are eligible for Medicaid/CHIP have higher per enrollee spending than other Medicaid children; therefore, per capita caps that limit spending per enrollee would disproportionately disadvantage this population who needs access to necessary and expensive services that are often unavailable through private insurance (Rudowitz et al., 2018). Furthermore, states should continue to promote Medicaid provider incentive programs, as many practitioners are less likely to accept Medicaid or may accept Medicaid patients at a slower rate due to low reimbursement.

Medicaid law requires that states provide medical services to its beneficiaries, including doctors' visits, hospitalizations, or institutional care. These are mandatory services. HCBS however, though critical to children with disabilities, are considered "optional" services and are not required by law. States choose to provide them to support the independence and health of children and adults with disabilities. A funding restructure of Medicaid would force states to lose federal funding and have to make difficult decisions to cut optional services in order to ensure that all beneficiaries are provided their mandatory care. Children with intellectual and developmental disabilities could lose access to HCBS and states may have to increase their use of institutionalization once again (Angeles, 2017). The unique needs of children with disabilities and their families must be considered in any proposal to restructure the funding of Medicaid and CHIP.

## Income Support

### Social Security Disability Insurance, Supplemental Security Income, and Temporary Assistance for Needy Families

Children with disabilities and their families receive income transfer payments through several different programs. The two largest federal programs that provide assistance to people with disabilities are Social Security Disability Insurance (SSDI) and SSI. SSDI, however, is not a major source of income to children with disabilities as it targets adults with a qualifying work history. SSI, on the other hand, can provide monthly payments to children with disabilities with low income without any work history. Many children with disabilities and their families are also supported through the Temporary Assistance for Needy Families (TANF) program, which is the largest cash assistance program for low-income families (Center on Budget and Policy Priorities, n. d.).

SSI is the only federal income support targeted specifically to families caring for children with disabilities. SSI is means-tested—based on an individual's income and assets—and provides monthly income to the aging population and to those with disabilities (Social Security Administration [SSA], n. d.-b). The cash provided is intended to meet basic needs for food, clothing, and shelter. Social Security considers children under 18 as *disabled* based on medically determined physical and mental impairments that result in "marked and severe functional limitations" and on having "lasted or can be expected to last for a continuous period of not less than 12 months" (SSA, n. d.-b). Though this is a federal program, state agencies make the disability decision. Parental income and assets relative to the family size are also considered in the eligibility process. In 2020, a single child with disabilities living in a two-parent home could receive SSI payments if parental income did not exceed $4,433 a month.

In 2017, roughly 1.2 million children with disabilities were receiving SSI benefits, averaging about $650 per month (SSA, n. d.-a), which equates to $7,800 a year. The federal poverty threshold for one person in 2017 was $12,060 (U.S. Department of Health and Human Services, 2020), meaning the SSI payment for one individual fell about 35% below the federal poverty line. Despite this limited level of support, SSI has lifted the children who qualify out of deep poverty (Ruffing, 2013). SSI helps to offset some of the extra costs of supporting a child with disabilities. Additionally, this added income from SSI can yield lasting gains. Evidence suggests that low-income children whose families receive a boost in income can do better in school and earn more as adults (Sherman, 2017).

Unfortunately, though, SSI has strict eligibility requirements. Qualified medical professionals such as physicians, licensed psychologists, or other experts must submit evidence of disability. Submissions by parents or teachers do not qualify. Evidence of the stringent criteria is noted in the fact that SSA rejects about 60% of applications for SSI for children with disabilities (Ruffing, 2013). Additionally, a child's eligibility must be reviewed once every three years, and these continuing disability reviews have led to termination for about 20% of children reviewed (SSA, n. d.-a).

## Recommendations for Income Support Policy

While SSI does mitigate hardship, many families who receive SSI remain poor, and because of the stringent eligibility criteria, many families with children with disabilities do not receive SSI at all. Income may not accurately portray the economic well-being of a family because of the high expenses that may be needed to care appropriately for their child. Additionally, many parents of children with disabilities must make the decision to work less in order to care for their child (Chung et al., 2007). Many parents, especially mothers, turn down promotions or work fewer hours in order to take their children to medical appointments, accommodate multiple school meetings, attend to emergencies, or provide the extra help that many children with disabilities need to succeed in daily activities. This long list of demands is daunting for any parent, regardless of SES, but especially for those who are low-income. Low-wage workers are also less likely to have a flexible schedule or paid family leave (Clemans-Cope et al., 2008). They may have less income for additional caregivers or transportation.

It is crucial therefore to protect and expand the effectiveness of this supplemental income program and support proposals that ensure the long-term solvency of the Social Security Trust Fund. Additionally, it is key to recognize that intellectual and developmental disabilities are lifelong disabilities and those who qualify for SSI under this diagnosis should not have their eligibility terminated at any time. Increasing the resource limit for qualifying for SSI will recognize the unique financial, time, and work demands that parents face when they raise a child with disabilities and will help to raise those families out of poverty.

Recently, the Achieving a Better Life Experience (ABLE) Act was passed to address this issue. Under this policy, ABLE accounts, which are tax-advantaged saving accounts for people with disabilities, can be created (ABLE National Resource Center, 2020). Contributions to the account can be made using post-taxed dollars and will not be tax deductible (ABLE National Resource Center, 2020). ABLE accounts are intended to meet the needs of people with disabilities who, in order to remain eligible for public benefits such as SSI, must remain relatively poor. The ABLE Act recognizes the extra costs of living with a disability or raising a child with a disability and allows these families to save money while still receiving their needed benefits. Many families and their providers are unaware of this crucial support, and public outreach surrounding ABLE accounts should be prioritized.

## USING KNOWLEDGE OF RISK, PROTECTION, AND RESILIENCE TO ACHIEVE SERVICE INTEGRATION IN DISABILITY POLICY

Policies and programs to support children with disabilities and their families are complex, fragmented, and rely heavily on the knowledge and advocacy abilities of parents. From the point of diagnosis, parents are expected to serve in the central role of providing care, accessing appropriate services and supports, leading an IEP team, and developing independent living and transition plans. With knowledge that the emotional and social well-being of caregivers and parents can serve as a protective factor in enhanced outcomes for their children, policies must specifically provide financial and emotional resources to assist them in being effective advocates and valuable partners. This may include increasing the breadth of services provided by federally funded parent training and information centers, ensuring access to early intervention in the most marginalized communities, or increasing the monthly SSI payments to families.

Fragmentation of services across education and health care systems are an ongoing challenge for people with disabilities and their families. To obtain appropriate services, families must go through multiple agencies and institutions, with stringent and differing eligibility criteria, complex paperwork, changing revenue sources, waitlists, and frequent application denials. This is even more challenging for families facing multiple adversities, especially poverty, which contributes to inequitable access to educational resources and networks, financial support, or transportation. Streamlined applications and coordination across government agencies that intend to protect children with disabilities must be prioritized moving forward. Children with access to adequate and inclusive medical, financial, and educational resources that prioritize inclusion, social support, and empowerment are more likely to have enhanced outcomes and better quality of life as they age with their disability.

## SUMMARY OF POLICY CONCLUSIONS AND RECOMMENDATIONS

We have reviewed the major public policies that affect the lives of children with disabilities and their families in the U.S. in education, early intervention, civil rights, health care, and income (Table 7.2). The extent to which knowledge of risk and protective factors have influenced the development of these policies remains unclear. However, despite variability in their effectiveness, these policies, brought forth by the tireless advocacy of disability self-advocates and parents of children with disabilities, have undoubtedly changed and improved outcomes for children with disabilities over the past couple decades.

Children with disabilities and their families are protected by many of these policies. The special education system and early intervention services are based on our knowledge of risk and protective factors; however, child and parental success in the system varies by race, ethnicity, SES, and parental education level. Schools should prioritize access to federal funded parent training and information centers and professional development and training related to student diversity. Evaluation instruments should be culturally, socially, and linguistically sensitive in order to address the overrepresentation of minority children in special education and the number of late diagnoses and misdiagnoses of children of color. Finally, Congress must prioritize fully funding the IDEA—as previously promised—to improve educational outcomes of children with disabilities.

Despite the significant gains that the ADA and the disability rights movement have achieved, gaps still remain. Discrimination and ableism still exist in employment, education, housing, and other areas of society. Disability is lifelong and children will be affected in all aspects of life if ableism remains a persistent and prevalent problem. The requirements and protections established in the ADA were necessary but are not sufficient for all children and youth with disabilities to truly thrive.

In terms of health care, the unique needs of children with disabilities and their families must be considered in any proposal to restructure the funding of Medicaid and CHIP. A funding restructure of Medicaid would force states to lose federal funding and have to make difficult decisions to cut services for children with intellectual and developmental disabilities. Medicaid and CHIP work to address disparities in health care access for children and families of color, especially those with disabilities. Finally, it is crucial to protect and expand SSI and support proposals that ensure the long-term solvency of the Social Security Trust Fund that backs it.

These policies offer some protective benefits, but these benefits are insufficient. As they stand, the benefits do not mitigate the challenges and costs associated with childhood disability. Additionally, no policy specifically supports the unique needs of children with disabilities who are also part of the LGBTQIA community nor do they explicitly protect against child maltreatment. Overall, it is crucial to integrate and coordinate the services and supports provided across government agencies and institutions to better support families and fill these gaps. Such efforts could reduce fragmentation in services and support parents and caregivers in their central role of coordinating and accessing appropriate care for their child.

In conclusion, the incidence and prevalence of disability is significantly rising. Because disability is lifelong, disability policies that support inclusion, caregiver well-being, and adequate and inclusive resources must be in place throughout the life course. Although principles of risk and protective factors relate deeply to each of the policy domains, they are applied in limited ways. Our systems remain fragmented and inadequately funded. Our recommendations are intended to improve access, mitigate disparities, and provide holistic care and support to children with disabilities and their families.

## REFERENCES

ABLE National Resource Center. (2020, August 17). [Website]. https://www.ablenrc.org/.

Access Living. (2020). *Ableism 101—What is ableism? What does it look like?* https://www.accessliving.org/newsroom/blog/ableism-101/.

ADA National Network. (n. d.). *What is the Americans with Disabilities Act (ADA)?* https://adata.org/learn-about-ada.

Adams, R. C., Tapia, C., & Council on Children with Disabilities (2013). Early intervention, IDEA Part C services, and the medical home: Collaboration for best practice and best outcomes. *Pediatrics, 132*(4), e1073–e1088.

Alquraini, T. A. (2013). An analysis of legal issues relating to the least restrictive environment standards. *Journal of Research in Special Educational Needs, 13*, 152–158.

Al-Yagon, M., & Mikulincer, M. (2004). Patterns of close relationships and socioemotional and academic adjustment among school-age children with learning disabilities. *Learning Disabilities Research & Practice, 19*, 12–19.

Angeles, J. (2017, October 11). *Ryan Medicaid Block Grant would cause severe reductions in health care and long-term care for seniors, people with disabilities, and children.* Center on Budget and Policy Priorities. https://www.cbpp.org/research/ryan-medicaid-block-grant-would-cause-severe-reductions-in-health-care-and-long-term-care.

Baird, R. M. (2009). *Disability: The social, political, and ethical debate.* Prometheus.

Ball-Brown, B., & Frank, Z. L. (1993). Disabled students of color. *New Directions for Student Services, 1993*(64), 79–88.

Bishop-Fitzpatrick, L., & Eisenbaum, E. (2016). Racial and ethnic disparities in the diagnosis and treatment of autism spectrum disorder. In K. Lomotey, P. X. Ruf, P. B. Jackson, V. C. Copeland, A. Huerta, N. Iglesias-Prieto, & D. L. Brown (Eds.), *People of color in the United States: Contemporary issues in education, work, communities, health, and immigration, Volume 3: Health and wellness* (pp. 25–30). ABC-CLIO.

Bruen, B., & Holahan, J. (2001). *Medicaid spending growth remained modest in 1998, but likely headed upward*. The Kaiser Commission on Medicaid and the Uninsured, the Henry J. Kaiser Family Foundation.

Cassidy, A. (2013). Health policy brief: Per capita caps in Medicaid. *Health Affairs*. http://www.healthaffairs.org/healthpolicybriefs/brief.php?brief_id=90

Center on Budget and Policy Priorities. (n. d.). *Temporary assistance for needy families*. https://www.cbpp.org/research/family-income-support/temporary-assistance-for-needy-families.

Centers for Disease Control and Prevention (CDC). (2019a). *Developmental disability fact sheet*. https://www.cdc.gov/ncbddd/developmentaldisabilities/facts.html

Centers for Disease Control and Prevention (CDC). (2019b). *Intellectual disability fact sheet*. https://www.cdc.gov/ncbddd/childdevelopment/facts-about-intellectual-disability.html?CDC_AA_refVal=https%3A%2F%2Fwww.cdc.gov%2Fncbddd%2Fdevelopmentaldisabilities%2F-facts-about-intellectual-disability.html

Centers for Medicare & Medicaid Services (n. d.). *Medicaid state waiver program demonstration projects: Medicaid waivers and demonstrations list*. http://www.medicaid.gov/Medicaid-CHIP-Program-Information/By-Topics/Waivers/Waivers.html

Centers for Medicare & Medicaid Services. (2019). *Medicaid state waiver program demonstration projects: Medicaid waivers and demonstrations list*. http://www.medicaid.gov/Medicaid-CHIP-Program-Information/By-Topics/Waivers/Waivers.html

Chung, P. J., Garfield, C. F., Elliott, M. N., Carey, C., Eriksson, C., & Schuster, M. A. (2007). Need for and use of family leave among parents of children with special health care needs. *Pediatrics, 119*(5), e1047–e1055.

Clemans-Cope, L., Perry, C. D., Kenney, G. M., Pelletier, J. E., & Pantell, M. S. (2008). Access to and use of paid sick leave among low-income families with children. *Pediatrics, 122*(2), e480–e486.

Dawkins, J. L. (1996). Bullying, physical disability and the pediatric patient. *Developmental Medicine and Child Neurology, 38*, 603–612.

De Brey, C., Musu, L., McFarland, J., Wilkinson-Flicker, S., Diliberti, M., Zhang, A., Branstetter, C., & Wang, X. (2019). *Status and trends in the education of racial and ethnic groups 2018 (NCES 2019-038)*. U.S. Department of Education, National Center for Education Statistics. https://nces.ed.gov/pubsearch/.

Dickenson, P., Keough, P., Courduff, J., & Sistek-Chandler, C. (2017). *Parents as partners in the special education process: A parent's perspective with suggestions for educators*. IGI Global.

Donohue, M. R., Childs, A. W., Richards, M., & Robins, D. L. (2019). Race influences parent report of concerns about symptoms of autism spectrum disorder. *Autism, 23*(1), 100–111.

Goode, S., Diefendorf, M., & Colgan, S. (2011). *The importance of early intervention for infants and toddlers with disabilities and their families*. The University of North Carolina, FPG Child Development Institute, National Early Childhood Technical Assistance Center.

Ferguson, P. M., & Asch, A. (1989). Lessons from life: Personal and parental perspectives on school, childhood, and disability. In D. Biklen, D. Ferguson, & A. Ford (Eds.), *Schooling and disability: Eighty-eighth yearbook of the National Society for the Study of Education: Part II* (pp. 108–141). University of Chicago Press.

Ferri, B. A., & Connor, D. J. (2005). In the shadow of brown: Special education and overrepresentation of students of color. *Remedial and Special Education, 26*(2), 93–100.

Georgetown University Center for Children and Families. (2017, April). *Snapshot of children's coverage by race and ethnicity*. https://ccf.georgetown.edu/wp-content/uploads/2018/05/Snapshot-of-Children%E2%80%99s-Coverage-by-Race-and-Ethnicity.pdf

Goss, A. C. (2019). Power to engage, power to resist: A structuration analysis of barriers to parental involvement. *Education and Urban Society, 51*(5), 595–612.

Ha, J. H., Greenberg, J. S., & Seltzer, M. M. (2011). Parenting a child with a disability: The role of social support for African American parents. *Families in Society, 92*(4), 405–411.

Health Resources and Services Administration. (2019, December 17). *Children with special health care needs*. https://mchb.hrsa.gov/maternal-child-health-topics/children-and-youth-special-health-needs

Hehir, T. (2009). Eliminating ableism in education. *Harvard Educational Review, 72*(1), 1–33.

Heyer, K. (2015). *Rights enabled: The disability revolution, from the US, to Germany and Japan, to the United Nations*. University of Michigan Press.

Holburn, C. S. (1997). A brief review of "Unforgotten Twenty-Five Years and Willowbrook" and a tribute to the forgotten. *Mental Retardation, 35*(5), 381.

Hugh-Jones, S., & Smith, P. K. (1999). Self-reports of short-and long-term effects of bullying on children who stammer. *British Journal of Educational Psychology, 69*(2), 141–158.

Institute of Medicine. (2003). *Unequal treatment: Confronting racial and ethnic disparities in health care*. National Academies Press.

Institute of Medicine. (2007). *The future of disability in America*. National Academies Press.

Jones, L., Bellis, M. A., Wood, S., Hughes, K., McCoy, E., Eckley, L., Bates, G., Mikton, C., Shakespeares, T., & Officer, A. (2012). Prevalence and risk of violence against children with disabilities: A systematic review and meta-analysis of observational studies. *The Lancet, 380*(9845), 899–907.

Kamalipour, Y. R., & Carilli, T. (1998). *Cultural diversity and the U.S. media*. State University of New York Press.

King, G., King, S., Rosenbaum, P., & Goffin, R. (1999). Family-centered caregiving and well-being of parents of children with disabilities: Linking process with outcome. *Journal of Pediatric Psychology, 24*(1), 41–53.

Krahn, G. L., Walker, D. K., & Correa-De-Araujo, R. (2015). Persons with disabilities as an unrecognized health disparity population. *American Journal of Public Health, 105*(Suppl 2), S198–S206.

Lipkin, P. H., & Okamoto, J. (2015). The Individuals with Disabilities Education Act (IDEA) for children with special educational needs. *Pediatrics, 136*(6), e1650.

Mandell, D. S., Ittenbach, R. F., Levy, S. E., & Pinto-Martin, J. A. (2007). Disparities in diagnoses received

prior to a diagnosis of autism spectrum disorder. *Journal of Autism and Developmental Disorders, 37*(9), 1795–1802.

Mandell, D. S., Wiggins, L. D., Carpenter, L. A., Daniels, J., DiGuiseppi, C., Durkin, M. S., Giarelli, E., Morrier, M. J., Nicholas, J. S., Pinto-Martin, J. A., Shattuck, P. T., Thomas, K. C., Yeargin-Allsopp, M., & Kirby, R. S. (2009). Racial/ethnic disparities in the identification of children with autism spectrum disorders. *American Journal of Public Health, 99*(3), 493–498.

Martin, E. W., Martin, R., & Terman, D. L. (1996). The legislative and litigation history of special education. *The Future of Children, 6*(1), 25–39.

Madaus, J. W., & Shaw, S. F. (2008). The role of school professionals in implementing Section 504 for students with disabilities. *Educational Policy, 22*(3), 363–378.

McDonnell, C. G., Boan, A. D., Bradley, C. C., Seay, K. D., Charles, J. M., & Carpenter, L. A. (2019). Child maltreatment in autism spectrum disorder and intellectual disability: Results from a population-based sample. *Journal of Child Psychology and Psychiatry, 60*(5), 576–584.

Miles, J. H. (2011). Autism spectrum disorders—a genetics review. *Genetics in Medicine, 13*(4), 278–294.

Mills v. Board of Education of District of Columbia, 348 F. Supp. 866 (D.D.C. 1972).

Movement Advancement Project. (2019, July). *LGBT people with disabilities*. https://www.lgbtmap.org/lgbt-people-disabilities

Musumeci, M. (2018). Medicaid's role for children with special health care needs. *The Journal of Law, Medicine & Ethics, 46*(4), 897–905.

National Academies of Sciences, Engineering, and Medicine (NASEM). (2015). *Mental disorders and disabilities among low-income children*. National Academies Press.

National Dissemination Center for Children with Disabilities (NICHCY). (2011). *NICHCY disability fact sheet #8: Intellectual disabilities*. Author.

National Education Association. (n. d.). *IDEA funding coalition offers proposal*. https://www.nea.org/student-success/smart-just-policies/special-education

Noonan, A., & Gomez, M. T. (2011). Who's missing? Awareness of lesbian, gay, bisexual and transgender people with intellectual disability. *Sexuality and Disability, 29*(2), 175–180.

O'Hara, N., Munk, T. E., Reedy, K., & D'Agord, C. (2016, May). *Equity, inclusion, and opportunity: Addressing success gaps* [White paper (Version 3.0)]. IDEA Data Center. Westat.

Palmer, S. B., Wehmeyer, M. L., Shogren, K., Williams-Diehm, K., & Soukup, J. (2012). An evaluation of the beyond high school model on the self-determination of students with intellectual disability. *Career Development for Exceptional Individuals, 35*(2), 76–84.

Pascoe, J. M., Wood, D. L., Duffee, J. H., Kuo, A., & Committee on Psychosocial Aspects of Child and Family Health. (2016). Mediators and adverse effects of child poverty in the United States. *Pediatrics, 137*(4), e1–17.

PARC v. Commonwealth. 343 F. Supp. 279; U.S. Dist. LEXIS 13874 (1972).

Park, J., Turnbull, A. P., & Turnbull, H. R. (2002). Impacts of poverty on quality of life in families of children with disabilities. *Exceptional Children, 68*(2), 151–170.

Pfeiffer, D. (1993). Overview of the disability movement: History, legislative record, and political implications. *Policy Studies Journal, 21*, 724–734.

Rosenfeld, S. (1996). *Section 504 and IDEA: Basic similarities and differences.* https://eric.ed.gov/?id=ED427487

Rousso, H. (1984). Fostering healthy self-esteem: Part one. *Exceptional Parent, 14*(8), 9–14.

Rudowitz, R., Hinton, E., & Antonisse, L. (2018, November 12). Medicaid enrollment & spending growth: FY 2018 & 2019. *Kaiser Family Foundation.* https://www.kff.org/medicaid/issue-brief/medicaid-enrollment-spending-growth-fy-2018-2019/.

Ruffing, K. (2013). *Rich man, poor man: Lawmakers should raise and index the SSI asset limits.* Center on Budget and Policy Priorities. https://www.cbpp.org/blog/rich-man-poor-man-lawmakers-should-raise-and-index-the-ssi-asset-limits.

Shapiro, J. P. (1994). *No pity: People with disabilities forging a new civil rights movement.* Times Books.

Sherman, A. (2017, November 15). Poverty in early childhood has long and harmful reach. *Center on Budget and Policy Priorities.* https://www.cbpp.org/blog/poverty-in-early-childhood-has-long-and-harmful-reach

Social Security Administration (SSA). (n. d.-a). *Social security red book.* https://www.ssa.gov/redbook/eng/overview-disability.htm

Social Security Administration (SSA). (n. d.-b). *SSI annual report.* https://www.ssa.gov/OACT/ssir/.

Sowers, J., & Powers, L. (1995). Enhancing the participation and independence of students with severe physical and multiple disabilities in performing community activities. *Mental Retardation, 33*, 209–220.

Spaulding, L. S., & Pratt, S. M. (2015). A review and analysis of the history of special education and disability advocacy in the United States. *American Educational History Journal, 42*(1/2), 91.

Trainor, A. A. (2010). Reexamining the promise of parent participation in special education: An analysis of cultural and social capital. *Anthropology & Education Quarterly, 41*, 245–63.

Turnbull, A., Turnbull, R., & Wehmeyer, M. (2010). *Exceptional lives.* Pearson.

Twyman, K. A., Saylor, C. F., Saia, D., Macias, M. M., Taylor, L. A., & Spratt, E. (2010). Bullying and ostracism experiences in children with special health care needs. *Journal of Developmental & Behavioral Pediatrics, 31*(1), 1–8.

U.S. Bureau of Labor Statistics. (2015, July 20). *People with a disability less likely to have completed a bachelor's degree.* https://www.bls.gov/opub/ted/2015/people-with-a-disability-less-likely-to-have-completed-a-bachelors-degree.htm

U.S. Department of Education. (2007, July). *25 year history of the IDEA.* https://www2.ed.gov/policy/speced/leg/idea/history.html

U.S. Department of Education. (2016, April). *Thirty-five years of progress in educating children with disabilities through IDEA.* https://www2.ed.gov/about/offices/list/osers/idea35/history/index_pg10.html.

U.S. Department of Education. (2018). *Sec. 300.8 child with a disability.* Individuals with Disabilities Education Act. https://sites.ed.gov/idea/regs/b/a/300.8.

U.S. Department of Education. (2019). *Guide to the individualized education program.* https://www2.ed.gov/parents/needs/speced/iepguide/index.html

U.S. Department of Education. (n. d.). *Statute and regulations.* Individuals with Disabilities Education Act. https://sites.ed.gov/idea/statuteregulations/.

U.S. Department of Health and Human Services. (2020). *Poverty guidelines.* ASPE. https://aspe.hhs.gov/poverty-guidelines.

Wehmeyer, M. L. (2005). Self-determination and individuals with severe disabilities: Reexamining meanings and misinterpretations. *Research and Practice for Persons with Severe Disabilities, 30*, 113–120.

Wehmeyer, M. L., Abery, B., Mithaug, D. E., & Stancliffe, R. J. (2003). *Theory in self-determination: Foundations for educational practice*. Charles C Thomas Publisher, LTD.

Wehmeyer, M. L., & Schwartz, M. (1997). Self-determination and positive adult outcomes: A follow-up study of youth with mental retardation or learning disabilities. *Exceptional Children, 63*, 245–255.

World Health Organization & World Bank. (2011). *World report on disability 2011*. World Health Organization.

Yell, M. L., & Bateman, D. F. (2017). Endrew F. v. Douglas County School District (2017). FAPE and the U.S. Supreme Court. *TEACHING Exceptional Children, 50*(1), 7–15.

Yell, M., Rogers, D., & Rogers, E. (1998). The legal history of special education: What a long, strange trip it's been! *Remedial and Special Education, 19*, 219–228. 10.1177/074193259801900405.

Zablotsky, B., Black, L. I., Maenner, M. J., Schieve, L. A., Danielson, M. L., Bitsko, R. H., Blumberg, S. J., Kogan, M. D., & Boyle, C. A. (2019). Prevalence and trends of developmental disabilities among children in the United States: 2009–2017. *Pediatrics, 144*(4), e20190811.

# 8

# POLICIES AND PROGRAMS FOR ADOLESCENT SUBSTANCE ABUSE

## Elizabeth K. Anthony, Jeffrey M. Jenson, and Matthew O. Howard

Adolescent substance abuse has been the subject of frequent discussion in local, state, and federal policy circles since the 1960s. Substance abuse among children and youth has also attracted the attention of the American public. The Centers for Disease Control and Prevention (CDC) reports that in 2018, more than 67,000 people died from drug overdoses, outpacing other injury-related deaths as a leading cause in the United States (CDC, 2020). Unlike some other injury-related deaths, substance abuse is preventable. Substance use contributes to an increase in the probability of dying by age 50 (Case & Deaton, 2015; Murphy et al., 2018); substance use is also a factor in several other social problems, including domestic violence, theft, and suicide (Johnston et al., 2019).

The visible and often devastating effects of substance use on individuals—coupled with the societal and economic costs associated with abuse—have been the targets of repeated social intervention in the past century. Significant increases in opioid-related deaths and in the overuse of prescription drugs by teenagers and young adults have raised new concerns in the past decade. The misuse of opioids was problematic before the recent public health crisis of the novel coronavirus (COVID-19) reached the United States in 2020. Unfortunately, the high number of COVID-19 cases in the country has also adversely affected access to opioid treatment and contributed to opioid overdoses (Becker & Fiellin, 2020). And while overall drug use is historically lower among Black and Brown adolescents, the COVID-19 pandemic—combined with current protests aimed at eliminating structural racism and promoting equity—has heightened concern about disparities in health and behavioral health outcomes among Black and Brown youth (Egede & Walker, 2020). Trent, Dooley, and Douge (2019) identify the systemic issues sustaining racism in child and adolescent health outcomes and limiting the ability of pediatric health professionals to address the disparities. They present research findings acknowledging the role of racism and attempt to proactively engage the health community through education, workforce development, and other structural approaches.

Demands for policy and program reform have come from a range of constituents and organizations. A report published at the beginning of the past decade by Physician

Leadership on National Drug Policy (2002) outlined the need for more policy directives aimed at preventing adolescent substance abuse in the United States. More recent reports from the National Institute on Drug Abuse (NIDA) and the Substance Abuse and Mental Health Services Administration (SAMHSA) place considerable emphasis on informing practitioners about efficacious ways to prevent and treat adolescent substance abuse (NIDA, 2014; SAMHSA, 2020a). It is significant that researchers and policy officials are working together to apply knowledge about the risk and protective factors associated with the onset and use of alcohol and illicit drugs to social interventions and policies for children and families (Catalano & Kellogg, 2020; Hawkins et al., 2015; Jenson & Bender, 2014; Liddle & Rowe, 2006; Scheier, 2010; Woolf, 2008).

In this chapter, we describe risk and protective factors related to substance use and abuse. In addition, we review past and current policy and program responses to treating and preventing substance abuse in adolescence. We also discuss disparities and inequities related to race, ethnicity, gender, sexual orientation, socioeconomic status, immigrant/citizenship status, and ability/disability. We emphasize the recommendations for those disproportionately impacted by substance use and the role of culturally relevant protective factors to impact resilience development. The utility of a public health framework that emphasizes risk, protection, and resilience for the development of innovative policy and programs is examined. We begin with a brief discussion of recent trends in adolescent substance use.

## TRENDS IN ADOLESCENT SUBSTANCE USE

Adolescent substance use exists on a continuum that includes no use, non-problematic use, abuse, and dependence. Substance abuse and dependence represent the most serious concerns to practitioners and policymakers. However, even low levels of drug use by children and youth can be problematic, given the many developmental tasks they encounter at school and in the community. Our review of trends in substance use, therefore, includes reports of experimental and regular use.

The nation's most accurate prevalence estimates for adolescent substance use come from the Monitoring the Future (MTF) study (Johnston et al., 2019), co-sponsored by NIDA and the University of Michigan. MTF is an annual assessment of alcohol and drug use in a random sample of about 16,000 public and private high school students. In-school surveys with nationally representative samples of high school seniors have been conducted since 1975. Students in Grades 8 and 10 have been surveyed since 1991.

There have been several notable trends in adolescent substance use since the 1970s. Lifetime illicit drug use—including the use of marijuana, hallucinogens, cocaine, heroin, and other opiates as well as stimulants, barbiturates, or tranquilizers that are not under a doctor's order—peaked among seniors in 1981. About 66% of twelfth graders in 1981 used an illicit drug at least once in their lives; 43% used an illicit drug other than marijuana. Lifetime use of illicit drugs reached its lowest point in 1992: Only 41% of high school seniors used any illicit drug and 25% used an illicit drug other than marijuana. In 1993, seniors reversed a decade-long pattern of declining illicit drug use.

Rates of illicit drug use rose for six consecutive years, and by 1999, 55% of high school seniors reported using illicit drugs. A 10-year trend of declining rates of illicit drug use among seniors began in 2000. By 2009, only 47% of seniors reported illicit drug use in their lifetime. This rate rose slightly to 50% by 2013.

Consistent with prior years, daily marijuana use increased among all adolescents in 2019, particularly among eighth graders. Other drugs demonstrating an increase in 2019 included LSD. The prevalence of other commonly used drugs such as marijuana and illicit drugs (hallucinogens, cocaine, ecstasy [MDMA], and heroin) showed little change in 2019.

On a positive note, several drugs that had increased in the past decade declined in 2019. These decreases included use of prescription drugs and nonmedical use of amphetamines and tobacco use in its many forms (Miech et al., 2019). Alcohol use, which has steadily declined since the 1980s, showed little change from previous years in 2019.

New trends in adolescent substance use have also emerged in the past several years. The most troubling new trend is that marijuana vaping has increased significantly among young people: 21% of twelfth graders, 19% of tenth graders, and 7% of eighth graders reported lifetime vaping use in 2019. Increases in vaping represent the single largest rise in drug use among all substances measured by MTF in the past 45 years (Miech et al., 2019). Similarly, nicotine vaping surged in both 2018 and 2019. Vaping is a relatively recent phenomenon and may require new preventive interventions and policies.

Adolescent males have typically used illicit drugs at higher rates than females; the last few years, however, have revealed fewer differences in rates of substance use between boys and girls (Johnston et al., 2019). In fact, girls in the eighth grade reported slightly higher use of inhalants, amphetamines, methamphetamines, and tranquilizers than boys. The use of tobacco products is consistently higher and almost exclusively used by males. Gender differences in use, with males still using at a higher rate for most substances, tend to stabilize as young people grow older. Historically, MTF results have indicated that alcohol and drug use are more prevalent among White students than among Black or Hispanic students.

Substance use also differentially impacts LGBTQIA+ (lesbian, gay, transgender, queer or questioning, intersex, and asexual or allied) adolescents. Rates of tobacco, alcohol, and cannabis use are generally higher among LGBTQIA+ adolescents than among cisgender/heterosexual adolescents (Watson et al., 2017). LGBTQIA+ youth experience a number of other adverse outcomes, including suicide, and efforts to reduce drug use should be tailored to their specific risk and protective factors (Aranmolate et al., 2017).

MTF results provide a fairly accurate picture of substance use among youth living in the United States. However, it is important to acknowledge that the MTF study may underestimate the magnitude of substance use among youth in the United States because it does not include school dropouts (an estimated 15% to 20% of students in this age group), a group at high risk for alcohol and drug use. Documentation status may also limit an adolescent's willingness to complete a survey about substance use for fear of repercussions.

It is also important to note that rates of adolescent substance use among Black and Brown youth are impacted by issues of equity and practices and policies characterized by structural racism. For example, White youth are more likely to use most illegal or "hard" drugs; however, Black youth are significantly more likely than White youth to go to prison for a drug offense (James & Jordan, 2018; Welty et al., 2016). Black youth and other ethnic minority groups are also more likely than White youth to have difficulty accessing substance abuse treatment (Alegria et al., 2011). More studies are needed to further examine racial and ethnic differences in substance use (Wu et al., 2011).

In sum, trends in adolescent substance use point to the need for a continuum of policy and practice responses. Prevention strategies are needed to delay initiation and to interrupt the progression of substance use that often begins with alcohol or tobacco and culminates with more serious drug use. Conversely, treatment options are necessary for individuals exhibiting symptoms of abuse or dependence. In recent years, policy and program approaches aimed at preventing and treating adolescent substance abuse have been based on etiological models that emphasize principles of risk, protection, and resilience.

# THE ETIOLOGY OF ADOLESCENT SUBSTANCE ABUSE: PRINCIPLES OF RISK, PROTECTION, AND RESILIENCE

Knowledge generated by investigations examining the relationship among risk and protective factors and adolescent substance use has led to significant advancements in the etiology, assessment, and prevention of drug abuse (for a review of such investigations, see Belcher & Shinitzky, 1998; Brook et al., 2006; Hawkins, Catalano, & Miller, 1992; Hawkins et al., 2015; Jenson & Bender, 2014; Kim, 2009; Schinke et al., 2008). Yet, definitions and policy applications underlying concepts of risk and protection are clouded with controversy. Most researchers, practitioners, and public health specialists agree that risk factors for adolescent substance use can be empirically identified. As noted in Chapter 1, there is considerably less agreement about the concept and definition of protection. Some authors (Luthar, 2003) have asserted that risk and protective factors act as polar opposites of one another. Other investigators (Fraser, 2004; Rossa, 2002; Rutter, 2000) have argued that protective factors are characteristics and conditions that moderate or mediate levels of risk for problem behaviors such as substance abuse. Identifying culturally based protective factors is an emerging area of research. The following discussion of protective factors, consistent with the interpretation presented in Chapter 1, is based on the view that protective factors are traits, conditions, and characteristics that influence or modify the risk of substance abuse.

# Risk Factors

Risk factors for adolescent substance abuse occur at environmental, interpersonal, social, and individual levels. These factors are summarized next and in Table 8.1.

## Table 8.1 Risk Factors for Adolescent Substance Abuse

### Environmental Factors

Low taxation and weak regulation of alcohol and drugs

Permissive cultural and social norms about substance use

Availability of alcohol and drugs

Poverty

Limited economic opportunity

Neighborhood disorganization

Low neighborhood attachment

High rates of residential mobility

High rates of adult criminality

High population density

### Interpersonal and Social Factors

Family conflict

Poor family management practices

Dysfunctional family communication patterns

Parent and sibling substance use

Poor parent–child bonding

School failure

Low commitment to school

Rejection by conforming peer groups

Association with drug-using friends

### Individual Factors

Family history of alcoholism

Sensation-seeking orientation

Poor impulse control

Attention deficits

Hyperactivity

*Source:* Table adapted from Jenson (2004) and Jenson & Bender (2014).

## Environmental Risk Factors

Community laws and norms favorable to drug use, such as low legal drinking ages and low taxes on alcoholic beverages, increase the risk of substance use during adolescence (Joksch, 1988). Studies examining the relationship between legal drinking age and adolescent drinking and driving have shown that lowering the drinking age increases underage drinking and teen traffic fatalities (Saffer & Grossman, 1987). Laws and norms that express intolerance for use of alcohol and illicit drugs by adolescents are associated with a lower prevalence of alcohol and drug use (Johnston, 1991).

Child poverty rates have increased in the last few years; 21% of children under the age of 18 lived in conditions of poverty in 2019 (defined as below the federal poverty threshold; National Center for Children and Poverty, 2019). Experts suggest that poverty rates are significantly higher (43%) if you consider basic living expenses for which the federal poverty threshold does not account. Poverty is associated with many adverse adolescent outcomes, including conduct problems, delinquency, and unwanted pregnancy (Cauce et al., 2003; Hannon, 2003; National Academies of Sciences, Engineering, and Medicine, 2019a, 2019b). Poverty may also have an indirect effect on adolescent substance use. Family income is associated with many other risk factors for drug use (e.g., parenting practices and academic difficulties); low family income may affect drug use indirectly through such risk factors.

Low neighborhood attachment, school transitions, and residential mobility are associated with drug and alcohol abuse (Murray, 1983). Neighborhoods with high population density and high rates of adult crime also have high rates of adolescent crime and drug use (Simcha-Fagan & Schwartz, 1986). Neighborhood disorganization may also indirectly affect risk for drug abuse by eroding the ability of parents to supervise and control their children.

## Interpersonal and Social Risk Factors

Interpersonal and social risk factors for adolescent substance abuse occur in family, school, and peer settings. Children whose parents or siblings engage in serious alcohol or illicit drug use are themselves at greater risk for these behaviors (Biederman et al., 2000). Children raised in families with lax supervision, excessively severe or inconsistent disciplinary practices, and little communication and involvement between parents and children are also at high risk for later substance abuse (Hill et al., 2000). Similarly, studies have shown that parental conflict is related to subsequent alcohol or drug use by adolescent family members (Brook et al., 1988).

School failure, low degree of commitment to education, and lack of attachment to school are school-related factors that increase the risk of substance abuse during adolescence (Holmberg, 1985). Adolescent drug users are more likely to skip classes, be absent from school, and perform poorly than those who are not drug users (Gottfredson, 1981).

Association with friends who use drugs is among the strongest predictors of adolescent substance abuse (Fergusson & Horwood, 1999; Reinherz et al., 2000). Peer rejection in elementary grades is associated with school problems and delinquency

(Coie, 1990; Kupersmidt et al., 1990), which are also risk factors for drug abuse. Some investigators have hypothesized that rejected children form friendships with other rejected children and that such groups become delinquent or engage in drug use during adolescence (Patterson, 2002; Patterson et al., 2002).

## Individual Risk Factors

Psychosocial and biological factors are related to drug and alcohol abuse during adolescence. For example, evidence from adoption, twin, and half-sibling studies supports the notion that alcoholism is an inherited disorder (Cadoret et al., 1980). Several studies have found that a sensation-seeking orientation predicts initiation and continued use of alcohol and other drugs (Cicchetti & Rogosch, 1999; Cloninger et al., 1988). Research also indicates that attention deficit disorders, hyperactivity, and poor impulse control before the age of 12 predict the age of onset of drinking and drug use (Shedler & Block, 1990).

Jenson and Potter (2003) found three distinct patterns of co-occurring mental health and substance use in a longitudinal investigation of detained youths. Adolescents who were most likely to abuse alcohol and other drugs also had high levels of self-reported depression, paranoia, hostility, and suicidal ideation. This and other investigations (Loeber et al., 1998; Vaughn, Freedenthal et al., 2007; Vaughn et al., 2008) suggest that mental health problems may play an important role in a youth's decision to experiment with and to persistently use alcohol or other drugs.

# Protective Factors

Many adolescents develop healthy relationships and succeed in school and the community despite being exposed to multiple risk factors. Empirical research devoted to identifying individual and environmental characteristics that protect youth from substance abuse has lagged behind similar efforts aimed at identifying risk factors for drug use. However, an increasing number of investigators have begun to examine the relationship between protective factors and substance use in recent years (Brook et al., 2006; Jenson, 2004). When identified in children and adolescents, protective factors can be established or enhanced to reduce risks for substance abuse. Protective factors for alcohol and other drug use are summarized next and in Table 8.2.

## Environmental, Interpersonal, and Social Protective Factors

Environmental, interpersonal, and social protective factors are attributes that buffer community, neighborhood, family, school, and peer risk factors. The most comprehensive study of protective factors among children was conducted by Werner and colleagues. Werner and Smith (1989) began following a cohort of high-risk children in Kauai, Hawaii, in 1955. Analysis of the children's outcomes as adolescents and adults has contributed to knowledge about factors that prevent youth from abusing alcohol and other drugs.

Werner (1994) found that being raised in a family with four or fewer children, experiencing low parental conflict, and being a firstborn child reduce the effects of

## Table 8.2 Protective Factors Against Adolescent Substance Abuse

### Environmental, Interpersonal, and Social Factors

Being a firstborn child

Being raised in a small family

Low parental conflict

Caring relationships with siblings

Caring relationships with extended family members

Attachment to parents

Social support from nonfamily members

Commitment to school

Involvement in conventional activities

Belief in prosocial norms

### Individual Factors

Social and problem-solving skills

Positive attitude

Positive temperament

High intelligence

Low childhood stress

Racial/ethnic/tribal identity

Sexual identity

Racial socialization

*Source:* Table adapted from Jenson (2004) and Jenson & Bender (2014).

poverty and other risk factors for substance abuse. Children who abstained from drug use during adolescence and early adulthood had positive parent–child relationships in early childhood and caring relationships with siblings and grandparents. Children who abstained from alcohol and other drugs also received social support and frequent counsel from teachers, ministers, and neighbors.

A positive family milieu and community supports are protective factors for drug abuse among children exposed to multiple risk factors. Garmezy (1985) found low childhood stress among high-risk children living in supportive family environments and among adolescents who had strong external support systems. Because stress increases the risk of drug use in later adolescence and early adulthood (Rutter, 2000), such findings have implications for preventing childhood and early adolescent drug abuse.

Strong social bonds to parents, teachers, and prosocial peers are significant factors in children's resistance to drug use (Berrueta-Clement et al., 1984). Four elements of the social bond have been found to be inversely related to adolescent drug abuse: (1) strong attachments to parents (Brook et al., 2006), (2) commitment to school (Friedman, 1983), (3) involvement in prosocial activities such as church or community organizations (Miller et al., 2000), and (4) belief in the generalized norms and values of society (Jenson & Howard, 1999).

Understanding the processes by which strong social bonds develop is necessary to develop strategies that increase healthy bonding in high-risk youth. Social learning (Bandura, 1989) and social development (Catalano & Hawkins, 1996) theorists have suggested that three conditions are critical to the formation of strong social bonds: (1) opportunities for involvement in prosocial activities, (2) possession of the requisite behavioral and cognitive skills necessary to achieve success in such activities, and (3) rewards or recognition for positive behaviors. To promote healthy bonds, policies should support intervention strategies that provide opportunities, enhance skills, and offer rewards to high-risk youth.

## Individual Protective Factors

Individual protective factors are psychosocial and biomedical characteristics that inhibit drug use. Competence in social and problem-solving situations is associated with abstinence and reductions in teenage drug use and delinquency. In a sample of high-risk urban children, Rutter (2000) found that problem-solving skills and strong self-efficacy were associated with successful adolescent outcomes. Youth who possessed adequate problem-solving skills and the ability to use skills were less likely to engage in drug use and delinquency. Jenson, Wells, Plotnick, Hawkins, and Catalano (1993) found that strong self-efficacy decreased the likelihood of drug use six months following drug treatment among adjudicated delinquents. These findings suggest that social and problem-solving skills moderate the effects of multiple risk factors for drug abuse and other adolescent outcomes.

Attitude and temperament are protective factors for substance abuse. Positive social orientation and positive temperament reduce the likelihood of adolescent drug abuse in several studies of high-risk youth (e.g., Jenson & Howard, 1999). Low intelligence (Werner, 1994) is also related to drug use.

Jones and Neblett (2016) identified racial identity, racial socialization, and Afrocentric worldview as racial/ethnic protective factors for substance use among Black children and adolescents. Similarly, Marsiglia, Kulis, Hecht, and Sills (2004) found that ethnicity and ethnic identity, including strong ethnic affiliation, attachment, and pride, were associated with lower substance use and stronger antidrug norms in young people. Goldbach and Steiker (2011) reported on the development of a culturally grounded, evidence-based substance abuse intervention for LGBTQIA-identified youth that utilizes culturally based protective factors. Further research is necessary to address the impact of specific cultural and ethnic protective factors on substance use outcomes for specific populations.

## Resilience

In Chapter 1 of this book, Hall, Lanier, Jenson, and Fraser note the importance of resilience—an individual's ability to succeed in the face of adverse life circumstances—in the prevention of adolescent problem behaviors such as substance abuse. Anecdotal accounts detailing a person's ability to overcome substance abuse and addiction are common in American popular literature (Burroughs, 2003; Hamill, 1994; Knapp, 1996). However, the concept of resilience as an empirical construct in the explanation, prevention, or treatment of adolescent substance use remains a relatively new area of investigation (Luthar, 2003; Meschke & Patterson, 2003).

Studies indicate that some children and adolescents display high levels of functioning despite being surrounded by adverse familial or environmental influences (Fergusson & Horwood, 2003; Zucker et al., 2003). Zucker and colleagues (2003) examined the relationship between levels of resilience and subsequent childhood and adolescent outcomes among sons of alcoholic fathers and found that resilient youth were significantly more likely to resist substance use and other antisocial behaviors than youth who are less resilient. Other studies have focused on the role of resilience in overcoming conditions of poverty (Cauce et al., 2003) and exposure to violence (Gorman-Smith & Tolan, 2003). Additional research is needed to better understand both the direct and indirect effects of resilient adaptation on substance use and, in turn, the effects of substance use on resilience. Investigators have made important progress in identifying cultural and ethnic protective factors for substance abuse. However, additional efforts are needed to apply this knowledge to preventive interventions, treatment strategies, and policies.

## Summary

Risk factors for substance use have been shown to be relatively stable over the past several decades. The factors summarized earlier consistently predict alcohol and drug use even though social norms about the acceptability of substance use have changed several times during this period. This suggests that policies and programs should encourage the development of strategies that target risk factors at multiple levels, including differential vulnerability, child-rearing practices, school achievement, social influences, social learning, and broad social norms.

Protection and resilience hold great promise in understanding, preventing, and treating substance abuse. Knowledge gained from studies examining the complex relationships among risk, protection, and resilience should be considered in policy and program design.

# RISK, PROTECTION, AND RESILIENCE IN SUBSTANCE ABUSE POLICY

## The Evolution of Drug Policy: A Brief Overview

Drug policy in the United States reflects cultural beliefs about the risks associated with substance use and the role of governmental regulation in people's personal and social lives. Cultural beliefs about substance use and opinions about the best way to prevent or treat substance abuse are in turn affected by a host of social, political, and economic conditions (DuPont & Voth, 1995). The evolving nature of these beliefs may best be seen in the underlying tension that is evident between policy approaches favoring control and regulation and those favoring prevention and treatment. The relative emphasis placed on control strategies versus prevention and treatment alternatives has a significant impact on the nature of available policies, programs, and services for children and adolescents at any given point in time (McBride et al., 2001; Musto, 1996). The good news for prevention and treatment advocates may be that increases in federal funding for adolescent health have led to a greater array of substance abuse prevention and treatment alternatives for children and youth (Dougherty, 1993; Irwin et al., 2002). Beginning in 2010, the Obama administration's approach to reducing drug use and the consequences of drug use have shifted the historical enforcement approach ("war on drugs") to the use of science and evidence-based public health and safety, focusing on prevention, treatment, and recovery (Office of National Drug Control Policy [ONDCP], 2014). In the current economic climate, however, there is considerable competition for funds, and efforts to reduce substance abuse among youth must demonstrate evidence of effectiveness. Major American drug policies of the past century are reviewed next and are shown in Table 8.3.

## Early Drug Policy

American drug policy emerged at the turn of the century with the passage of several important acts. The Pure Food and Drug Act of 1906 required the labeling of all drugs sold in the country. The Harrison Narcotics Act of 1914 and the 1919 Volstead Act prohibited the sale of narcotics and alcohol (DuPont & Voth, 1995). Prohibition against illicit drugs was used as a public policy approach well into the 1950s, when the federal government implemented drug trafficking laws and enacted strict penalties for drug violations.

## 1960–1980

The "drug revolution" of the 1960s and 1970s created an increase in demand for illicit drugs that was unparalleled in prior years. Changing social norms reflecting greater tolerance for experimental drug use led to a shift from the predominantly punitive stance that was common before 1960 to an interest in decriminalizing marijuana and other less serious drugs. As recreational and experimental drug use became more common, increased public awareness of the health risks associated with substance use coincided with the development of prevention and treatment strategies for illicit drug abuse (McBride et al., 2001). Passage of the Narcotic Addict Rehabilitation Act of 1966 reflected society's desire to help individuals suffering from addiction. And in 1967, the American Medical Association endorsed the disease theory as the predominant explanation of alcohol addiction, a change that was to have a profound effect on American social policy (Freeman, 2001).

| Table 8.3 | Major Federal Substance Abuse Policies for Children and Families, 1900 to Present |
|---|---|
| **Legislation** | **Purpose** |
| 1906 Pure Food and Drug Act | Required the patent medicine industry to list product ingredients |
| 1914 Harrison Narcotics Act | Prohibited the manufacture, sale, and possession of narcotics |
| 1919 Volstead Act and Eighteenth Amendment to the Constitution | Prohibited the sale of alcohol |
| 1937 Marijuana Tax Act | Prohibited the nonmedical use of marijuana |
| 1966 Narcotic Addict Rehabilitation Act | Established civil commitment system (treatment) for federal offenders rather than prosecution |
| 1970 Comprehensive Drug Abuse Prevention and Control Act | Consolidated previous drug laws and reduced penalties for marijuana possession; included the Controlled Substances Act, which established five schedules for regulating drugs based on medicinal value and potential for addiction or abuse |
| 1986 and 1988 Anti-Drug Abuse Acts | Emphasized law enforcement in general, with the 1988 act also attending to treatment and prevention; created the Office of National Drug Control Policy (ONDCP) and the Substance Abuse and Mental Health Services Administration (SAMHSA) |
| 1997 Title XXI (Social Security Administration), State Children's Health Insurance (SCHIP) established | Expanded health insurance coverage for children and allowed flexibility in resource distribution |
| 2008 Mental Health Parity and Addiction Equity Act (MHPAEA) | Required equity with all medical/surgical benefits for financial requirements and treatment limitations for mental health or substance use disorder benefits |
| Patient Protection and Affordable Care Act (ACA) of 2010 | Among the other major changes to national health care delivery, the 2014 expansion built on the MHPAEA and required coverage of mental health and substance use disorder services at parity with medical and surgical benefits for all new small group and individual market plans. |
| 2017–2018 H.R.6: The Substance Use Disorder Prevention that Promotes Opioid Recovery and Treatment (SUPPORT) for Patients and Communities Act | Afforded practitioners greater flexibility in the provision of medication-assisted treatment |
| Drug Addiction Treatment Act (DATA) of 2000 | DATA 2000, part of the Children's Health Act of 2000, permits physicians who meet certain qualifications to treat opioid dependency with narcotic medications approved by the Food and Drug Administration (FDA), including buprenorphine in treatment settings other than Opioid Treatment Programs (OTPs) |
| HEAL (Healing to End Addiction Long-Term) Initiative, 2018 | Initiative funded by Congress to National Institutes of Health (NIH). Offers scientific solutions to the national opioid overdose crisis, including treatment |

The 1970s witnessed several key pieces of drug-related legislation. Predating President Richard Nixon's declaration calling for a "war on drugs" by only one year, Congress passed the Comprehensive Drug Abuse Prevention and Control Act in 1970. The act consolidated several previous federal laws and categorized addictive drugs for purposes of control and regulation. While reducing the penalties for certain types of possession offenses, the act also strengthened law enforcement efforts. The emphasis on rehabilitation, however, remained an important part of the 1970 legislation.

## 1980–Present

An increase in drug use among the nation's youth at the end of the 1970s marked a reversal in public opinion about the nature of substance use policy. "Get-tough" approaches began to replace policies favoring community-based treatment, and the subsequent passage of the Anti-Drug Abuse Acts of 1986 and 1988 reinforced a return to policies favoring law enforcement and control (McBride et al., 2001). The federal ONDCP was created in 1988 to better coordinate drug policy across states and international borders. By the late 1980s, all states raised the legal drinking age to 21 in response to growing concerns about the dangers and consequences of adolescent alcohol abuse. Arrest, conviction, and incarceration rates for drug-related offenses—particularly among poor youth and Black and Brown youth—increased following tougher policy provisions passed in the 1980s (Snyder, 1990).

Some policy experts noted a return to drug policies favoring prevention and rehabilitation in the next decade (Physician Leadership on National Drug Policy, 2002). As one important example, treatment parity with other health conditions from an insurance perspective has long been sought by mental health and substance-related disorder advocates. When the Mental Health Parity Act was first introduced in 1996, it provided parity for mental health benefits, in terms of aggregate lifetime and annual dollar limits, when compared with medical/surgical benefits. Substance abuse or chemical dependency was excluded, however. When the Mental Health Parity and Addiction Equity Act (MHPAEA) was passed in 2008, it required equity for mental health and substance use disorder benefits when these services are provided. Specifically, the financial requirements such as co-pays or deductibles and limitations set on treatment must be "no more restrictive" than the limitations set for all medical/surgical benefits (U.S. Department of Labor, 2010). Building on the MHPAEA and beginning in 2014, the implementation of the Patient Protection and Affordable Care Act (2010) required coverage of mental health and substance use disorder services and required that these services be provided at parity with medical and surgical benefits by insurers and group health plans (Beronio et al., 2013).

This change coincided with a newfound interest in viewing adolescent substance abuse as a public health problem and applying principles of risk and protection to substance policy and programs. The Obama administration's reform of drug policy that began in 2010 emphasized the prevention of drug abuse as a public health issue in addition to a criminal justice issue. As a consequence, federal drug-control spending decreased funds for supply reduction while increasing funds for demand reduction (ONDCP, 2014).

President Trump and his administration focused their drug control efforts on reducing the number of deaths from opioid drug overdoses and increasing access to opioid treatment (ONDCP, 2020). The Trump administration also supported supply-side efforts to stop the flow of drugs into the country. Some scholars have noted that too strong of a focus on supply-side strategies may undermine or reverse recent progress in viewing substance use as a public health problem as opposed to an individual failing, thereby de-emphasizing the importance of harm reduction policies (Nadelmann & LaSalle, 2017). Also, the national drug control budget under President Trump's term increased funding for treatment and law enforcement while decreasing funding for prevention (ONDCP, 2020). Next, we discuss specific federal policies across the domains of law enforcement, prevention, and treatment. These selected policies highlight major trends in policy approaches aimed at adolescent substance abuse.

## Domestic Law Enforcement

Law enforcement has always been a critical component of American drug policy (Morin & Collins, 2000; Physician Leadership on National Drug Policy, 2002). Funding for law enforcement efforts aimed at combating adolescent substance abuse has increased substantially nearly every year since 1980. Federal spending for the control of illicit drugs alone increased from $1.5 billion in 1981 to $17.9 billion in 1999 (Robert Wood Johnson Foundation, 2001). Historically, more than 75% of federal funds distributed to state and local communities for the control of illicit drug use were devoted to law enforcement activities (Kleiman, 1998).

The 2021 National Drug Control Strategy earmarks approximately 48% of the $35,695 million drug control budget for the supply-reduction strategies of international and domestic law enforcement. The remaining 52% of the overall budget was allocated to prevention and treatment (ONDCP, 2021). Federal spending has shifted over recent years to prevention and treatment; however, the funds allocated to prevention are consistently low compared to treatment.

Domestic and international law enforcement and interdiction policies constitute what is known as a *supply-reduction strategy*. Intended to disrupt the drug trade market and to limit access to drugs, supply reduction relies on practices such as taxation and law enforcement to control alcohol and illicit drug use. Initiatives to dismantle illicit drug trafficking networks are also included in supply-reduction strategies. The federal drug-control budget provides funding through various initiatives to increase the capacity of organizations such as the Drug Enforcement Administration, Federal Bureau of Investigation, U.S. Customs Service, Border Patrol, and Coast Guard to implement these approaches (see Figure 8.1).

The effectiveness of law enforcement and drug interdiction can be evaluated by assessing the cost of illicit drugs and by monitoring rates of adolescent substance use. Based on these outcome measures, the results of law enforcement and drug interdiction efforts have achieved limited success. Although the United States has spent more than $18 billion a year on international law enforcement and interdiction, evidence suggests that the relative price of many "hard drugs" has actually decreased in recent

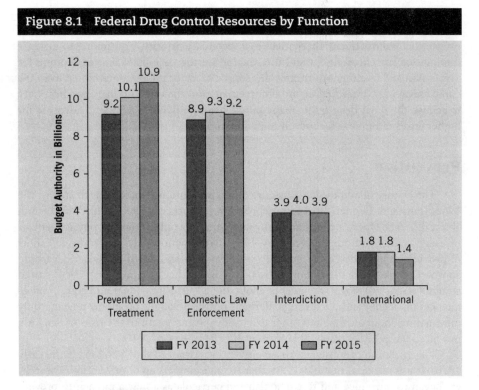

**Figure 8.1   Federal Drug Control Resources by Function**

*Source:* This figure is adapted from the National Drug Control Budget, FY 2015 Funding Highlights, by ONDCP, 2014, Washington, DC: The White House.

years (Bach & Lantos, 1999; Kleiman, 1998) and that access to illicit drugs has not diminished (Robert Wood Johnson Foundation, 2001). In 2013, about 50% of adolescents had tried an illicit substance by the time they graduated from twelfth grade (Johnston et al., 2013), a finding that offers at least cursory evidence to suggest that law enforcement and interdiction efforts alone are not effective in reducing adolescent substance use.

Supply-reduction strategies restricting access and increasing taxes for alcohol and other drugs appear to have produced greater success in reducing substance abuse. For example, an increase in the minimum drinking age is associated with a decline in alcohol consumption and in alcohol-related auto fatalities (Cook & Tauchen, 1984). Furthermore, federal taxes on alcohol and tobacco have generated government revenue that has been used to fund efficacious prevention and treatment services in many states (Robert Wood Johnson Foundation, 2001).

Many experts assert that policy debates about the merits of supply reduction strategies do not lie in the specific findings regarding the effectiveness of law enforcement, interdiction, taxation, and restrictive access strategies (Caulkins et al., 2005; Kleiman,

1998; Morin & Collins, 2000). Rather, the primary concern of many policy officials is the disproportionate allocation of federal funding, which has historically relegated prevention and treatment alternatives to a secondary priority. Continuing to increase funding for law enforcement and interdiction during periods of limited funding for prevention and treatment illustrates this source of major policy contention. Given the enormous cost of interdiction and enforcement and the ongoing increases necessary to reduce the illicit drug trade, many public health officials continue to advocate for higher levels of funding for prevention and treatment.

## Prevention

The history of adolescent substance abuse prevention efforts dates to at least the 1960s (Jenson & Bender, 2014). Early prevention efforts educated children and youth about different types of drugs and informed young people about the physical effects of using alcohol and other substances. These "information only" programs fell short of providing interactive experiences to young people and relied on didactic learning approaches to educate them about substance abuse. Other programs employed "scared straight" tactics to warn adolescents about the adverse individual and social consequences of alcohol and illicit drugs. Perhaps not surprisingly, programs relaying only information about alcohol and other drugs or exposing youth to the risks of drug use produced few positive results (Hawkins et al., 2015; Jenson, 2010).

The evolution of substance abuse prevention advanced slowly following the early 1970s. It was not until the mid-1980s that an emerging group of prevention researchers began to introduce and test school-based curricula as a new approach to prevent substance abuse (Botvin, 2004; Catalano, 2007). These curricula were based on known correlates of substance abuse and relied on interactive and structured activities that involved children in the concept of prevention. Subsequent longitudinal studies of these interventions revealed that well-designed prevention curricula could effectively prevent the initiation of drug use among young people (e.g., Hansen, 1992). The common thread among the programs was the use of a risk and protective factor framework as a guiding source of program design.

Policies and programs supporting substance abuse prevention have increased significantly since the initial program evaluations of the mid-1980s. The fiscal year (FY) 2015 national drug-control budget proposed a 4.5% increase ($58.1 million) over the FY 2014 budget for prevention efforts (ONDCP, 2014). It is widely agreed that the adoption of the risk-based prevention paradigm is largely responsible for the increased attention to prevention policy and prevention research (Robertson et al., 2003). NIDA, SAMHSA, and governmental entities such as the Office of Juvenile Justice and Delinquency Prevention (OJJDP) all recognize the utility of a public health framework for prevention and have taken efforts to implement principles of risk, protection, and resilience in their program and policy initiatives (Howell, 2003; Robertson et al., 2003; Schinke et al., 2002). Programs targeting factors that increase and guard against the risk of substance abuse now undergird the most effective prevention strategies in the United States (CDC, 2008; National Academies of Sciences, Engineering, and

Medicine, 2019b; National Research Council and Institute of Medicine, 2009; Office of the Surgeon General, 2016). The results from a number of longitudinal investigations of risk- and protection-based prevention programs implemented in school, family, and community settings reveal positive outcomes with regard to substance use (Biglan, 2015; Elliott & Fagan, 2017; Hawkins et al., 2015; Jenson & Bender, 2014; Pentz, 2010).

## Federal Policy Initiatives

Several important federal policy directives support the use of a public health framework for substance abuse prevention. The Drug-Free Communities Program, initiated in 1997, supports community and antidrug coalitions that create collaborative efforts among prevention agencies and organizations (ONDCP, 2010). The Department of Education and SAMHSA provide funds for school- and community-based prevention programs under this initiative.

Changing social norms about substance use is a primary objective of several media campaigns and education programs that have received generous federal support. In 1998, the National Youth Anti-Drug Media Campaign received $195 million in federal funding and $2 billion in public and private funds to combat media images promoting substance use (Kelder et al., 2000).

The National Youth Anti-Drug Media Campaign has been one of the most visible and widespread prevention strategies in the country. Partnership for Drug-Free Kids (formerly known as Partnership for a Drug-Free America) was founded in 1987 as a collaboration with the Ad Council. The program's primary objective was to educate children, youth, and parents about drug use and to promote young people's ability to reject illegal drugs through personal and social skill development (ONDCP, 1997). The campaign aimed to change social norms about drug use by communicating messages about youth who do not use substances, discussing the negative effects of drugs, and portraying the positive aspects of a drug-free lifestyle. An evaluation of the campaign revealed that nearly 80% of youth and 70% of parents who were polled about the campaign recalled seeing at least one message delivered through media sources each week (Westat & the Annenberg School for Communication, 2003). However, like the information-only effort before it, the media campaign in this format produced little direct evidence of reducing substance use. Some modifications have been made to the overall strategy since 2005 through the Above the Influence (ATI; http://www.abovetheinfluence.com/) teen-targeted campaign, which is based on commercial advertising and marketing principles (ONDCP, 2012). The ad and campaign messages were developed and tracked through research and testing phases. The 2010 relaunch increased the scope of the ATI brand with national television, print, and internet exposure in addition to local advertising. The results of several evaluations suggested that exposure to ATI predicted a reduction in the initiation of marijuana use (Slater et al., 2011); a reduction in marijuana use among eighth grade girls (Carpenter & Pechmann, 2011; Farrelly et al., 2005); and improvements in antidrug beliefs, drug use intentions, and marijuana use for the target audience of the ATI campaign (Scheier et al., 2011).

Public schools have been a primary location of substance abuse prevention activities. Funding for school-based drug education formally began in the 1980s, when Congress allocated about $500 million a year for prevention activities (Burke, 2002; Wyrick et al., 2001). Federal government involvement in substance abuse prevention, however, has had an uneven history. In the late 1980s and early 1990s, significant government dollars were devoted to a drug abuse resistance education program called Project D.A.R.E. The popular program brought police officers and law enforcement officials to school classrooms. Officers warned children about the dangers of alcohol and other drugs and worked to reduce negative stereotypes of law enforcement. Evaluations of Project D.A.R.E. revealed that the program was no more effective than the routine prevention approaches being used in the nation's schools and classrooms to prevent substance use (Lynam et al., 1999). To their credit, the developers of D.A.R.E. used these findings to retool the program to include more interactive and skills-based teaching strategies in the curriculum. Still, the enormous sum of money allocated to an ineffective program has been a stark lesson to policymakers about the risk of funding untested prevention approaches.

Other school-based prevention programs targeting ethnic and cultural risk and protective factors have reported positive results. Keepin' It REAL is a culturally grounded school-based program that teaches resistance and other social skills to prevent substance use (Hecht et al., 2003; Kulis et al., 2005). The Healing of the Canoe Project is an example of a culturally grounded substance abuse preventive intervention for Native Youth that also seeks to promote tribal identity as a protective factor against drug use and other adverse outcomes (Donovan et al., 2015).

In 1997, the U.S. Department of Education's Safe and Drug-Free School and Communities Program took an important step in prevention policy by requiring all programs that receive federal funds to select and implement interventions that had demonstrated some degree of effectiveness in preventing substance use. Efforts to increase the number of empirically supported interventions in prevention settings have positively affected the quality and outcomes of school-based prevention programs since 1997 (Burke, 2002). NIDA supports considerable substance abuse prevention research and has developed specific action steps for school and community-based programs that are founded on principles of risk and protection (Robertson et al., 2003).

Prevention research continues to advance what is known about effective ways to delay or prevent substance use initiation. Efforts are now underway to implement efficacious programs on a larger scale across school districts and communities (Fagan et al. 2019; Hawkins et al., 2015; Jenson, 2020). No matter how effective such efforts become, the need for treatment services for children and youth experiencing more serious substance use problems must also be an important part of a policy and program continuum.

## Treatment

As the Affordable Care Act is fully implemented, more adolescents should become eligible for substance use disorder services as an identified essential health benefit via expansion of dependent coverage, Medicaid and Children's Health Insurance Program (CHIP), and the health insurance marketplace (Pilkey et al., 2013). Health insurance eligibility is an important part of substance abuse treatment services; however, several other treatment barriers still exist. Several public health organizations, including Physician Leadership on National Drug Policy and the American Academy of Pediatrics (2000), were at the forefront of advocacy efforts aimed at increasing funding for substance abuse treatment. A position paper on adolescent drug policy that was published by Physician Leadership on National Drug Policy (2002) called for the use of evidence-based interventions in drug treatment. The group also suggested that levels of substance abuse funding should be similar to funds provided for diseases such as diabetes and heart disease. Physician Leadership on National Drug Policy continues to argue that the long-standing federal emphasis on law enforcement policy has mitigated the potential of treatment as a means of reducing substance abuse problems. Importantly for prevention and treatment efforts, the Obama administration's approach to drug control acknowledges drug addiction as a preventable and treatable disease rather than a moral failing (ONDCP, 2014).

There is currently no national standard of care for treating adolescent substance abusers in the United States. Substance abuse treatment varies by region, state, and locality and is generally considered to be poorly funded and difficult to access. Recent estimates from SAMHSA's National Survey on Drug Use and Health reveal that about 1.6 million young people require treatment for an illicit drug or alcohol use problem annually but only 157,000 received treatment in a specialty facility (SAMHSA, 2013). Other reports have indicated that as few as one in every 10 adolescents who need substance abuse treatment actually receive it and that only 25% of those participating in treatment receive the appropriate type and level of assistance (Center for Substance Abuse Treatment, 2002; NIDA, 2009). Historically, access to care appears to be strongly related to inadequate health insurance coverage and to complicated managed-care regulations that limit time allotted for treatment (American Academy of Pediatrics, 2001). While the Patient Protection and Affordable Care Act (2010) expands health insurance coverage for uninsured adolescents and school-based health centers under the act show promise for access to treatment, there are many barriers to providing treatment that is tailored to the needs of adolescents.

A major concern affecting access to care for many children and adolescents is the fragmented nature of substance abuse treatment. Policies and programs supporting adolescent substance abuse treatment come from such disparate domains as education, juvenile justice, child welfare, labor, and health. Each system has its own eligibility criteria, and each operates independently from the other. The result is a fragmented system of care in which many youth may be shuffled from program to program with little coordination across service sectors.

Youth with substance abuse problems are also more likely to experience other mental health problems. In many cases, treatment facilities in one system are not equipped to handle multiple problems. For example, estimates indicate that 60% to 80% of youth involved in the juvenile justice system also have a substance use disorder (Washburn et al., 2008). Few resources currently exist to treat youth who have multiple problems.

Public sources provide funding for alcohol and drug treatment through a combination of Medicaid and state and local funds. Funds for public substance abuse treatment are limited, and restrictions placed on the type of eligible service often prevent integration across systems of care (Physician Leadership on National Drug Policy, 2002). The Medicaid program provides health insurance coverage for more than 16.4 million children. However, Medicaid programs display considerable variation in the services they fund, ranging from comprehensive treatment benefits in some states to only inpatient detoxification in other states (Gehshan, 1999). Medicaid reimbursement rates are also typically quite low, which has led to fewer incentives to provide treatment services (American Academy of Pediatrics, 2001).

Expansion of health care coverage for low-income children was included as a provision in a 1997 bill that created the State Children's Health Insurance Program (SCHIP), now simply referred to as CHIP. This program allows states to access federal funds for children who are not eligible for other coverage. Funds are provided via the Medicaid program or through a separate program established specifically for CHIP participants. Although coverage still varies considerably by state, all states using CHIP have generally paid for detoxification and for some type of outpatient substance abuse treatment (Gehshan, 1999).

Medicaid and CHIP are required to implement the Early and Periodic Screening, Diagnostic, and Treatment (EPSDT) program. Many experts believe that EPSDT could be an effective way to increase substance abuse treatment services for troubled youth (Rosenbaum et al., 1998). However, a general lack of awareness about EPSDT in the professional community has led to underutilization. Weak coordination between Medicaid and CHIP has also limited use of EPSDT as a referral source for substance abuse treatment.

Federal block grants provide resources that seek to improve access to substance abuse treatment services. These grants typically provide funds that are channeled through federal and state agencies. For example, prevention services funded by the Substance Abuse Prevention and Treatment Block Grant are administered by the Center for Substance Abuse Prevention. Corresponding treatment services are funded and administered by the Center for Substance Abuse Treatment, SAMHSA, and the U.S. Department of Health and Human Services. With many states rolling block-grant money into specialty "carve-out" arrangements, one policy concern is that substance abuse services may be inappropriately offered by mental health providers rather than by trained substance abuse treatment specialists.

The most recent federal funding efforts for substance abuse treatment focus primarily on the well-documented opioid crisis of the past decade. These efforts include passage of the Substance Use Disorder Prevention that Promotes Opioid Recovery and Treatment (SUPPORT) for Patients and Communities Act of 2018, the Drug Addiction Treatment Act (DATA) of 2000, and the Healing to End Addiction Long Term (HEAL) Initiative of 2018. All of these acts generally seek to provide additional treatment services for opioid use. SUPPORT is a bipartisan bill focused on addressing the opioid overdose epidemic through teaching the workforce, standardizing delivery of care, and ensuring comprehensive treatment (SAMHSA, 2020b). DATA is part of the overall Children's Health Act and expands treatment options by allowing qualified physicians to treat opioid addiction with certain narcotic medications approved by the Food and Drug Administration (FDA) in general practice settings (SAMHSA, 2020b). Lastly, the National Institutes of Health's HEAL is a long-term initiative to engage most National Institutes of Health (NIH) centers in scientific efforts to understand and manage pain and improve opioid misuse and addition (NIH, 2020).

Finally, financial barriers to substance abuse treatment exist. The Affordable Care Act of 2010 required parity for mental health and substance use disorder services; however, access to services and availability of developmentally appropriate services is still a concern. It remains unclear how funding for general treatment of substance abuse will look in the coming years with changes proposed under the Trump administration's efforts to overturn the Affordable Care Act and the Biden administration's efforts to restore the protections provided under President Obama. Opioid use is a major concern, there are many other forms of substance use that are problematic and require access to treatment. Several public health organizations have recently made policy recommendations calling for a more thoughtful and integrated continuum of care in adolescent substance abuse prevention and treatment (American Academy of Pediatrics, 2010; Robert Wood Johnson Foundation, 2010). We explore these and other ideas more fully in the next section.

# USING KNOWLEDGE OF RISK, PROTECTION, AND RESILIENCE TO ACHIEVE SERVICE INTEGRATION

Principles of risk, protection, and resilience are key components of effective substance abuse intervention. The potential of these principles for public policy has yet to be fully realized. To be effective, knowledge of risk, protection, and resilience should undergird policy and programs in all systems of care for children and youth.

## A Continuum of Substance Abuse Policy

Substance use disorders are prevalent among children and youth in nearly all public sectors of care in the United States. Aarons, Brown, Hough, Garland, and Wood (2001) examined prevalence rates for substance use disorders among adolescents who were receiving care in five service systems in San Diego County. Prevalence estimates ranged from 19% for youth in the child welfare system to 41% and 62% for adolescents in the mental health and juvenile justice systems, respectively. More recent estimates reveal that as many as 49% of children in foster care (Vaughn, Ollie et al., 2007), 80% of youth in the juvenile justice system (Washburn et al., 2008), and 50% of youth with serious mental health problems use alcohol and illicit drugs (James, 2007). The high prevalence of substance abuse across systems of care points to the need for better integration and coordination of prevention and treatment policy and programs.

Policies aimed at adolescent substance abuse, similar to policies targeting other childhood and adolescent problems, have largely been incremental and fragmented. That is, programs and interventions tend to develop as a result of localized conditions that fail to consider national trends vis-à-vis substance abuse or empirical evidence regarding the relative effectiveness of prevention and treatment approaches. To confound matters, service sectors for high-risk youth develop responses to problems that tend to be very similar to one another. Creating an integrated continuum of care must begin with assessment and screening policies and practices.

## Assessment and Screening Policies

An integrated system of care for children and youth must first acknowledge the need to assess and screen youth for a variety of problem behaviors, including substance abuse. Once appropriate assessment data are collected, appropriate placements and sanctions can be more easily determined. Policies are needed to create centralized assessment centers that serve diagnostic and referral needs across major service systems for children and adolescents. Provisions of these policies should include standardized diagnostic tools that offer interpretative guidelines for juvenile justice, mental health, child welfare, and substance abuse practitioners. Standardized assessment procedures might also lead to more systematic placement criteria and decision making and would allow cross-system comparisons of risk and protective factors found to be prevalent among youth and their family members. Knowledge of these factors, in turn, could be used to inform the direction of prevention and treatment programs.

## Prevention Policies

Perhaps the single greatest policy gap in combatting substance abuse lies in the need to increase prevention funding. Prevention has historically been underfunded when compared with competing demands made by treatment providers and law enforcement personnel (Catalano, 2007; Hawkins et al., 2015; Jenson & Bender, 2014). Evidence indicates there are currently more than 60 tested and effective prevention programs ready for implementation in school, family, and community settings (Hawkins et al., 2015; Jenson, 2018). In addition to being effective, these programs are also more cost-effective than the vast majority of treatment and law enforcement approaches used to combat substance use (Aos et al., 2004; Jenson, 2018). The availability of tested and effective programs through the dissemination efforts of entities such as the Blueprints for Healthy Youth Development initiative at the University of Colorado-Boulder (Blueprints for Healthy Youth Development, 2020) and by interdisciplinary groups dedicated to advancing evidence-based practice such as the Cochrane Collaboration and the Campbell Collaboration is further argument for the adoption of prevention practice and policy as a national priority for children and families.

Recent efforts by the Coalition for the Promotion of Behavioral Health (CPBH) to increase the implementation of effective prevention programs exemplify the need to increase infrastructure for delivering preventive interventions at the community, state, and federal levels (CPBH, 2020; Hawkins et al., 2015; Jenson & Hawkins, 2018). Members of the CPBH have used seven action steps to work with states and communities to build infrastructure and increase the use of tested and effective prevention programs. These seven steps are described in the CPBH's guiding framework, *Unleashing the Power of Prevention* (see Box 8.1).

---

### Unleashing the Power of Prevention!

The Coalition for the Promotion of Behavioral Health (CPBH) is working to increase awareness and use of tested and effective preventive interventions in communities, settings, and states. Its work is guided by seven action steps described in CPBH's framework, called *Unleashing the Power of Prevention*:

1. Develop and increase public awareness of the advances and cost savings of effective preventive interventions that promote healthy behaviors for all.

2. Ensure that 10% of all public funds spent on young people support effective prevention programs.

3. Implement community-assessment and capacity-building tools that guide communities to systematically assess and prioritize risk and protective factors, and select and implement evidence-based prevention programs that target prioritized factors.

4. Establish and implement criteria for preventive interventions that are effective, sustainable, equity enhancing, and cost beneficial.

5. Increase infrastructure to support the high-quality implementation of preventive interventions.

6. Monitor and increase access of children, youth, and young adults to effective preventive interventions.

7. Create workforce development strategies to prepare social work graduates and allied practitioners for new roles in promotion and preventive interventions.

See the CPBH's website (https://www.coalitionforbehavioralhealth.org/) for more information about promoting prevention programs and policies.

---

To reach more children and families, prevention policy must bring effective programs to scale at the school, neighborhood, and community levels. One method of increasing the use of effective programs in community settings is found in the Communities That Care (CTC) intervention (Fagan et al., 2019; Hawkins, Catalano, & Associates, 1992). In the CTC model, coalitions are formed to engage in systematic prevention planning that requires communities to identify prevalent risk and protective factors for adolescent problems in their localities. Following the assessment of such factors, communities are encouraged to select, implement, and evaluate prevention strategies on the basis of available empirical evidence. Findings from a longitudinal study called the Community Youth Development Study, a randomized trial that uses principles of CTC, have revealed significantly lower rates of delinquency and drug use among students in experimental communities compared with control communities (Fagan et al., 2019). These promising results have led the Center for Substance Abuse Prevention (2010) to recommend CTC as a key component in its overall prevention strategy. See Box 8.2 for an example of a prevention case that uses the CTC model.

## A Prevention Case Example

Bishopville, a (fictitious) suburban community on the East Coast, has recently become alarmed about increases in adolescent substance abuse. Anecdotal reports about all-night drug parties (i.e., raves) involving alcohol, marijuana, and hallucinogens have surfaced in local schools and neighborhoods. A recent party led to the arrest of six teenagers and alerted officials that action steps were necessary.

Officials chose the Communities That Care (CTC) model (Hawkins, Catalano, & Miller, 1992) as a means of better understanding and addressing the problem of adolescent substance abuse in Bishopville. Using the model, Bishopville employed the following action steps that led to the creation of a citywide prevention policy:

Step 1: *Organizing and mobilizing.* Leaders of Bishopville selected key individuals to guide the prevention planning process. These included the mayor, educators, business representatives, and other elected officials. The group subsequently formed a community prevention board that was charged with organizing and mobilizing other community advocates and constituency groups.

Step 2: *Developing a community profile of strengths, resources, and challenges.* Risk and protective factors for adolescent substance use were assessed using a CTC survey with a random sample of children and adolescents in Grades 6 to 12. Survey results were used to rank the most common risk and protective factors found among children and youth in Bishopville. A community-needs assessment aimed at identifying existing and needed services for children and youth was also conducted in this phase.

Step 3: *Creating a strategic prevention plan.* In this phase, the Bishopville Community Prevention Board reviewed and selected several efficacious prevention strategies that will be implemented in their local schools and neighborhoods. A school-based curriculum that targets the early onset of substance use and a community-level media campaign were among the strategies selected for implementation.

Step 4: *Evaluating and monitoring the plan.* Steps were identified to monitor and evaluate the prevention strategies selected by the board. Outcome measures and other methodological decisions were made in consultation with local and national experts to ensure a rigorous evaluation process.

Please see Hawkins, Catalano, and Associates (1992) for a more detailed description of using the CTC model in a community setting.

## Treatment Policies

Historically, treatment for young people has mirrored that for adults; 12-step and self-help interventions based on a disease model of addiction have dominated the field (Liddle & Rowe, 2006). Reviews of adolescent substance abuse treatment have identified relatively few controlled trials in the past two decades (Deas & Thomas, 2001; Jenson et al., 2004; Vaughn & Howard, 2004). Meta-analytic studies assessing treatment outcomes for young drug abusers have suggested that cognitive-behavioral interventions promoting skill development and family-based therapeutic approaches are among the most effective treatment strategies for adolescents (Vaughn & Howard, 2004). Additional controlled studies of adolescent substance use treatment are needed to create the knowledge base necessary to recommend and disseminate efficacious programs to the practice community. Only limited empirical evidence is available to form the basis of a policy continuum reflecting different levels of treatment for adolescent substance abuse. Standards of care for treatment connected to evidence-based interventions also need to be made available to professionals in the treatment community.

Years of anecdotal evidence suggest that a lack of communication between drug treatment agencies and poor coordination across service systems have interacted to create a mix of programs that have not adequately met the needs of adolescent substance abusers, like the case shown here (Box 8.3). Several treatment initiatives have shown promise with regard to improving the disjointed treatment system. Drug courts, an initiative funded by the federal government under the National Drug Control Strategy (ONDCP, 2009) are one alternative for juvenile offenders with substance abuse problems. As part of the program, youth may be referred to treatment and receive mandatory drug sanctions in lieu of traditional case-processing. The Tribal Youth program administered by OJJDP (2000) emerged in response to the problem of violent crime and co-occurring substance use disorders among American Indian youth. The departments of Health and Human Services, Education, Interior, and Justice collaborated to design the program. Program objectives include providing a range of assessment and treatment strategies aimed at addressing the unique needs of substance-abusing American Indian youth. The Tribal Youth initiative represents the type of cross-system coordination needed to implement integrated policies and services for troubled youth.

These initiatives represent only the surface of adolescent substance abuse treatment needs in the United States. Efficacy trials of treatment approaches, community advocacy efforts, and standards of care are needed to inform the direction of substance abuse treatment. Coordination across agencies and the development of systems of care should be a top priority in treatment policy discussions.

## SUMMARY

Principles of risk, protection, and resilience hold great promise for substance abuse programs and policies. A prevention and treatment continuum based on risk and protective factors offers a cogent solution to legislators and policy officials charged with developing effective ways to prevent and reduce adolescent substance abuse. A public health model that incorporates risk and protection as guiding principles is also consistent with the current evidence-based practice movement. Protective factors in particular can be used to address the racial disparities in prevention and treatment. Uncovering cultural and ethnic protective factors against substance use holds great promise for fighting the systematic racism that has disproportionately impacted Black and Brown youth.

Efforts toward integrating substance abuse policy might benefit by examining overlapping initiatives in juvenile justice and mental health (see Box 8.3).

Co-occurring drug use and mental health problems are well documented among young people. Many young people with concomitant problems are subsequently placed in the nation's juvenile justice and mental health systems. Efforts to improve coordination must also include the array of treatment providers who contract for services with public agencies. Community-based programs that offer outpatient care, day treatment, and residential care must be added to policy discussions across the multiple service systems for children, youth, and families. A public health approach emphasizing risk, protection, and resilience may provide a common language and effective organizing framework for adolescent substance programs and policies.

## BOX 8.3

### A Treatment Case Example

*A case history.* Johnny is a 16-year-old boy who is currently under the jurisdiction and supervision of the juvenile justice system. He has a history of property offending dating back some six years to when he was arrested for stealing. In recent years, Johnny's behavior escalated to more serious offenses, including assault. He first experimented with alcohol and marijuana at age 12 and now admits to using marijuana, cocaine, and hallucinogens "whenever and wherever" they are available. Johnny was placed in the juvenile justice system for assaulting a boy in his neighborhood. He reports that he had been drinking and was high on cocaine at the time of the incident.

Johnny's family life had been unstable. His father left home when Johnny was 5 years old; the family has had relatively little contact with him since that time. Johnny has heard from other relatives that his father frequently uses alcohol and that he has been incarcerated on several occasions. Johnny's mother has worked a series of low-paying jobs but has no history of substance abuse. Two years ago, his mother invited her boyfriend into the family home. Johnny was initially resentful of this decision and has adapted to the situation by largely ignoring the boyfriend. Johnny has two sisters, both of whom are younger. Johnny's mother reports that Johnny tends to be withdrawn and sad much of the time. He spends long periods of time alone in his room and has recently stopped seeing many of his friends.

*System response.* Johnny's case represents a profile that is common among youth in the juvenile justice system. Perhaps what is most typical is the presence of multiple and overlapping behavior problems. Johnny's problems include antisocial conduct, substance abuse, and undiagnosed symptoms of depression.

Theoretically, the presence of these problems could logically lead to placement in the juvenile justice system for antisocial conduct, the substance abuse treatment network for drug-using behaviors, or the mental health system for symptoms of depression. The challenge for treating Johnny—and the thousands of young people like him—lies in integrating system responses and treatments in a manner that addresses Johnny's multiple problems. In Johnny's case, policies that create and support a centralized assessment process might best lead to a coordinated response across multiple service systems.

## QUESTIONS FOR DISCUSSION

1. What have been the dominant public policy approaches to adolescent substance abuse in the past four decades? Which strategy has received the greatest percentage of funding?

2. What are the financial and organizational implications of a shift to a public health approach to substance abuse prevention and treatment?

3. What are the challenges in integrating service systems for the delivery of adolescent substance abuse treatment and prevention?

4. What are the distinct challenges faced by prevention approaches in an anti-scientific governmental climate? How do we combat misinformation in the media that undermines experts' messages to parents, educators, and policymakers?

5. What policy recommendations would you make to address the racial disparities in adolescent substance use treatment and prevention?

6. What policy recommendations would you make to address the disjointed delivery system?

## REFERENCES

Aarons, G. A., Brown, S. A., Hough, R. L., Garland, A. F., & Wood, P. A. (2001). Prevalence of adolescent substance use across five sectors of care. *Journal of the American Academy of Child & Adolescent Psychiatry, 40*, 419–426.

Alegria, M., Carson, N. J., Goncalves, M., & Keefe, K. (2011). Disparities in treatment for substance use disorders and co-occurring disorders for ethnic/racial minority youth. *Journal of the American Academy of Child & Adolescent Psychiatry, 50*(1), 22–31.

American Academy of Pediatrics. (2000). Insurance coverage of mental health and substance abuse services for children and adolescents: A consensus statement. *Pediatrics, 106*, 860–862.

American Academy of Pediatrics. (2001). Improving substance abuse prevention, assessment, and treatment financing for children and adolescents. *Pediatrics, 108*, 1025–1029.

American Academy of Pediatrics. (2010). *About us.* http://www.aap.org/visit/cmte35.htm

Aos, S., Lieb, R., Mayfield, J., Miller, M., & Pennucci, A. (2004). *Benefits and costs of prevention and early intervention programs for youth.* Washington State Institute for Public Policy.

Aranmolate, R., Bogan, D. R., Hoard, T., & Mawson, A. R. (2017). Suicide risk factors among LGBTQ youth: Review. *JSM Schizophrenia*, *2*(2), 1011.

Bach, P. B., & Lantos, J. (1999). Methadone dosing, heroin affordability and the severity of addiction. *American Journal of Public Health*, *89*, 662–665.

Bandura, A. (1989). Human agency in social cognitive theory. *American Psychologist*, *14*, 1175–1184.

Becker, W. C., & Fiellin, D. A. (2020). When epidemics collide: Coronavirus disease and the opioid crisis. *Annals of Internal Medicine*, *173*(1), 59–60. https://doi.org/10.7326/M20-1210

Belcher, H. M., & Shinitzky, H. E. (1998). Substance abuse in children: Prediction, protection, and prevention. *Archives of Pediatrics and Adolescent Medicine*, *152*, 952–960.

Beronio, K., Po, R., Skopec, L., & Glied, S. (2013). *Affordable Care Act will expand mental health and substance use disorder benefits and parity protections for 62 million Americans* [ASPE Research Brief]. Department of Health and Human Services, Office of the Assistant Secretary for Planning and Evaluation.

Berrueta-Clement, J. R., Schweinhart, L. J., Barnett, W. S., Epstein, A. S., & Weikhard, D. P. (1984). *Changed lives: The effects of the Perry Preschool program on youths through age 19.* High/Scope Press.

Biederman, J., Faraone, S. V., Monuteaux, M. C., & Feighner, J. A. (2000). Patterns of alcohol and drug use in adolescents can be predicted by parental substance use disorders. *Pediatrics*, *106*, 792–797.

Biglan, T. (2015). *The nurture effect: How the science of human behavior can improve our lives and our world.* New Harbinger Publications.

Blueprints for Healthy Youth Development. (2020). [Website]. https://www.blueprintsprograms.org

Botvin, G. J. (2004). Advancing prevention science and practice: Challenges, critical issues, and future directions. *Prevention Science*, *5*, 69–72.

Brook, J. S., Brook, D. W., & Pahl, K. (2006). The developmental context for adolescent substance abuse intervention. In H. A. Liddle & C. L. Rowe (Eds.), *Adolescent substance abuse: Research and clinical advances* (pp. 25–51). Cambridge University Press.

Brook, J. S., Whiteman, M., Gordon, A. S., & Brook, D. W. (1988). The role of older brothers in younger brothers' drug use viewed in the context of parent and peer influences. *Journal of Genetic Psychology*, *151*, 59–75.

Burke, M. R. (2002). School-based substance abuse prevention: Political finger-pointing does not work. *Federal Probation*, *66*, 66–71.

Burroughs, A. (2003). *Dry: A memoir.* St. Martin's Press.

Coalition for the Promotion of Behavioral Health (CPBH). (2020). [Website]. https://www.coalitionforbehavioralhealth.org/

Cadoret, R. J., Cain, C. A., & Grove, W. M. (1980). Development of alcoholism in adoptees raised apart from alcoholic biologic relatives. *Archives of General Psychiatry*, *37*, 561–563.

Carpenter, C. S., & Pechmann, C. (2011). Exposure to the "Above the Influence" antidrug advertisements and adolescent marijuana use in the United States, 2006–2008. *American Journal of Public Health*, *101*(5), 948–54.

Case, A., & Deaton, A. (2015). Rising morbidity and mortality in midlife among White non-Hispanic Americans in the 21st century. *Proceedings of the National Academy of Sciences*, *112*(49), 15078–15083.

Catalano, R. F. (2007). Prevention is a sound public and private investment. *Criminology and Public Policy*, *6*, 377–398. 10.1111/j.1745-9133.2007.00443.x

Catalano, R. F., & Hawkins, J. D. (1996). The social development model: A theory of antisocial behavior. In J. D. Hawkins (Ed.), *Delinquency and crime: Current theories* (pp. 149–197). Cambridge University Press.

Catalano, R. F., & Kellogg, E. (2020). Fostering healthy mental, emotional, and behavioral development in children and youth: A national agenda. *Journal of Adolescent Health*, *66*, 265–267.

Cauce, A. M., Stewart, A., Rodriguez, M. D., Cochran, B., & Ginzler, J. (2003). Overcoming the odds? Adolescent development in the context of urban poverty. In S. S. Luthar (Ed.), *Resilience and vulnerability: Adaptation in the context of childhood adversities* (pp. 343–363). Cambridge University Press.

Caulkins, J. P., Reuter, P., Iguchi, M. Y., & Chiesa, J. (2005). *How goes the "war on drugs"? An assessment of U.S. drug problems and policy.* RAND Corporation.

Center for Substance Abuse Prevention. (2010). *Communities That Care® community planning system*. Author.

Center for Substance Abuse Treatment. (2002). *Treatment episode data set, 2002*. http://www.icpsr.umich.edu/SAMHDA/das.html

Centers for Disease Control and Prevention (CDC). (2008). *Understanding youth violence: Fact sheet*. Author.

Centers for Disease Control and Prevention (CDC). (2020). *Opioid overdose*. https://www.cdc.gov/drugoverdose/index.html

Cicchetti, D., & Rogosch, F. A. (1999). Psychopathology as risk for adolescent substance use disorders: A developmental psychopathology perspective. *Journal of Clinical Child Psychology, 28*, 355–365.

Cloninger, C. R., Sigvardsson, S., & Bohman, M. (1988). Childhood personality predicts alcohol abuse in young adults. *Alcoholism: Clinical and Experimental Research, 12*, 494–503.

Coie, J. D. (1990). Towards a theory of peer rejection. In S. R. Asher & J. D. Coie (Eds.), *Peer rejection in childhood* (pp. 365–398). Cambridge University Press.

Cook, P. J., & Tauchen, G. (1984). The effect of minimum drinking age legislation on youthful auto fatalities, 1970–1977. *Journal of Legal Studies, 13*, 169–190.

Deas, D., & Thomas, S. E. (2001). An overview of controlled studies of adolescent substance abuse treatment. *The American Journal on Addictions, 10*, 178–189.

Donovan, D. M., Rey Thomas, L., Sigo, R. L. W., Price, L., Lonczak, H., Lawrence, N., Ahvakana, K., Austin, L., Lawrence, A., Price, J., Purser, A., & Bagley, L. (2015). Healing of the canoe: Preliminary results of a culturally grounded intervention to prevent substance abuse and promote tribal identity for native youth in two Pacific Northwest tribes. *American Indian Alaska Native Mental Health Research, 22*(1), 42–76.

Dougherty, D. M. (1993). Adolescent health: Reflections on a report to the U.S. Congress. *American Psychologist, 48*, 193–201.

DuPont, R. L., & Voth, E. A. (1995). Drug legalization, harm reduction, and drug policy. *Annals of Internal Medicine, 123*, 461–465.

Egede, L. E., & Walker, R. J. (2020). Structural racism, social risk factors, and Covid-19—A dangerous convergence for Black Americans. *The New England Journal of Medicine.* 10.1056/NEJMp2023616

Elliott, D., & Fagan, A. (2017). *The prevention of crime*. John Wiley & Sons.

Fagan, A. A., Hawkins, J. D., Catalano, R. F., & Farrington, D. P. (2019). *Communities that care: Building community engagement and capacity to prevent youth behavior problems*. Oxford University Press.

Farrelly, M. C., Davis, K. C., Haviland, M. L., Messeri, P., & Healton, C. G. (2005). Evidence of a dose-response relationship between "truth" antismoking ads and youth smoking prevalence. *American Journal of Public Health, 95*(3), 425–431.

Fergusson, D. M., & Horwood, L. J. (1999). Prospective childhood predictors of deviant peer affiliations in adolescence. *Journal of Child Psychology and Psychiatry and Allied Disciplines, 40*, 581–592.

Fergusson, D. M., & Horwood, L. J. (2003). Resilience in childhood adversity: Results of a 21-year study. In S. S. Luthar (Ed.), *Resilience and vulnerability: Adaptation in the context of childhood adversities* (pp. 130–155). Cambridge University Press.

Fraser, M. W. (Ed.). (2004). *Risk and resilience in childhood: An ecological perspective* (2nd ed.). NASW.

Freeman, E. M. (2001). *Substance abuse intervention, prevention, rehabilitation, and systems change strategies: Helping individuals, families, and groups to empower themselves*. Columbia University Press.

Friedman, A. S. (1983). *Clinical research notes*. National Institute on Drug Abuse.

Garmezy, N. (1985). Stress-resistant children: The search for protective factors. In J. E. Stevenson (Ed.), *Recent research in developmental psychology* (pp. 213–233). Pergamon Press.

Gehshan, S. (1999). *Substance abuse treatment in state children's health insurance programs*. National Conference of State Legislatures.

Goldbach, J. T., & Steiker, L. K. (2011). An examination of cultural adaptations performed by LGBT-identified youths to a culturally grounded, evidence-based substance abuse intervention. *Journal of Gay & Lesbian Social Services, 23* (2), 188–203.

Gorman-Smith, D., & Tolan, P. H. (2003). Positive adaptation among youth exposed to community violence. In S. S. Luthar (Ed.), *Resilience and vulnerability: Adaptation in the context of childhood adversities* (pp. 392–413). Cambridge University Press.

Gottfredson, G. D. (1981). Schooling and delinquency. In S. E. Martin, L. B. Sechrest, & R. Redner (Eds.), *New directions in the rehabilitation of criminal offenders* (pp. 424–469). National Academy Press.

Hamill, P. (1994). *A drinking life: A memoir*. Little, Brown.

Hannon, L. (2003). Poverty, delinquency, and educational attainment: Cumulative disadvantage or disadvantage saturation? *Sociological Inquiry, 73*, 576–594.

Hansen, W. B. (1992). School-based substance abuse prevention: A review of the state of the art in curriculum: 1980–1990. *Health Education Research, 7*, 403–430.

Hawkins, J. D., Catalano, R. F., & Associates. (1992). *Communities That Care: Action for drug abuse prevention*. Jossey-Bass.

Hawkins, J. D., Catalano, R. F., & Miller, J. Y. (1992). Risk and protective factors for alcohol and other drug problems in adolescence and early adulthood: Implications for substance abuse prevention. *Psychological Bulletin, 112*, 64–105.

Hawkins, J. D., Jenson, J. M., Catalano, R., Fraser, M. W., Botvin, G. J., Shapiro, V., Brown, C. H., Beardslee, D., Brent, D., Leslie, L. K., Rotheram-Borus, M. J., Shea, P., Shih, A., Anthony, E. K., Haggerty, K., Bender, K. Gorman-Smith, D., Casey, E., & Stone, S. (2015). *Unleashing the power of prevention* [Discussion paper]. Institute of Medicine and National Research Council. http://nam.edu/perspectives-2015-unleashing-the-power-of-prevention/

Hecht, M. L., Marsiglia, F., Elek, E., Wagstaff, D. A., Kulis, S., Dustman, P., & Miller-Day, M. (2003). Culturally grounded substance use prevention: An evaluation of the Keepin' It R.E.A.L. curriculum. *Prevention Science, 4*, 233–248.

Hill, S. Y., Shen, S., Lowers, L., & Locke, J. (2000). Factors predicting the onset of adolescent drinking in families at high risk for developing alcoholism. *Biological Psychiatry, 48*, 265–275.

Holmberg, M. B. (1985). Longitudinal studies of drug abuse in a fifteen-year-old population. I. Drug career. *Acta Psychiatrica Scandinavia, 71*, 67–79.

Howell, J. C. (2003). *Preventing and reducing juvenile delinquency: A comprehensive framework*. SAGE.

Irwin, C. E., Burg, S. J., & Cart, C. U. (2002). America's adolescents: Where have we been, where are we going? *Journal of Adolescent Health, 31*, 91–121.

James, A. (2007). Mental health in childhood and adolescence. *The Lancet, 369*, 1251–1252.

James, K., & Jordan, A. (2018). The opioid crisis in black communities. *The Journal of Law, Medicine & Ethics, 46*(2), 404–421.

Jenson, J. M. (2004). Risk and protective factors for alcohol and other drug use in childhood and adolescence. In M. W. Fraser (Ed.), *Risk and resilience in childhood: An ecological perspective* (2nd ed., pp. 183–208). NASW.

Jenson J. M. (2010). Advances in preventing childhood and adolescent problem behavior. *Research on Social Work Practice, 20*(6), 701–713. 10.1177/1049731509349105

Jenson, J. M. (2018, May 1). *Seven ways to unleash the power of prevention* [Keynote presentation]. The Blueprints for Healthy Youth Development Conference, Denver, CO, United States.

Jenson, J. M. (2020). Improving behavioral health in young people: It is time for social work to adopt prevention. *Research on Social Work Practice, 30*, 707–711.

Jenson, J. M., & Bender, K. A. (2014). *Preventing child and adolescent problem behavior: Evidence-based strategies in schools, families, and communities*. Oxford University Press.

Jenson, J. M., & Hawkins, J. D. (2018). Ensuring healthy development for all youth: Unleashing the power of prevention. In R. Fong, J. Lubben, & R. P. Barth (Eds.), *Grand challenges for social work and society: Social progress engineered by science* (pp. 18–35). Oxford University Press.

Jenson, J. M., & Howard, M. O. (1999). Hallucinogen use among juvenile probationers: Prevalence and characteristics. *Criminal Justice and Behavior, 26*, 357–372.

Jenson, J. M., Howard, M. O., & Vaughn, M. G. (2004). Assessing social work's contribution to controlled studies of adolescent substance abuse treatment. *Journal of Social Work in the Addictions, 4*, 54–66.

Jenson, J. M., & Potter, C. C. (2003). The effects of cross-system collaboration on mental health and substance abuse problems of detained youth. *Research on Social Work Practice, 13*, 588–607.

Jenson, J. M., Wells, E. A., Plotnick, R. D., Hawkins, J. D., & Catalano, R. F. (1993). The effects of skills and intentions to use drugs on posttreatment drug use of adolescents. *American Journal of Drug and Alcohol Abuse*, *19*, 1–17.

Johnston, L. D. (1991). Toward a theory of drug epidemics. In L. Donohew, H. E. Sypher, & W. J. Bukoski (Eds.), *Pervasive communication and drug abuse prevention* (pp. 93–131). Lawrence Erlbaum.

Johnston, L. D., Miech, R. A., O'Malley, P. M., Bachman, J. G., Schulenberg, J. E., & Patrick, M. E. (2019). *Monitoring the future. 2019 overview: Key findings on adolescent drug abuse*. National Institute of Drug Abuse.

Johnston, L. D., O'Malley, P. M., Bachman, J. G., & Schulenberg, J. E. (2013). *Demographic subgroup trends among adolescents for fifty-one classes of licit and illicit drugs, 1975–2012*. Institute for Social Research, The University of Michigan.

Joksch, H. C. (1988). *The impact of severe penalties on drinking and driving*. AAA Foundation for Traffic Safety.

Jones, S., & Neblett, E. W. (2016). Racial-ethnic protective factors and mechanisms in psychosocial prevention and intervention programs for Black youth. *Clinical Child and Family Psychology Review*, *19*, 134–161.

Kelder, S. H., Maibach, E., Worden, J. K., Biglan, A., & Levitt, A. (2000). Planning and initiation of the ONDCP National Youth Anti-Drug Media Campaign. *Journal of Public Health Management Practice*, *6*, 14–26.

Kim, K. J. (2009). Risk and protective factors for drug use among American youth. In J. A. Mancini & K. A. Roberto (Eds.), *Pathways of human development: Explorations of change* (pp. 113–126). Lexington Books.

Kleiman, M. A. (1998). Drugs and drug policy: The case for a slow fix. *Issues in Science and Technology*, *15*, 45–52.

Knapp, C. (1996). *Drinking: A love story*. Delta.

Kulis, S., Marsiglia, F. F., Elek, E., Dustman, P., Wagstaff, D. A., & Hecht, M. L. (2005). Mexican/Mexican American adolescents and Keepin' It REAL: An evidence-based substance use prevention program. *Children & Schools*, *27*(3), 133–145.

Kupersmidt, J. B., Coie, J. D., & Dodge, K. A. (1990). The role of poor peer relationships in the development of disorder. In S. R. Asher & J. D. Coie (Eds.), *Peer rejection in childhood* (pp. 274–305). Cambridge University Press.

Liddle, H. A., & Rowe, C. L. (Eds.). (2006). *Adolescent substance abuse: Research and clinical advances*. Cambridge University Press.

Loeber, R., Farrington, D. P., Stouthamer-Loeber, M., & van Kammen, W. B. (1998). *Antisocial behavior and mental health problems: Explanatory factors in childhood and adolescence*. Lawrence Erlbaum.

Luthar, S. S. (Ed.). (2003). *Resilience and vulnerability: Adaptation in the context of childhood adversities*. Cambridge University Press.

Lynam, D. R., Milich, R., Zimmerman, R., Novak, S. P., Logan, T. K., Martin, C., Leukefeld, C., & Clayton, R. (1999). Project DARE: No effects at 10-year follow-up. *Journal of Consulting and Clinical Psychology*, *67*, 590–593.

Marsiglia, F. F., Kulis S., Hecht, M. L., & Sills, S. (2004). Ethnicity and ethnic identity as predictors of drug norms and drug use among preadolescents in the US Southwest. *Substance Use & Misuse*, *39*(7), 1061–1094.

McBride, D. C., VanderWaal, C. J., & Terry-McElrath, Y. M. (2001). *The drugs–crime wars: Past, present and future directions in theory, policy and program interventions* (Research Paper Series 14). The National Institute of Justice.

Meschke, L. L., & Patterson, J. M. (2003). Resilience as a theoretical base for substance abuse prevention. *The Journal of Primary Prevention*, *23*, 483–514.

Miech, R. A., Johnston, L. D., O'Malley, P. M., Bachman, J. G., Schulenberg, J. E., & Patrick M. E. (2019). *Monitoring the future: National survey results on drug use, 1975–2019*. National Institute of Drug Abuse.

Miller, L., Davies, M., & Greenwald, S. (2000). Religiosity and substance use and abuse among adolescents in the National Comorbidity Survey. *Journal of the American Academy of Child and Adolescent Psychiatry*, *39*, 1190–1197.

Morin, S. F., & Collins, C. (2000). Substance abuse prevention: Moving from science to policy. *Addictive Behaviors*, *25*, 975–983.

Murphy, S. L., Xu, J., Kochanek, K. D., & Arias, E. S. (2018). Mortality in the United States, 2017. *NCHS Data Brief, 328*. National Center for Health Statistics.

Murray, C. A. (1983). The physical environment and community control of crime. In J. Q. Wilson (Ed.), *Crime and public policy* (pp. 67–91). Institute for Contemporary Studies.

Musto, D. F. (1996). Alcohol in American history. *Scientific American, 274*, 78–82.

Nadelmann, E., & LaSalle, L. (2017). Two steps forward, one step back: Current harm reduction policy and politics in the United States. *Harm Reduction Journal, 14*, 37. https://doi.org/10.1186/s12954-017-0157-y

National Academies of Sciences, Engineering, and Medicine (2019a). *The promise of adolescence: Realizing opportunity for all youth.* The National Academies Press. https://doi.org/10.17226/25388.

National Academies of Sciences, Engineering, and Medicine (2019b). *Fostering healthy mental, emotional, and behavioral development in children and youth: A national agenda.* The National Academies Press. https://doi.org/10.17226/25201.

National Center for Children and Poverty. (2019). *Child poverty.* Author.

National Institute on Drug Abuse (NIDA). (2009). *Principles of drug addiction treatment: A research-based guide* (3rd ed.). National Institutes of Health, U. S. Department of Health and Human Services.

National Institute on Drug Abuse (NIDA). (2014). *Principles of adolescent substance use disorder treatment: A research-based guide.* U.S. Department of Health and Human Services.

National Institutes of Health (NIH). (2020). *About.* https://heal.nih.gov/about

National Research Council and Institute of Medicine (2009). *Preventing mental, emotional, and behavioral disorders among young people: Progress and possibilities.* The National Academies Press.

Office of Juvenile Justice and Delinquency Prevention (OJJDP). (2000). *Tribal youth program.* U.S. Department of Justice, Office of Justice Programs, OJJDP.

Office of National Drug Control Policy (ONDCP). (1997). *The national youth anti-drug media campaign: Communication strategy statement.* Author.

Office of National Drug Control Policy (ONDCP). (2009). *The president's national drug control strategy, 2009.* Executive Office of the President.

Office of National Drug Control Policy (ONDCP). (2010). *Drug free communities support program.* http://www.whitehouse.gov/ondcp/drug-free-communities-support-program

Office of National Drug Control Policy (ONDCP). (2012). *Above the influence.* http://www.whitehouse.gov/sites/default/files/page/files/ati_fact_sheet_6-26-12.pdf

Office of National Drug Control Policy (ONDCP). (2014). *2013 national drug control strategy.* www.whitehouse.gov/ondcp/national-drug-control-strategy

Office of National Drug Control Policy (ONDCP). (2020). *The president's national drug control strategy, 2020.* Executive Office of the President.

Office of National Drug Control Policy (ONDCP). (2021). *The president's national drug control strategy, 2021.* Executive Office of the President.

Office of the Surgeon General. (2016). *Facing addiction in America: The Surgeon General's report on alcohol, drugs, and health.* HHS.

Patient Protection and Affordable Care Act, PL 111-148, §2702, 124 Stat. 199, 318–319 (2010).

Patterson, G. R. (2002). The early development of coercive family process. In J. B. Reid, G. R. Patterson, & J. Snyder (Eds.), *Antisocial behavior in children and adolescents: A developmental analysis and model for intervention* (pp. 25–44). American Psychological Association.

Patterson, G. R., Reid, J. B., & Eddy, J. M. (2002). A brief history of the Oregon model. In J. B. Reid, G. R. Patterson, & J. Snyder (Eds.), *Antisocial behavior in children and adolescents: A developmental analysis and model for intervention* (pp. 3–24). American Psychological Association.

Pentz, M. A. (2010). Translating research into practice and practice into research for drug use prevention. In L. Scheier (Ed.), *Handbook of drug use etiology: Theory, methods, and empirical findings* (pp. 581–596). American Psychological Association.

Physician Leadership on National Drug Policy. (2002). *Adolescent substance abuse: A public health priority: An evidence-based, comprehensive, and integrative approach.* Brown University, Center for Alcohol and Addiction Studies.

Pilkey, D., Skopec, L., Gee, E., Finegold, K., Amaya, K., & Robinson, W. (2013). *The Affordable Care Act and adolescents. ASPE Research Brief.* U. S. Department of Health & Human Services, Office of the Assistance Secretary for Planning and Evaluation.

Reinherz, H. Z., Giaconia, R. M., Hauf, A. M., Wasserman, M. S., & Paradis, A. D. (2000). General and specific childhood risk factors for depression and drug disorders by early childhood. *Journal of the American Academy of Child and Adolescent Psychiatry, 39*, 223–231.

Robert Wood Johnson Foundation. (2001). *Substance abuse: The nation's number one health problem. Key indicators for policy*. Author.

Robert Wood Johnson Foundation. (2010). *Publications and research: Addictions*. http://www.rwjf.org/pr/topic.jsp?topicid=1006

Robertson, E. B., David, S. L., & Rao, S. A. (2003). *Preventing drug use among children and adolescents: A research-based guide for parents, educators, and community leaders* (2nd ed.). U.S. Department of Health and Human Services.

Rosenbaum, S., Johnson, K., Snonsky, C., Markus, A., & DeGraw, C. (1998). The children's hour: The state of children's health insurance program. *Health Affairs, 17*, 75–89.

Rossa, M. W. (2002). Some thoughts about resilience versus positive development, main effects, versus interaction effects and the value of resilience. *Child Development, 71*, 567–569.

Rutter, M. (2000). Psychosocial influences: Critiques, findings, and research needs. *Development and Psychopathology, 12*, 375–405.

Saffer, H., & Grossman, M. (1987). Beer taxes, the legal drinking age, and youth motor vehicle fatalities. *Journal of Legal Studies, 16*, 351–374.

Scheier, L. (Ed.). (2010). *Handbook of drug use etiology: Theory, methods, and empirical findings*. American Psychological Association.

Scheier, L. M., Grenard, J. L., & Holtz, K. D. (2011). An empirical assessment of the "Above the Influence" advertising campaign. *Journal of Public Health, 95*(3), 425–431.

Schinke, S., Brounstein, P., & Gardner, S. (2002). *Science-based prevention programs and principles, 2002* (DHHS Pub No. SMA 03-3764). Substance Abuse and Mental Health Services Administration.

Schinke, S. P., Fang, L., & Cole, K. C. A. (2008). Substance use among early adolescent girls: Risk and protective factors. *Journal of Adolescent Health, 43*, 191–194.

Shedler, J., & Block, J. (1990). Adolescent drug use and psychological health: A longitudinal inquiry. *American Psychologist, 45*, 612–630.

Simcha-Fagan, O., & Schwartz, J. E. (1986). Neighborhood and delinquency: An assessment of contextual effects. *Criminology, 24*, 667–703.

Slater, M. D., Kelly, K. J., Lawrence, F. R., Stanley, L. R., & Cornello, M. L. (2011). Assessing media campaigns linking marijuana non-use with autonomy and aspirations: "Be Under Your Own Influence" and ONDCP's "Above the Influence." *Prevention Science, 12*(1), 12–22.

Snyder, H. (1990). *Growth in minority detentions attributed to drug law violators*. Office of Juvenile Justice and Delinquency Prevention.

Substance Abuse and Mental Health Services Administration (SAMHSA). (2013). *Results from the 2012 National Survey on Drug Use and Health: Summary of national findings*, NSDUH Series H-46, HHS Publication No. (SMA) 13-4795. Author.

Substance Abuse and Mental Health Services Administration (SAMHSA). (2020a). *Evidence-based resource center*. https://www.samhsa.gov/ebp-resource-center

Substance Abuse and Mental Health Services Administration (SAMHSA). (2020b). *About us*. https://www.samhsa.gov/about-us/who-we-are/laws-regulations

Trent, M., Dooley, D. G., & Douge, J. (2019). The impact of racism on child and adolescent health. *Pediatrics, 144* (2), 1–16.

U.S. Department of Labor. (2010). *Frequently asked questions about the Mental Health Parity Act*. http://www.dol.gov/ebsa/faqs/faq_consumer_mentalhealthparity.html

Vaughn, M. G., Freedenthal, S., Jenson, J. M., & Howard, M. O. (2007). Psychiatric symptoms and substance use among juvenile offenders. *Criminal Justice and Behavior, 34*, 1296–1312.

Vaughn, M. G., & Howard, M. O. (2004). Adolescent substance abuse treatment: A synthesis of controlled evaluations. *Research on Social Work Practice, 14*, 325–335.

Vaughn, M. G., Ollie, M. T., McMillen, J. C., Scott, L., & Munson, M. (2007). Substance use and abuse among older youth in foster care. *Addictive Behaviors, 32*, 1929–1935.

Vaughn, M. G., Wallace, J. M., Davis, L., Fernandes, G. T., & Howard, M. O. (2008). Variations in mental health problems, substance use, and delinquency between African American and Caucasian juvenile offenders. *International Journal of Offender Therapy and Comparative Criminology, 52*, 311–329.

Washburn, J. J., Teplin, L. A., Voss, L. S., Simon, C. D., Abram, K. M., & McCelland, G. M. (2008). Psychiatric disorders among detained youths: A comparison of youths processed in juvenile court and adult criminal court. *Psychiatric Services, 59*, 965–973.

Watson, R. J., Goodenow, C., Porta, C., Adjei, J., & Saewyc, E. (2017). Substance use among sexual minorities: Has it actually gotten better? *Substance Use & Misuse, 53* (7), 1221–1228.

Welty, L. J., Harrison, A. J., Abram, K. M., Olson, N. D., Aaby, D. A., McCoy, K. P., Washburn, J. J., & Teplin, L. A. (2016). Health disparities in drug-and alcohol use disorders: A 12-year longitudinal study of youth after detention. *American Journal of Public Health, 106*(5), 872–880.

Werner, E. E. (1994). Overcoming the odds. *Developmental and Behavioral Pediatrics, 15*, 131–136.

Werner, E. E., & Smith, R. S. (1989). *Vulnerable but invincible: A longitudinal study of resilient children and youth.* Adams, Bannister, and Cox.

Westat & the Annenberg School for Communication. (2003). *Evaluation of the National Youth Anti-Drug Media Campaign: 2003 report of findings executive summary* (Contract No: N01DA-8-5063). National Institute on Drug Abuse.

Woolf, S. H. (2008). The power of prevention and what it requires. *Journal of the American Medical Association, 299*, 2437–2439.

Wu, L., Woody, G. E., Yan, C., Pan, J., & Blazer, D. G. (2011). Racial/ethnic variations in substance-related disorders among adolescents in the United States. *Arch Gen Psychiatry, 68*(11), 1176–1185.

Wyrick, D., Wyrick, C. H., Bibeau, D. L., & Fearnow-Kenney, M. (2001). Coverage of adolescent substance use prevention in state frameworks for health education. *Journal of School Health, 71*, 437–442.

Zucker, R. A., Wong, M. M., Puttler, L. I., & Fitzgerald, H. E. (2003). Resilience and vulnerability among sons of alcoholics: Relationship to developmental outcomes between early childhood and adolescence. In S. S. Luthar (Ed.), *Resilience and vulnerability: Adaptation in the context of childhood adversities* (pp. 76–103). Cambridge University Press.

# ADDITIONAL READING

Springer, D. W., & Rubin, A. (Eds.). (2009). *Substance abuse treatment for youth and adults.* John Wiley.

Tolan, P., Szapocznik, J., & Sambrano, S. (Eds.). (2007). *Preventing youth substance abuse: Science-based programs for children and adolescents.* American Psychological Association.

# WEB-BASED RESOURCES

Blueprints for Healthy Youth Development: http://www.blueprintsprograms.org

Coalition for the Promotion of Behavioral Health: http://www.coalitionforbehavioralhealth.org

The Center for Communities That Care: https://www.communitiesthatcare.net

Monitoring the Future: https://www.drugabuse.gov/drug-topics/trends-statistics/monitoring-future

National Institute on Drug Abuse: https://www.drugabuse.gov

National Prevention Science Coalition to Improve Lives: http://www.npscoalition.org/

Physicians and Leadership for National Drug Policy: http://www.plndp.org

Robert Wood Johnson Foundation: https://www.rwjf.org

Social Development Research Group (SDRG): https://www.washington.edu/research/research-centers/social-development-research-group-sdrg/

Substance Abuse and Mental Health Services Administration (SAMHSA): https://www.samhsa.gov

# 9

# SOCIAL POLICY FOR IMMIGRANT CHILDREN AND FAMILIES

Megan Finno-Velasquez, Anayeli Lopez, Sophia Sepp, and Marianna Corkill

## INTRODUCTION

The United States (U.S.) is a nation that was founded, built, and transformed by immigrants' social and human capital (Mendoza & Festa, 2013). An *immigrant* is an individual who leaves their country of origin to permanently settle in another country (Bolter, 2019). In the U.S., these include all foreign individuals who are living in this country. Throughout its history, complicated and at times conflicting values have guided policies that legally define an immigrant (Garcia et al., 2012), establish their eligibility for services, and influence migration trends (Morrison & Thronson, 2010). In today's heightened sociopolitical climate regarding immigration, it is crucial to understand how immigration policies impact our most vulnerable children and families as well as our public systems more generally (Eikenberry, 2017; Torres, 2017).

Even though immigrants are vital assets to the country's social fabric and economy, throughout history, U.S. social policies and public systems have repeatedly neglected to effectively and equitably serve this population. Our country's social systems continue to fail to address some of the common challenges experienced by immigrant families and children. Major issues that impact immigrant families include immigration status, cultural differences and acculturation, past trauma, language challenges, distrust of government, and other risk factors that stem from poverty and a disadvantaged socioeconomic background (Earner, 2010).

This chapter provides a description of U.S. immigrant populations and an overview of how U.S. social policies have been exclusive or inclusive of immigrant children and families, serving as risk or protective factors for the well-being of this population. In examining the nation's evolving immigration policies, the chapter will (1) analyze how inconsistent and punitive policies infringe on the human rights and dignity of immigrant children and families and (2) discuss the impact of an anti-immigrant political climate on health, family unity, essential needs, and freedom. To conclude, this chapter offers solutions and policy recommendations for supporting immigrant children, families, and communities within our society.

# DEMOGRAPHICS OF IMMIGRANT FAMILIES AND CHILDREN IN THE UNITED STATES

In 2018, there were more than 43 million immigrants in the U.S., accounting for 13.7% of the country's population. According to Migration Policy Institute estimates, approximately 18 million children under age 18 live with at least one immigrant parent, representing 25.9% of the 69.5 million children under age 18 in the U.S. (Batalova et al., 2020). The majority of these children are born in the U.S. and live in a *mixed-status household*, meaning that at least one of their family members is an unauthorized immigrant. In 2017, there were 5.1 million children under age 18 with an immigrant parent who lacked legal status, accounting for 30% of all children of immigrants and 7% of all children in the U.S. This situation poses unique challenges to immigrant families when engaging with social and public systems.

While immigrant population growth is likely to continue, demographic trends are rapidly changing in regard to where immigrants are coming from (country of origin) and where they are settling. Since 2010, more immigrants are likely to come from India, China, the Philippines, El Salvador, Cuba, the Dominican Republic, Guatemala, and Venezuela (Batalova et al., 2020). More and more immigrants, mainly refugees, are also coming from other destinations, including the Democratic Republic of Congo, Iraq, Syria, Somalia, Burma, and Bhutan (Kishi, 2017). *Refugees* are individuals located outside the U.S. who are unable or unwilling to return to their home country due to a "well-founded fear of persecution" based on their race, religion, nationality, political opinion, or membership in a particular social group (American Immigration Council [AIC], 2020a).

Today, immigrants are also more dispersed throughout the country as opposed to clustering in a few traditional destination states as in past decades, such as California, Texas, New York, New Jersey, and Florida (Batalova et al., 2020). Immigrant families are moving to new destination states for various reasons, such as family connections, social networks, employment opportunities, and quality educational systems (Held et al., 2018). States experiencing the fastest growth rates in immigrant populations in recent years include Alabama, South Carolina, Tennessee, Arkansas, Kentucky, North Dakota, South Dakota, Minnesota, Delaware, and Iowa (Batalova et al., 2020).

In recent years, unaccompanied migrant children have arrived at the U.S.–Mexico border region in record numbers from an area known as the *Northern Triangle*, comprised of Guatemala, Honduras, and El Salvador (Chishti & Hipsman, 2016). The number of young children and families seeking refuge in the U.S. has increased significantly in recent years, also originating from the aforementioned Central American countries, in response to ongoing poverty, homicide, gang violence, domestic violence, and kidnapping, especially toward women and children (Chishti & Hipsman, 2016; Held et al., 2018). For example, the number of family units encountered by border patrol at the U.S.–Mexico border increased from 107,212 in the 2018 fiscal year to 473,682 in 2019 (U.S. Customs and Border Protection, 2018, 2019). The shifting trends in countries of origin and new settlement locations illuminate the need for consideration of immigrant children and families living within their jurisdictions as state and local governments make decisions about policies, practices, and programs that serve them.

# RISK AND RESILIENCE IN IMMIGRANT FAMILIES

## Risk

The landmark study on adverse childhood experiences highlights the factors that increase children's risk for developing adverse emotional and behavioral problems (Felitti et al., 1998). Its findings indicate that encountering multiple cumulative risk factors related to abuse, neglect, and household dysfunction can be potentially damaging for children, including exposure to physical and emotional abuse and neglect, sexual abuse, mental illness, substance abuse, domestic violence, and parental incarceration. Experiencing early childhood adversities can also have a negative impact on the physical, mental, and behavioral health of children later in life. Research finds that trauma and toxic stress can result in risky behavior (e.g., drug and alcohol use) as well as serious health conditions (e.g., cardiovascular disease, cancer, asthma, pulmonary disease, autoimmune diseases, poor dental health, and depression; Shonkoff et al., 2012).

A wealth of literature documents the challenges that immigrant children and families face before, during, and following migration, with potential negative consequences for their physical and mental well-being (Pumariega & Rothe, 2010). Unsafe and impoverished environments in other countries often drive the decision to migrate to the U.S. A primary reason for fleeing home countries is the high levels of violence, which is a source of trauma for many unaccompanied children, families, and individuals before they even begin the migration journey (Held et al., 2018; Keller et al., 2017). The Northern Triangle countries have among the highest homicide rates in the world, with Honduras, El Salvador, and Guatemala ranked first, fourth, and fifth in the world in homicide incidence (UNICEF Child Alert, 2018). This region also has some of the highest rates of gender-based violence that are often left unprosecuted (Geneva Declaration Secretariat, 2015; Nowak, 2012).

Not only do immigrants experience violence, trauma, and other risks and adversities in their home countries that often prompt their decisions to migrate but they also experience similar and re-traumatizing risk factors during the migration journey. Without many viable options for legal entry into the U.S. (discussed later in this chapter), many immigrants, especially those from Latin America, are faced with a treacherous journey north marked by additional violence, extortion, and physical hardship (DeLuca et al., 2010; Infante et al., 2012). They are at risk of becoming victims of human trafficking, kidnapping, and sexual assault (UNICEF Child Alert, 2018), potentially contributing to toxic stress levels documented even prior to arriving to the U.S. (Derluyn & Broekaert, 2008). Immigrants are exposed to threats, verbal abuse, physical assaults, and sexual violence (Infante et al., 2012), which, when combined with factors such as premigration poverty, increase their trauma exposure and subsequent development of post-traumatic stress disorder (PTSD) symptoms (Perreira & Ornelas, 2013).

Once in the U.S., immigrant children and families experience a wide range of challenges after having already experienced stressful and often traumatic events prior to their arrival. These children and families must navigate the difficult *acculturation process*—a process of change and adaptation by which immigrants integrate into a new culture, adopting some of the values and practices of the new culture while also retaining elements of their own culture (Cole, 2019). This process is influenced not only by individual traits, such as age, gender, personality, language, education level, religious beliefs, family structure, and economic stability, but also by cultural differences related to those same characteristics (Padilla & Perez, 2003). The process of acculturation can be more difficult for immigrants coming from countries whose cultural norms are substantially different from those of the country of settlement. Stressors associated with acculturation may include navigating systems in a new country, racial discrimination, language barriers, changes in family structure, and neighborhood environment—all of which can exacerbate the risk for physical and psychological health issues (Ornelas & Perreira, 2011). Some of the issues experienced during the acculturation process may lessen as families integrate into their new communities; however, the opposite can be true for families in which not all family members obtain legal immigration status because their stress can accumulate over time (Kris & Skivenes, 2012; Mendoza & Festa, 2013; Morrison & Thronson, 2010).

Parental legal immigration status has spillover effects on all members of mixed-status families (Dreby, 2015; Menjívar & Cervantes, 2016). Children in mixed-status families experience various contextual risk factors associated with a parent's lack of legal status that has direct and indirect implications for the entire family system (Yoshikawa et al., 2016). Undocumented immigrant parents are more likely to earn low wages, be susceptible to dangerous job conditions and labor exploitation, and lack legal protections or rights (De Genova & Peutz, 2010). Parents' economic hardships impact the living conditions of children who are U.S. citizens. Children in mixed-status households are more likely to suffer from poverty and food insecurity than children of U.S. citizens (Kalil & Chen, 2008; Ortega et al., 2009).

Studies have also found that parental undocumented status can have a negative impact on children's psychological well-being and development even if they are still in the country and have not been previously deported (Yoshikawa, 2011; Yoshikawa et al., 2016). Children living in mixed-status households may live in constant fear of their parent's possible deportation and may suffer by having to continuously hide their parent's legal status. This can lead to mental health problems in children, including depression, anxiety, and behavioral issues (Delva et al., 2013).

A parent's undocumented status can lead to arrest, detention, and deportation, significantly altering their children's lives and detrimentally impacting their mental health (Zayas, 2015). The majority of individuals who are deported are men, often leaving women as single mothers (Dreby, 2012). In addition to the emotional stress of separation, many single mothers are left with financial hardship and heightened childcare responsibilities (Dreby, 2015). In the short term, mental and behavioral consequences for children can include anxiety, difficulty sleeping, crying, withdrawal, and clinginess (Chaudry et al., 2010). Frequently, these separations are indefinite, leading to long-term consequences for children that may include alterations in family roles, routines, responsibilities, and childcare arrangements (Dreby, 2015).

## Resilience

Despite immigrant children and families' exposure to multiple risks before, during, and after their migration journey, these experiences do not necessarily result in adverse outcomes (Carlson et al., 2012). In fact, various health indices indicate that immigrants fare better in physical and mental health than U.S.–born populations upon early arrival from their home countries (Mehta & Elo, 2012; Singh et al., 2013). This phenomenon is known as the "immigrant health paradox." Evidence of the immigrant health paradox has been observed in numerous health (e.g., self-reported health status, chronic disease, obesity, pregnancy outcomes) and psychosocial (e.g., mental health status, antisocial behavior, intimate partner violence) indicators across immigrants from various parts of the world and in multiple receiving countries (Kennedy et al., 2015; Salas-Wright et al., 2014). This immigrant health paradox also holds true for newcomer children and adolescents in the U.S. However, as immigrant children and adolescents acculturate to the U.S. over time and through generations, they are exposed to more adverse experiences (Villamil et al., in press) and their developmental outcomes become less optimal (Marks et al., 2014).

One explanation for this paradox is that traditional cultural values and strong ethnic identities may protect immigrants from adverse outcomes associated with socioeconomic and other contextual risk factors (Flores, 2013). Immigrants who have lived longer in the U.S. and children of immigrants may suffer from eroded connections to cultural values and traditions that buffer against health issues and other adverse outcomes (Alegría et al., 2007). In addition, children of immigrants may have a stronger connection to dominant U.S. culture, allowing them to perceive discrimination and be more vulnerable than their foreign-born parents (Viruell-Fuentes, 2007). However, there remain questions as to whether the protective factors associated with the immigrant health paradox hold true for immigrants with different immigration statuses, particularly those with an undocumented legal status.

Resilience theory offers another perspective on the immigrant experience (specifically for children) and adaptation in the U.S. as it posits that individuals have the ability to adapt to adversities and challenges, highlighting that not all children exposed to cumulative risks develop adverse outcomes later in life. Children who are resilient not only avoid poor outcomes but also thrive, despite their exposure to multiple adversities (Masten, 2014). Much of the existing literature on refugee children and youth notes that despite their exposure to traumatic events and chronic stress, they display resilience and function at high levels (Derluyn & Broekaert, 2008; Kohli & Mather, 2003) by using their skills and intelligence to survive overwhelming stressors (Carlson et al., 2012).

Characteristics that may link to resilience in immigrant and refugee children include healthy coping skills, mild temperament, and connection to a higher power or religiosity (Masten et al., 2019). One study found that immigrant and refugee children who had secure relationships with their parents were able to adapt better than those who had been in insecure relationships (Juang et al., 2018). A positive relationship with extended family members can also help children in the adaptation process, particularly for children without parental figures in their lives. Beyond familial supports, social support from prosocial organizations, school mentors, church members, or community groups have also been found to protect children from adverse outcomes later in life (Carlson et al., 2012). Indeed, positive relationships are protective for children, as are adaptive coping strategies—such as talking with family members, friends, and classmates—as well as playing sports and going to church (Cardoso, 2018).

# IMMIGRANT DISPARITIES IN ACCESS TO SERVICES

In spite of relatively low rates of health and mental health problems among immigrant children and families, research has documented a number of disparities that often limit immigrant children and families' access to food, housing, education, and physical and psychological health services (Chang, 2019; Franzini et al., 2001; Gushulak et al., 2011). In addition, compared to the U.S.–born population, immigrant children and families face greater disparities in their use of formal services and programs as they are exposed to unequal treatment in a multitude of ways based on their race and language alone (Chang, 2019). As we will discuss, policies that systematically exclude many immigrants from eligibility for assistance also contribute greatly to these disparities.

## Public Assistance and Early Childhood Programs

Even when immigrant families meet income eligibility criteria for federal public assistance programs (e.g., food stamps), they are less likely to access those programs due to a multitude of factors that thwart their ability to meet essential human needs (Yoshikawa et al., 2014). A primary reason is the lack of clarity about program eligibility requirements among agencies and immigrant families (Gelatt & Koball, 2014). Many eligible immigrants assume they do not qualify for services; public eligibility workers have also mistakenly denied benefits to eligible immigrants. Language difficulties are another significant barrier that prevents immigrants from receiving public benefits when eligible. Even though federally funded programs must assure interpretation and translation services to limited-English proficient (LEP) immigrants, compliance with the requirement varies, and some immigrants still face linguistic and cultural barriers in obtaining benefits (Gelatt & Koball, 2014). In addition to the language barriers, immigrants typically come from less-developed countries and rural communities that tend to have minimal formal schooling and lower literacy levels (Perreira et al., 2012). This can further complicate the application process and comprehension of outreach materials if not translated in plain and reader-friendly English.

Undocumented legal status of even one family member adds an additional barrier to accessing services among all members of mixed-status families. Studies have found that undocumented parents are less likely to seek and access available government-based services and programs for their children, including prekindergarten programs, Medicaid, Children's Health Insurance Program (CHIP), food stamps, public housing, Supplemental Nutrition Assistance Program (SNAP), Social Security, and other forms of public assistance, even if their children are eligible based on their U.S. citizenship status (Brabeck et al., 2015). As cited by immigrant mothers, the leading reason for this is fear of being reported to immigration authorities (Xu & Brabeck, 2012). Another study found that undocumented mothers are deterred from enrolling in Women, Infants, and Children (WIC) programs due to fear of detainment and deportation (Vargas & Pirog, 2016). Undocumented parents are also less likely than legal permanent resident or citizen parents to enroll their young children in public preschool programs and other early childhood development programs (Kalil & Chen, 2008; Kalil & Crosnoe, 2009).

## Health Care

Immigrants encounter many structural barriers to accessing health care, including lack of insurance coverage, high costs, immigration status, limited English proficiency, and lack of transportation (Perreira & Pedroza, 2019). Because of the structure of the U.S. health care system, the health insurance status of the population can be divided into three categories: those with employer-sponsored insurance, those with public health insurance or government-subsidized coverage (e.g., Medicare, Medicaid, CHIP, and the Affordable Care Act [ACA] marketplace plans), and those who lack insurance coverage. Almost half (45%) of the undocumented immigrant population and 23% of legal permanent residents in the U.S. lack health insurance compared to 9% of naturalized citizens (Artiga & Diaz, 2019; Kaiser Family Foundation, 2020b). Citizen children with at least one foreign-born parent are also more likely to be uninsured compared to those with citizen parents (Kaiser Family Foundation, 2020a). The lack of health insurance coverage among the immigrant population also varies depending on the country of origin. For example, only 7% of immigrants from Germany lack insurance coverage compared to 58% of immigrants from Guatemala (Carrasquillo et al., 2000). This inequitable system exacerbates health disparities and creates structural barriers to accessing affordable health care services for immigrant families and children (Chang, 2019). The high number of uninsured rates among immigrant families reflects the limited access to employer-sponsored health insurance and eligibility restrictions preventing immigrants in different legal status categories from participating in government-based health insurance programs.

While the ACA aimed to extend health insurance coverage to many uninsured individuals and improve access to and quality of care in the U.S., the number of vulnerable immigrants without access to health care continues to grow (Blumenthal et al., 2015; Bustamante et al., 2019). Due to structural and cultural barriers in accessing health care, such as high uninsured rates, many undocumented immigrants resist or delay seeking and receiving needed health care. For the same reasons, undocumented parents are also less likely to take their children for routine visits to medical doctors, mental health providers, and dentists (Brabeck et al., 2015). While immigrants who lack legal status can obtain care from community health centers for free or reduced cost, services are often limited to preventive and primary care, leaving immigrants without access to specialized health care. Fear tactics in shifting immigration policies, such as the public charge rule, further discourage families from utilizing health care programs and services such as Medicaid and CHIP for themselves and their U.S.–born children, even though they are eligible. The public charge rule, which we explain in detail later in the chapter, enables U.S. Citizenship and Immigration Services (USCIS) to deny individuals admission to the U.S. or legal permanent resident status if they are determined to be likely to depend on the government as a primary source of support. The definition of public charge was expanded under the Trump administration, threatening to exclude even more immigrants from obtaining legal status.

In addition to lack of insurance coverage, the high cost of health services, and an undocumented status, there are nonfinancial obstacles that prevent immigrants from accessing health care. These obstacles include limited or lack of transportation, inflexible work schedules, language challenges, and cultural beliefs and norms about health care and illness conditions (Chang, 2019). Immigrant adults with limited English proficiency and their children are less likely to have insurance coverage and to access health care than those who speak English. Even though federally funded health care facilities are mandated by law to provide interpretation for patients, the funding mechanisms at the state level are inadequate (Luque et al., 2018). Studies have found that patients who experience language barriers have poorer health outcomes compared to those who speak the native language (Divi et al., 2007; Squires, 2017). The lack of coverage and barriers to health care among immigrant families and children can have an impact on the healthy development of future generations.

## Mental Health Services

Although immigrants experience fewer mental health problems overall compared to U.S.–born individuals, unique stressors related to the immigration and resettlement experiences may cause mental health problems, including PTSD, general anxiety, depression, and behavioral problems (Rousseau & Frounfelker, 2019). However, the rate of access to behavioral health services by immigrants is far below that of the U.S.–born population, placing them at higher risk for untreated mental health conditions (Derr, 2016). A study of Asian and Latinx immigrants showed that only 6% of immigrant participants in the study had ever utilized a mental health service, indicating that they were 40% less likely than the general population to access services (Chen & Vargas-Bustamante, 2011; Lee & Matejkowski, 2011). When left untreated, mental health problems can contribute to other concerning behaviors, such as substance abuse and criminal behavior (Salami et al., 2018). Another study found that 15% of Mexican immigrants with diagnosed mental health problems utilized services compared with 38% of U.S.–born Mexican Americans who had similar mental health needs (Derr, 2016). Because of the traumatic events experienced throughout their migration journey, refugees, asylum seekers, and undocumented immigrants may need more mental health supports than others (Salami et al., 2018).

In general, studies indicate that barriers to mental health care can be both cultural (e.g., stigma and cultural norms about mental illness) and structural (e.g., cost, insurance status, transportation, immigration status, limited English proficiency). One of the most common cultural barriers to services is stigma. In a study that included African and Latino women, stigma was reported as a barrier to accessing mental health services (Nadeem et al., 2009). Another study on older Korean immigrants cited stigma and misconceptions about mental illnesses as the most frequent cultural barrier to using mental health services (Jang et al., 2009). Research about the experiences of immigrants, especially women, in accessing mental health care services indicates significant barriers due to cultural differences, social stigma, and unfamiliarity with Western treatment options; spiritual beliefs and practices; and provider–client relationships (O'Mahony & Donnelly, 2007). Other cultural factors that often impede mental health service seeking and receipt include cultural beliefs that mental health issues indicate weakness of character or presence of evil spirits or reflect poorly upon the family (Abdullah & Brown, 2011). For example, in the Latino culture, the perception of mental illness as a weakness conflicts with the cultural values of *marianismo* (the belief that women should be self-sacrificing and tolerate suffering with dignity) and *machismo* (the belief that men should be strong and self-reliant), creating stigma. In other cultures, such as many African belief systems, people perceive mental health problems as interference by ancestors or as the result of bewitchment or curses, preferring to seek traditional spiritual healers and religious advisors as opposed to Western treatment providers (Sorsdahl et al., 2009).

These cultural factors and their associated stigmas coincide with significant structural barriers to create further challenges for immigrant populations in accessing services for mental health care. Some of the most frequent structural barriers related to mental health service use include lack of insurance coverage, cost of services, accessibility, long wait times, lack of cultural services in native languages, and fears related to unauthorized legal status (Chen & Vargas-Bustamante, 2011; Hansen & Cabassa, 2012; Kaltman et al., 2014; Leung et al., 2012). Other frequent barriers to seeking mental health services include the lack of knowledge about mental health resources, limited English proficiency, and lower levels of acculturation (Salami et al., 2018).

# OVERVIEW OF FEDERAL SOCIAL POLICY IMPACTS ON IMMIGRANTS

Federal social policy dictates program funding, service access, and benefits eligibility in the U.S. For the most part, rather than improving conditions and outcomes for immigrant children, youth, and families, U.S. social policies have caused and perpetuated the risks and disparities identified above. Major federal policies implemented over the past several decades have contributed to the present precarious situation for immigrant children and families.

## Personal Responsibility and Work Opportunity Reconciliation Act of 1996

Despite high levels of poverty among immigrant and mixed-status families, their access to many public benefits has been severely restricted. The Personal Responsibility and Work Opportunity Reconciliation Act (PRWORA) of 1996, instituted by the Clinton administration, was a bipartisan welfare reform plan requiring work in exchange for time-limited assistance (Assistant Secretary for Planning and Evaluation, 2016). However, PRWORA was partially designed to address the idea of the "pull factor" that allegedly incentivized immigrants to come to the U.S. in order to take advantage of public benefits (Fix & Passel, 2002). As such, select provisions of the reform significantly restricted eligibility for public benefits among legal immigrants, refugees, citizen children, and other populations who had previously been eligible in an effort to disincentivize illegal immigration (Broder et al., 2015; Speiglman et al., 2013). The law created two categories of immigrants to determine eligibility—*qualified* and *not qualified*. The qualified immigrant category includes lawful permanent residents (LPR), refugees and asylum grantees, certain abused immigrants and their children and/or parents, certain survivors of trafficking, and some others (Broder et al., 2015). The not-qualified immigrant category includes all other immigrants, including undocumented immigrants and some immigrants who are legally present in the U.S. When PRWORA was enacted, 935,000 noncitizens lost benefits (Fix & Passel, 2002). PRWORA removed the responsibility of providing immigrants with the public benefits from the federal level and placed it on individual states, resulting in widespread variation in immigrant eligibility determination and benefit provision practices (Zimmermann & Tumlin, 1999).

The U.S. Department of Health and Human Services (HHS) is the primary federal agency that controls and provides partial funding for public health and social services. HHS has designated 31 programs as federal public benefits, including adoption assistance, the Child Care and Development Fund, CHIP, foster care, Medicaid, Medicare, Temporary Assistant to Needy Families (TANF), and the Low-Income Home Energy Assistance Program (Broder et al., 2015). PRWORA prevents not-qualified immigrants from enrolling in most federal public benefit programs, with some exceptions; furthermore, even qualified immigrants—including LPR—are prohibited from accessing public benefit programs (i.e., Medicaid, CHIP, TANF, SNAP, and Supplemental Security Income [SSI]) for their first five years in the U.S. if they entered the U.S. on or after 1996 (Broder et al., 2015; Speiglman et al., 2013). Due to other PRWORA restrictions, undocumented children of immigrants are not eligible for federally funded foster care. Federal policies regarding children in foster care prevent federal reimbursement of some costs for undocumented immigrant children (i.e., Medicaid and Title IV-E payments) to states. In these situations, foster care and other services must be paid for through local funds, which are frequently limited and subjected to cuts by state legislatures or by agencies who must stretch their financial resources and make arrangements to meet client needs (Rajendran & Chemtob, 2010).

PRWORA created the TANF block grant to replace the Aid to Families with Dependent Children (AFDC) program, which resulted in a major decline in "aided-adult" cases in which adults receive benefits and an increase in "child-only" cases in which only the child receives benefits because the caregiver is deemed ineligible (Speiglman et al., 2013). PRWORA also ushered in a new categorization of ineligible immigrant parents (IIPs), with 25% of the country's child-only cases being children of IIPs. From 1994 to 1999, there was a decrease of 53% among low-income LPR families in children receiving TANF benefits and a decrease of 78% among refugee families receiving TANF benefits (Fix & Passel, 2002).

There are some exceptions to the restrictions imposed by PRWORA. Not-qualified immigrants can access emergency Medicaid and some public health programs in order to receive immunizations and treatment for communicable diseases (Broder et al., 2015). Additionally, children may utilize free or reduced-price school breakfast and lunch programs regardless of their immigration status, and every state has chosen to provide access to the Special Supplemental Nutrition Program for WIC. Nonetheless, the restrictions from PRWORA resulted in reduced utilization of benefits not only by noncitizens but also by mixed-status families, including families with U.S.–citizen children (Fix & Passel, 2002).

## The Patient Protection and Affordable Care Act

Even with the implementation of the 2010 ACA (colloquially known as "Obamacare") intended to expand access to health insurance, immigrant populations continued to face significant barriers in accessing insurance coverage due to immigration status. Although the ACA offered the expansion of Medicaid coverage to individuals below 138% of the federal poverty guideline beginning January 2014, federal Medicaid eligibility restrictions for immigrants were maintained, including the five-year ban such that LPR and other legally residing immigrants are prevented from accessing Medicaid within those five years (National Alliance of State and Territorial AIDs Directors, 2014). Furthermore, the decision to offer this expansion was left up to each individual state. As of September 2020, 38 states have elected to expand Medicaid, leaving 12 states that have not adopted the expansion, and the 38 adopters have varied with respect to their implementation timelines (Kaiser Family Foundation, 2020c). Under the ACA, LPRs do have access to the ACA's qualified health plans and subsidies within the five-year ban. However, undocumented immigrants continue to be ineligible for enrollment in Medicare, Medicaid, and CHIP; are unable to purchase qualified health plans within the ACA marketplaces; and do not qualify for subsidies, tax credits, or cost-sharing reductions (Artiga & Diaz, 2019). Furthermore, individuals with Deferred Action for Childhood Arrivals (DACA) status remain ineligible for coverage options, including Medicaid, CHIP, and other ACA benefits (National Alliance of State and Territorial AIDs Directors, 2014). The Immigrant Children's Health Improvement Act, part of the

Medicaid and CHIP Reauthorization Act of 2009, does provide states with the option of expanding Medicaid and CHIP coverage to legally residing immigrant children and pregnant women who are within the five-year waiting period. As of January 1, 2020, 35 states provide the expansion to immigrant children and 25 states provide the expansions to pregnant immigrant women (Kaiser Family Foundation, 2020c).

## Access to Housing Assistance and Education

Despite the restrictions imposed by PRWORA on immigrants' access to many public benefits, the attorney general identified exceptions to certain programs and benefits, including some housing programs, which are deemed "necessary for the protection of life and safety" (Lynch et al., 2016). These housing programs, available regardless of immigration status, include short-term shelter or housing assistance for the homeless; for victims of domestic violence; or for runaway, abused, or abandoned children as well as programs, services, or assistance for persons during periods of heat, cold, or other adverse weather conditions (McCarty & Siskin, 2015). In 2000, it was determined that Department of Housing and Urban Development (HUD) programs are not considered to be federal means-tested public benefits, and as such, the stricter eligibility requirements (i.e., the five-year waiting period) do not apply to HUD programs. As long as one household member is a citizen or eligible citizen (e.g., LPR), a family may apply for HUD public housing and Section 8 programs.

The McKinney-Vento Homeless Assistance Act of 1987 established a federal program to provide services to people experiencing homelessness, including various housing assistance (i.e., emergency shelter and transitional housing; National Coalition for the Homeless, 2006). Title VII of the act ensures that all children have the right to go to school regardless of whether or not they are experiencing homelessness. This right and the services under the act apply to immigrant children as well, regardless of immigration status, as long as they meet the definition of *homeless* (National Center for Homeless Education, 2017). This law provides important access to supportive educational services for immigrant children and families, who disproportionately experience poverty, which often results in homelessness.

Additional seminal policies protect the educational rights of immigrant children. The 1982 *Plyler v. Doe* Supreme Court decision ensured that all children in the U.S. have access to free public education, including immigrant children. This decision established that states cannot deny students free public education on the basis of their immigration status (AIC, 2016). The Family Educational Rights and Privacy Act, which protects the privacy of student education records, also applies to protecting immigrant students as it prevents schools from disclosing information in student files without parental consent, including to federal agents (e.g., immigration officials).

## Public Charge Ground of Inadmissibility

Another significant policy-related factor negatively impacting immigrant families and children in the U.S. is the public charge ground of inadmissibility. *Public charge* is a concept within federal immigration law created to identify individuals who are likely to depend on the government as a primary source of support. If the government determines that an individual is likely to become a public charge, it can deny that individual admission to the U.S. or LPR status. In the past, determinations of public charge primarily considered an individual's receipt of public cash assistance and long-term institutionalization at the government's expense and did not consider the utilization of health care, housing, nutrition programs, or other such benefits (Quinn & Kinoshita, 2020). However, on August 14, 2019, the Department of Homeland Security (DHS) issued a final rule altering the definition of *public charge* and expanding the array of public benefits considered in a determination, which went into effect February 24, 2020. The Department of State (DOS) also implemented its own similar rule to apply to cases (e.g., visa applications processed at a U.S. consulate or embassy).

The definition of public charge now includes an individual who utilizes more than 12 months of public benefits in aggregate over a three-year time period (Quinn & Kinoshita, 2020). The public benefits considered under the new rule include the following: cash assistance, SSI, TANF, and similar state and local programs; federally funded Medicaid (with exceptions for Medicaid used during pregnancy and up to 60 days after birth, emergency Medicaid use, and Medicaid for those under 21); SNAP; and federally subsidized housing and Section 8 housing assistance. However, it should be noted that receiving any one of these benefits does not automatically qualify an individual as a public charge, and multiple other factors (e.g., age, health, family status, assets, resources, financial status, education, and skills) are also considered in the determination. In the wake of the COVID-19 pandemic, on July 29, 2020, the Second U.S. Circuit Court of Appeals issued a nationwide injunction barring the government from implementing the new public charge rule during the COVID-19 public health emergency. The USCIS also announced that COVID-19 testing, treatment, and prevention would not be considered in a public charge determination.

## COVID-19 and the CARES Act

In response to the COVID-19 public health emergency, Congress passed the 2.2 trillion-dollar Coronavirus Aid, Relief, and Economic Security (CARES) Act in March 2020. The CARES Act included a number of relief components that were largely unavailable to immigrants, some of whom are the most gravely impacted by the pandemic. The Pandemic Unemployment Assistance (PUA) program of the CARES Act enabled self-employed workers, such as gig workers, contractors, and freelancers, who typically cannot apply for unemployment to access relief (Chishti & Bolter, 2020). However, the PUA program did not extend to undocumented workers. The CARES Act also authorized one-time payments of $1,200 to individuals who earned less than $75,000. However, in order to receive that payment, including a $500 per child additional relief, individuals must have filed taxes for 2018 or 2019 using a Social Security number (SSN), consequently excluding most unauthorized immigrants, even those who file taxes utilizing an Individual Tax Identification Number (ITIN) from the Internal Revenue Service. Mixed-status families were also excluded from accessing this relief as any person filing jointly with an ITIN filer is ineligible, yielding entire families ineligible if they have even one member utilizing an ITIN—an estimated 15.4 million individuals. However, immigrants with work authorization (i.e., DACA and temporary protected status [TPS]) were able to access this relief.

Congress also passed the Families First Coronavirus Relief Act and the Paycheck Protection Program and Health Care Enhancement Act to authorize COVID-19 testing to be covered by Medicaid and to provide funding via Medicaid for testing for the uninsured. However, as discussed previously, only certain immigrants in the qualified category are eligible for Medicaid, leaving those not-qualified immigrants without coverage for testing and treatment of COVID-19. This issue was partially addressed when HHS announced that an undisclosed portion of a $100 billion allotment of the CARES Act funding would go toward reimbursing hospitals for treating uninsured patients, regardless of immigration status (Chishti & Bolter, 2020).

## U.S. IMMIGRATION POLICY

Federal immigration policies play a dual role in the lives of children of immigrant families because they govern both the enforcement of immigration laws and paths to legal entry to the U.S. as well as immigration relief available to individuals with special circumstances or hardships. Immigrants are primarily able to immigrate to the U.S. and obtain legal status via the following channels: family-based immigration, employment-based immigration, the diversity-based visa program, as a refugee or asylee, or through other forms of humanitarian relief. However, each of these channels has its own procedures, timelines, and quotas, which have become increasingly restrictive and difficult to navigate.

The family-based immigration system is one of the most common ways in which individuals obtain legal status in the U.S. Through this system, a family member who is a U.S. citizen or LPR can petition for their family member to immigrate to the U.S. and apply for legal permanent residency. An individual may qualify for family-based immigration if they are the immediate relative of a U.S. citizen. To be considered an *immediate relative*, one must be a spouse, an unmarried child under 21 years old, or a parent (if the U.S. citizen is 21 or older). The second pathway for family-based immigration is through four family preference categories: (F1) unmarried sons and daughters (21 years of age and older) of U.S. citizens; (F2A) spouses and children (unmarried and under 21 years of age) of LPRs; (F2B) unmarried sons and daughters (21 years of age and older) of LPRs; (F3) married sons and daughters of U.S. citizens; and (F4) brothers and sisters of U.S. citizens (if the U.S. citizen is 21 years of age and older; USCIS, 2020a, 2020b). Individuals who meet the criteria for these categories may apply for a green card, but their applications are processed according to the visa bulletin established by the DOS. Applications are based on country of origin and there are a limited number available per category each year. For example, if someone falls into the F1 category and their home country is Mexico, in 2020, the USCIS is currently processing applications that were submitted in December 1997 (U.S. Department of State, 2020). However, if one falls in the same F1 category but originates from China, India, or any other country (except Mexico or the Philippines) the USCIS is processing applications from August 2014. This illustrates the reality of a severe backlog that makes the option of family-based, legal immigration virtually impossible for many people, depending on their country of origin. A similar visa bulletin exists for processing employment-based applications. There are also annual limits set on the number of immigrants permitted visas from any one country in addition to the category and preference limits (AIC, 2019b). Nonimmigrant visas, such as student and tourist visas, do not have a numerical limit and are only subject to the criteria for the respective visa type.

Several other forms of immigration relief, identified in Table 9.1, offer pathways to legal permanent residency and citizenship for immigrants who meet extensive criteria. However, the number of visas available for different forms of relief have been severely restricted, in some cases to almost none in recent years, and they are also subject to increasing backlog due to a shortage of resources allocated to process applications.

In addition to these humanitarian forms of immigration relief, another form of relief is known as Cancelation of Removal for Non-Permanent Residents. This offers some immigrants faced with immigration enforcement the option to obtain permanent residence if they have lived in the U.S. for at least 10 years and have a parent, spouse, or child who is a legal resident or citizen who would suffer hardship if they were deported. To qualify, an individual must also have had good moral character for 10 years and must not have been convicted of certain offenses. There is a limit of 4,000 cancellations of removal per year (U.S. Congress, 1996).

Another important form of immigration relief is the DACA program. Created in 2012 by the Obama administration, it has enabled over 650,000 young immigrants who were brought to the U.S. as children by their parents (also known as "DREAMers") to obtain temporary work authorization and reprieve from deportation. However, in recent years, the program and its recipients have faced ongoing threats. In September 2017, under the Trump administration, the DHS announced the recission of the DACA program, resulting in multiple lawsuits. In June 2020, the Supreme Court overturned the recission on the grounds that it was improperly rescinded. DHS responded in July 28, 2020, with a memorandum limiting the availability of DACA (National Immigration Law Center [NILC], 2020). This memorandum instructed the USCIS to (1) reject any first-time DACA applications; (2) reject applications for advance parole from DACA recipients except in exceptional circumstances; and (3) continue processing DACA renewals but shorten the renewal and work authorization period from the previous two years to one year (DHS, 2020). In December 2020, a U.S. District Court in New York directed DHS to fully restore the DACA program (American Immigration Lawyers Association [AILA], 2021b). Upon taking office in January 2021, the Biden administration issued an executive order instructing the Secretary of Homeland Security to "preserve and fortify DACA" (The White House, Office of the Press Secretary [WH OPS], 2021). The Biden administration has also prioritized DREAMers and DACA recipients in proposed immigration reform legislation known as the U.S. Citizenship Act (2021), which would provide them the ability to immediately adjust to LPR status and offer a streamlined, three-year pathway to citizenship. This proposed legislation is discussed more in depth below.

# Table 9.1  Select Immigration Relief Policies

| Relief Form | Description and Purpose | Numerical Limit |
|---|---|---|
| **Asylum** | Asylum status is provided to those who can prove past persecution or fear of future persecution due to race, religion, nationality, membership in a particular social group, or political opinion.<br><br>Asylees may apply at a port of entry or within one year of arriving to the U.S. | There are no numerical limits on granting asylum cases. However, there are many restrictions and backlogs impacting the process (AIC, 2019b). |
| **Refugee** | Refugees may be admitted to the U.S. due to an inability to return to their home countries because of a "well-founded fear of persecution" based on their race, membership in a particular social group, political opinion, religion, or national origin. Refugees apply for admission from outside of the United States. | 2017: 110,000<br><br>2018: 45,000<br><br>2019: 30,000<br><br>2020: 18,000<br><br>These limits are determined by the president and Congress and are further allocated according to region (i.e., Africa, East Asia, Europe/Central Asia, Latin America/Caribbean, Near East/South Asia; AIC, 2019b). |
| **Special Immigrant Juvenile Status (SIJS)** | SIJS provides lawful permanent residency to children who are under the jurisdiction of a juvenile court and who will not be reunified with their parents due to abuse, neglect, or abandonment. | SIJS applications are subject to a quota based on category and country of origin. They fall under the employment-based fourth preference category in the visa bulletin. This category is limited to 7.1% of 140,000 employment-based preference immigrants. The categories for El Salvador, Guatemala, Honduras, and Mexico have become oversubscribed in recent years. Currently, applications from June 2018 are being accepted for Mexico and from April 2017 for the others (DOS, 2020). |
| **U Visa** | Victims of certain designated crimes (including domestic violence and sexual assault) may be eligible for a U visa. The victim must be willing to work with law enforcement to cooperate in the investigation and prosecution of the crime. | 10,000 U visas are permitted to be issued each year. The number of U visa petitions has outpaced this limit for many years, creating a long backlog (multiple years). However, once individuals are added to the U visa wait-list, they are eligible for employment authorization (AIC, 2019a). |

| Relief Form | Description and Purpose | Numerical Limit |
| --- | --- | --- |
| T Visa | Victims of human trafficking may be eligible for a T visa, allowing them to live and work temporarily in the United States, generally upon agreeing to aid in the prosecution of their traffickers. | There is a limit of 5,000 T visas per year, but this cap has never been reached (Kamhi & Prandini, 2017). |
| Violence Against Women Act (VAWA) | VAWA provides a self-petition process to protect immigrant victims married to an abuser who is a U.S. citizen or legal permanent resident and uses the victim's undocumented status to exert power and control. | There is no limit on the number of VAWA visas available (AIC, 2019a). |
| Temporary Protected Status (TPS) | TPS is for noncitizens from certain countries who have experienced natural disasters, civil wars, or other destabilizing events. | TPS designations are time limited to 6, 12, or 18 months, at which point they may be extended or terminated. There is also no pathway to LPR status for TPS designees unless they are otherwise eligible. TPS designation for several countries, including Sudan, Haiti, Nicaragua, and El Salvador, were ended by the Trump administration (AIC, 2019b). |

# History of Immigration Enforcement

To some extent, legal immigration relief categories are meant to protect the most vulnerable. However, with nearly 22 million noncitizens and 11 million undocumented people residing in the U.S., apart from ineligibility for many federal benefits, many live with daily vulnerability to deportation and separation from their families and communities (U.S. Census Bureau, 2018). This modern era of immigration enforcement policies began with the Illegal Immigration Reform and Immigrant Responsibility Act (IIRIRA) of 1996.

The IIRIRA, signed into law by President Clinton, marked the beginning of a legacy of immigrant criminalization and immigration enforcement priorities that have pervaded U.S. immigration policy and practice over the last several decades. The act is divided into six main sections: (1) improvements to border control and facilitation of legal entry and interior enforcement; (2) enhanced enforcement and penalties against alien smuggling and document fraud; (3) inspection, apprehension, detention, adjudication, and removal of inadmissible and deportable aliens; (4) enforcement of restrictions against employment; (5) restrictions on benefits for aliens; and (6) miscellaneous provisions (U.S. Congress, 1996). The act authorized significant funding and expansion of immigration enforcement mechanisms at the border as well as in the interior of the U.S. (Kerwin, 2018). It expanded the number of crimes that would qualify an individual for deportation; created procedures of "expedited removals" and "reinstatement of removals," which have dramatically increased as a percentage of overall removals since IIRIRA; and expanded mandatory detention of noncitizens and asylum seekers. IIRIRA also created a three-year bar for individuals who are unlawfully present in the U.S. for 180–365 days and a 10-year bar for individuals unlawfully present for more than a year before they can pursue legal status again (Siskind Susser PC, 1996). It also introduced additional restrictions and exclusions to legal immigration processes, including additional barriers to seeking asylum (Acer & Byrne, 2017).

IIRIRA also founded the 287(g) program, which enables local law enforcement agencies to cooperate with Immigration and Customs Enforcement (ICE) and effectively deputizes local police officers as ICE agents, giving them the ability to investigate the immigration status of individuals detained in their jurisdiction (Juárez et al., 2018). By prioritizing the removal of individuals already in the U.S. and expanding the grounds for deportation, IIRIRA and the immigration enforcement practices it initiated have led to decades of family separation and restructuring, a legacy that the Trump administration continued to build upon (Abrego et al., 2017; Kerwin, 2018).

Immigration enforcement activities conducted by ICE have resulted in an unprecedented number of deportations over the past 20 years. A large increase in enforcement efforts occurred between 2005 and 2008, highlighted by several large worksite enforcement operations (Dettlaff & Finno-Velasquez, 2013). In the wake of harsh criticism by child advocates and the change in federal administration, major worksite enforcement operations mostly stopped in 2008, and ICE developed a set of humanitarian guidelines that applied to enforcement actions (DHS, 2009; Dettlaff, 2012). Those guidelines encouraged the identification and timely release of individuals who are the sole caregivers of minor children or who have other humanitarian concerns, including individuals with serious medical conditions, nursing mothers, pregnant women, or caregivers of spouses or relatives with serious medical conditions (DHS, 2009). Research found that when appropriately executed, those guidelines have been effective in preventing or minimizing parent–child separations (Chaudry et al., 2010). However, those guidelines do not apply to enforcement actions impacting small groups or individuals.

Despite the fact that worksite raids halted under the Obama administration, that administration oversaw the highest number of deportations in recent history. Between 2009 and 2013, almost half a million parents were deported from the U.S. (AIC, 2017). In fiscal year 2016 alone, almost a quarter million immigrants were deported (López & Bialik, 2017). The majority of deportations were of individuals whose home countries included Mexico, Honduras, Guatemala, and El Salvador (Lesser & Batalova, 2017). Between 2015 and 2017, the number of deportations of parents of U.S.–citizen children declined slightly from 31,411 in 2015 to 28,860 in 2016 to 27,080 in 2017 (Buiano, 2018). However, this number has started to rise again, jumping to 32,132 for 2018, the most recent available data from ICE (ICE, 2019a, 2019b). Worksite raids and deportations have significant impacts on immigrant families and children, including family economic hardship, psychological trauma to children, difficulty accessing social services because of language barriers, difficulty documenting eligibility, mistrust and fear, and family separation (Campetella et al., 2015).

These trends in increased detention and deportation have been prompted by expanded interior enforcement operations, such as fugitive operations, small worksite raids, Customs and Border Patrol traffic stops, and increased cooperation between local law enforcement and the DHS. In 2007, the ICE Agreements of Cooperation in Communities to Enhance Safety and Security initiative combined several programs as a part of a strategy prioritizing the apprehension of immigrants who have committed criminal offenses. This included the expansion of the 287(g) program, one of the most notorious of the programs that authorizes collaboration between ICE and local officials to allow local police to be deputized to enforce immigration laws. Currently, ICE has 287(g) agreements with 75 law enforcement agencies in 21 states, and ICE officers have certified over 1,800 local officers to enforce immigration law (ICE, 2020). A similar program, Secure Communities, utilizes local jails to identify immigrants for deportation by sharing Federal Bureau of Investigation fingerprint data with ICE, determining the arrested individual's immigration status. If the arrested individual is identified as a noncitizen, ICE can ask local authorities to detain that individual until ICE moves them to an immigration detention center. On the surface, these programs tout the removal of individuals who threaten public safety and national security by targeting those with an aggravated felony conviction or multiple felonies. However, in reality, Secure Communities has resulted in the deportation of thousands of immigrants without any criminal convictions or with simple misdemeanors such as driving without a license (AILA, 2011). While Secure Communities was temporarily suspended between November 2014 and January 2017, the Trump administration reactivated the program through its executive order on enhancing public safety in the interior of the U.S.

In the midst of anti-immigrant sentiment, several states have pursued their own immigration enforcement initiatives outside of these federal enforcement programs. Arizona's Senate Bill (SB) 1070 (Support our Law Enforcement and Safe Neighbors Act, 2010) imposed penalties on immigrants who failed to provide immigration documentation and enabled law enforcement officers to inquire about immigration legal status from suspected undocumented immigrants. Many states followed suit and adopted similar laws, including Utah, Georgia, Indiana, Alabama, and South Carolina, which passed SB 1070-style legislation (Lacayo, 2011). However, these laws have since been challenged in court, with the Supreme Court blocking most of their provisions (Liptak, 2012).

In spite of increasing immigration enforcement trends during the Obama administration, there were also some successful efforts to address the collateral consequences of enforcement for children. With pressure from child protection and immigrant rights groups, ICE increased its use of prosecutorial discretion to release parents in deportation cases, consequently decreasing the number of removal of parents of children legally present in the U.S. (Trevizo, 2016). In 2011, ICE announced its "sensitive locations" policy, which stipulated that ICE personnel should refrain from conducting enforcement actions at certain "sensitive locations" including churches, schools, childcare programs, hospitals, public religious ceremonies (e.g., weddings and funerals), and public demonstrations (e.g., marches and parades; ICE, 2011). One of the largest victories for children during the Obama administration was ICE's 2013 Parental Interests Directive, which aimed to create a balance between the enforcement of immigration laws and respect for a parent/guardian's rights and responsibilities as a caregiver. The Parental Interests Directive provided specific guidelines for handling cases involving primary caretakers, parents, or legal guardians of minor children, especially those involved in family court or child welfare proceedings. It encouraged better tracking of these immigration cases, taking children into account when determining detention placement locations, accounting for court participation needs, and allowing for parent–child visitation. Consequently, it also increased the ability of detained parents to make decisions for the care of their children and to participate in child welfare proceedings. While families continued to be separated by immigration enforcement, the Parental Interests Directive reduced the chances that a family would become involved with the child welfare system as a result of immigration enforcement.

Harsh border enforcement priorities were re-implemented in 2014 by the Obama administration in response to the influx of unaccompanied immigrant children fleeing to the U.S. to escape violence and persecution in their home countries (Kandel, 2017). An aggressive new deterrence strategy resulted in increased apprehensions of children and individuals seeking asylum at the U.S.–Mexico border from Mexico and other Central American countries (WH OPS, 2014). This influx led to the expansion of detention of all immigrants, including the detention of mothers and children, and an increase in the separation of children from their parents at the border (Detention Watch Network, n. d.). HHS's Office of Refugee Resettlement (ORR) became responsible for the care and placement of these thousands of unaccompanied children, facilitating their release to parents or relative sponsors while the children awaited decisions in their immigration cases. However, the ORR licensing and monitoring process for placements of unaccompanied minors is generally less stringent than the regulation and oversight required in state foster care licensing. In a majority of cases, federal protective jurisdiction over unaccompanied children ends following a brief home assessment and release to sponsors. At that point, those placements are no longer monitored. Furthermore, unaccompanied minor children do not have access to health insurance, public assistance, or other health or support services normally available to children in state foster care, leaving the placements at risk of disruption, exploitation, and maltreatment.

## Immigration Policy During the Trump Administration

Draconian policies by the Trump administration have intensified concerns for immigrant children due to family separation and immigration enforcement. Previous discretion and enforcement priorities that had safeguarded many parents were eliminated—a much larger group of immigrants became targeted for deportation. Shortly after taking office, President Trump announced two executive orders on enhancing public safety in the interior of the U.S. and border security and immigration enforcement improvements, detailing a new set of immigration enforcement priorities extending removability to anyone who has committed a chargeable offense, such as entering the country illegally (WH OPS, 2017). This placed nearly 11 million undocumented individuals and many legal permanent residents at risk of deportation and led to an increase in ICE activity in communities across the country. These orders also encouraged the furtherance of 287(g) agreements to enlist state and local law enforcement officers in the execution of federal immigration law and ordered the reinstitution of the Secure Communities program.

In 2017, the 2013 Parental Interests Directive was also replaced with the Detained Parents Directive, which significantly weakened the protections of the 2013 directive, eliminating the language of prosecutorial discretion previously applied to cases with children. In June of 2017, the Trump administration also announced that it would arrest and deport undocumented parents, guardians, and relative sponsors of unaccompanied children (Burke, 2017). Not only does this policy punish individuals who have come forward in good faith to care for unaccompanied children, but it also leaves children with fewer relative and kin options for sponsors, placing them at higher risk of disruption in placement and increased risk for entry into state foster care.

In May 2018, the Department of Justice implemented a zero-tolerance policy toward illegal border crossing that required prosecuting all adults who were apprehended while crossing the border illegally. Criminal prosecution of adults required detaining them in federal criminal facilities where children are not permitted, thus leading to the separation of thousands of children from their parents. These children were then processed as unaccompanied minors and transferred to the custody of ORR (Kandel, 2019). The Trump administration also attempted to terminate the Flores Agreement, which is a policy that set certain conditions for the detention, treatment, and release of minors, including a 20-day cap on detention. However, a federal judge ruled against this termination. In December 2018, the Migrant Protection Protocols were instituted, allowing for individuals seeking asylum in the U.S. to be returned to Mexico to await their asylum court hearing. This has resulted in between 57,000 to 62,000 asylum seekers being returned to Mexico (AIC, 2020b). Additional policies, including "metering" (a practice by which U.S. Customs and Border Protection limits the number of individuals allowed to present for asylum on a given day) and a ban on asylum for individuals who traveled through Mexico before arriving at the U.S.–Mexico border, have further restricted asylum opportunities under the Trump administration. New proposed rules in June 2020 would create even more barriers to asylum, particularly for Central Americans fleeing gang violence, women fleeing domestic violence, and lesbian, gay, bisexual, transgender, or queer (LGBTQ) individuals (Executive Office for Immigration Review & DHS, 2020).

## IMPACT OF IMMIGRATION POLICY ON CHILDREN AND FAMILIES

Research has documented how immigration enforcement activities and parental detention and deportation result in child trauma and mental health issues, increased family instability, and heightened risk for child welfare system involvement (Koball et al., 2015). U.S.–citizen children whose parents have been detained and deported experience increased levels of psychological distress, trauma, and PTSD symptoms in comparison to their peers whose parents have not been impacted by immigration enforcement (Rojas-Flores et al., 2017). These children also demonstrate higher levels of depression and anxiety, lower academic performance, and greater behavioral problems. In addition to persistent fear of immigration enforcement, children in Latinx immigrant families also experience negative outcomes related to ethnic identity challenges and stigma as well as conflation of ICE with law enforcement (Dreby, 2012).

The negative impacts of immigration enforcement can expand beyond children and impact the entire family system. One study found that spouses/partners of detained or deported individuals experienced increased feelings of depression and social isolation, which are, in turn, associated with negative cognitive and behavioral outcomes for children (Koball et al., 2015). The loss of income from a detained or deported family member not only contributes to family insecurity regarding finances, housing, and food but also to a broader lack of access to social services due to the resulting fear of coming into contact with government officials (Brabeck et al., 2016; Dreby, 2012). Immigrant parents experience acculturative stress and must navigate the loss and adaptation that come with the immigration experience—all of which is compounded by daily concerns about detection by authorities, deportation, and separation from family members in their new country. As discussed earlier in this chapter, immigrant parents are also more likely to have experienced some form of trauma (e.g., physical or sexual assault, robbery, threats, extortion, witness to murder) either in their home countries or along their migration journeys. These stressors are often compounded by predatory and discriminatory treatment in the U.S.; for example, a parent may face unfair or unsafe work conditions but may not voice their concerns due to fear of retribution. All of these stress-related factors contribute to parents' coping abilities, which impact their caregiving capacities. The many burdens of immigration enforcement, including financial distress, stressful events, and social isolation, may contribute to child maltreatment and involvement with the child welfare system (Dettlaff & Finno-Velasquez, 2013). The grimmest repercussions are parents losing the right to be parents to their children.

Although child-serving systems do not have the mechanisms to systematically track families who have interacted with the immigration system, experts remain concerned that this problem is likely to grow as a result of increasingly harsh and punitive immigration enforcement policies. In fact, some legal scholars assert that immigration law operates to intentionally hinder family unity and ignores the best interests of children, going against core child welfare principles (Morrison & Thronson, 2010). For example, parental immigration status is sometimes used as a basis for terminating parental rights in child welfare cases by arguing that parents' undocumented status will create instability for the child. Family courts are rarely equipped to address the complex issues impacting mixed-status families, and courts have historically discriminated against undocumented immigrant parents (Rogerson, 2013). This discrimination can also extend to undocumented family members when fear of deportation hinders them from coming forward to act as kin caregivers. In the worst scenarios, when parents are deported, their children may either become exiles, forced to leave with their parents to another country that they often have never known, or orphans, forced to remain in the care of others in the U.S. or in the child welfare system.

# APPROACHES TO SUPPORT RESILIENCE AMONG IMMIGRANTS

Despite multiple layers of discrimination in U.S. immigration policy, immigrants have demonstrated great resilience. They contribute roughly $2 trillion to the economy each year, with undocumented immigrant contributions making up about 2.6% of gross domestic product (i.e., the monetary value of all goods and services produced in the U.S.; Blau & Mackie, 2017; Edwards & Ortega, 2017). Immigrant workers dominate the service, construction, transportation, production, and farming labor sectors (Nunn et al., 2018). They provide greater opportunities for their children, who often become better off financially than their parents. However, as mentioned in the beginning of this chapter, acculturation to the U.S. takes its toll, as we see rising rates of health and behavioral issues, criminal behaviors, and other challenges in subsequent generations.

## Federal Policy Approaches to Promote Resilience

In order for policy to effectively serve and support immigrant children and families, it must integrate the voices of immigrants themselves. Policymakers must prioritize the well-being of children and families over institutional inertia and bureaucracy as well as the legal and economic rationales that overwhelmingly dictate policymaking (Cervantes, personal communication, 2017; Kohler & Sola-Visner, 2014). In order to work toward improving outcomes for immigrant children and families and to ensure that these outcomes are appropriate, feasible, and long-lasting, policy and social change must be driven and informed by the voices of those impacted.

In the past 20 years, there have been several pushes for comprehensive immigration reform with a path to citizenship for those who have not committed serious or violent crimes as well as work authorization and access to health care and education. In 2013, legislators came close to substantial immigration reform, when the largely Democratic Senate passed a bill that included a path to citizenship for undocumented immigrants. However, this bill did not survive the Republican-led House of Representatives. After almost a decade of stagnation, the Biden administration renewed efforts to reform the U.S. immigration system with the U.S. Citizenship Act (2021), which has been introduced in both the Senate and House. Key elements of the U.S. Citizenship Act include immediate eligibility for LPR status and a three-year pathway to citizenship for DACA, TPS, and deferred enforced departure (DED) recipients and agricultural workers; an eight-year pathway to citizenship for undocumented immigrants; addressing immigration court backlog; increasing the cap on U visas and diversity visas; and other provisions to improve the family-based, employment-based, and humanitarian immigration systems and support unaccompanied children and asylum seekers.

The Development, Relief, and Education for Alien Minors (DREAM) Act was initially introduced in 2001 in an attempt to provide a pathway to citizenship for children brought to the U.S. unlawfully by their parents, known as *DREAMers*. Despite at least 10 iterations of the act since its initial introduction, it has continued to fail in garnering enough support to be enacted into law. In 2019, the Dream and Promise Act, which would provide a pathway to permanent legal status for DREAMers as well as TPS and DED beneficiaries was introduced but was also ultimately unable to obtain sufficient support. Meanwhile, the DACA program initiated by President Obama to provide protections for DREAMers underwent various threats by the Trump administration, which ended the program in 2017. Litigation and actions by federal judges enabled current DACA recipients to continue renewing their status, but no new applications were being accepted. While the Supreme Court blocked the Trump administration's attempt to end the program in June 2020, the Trump administration responded with new restrictions to the program. However, in December 2020, DHS was ordered to fully restore the DACA program, and once in office, the Biden administration issued its executive order to "preserve and fortify DACA" (AILA, 2021b; WH OPS, 2021). Then on March 3, 2021, the Dream and Promise Act, which would provide a path to citizenship for DREAMers as well as TPS and DED recipients, was reintroduced in the House (AILA, 2021a).

## State Policy Approaches to Promote Resilience

In the absence of action by the federal government to address the broken U.S. immigration system and provide immigrants with a path to citizenship and integration into U.S. society, some states and local governments have responded with their own policies and community-led efforts to support their immigrant members. Many jurisdictions have adopted "sanctuary policies" in an effort to provide safety and security to all their community members, regardless of immigration status. These sanctuary policies take a variety of forms. For example, some prohibit 287(g) agreements to ensure that local law enforcement officers are not playing dual roles and enforcing federal immigration laws. Some restrict law enforcement from asking or collecting information about immigrations status or create specific protections for sensitive information. Some sanctuary policies further reiterate and enforce the sensitive locations policy to ensure that immigration enforcement does not occur in schools, hospitals, churches, and other venues. Many states have also created the ability for individuals to obtain drivers licenses regardless of immigration status. Research has found that jurisdictions with sanctuary policies are safer and have better economic outcomes than non-sanctuary jurisdictions, including lower crime, higher median income, lower poverty and unemployment levels, and less reliance on public assistance (AIC, 2017).

Some states have also taken steps toward ensuring that all their residents, regardless of immigration status, have access to health care. States have become creative in extending coverage to populations who do not otherwise qualify for federal health care coverage by broadening statutory language and utilizing state funds (Taylor, 2018). Many states have elected to provide medical coverage to lawfully residing immigrants, especially children and pregnant women, who have not yet met the five-year waiting period to qualify for federal public benefits such as Medicaid. Some states, including California, Illinois, Massachusetts, New Jersey, New York, Oregon, and the District of Columbia, have made medical coverage available to all children regardless of immigration status (NILC, 2015). Many states also make prenatal care available regardless of immigration status. In June 2019, California became the first state to decide to offer Medicaid coverage to undocumented adults. Those who are between the ages of 19 and 25 and would otherwise qualify for California Medicaid according to income are eligible (Allyn, 2019). California has also made its state Medicaid program available to DACA recipients with qualifying incomes (McConville et al., 2015). More local initiatives, such as Health San Francisco, offer medical coverage to community members who do not qualify for Medicaid or Medi-Cal, regardless of immigration status (HealthySF, 2020).

Other safety net health care options for immigrants, regardless of immigration status, include Federally Qualified Health Centers (FQHC), which include Community Health Centers and Migrant Health Centers. FQHCs receive funds from the Health Resources and Services Administration to provide primary care in underserved areas regardless of ability to pay and immigration status and thus offer one of the most feasible ways to extend medical coverage to undocumented populations in the current public and social policy landscape (Taylor, 2018).

## Community-Based Approaches to Promote Resilience

Where specific policy to support and protect immigrant children and families is absent, we see community groups and faith groups stepping up. These groups are often at the forefront, advocating for expanding access to essential rights and services to immigrants, especially those without legal status. Advocacy organizations are able to bring important issues to the attention of stakeholders and key decision makers in order to effect policy changes. Community-organizing and faith-based groups are also unique in that they empower immigrants to be able to actively participate in organizing efforts (Wood & Warren, 2002). Whether due to immigration status or fear of encountering government officials, immigrants are often cut out of the arenas where many of the policies that impact their lives are forged, making these groups an essential modality for engaging this population in social change efforts.

# RECOMMENDATIONS FOR POLICY AND PRACTICE WITH IMMIGRANTS

Immigration enforcement policies play a detrimental role in causing negative outcomes for the entire family system. As such, any efforts toward improving the lives and well-being of immigrant children and families in the U.S. must include stipulations to address our increasingly punitive immigration enforcement policies and practices and lessen their impact to families. Without major changes in this area, the children and families confronted by the intersections of our immigration, criminal justice, and child welfare systems will continue to suffer separation and irreparable harm (Hidalgo, 2013). The path to just and equitable treatment of immigrants in the U.S. requires a transition from enforcement-based, criminality-focused approaches to an equitable, humanitarian-based system centered on principles of family unity. This transition requires some critical changes in border enforcement policy and procedures: (1) timely and fair asylum processing, (2) supervised release (pending asylum decisions), (3) reconfiguring U.S. Customs and Border Protection strategies and operations, and (4) regional cooperation in migration management and in tackling root causes of migration (e.g., limited economic opportunities in less-developed nations, violence related to the distribution of illicit drugs to the U.S., and inadequate human rights protections in developing nations; Capps et al., 2019, pp. 2–3). When it comes specifically to children, advocates and experts recommend incorporating a "best interest of the child" standard into border patrol decision-making protocols, replacing or supplementing current border patrol screening protocols with specific child welfare screenings, and implementing due process protection and resources (AIC, 2015).

Some advocates call for the complete defunding of ICE (the enforcement arm of DHS) that was established and funded to combat extremist terrorism after the September 11th attacks (Hong, 2019). This call to "abolish ICE" gained popularity, especially in the wake of the Trump administration's zero-tolerance policy and family separation catastrophe. There is no central or official definition of what this would entail, and proposals span the range from completely eliminating the agency to restructuring or replacing it. Hong (2019) contends that the idea of defunding or abolishing ICE centers around defunding the Enforcement and Removal Operations branch of the agency, which primarily apprehends individuals without any criminal convictions or with minor offenses, while the Homeland Security Investigations branch is tasked with investigating criminal enterprises such as drug trafficking, spending tens of millions of taxpayer dollars annually.

At the very minimum, we should advocate for establishing more humane prosecutorial processes, increasing the number of immigration judges, and allowing greater judicial discretion over immigration cases when children are involved. It is also recommended to pursue legislation that would require immigration enforcement personnel to follow designated timelines from initial detention to making a custody determination in order to reduce the separation times between family members. Policy to ensure consistent implementation of the few protections in place for immigrant children and families (i.e., the Detained Parents Directive and Sensitive Locations Policy) is also needed, as these policies are often not enforced or executed consistently. Addressing DHS's contracts with for-profit detention centers and reforming immigration enforcement criteria to refocus on the most dangerous offenders (as opposed to all undocumented individuals in general) are other areas that require attention in order to address the complex factors and systems perpetuating our criminalized immigration system.

Even without broader changes to immigration enforcement policy, protocols and services within our immigration enforcement and detention mechanisms could be significantly improved to address the needs and interests of detained parents. For example, these systems could expand current policy to include specific protocols to screen individuals in order to identify whether they have children or are a primary caretaker in order to give all parents time to arrange for caretakers for their children at the time of arrest or detention and to ensure that culturally and linguistically appropriate information is provided to immigrants while they are detained. Culturally and linguistically appropriate services (e.g., medical, educational, family services) should be provided to immigrants while detained, which would also improve outcomes for family reunification when the child welfare system is involved. There may also be appropriate alternatives to detention for caregiving parents, particularly if detention will result in child welfare system involvement, by using parole, electronic monitoring, or family-based facilities. Immigration detention facilities should also improve their compliance with telephonic and video appearances and establish consistent procedures and protocols for parents to appear in person in court.

Collaboration among the various systems impacting children with respect to immigration enforcement is also key. Creating liaison positions within ICE regional offices to connect with service providers (e.g., social services, child welfare services, and juvenile services) and establishing communication and coordination protocols would provide essential points-of-contact and improve timeliness of response when immigration-related issues arise. Establishing relationships between service providers and local advocates and experts (e.g., low-cost legal service providers) can help support children and their family members, especially those who may be victims of crime, to explore and apply for immigration relief options. Furthermore, developing formal working relationships and agreements (i.e., Memoranda of Understanding [MOU]) between service-providing agencies, detention centers, and foreign consulates improves coordination in dealing with potential deportation and/or in ensuring that children are provided available resources for safe family reunification. Early childhood education programs are also uniquely positioned to leverage their relationships with parents in order to mitigate risks to children in immigrant and refugee families (Park et al., 2018). Policy and practice recommendations also include the implementation of universal protections of confidentiality for any collection of, access to, or sharing of data on immigrant youth or families to prevent complications with law or immigration enforcement agencies as well as the strengthening of anti-discrimination policies at the federal level and beyond.

Ongoing training is also an essential component of ensuring ethical and informed practice by the various professionals who serve immigrant children and families in varying capacities. This may include mandatory and regular trainings for judges, attorneys, guardians ad litem, domestic violence advocates, caseworkers, and social workers regarding immigration-related issues, including immigration detention and deportation proceedings and the ICE prosecutorial discretion policies, so that they are aware and informed about the various systems impacting their clients. Service providers should ensure that they are familiar with the ICE locator service to help their clients maintain contact with detained family members. Deportation officers and immigration detention facility personnel should also be educated about the unique challenges facing detained parents with children as well as the policies in place to offer them protection (e.g., Detained Parents Directive).

Child welfare and other child-serving systems also have important roles to play in addressing the needs of their immigrant constituencies. Child welfare policy should create exceptions to the termination of parental rights timeline to account for the unique challenges of detained and deported parents. California has taken important steps toward this end with SB 1064 and Assembly Bill 2015 Call for Kids Act. SB 1064 is the first in the country to address systemic problems and specific barriers that prevent family reunification for immigrant families involved with the child welfare system. It addresses and provides guidelines for reasonable efforts to facilitate reunification, extended timelines for reunification, relative placement, immigration relief, and consulate MOU—all toward protecting children impacted by immigration enforcement (Zayas & Bradlee, 2014). California's Assembly Bill 2015 Call for Kids Act requires law enforcement officers to inform detainees of their right to three free local phone calls in order to arrange for childcare to prevent children from being suddenly abandoned or left without supervision if their parents are detained. These policies provide important examples that other states and jurisdictions can replicate in order to protect family unity among their immigrant populations, especially amid the current political landscape and absence of comprehensive immigration reform. Continued research on pro- and anti-immigrant policies and their consequences as well as state-specific policy initiatives to address immigrants' needs, especially in the child welfare system, are needed in order to better assess the impact of current policies and systems and the potential for effective replication.

Several strategies could be implemented to improve the service engagement among immigrants within child- and family-serving systems at federal, state, and/or local levels. For example, to improve benefits eligibility and service access, agencies should create simple application processes and ensure eligibility for preventive services and supports regardless of immigration status, when possible. Agencies should implement firewalls to protect sensitive information and prevent information sharing with immigration enforcement officials. When appropriate, agencies may collect data addressing immigration status (contingent upon firewalls) and racial/ethnic disparities in order to target and provide adequate services for family needs. Organizations can also support the implementation of best practice approaches in casework, courts, and treatment interventions by pursuing adequate funding and codification of practices in agency policy. To improve cultural competency and address disparity, agencies can implement incentives or penalties to ensure that all immigrant children and families receive linguistically appropriate translation and/or interpretation, and they can incorporate adequate cultural competency/sensitivity training into standard staff requirements.

Governmental and community-based organizations can also support immigrant families by creating safe organizational environments. Organizations can inform and assist families in creating safety or contingency plans and outlining the family's plan in the event of detention or deportation, including power of attorney and caregiving plans. Organizations can further promote safe environments by ensuring that all personnel are familiar with the ICE sensitive locations policy and other internal safety procedures; placing signs and banners in multiple languages in agency buildings announcing and explaining agency policies; and distributing cards explaining the agency policies and related "Know Your Rights" information to parents, children, and agency staff. Collaboration with trusted community partners can help organizations reach out to families/clients and provide needed services. Organizations should also be aware of and incorporate ICE Sensitive Locations Policy (Policy Number: 10029.2) and Detained Parents' Directive (Policy Number 11064.2) into agency policy as well as develop clear policies on confidentiality and sharing information with immigration authorities. They should commit to ongoing policy review and development to improve responsiveness to these families. Where appropriate, agencies should have screening tools to determine eligibility for immigration relief options, such as Special Immigrant Juvenile Status, U visas, and Violence Against Women Act visas. This is also an area where collaboration with other community partners can be helpful. Organizations may also consider having specific staff members or task forces trained on immigration-related issues (e.g., immigration liaison). At the very least, agencies should ensure that all documents and forms are language-accessible to clients.

## CONCLUSION

As this chapter illustrates, policies impacting immigrants in the U.S. are some of the most discriminatory against a specific population of people, reflective of a culture of moral superiority, white supremacy, and xenophobia that continues to pervade social policy and political rhetoric. Exclusionary, punitive, and inhumane immigration policies will undoubtedly have negative impacts on child and family well-being for generations to come. Nevertheless, immigrants to the U.S. persist in establishing thriving communities, running successful businesses, educating their children, and becoming productive members of U.S. society. The path to justice and equity for immigrants is multifaceted and requires fundamental reform from an enforcement-based, crime-and-punishment system to a humanitarian one that recognizes the contributions of immigrants to the U.S. economy and social fabric and that values the lives of children and families.

## REFERENCES

Abdullah, T., & Brown, T. L. (2011). Mental illness stigma and ethnocultural beliefs, values, and norms: An integrative review. *Clinical Psychology Review, 31*(6), 934–948.

Abrego, L., Coleman, M., Martínez, D. E., Menjívar, C., & Slack, J. (2017). Making immigrants into criminals: Legal processes of criminalization in the post-IIRIRA era. *Journal on Migration and Human Security, 5*(3), 694–715.

Acer, E., & Byrne, O. (2017). How the Illegal Immigration Reform and Immigrant Responsibility Act of 1996 has undermined US refugee protection obligations and wasted government resources. *Journal on Migration and Human Security, 5*(2), 356–378.

Alegría, M., Sribney, W., Woo, M., Torres, M., & Guarnaccia, P. (2007). Looking beyond nativity: The relation of age of immigration, length of residence, and birth cohorts to the risk of onset of psychiatric disorders for Latinos. *Research in Human Development, 4*(1), 19–47.

Allyn, B. (2019). California is 1st state to offer health benefits to adult undocumented immigrants. *NPR.* https://www.npr.org/2019/07/10/740147546/california-first-state-to-offer-health-benefits-to-adult-undocumented-immigrants

American Immigration Council (AIC). (2015). *A guide to children arriving at the border: Laws, policies and responses.* https://www.americanimmigrationcouncil.org/research/guide-children-arriving-border-laws-policies-and-responses

American Immigration Council (AIC). (2016). *Public education for immigrant students: Understanding Plyler v. Doe.* https://www.americanimmigrationcouncil.org/research/plyler-v-doe-public-education-immigrant-students

American Immigration Council (AIC). (2017). *Sanctuary policies: An overview.* https://www.americanimmigrationcouncil.org/research/sanctuary-policies-overview

American Immigration Council (AIC). (2019a). *Fact sheet: Violence Against Women Act (VAWA) provides protections for immigrant women and victims of crime.* https://www.americanimmigrationcouncil.org/research/violence-against-women-act-vawa-immigration

American Immigration Council (AIC). (2019b). *How the United States immigration system works.* https://www.americanimmigrationcouncil.org/research/how-united-states-immigration-system-works

American Immigration Council (AIC). (2020a). *An overview of U.S. refugee law and policy.* http://www.americanimmigrationcouncil.org/research/overview-us-refugee-law-and-policy

American Immigration Council (AIC). (2020b). *Policies affecting asylum seekers at the border the Migrant Protection Protocols, prompt asylum claim review, humanitarian asylum review process, metering, asylum transit ban, and how they interact.* https://www.americanimmigrationcouncil.org/research/policies-affecting-asylum-seekers-border

American Immigration Lawyers Association (AILA). (2011). *In abrupt shift, ICE announces Secure Communities to be imposed on states* [Press release]. https://www.aila.org/advo-media/press-releases/2011/ice-announces-secure-communities-imposed-on-states

American Immigration Lawyers Association (AILA). (2021a). *House bill: American dream and promise act of 2021.* https://www.aila.org/infonet/house-bill-american-dream-and-promise-act-of-2021

American Immigration Lawyers Association (AILA). (2021b). *Practice alert: President Biden protects DACA.* https://www.aila.org/advo-media/aila-practice-pointers-and-alerts/aila-practice-alert-filing-daca-renewal

Artiga, S., & Diaz, M. (2019, July 15). Health coverage and care of undocumented immigrants. *Kaiser Family Foundation.* https://www.kff.org/disparities-policy/issue-brief/health-coverage-and-care-of-undocumented-immigrants/

Assistant Secretary for Planning and Evaluation. (2016). *The Personal Responsibility and Work Opportunity Reconciliation Act of 1996.* U.S. Department of Health and Human Services. aspe.hhs.gov/report/personal-responsibility-and-work-opportunity-reconciliation-act-1996.

Batalova, J., Blizzard, B., & Bolter, J. (2020, February 14). *Frequently requested statistics on immigrants and immigration in the United States.* Migration Policy Institute. https://www.migrationpolicy.org/article/frequently-requested-statistics-immigrants-and-immigration-united-states

Blau, F. D., & Mackie, C. (2017). *The economic and fiscal consequences of immigration.* National Academies Press.

Blumenthal D., Abrams M., & Nuzum, R. (2015). The Affordable Care Act at 5 years. *Massachusetts Medical Society, 372,* 2451–2458.

Bolter, J. (2019). Explainer: Who is an immigrant? *Migration Policy Institute.* https://www.migrationpolicy.org/content/explainer-who-immigrant

Brabeck, K., Lykes, M. B., & Hunter, C. (2015). The psychosocial impact of detention and deportation on U.S. migrant children and families. *American Journal of Orthopsychiatry, 84*(5), 496–505

Brabeck, K. M., Sibley, E., & Lykes, M. B. (2016). Authorized and unauthorized immigrant parents: The impact of legal vulnerability on family contexts. *Hispanic Journal of Behavioral Sciences*, *38*, 3–30.

Broder, T., Moussavian, A., & Blazer, J. (2015, December). Overview of immigrant eligibility for federal programs. *National Immigration Law Center*. https://www.nilc.org/issues/economic-support/overview-immeligfedp

Buiano, M. (2018). ICE data: Tens of thousands of deported parents have US citizen kids. *Center for Public Integrity*. https://publicintegrity.org/inequality-poverty-opportunity/immigration/ice-data-tens-of-thousands-of-deported-parents-have-u-s-citizen-kids/

Burke, G. (2017, June 30). *Feds will now target relatives who smuggled in children.* The Associated Press website https://apnews.com/291d565801984005886f5a22c800fee6/Feds-will-now-target-re

Bustamante, A. V., Chen, J., McKenna, R. M., & Ortega, A. N. (2019). Health care access and utilization among US immigrants before and after the Affordable Care Act. *Journal of Immigrant and Minority Health*, *21*(2), 211–218.

Campetella, A., Capps, R., Hooker, S., Koball, H., Pedroza, J. M., & Perreira, K. (2015). Research report: Implications of immigration enforcement activities for the well-being of children in immigrant families. *Migration Policy Institute and Urban Institute*. https://www.urban.org/sites/default/files/alfresco/publication-exhibits/2000405/2000405-Implications-of-Immigration-Enforcement-Activities-for-the-Well-Being-of-Children-in-Immigrant-Families.pdf

Capps, R., Meissner, D., Soto, A. G. R., Bolter, J., & Pierce, S. (2019). *From control to crisis: Changing trends and policies reshaping US–Mexico border enforcement.* Migration Policy Institute.

Cardoso, J. B. (2018). Running to stand still: Trauma symptoms, coping strategies, and substance use behaviors in unaccompanied migrant youth. *Children and Youth Services Review*, *92*, 143–152.

Carlson, B. E., Cacciatore, J., & Klimek, B. (2012). A risk and resilience perspective on unaccompanied refugee minors. *Social Work*, *57*(3), 259–269.

Carrasquillo, O., Carrasquillo, A. I., & Shea, S. (2000). Health insurance coverage of immigrants living in the United States: Differences by citizenship status and country of origin. *American Journal of Public Health*, *90*(6), 917–923.

Chang, C. D. (2019). Social determinants of health and health disparities among immigrants and their children. *Current Problems in Pediatric and Adolescent Health Care*, *49*(1), 23–30.

Chaudry, A., Capps, R., Pedroza, J. M., Castañeda, R. M., Santos, R., & Scott, M. M. (2010). Facing our future: Children in the aftermath of immigration enforcement. *Urban Institute*.

Chen, J., & Vargas-Bustamante, A. (2011). Estimating the effects of immigration status on mental health care utilization in the United States. *Journal of Immigrant and Minority Health*, *13*(4), 671–680.

Chishti, M., & Bolter, J. (2020). Vulnerable to COVID-19 and in frontline jobs, immigrants are mostly shut out of U.S. relief. *Migration Policy Institute*. https://www.migrationpolicy.org/article/covid19-immigrants-shut-out-federal-relief

Chishti, M., & Hipsman, F. (2016, February 18). Increased Central American migration to the United States may prove an enduring phenomenon. *Migration Policy Institute*. https://www.migrationpolicy.org/article/increased-central-american-migration-united-states-may-prove-enduring-phenomenon

Cole, N. L. (2019). *Understanding acculturation and why it happens.* https://www.thoughtco.com/acculturation-definition-3026039

de Genova, N., & Peutz, N. (2010). *The deportation regime.* Duke University Press.

DeLuca, L. A., McEwen, M. M., & Keim, S. M. (2010). United States–Mexico border crossing: Experiences and risk perceptions of undocumented male immigrants. *Journal of Immigrant and Minority Health*, *12*(1), 113.

Delva, J., Horner, P., Sanders, L., Lopez, W., & Doering-White, J. (2013). Mental health problems of children of undocumented parents in the United States: A hidden crisis. *Journal of Community Positive Practices*, *XIII*(3), 25–35.

Derluyn, I., & Broekaert, E. (2008). Unaccompanied refugee children and adolescents: The glaring contrast between a legal and a psychological perspective. *International Journal of Law and Psychiatry*, *31*(4), 319–30.

Derr, S. A. (2016). Mental health service use among immigrants in the United States: A systematic review. *Psychiatric Services, 67*(3), 265–274.

Detention Watch Network. (n. d.). *Family detention.* https://www.detentionwatchnetwork.org/issues/family-detention

Dettlaff, A. J. (2012). Immigrant children and families and the public child welfare system: Considerations for legal systems. *Juvenile and Family Court Journal, 63*(1), 19–30.

Dettlaff, A. J., & Finno-Velasquez, M. (2013). Child maltreatment and immigration enforcement: Considerations for child welfare and legal systems working with immigrant families. *Children's Legal Rights Journal, 33,* 37–63.

Divi, C., Koss, R. G., Schmaltz, S. P., & Loeb, J. M. (2007). Language proficiency and adverse events in U.S. hospitals: A pilot study. *International Journal of Quality in Health Care, 19,* 60–67.

Dreby, J. (2012). The burden of deportation on children in Mexican immigrant families. *Journal of Marriage and Family, 74*(4), 829–845.

Dreby, J. (2015). *Everyday illegal: When policies undermine immigrant families.* University of California Press.

Earner, I. (2010). Double risk: Immigrant mothers, domestic violence and public child welfare services in New York City. *Evaluation and Program Planning, 33,* 288–293.

Edwards, R., & Ortega, F. (2017). The economic contribution of unauthorized workers: An industry analysis. *Regional Science and Urban Economics, 67,* 119–134.

Eikenberry, D. (2017, June). Proposed policies target children for deportation. *National Immigrant Justice Center.* https://immigrantjustice.org/sites/default/files/content-type/research-item/documents/2017-06/NIJC-brief_Trumpadminpolicies_June2017-FINAL2.pdf

Executive Office for Immigration Review & the Department of Homeland Security. (2020, June). Procedures for asylum and withholding of removal; credible fear and reasonable fear review. *Federal Register.* https://www.federalregister.gov/documents/2020/06/15/2020-12575/procedures-for-asylum-and-withholding-of-removal-credible-fear-and-reasonable-fear-review

Felitti, V. J., Anda, R. F., Nordenberg, D., Williamson, D. F., Spitz, A. M., Edwards, V., & Marks, J. S. (1998). Relationship of childhood abuse and household dysfunction to many of the leading causes of death in adults: The Adverse Childhood Experiences (ACE) Study. *American Journal of Preventive Medicine, 14*(4), 245–258.

Fix, M. E., & Passel, J. (2002). The scope and impact of welfare reform's immigrant provisions. *Urban Institute.* http://webarchive.urban.org/publications/410412.html

Flores, Y. G. (2013). *Chicana and chicano mental health: Alma, mente y corazón.* University of Arizona Press.

Franzini, L., Ribble, J. C., & Keddie, A. M. (2001). Understanding the Hispanic paradox. *Ethnicity & Disease, 11*(3), 496–518.

Garcia, A., Aisenberg, E., & Harachi, T. (2012). Pathways to service inequalities among Latinos in the child welfare system. *Children and Youth Services Review, 34*(5), 1060–1071.

Gelatt, J., & Koball, H. (2014). Immigrant access to health and human services. *Urban Institute.* http://www.urban.org/sites/default/files/publication/33551/2000012-Immigrant-Access-to-Health-and-Human-Services.pdf

Geneva Declaration Secretariat. (2015). Lethal violence against women and girls. In *Global burden of armed violence 2015: Every body counts.* http://www.genevadeclaration.org/measurability/global-burden-of-armed-violence/global-burden-of-armed-violence-2015.html

Gushulak, B. D., Pottie, K., Hatcher R. J., Torres, S., & DesMeules, M. (2011). Migration and health in Canada: Health in the global village. *CMAJ, 183*(12), E952–8.

Hansen, M. C., & Cabassa, L. J. (2012). Pathways to depression care: Help-seeking experiences of low-income Latinos with diabetes and depression. *Journal of Immigrant and Minority Health, 14*(6), 1097–1106.

HealthySF. (2020). Are you eligible? *Healthy San Francisco.* https://healthysanfrancisco.org/visitors/are-you-eligible/

Held, M. L., Allmang, S., Galarza, J., Scott, J., & De La Rosa, I. A. (2018). Why do people Migrate? The context of migration from Central America and Mexico to the United States. *Center on Immigration and Child Welfare.* https://cimmcw.org/wp-content/uploads/Migration-Reasons_Research-Brief-1.pdf

Hidalgo, R. (2013). Crossroads: The intersection of immigrant enforcement and the child welfare system. *Juvenile and Family Court Journal, 64* (4), 35–44.

Hong, K. E. (2019). 10 reasons why congress should defund ICE's deportation force. *NYU Review of Law & Social Change Harbinger, 43.*

Infante, C., Idrovo, A. J., Sánchez-Domínguez, M. S., Vinhas, S., & González-Vázquez, T. (2012). Violence committed against migrants in transit: Experiences on the Northern Mexican border. *Journal of Immigrant and Minority Health*, *14*(3), 449–459.

Jang, Y., Chiriboga, D. A., & Okazaki, S. (2009). Attitudes toward mental health services: Age-group differences in Korean American adults. *Aging and Mental Health*, *13*(1), 127–134.

Juang, L., Simpson, J., Lee, R., Rothman, A., Titzmann, P., Schachner, M., Korn, L., Heinemeier, D., & Betsch, C. (2018). Using attachment and relational perspectives to understand adaptation and resilience among immigrant and refugee youth. *American Psychologist*, *73*(6), 797–811.

Juárez, M., Gómez-Aguiñaga, B., & Bettez, S. P. (2018). Twenty years after IIRIRA: The rise of immigrant detention and its effects on Latinx communities across the nation. *Journal on Migration and Human Security*, *6*(1), 74–96.

Kaiser Family Foundation. (2020a). *Medicaid/CHIP coverage of lawfully residing immigrant children and pregnant women*. Author. https://www.kff.org/health-reform/state-indicator/medicaid-chip-coverage-of-lawfully-residing-immigrant-children-and-pregnant-women/?current Timeframe=0&sortModel=%7B%22colId%22:%22Lo cation%22,%22sort%22:%22asc%22%7D

Kaiser Family Foundation. (2020b, March 18). *Health coverage of immigrants*. Author. https://www.kff.org/racial-equity-and-health-policy/fact-sheet/health-cover age-of-immigrants/

Kaiser Family Foundation. (2020c, August 5). *Status of state Medicaid expansion decision: Interactive map*. Author. https://www.kff.org/medicaid/issue-brief/status-of-state-medic aid-expansion-decisions-interactive-map/

Kalil, A., & Chen, J. (2008). Family citizenship status and food insecurity among low-income children of immigrants. *New Directions in Child and Adolescent Development*, *121*, 43–62.

Kalil, A., & Crosnoe, R. (2009). Two generations of educational progress in Latin American immigrant families in the United States. In E. Grigorenko & R. Takanishi (Eds.), *Immigration, diversity, and education* (pp. 188–204). Routledge.

Kaltman, S., Hurtado de Mendoza, A., Gonzalez, F. A., & Serrano, A. (2014). Preferences for trauma-related mental health services among Latina immigrants from Central America. South America, and Mexico. *Psychological Trauma: Theory, Research, and Practice*, *6*(1), 83–91.

Kamhi, A., & Prandini, R. (2017). T-visas: What they are and how they can help your clients. *Immigrant Legal Resource Center*. https://www.ilrc.org/sites/default/files/resources/t_visa_advisory-20170509.pdf

Kandel, W. A. (2017, January 18). Unaccompanied alien children: An overview (CRS Report No. R43599). *Congressional Research Services*. https://www.every-crsreport.com/files/20170118_R43599_9badd1b2c-964c6418e27f824f0d2435f5b679156.pdf

Kandel, W. A. (2019, October 9). Unaccompanied alien children: An overview (CRS Report No. R43599). *Congressional Research Services*. https://fas.org/sgp/crs/homesec/R43599.pdf

Keller, A., Joscelyne, A., Granski, M., & Rosenfeld, B. (2017). Pre-migration trauma exposure and mental health functioning among Central American migrants arriving at the US border. *PLoS One*, *12*(1), e0168692.

Kennedy, S., Kidd, M. P., McDonald, J. T., & Biddle, N. (2015). The healthy immigrant effect: Patterns and evidence from four countries. *Journal of International Migration and Integration*, *16*(2), 317–332.

Kerwin, D. (2018). From IIRIRA to Trump: Connecting the dots to the current us immigration policy crisis. *Journal on Migration and Human Security*, *6*(3), 192–204.

Kishi, K. (2017). Most refugees who enter the U.S. as religious minorities are Christians. *Pew Research Center*. https://www.pewresearch.org/fact-tank/2017/02/07most-refugees-who-enter-the-u-s-as-religious-minorities-are-christians/

Koball, H., Capps, R., Hooker, S., Perreira, K., Campetella, A., Pedroza, J. M., Monson, W., & Huerta, S. (2015). Health and social service needs of U.S. citizen children with detained or deported immigrant parents. *Migration Policy Institute*. http://www.migrationpolicy.org/research/health-and-socialservice-needs-us-citizen-children-de tained-or-deported-immigrant-parents

Kohler, J. R., & Sola-Visner, M. (2014). The silent crisis: Children hurt by current immigration enforcement policies. *Journal of American Medical Association*, *168*(2), 103–104.

Kohli, R., & Mather, R. (2003). Promoting psychosocial well-being in unaccompanied asylum-seeking young people in the United Kingdom. *Child and Family Social Work*, *8*, 201–212.

Kris, K., & Skivenes, M. (2012). How child welfare workers perceive their work with undocumented immigrant families: An explorative study of challenges and coping strategies. *Children and Youth Services Review, 34*, 790–979.

Lacayo, E. (2011). *One year later: A look at SB 1070 and copycat legislation*. National Council of La Raza. http://publications.unidosus.org/handle/123456789/666

Lee, S., & Matejkowski, J. (2011). Mental health service utilization among noncitizens in the United States: Findings from the National Latino and Asian American Study. *Administration and Policy in Mental Health, 39*(5), 406–418.

Lesser, G., & Batalova, J. (2017). *Central American immigrants in the United States*. http://www.migrationpolicy.org/article/central-american-immigrants-united-states

Leung, P., Cheung, M., & Tsui, V. (2012). Help-seeking behaviors among Chinese Americans with depressive symptoms. *Social Work, 57*(1), 61–71.

Liptak, A. (2012, June 25). Blocking parts of Arizona law, justices allow its centerpiece. *New York Times*. https://www.nytimes.com/2012/06/26/us/supreme-court-rejects-part-of-arizonaimmigration-law.html

López, G., & Bialik, K. (2017, May 3). Key findings about U.S. immigrants. *Pew Research Center*. http://www.pewresearch.org/facttank/2017/05/03/key-findings-about-u-s-immigrants/

Luque, J. S., Soulen, G., Davila, C. B., & Cartmell, K. (2018). Access to health care for uninsured Latina immigrants in South Carolina. *BMC Health Services Research, 18*(1), 310.

Lynch, L. E., Burwell, S. M., & Castro, J. (2016). *Joint letter from HUD, HSS, and DOJ on immigrant access to shelter and transitional housing*. U.S. Department of Justice, U.S. Department of Health and Human Services, U.S. Department of Housing and Urban Development. http://niwaplibrary.wcl.american.edu/wp-content/uploads/Joint-Letter-from-HUD-HHS-ad-DOJ-on-Immigrant-Access-to-Shelter-and-Transitional-Housing-Aug-2016.pdf

Marks, A. K., Ejesi, K., & Coll, C. G. (2014). Understanding the U.S. immigrant paradox in childhood and adolescence. *Child Development Perspectives 8*(2), 59–64.

Masten, A. S. (2014). *Ordinary magic: Resilience in development*. Guilford Press.

Masten, A. S., Motti-Stefanidi, F., & Rahl-Brigman, H. A. (2019). Developmental risk and resilience in the context of devastation and forced migration. In R. D. Parke & G. H. Elder Jr. (Eds.), *Children in changing worlds: Sociocultural and temporal perspectives* (pp. 84–111). Cambridge University Press.

McCarty, M., & Siskin, A. (2015, December 8). Immigration: Noncitizen eligibility for needs-based housing programs. *Congressional Research Services*. https://fas.org/sgp/crs/homesec/RL31753.pdf

McConville, S., Hill, L., Ugo, I., & Hayes, J. (2015). Health coverage and care for undocumented immigrants. *Public Policy Institute of California*. https://www.ppic.org/publication/health-coverage-and-care-for-undocumented-immigrants/#:~:text=Undocumented%20immigrants%20are%20currently%20not,women%20and%20limited%20other%20services

Mehta, N. K., & Elo, I. T. (2012). Migrant selection and the health of U.S. immigrants from the former Soviet Union. *Demography. 49*(2), 425–47.

Mendoza, F. S., & Festa, N. K. (2013). New American Children. *Journal of the American Medical Association, 167*(1), 12–13.

Menjívar, C., & Cervantes, A. G. (2016). The effect of parental undocumented status on families and children. *American Psychological Association*. http://www.apa.org/pi/families/resources/newsletter/2016/11/undocumented-status.aspx

Morrison, A. D., & Thronson, D. B. (2010). Beyond status: Seeing the whole child. *Evaluation and Program Planning, 33*, 281–287.

Nadeem, E., Lange, J. M., & Miranda, J. (2009). Perceived need for care among low-income immigrant and U.S.–born black and Latina women with depression. *Journal of Women's Health, 18*(3), 369–375.

National Alliance of State and Territorial AIDs Directors. (2014). Health reform issue brief: Immigrants and the Affordable Care Act. *The Center for HIV Law and Policy*. https://www.hivlawandpolicy.org/sites/default/files/Health%20Reform%20Issue%20Brief%20-%20Immigrants%20and%20the%20ACA%20%28NASTAD%29.pdf

National Center for Homeless Education. (2017, December). *Supporting the education of immigrant students experiencing homelessness*. https://nche.ed.gov/wp-content/uploads/2018/10/imm_lia.pdf

National Coalition for the Homeless. (2006). *McKinney-Vento Act*. https://www.nationalhomeless.org/publications/facts/McKinney.pdf

National Immigration Law Center (NILC). (2015). *Medical assistance programs for immigrants in various states*. https://www.nilc.org/wp-content/uploads/2015/11/med-services-for-imms-in-states.pdf

National Immigration Law Center (NILC). (2020). *DACA*. https://www.nilc.org/issues/daca/

Nowak, M. (2012). *Femicide: A global problem*. Small Arms Survey.

Nunn, R., O'Donnell, J., & Shambaugh, J. (2018). *A dozen facts about immigration*. The Hamilton Project. https://www.brookings.edu/wp-content/uploads/2018/10/ImmigrationFacts_Web_1008_540pm.pdf

O'Mahony, J. M., & Donnelly, T. T. (2007). The influence of culture on immigrant women's mental health care experiences from the perspectives of health care providers. *Issues in Mental Health Nursing, 28*(5), 453–471.

Ornelas, I. J., & Perreira, K. M. (2011). The role of migration in the development of depressive symptoms among Latino immigrant parents in the U.S. *Social Science & Medicine, 73*(8), 1169–1177.

Ortega, A. N., Horwitz, S. M., Fang, H., Kuo, A. A., Wallace, S. P., & Inkelas, M. (2009). Documentation status and parental concerns about development in young U.S. children of Mexican origin. *Academic Pediatrics, 9*(4), 278–282.

Padilla, A. M., & Perez, W. (2003). Acculturation, social identity, and social cognition: A new perspective. *Hispanic Journal of Behavioral Sciences, 25*(1), 35–55.

Park, M., Katsiaficas, C., & McHugh, M. (2018). *Responding to the ECEC needs of children of refugees and asylum seekers in Europe and North America*. Migration Policy Institute.

Perreira, K. M., Crosnoe, R., Fortuny, K., Pedroza, J. M., Ulvestad, K., Weiland, C., Yoshikawa, H., & Chaudry, A. (2012). Barriers to immigrants' access to health and human services programs. *Urban Institute*. http://www.urban.org/publications/413260.html

Perreira, K. M., & Ornelas, I. (2013). Painful passages: Traumatic experiences and post-traumatic stress among immigrant Latino adolescents and their primary caregivers. *The International Migration Review, 47*(4), 976–1005.

Perreira, K. M., & Pedroza, J. M. (2019). Policies of exclusion: Implications for the health of immigrants and their children. *Annual Review of Public Health, 40*, 147–166.

Pumariega, A. J., & Rothe, E. (2010). Leaving no children or families outside: The challenges of immigration. *American Journal of Orthopsychiatry, 80*(4), 505–515.

Quinn, E., & Kinoshita, S. (2020). An overview of public charge and benefits. *Immigrant Legal Resource Center*. https://www.ilrc.org/sites/default/files/resources/overview_of_public_charge_and_benefits-march2020-v3.pdf

Rajendran, K., & Chemtob, C. M. (2010). Factors associated with service use among immigrants in the child welfare system. *Evaluation and Planning, 33*, 317–323.

Rogerson, S. (2013). Lack of detained parents' access to the family justice system and the unjust severance of the parent–child relationship. *Family Law Quarterly, 47*(2), 141–172.

Rojas-Flores, L., Clements, M. L., Hwang Koo, J., & London, J. (2017). Trauma and psychological distress in Latino citizen children following parental detention and deportation. *Psychological Trauma: Theory, Research, Practice, and Policy, 9*(3), 352–361.

Rousseau, C., & Frounfelker, R. L. (2019). Mental health needs and services for migrants: An overview for primary care providers. *Journal of Travel Medicine, 26*(2).

Salami, B., Salma, J., & Hegadoren, K. (2018). Access and utilization of mental health services for immigrants and refugees: Perspectives of immigrant service providers. *International Journal of Mental Health in Nursing, 28*(1), 152–161.

Salas-Wright, C. P., Vaughn, M. G., Clark, T. T., Terzis, L. D., & Córdova, D. (2014). Substance use disorder among first- and second-generation immigrant adults in the United States: Evidence of an immigrant paradox? *Journal of Studies on Alcohol and Drugs 75*(6), 958–967.

Shonkoff, J. P., Garner, A. S., Siegel, B. S., Dobbins, M. I., Earls, M. F., McGuinn, L., Pascoe, J., Wood, D. L., & Committee on Early Childhood, Adoption, and Dependent Care. (2012). The lifelong effects of early childhood adversity and toxic stress. *Pediatrics, 129*(1), e232–e246.

Singh, G. K., Yu, S. M., & Kogan, M. D. (2013). Health, chronic conditions, and behavioral risk disparities among U.S. immigrant children and adolescents. *Public Health Reports, 128*(6), 463–79.

Siskind Susser PC. (1996). *IIRIRA 96—A summary of the new immigration bill*. https://www.visalaw.com/iirira-96-a-summary-of-the-new-immigration-bill/

Sorsdahl, K., Stein, D. J., Grimsrud, A., Seedat, S., Flisher, A. J., Williams, D. R., & Myer, L. (2009). Traditional healers in the treatment of common mental disorders in South Africa. *The Journal of Nervous and Mental Disease*, *197*(6), 434–441.

Speiglman, R., Castaneda, R. M., Brown, H., & Capps, R. (2013). Welfare reform's ineligible immigrant parents: Program reach and enrollment barriers. *Journal of Children and Poverty*, *19*(2), 91–106.

Squires, A. (2017). Evidence-based approaches to breaking down language barriers. *The Peer-Reviewed Journal of Clinical Excellence*, *47*(9), 34–40.

Taylor, B. A. (2018). Undocumented, untreated, unhealthy: How the expansion of FQHCs can fill the gaps of basic healthcare for undocumented immigrants. *Buffalo Human Rights Law Review*, *25*, 139–162.

Torres, K. (2017). Children of immigrants forced into the shadows. *First Focus*. https://firstfocus.org/blog/children-of-immigrants-forced-into-the-shadows

Trevizo, P. (2016, January 2). Fewer parents of US-citizen kids being deported. *Arizona Daily Star*. http://tucson.com/news/fewer-parents-of-us-citizen-kidsbeing-deported/article_e45be3ba-b66e-5017-ab9c-9e0905b35c87.html

UNICEF Child Alert. (2018). *Uprooted in Central America and Mexico: Migrant and refugee children face a vicious cycle of hardship and danger*. https://www.unicef.org/publications/files/UNICEF_Child_Alert_2018_Central_America_and_Mexico.pdf

U.S. Census Bureau. (2018). *Selected social characteristics in the United States: 2018 American Community Survey 1-Year estimates*. https://data.census.gov/cedsci/table?q=Native%20and%20Foreign%20Born&tid=ACSDP1Y2018.DP02&vintage=2018&hidePreview=true

U.S. Citizenship Act, S. 348, 117th Cong. (2021). https://www.menendez.senate.gov/imo/media/doc/USCitizenshipAct2021BillText.pdf

U.S. Citizenship and Immigration Services (USCIS). (2020a, August 4). *Green card for family preference immigrants*. https://www.uscis.gov/green-card/green-card-eligibility/green-card-for-family-preference-immigrants

U.S. Citizenship and Immigration Services (USCIS). (2020b, June 16). *Green card for immediate relatives of U.S. Citizen*. https://www.uscis.gov/green-card/green-card-eligibility/green-card-for-immediate-relatives-of-us-citizen

U.S. Congress. (1996). Illegal Immigration Reform and Immigrant Responsibility Act (IR) of 1996. *Pub. L*, 104–208. https://www.govinfo.gov/content/pkg/PLAW-104publ208/pdf/PLAW-104publ208.pdf

U.S. Customs and Border Protection. (2018). *Southwest border migration FY 2018*. https://www.cbp.gov/newsroom/stats/sw-border-migration/fy-2018

U.S. Customs and Border Protection. (2019). *Southwest border migration FY 2019*. https://www.cbp.gov/newsroom/stats/sw-border-migration/fy-2019

U.S. Department of Homeland Security (DHS). (2009). *Fact sheet: Worksite enforcement strategy*. https://www.aila.org/infonet/ice-fact-sheet-new-worksite-enforcement-strategy

U.S. Department of Homeland Security (DHS). (2020, July 28). *Reconsideration of the June 15, 2012 memorandum entitled "Exercising prosecutorial discretion with respect to individuals who came to the United States as children."* https://www.dhs.gov/sites/default/files/publications/20_0728_s1_daca-reconsideration-memo.pdf

U.S. Department of State (DOS). (2020, July 8). *Visa bulletin for August 2020*. https://travel.state.gov/content/travel/en/legal/visa-law0/visa-bulletin/2020/visa-bulletin-for-august-2020.html

U.S. Immigration and Customs Enforcement (ICE). (2011). *Enforcement actions at or focused on sensitive locations*. U.S. Department of Homeland Security. https://www.ice.gov/doclib/ero-outreach/pdf/10029.2-policy.pdf

U.S. Immigration and Customs Enforcement (ICE). (2019a). *Removal of aliens claiming U.S.–born children first half, calendar year 2018*. U.S. Department of Homeland Security. https://www.dhs.gov/sites/default/files/publications/ice_-_removal_of_aliens_claiming_u.s.-born_children_first_half_cy_2018.pdf

U.S. Immigration and Customs Enforcement (ICE). (2019b). *Removal of aliens claiming U.S.–born children second half, calendar year 2018*. U.S. Department of Homeland Security. https://www.dhs.gov/sites/default/files/publications/ice_-_removal_of_aliens_claiming_u.s.-born_children_second_half_cy_2018.pdf

U.S. Immigration and Customs Enforcement (ICE). (2020). *Delegation of immigration authority Section 287(g) Immigration and Nationality Act*. U.S. Department of Homeland Security. https://www.ice.gov/287g

Vargas, E., & Pirog, M. (2016). Mixed-status families and WIC uptake: The effects of risk of deportation on program use. *Social Science Quarterly, 97*(3), 556–574.

Villamil, C., Finno-Velasquez, M., Unger, J., & Cederbaum, J. (in press). Adverse childhood experiences among Latinx youth: Does adversity worsen across generations? *Journal of Preventive Medicine.*

Viruell-Fuentes, E. A. (2007). Beyond acculturation: Immigration, discrimination, and health research among Mexicans in the United States. *Social Science & Medicine, 65*(7), 1524–1535.

White House, Office of the Press Secretary (WH OPS). (2014, June 30). *Letter from the president—Efforts to address the humanitarian situation in the Rio Grande Valley areas of our nation's Southwest border* [Press release]. https://obamawhitehouse.archives.gov/the-pressoffice/2014/06/30/letter-president-efforts-address-humanitarian-situation-rio-grandevalle

White House, Office of the Press Secretary (WH OPS). (2017, January 25). *Executive order: Enhancing public safety in the interior of the United States* [Press release]. https://www.whitehouse.gov/the-pressoffice/2017/01/25/presidential-executive-order-enhancing-public-safety-interiorunited

White House, Office of the Press Secretary (WH OPS). (2021, January 20). *Executive order: Preserving and fortifying Deferred Action for Childhood Arrivals (DACA)* [Press release]. https://www.whitehouse.gov/briefing-room/presidential-actions/2021/01/20/preserving-and-fortifying-deferred-action-for-childhood-arrivals-daca/

Wood, R. L., & Warren, M. R. (2002). A different face of faith-based politics: Social capital and community organizing in the public arena. *International Journal of Sociology and Social Policy, 22*(11/12), 6–54.

Xu, Q., & Brabeck, K. (2012). Service utilization for Latino children in mixed-status families. *Social Work Research, 36*(3), 209–221.

Yoshikawa, H. (2011). *Immigrants raising citizens: Undocumented parents and their children.* Russell Sage Foundation.

Yoshikawa, H., Suárez-Orozco, C., & Gonzales, R. (2016). Unauthorized status and youth development in the United States: Consensus statement of the society for research on adolescence. *Journal of Research on Adolescence, 27,* 4–19.

Yoshikawa, H., Weiland, C., Ulvestad, K., Perreira, K. M., Crosnoe, R., & Chaudry, A. (2014). Improving access of low-income immigrant families to health and human services: The role of community-based organizations. *Urban Institute.* http://www.urban.org/publications/413265.html

Zayas, L. H. (2015). *Forgotten citizens: Deportation, children, and the making of American exiles and orphans.* Oxford.

Zayas, L. H., & Bradlee, M. H. (2014). *Exiling children, creating orphans: When immigration policies hurt citizens.* National Association of Social Workers.

Zimmermann, W., & Tumlin, K. (1999). Patchwork policies: State assistance for immigrants under welfare reform. *Urban Institute.* http://webarchive.urban.org/publications/309007.html

# 10

# JUVENILE JUSTICE POLICIES AND PROGRAMS

Amy Wilson, Jonathan Phillips, Melissa Villodas, Anna Parisi, and Ehren Dohler

## INTRODUCTION

### History of Juvenile Justice Policy

Descriptions of the juvenile justice system in the United States (U.S.) often begin with the creation of the first juvenile court in 1899 in Chicago, Illinois (Hess et al. 2012; Mallett & Tedor, 2018). The establishment of the court marks the beginning of the modern-day juvenile justice system, which represents the most recent—but by no means the first—justice reform initiative for young people and their families.

During the early years of the U.S., the same laws and policies were used for children and adults. This meant that when problems arose, children were placed in almshouses, indentured servitude, and jails just as adults were (Mallett & Tedor, 2018). During the middle of the 19th century, reformers began to advocate for separate treatment of children, who they saw as less morally and cognitively developed than adults. These efforts led to a reframing of juvenile delinquency as a social problem resulting from children's environments rather than a moral failure on the part of the child. This redefining of juvenile delinquency resulted in the development of several responses to delinquency in the late 19th century that focused on out-of-home placements such as reform schools, which proliferated during this time period. Unfortunately, as with many social initiatives of this time, most out-of-home placement options were underfunded, overcrowded, and mismanaged. As a result, these placements failed to live up to their promise for curbing juvenile delinquency and they resulted in children suffering high levels of abuse and living in unacceptable circumstances (Mallett & Tedor, 2018).

The development of juvenile courts grew out of reformers' focus on children as distinct from adults and more amenable to rehabilitation (Hess et al., 2012; Mallett & Tedor, 2018). As such, juvenile courts came to represent an extension of earlier efforts to remove children from systems that were created to handle adult offenders. However, these courts went further than earlier reform efforts by creating an entirely separate justice system for juveniles. The stated mission of this new system was to protect the best interest of the child, which shifted the focus of our modern-day juvenile justice system back to rehabilitation. Yet, despite their idealism and promise, juvenile courts—like all institutional structures—operate within the context of larger societal forces that shape their focus and operations. Thus, the development and operations of juvenile courts and the larger juvenile justice system in the U.S. are best understood when examined within the context that shaped them.

The development of our modern-day juvenile justice system in the U.S. can be broken into five eras, which are outlined in Table 10.1: (1) establishment of the juvenile courts, (2) confinement of juvenile delinquents, (3) juvenile justice and individuals' rights, (4) the tough-on-crime era, and (5) evidence-based practice. A brief description of each era is provided next.

## Table 10.1  History of Juvenile Justice Policy

### Prior to Juvenile Courts

| | |
|---|---|
| 1750–1850 | Almshouses, the Child Savers, and houses of refuge |
| 1847–1899 | Proliferation of training and reform schools |

### Juvenile Courts Era (1899–1920s)

| | |
|---|---|
| 1899 | The Act to Regulate the Treatment and Control of Dependent, Neglected, and Delinquent Children in Illinois establishes the first juvenile court |
| 1912 | The U.S. Children's Bureau is established as the first federal agency dedicated to the welfare of children and families. The bureau helps establish juvenile justice courts, child labor laws, and the modern child welfare system. |
| 1899–1925 | All but two states establish a juvenile court system. |

### Confinement of Juvenile Delinquents (1920s–1960s)

| | |
|---|---|
| 1935 | The Social Security Act passes, which includes funding for programs aimed at dependent, neglected, exploited, abused, and delinquent youth. |
| 1938 | The Federal Juvenile Justice Act is the first federal legislation providing special treatment for a juvenile accused of a crime. |
| 1945 | All states have established a juvenile court system. |
| 1951 | The Federal Youth Correction Act creates the Juvenile Delinquency Bureau under the auspice of the Department of Health, Education, and Welfare. |
| 1958 | *Shioutakon v. District of Columbia* establishes the right to counsel in juvenile court proceedings. |

### Juvenile Justice and Individuals' Rights (1960s–1980s)

| | |
|---|---|
| 1966–1967 | In *Kent v. United States* (*1966*) and *In re Gault* (*1967*), the Supreme Court confers a greater number of due process rights to youth. |
| 1968 | The Delinquency Prevention and Control Act and Uniform Juvenile Court Act fund and oversee preventative and rehabilitative services for youth and families. |

| Juvenile Justice and Individuals' Rights (1960s–1980s) | |
|---|---|
| 1970 | *In re Winship* requires proof beyond reasonable doubt for non-status offenses for juveniles. |
| 1974 | The Juvenile Justice and Delinquency Prevention Act (JJDPA) seeks to remove status offenders from detention facilities and requires that youth and adults be separated in correctional facilities. |
| 1974 | Creation of the Office of Juvenile Justice and Delinquency Prevention (OJJDP) under the JJDPA. The OJJDP funds and disseminates research about juvenile crime. |
| **Tough-on-Crime Era (1980s–2000s)** | |
| 1984 | *Schall v. Martin* confirms a state's right to use preventive detention. |
| 1986 | Reagan signs the Anti-Drug Abuse Act of 1986, which is foundational to the "war on drugs" and establishes mandatory minimum sentencing for some drug offenses. |
| 1988 | Amendment of JJDPA requires states to investigate disproportionate minority confinement (DMC) |
| 1992 | JJDPA reauthorization establishes grants to fund boot camps for youth and calls for an examination of gender bias in juvenile justice programming. |
| 1994 | Clinton signs the Violent Crime Control and Law Enforcement Act and the Gun-Free Schools Act, which lowers the age at which a youth could be tried as an adult, creates harsher punishments for drug crimes, and makes the possession of firearms a federal crime. |
| **Evidence-Based Practice Era (2000s–present)** | |
| 2002 | The JJDPA expands DMC to include all parts of the juvenile justice process. As a result, *DMC* comes to mean disproportionate minority *contact*. |
| 2002 | *Atkins v. Virginia* abolishes the death penalty for juveniles and adults with an intellectual impairment. |
| 2005 | *Roper v. Simmons* abolishes death penalty for all juveniles. |
| 2010 | *Graham v. Florida* establishes that juveniles cannot be sentenced to life without parole for non-homicide offenses. |
| 2012 | *Miller v. Alabama* rules that state mandatory sentencing of life without parole for youth is unconstitutional, regardless of the crime. |
| 2016 | *Montgomery v. Louisiana* requires that the *Miller* decision be applied retroactively. |
| 2018 | The latest reauthorization of the JJDPA emphasizes reducing racial and ethnic disparities throughout the juvenile justice process. |

## First Era: The Establishment of Juvenile Courts, 1899–1920s

Many social reform movements were born out of the sociopolitical landscape of the Progressive Era during the late nineteenth century. Among them were the so-called Child Savers, whose mission was to improve the treatment of delinquent youth. The Child Savers saw troubled youth not as criminals but as victims of their environment. Accordingly, the Child Savers believed that troubled youth were capable of reform and should not be held to the same standards of culpability as adults (Hess et al., 2012). This reframing of delinquency not only spurred the proliferation of reform schools and houses of refuge throughout the latter half of the 19th century but also helped establish the early juvenile courts.

The first juvenile court was established in Chicago in 1899 after the Illinois legislature passed the Act to Regulate the Treatment and Control of Dependent, Neglected, and Delinquent Children. Over the next decade, 20 states would adopt similar legislation that established juvenile courts; every state in the country had such a court by the end of World War II (Merlo et al., 2016). In addition to establishing juvenile courts generally, the 1899 Illinois legislation dictated that probation acts in both an investigative as well as restorative capacity when working with juveniles (Hess et al., 2012).

Borrowing from the paradigm of the Child Savers movement, early juvenile courts were driven by the recognition that childhood development was marked by distinct life stages (Mallett & Tedor, 2018). Accordingly, new courts sought to function as social welfare agencies, tasked with addressing the needs of youth. As a result, adolescents in the juvenile justice system came to be seen as wards of the state. Though the juvenile court was often considered more humane than the adult justice system, juveniles were not afforded many of the rights that justice-involved adults were, including indictments, pleadings, juries, rules of evidence, or written judgements during this early era (Burton, 2019; Hess et al., 2012).

Although the establishment of the juvenile courts was largely driven by state efforts, federal policy would soon follow. In 1912, the U.S. Children's Bureau was established as the first federal agency seeking to improve child and family welfare. The passage of the Social Security Act in 1935 earmarked funding that allowed the Children's Bureau to develop programs for dependent, neglected, exploited, abused, and delinquent youths (Hess et al., 2012; Merlo et al., 2016). While all but two states had established juvenile courts by 1925, the passage of the federal Juvenile Court Act in 1938 outlined the rights of juveniles accused of federal crimes (U.S. Department of Justice Archives, 2020).

The development of juvenile courts is often framed as an effort to look out for youth welfare. However, it is important to note several criticisms of this era. In his 1969 canonical text, *Child Savers: The Invention of Delinquency*, Anthony Platt suggests that the establishment of the juvenile court system represents an expansion, rather than a reformation, of the social control of middle-class Anglo norms over lower-class and immigrant families (Platt, 1969, 1977). He further asserts that the construction of the notions surrounding delinquency and juvenile justice represents a "middle-class compromise of social control and sectarian interest groups driven by concerns with crime more than by concerns with treatment" (Burton, 2019, p. 1258). Therefore, it is important to keep in mind that these early reform efforts were born out of dominant contemporary social mores and were informed, at least in part, by the eugenics movement that flourished between the late 19th and early 20th century.

## Second Era: Confinement of Juvenile Delinquents, 1920s–1960s

Despite the stated goal of education and reformation, the decades following the establishment of the early juvenile court systems saw vast increases in the institutionalization of young people. In the newly created juvenile justice system, the de facto conclusion of an adjudicated youth was most often a sentence to confinement. As a result, the number of youths placed in correctional facilities quadrupled between the 1940s and 1960s, increasing from 100,000 to 400,000 (Mallett & Tedor, 2018). Detention facilities were susceptible to the same problems that plagued many institutions for adults: underfunding, overcrowding, and substandard living conditions. The proliferation of this type of confinement, coupled with the lack of legal rights afforded to youth, created a situation in which youth were essentially imprisoned without due process (Merlo et al., 2016). Encouraged by the growing civil rights movement, the U.S. Supreme Court ruled on several key cases over the next several decades that granted youths' rights in juvenile courts and proceedings. The first of these was *Shioutakon v. District of Columbia* in 1958, which established the right to legal counsel in juvenile court proceedings (Hess et al., 2012).

## Third Era: Juvenile Justice and Individual Rights, 1960s–1980s

Whereas the progressive era viewed youth as developmentally distinct from adults and reframed delinquency as a social problem, the civil rights era focused on the lack of rights that the juvenile justice systems afforded youth. The 1960s through the 1980s is considered a pivotal time for juvenile justice policy and procedures. Hess, Orthman, and Wright (2013), in discussing earlier work by the well-known sociologist LaMar Empey, define this period in juvenile justice's history by the "four *D*s": *deinstitutionalization, diversion, decriminalization*, and *due process*. Each of these reform efforts occurred at both the state and federal levels. For example, California and New York were among the first states to separate status offenses from other delinquent categories (Hess et al., 2012). At the federal level, recommendations from a juvenile delinquency committee appointed by the Kennedy administration in 1961 sought to renew the framing of delinquency within the context of broader social problems and expand the use of diversion away from juvenile adjudication (Mallett & Tedor, 2018). In 1967, the President's Commission on Law Enforcement and Administration of Justice under Lyndon B. Johnson continued to point out the injustice, disenfranchisement, and physical and psychological damage that was inflicted upon many youths through detention and confinement (Hess et al., 2012). The notion that harsh punishments for juvenile offenders would deter crime became increasingly scrutinized; federal and local government agencies feared that a punitive juvenile justice system might compel youth into a life of crime. Increasingly, resources were allocated for preventative services and community-based alternative to institutionalization, including probation, foster care, and group homes (Hess et al., 2012; Mallett & Tedor, 2018). The establishment of federal and local youth service bureaus sought to coordinate these efforts, and additional resources were made available to support families and prevent at-risk youth from entering the juvenile justice system under the Uniform Juvenile Court Act in 1968 (Hess et al., 2012; Jenson & Howard, 1998).

Against the backdrop of the civil rights movement, the Supreme Court heard several cases that formally established due process in the juvenile justice system. For the first time, in *Kent v. United States* (1966), procedural standards were outlined for transferring adolescents to adult criminal courts. Due process rights for youth would be further codified by the Supreme Court a year later in *In re Gault*, a case involving a 15-year-old boy from Arizona who was charged and sentenced to six years in a state industrial school for making an obscene phone call. The initial court proceedings lacked several key aspects that would have been afforded in an adult court, including a complaining witness, sworn testimony, legal representation for the defendant, and an official record of the proceeding (Hess et al., 2012). The Supreme Court subsequently overruled Gault's sentence and, in the process, established that youth were to be afforded the due process rights that adults were under the Fifth and Sixth Amendments of the Constitution.

Efforts to rehabilitate delinquent youth, support youth and their families, and reform the juvenile justice system continued into the 1970s. In 1974, Congress established the Office of Juvenile Justice and Delinquency Prevention (OJJDP) through the passage of the Juvenile Justice and Delinquency Prevention Act (JJDPA; Hess et al., 2012). The JJDPA also allocated resources for states to deinstitutionalize status offenders and establish alternative diversion programs. While these efforts were successful in diverting offenders away from adjudication and into community-based alternatives, critics pointed to pre-adjudication diversion as a form of "net-widening" by police and probation departments. These diversion programs, they argued, did not adhere to the due process that was now legally required in juvenile adjudication proceedings (Hess et al., 2012). In fact, some research suggests that diversion programs encourage authorities to bring youth into the system who would have otherwise been released, thus increasing the number of justice-involved youth overall. Furthermore, the failure of youth and families to comply with diversion program requirements can lead to increases in future justice involvement (Decker, 1985; Elrod & Ryder, 2013; Mears et al., 2016).

Over the next several decades, a number of amendments and reauthorizations of the JJDPA significantly impacted the juvenile justice system. Among them was a 1980 amendment that called for the separation of youth and adults in correctional institutions; in 1988, the disproportionate minority confinement (DMC) provision was added. The DMC was among the earliest attempts to address the disproportionate representation of racial and ethnic minorities in secure confinement settings, despite such disproportionality being established decades earlier (Thornberry, 1973, 1979). The DMC provision mandated that states establish and deploy plans to address racial and ethnic disproportionality in youth confinement in order to receive federal funds under the JJDPA. Unfortunately, the potential impact of this provision was tempered by increasing concern about levels of youth crime, which was on the rise during the 1970s and was exacerbated by the lack of widely deployed alternatives to traditional punitive models (Hess et al., 2012; Mallett & Tedor, 2018). The result was a law-and-order sociopolitical landscape and policies that would come to define the tough-on-crime era (Mallett & Tedor, 2018).

## Fourth Era: Tough on Crime, 1980s–2000s

The tough-on-crime era of the 1980s and 1990s stemmed from a paradigm shift toward youth culpability and individual responsibility for crime and delinquency. This shift was driven by several social and political factors, many of which proved to be short-lived or misguided. For example, the number of youths arrested for robbery, forcible rape, aggravated assault, and homicide increased by 64% between 1985 and 1993 (Mallett & Tedor, 2018). Although these increases were relatively short-lived and would decrease drastically in the subsequent decade, this uptake in violent crimes was concerning to the communities in which they were happening—largely socioeconomically disadvantaged communities and communities of color. They caught the attention of scholars and politicians alike. John Dilulio (1995) coined and popularized the term *super predator* in response to the increase in violent crime among juveniles during this time period. Dilulio asserted that this term described a new type of offender, one that lacked respect for human life and a future orientation. Dilulio's idea of an impending generation of super predators led to dire predictions, which fueled politicians' calls for and development of a wave of punitive policies in the juvenile justice system. But the assumptions Dilulio and others were using in their predictions were erroneous and, therefore, so were their predictions. For example, while there was a sharp increase in homicides among adolescents and young adults in the late 1980s (Cook & Laub, 1998), the reality was that only 6% of all juvenile arrests were for violent crimes during this time period and less than one-tenth of 1% of these arrests were for homicide (McCord et al., 2001).

Other forces that fueled the tough-on-crime era included the "nothing works" movement, which was inspired by research by Martinson and his colleagues and cast doubt on the effectiveness of therapeutic interventions and juvenile justice policy more generally (Lipton et al., 1975; Martinson, 1974). While findings from Martinson's research were eventually proven false, they led to the development of more punitive and harmful measures and sentencing policies (Lipsey et al., 2010).

Juvenile justice scholar Barry C. Feld (2019) notes that the tough-on-crime policy shifts stemmed in part from a response to the previous civil and individual's rights era. During this time, law-and-order rhetoric was being increasingly used by conservative politicians to appeal to voters who saw civil rights protests as indicative of unrest and crime and who were averse to racial justice and integration. According to Feld, "conservatives rejected structural root-cause explanations of crime and poverty and instead attributed them to individuals' bad choices, personal character failings, and cultural shortcomings" (p. 12).

The results of tough-on-crime policies would include an era of mass incarceration in the adult justice system, increases in youth detention and transfers to adult corrections systems, the expansion of mandatory minimum sentencing in the juvenile justice systems, harsher dispositions for female juvenile offenders, and the solidification of the school-to-prison pipeline (Feld, 2019; Mallett & Tedor, 2018). By the early 1990s, most states had adopted policies that helped drive these trends.

The tough-on-crime policies mark such a dramatic departure from the previous era that Hess, Orthman, and Wright (2013) suggest the two Ds most emblematic of this period were *deterrence* and *deserts*. *Deterrence* was thought to be achieved by locking up current offenders so they could not engage in future crime. It was also seen as having the added benefit of sending a message to other youth that crimes have consequences. *Deserts* (i.e., just deserts) were based on the notion that justice was achieved not by rehabilitation but through retribution and punitive sentencing (Hess et al., 2012; Mallett & Tedor, 2018). The widespread adoption of these policies culminated into far-reaching federal legislation passed under the Clinton administration in 1994: the Violent Crime Control and Law Enforcement Act and the Gun-Free Schools Act (Mallett & Tedor, 2018). These laws lowered the age of adult prosecution to 13 for some federal offenses; provided resources to expand punitive boot camps; dramatically increased the punishment for drug possession near schools, playgrounds, and youth centers; and made the possession of firearms a federal crime (Bartollas, 2010; Mallett & Tedor, 2018).

## Fifth Era: Evidence-Based Practice, 2000s–Present

Despite the changes brought on by the tough-on-crime era, rehabilitation continued to be central to the mission of the juvenile justice system (Lipsey et al., 2010). Several factors influenced the shift back to a rehabilitative focus during the present era of evidence-based practice. First, the economic realities associated with large state deficits created incentives for states to find alternatives to incarceration for juveniles (Howell et al., 2014). Toward the end of the 1990s, it also became increasingly apparent that most young people involved in the juvenile justice system were not serious or chronic offenders and that harsh punishments as a means of *deterrents* and *deserts* generally did more harm than good (Mallett & Tedor, 2018). In a landmark study published in 1993, psychologist Terrie Moffitt made the distinction between *adolescent-limited* and *life-course persistent* antisocial behavior. According to Moffitt, the majority of delinquency is short-lived; in fact, "rates of illegal behavior soar so high during adolescence that participation in delinquency appears to be a normal part of teen life" (Moffitt, 1993, p. 675).

Additionally, researchers began using advanced analytic tools, such as meta-analytic techniques to re-examine evidence around the effectiveness of rehabilitative programs in juvenile justice settings. These analyses revealed that when implemented correctly, certain therapeutic programs demonstrated the ability to reduce delinquent behavior (Cullen, 2005; Lipsey & Cullen, 2007). This work helped to swing the pendulum back from punishment to programing. Moffitt's work called for a recontextualization of delinquency within broader developmental and social contexts and the work of Lipsey, Cullen, and others built the evidence base needed to identify practices and programs that could be used to prevent and, when needed, remediate delinquent behaviors. These efforts helped to refocus efforts in the juvenile justice system on the use of evidence-based programs (EBPs) and practices throughout the system.

Many of the efforts to engage evidence-based practices in the juvenile justice system have been led by private foundations, including the MacArthur Foundation's Models for Change Initiative and the Annie E. Casey Foundation's Juvenile Detention Alternatives Initiative (JDAI). These and other initiatives have led to the development and implementation of a number of EBPs that focus on decreasing the use of punitive measures for young offenders and increasing the use of rehabilitative approaches. (See Models for Change [http://www.modelsforchange.net/] and The Annie E. Casey Foundation Juvenile Justice site [https://www.aecf.org/work/juvenile-justice/] for more detail on these initiatives.) Citing new research on the psychological and neurocognitive development of adolescence, states have increasingly shifted resources away from detention and incarceration and into the wider adoption of community alternatives driven by EBP models (Feld, 2019; Mallett & Tedor, 2018). Over time, EBPs in the juvenile justice system expanded beyond treatment and prevention programs to include evidence-based tools that assess risks and treatment needs; disposition matrices that inform programming, placement, and supervision-level decisions and out-of-home placement; and case planning tools that use each child's risk/need profile to match them to EBPs and services (Howell et al., 2014; Lipsey et al., 2010).

Additionally, legislative trends at the state level during this time expanded due process protections for young people and increased review of a youth's ability to understand the legal process (Mallett & Tedor, 2018). Finally, state laws have been slowly raising the age at which a juvenile can be transferred to the adult courts. As of July 2020, 44 states have set the maximum juvenile court jurisdiction age at 17. Moreover, Missouri and Michigan are preparing to raise this age to 17 by 2021. The maximum age of juvenile jurisdiction is 16 in three states: Georgia, Texas, and Wisconsin, with Vermont being the first state to expand the age to 18 (Teigen, 2020).

Though many of the most impactful justice reforms took place at the state level, the federal government also took several legislative and judiciary actions during the early 2000s that helped catalyze changes in the juvenile justice system. For example, amendments to the JJDPA in 2002, and most recently in 2018, expanded the scope of disproportionate minority *confinement* (DMC) to include all steps in the juvenile justice process, including arrest, diversion, and probation. Thus, DMC became an acronym for disproportionate minority *contact* (Coalition for Juvenile Justice, 2014; Soler & Garry, 2009). The core provisions of the act today include a focus on reducing racial and ethnic disparities throughout the juvenile justice process, ensuring that juveniles awaiting trial as adults have sight and sound separation from adults, and capping the length that a status offender can be detained to seven days (Coalition for Juvenile Justice, n. d.).

Finally, the Supreme Court ruled on several important cases that recognized youth as developmentally distinct from, and therefore less culpable than, adults. In the 2002 case of *Atkins v. Virginia*, the court ruled that a developmentally delayed 15-year-old boy, Daryl Atkins, could not be sentenced to death under the Constitution's Eighth Amendment. This case set the precedent that juveniles and adults with impaired intellectual functioning lacked the impulse control and "moral culpability that characterizes the most serious adult criminal conduct" (*Atkins*, 536 U.S., 304, p. 306; Mallet & Tedor, 2018). Three years later, the Supreme Court would effectively eliminate the death penalty for all juvenile offenders in *Roper v. Simmons*, citing that lack of maturity and susceptibility to peer and other social influences diminishes a youth's culpability in the most serious crimes, including homicide (Mallet & Tedor, 2018). In the 2010 *Graham* case, the Supreme Court would apply this same reasoning in eliminating life without parole (LWOP) for juvenile offenders, except in cases of homicide. In applying language reminiscent of Moffitt, the court ruled that it was impossible "to differentiate between the juvenile offender whose crime reflects unfortunate yet transient immaturity, and the rare juvenile offender whose crime reflects irreparable corruption" (*Graham* 560 U.S. 48, p. 2026; Mallet & Tedor, 2018). Finally, the decisions of *Miller v. Alabama* (2012) and *Montgomery v. Louisiana* (2016) abolished LWOP for all juvenile offenders and ruled that this standard must be applied retroactively to all individuals who received LWOP before they were 18 years old (Mallett & Tedor, 2018).

The legislative, judiciary, and programmatic efforts implemented in the 2000s have been successful in decreasing the number of youths who become involved in the juvenile justice system. From 2000 to 2012, juvenile arrests decreased by 31% and juvenile commitments fell by 44% (Mallett & Tedor, 2018). As discussed below, juvenile justice system policies continue to show promising trends in reductions of youth adjudication and commitments. However, racial and ethnic disparities continue to persist across each step of the juvenile justice process. For example, despite promising trends in rates of juvenile adjudication and detention, the gap between White and Black youth in secure commitment increased by 15% between 2003 and 2013 (Rovner, 2016).

# AN OVERVIEW OF THE JUVENILE JUSTICE SYSTEM

In the U.S., both juvenile and adult criminal justice systems are often referred to as *unified systems*. Yet, the reality is that both systems are created and operated at the state or local level. In practical terms, this means that the U.S. has 50 different juvenile justice systems that vary in terms of their structure, content, and operations. Despite the variations that exist across states in terms of the laws that govern the operation of their juvenile justice systems, each shares a common series of decision points. The Center for Juvenile Justice (Hockenberry & Puzzanchera, 2020) has created a general framework that describes six key decision points in juvenile justice systems: (1) intake, (2) petitioning, (3) judicial waiver, (4) adjudication, (5) disposition, and (6) detention. Each is described briefly below.

*Intake* is the first point of contact with the juvenile justice system, which is referred to as *juvenile court processing* in this framework (Hockenberry & Puzzanchera, 2020). Most juveniles come to the attention of intake departments through an arrest or petition. Intake departments can be located within the juvenile court system or be operated by an entity outside of the court. Regardless of their location, the central focus of an intake department is to screen all cases referred to juvenile courts and decide whether cases should be sent on for formal processing. Intake departments also have the power to dismiss or resolve cases informally. Informal resolutions can take many forms and include options such as referral to social services, informal probation, or some type of fine, community service, or restitution.

When intake departments make a determination that a case requires formal juvenile court processing, they initiate the next step in the process by *petitioning* the juvenile court for one of two types of hearings: judicial waiver or adjudication. *Judicial waiver* hearings happen when the intake department asks the juvenile court to transfer cases to adult criminal courts. It is important to note that there are three different forms of judicial waivers (i.e., mandatory, presumptive, and discretionary), which limit the amount of discretion judges and intake departments have in making determinations of transfer. In cases where judicial waivers are granted (or mandated by law) the juvenile's case is transferred to adult criminal court for all further processing (Hockenberry & Puzzanchera, 2020).

When the juvenile's case has an *adjudication* hearing, the case remains in the juvenile court system and the judge has a number of options available at this hearing. The judge can dismiss the case or continue the case. These decisions are made with the goal of providing the juvenile with a chance to complete tasks to warrant a case dismissal. Alternatively, judges can adjudicate a young person as "delinquent" and schedule the case for a *disposition* hearing. These hearings are the point in a case where the juvenile court judge determines the type of sanctions to impose. The number and type of sanctions available to the judge at the disposition hearing vary widely across locales but typically include options such as secure detention and other out-of-home placements, probation, referral to community corrections programming and other social services, community service, and fines and/or restitution. Once a case has a disposition, juvenile court judges can hold regular review hearings while the child is under supervision of the court to determine how the case is progressing and to make modifications to the disposition as needed (Hockenberry & Puzzanchera, 2020).

The final aspect of the Center for Juvenile Justice's general framework for juvenile court processing is *detention*. Notably, juveniles can be placed in detention facilities at multiple points in their involvement with the juvenile courts, starting at initial contact with the intake department to adjudication and disposition. The specific nature of detention facilities and practices related to detention vary widely across systems. As such, the use of detention in juvenile courts is monitored closely on the local, state, and national levels because of the deleterious conditions associated with detention centers both in terms of the physical conditions of the facilities and the negative impact they have on the health and well-being of youth, the long-standing disparities in the confinement of youth of color, and abuses of power that judges have engaged in concerning the use of detention in recent years (see Peralta, 2011, for example).

## Who Is Involved in the Juvenile Justice System?

When considering rates of involvement in the juvenile justice system, it is important to understand that young people are generally referred to the juvenile court system for both delinquent and status offenses. *Delinquent offenses* include actions that would be considered as crimes if they were committed by an adult. Conversely, *status offenses* are specific to juveniles because they include behaviors that are law violations based on the age of the person committing them (e.g., running away from home, truancy, ungovernability). Status offenses are seen as less-serious offenses that most often indicate a need for supervision or support. Thus, responses to these two types of offenses tend to vary in terms of the provision of social services versus punishment that are afforded offenders.

Another factor that must be considered when examining rates of involvement with the juvenile justice system is the substantial body of evidence related to the "age–crime curve" (Loeber et al., 2012). This research has found that the number of children who engage in delinquent behavior starts to increase in late childhood (ages 7–12), crests in mid-adolescence (ages 13–16) and begins to decline in late adolescence/early adulthood (ages 17–25). Additionally, research on the age–crime curve has found that a very small proportion of juveniles (6%) account for a large proportion of all offenses committed by juveniles (Howell et al., 2014).

The number of children involved in the juvenile justice system is reported in two ways: (1) the number of cases processed by juvenile court systems across the country each year and (2) the number of children under the supervision of the juvenile justice systems each year. According to research by the National Center for Juvenile Justice, in 2018 (the most recent year for which this data is available), 31 million youth were under the supervision of the juvenile justice system, with 79% of these youth falling between the ages of 10–15 (Hockenberry & Puzzanchera, 2020). In terms of gender, 73% of the delinquency cases in 2018 involved males, a proportion that has remained stable since 2005, with the overall decline in cases in the juvenile justice system being equivalent for males and females (55%).

Additionally, the National Center for Juvenile Justice reports that juvenile courts in the U.S. processed 744,500 cases in 2018. This represents a 55% reduction in the number of cases processed since 2005, with a 20% reduction in case processing occurring in the past five years alone. Of the 744,500 cases processed by juvenile courts in 2018, 57% were handled formally through a petition, of which 1% involved a petition for a judicial waiver. Of the remaining adjudication petitions, 52% were adjudicated delinquent. Of the cases that were adjudicated delinquent, 28% resulted in an out-of-home placement, 62% resulted in probation, and 9% resulted in other sanctions. Among the 43% of cases that the intake department did not send on for formal processing, 40% were dismissed, 15% received probation, and 44% received some other sanction (Hockenberry & Puzzanchera, 2020).

Collectively, these numbers demonstrate that the juvenile justice system has a large footprint in the U.S. However, the reality is that the size of the juvenile justice system has also shrunk dramatically over the past 15 years, with over a 50% decrease in both the number of cases being processed by juvenile courts and the number of children under supervision during this time period (Hockenberry & Puzzanchera, 2020). These accomplishments are remarkable given the fact that they began during a time when the number of adults involved in the criminal justice system was continuing to increase. While these trends are encouraging and will be discussed further in the last section of this chapter, more work is needed to reduce both the size of the juvenile justice system and the disproportionate contact and disparities in outcomes that youth of color have with this system.

## Racial and Ethnic Disparities
## in the Juvenile Justice System

It is important to note that there is significant variation in how race and ethnicity are measured in studies involving young offenders, and that this variation often affects how youth are labeled, processed, and categorized in the juvenile justice system. We believe that the use of language should be intentional, so we will use the terms *African American*, *Latinx*, and *Native American* in the discussion that follows. Recent data reveal that the long-standing disproportionate representation of African American youth that has been present since the inception of the juvenile justice system continues today. For example, in 2018, 35% of cases in the juvenile justice system involved African American youth, even though only 14% of 12- to 17-year-olds in the U.S. were African American (Annie E. Casey Foundation, 2020; Hockenberry & Puzzanchera, 2020). Furthermore, research shows that the share of all cases that involve African American and Latinx youth has actually risen 2% since 2005, while the share of cases involving White youth has decreased (Hockenberry & Puzzanchera, 2020).

Racial and ethnic disparities exist at all key decision points in the juvenile justice system. The latest national data show that 64% of African American youth and 55% of Latinx youth in the juvenile justice system have their cases formally petitioned, compared to 52% of White youth (Hockenberry & Puzzanchera, 2020). Though a rare occurrence overall, national data indicate that African American youth are waived to adult court at higher rates than other racial groups and at twice the rate of White youth for crimes against persons. Although the differences in percentages waived to adult court by race are relatively small, the cumulative effect of disparities combined with the slightly higher share of African American youth waived to adult court resulted in 700 more African American youth in total waived to adult court than White youth in 2018.

Native American youth are adjudicated delinquent at higher rates than any other racial or ethnic group (59%), followed closely by Latinx youth (57%), while African American youth are adjudicated delinquent at the lowest rate of all youth (49%; Hockenberry & Puzzanchera, 2020). However, once adjudicated, African American and Latinx youth experience the highest levels of out-of-home placements (32%). Given the disproportionate number of African American youth involved in the juvenile justice system, the disparities experienced in out-of-home placement both before and after adjudication means that more African American youth experienced out-of-home placements in 2018 than any other racial group.

This point is illustrated by a study conducted by the W. Haywood Burns Institute (2020), which found that African American youth were five times more likely to be incarcerated than White youth in 2015 (calculated by comparing incarceration rates per 1,000 youth nationally). This disparity has remained virtually unchanged since 1997, even though overall incarceration and delinquency case rates have fallen precipitously during this period. In a small bright spot, the disparity in likelihood of incarceration among Latinx youth compared to White youth has fallen since 1997, though Latinx youth are still 1.6 times more likely than White youth to be incarcerated.

# RISK AND PROTECTIVE FACTORS FOR JUVENILE JUSTICE SYSTEM INVOLVEMENT

Risk factors for adolescent delinquency are typically defined as individual-, social-, and community-level characteristics that elevate the likelihood of future delinquent behavior or criminal offending (Bonta & Andrews, 2017). However, definitions of protective factors are generally more ambiguous. Some researchers and youth development experts consider protective factors to be characteristics and conditions that reduce or buffer the impact of a risk factor. Others suggest that protective factors simply denote low levels of risk factors (Shepherd et al., 2016) or are, conversely, unique variables that predict low probabilities of reoffending (Loeber & Stouthamer-Loeber, 2008). Still other researchers consider protective factors to be variables associated with adaptive outcomes only in the presence of a risk factor (e.g., Fraser et al., 2004). Common risk and protective factors for juvenile justice involvement are shown in Table 10.2.

**Table 10.2  Risk and Protective Factors for Juvenile Justice Involvement**

| Level | Risk Factors | Protective Factors |
|---|---|---|
| Individual | Male gender[j] | Female gender[j] |
| | Low intelligence[a,d,h,i] | High intelligence[e] |
| | Egocentrism[b,f] | Easy temperament[e] |
| | Aggressive behavior[a,b,i] | Self-efficacy[e] |
| | Antisocial cognitions[b] | Self-esteem[e] |
| | Prior antisocial behavior[a,j] | |
| | Alcohol and drug use[a,b,dj,i] | |
| | Conduct disorders[b,d,i] | |
| | Attention deficit hyperactivity disorder[a,d,h,i] | |
| | Impulsivity[d,h,i] | |
| | Psychopathy[a,b,f,i,j] | |
| | Exposure to trauma[d,h,i] | |
| | Poor use of time[b] | |
| | Emotional and behavioral problems[a] | |
| | Psychopathy[b,f,i] | |
| | Sexual behavior[a] | |
| Family | Family conflict[b,c,d,h,j] | High levels of parental attachment[d,i] |
| | Low levels of attachment with parents[b,d,i] | Parental support[g,i] |
| | Poor parental supervision[b,c,g,h,i] | High-quality parental supervision[d,i] |
| | Poor parental discipline practices[b,g,j] | High socioeconomic status[d] |
| | Child maltreatment[i] | |
| | Parental history of crime[h,j] | |

| Level | Risk Factors | Protective Factors |
|---|---|---|
| | Parental drug use[h] | |
| | Poor parental education[c,d] | |
| | Disrupted family[d,h,j] | |
| | Large family[c,d,h,j] | |
| | Low socioeconomic status[d,h,j,i] | |
| | Child-rearing skills[c,d] | |
| | Teenage mother[d] | |
| | Witnessing family violence[d] | |
| Social | Involvement with antisocial peers[a,b,d,j,i] | Prosocial peers[d] |
| | Gang involvement[d] | Close relationships with prosocial adults[d] |
| | Social isolation[b,j] | |
| School/ Employment | Poor performance[a,b,d,h,j,i] | High academic achievement[b,d,e] |
| | Low commitment to school[a,b,i,j] | Opportunities for education and/or employment[e] |
| | Truancy[a,i] | |
| | Difficulty obtaining or maintaining employment[a,b] | Commitment to school[b,d,i] |
| Community | Neighborhood problems[a,j,i] | Good neighborhood[d,i] |
| | High community crime levels[a] | Collective efficacy[d,e] |
| | Living in an urban area[d] | |
| | Concentrated economic disadvantage[d] | |
| | Low levels of informal social control and cohesion[d] | |

[a]Assink, M., van der Put, C. E., Hoeve, M., de Vries, S. L., Stams, G. J. J., & Oort, F. J. (2015). Risk factors for persistent delinquent behavior among juveniles: A meta-analytic review. *Clinical Psychology Review*, 42, 47–61.

[b]Bonta, J., & Andrews, D. A. (2017). *The psychology of criminal conduct*. Routledge.

[c]Derzon, J. H. (2010). The correspondence of family features with problem, aggressive, criminal, and violent behavior: A meta-analysis. *Journal of Experimental Criminology*, 6(3), 263–292.

[d]Farrington, D. P., Loeber, R., & Ttofi, M. M. (2012). Risk and protective factors for offending. In B. C. Welsh & D. P. Farrington (Eds.), *The Oxford handbook of crime prevention* (pp. 46–69). Oxford University Press.

[e]Fraser, M. W., Kirby, L. D., & Smokowski, P. R. (2004). Risk and resilience in childhood. In M. W. Fraser (Ed.), *Risk and resilience in childhood: An ecological perspective* (2nd ed., pp. 13–66). NASW Press.

[f]Geerlings, Y., Asscher, J. J., Stams, G. J. J. M., & Assink, M. (2020). The association between psychopathy and delinquency in juveniles: A three-level meta-analysis. *Aggression and Violent Behavior, 50*.

[g]Hoeve, M., Dubas, J. S., Eichelsheim, V. I., Van der Laan, P. H., Smeenk, W., & Gerris, J. R. (2009). The relationship between parenting and delinquency: A meta-analysis. *Journal of Abnormal Child Psychology*, 37(6), 749–775.

[h]Jolliffe, D., Farrington, D. P., Piquero, A. R., Loeber, R., & Hill, K. G. (2017). Systematic review of early risk factors for life-course-persistent, adolescence-limited, and late-onset offenders in prospective longitudinal studies. *Aggression and Violent Behavior*, 33, 15–23.

[i]Kennedy T. D., Detullio D., & Millen D. H. (2020). Risk and protective factors for delinquency. In T. D. Kennedy, D. Detullio, & D. H. Millen (Eds.), *Juvenile delinquency* (pp. 47–81). Springer.

[j]Lipsey, M. W., & Derzon, J. H. (1998). Predictors of violent or serious delinquency in adolescence and early adulthood: A synthesis of longitudinal research. In R. Loeber & D. P. Farrington (Eds.), *Serious & violent juvenile offenders: Risk factors and successful interventions* (pp. 86–105). SAGE.

Although a substantial body of research has evaluated the association between risk factors and delinquent behavior, far fewer have reviewed protective factors (Basto-Pereira et al., 2016). Thus, the protective factors discussed here should be considered in light of the relative scarcity of research on protection.

The assessment of risk factors is an ever-evolving field that can be organized within four distinct generations. Prior to the 1980s, risk factors were assessed by individual clinicians, who determined levels of risk based on their subjective and unstructured clinical judgements. With time, this first-generation practice was replaced by second-generation instruments that used assessment tools to measure static (i.e., unchangeable) risk factors such as gender or number of prior arrests (Andrews et al., 2006). Whereas research has consistently demonstrated the weak predictive validity of first-generation assessments, second-generation assessments have been found to perform well in predicting general offending. Nevertheless, a major limitation of second-generation instruments is that they are unable to capture natural changes in risk levels that occur with the passage of time. By contrast, third-generation instruments are distinguished from their predecessors through their inclusion of dynamic or changeable risk factors, such as school performance or substance abuse. More recently, fourth-generation instruments have emerged, which assess static and dynamic risk factors as well as specific case-management needs. These instruments are capable of measuring delinquency risk while also providing a practical assessment of general treatment and case management needs. As a result, fourth-generation instruments provide practical guidance for correctional services delivered to adolescents involved in the criminal justice system. One example of a commonly used fourth-generation assessment is the Youth Level of Service/Case Management Inventory 2.0 (YLS/CMI 2.0™), which is a strengths-focused risk assessment tool that has been found to reliably and accurately predict the likelihood of re-offending within juvenile justice populations (Hoge & Andrews, 2006).

Risk and protective factors may be categorized within various ecological levels. For the purpose of this overview, we have organized them in Table 10.2 into individual, family, social, school/employment, and community levels of influence. Notably, many correctional theories emphasize the role of individual factors rather than systemic factors. For example, one of the most influential frameworks guiding the assessment of risk factors in justice settings is the risk–need–responsivity (RNR) model (Bonta & Andrews, 2017). Briefly, the RNR model comprises three core principles: risk, need, and responsivity. The *risk* principle asserts that the correctional services will be most effective when they are matched to an individual's risk for reoffending, which should be assessed using structured, fourth-generation risk assessment tools. The *need* principle asserts that correctional interventions should target the changeable risk factors that have been found to have the strongest relationship to criminal offending. The *responsivity* principle calls for services to be tailored to the learning and treatment needs of individuals receiving services.

The RNR model is grounded in a general personality and cognitive social learning (GPCSL) theory, which posits that criminal behavior is learned through complex interactions between individuals and their immediate social environments (Bonta & Andrews, 2017). Although GPCSL theory acknowledges that these interactions are situated within broader social contexts, these broader factors are assumed to minimally impact criminal behavior after accounting for the key individual variables. Moreover, dynamic risk factors that occur at the individual level have the added advantage of serving as treatment targets for interventions delivered to adolescents and their families. By contrast, changing broader neighborhood or community-level variables often necessitates resources that expand beyond the scope of individual service providers. Nevertheless, many studies have identified the importance of risk factors that occur at broader structural levels, highlighting their importance for correctional research, theory, and practice.

# EVIDENCE-BASED PROGRAMS AND POLICIES

The juvenile justice system combines the goal of public safety with improving the chances that juveniles will grow up to prosper as productive citizens. To achieve this goal, the system requires a spectrum of EBPs that span from prevention to intervention (Lipsey et al., 2010). To assist communities in their efforts to address juvenile delinquency, the OJJDP developed a comprehensive strategy to combat juvenile delinquency that includes a system-level framework with five general operating principles: (1) strengthen families, (2) support core social institutions (i.e., schools, churches, community organizations), (3) promote prevention programs, (4) intervene immediately and effectively when delinquency occurs, and (5) identify and control the small group of serious, violent, and chronic juvenile offenders (Wilson & Howell, 1993).

The OJJDP's comprehensive strategy includes the mantra that the juvenile justice system must deliver the "right services, to the right youth, at the right time" (Howell et al., 2014, p. 9). To accomplish this goal, the comprehensive framework has two tiers. The first tier focuses on preventing delinquency through a wide range of programs for at-risk youth, including delinquency prevention, youth development, and early intervention programs. When prevention efforts fail, the juvenile justice system intervenes as the second tier of this framework. In this model, the juvenile justice system proactively responds to delinquency by addressing youth risk factors for delinquency and their associated needs using a continuum of services that include immediate interventions, graduated sanctions, confinement, and community aftercare (Howell et al. 2014; Wilson & Howell, 1993).

According to Lipsey and colleagues (2010), prevention services are an essential part of an effective strategy to address juvenile delinquency. They define *prevention services* as "community-based activities aimed at helping youth avoid delinquent behavior" (p. 11) and note that these programs generally operate in schools, public health agencies, and other social services that work with youth who are not yet involved in the justice system.

Juvenile justice interventions include two key components: supervision and treatment. Supervision involves monitoring young people's activities and constraining their actions in some way, while treatment centers around activities or services such as counseling, education, and vocational training that aim to facilitate positive behavioral changes. At least one of these two intervention components are typically present in juvenile justice interventions (Lipsey et al., 2010). Research on the effectiveness of juvenile justice interventions that employ evidence-based treatment and supervision strategies include three central findings. First, research has found that at best, supervision through probation and other monitoring strategies has a modest positive impact on recidivism among juveniles (Lipsey & Cullen, 2007; Petrosino et al., 2010). Second, deterrence-oriented programs such as Scared Straight, D.A.R.E, or large detention facilities and boot camps that rely on the threat of punishment and surveillance have not been found to reduce recidivism and can increase it (Lipsey, 2009). Third, significant evidence exists related to what forms of treatment are effective at reducing recidivism for juveniles involved with the system (Cullen, 2005; Lipsey, 2009; Lipsey & Cullen, 2007).

Programs, interventions, and strategies are constantly being updated and revised in the era of EBPs as new evidence continues to emerge. As a result, creating a list of specific EBPs has limited utility. There are a number of valuable resources for educators, policymakers, and practitioners who are interested in learning about EBPs in juvenile justice settings, which keep up-to-date listings of EBPs. One such program is the OJJDP's Model Programs Guide (https://www.ojjdp.gov/mpg). This site curates a comprehensive listing of juvenile justice and youth prevention, intervention, and reentry programs, which include descriptions of the programs, information on populations and settings where they have been used, and evidence on effectiveness. Additional resources on EBPs for both offenders and young people at risk for involvement in the justice system can be found at the Blueprints for Healthy Youth Development registry (https://www.blueprintsprograms.org/). Each of these program registries use different criteria and ranking systems to review, classify, and identify effective programs, practices, and policies. Finally, it is also important to note that the effectiveness ratings provided by registries are dependent on an organization's ability to implement an intervention with fidelity to the original model. In some cases, this may limit the reach of EBPs due to the practical challenges associated with implementing EBPs in real-world practice settings (Lipsey et al., 2010).

## CURRENT AND FUTURE POLICY CHALLENGES

The juvenile justice system has seen major reductions in its scope of operations over a very short time period. It is too soon to tell if these reductions are part of a larger decarceration trend in the juvenile justice system or if these reductions will even be maintained over time. That said, the successes that the juvenile justice system have achieved in this area are notable and require further discussion and study.

The reductions in the size of the juvenile justice system are so recent that scholars cannot say with certainty what factors caused the steep decline in case rates in the juvenile justice system. Despite this uncertainty, it is important to point out several factors that have likely played a role in recent declines in juvenile justice cases. First and most important, juvenile crime rates have dropped precipitously in the past 15 years. These reductions occurred at a time when state budgets experienced significant financial cuts following a major economic recession that began in 2008. Taken together, these two dynamics likely lessened the demand for services from the juvenile justice system at a time when the system was incentivized to find new, less costly alternatives to confinement and other formal interventions.

Additionally, unlike the adult criminal justice system, which is made up of at least four separate systems, the juvenile system operates for the most part as a singular system, with the courts providing strong oversight to most if not all of the activities that take place within the system. This structure makes it much easier—albeit not simple—to create systemwide reforms similar to the ones described here. It is also likely that the structure of the juvenile justice system has allowed for reform efforts that focus on embedding evidence-based practices at all of the major decision points in this system in a coordinated fashion. In our opinion, the significance of this approach to evidence-based practices cannot be understated. Another recent notable reform element is the work of both private foundations and governmental agencies in promoting programs and policies that improve outcomes for young people (Horowitz, 2017; National Research Council, 2014; Stanfield, 1999; Stevens et al., 2016).

Furthermore, developments in neuropsychology related to the brain development of adolescents and young adults have also informed efforts to improve outcomes for adolescents in the juvenile justice system. These developments have normalized some of the social and behavioral struggles that adolescents face. Further, they have made society once again more amenable to rehabilitative interventions for youth. But these advances would not have been successful if not for the research debunking the polarizing claims associated with the "nothing works" movement and the tough-on-crime era while also providing a solid evidence base pertaining to programs that are effective at reducing recidivism through the use of interventions that engage positive behavioral change.

## Reducing Disproportionate Contact and Racial and Ethnic Disparities in Juvenile Justice

Disproportionate contact and disparities in outcomes continue to exist for youth of color across all major points of contact with the juvenile justice system. This alarming pattern continues to exist despite decades of legislative efforts aimed at reducing these disparities (Coalition for Juvenile Justice, 2014; Rovner, 2016; Soler & Garry, 2009). In terms of arrest and confinement, the disparities between African American youth and White youth have increased in the past 20 years. These facts raise more questions than answers. For example, questions abound related to the implementation of legislation focused on disproportionate contact. Local efforts have also faced challenges in reducing racial and ethnic disproportionality in the juvenile justice system. The final report evaluating the recent Models for Change initiative, for instance, indicated that some participating localities avoided addressing racial disparities head-on due to defensiveness among some stakeholders (Stevens et al., 2016).

Another set of discussions about the failure to decrease disproportionate contact in the juvenile justice system focuses on whether the disparities in outcomes related to arrest and confinement of African American youth are caused by differences in the types of crimes that African American youth commit as compared to White youth. The Sentencing Project addresses this issue by pointing to research that has found few differences in the types of things that African American and White youth are arrested for (Rovner, 2016). This report notes that while African American youth are 2.3 times more likely to be arrested than their White peers, the two groups of youth have similar odds of engaging in the behaviors that youth typically get arrested for (i.e., fighting, stealing, using or selling drugs, skipping school). The report also notes that while African American youth are more likely than their White peers to commit violent offenses, arrests for these offenses account for less than 5% of all juvenile arrests and, therefore, cannot explain the scope of racial disparities in the juvenile justice system, both generally or in terms of the use of confinement specifically. Based on the research cited here, it seems clear that differences in the types of crimes committed by African American and White youth do not explain the disparities that are present in the juvenile justice system.

A well-established body of research demonstrates that disparities in outcomes for youth of color are a pervasive part of the juvenile justice system. It is our assertation that good intentions are simply not enough to address these disparities. In fact, the precipitous drops in arrest, adjudication, and confinement among White youth suggest that these youth are the primary beneficiaries of the reform efforts that have been initiated in the juvenile justice system, including those focused on reducing disproportionate minority contact (Rovner, 2016). While this fact is not altogether surprising, given the history of racial disparities in our country more generally, they should serve as a wake-up call to the nation. Good intentions and several legislative initiatives alone are not enough to dismantle centuries of racism and institutional oppression.

In her seminal text, *The New Jim Crow*, Michele Alexander (2012) notes that the "more things change, the more they stay the same" (p. 1). She is referencing the fact that the modern-day criminal justice system is only the latest set of tactics that society has used to exclude and discriminate against African Americans. While Alexander's work focused mostly on the adult criminal justice system, the entrenched and pervasive nature of disproportionate contact and disparate outcomes of African American youth in the juvenile justice system suggests that her analysis could and should be extended to the juvenile justice system as well.

The relevance of Alexander's (2012) work to the juvenile justice system is supported by another important body of scholarship, which reveals that the social construct of *childhood* that undergirds the foundation of the modern-day juvenile justice system was grounded in prevailing notions of White middle-class "childlikeness." As a result, African American youth were seen as "inferior, less malleable, and not suitable for the civic-education function of rehabilitative juvenile justice" (Burton, 2019, p. 1261). This led to African American adolescents being disproportionately tried in the adult court system, receiving longer periods in detention, and facing higher rates of corporal punishment than their White counterparts (Burton, 2019; Mallett & Tedor, 2018). The continued disparities in outcomes for African American children in the juvenile justice system today raise questions about the value and fairness of continuing to base the operations of the juvenile justice system around social norms that continue to be defined by a dominant culture centered on whiteness. As scholar Michael J. Dumas notes, "Black boyhood is socially unimagined and unimaginable, largely due to the devalued position and limited consideration of Black girls and boys within the broader social conception of childhood" (Dumas & Nelson, 2016, p. 27).

Some scholars have noted that it is difficult to study racial disparities in the juvenile justice system because of the strong relationship between crime and the social factors that affect communities where many young people of color live (Robles-Ramamurthy & Watson, 2019). For example, African American and Latinx families experience higher rates of poverty than White families. And African American students are more likely to be subjected to arrest due to the fact that they are more likely to go to schools that have strong law enforcement presences and zero-tolerance policies.

Juvenile delinquency is considered by many to be a social rather than an individual problem. In this regard, it is past time to move beyond individual-level explanations for disparities in juvenile justice referrals, dispositions, and outcomes that may only serve to reinforce commonly held stereotypes about race and ethnicity. It is also necessary to re-examine the utility and fairness of some of the assumptions on which juvenile justice is based. For example, the social and demographic makeup of our country has changed drastically over the past 100 years, yet the assumptions about appropriate behavior and family life continue to be routed in middle-class White notions of the early 20th century. One important step toward creating a fair and equitable juvenile justice system is to center the operations of the system on children and families with the greatest needs. Considering the scope and nature of the disparities in the juvenile justice system, it seems that the fair and equitable approach to operating this system should include re-centering its operations around the needs of children of color. Given the research around the important role that community context plays in perpetuating racial disparities in the juvenile justice system, re-centering the system around the needs of children of color could lead to a greater focus on programming that attends to their basic needs while creating programming that generates economic and vocational opportunities.

Another practical step that the juvenile justice system could take to address the impact that racism has on the lives of African American, Native American, and Latinx youth is to acknowledge that racism is a risk factor for involvement in the criminal justice system and to create risk assessment tools that are capable of measuring its impact on the lives of youth at the individual, community, and system levels. While the suggestions offered here will not solve the disproportionate contact and racial disparities present in the juvenile justice system, we offer them as a starting place and hope that they spur more conversations about new approaches that can be taken to address this long-standing injustice.

## Improving the Responsivity of the Juvenile Justice System

The development and implementation of EBPs is contingent on the ability of these services to address the needs of *everyone* in the juvenile justice system. However, research has found that there are particular populations that may have needs and experiences warranting special consideration; specifically, developing programs and services that (1) are gender-responsive, attending to the experiences and needs of girls; (2) acknowledge the issues and needs of lesbian, gay, bisexual, transgender, and queer (LGBTQ) youth; and (3) consider the impact of adverse childhood experiences and mental health challenges. These are necessary to create socially just systems and improve outcomes for all young people and their families.

## Gender-Responsive Services

Because girls comprise less than one third of all youth arrests, the majority of correctional literature has focused on the treatment needs of boys (Hockenberry & Puzzanchera, 2020; Zahn et al., 2009). However, research has found significant gender differences in the experiences and treatment needs of boys and girls in the juvenile justice system (Walker et al., 2015). For example, compared to justice-involved boys, girls in the juvenile justice system are more likely to experience mental health problems (Belknap & Holsinger, 2006); have histories of physical, sexual, and emotional abuse (Belknap & Holsinger, 2006; Bloom et al., 2002; DeHart & Moran, 2015); report unstable and dysfunctional family relationships (Belknap & Holsinger, 2006); and have higher rates of substance misuse (Chesney-Lind et al., 2008). These differences are notable as research has found that certain life events may have more of an impact on the delinquent behavior of girls than boys (Development Services Group [DSG], 2018).

Evidence for gender differences between justice-involved boys and girls has prompted several researchers to suggest that girls may benefit from specialized services that consider their unique needs and experiences (Walker et al., 2015; Zahn et al., 2009). These services, often referred to as *gender-responsive* or *gender-specific* services, strive to account for girls' unique life experiences and pathways into crime while addressing their physical, psychological, and social treatment needs (Anderson et al., 2019; Bloom et al., 2006). Although there is no consistent definition of what constitutes a gender-responsive service, these programs are typically comprehensive, community-based services that focus on safety, empowerment, family, and relationship support (Matthews & Hubbard, 2008; Watson & Edelman, 2012).

## LGBTQ Issues

LGBTQ youth represent another growing and vulnerable population within the U.S. juvenile justice system. Although only 7% to 9% of youth identify as LGBTQ nationally, estimates have found that as many as 39% of girls and 3% of boys in U.S. juvenile detention and correctional facilities identify as LGBTQ (Wilson et al., 2017). The disproportionate representation of LGBTQ youth is particularly pronounced among youth of color—one 2016 survey of juvenile detention and correctional facilities in California found that 19% of incarcerated youth identified as LGBTQ or gender nonconforming, 90% of whom were youth of color (Irvine et al., 2017). LGBTQ youth enter the juvenile justice system for a number of reasons, many of which are unrelated to their sexual orientation or gender identity. However, this population faces numerous challenges associated with their sexual orientation and gender identities that can negatively impact their transition to adulthood and increase their risk of future criminal justice involvement (DSG, 2018; Garnette et al., 2011). For example, LGBTQ youth are more likely than their non-LGBTQ peers to experience stigma and harassment in their school environments and home environments, placing them at an elevated risk of early school dropout, truancy, and homelessness (Dank et al., 2015; Garnette et al., 2011; Majd et al., 2009).

Once referred to the juvenile justice system, many LGBTQ youth may not feel safe disclosing their identities (Garnette et al., 2011). Moreover, because LGBTQ youth are more likely than their non-LGBTQ peers to experience sexual and gender-identity related problems in their families and schools, they often report higher levels of family discord and poor school attendance. Because many risk assessment instruments include family relationships and school performance as risk factors, LGBTQ youth assessed as being high risk in these categories may be more likely to be placed in more secure settings and intensive services than their counterparts (Irvine, 2010).

The disparate treatment and outcomes of LGBTQ youth in the juvenile justice system has spurred the development of new laws, standards, and policies aimed at supporting the health and well-being of this population. In 2003, Congress enacted the Prison Rape Elimination Act (PREA), which remains the most comprehensive federal statute governing the treatment of this population in secure correctional facilities. However, although PREA contains explicit protections for LGBTQ youth, there is a significant need for further research examining effective treatment and rehabilitation practices among this population (Irvine et al., 2017).

### Adverse Childhood Experiences and Mental Health Challenges

Another important area for increased responsivity in EBPs in the juvenile justice system is related to a body of work known as adverse childhood experiences (ACEs). ACEs are defined simply as "potentially traumatic events that occur in childhood" (Centers for Disease Control and Prevention [CDC], 2020). ACEs often include aspects of a child's environment that threaten their safety and stability. Some examples include experiencing or witnessing violence in the home or community and instability due to parental separation or family members being incarcerated, among others. Though predominantly studied as predictors of adult outcomes, the impacts of ACEs are observed as early as childhood. This is evidenced by its prevalence among youth involved in the juvenile justice system. Youth involved in the juvenile justice system are reportedly more likely to have been exposed to one or more ACEs than the general population (Baglivio et al., 2014; Logan-Greene et al., 2017).

Higher ACEs scores (an aggregate of exposures to adverse events), specifically those related to maltreatment and exposure to household challenges, have been linked to increased odds of general delinquency and violent offending by more than 200% and have been found to increase recidivism within a shorter time span (Artz et al., 2014; Baglivio et al., 2015; Lattimore et al., 1995; Maxfield & Widom, 1996; Steketee et al. 2019; Teague et al., 2008), to be associated with childhood and adolescent aggression (Raine et al., 1997; Shaw & Winslow, 1997), and to be identified as a causative factor of lifelong antisocial behavior (Moffitt, 1993; Widom, 1989). Family dynamics—including household members with mental illness, parental separation and divorce, substance abuse in the home, and domestic violence—are risk factors that increase the likelihood that a child will engage in antisocial and criminal behavior (Braungart-Rieker et al., 1995; Cadoret et al., 1995; Widom & Morris, 1997). Childhood exposure to parental incarceration is also associated with delinquency and maladaptive behaviors and has predicted antisocial delinquent outcomes beyond other types of parental separation (Baglivio & Epps, 2015; Geller et al., 2009; Murray & Farrington, 2005; Parke & Clarke-Stewart, 2014).

Racism is an emerging ACE that should be considered within the context of responsivity of EBPs in the juvenile justice system, as it has been identified as a stressor among racial minority youth. In a 2020 research brief, when including interpersonal and individual racism while assessing ACEs, racism was significantly associated with all other ACEs and increased the risks of experiencing household challenges (Lanier, 2020), which is noted above as a risk factor for criminal behavior. Furthermore, increases in perceived racial discrimination, which is one form of racism, are also positively linked with conduct problems among youth (Brody et al., 2006). With the increased research on racism as an ACE, researchers must begin building more explicit investigations to understand the impacts of individual, interpersonal, institutional, and structural racism on children of color and how these experiences contribute to disproportionate juvenile justice involvement.

Finally, the ACEs discussed here have documented impacts on child mental health. For example, in addition to justice-related outcomes, child maltreatment has been identified as the strongest contributor to mental health problems (Logan-Green et al., 2017). Mental illness has been identified as one of the most reliable correlates of recidivism among justice-involved youth, and justice-involved youth have been documented to suffer from higher rates of mental illness than youth in the general population (Barret et al., 2013; Logan-Greene et al., 2017; Teplin et al., 2005). This has important responsivity implications for EBPs in the areas of research, policy, and practice for youth who are involved in the juvenile justice system and who are also experiencing mental illness. Youth who are socially disadvantaged and less likely to receive mental health care to address the impacts of ACEs become particularly vulnerable to involvement in the juvenile justice system. Research on the role of ACEs in predicting juvenile justice involvement and its impact on mental health challenges is key to the development of responsive policies, initiatives, and interventions aimed at prevention efforts and reducing recidivism.

## SUMMARY

Significant strides have been made in the juvenile justice system. This is evidenced by both a large decrease in the number of youths involved in the system as well as the increased deployment of EBPs at key points throughout the system. Yet, as noted previously, these changes are relatively recent and much is to be learned about how research, policy, and programming will need to be leveraged in order to sustain, and equitably build on, this progress. First and foremost, we need to create new strategies for addressing the long-entrenched racial and ethnic disparities that exist throughout the juvenile justice system. This work will involve a re-centering of the operations of the existing juvenile justice system and a re-examination and possible reimagining of the focus and content of intervention points and programming. Second, it is critical that we ensure that prevention and intervention programming is responsive to the needs of all youth who have contact with the juvenile justice system. Finally, efforts to reduce involvement in the juvenile justice system would benefit from a greater incorporation of protective factors and resiliency in both research and programming.

In order to empower youth and their families, and to minimize the deleterious effects associated with involvement in punitive justice systems, the juvenile justice system will need to continue to champion evidence-based policies and programming. As recent history shows us, in the juvenile justice system, this requires the deployment of a coordinated array of services. In order to support and build on the recent gains in this system, EBP efforts need to expand to include programming and services that support healthy youth development across multiple life domains, respond to delinquency in a way that acknowledges normal youth neurocognitive development, and foster the types of environments that prevent delinquency before it happens.

# REFERENCES

Alexander, M. (2012). *The new Jim Crow: Mass incarceration in the age of colorblindness*. The New Press.

Anderson, V. R., Walerych, B. M., Campbell, N. A., Barnes, A. R., Davidson, W. S., II, Campbell, C. A., Onifade, E., & Petersen, J. L. (2019). Gender-responsive intervention for female juvenile offenders: A quasi-experimental outcome evaluation. *Feminist Criminology*, *14*(1), 24–44.

Andrews, D. A., Bonta, J., & Wormith, J. S. (2006). The recent past and near future of risk and/or need assessment. *Crime & Delinquency*, *52*(1), 7–27.

Annie E. Casey Foundation. (2020, September). *Child population by race and age group in the United States*. https://datacenter.kidscount.org/data/tables/8446-child-population-by-race-and-age-group

Artz, S., Jackson, M. A., Rossiter, K. R., Nijdam-Jones, A., Géczy, I., & Porteous, S. (2014). A comprehensive review of the literature on the impact of exposure to intimate partner violence for children and youth. *International Journal of Child, Youth and Family Studies*, *5*(4), 493–587.

Atkins v. Virginia, 536 U.S. 304 (2002). https://scholar.google.com/scholar_case?case=2043469055777796288&hl=en&as_sdt=6&as_vis=1&oi=scholarr

Baglivio, M. T., & Epps, N. (2015). The interrelatedness of adverse childhood experiences among high-risk juvenile offenders. *Youth Violence and Juvenile Justice*, *14*(3), 179–198.

Baglivio, M. T., Epps, N., Swartz, K., Huq, M. S., Sheer, A., & Hardt, N. S. (2014). The prevalence of adverse childhood experiences (ACE) in the lives of juvenile offenders. *Journal of Juvenile Justice*, *3*(2).

Baglivio, M. T., Wolff, K. T., Piquero, A. R., & Epps, N. (2015). The relationship between adverse childhood experiences (ACEs) and juvenile offending trajectories in a juvenile offender sample. *Journal of Criminal Justice*, *43*(3), 229–241.

Barrett, D. E., Katsiyannis, A., Zhang, D., & Zhang, D. (2013). Delinquency and recidivism: A multicohort, matched-control study of the role of early adverse experiences, mental health problems, and disabilities. *Journal of Emotional and Behavioral Disorders*, *22*(1), 3–15.

Bartollas, C. (2010). *Juvenile justice in America*. Pearson.

Basto-Pereira, M., Miranda, A., Ribeiro, S., & Maia, A. (2016). Growing up with adversity: From juvenile justice involvement to criminal persistence and psychosocial problems in young adulthood. *Child Abuse & Neglect*, *62*, 63–75.

Belknap, J., & Holsinger, K. (2006). The gendered nature of risk factors for delinquency. *Feminist Criminology*, *1*(1), 48–71.

Bloom, B. E., Owen, B., & Covington, S. (2006). A summary of research, practice and guiding principles for women offenders. National Institute of Corrections.

Bloom, B. E., Owen, B., Deschenes, E. P., & Rosenbaum, J. (2002). Improving juvenile justice for females: A statewide assessment in California. *Crime & Delinquency*, *48*(4), 526–552.

Bonta, J., & Andrews, D. A. (2017). *The psychology of criminal conduct* (6th ed.). Taylor & Francis.

Braungart-Rieker, J., Rende, R. D., Plomin, R., DeFries, J. C., & Fulker, D. W. (1995). Genetic mediation of longitudinal associations between family environment and childhood behavior problems. *Development and Psychopathology*, *7*(2), 233–245.

Brody, G. H., Chen, Y. F., Murry, V. M., Ge, X., Simons, R. L., Gibbons, F. X., Gerrard, M., & Cutrona, C. E. (2006). Perceived discrimination and the adjustment of African American youths: A five-year longitudinal analysis with contextual moderation effects. *Child Development*, *77*(5), 1170–1189.

Burton, C. S. (2019). Child savers and unchildlike youth: Class, race, and juvenile justice in the early twentieth century. *Law & Social Inquiry*, *44*(4), 1251–1269.

Cadoret, R. J., Yates, W. R., Troughton, E., Woodworth, G., & Stewart, M. A. (1995). Adoption study demonstrating two genetic pathways to drug abuse. *Archives of General Psychiatry*, *52*(1), 42–52.

Centers for Disease Control and Prevention (CDC). (2020, April 3). *Preventing Adverse Childhood Experiences*. https://www.cdc.gov/violenceprevention/aces/fastfact.html

Chesney-Lind, M., Morash, M., & Stevens, T. (2008). Girls' troubles, girls' delinquency, and gender responsive programming: A review. *Australian & New Zealand Journal of Criminology*, *41*(1), 162–189.

Coalition for Juvenile Justice. (2014). *Disproportionate minority contact and status offenses*. https://www.juvjustice.org/sites/default/files/resource-files/DMC%20Emerging%20Issues%20Policy%20Brief%20Final_0.pdf

Coalition for Juvenile Justice. (n. d.). *Summary of the Juvenile Justice Reform Act of 2018*. https://www.juvjustice.org/sites/default/files/resource-files/Summary%20of%20the%20Juvenile%20Justice%20Reform%20Act%20of%202018.pdf

Cook, P. J., & Laub, J. H. (1998). The unprecedented epidemic in youth violence. *Crime and Justice*, *24*, 27–64.

Cullen, F. T. (2005). The twelve people who saved rehabilitation: How the science of criminology made a difference: The American Society of Criminology 2004 Presidential Address. *Criminology*, *43*(1), 1–42.

Dank, M., Yahner, J., Madden, K., Bañuelos, I., Yu, L., Ritchie, A., Mora, M., & Conner, B. M. (2015). *Surviving the streets of New York: Experiences of LGBTQ youth, YMSM, and YWSW engaged in survival sex*. The Urban Institute.

Decker, S. H. (1985). A systematic analysis of diversion: Net widening and beyond. *Journal of Criminal Justice*, *13*(3), 207–216.

DeHart, D. D., & Moran, R. (2015). Poly-victimization among girls in the justice system: Trajectories of risk and associations to juvenile offending. *Violence Against Women*, *21*(3), 291–312.

Development Services Group, Inc. (DSG). (2018). Specialized responses for girls in the juvenile justice system. Literature review. *Office of Juvenile Justice and Delinquency Prevention*. https://www.ojjdp.gov/mpg/litreviews/Specialized-Responses-for-Girls-in-the-Juvenile-Justice-System.pdf

Dilulio, John J., Jr. (1995). The coming of the super-predators. *The Weekly Standard*, *1*(11), 23–28.

Dumas, M. J., & Nelson, J. D. (2016). (Re)Imagining Black boyhood: Toward a critical framework for educational research. *Harvard Educational Review*, *86*(1), 27–47.

Elrod, P., & Ryder, R. S. (2013). *Juvenile justice: A social, historical, and legal perspective* (4th ed.). Jones & Bartlett Publishers.

Feld, B. C. (2019). *The evolution of the juvenile court: Race, politics, and the criminalizing of juvenile justice* (Vol. 4). NYU Press.

Fraser, M. W., Kirby, L. D., & Smokowski, P. R. (2004). Risk and resilience in childhood. In M. W. Fraser (Ed.), *Risk and resilience in childhood: An ecological perspective* (2nd ed., pp. 13–66). NASW Press.

Garnette, L., Irvine, A., Reyes, C., & Wilber, S. (2011). Lesbian, gay, bisexual, and transgender (LGBT) youth and the juvenile justice system. In F. T. Sherman & F. H. Jacobs (Eds.), *Juvenile justice: Advancing research, policy, and practice* (pp. 156–173). John Wiley & Sons.

Geller, A., Garfinkel, I., Cooper, C. E., & Mincy, R. B. (2009). Parental incarceration and child well-being: Implications for urban families. *Social Science Quarterly, 90*(5), 1186–1202.

Graham v. Florida, 560 U.S. 48 (2010). https://scholar.google .com/scholar_case?case=5709058278308728322&q=Gra ham+560+U.S.+48&hl=en&as_sdt=6,34&as_vis=1

Hess, K. M., Orthmann, C. H., & Wright, J. P. (2013). *Juvenile justice* (6th ed.). Cengage Learning.

Hockenberry, S., & Puzzanchera, C. (2020). *Juvenile court statistics 2018*. National Center for Juvenile Justice. https:// www.ojjdp.gov/ojstatbb/njcda/pdf/jcs2018.pdf

Hoge, R. D., & Andrews, D. A. (2006). *Youth level of service/case management inventory (YLS/CMI)*. Multi-Heath Systems.

Horowitz, J. (2017). *States take the lead on juvenile justice reform.* The PEW Charitable Trusts. https:// www.pewtrusts.org/en/research-and-analysis/articles/ 2017/05/11/states-take-the-lead-on-juvenile-justice- reform

Howell, J. C., Lipsey, M. W., Wilson, J. J., & Howell, M. Q. (2014). A practical approach to evidence-based juvenile justice systems. *Journal of Applied Juvenile Justice Services, 1*, 1–21.

Irvine, A. (2010). We've had three of them: Addressing the invisibility of lesbian, gay, bisexual, and gender non-conforming youths in the juvenile justice system. *Columbia Journal of Gender and Law, 19*, 675.

Irvine, A., Canfield, A., & Roa, J. (2017). Lesbian, bisexual, questioning, gender-nonconforming, and transgender (LBQ/GNCT) girls in the juvenile justice system. In

C. C. Datchi & J. R. Ancis (Eds.), *Gender, psychology, and justice: The mental health of women and girls in the legal system* (p. 200). New York University Press.

Jenson, J. M., & Howard, M. O. (1998). Youth crime, public policy, and practice in the juvenile justice system: Recent trends and needed reforms. *Social Work, 43*(4), 324–334.

Lanier, P. (2020, July 2). Racism is an adverse childhood experience (ACE). *Jordan institute for families*. https:// jordaninstituteforfamilies.org/2020/racism-is-an-ad verse-childhood-experience-ace/

Lattimore, P. K., Visher, C. A., & Linster, R. L. (1995). Predicting rearrest for violence among serious youthful offenders. *Journal of Research in Crime and Delinquency, 32*(1), 54–83.

Lipsey, M. W. (2009). The primary factors that characterize effective interventions with juvenile offenders: A meta-analytic overview. *Victims and Offenders, 4*(2), 124–147.

Lipsey, M. W., & Cullen, F. T. (2007). The effectiveness of correctional rehabilitation: A review of systematic reviews. *Annual Review of Law and Social Science, 3*, 297–320.

Lipsey, M. W., Howell, J. C., Kelly, M. R., Chapman, G., & Carver, D. (2010). *Improving the effectiveness of juvenile justice programs*. Center for Juvenile Justice Reform at Georgetown University.

Lipton, D. S., Martinson, R., & Wilks, J. (1975). *The effectiveness of correctional treatment: A survey of treatment evaluation studies*. Praeger Publishers.

Loeber, R., Farrington, D. P., Howell, J. C., & Hoeve, M. (2012). Overview, conclusions, and key recommendations. In R. Leober & D. P. Farrington (Eds.), *Juvenile delinquency to adult crime* (pp. 315–383). Oxford University Press.

Loeber, R., & Stouthamer-Loeber, M. (2008). A cumulative developmental model of risk and promotive factors. In R. Loeber, N. W. Slot, P. H. van der Laan, & M. Hoeve (Eds.), *Tomorrow's criminals: The development of child delinquency and effective interventions* (pp. 133–164). Ashgate.

Logan-Greene, P., Tennyson, R. L., Nurius, P. S., & Borja, S. (2017, December). Adverse childhood experiences, coping resources, and mental health problems among court-involved youth. *Child & Youth Care Forum, 46*(6), 923–946.

Mallett, C. A., & Tedor, M. F. (2018). *Juvenile delinquency: Pathways and prevention*. SAGE.

Majd, K., Marksamer, J., & Reyes, C. (2009). Hidden injustice: Lesbian, gay, bisexual, and transgender youth in juvenile courts. Equity Project.

Martinson, R. (1974). What works? Questions and answers about prison reform. *The Public Interest, 35*, 22.

Matthews, B., & Hubbard, D. J. (2008). Moving ahead: Five essential elements for working effectively with girls. *Journal of Criminal Justice, 36*(6), 494–502.

Maxfield, M., & Widom, C. (1996). The cycle of violence: Revisited 6 years later. *Archives of Pediatrics & Adolescent Medicine, 150*(4), 390–395.

McCord, J., Widom, C. S., & Crowell, N. A. (2001). *Juvenile crime, juvenile justice*. Panel on Juvenile Crime: Prevention, Treatment, and Control, National Academy Press.

Mears, D. P., Kuch, J. J., Lindsey, A. M., Siennick, S. E., Pesta, G. B., Greenwald, M. A., & Blomberg, T. G. (2016). Juvenile court and contemporary diversion: Helpful, harmful, or both? *Criminology & Public Policy, 15*(3), 953–981.

Merlo, J., Benekos, P., & Champion, D. J. (2016). *The juvenile justice system: Delinquency, processing, and the law*. Pearson.

*Miller v. Alabama*, 132 S. Ct. 2455, 567 U.S. 460, 183 L. Ed. 2d 407 (2012).

Moffitt, T. E. (1993). Adolescence-limited and life-course-persistent antisocial behavior: A developmental taxonomy. *Psychological Review, 100*(4), 674–701.

*Montgomery v. Louisiana*, 136 S. Ct. 718, 577 U.S. 460, 193 L. Ed. 2d 599 (2016).

Murray, J., & Farrington, D. P. (2005). Parental imprisonment: Effects on boys' antisocial behaviour and delinquency through the life-course. *Journal of Child Psychology and Psychiatry, and Allied Disciplines, 46*(12), 1269–1278.

National Research Council. (2014). *Implementing juvenile justice reform: The federal role*. The National Academies Press.

Parke, R. D., & Clarke-Stewart, A. (2014). *Effects of parental incarceration on young children*. United States Department of Health and Human Services.

Peralta, E. (2011, August 11). Pa. judge sentenced to 28 years in massive juvenile justice bribery scandal. *NPR*. https://www.npr.org/sections/thetwo-way/2011/08/11/139536686/pa-judge-sentenced-to-28-years-in-massive-juvenile-justice-bribery-scandal

Petrosino, A., Turpin-Petrosino, C., & Guckenburg, S. (2010). Formal system processing of juveniles: Effects on delinquency. *Campbell Systematic Reviews, 6*(1), 1–88.

Platt, A. M. (1969). *The child savers: The invention of delinquency*. University of Chicago.

Platt, A. M. (1977). *The child savers: The invention of delinquency*. University of Chicago.

Prison Rape Elimination Act (PREA); 42 U.S.C. §§ 15601.

Raine, A., Buchsbaum, M., & Lacasse, L. (1997). Brain abnormalities in murderers indicated by positron emission tomography. *Biological Psychiatry, 42*(6), 495–508.

Robles-Ramamurthy, B., & Watson, C. (2019). Examining racial disparities in juvenile justice. *The Journal of the American Academy of Psychiatry and the Law, 47*(1), 48–52.

Rovner, J. (2016). Racial disparities in youth commitments and arrests. *The Sentencing Project*. https://www.sentencingproject.org/publications/racial-disparities-in-youth-commitments-and-arrests/

Shaw, D. S., & Winslow, E. B. (1997). Precursors and correlates of antisocial behavior from infancy to preschool. In D. M. Stoff, J. Breiling, & J. D. Maser (Eds.), *Handbook of antisocial behavior* (pp. 148–158). John Wiley & Sons Inc.

Shepherd, S. M., Luebbers, S., & Ogloff, J. R. (2016). The role of protective factors and the relationship with recidivism for high-risk young people in detention. *Criminal Justice and Behavior, 43*(7), 863–878.

Soler, M., & Garry, L. M. (2009). *Disproportionate minority contact*. U.S. Department of Justice. Office of Juvenile Justice and Delinquency Prevention. https://www.ncjrs.gov/pdffiles1/ojjdp/218861.pdf

Stanfield, R. (1999). *Pathways to juvenile detention reform: The JDAI story building a better juvenile detention system*. Annie E. Casey Foundation.

Steketee, M., Aussems, C., & Marshall, I. H. (2019). Exploring the impact of child maltreatment and interparental violence on violent delinquency in an international sample. *Journal of Interpersonal Violence*.

Stevens, B., Sattar, S., Morzuch, M., Young, D., Ruttner, L., Stein, J., Hargreaves, M., & Foster, L. (2016). *Final report from the model of change evaluation*. MacArthur Foundation. https://www.macfound.org/media/files/Models_for_Change_Initiative_Report_Final.pdf

Teague, R., Mazerolle, P., Legosz, M., & Sanderson, J. (2008). Linking childhood exposure to physical abuse and adult offending: Examining mediating factors and gendered relationships. *Justice Quarterly, 25*(2), 313–348.

Teigen, A. (2020). *Juvenile age of jurisdiction and transfer to adult court laws.* National Conference of State Legislatures. https://www.ncsl.org/research/civil-and-criminal-justice/juvenile-age-of-jurisdiction-and-transfer-to-adult-court-laws.aspx

Teplin, L. A., McClelland, G. M., Abram, K. M., & Mileusnic, D. (2005). Early violent death among delinquent youth: A prospective longitudinal study. *Pediatrics, 115*(6), 1586–1593.

Thornberry, T. P. (1973). Race, socioeconomic status and sentencing in the juvenile justice system. *The Journal of Criminal Law and Criminology, 64*(1), 90–98.

Thornberry, T. P. (1979). Sentencing disparities in the juvenile justice system. *The Journal of Criminal Law and Criminology, 70*(2), 164–171.

U.S. Department of Justice Archives. (2020, January 22). *Juvenile delinquency prosecution.* https://www.justice.gov/archives/jm/criminal-resource-manual-116-juvenile-delinquency-prosecution-introduction#:~:text=In%201938%2C%20the%20Federal%20Juvenile,the%20age%20of%20twenty%2Done.

W. Haywood Burns Institute. (2020). *United States of disparities.* https://usdata.burnsinstitute.org/#comparison=2&placement=1&races=2,3,4,5,6&offenses=5,2,8,1,9,11,10&year=2017&view=map

Walker, S. C., Muno, A., & Sullivan-Colglazier, C. (2015). Principles in practice: A multistate study of gender-responsive reforms in the juvenile justice system. *Crime & Delinquency, 61*(5), 742–766.

Watson, L., & Edelman, P. (2012). *Improving the juvenile justice system for girls: Lessons from the states.* Georgetown Center on Poverty, Inequality and Public Policy.

Widom, C. S. (1989). Child abuse, neglect, and adult behavior: Research design and findings on criminality, violence, and child abuse. *American Journal of Orthopsychiatry, 59*(3), 355–367.

Widom, C. S., & Morris, S. (1997). Accuracy of adult recollections of childhood victimization, Part 2: Childhood sexual abuse. *Psychological Assessment, 9*(1), 34–46.

Wilson, B. D., Jordan, S. P., Meyer, I. H., Flores, A. R., Stemple, L., & Herman, J. L. (2017). Disproportionality and disparities among sexual minority youth in custody. *Journal of Youth and Adolescence, 46*(7), 1547–1561.

Wilson, J. J., & Howell, J. C. (1993). *A comprehensive strategy for serious, violent, and chronic juvenile offenders.* U.S. Department of Justice. https://ojjdp.ojp.gov/library/publications/serious-violent-and-chronic-juvenile-offenders-comprehensive-strategy

Zahn, M. A., Day, J. C., Mihalic, S. F., & Tichavsky, L. (2009). Determining what works for girls in the juvenile justice system: A summary of evaluation evidence. *Crime & Delinquency, 55*(2), 266–293.

# WEB-BASED RESOURCES

Annie E. Casey Foundation Juvenile Justice Strategy: https://www.aecf.org/work/juvenile-justice/

Blueprints for Healthy Youth Development: https://www.blueprintsprograms.org/

MacArthur Foundation Models of Change Program: http://www.modelsforchange.net/

Model Programs Guide: https://www.ojjdp.gov/mpg

The Sentencing Project: https://www.sentencingproject.org/issues/juvenile-justice/

# 11

# FIREARM FATALITIES AND INJURIES IN THE UNITED STATES

An Unnecessary Epidemic?

## Chris A. Rees and Eric W. Fleegler

Since the founding of the United States (U.S.), 1,304,681 American military fatalities have occurred in all of the major conflicts fought from 1775 to 2020 (Statista, 2020). Between 1981 and 2018, 1,272,575 firearm fatalities occurred in the U.S. (Centers for Disease Control and Prevention [CDC], 2020). Given that almost 40,000 firearm fatalities occur annually, the cumulative number of U.S. civilian deaths in the past 38 years surpassed all historic military deaths midway through 2019. Among these deaths, 311,270 (24%) were children, adolescents, and emerging adults aged 0 to 24 years.

How did we get here? Why do all of these firearm fatalities occur with such frequency in the U.S.? The reasons are myriad. These fatalities are unquestionably related to the ease and mass availability of firearms. Many would argue that the right to own these firearms is enshrined in our Bill of Rights. To debate this is typically nonproductive and unlikely to diminish the number of unnecessary deaths that occur each year. Rather, we must understand *who* owns and *why* people own guns. We need to understand the *who*, *what*, *where*, and *why* people die from firearms. We need to understand which interventions, including policies, reduce firearm fatalities and figure out a way to maximize the safety of all people in the U.S. All of this occurs within the context of a society mixed with people, including those who do not own nor desire guns and those who broadly embrace a diverse set of gun cultures (Boine et al., 2020).

Given the emphasis of this book, children, youth, and families are the focus of this chapter. However, given the importance of the historical and social context of firearms in America, we begin with an overview of gun ownership and then discuss the epidemiology of firearm violence and prevention.

## GUN OWNERSHIP

According to a national Gallup poll in 2019, about 37% of American households own guns, down from a peak of 51% in 1994 (Gallup, 2020). Ownership varies enormously by race/ethnicity, sex, and political affiliation. White families own firearms at 50% higher rates than Black families and more than twice the rate of Hispanic families (49% vs. 32%. vs. 21%, respectively). Males own guns at nearly double the rate of females (39% vs. 22%). People who affiliate themselves with the Republican party own guns at more than twofold higher rates than those affiliated with the Democratic party (41% vs. 16%; Parker et al., 2017). Though gun purchases have increased under each of the past three presidential administrations (8.5 million firearm background checks in 2000 to 28 million firearm background checks in 2019), the largest volume of gun purchases in history, and likely the largest shift in first-time gun ownership ever, occurred during the 2020 COVID-19 pandemic (Mannix et al., 2020) with nearly 40 million firearm background checks performed, an albeit imperfect but reasonable approximation of trends in gun sales (Federal Bureau of Investigation [FBI], 2020).

While this variability exists across demographic groups, the greatest variability exists across states. Since the federal law known as the Firearm Owners Protection Act (FOPA) prohibits maintaining a central registry of firearms owned by private citizens, it is a challenge to know exactly how many firearms are in the U.S. or how many households own firearms. Best estimates suggest there are 350–400 million guns in 45 million homes in the U.S. (Siegel et al., 2014). A range of proxy values have been developed to estimate how many households own firearms in each state, all based on the principle that the ratio of firearm suicides to total suicides closely approximates the number of households owning firearms. The most recent and refined calculation was developed by the RAND Corporation. By this estimate, in 2016, the household firearm ownership rates varied from a low in New Jersey, Massachusetts, and Hawaii of 9% to greater than 60% in West Virginia, Montana, and Wyoming (Figure 11.1; Schell et al., 2020). This geographic trend is also reflected by urbanicity; the firearm ownership rate in urban households is 29% and in rural households is 58% (Parker et al., 2017).

Approximately 22.6 million children live in households with firearms (Azrael et al., 2018). Among them, 4.6 million children (7% of all U.S. children) are exposed to at least one gun that is loaded and unlocked, which is the most dangerous storage environment. Another 11.4 million children live in households with the gun loaded and locked or unloaded and unlocked, each a dangerous storage method. In children with a history of self-harm risk factors, 44% live in a household with a firearm present (Scott et al., 2018).

The reason why people own firearms has changed in the past four decades from predominately hunting and sport to safety and home protection. Beliefs around the safety of guns in the home have shifted since 2000, when 35% of Americans felt guns made a house safer and 51% of Americans felt guns made a home more dangerous (Parker et al., 2017). By 2014, these opinions had completely flipped—63% felt guns made homes safer and 30% felt guns made homes more dangerous. Two thirds of gun owners stated they owned their gun for protection and only a third owned them for hunting or sport. Three quarters of all gun owners state that their firearm is essential to their personal freedom and 50% say that their firearm is important to their overall identity. A study in the U.S. showed three major gun cultures that vary substantially between states: recreation, self-defense, and Second Amendment activism. Over time, the recreational gun culture variation has decreased whereas the self-defense culture

Figure 11.1   Firearm Ownership Rates by States, 2016

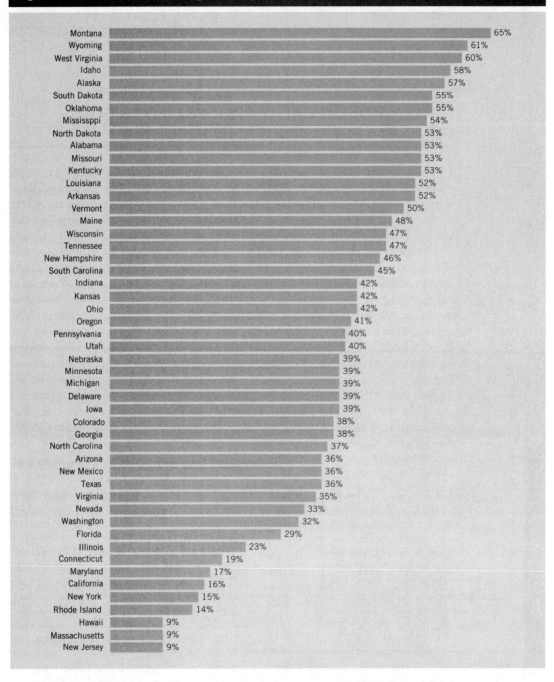

Montana 65%
Wyoming 61%
West Virginia 60%
Idaho 58%
Alaska 57%
South Dakota 55%
Oklahoma 55%
Mississppi 54%
North Dakota 53%
Alabama 53%
Missouri 53%
Kentucky 53%
Louisiana 52%
Arkansas 52%
Vermont 50%
Maine 48%
Wisconsin 47%
Tennessee 47%
New Hampshire 46%
South Carolina 45%
Indiana 42%
Kansas 42%
Ohio 42%
Oregon 41%
Pennsylvania 40%
Utah 40%
Nebraska 39%
Minnesota 39%
Michigan 39%
Delaware 39%
Iowa 39%
Colorado 38%
Georgia 38%
North Carolina 37%
Arizona 36%
New Mexico 36%
Texas 36%
Virginia 35%
Nevada 33%
Washington 32%
Florida 29%
Illinois 23%
Connecticut 19%
Maryland 17%
California 16%
New York 15%
Rhode Island 14%
Hawaii 9%
Massachusetts 9%
New Jersey 9%

*Source:* Schell et al. (2020).

has increased, and a new mobilization around the Second Amendment has arisen (Boine et al., 2020).

Most youth in the U.S. support guns in the home. A national text message survey of U.S. youth reported 66% were "pro" or "conditionally pro" having guns in the home. They cite the Second Amendment as well as wanting guns for protection and hunting as reasons for wanting to have a gun (Van Sparrentak et al., 2018).

## EPIDEMIOLOGY AND RISK FACTORS FOR FIREARM FATALITIES AND INJURIES

Firearms are the cause of significant morbidity and mortality in the U.S. There are more than 100 firearm deaths per day in the U.S. (Brady, 2019). In 2018 alone, there were nearly 40,000 firearm-related fatalities, 12.2 per 100,000 individuals (CDC, 2019). This is the highest number of annual firearm-related fatalities in the U.S. since the CDC began tracking injury fatalities in 1981. There is evidence to suggest that overall rates of firearm fatalities are increasing, and dramatic increases in firearm-related suicides may be a key driver (Goldstick et al., 2019; Kegler et al., 2018). Firearm-related fatalities are now the third leading cause of injury-related deaths in Americans age 15–24 years. In fact, firearms account for more than 22% of all deaths in this age group (CDC, 2017a; Lee & Mannix, 2018). Though younger children have lower firearm fatality rates (0.8 per 100,000 for children aged 1–14), firearms still account for 5% of all childhood fatalities. Among adults 20 years and older, firearm fatalities are 56% suicides, 42% homicides, 1% unintentional, and 1% legal intervention (i.e., inflicted by law enforcement; CDC, 2016). In children, these numbers are flipped: 40% suicides, 56% homicide, 3% unintentional, and 1% legal intervention.

There are multiple risk factors associated with firearm fatalities in the U.S. First, males make up 86% of all firearm-related deaths, which is 6.5 times more than females. Furthermore, the shooter in 97% of firearm-related homicides is male. Second, race and ethnicity are associated with disparate rates in firearm fatalities. Specifically, young and middle-age Black and Hispanic males and females have much higher rates of firearm-related fatalities than White males and females (Beard et al., 2017; Hawes et al., 2016; Pear et al., 2018; Riddell et al., 2018; Tuan & Frey, 2017). See Figure 11.2 for firearm fatality rates by age and race/ethnicity and Figure 11.3 for child, adolescent, and emerging adult fatalities over time. Third, people 65 years or older may be less likely to attempt suicide than persons less than 25 years old but were more likely to die by suicide (Conner et al., 2019), conferring a higher risk of firearm-related fatalities among older adults in the U.S. Fourth, county-level poverty has been associated with increased rates of firearm-related unintentional deaths and suicides (Hoffmann et al., 2020; Karb et al., 2016). In counties with high levels of poverty (≥ 20% of the population living below the federal poverty level [FPL]), the youth firearm fatality rate (age 5–24 years) is 4.6 times higher than in counties with the lowest poverty levels (< 5% living below FPL; Barrett et al., 2020). A study in Philadelphia demonstrated that firearm injuries were highest in areas historically zoned for people of color (Jacoby et al., 2018).

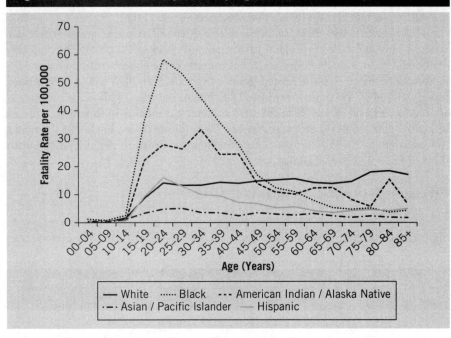

**Figure 11.2  Firearm Fatality Rates by Age and Race/Ethnicity, 2018**

*Source:* CDC (2020).

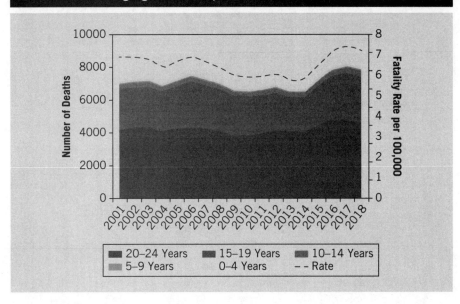

**Figure 11.3  Firearm Fatalities Over Time by Age Group (Infancy to Emerging Adulthood)**

*Source:* CDC (2020).

One of the top predictors of where firearm fatalities occur is where firearm ownership rates are the highest. As state-level firearm ownership rates increase, both firearm homicides and firearm suicides increase (see Figure 11.4).

Not all events with firearms in the U.S. are fatal. There are approximately two nonfatal firearm injuries for each firearm fatality (Fowler et al., 2015). The reporting of nonfatal firearm-related injury rates has recently come under scrutiny, given a 37% increase in nonfatal firearm-related injuries from 2015 to 2016 with a concomitant increase of only 6.6% in firearm-related fatalities as reported by the CDC (Spitzer et al., 2020). However, if the CDC data are accurate, the lethality of firearm injuries are decreasing. However, other studies suggest the opposite (Cook et al., 2017; Kalesan, Adhikarla et al., 2017). The risk factors for nonfatal firearm-related injuries mirror those of firearm-related fatalities.

## Firearm Homicide and Assaults

In 2018, there were 18,830 Americans killed by homicide, and firearms were implicated in nearly 75% of these deaths (Kochanek et al., 2019). Firearm-related

**Figure 11.4  State-Level Firearm Homicide and Suicide Rates (2018) Relative to Firearm Ownership Rates (2016)**

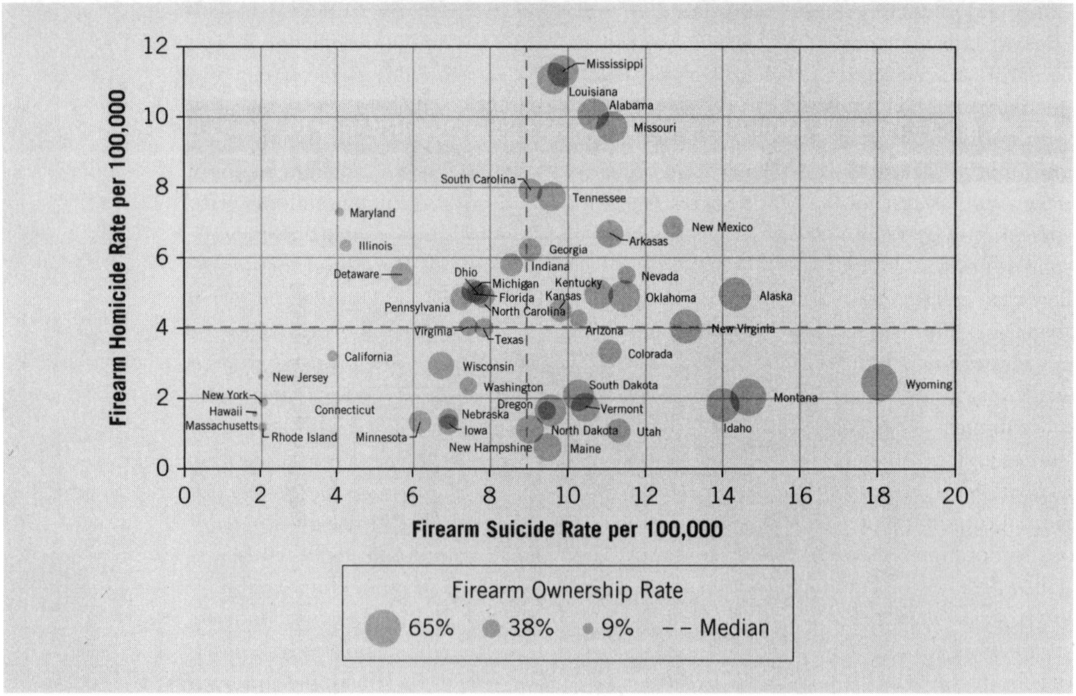

*Sources:* Azrael et al. (2018); Scott et al. (2018)

homicide rates are higher in the U.S. than any other country in the world, with the U.S. accounting for more than 90% of all firearm-related homicides among high-income countries (Grinshteyn & Hemenway, 2016). Though firearm-related fatalities have decreased since 1993, recent data suggest an increase in firearm-related homicides (CDC, 2017b). From 2013 to 2017, firearm-related homicides increased 37%, suggesting that the overall declining trend in firearm-related homicides has reversed. Non-firearm–related homicides decreased by 11% during the same time period.

In 2016, firearms were the second leading cause of all child and adolescent deaths (3,143 total firearms deaths, 15.4% of all deaths), with firearm homicides the leading cause of firearm deaths (1,865 firearm homicides, 59.3% of all firearm deaths). Firearm mortality rates had hit a nadir in 2013 but have risen since then to near-record highs (CDC, 2020). The youngest children are frequently killed by their fathers whereas older children are victims of interpersonal violence.

For all ages, firearm-related homicides are sixfold greater among males compared to females (CDC, 2017b). Firearm-related homicides disproportionately affect individuals living in urban communities when compared to people living in rural communities in the United States. State-level firearm ownership rates are a strong predictor of firearm homicide rates: For every 1% increase in firearm ownership, the firearm homicide rate increases 0.9% (Siegel et al., 2013).

Furthermore, Black individuals have significantly higher rates of firearm-related homicides than other racial groups. Firearm-related homicides rates are as high as eight times higher among Black people compared to other racial groups in the U.S. (CDC, 2017b). See Figure 11.5 for child and adolescent firearm homicides by race/ethnicity over time. Such disparities in firearm-related homicide rates are, in part, due to structural racism and community-level segregation (Beard et al., 2017; Kalesan et al., 2016).

Nonfatal firearm assault injuries are also common in the U.S. Estimates suggest that for each firearm-related homicide, there are seven other nonfatal firearm-related assaults (CDC, 2017b). This is likely even in the face of underreporting of nonfatal firearm-related assault injuries. Every year, approximately 12,500 nonfatal firearm assault injuries among adolescents occur in the U.S. and are treated in emergency departments. Males and Black individuals in the U.S. are similarly at increased risk of nonfatal firearm-related assaults when compared to females and nonblack individuals.

Individuals who sustain intentional firearm-related assaults have a greater risk of subsequent and repeated interpersonal violence (Carter et al., 2015; Rowhani-Rahbar et al., 2015), making incidents of nonfatal firearm-related injuries potential points for intervention to reduce subsequent episodes. Additionally, children and adolescents who are involved in nonfatal firearm-related injuries have greater risk of mental illness (e.g., post-traumatic stress disorder, substance use disorders) and subsequent arrest and incarceration (Carter et al., 2018; Rowhani-Rahbar et al., 2015; Walton et al., 2017).

## Access to Firearms and Suicide

Depression is a major risk factor for suicide, which is the second leading cause of death in those 10–24 years old (CDC, 2017b). By early adolescence, approximately

## Figure 11.5    Firearm Homicide Rates by Race/Ethnicity, Ages 1–19 Years

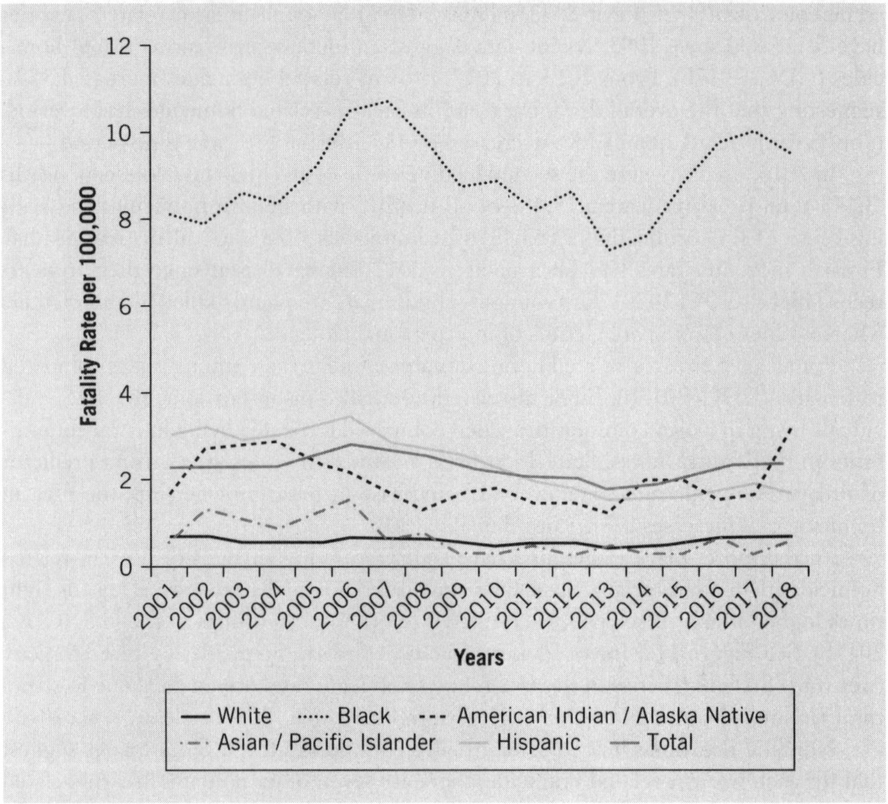

Source: CDC (2020).

5% of youth will experience a depressive episode in a given year, and by the age of 24, up to 20% of young people will have experienced at least one episode of depression in their life (Costello et al., 2005; Costello et al., 2006; Hankin et al., 1998; Lewinsohn et al., 1999). However, only 50% of adolescent suicide victims had a diagnosis of depression at the time of their death (Hawton & van Heeringen, 2009). Among suicides in adolescents with no apparent psychiatric disorder (compared to suicides with known mental health problems), there is a 14-fold higher rate of loaded guns stored in the home (Brent et al., 1993). Firearms are the cause of death in a third of suicides among those 10- to 14-years-old and by the age of 20–24 years, firearms are used in half of all suicides. While males have the highest rates of total and firearm-related suicide, among female adolescent suicides, firearms are used 27% of the time (CDC, 2020).

Firearm ownership at the state level is related to both adolescent and emerging adult suicide rates. For each 10% increase in the state firearm ownership rate, there is a 27% to 39% increase in adolescent firearm suicides, which contribute to an overall 7%

increase in total adolescent suicides (Kivisto et al., 2020; Knopov et al., 2019). Firearm suicide rates at the state level are independent of suicidal ideation and depression but are directly correlated with the presence of firearms in the home. A firearm in the home imposes an increase in suicide risk (Miller et al., 2013).

When a firearm is used in a pediatric suicide, among 10- to 14-year-olds and 15- to 19-year-olds, parents owned the firearm 66% and 51% of the time, respectively. Importantly, in these same age groups, the victims themselves owned the firearm 10% and 25% of the time, respectively (Azad, Monuteaux et al., 2020). Firearm storage matters. For suicides among 10- to 14-year-olds and 15- to 19-year-olds, the gun was stored loaded and unlocked 42% and 35% of the time, respectively, or unloaded and unlocked 38% and 39% of the time, respectively. Added together, over three quarters of these suicides occurred when there was ready access to the unlocked gun and ammunition.

Major disparities exist in adolescent firearm suicidality by sex and race/ethnicity. Females experience depression at twice the rate of males (Hyde et al., 2008), but males have fourfold higher rates of suicide and sevenfold higher rates of firearm-related suicide (CDC, 2020). Firearm suicide rates are highest among American Indian/Alaskan Native males followed by White males. Over the past decade, both male and female firearm suicide rates have risen to all-time highs, with overall male firearm suicides increasing 50% and female firearm suicides more than doubling (CDC, 2020). See Figure 11.6 for changes in youth (age 15–24) firearm suicide rates over time.

An important element of suicide reduction is lethal means restriction, aimed at the restriction of access to the most lethal agents of harm (Barber & Miller, 2014). A firearm in the home does not make people more suicidal, but the presence of a firearm does increase the likelihood of death. Suicidal adolescents typically use the method most conveniently available, and what matters at that moment is both whether they have the opportunity for regret as well as the lethality of the action. If an adolescent takes an overdose of medications, they have time to think it over and ask for help. They can call a friend, a family member, or a suicide hotline. Overall, overdoses are treatable and have a mortality rate of 3% (Miller et al., 2004). Unfortunately, with firearms, once the trigger is pulled, there is no opportunity for regret, and 91% of firearm suicide attempts will result in death.

## Unintentional Firearm Injuries

Though the majority of firearm injuries and fatalities in the U.S. are intentional, unintentional firearm injuries and fatalities (which include accidental firing while cleaning or playing) disproportionately affect younger children. Indeed, unintentional firearm fatalities represent 1% of all firearm-related fatalities (CDC, 2017b), but among children age 0–19 years, they represent 3.5% of total firearm deaths; over 100 children die annually from unintentional firearm injuries (Fowler et al., 2015). Unintentional firearm injuries carry a much lower fatality rate (5%) than assaults (19%) or self-inflicted injuries (85%–91%; Miller et al., 2004). Consequently, young people (ages 0–24 years) experience on average over 4,000 unintentional nonfatal firearm injuries annually (Fowler et al., 2015).

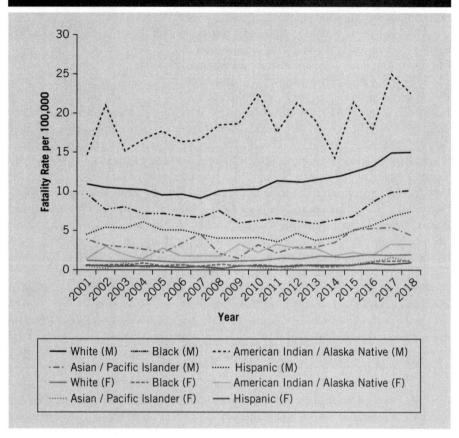

**Figure 11.6 Firearm Suicide Rates by Race/Ethnicity and Sex, Ages 15–24 Years**

*Source:* CDC (2020).

Similar to homicides, males account for the majority of unintentional firearm fatalities. Unlike firearm homicides, unintentional firearm fatalities are more common in rural areas than in urban communities. Though not nearly as pronounced as is the case in firearm-related homicides, the rates of unintentional firearm-related fatalities among Black children are double that of White children and four times higher than among Hispanic children. Rates among American Indian/Alaskan Native children are small enough (< 10 per year) that the actual annual rate is unstable, though clearly higher than other racial/ethnic groups. See Figure 11.7 for firearm unintentional fatality rates.

Most unintentional firearm injuries occur in the home, where children can gain access to caregivers' firearms if they are available and if they are stored unsafely (though even "safely stored" firearms are used in firearm fatalities every year). Approximately

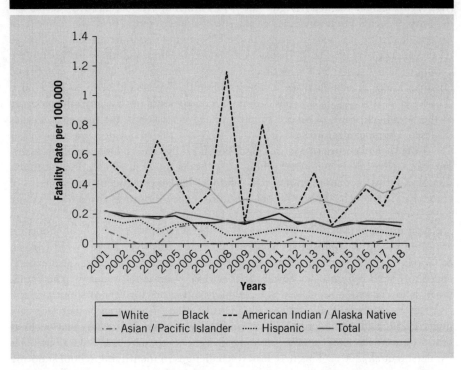

*Source:* CDC (2020).

one third of households in the U.S. have at least one firearm and many have more than one firearm. Greater than one in five households with firearms store them unlocked and loaded, which is the least safe way of storing firearms. Children are often aware of where firearms are stored in the home, and 36% of children have handled a firearm in the home (Baxley & Miller, 2006). One in five caregivers were unaware that their child had handled a firearm in the home. Children as young as 3 years old are able to generate enough force to pull the trigger of firearms (Naureckas et al., 1995). Lastly, in studies simulating home settings where children were observed behind one-way glass, researchers found that when boys discovered a firearm (unloaded and designed to detect a trigger pull), the vast majority of them picked up and played with the firearm, including pulling the trigger while pointing the firearm at another child (Jackman et al., 2001).

## School Shootings

*School shootings* are broadly defined as acts of violence carried out with firearms in which schools are deliberately chosen as the site of violence. Though mass school shootings, such as the tragic events at Columbine High School in Littleton, Colorado, in 1999; Sandy Hook Elementary School in Newtown, Connecticut, in 2012; and Marjory Stoneman Douglas High School in Parkland, Florida, in 2018 receive the majority of media attention (Rees et al., 2019; Towers et al., 2015), the majority of firearm deaths from school shootings in the U.S. are not due to mass school shootings (Gun Violence Archive, 2020). Instead, single-victim school shootings are much more common than mass school shootings. Fatalities from school shootings comprised less than 1% of firearm fatalities among children 0–17 years old between 1999–2016 (Fowler et al., 2017). The U.S. has had more school shootings than any other country in the world, and rates of school shootings have increased in the past two decades (Kalesan, Lagast et al., 2017).

More than two thirds of victims in school shootings are students and the remaining third are teachers and other school staff (Anderson et al., 2001). Furthermore, school shootings are more common in schools where most students are students of color than in majority-White schools, despite school shootings at majority-White schools receiving more media attention (Livingston et al., 2019). School shootings are typically intentional (Newman et al., 2008). Perpetrators of school shootings are often young, as almost half of perpetrators are less than 20 years old (Brown & Goodin, 2018). States that have higher rates of firearm ownership also experience more school shootings (Towers et al., 2015). Despite these alarming statistics, much is unknown about school shootings. Risk factors for school shootings and risk factors that would allow the early identification of potential perpetrators are not well elucidated. This may be because firearm injuries and deaths that occur at schools are not labeled as *school shootings* in reports to state and federal agencies (Anderson et al., 2001). This may lead to challenges in identifying school shooting victims and perpetrators in the current federal health care system and criminal justice data sources.

More than half of all school shootings in the U.S. are preceded by a warning sign, indicating the likelihood for impending violence (Anderson et al., 2001). Mental illness is often blamed for school shootings, with as many as 54% of assailants having had some mental health disorder prior to their violent acts at schools (Brown & Goodin, 2018). Epidemiologic data also support this, as states with higher budgets for care for patients with mental illness have fewer school shootings (Kalesan, Lagast et al., 2017). There is also evidence to suggest that patients with mental health disorders are more likely to be victims rather than perpetrators of violent acts (Hiroeh et al., 2001; Stuart, 2003). School shootings are often modeled by others through a "copycat effect." Modeling studies suggest there is significant evidence of school shooting contagion, as rates of school shootings are higher within two weeks of previous school shootings than baseline rates of school shootings (Towers et al., 2015).

There are many risk factors for being involved in firearm violence in terms of perpetration and victimization. Table 11.1 shows risk factors at the individual, family, peer and school, and community levels. Very little research has been conducted about factors that protect young people from firearm injuries or fatalities.

| Table 11.1 Risk Factors for Youth Involvement in Firearm Violence |
|---|
| **Individual Factors** |
| Carrying a firearm |
| History of delinquency |
| Substance use/abuse (alcohol and illicit drugs) |
| Prior involvement with violence (victimization, witnessing, fighting) |
| History of mental illness, including depression (primarily a risk factor for suicide) |
| **Family Factors** |
| Having a firearm in the home |
| Unsafe firearm storage |
| Poor parent–child relationship |
| Low levels of parental supervision |
| Parental/caregiver history of drug use |
| **Peer and School Factors** |
| Affiliation with peers who own or use firearms |
| Truancy |
| Low academic achievement |
| **Community Factors** |
| Living in a disadvantaged and disorganized neighborhood |
| Exposure to community violence |
| Availability of firearms |

*Source:* Schmidt et al. (2019).

# PREVENTION OF FIREARM INJURIES AND FATALITIES

Prevention strategies to reduce firearm-related injuries and fatalities are many. The most effective measure to prevent firearm-related injuries in the home is to not have firearms in the household (Dowd et al., 2012). However, given the widespread ownership of firearms in the U.S., alternative methods for safe storage are needed. The safest way to store a firearm in the home is unloaded, locked, and stored separately from the locked ammunition. Studies suggest that safe storage of firearms in the home could reduce up to 32% of firearm injuries and suicides (Monuteaux et al., 2019).

Though some advocate for firearm handling education for children, firearm safety education may not instill consistent and safe firearm handling habits in children and may actually provide parents with a false sense of security about the safety of their readily available firearms. On the epidemiologic level, states with more stringent child access prevention laws—laws that hold firearm owners accountable if a child could or does access a firearm—tend to have lower rates of firearm-related fatalities (Azad, Rees et al., 2021).

## Safety Devices for Firearms

Beyond policy aimed to limit access to firearms or to regulate the purchase of firearms, other mechanical safety devices have been developed to prevent the accidental (unintentional) firing of a firearm. Mechanical safety devices can be thought of as either *passive*, which would not require any sort of activation by the shooter to use the firearm, or *active*, which requires action by the shooter to deactivate the safety device and subsequently fire the firearm (Dodington, 2021). Passive safety devices are designed such that a firearm will only fire when the trigger is engaged and not when the firearm is dropped on the ground, for example. Active safety devices include pivot safeties, grip safeties, trigger locks, and cable locks. All of these mechanical devices require manipulation or removal prior to firing the firearm.

Another example of an active safety device is "smart gun technology." With smart gun technology, a firearm can only be fired when an authorized user is handling the firearm. The authorized user can be identified by their fingerprints or another device, such as a wristwatch that must be worn in order for the firearm to be fired or a radio-frequency identification (RFID) ring (Simonetti et al., 2017). Despite seeming to promise to reduce firearm fatalities and injuries, the effect of smart gun technology on reducing firearm-related fatalities and injuries has yet to be studied. This is primarily because of opposition by a small but vocal group that are concerned about any restrictions, including safety, related to firearms. However, a majority of firearm owners are interested in having smart guns available for sale and many would consider exchanging their current firearms for ones with a built-in safety feature (Wallace, 2016). Some of the biggest concerns related to smart gun technologies are the additional costs, which can potentially be subsidized (such as occurred with the introduction of electric cars) and/or would change over time as market pressures are exerted and technologies advance (Crifasi et al., 2019). There is an estimate that smart gun technology could reduce up to 37% of deaths based on a study of just over 100 firearm fatalities (Vernick et al., 2003).

Studies have shown that distributing mechanical safety devices for firearms can increase safe firearm storage. In a randomized trial comparing pediatric office-based counseling on safe firearm storage and provision of locking devices to no intervention, rates of safe firearm storage increased by 10% among more than 130 pediatric practices (Barkin et al., 2008). Participants who did not receive counseling or a mechanical safety device had a decrease in safe firearm storage practices during the study period. Another study showed that distributing free metal firearm cabinets in Alaska reduced the proportion of unlocked firearms stored in the home from 95% to 35% (Grossman et al., 2012).

## Firearm Legislation

There are over 300 different firearm laws at the federal and state levels. At the federal level, there are a limited number of laws that have evolved over the past 90 years. They primarily regulate licensing and requirements of gun makers, distributers, and licensed dealers. Early legislation still in effect includes the National Firearms Act of 1934, which regulates the sales and possession of guns as a way to reduce organized crime, and the Gun Control Act of 1968, which prohibits certain groups of people from owning guns (e.g., individuals convicted of certain crimes, undocumented immigrants, and people with severe mental illness) and came about after the assassinations of Reverend Martin Luther King Jr. and Senator Robert Kennedy. These laws regulate the manufacture, transfer, and possession of firearms (Foster, 2019). The Brady Handgun Violence Prevention Act—enacted in 1994 and named after James Brady, who was shot and wounded during the assassination attempt of President Ronald Reagan in 1981—requires background checks when guns are sold through licensed dealers and sets out further criteria about who may or may not purchase a firearm (Lyneé Madeira, 2021). It led to the establishment of the federal criminal background check system in 1998. In 2021, Congress is considering laws that would expand background checks to all firearm sales whether by licensed dealers or private individuals.

There are considerations about the ability to regulate firearms in the context of the Second Amendment. The Second Amendment states, "[A] well-regulated Militia, being necessary to the security of a free State, the right of the people to keep and bear arms, shall not be infringed." Historically, firearm legislation passed by Congress and at the state level has been upheld in the courts; however, under *District of Columbia v. Heller* in 2008, a law regulating handgun possession was overturned under the rubric of protecting the right to possess firearms for historically lawful purposes. Other key federal laws and regulations include the 1986 FOPA, which prohibited a national registry of guns sales, allowed licensed dealers to sell firearms at gun shows, and loosened regulations related to ammunition. In 1994, the Federal Assault Weapons Ban was passed but expired without renewal in 2004. In 2005, the Protection of Lawful Commerce in Arms Act banned lawsuits against firearm manufacturers from victims of firearm crimes. In addition, firearms are completely exempt from safety regulation ever since the establishment of the Consumer Product Safety Commission in 1972, which makes firearms the only product in the U.S. not regulated for safety.

At the state level, policy covers a wide range of rules and regulations that have been captured succinctly in a database maintained by the Boston University School of Public Health that is available for free at http://statefirearmlaws.org. The laws in each state from 1991 to present are quantified and qualified, allowing for comparison. The laws are categorized into 15 groups, each with multiple subcategories, including ammunition regulations, assault weapons and large capacity magazines, background checks, buyer regulations, child access prevention, concealed carry permitting, dealer regulations, domestic violence, gun trafficking, immunity, possession regulations, preemption, prohibitions for high-risk gun possession, and stand your ground laws (Siegel, 2020; Siegel, Pahn et al., 2017).

There is enormous variation across states in the passage of legislation, the actual implementation of these laws, and the enforcement and penalties associated with them. The volume of firearm legislation is highly variable, with some states only having one firearm law (e.g., Idaho) and other states with more than 100 laws (e.g., California and Massachusetts; see Figure 11.8; Siegel, 2020).

In the context of policy effectiveness, an important question exists: Does firearm legislation make a difference in decreasing fatalities in the U.S.? Unlike the relatively straightforward measurement of the effectiveness of implementing a single law such as booster seat legislation, bicycle helmet laws, and seatbelt laws, which all lead to lower fatality rates (Lee et al., 2015; Mannix et al., 2012; Meehan et al., 2013), firearm laws are more complicated to evaluate. Overall, states with more firearm legislation have up to 42% lower firearm fatality rates than states with minimal legislation (Fleegler et al., 2013). See Figure 11.9 for the relationship between the number of state laws and firearm-related homicide and suicide rates. When these laws have been examined individually, the evidence shows that many (but not all) laws reduce the rate of firearm-related homicides (Lee et al., 2017; Siegel et al., 2019; Siegel, Xuan et al., 2017) and firearm-related suicides (Santaella-Tenorio et al., 2016). The laws with the strongest demonstration of reducing firearm fatalities are those related to universal background checks and violent misdemeanor laws (Siegel et al., 2019). Laws associated with increased fatality rates include "shall issue" laws (e.g., require that a firearm license be given to an individual as opposed to "may issue" guidelines that leave the issuing of a license to the discretion of the police) and "stand your ground" laws that allow a person to shoot if they feel threatened (Humphreys et al., 2017; Siegel, Xuan et al., 2017; Siegel et al., 2019).

Specifically relevant to families are laws that remove firearms from people with domestic violence restraining orders; these have been shown to reduce intimate partner firearm homicides by 14% (Díez et al., 2017). Multiple states have passed child access prevention legislation, which, as of 2020, mandate safe firearm storage in 16 states (Azad, Monuteaux et al., 2020). So-called negligence laws hold the parent responsible if their child uses the firearm, accesses the firearm, and—in the most rigorous examples—*could* access the firearm. In states that have passed these laws (controlling for multiple factors, including the rate of firearm ownership), child firearm fatality rates are 13% lower, and these effects cross homicides, suicides, and unintentional deaths. Another type of child access prevention law is a "recklessness" law that only holds the gun owner responsible if they give a loaded gun to a child and that child hurts or kills someone. Nine states have passed this kind of law, but they do not appear to decrease fatality rates. See Figure 11.10 for which states have passed these laws.

Over the last 10 years, support has increased for stricter firearm laws. This is consistent with increasing dissatisfaction with U.S. gun policy: 36% of Americans were very dissatisfied and only 17% of Americans were very satisfied with strict firearm legislation in 2019 (Gallup, 2020). This is compared to 2008, when 21% of Americans

**Figure 11.8    Number of State Firearm Laws, 2020**

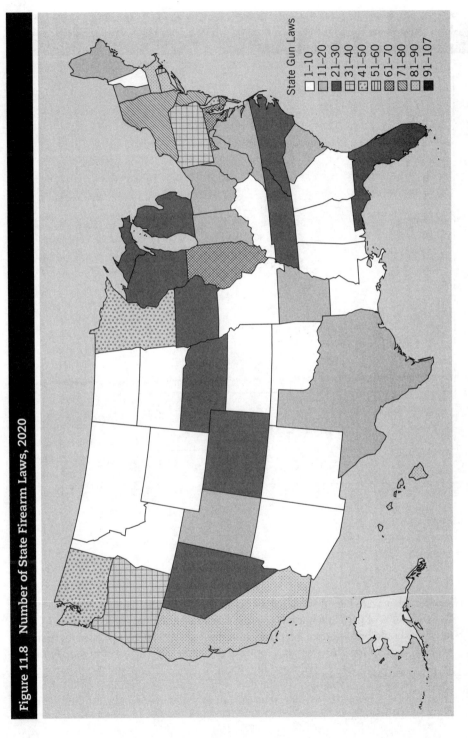

State Gun Laws

1–10
11–20
21–30
31–40
41–50
51–60
61–70
71–80
81–90
91–107

Source: Siegel (2020).

379

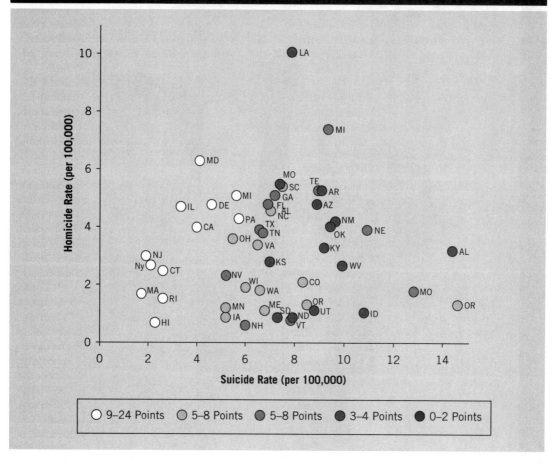

**Figure 11.9** Number of State Firearm Laws by Rates of Firearm-Related Homicides and Suicides in 2010

*Source:* Fleegler et al. (2013).

reported they were very dissatisfied and 14% were very satisfied with U.S. gun policy. By 2019, 64% of people felt laws covering firearms should be stricter versus 7% who felt they should be less strict. Americans are divided on what type of laws there should be: 29% want to ban the possession of handguns and 47% want to ban semiautomatic guns (i.e., "assault rifles"). Almost all Americans (96%) favor universal background checks for all gun purchases, 75% favor enacting a 30-day waiting period for all gun sales, and 70% favor the requirement that all privately owned guns should be registered with the police.

**Figure 11.10 Child Access Prevention Laws, 1989–2020**

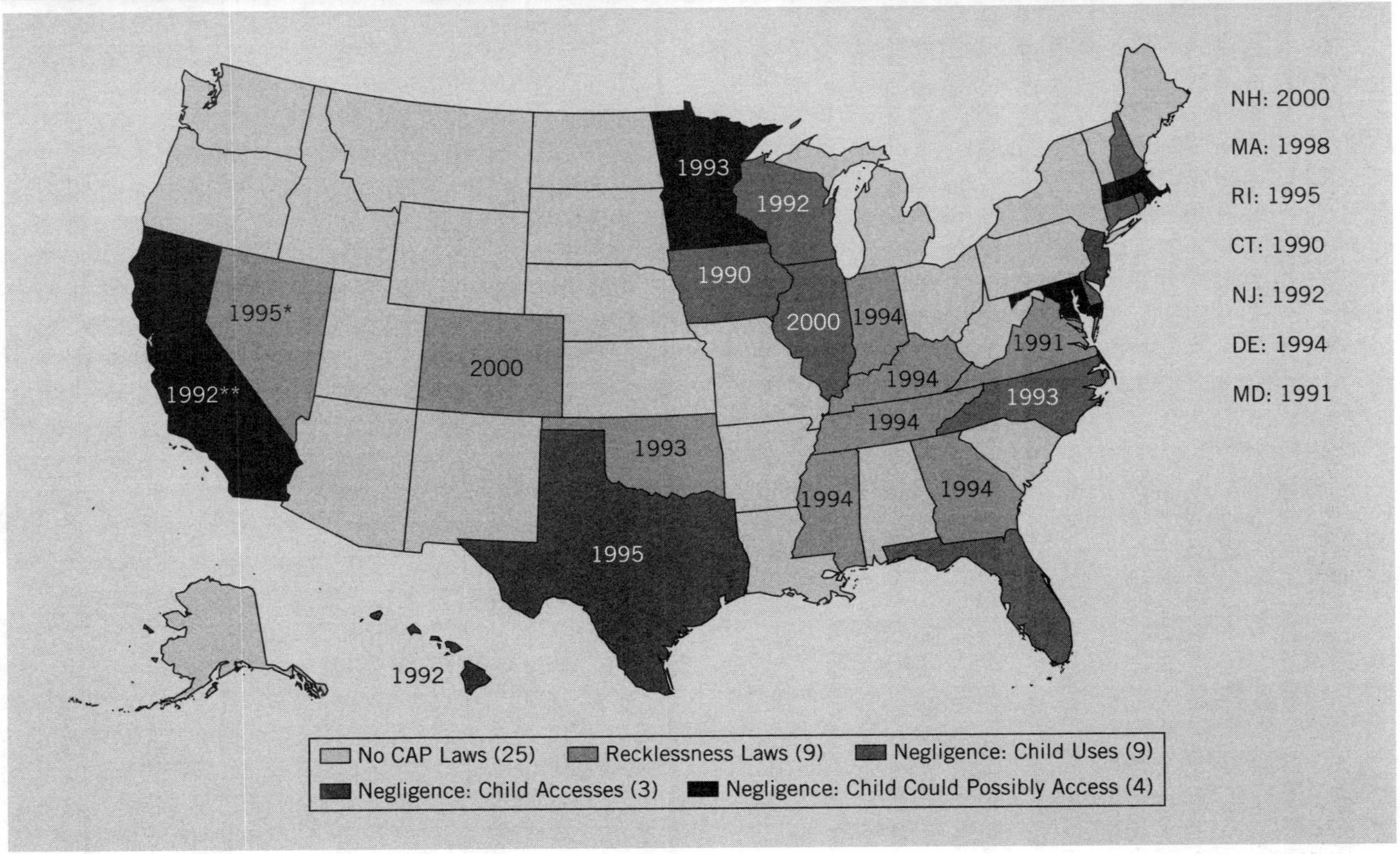

1993
1992
1990
2000
1994
1995*
2000
1992**
1994
1991
1993
1994
1993
1994
1994
1995
1992
NH: 2000
MA: 1998
RI: 1995
CT: 1990
NJ: 1992
DE: 1994
MD: 1991
No CAP Laws (25)
Recklessness Laws (9)
Negligence: Child Uses (9)
Negligence: Child Accesses (3)
Negligence: Child Could Possibly Access (4)


*Source:* Azad et al., 2020b

## SUMMARY

This chapter provided an overview of gun ownership in the U.S.; prevalence, disparities, and risk factors for firearm fatalities and injuries; and preventive strategies in terms of gun and ammunition storage, safety devices, and firearm legislation. Here are some key points to remember:

- There are currently more firearms in the U.S. than there are people.

- Firearm ownership across states varies sevenfold, with some states as low as 9% ownership and others as high as 65% ownership. As firearm ownership rates increase at the state level, so do the rates of firearm homicide and firearm suicide.

- Gun ownership varies significantly by sex, race/ethnicity, urbanicity, and political affiliation.

- Firearm deaths account for 5% of child fatalities and 22% of emerging adult fatalities and are the second leading cause of death for young people.

- Significant disparities exist, with males dying by firearms at multiple times the rate of females. There are large disparities by race, with Black children dying at the highest rates by firearm homicide and unintentional firearm shootings; American Indians/Alaskan Natives have the highest rates of firearm suicide.

- Guns in the home are the highest risk factor for adolescent firearm suicides; unsafe storage (loaded and unlocked or unloaded and unlocked) increase the risk of a firearm suicide.

- Gun fatalities are not inevitable—the choice to keep a gun in the home is a personal decision. If a firearm is kept in the home, there are multiple devices (e.g., locked boxes and trigger locks) that can store the gun in a safer manner. "Smart gun technology" has the potential to reduce firearm deaths; however, special interest groups have prevented their sale in the U.S.

- Firearm legislation can reduce firearm deaths among children, adolescents, and adults. However, states vary dramatically in the number of laws passed and the enforcement of these laws. Universal laws related to child access prevention and domestic violence have the potential to improve the safety of families.

## REFERENCES

Anderson, M., Kaufman, J., Simon, T. R., Barrios, L., Paulozzi, L., Ryan, G., Hammond, R., Modzeleski, W., Feucht, Potter, L., & School-Associated Violent Deaths Study Group. (2001). School-associated violent deaths in the United States, 1994–1999. *JAMA, 286*(21), 2695–2702.

Azad, H. A., Rees, C., Monuteaux, M. C., Hoffmann, J., Mannix R., Lee, L. K., & Fleegler, E. W. (2021). *Firearm violence in children and teenagers: The source of the firearm* [Manuscript under review].

Azad, H. A., Monuteaux, M. C., Rees, C. A., Siegel, M., Mannix, R., Lee, L. K., Sheehan, K. M., & Fleegler, E. W. (2020). Child access prevention firearm laws and firearm fatalities among children aged 0 to 14 years, 1991–2016. *JAMA Pediatrics, 174*(5), 463–469.

Azrael, D., Cohen, J., Salhi, C., & Miller, M. (2018). Firearm storage in gun-owning households with children: Results of a 2015 national survey. *Journal of Urban Health, 95*(3), 295–304.

Barber, C. W., & Miller, M. J. (2014). Reducing a suicidal person's access to lethal means of suicide: A research agenda. *American Journal of Preventive Medicine*, *47*(3 Suppl. 2), S264–S272.

Barkin, S. L., Finch, S. A., Ip, E. H., Scheindlin, B., Craig, J. A., Steffes, J., Weiley, V., Slora, E., Altman, D., & Wasserman, R. C. (2008). Is office-based counseling about media use, timeouts, and firearm storage effective? Results from a cluster-randomized, controlled trial. *Pediatrics*, *122*(1), e15–25.

Barrett, J. T., Lee, L. K., Monuteaux, M. C., & Hoffmann, J. A. (2020). *County-level poverty and inequalities in firearm-related mortality in U.S. youth* [Manuscript under review].

Baxley, F., & Miller, M. (2006). Parental misperceptions about children and firearms. *Archives of Pediatrics & Adolescent Medicine*, *160*(5), 542–547.

Beard, J. H., Morrison, C. N., Jacoby, S. F., Dong, B., Smith, R., Sims, C. A., & Wiebe, D. J. (2017). Quantifying disparities in urban firearm violence by race and place in Philadelphia, Pennsylvania: A cartographic study. *American Journal of Public Health*, *107*(3), 371–373.

Boine, C., Siegel, M., Ross, C., Fleegler, E. W., & Alcorn, T. (2020). What is gun culture? Cultural variations and trends across the United States. *Humanities and Social Sciences Communications*, *7*(21).

Brady. (2019). *Key gun violence statistics: The facts that make us act.* https://www.bradyunited.org/key-statistics

Brent, D., Perper, J., Moritz, G., Baugher, M., & Allman, C. (1993). Suicide in adolescents with no apparent psychopathology. *Journal of the American Academy of Child & Adolescent Psychiatry*, *32*(3), 494–500.

Brown, J. D., & Goodin, A. J. (2018). Mass casualty shooting venues, types of firearms, and age of perpetrators in the United States, 1982–2018. *American Journal of Public Health*, *108*(10), 1385–1387.

Carter, P. M., Dora-Laskey, A. D., Goldstick, J. E., Heinze, J. E., Walton, M. A., Zimmerman, M. A., Roche, J. S., & Cunningham, R. M. (2018). Arrests among high-risk youth following emergency department treatment for an assault injury. *American Journal of Preventive Medicine*, *55*(6), 812–821.

Carter, P. M., Walton, M. A., Roehler, D. R., Goldstick, J., Zimmerman, M. A., Blow, F. C., & Cunningham, R. M. (2015). Firearm violence among high-risk emergency department youth after an assault injury. *Pediatrics*, *135*(5), 805–815.

Centers for Disease Control and Prevention (CDC). (2016). *Deaths, percent of total deaths, and death rates for the 15 leading causes of death in 5-year age groups, by race and sex: United States, 1999–2015.* https://www.cdc.gov/nchs/nvss/mortality/lcwk1.htm

Centers for Disease Control and Prevention (CDC). (2017a). *10 leading causes of injury deaths by age group highlighting unintentional injury deaths, United States—2017.* https://www.cdc.gov/injury/wisqars/pdf/leading_causes_of_injury_deaths_highlighting_unintentional_2017-508.pdf

Centers for Disease Control and Prevention (CDC). (2017b). *Web-based injury statistics query and reporting system (WISQARS): Fatal injuries reports, national, regional, and state 1981–2016.* https://webappa.cdc.gov/sasweb/ncipc/mortrate.html

Centers for Disease Control and Prevention (CDC). (2019). *All injuries.* https://www.cdc.gov/nchs/fastats/injury.htm

Centers for Disease Control and Prevention (CDC). (2020). *Injury prevention & control: Data and statistics (WISQARS).* https://www.cdc.gov/injury/wisqars

Conner, A., Azrael, D., & Miller, M. (2019). Suicide case-fatality rates in the United States, 2007 to 2014: A nationwide population-based study. *Annals of Internal Medicine*, *171*(12), 885–895.

Cook, P. J., Rivera-Aguirre, A. E., Cerdá, M., & Wintemute, G. (2017). Constant lethality of gunshot injuries from firearm assault: United States, 2003–2012. *American Journal of Public Health*, *107*(8), 1324–1328.

Costello, E., Egger, H., & Angold, A. (2005). 10-year research update review: The epidemiology of child and adolescent psychiatric disorders: I. Methods and public health burden. *Journal of the American Academy of Child & Adolescent Psychiatry*, *44*(10), 972–986.

Costello, E., Erkanli, A., & Angold, A. (2006). Is there an epidemic of child or adolescent depression? *Journal of Child Psychology and Psychiatry*, *47*(12), 1263–1271.

Crifasi, C. K., O'Dwyer, J. K., McGinty, E. E., Webster, D. W., & Barry, C. L. (2019). Desirability of personalized guns among current gun owners. *American Journal of Preventive Medicine*, *57*(2), 191–196.

Díez, C., Kurland, R. P., Rothman, E. F., Bair-Merritt, M., Fleegler, E., Xuan, Z., Galea, S., Ross, C. S., Kalesan, B., Goss, K. A., & Siegel, M. (2017). State intimate partner violence-related firearm laws and intimate partner homicide rates in the United States, 1991 to 2015. *Annals of Internal Medicine, 167*(8), 536–543.

Dodington, J. (2021). Safety devices for firearms. In L. K. Lee & E. W. Fleegler (Eds.), *Pediatric firearm injuries and fatalities: The clinician's guide to policies and approaches to firearm harm prevention* (pp. 179–192). Springer International Publishing.

Dowd, M. D., Sege, R. D., & the Council on Injury, Violence and Poison Prevention Executive Committee of the American Academy of Pediatrics. (2012). Firearm-related injuries affecting the pediatric population. *Pediatrics, 130*(5), e1416–1423.

Federal Bureau of Investigation (FBI). (2020). *NICS firearm checks: Month/year.* https://www.fbi.gov/file-repository/nics_firearm_checks_-_month_year.pdf/view

Fleegler, E. W., Lee, L. K., Monuteaux, M. C., Hemenway, D., & Mannix, R. (2013). Firearm legislation and firearm-related fatalities in the United States. *JAMA Internal Medicine, 173*(9), 732–740.

Foster, M. A. (2019). Federal firearms laws: Overview and selected legal issues for the 116th Congress. *Congressional Research Service.* https://crsreports.congress.gov/product/pdf/R/R45629

Fowler, K. A., Dahlberg, L. L., Haileyesus, T., & Annest, J. L. (2015). Firearm injuries in the United States. *Preventive Medicine, 79,* 5–14.

Fowler, K. A., Dahlberg, L. L., Haileyesus, T., Gutierrez, C., & Bacon, S. (2017). Childhood firearm injuries in the United States. *Pediatrics, 140*(1), e20163486.

Gallup. (2020). *Guns.* https://news.gallup.com/poll/1645/guns.aspx

Goldstick J. E., Zeoli, A., Mair, C., & Cunningham, C. R. (2019). US firearm-related mortality: National, state, and population trends, 1999–2017. *Health Affairs, 38*(10), 1646–1652.

Grinshteyn, E., & Hemenway, D. (2016). Violent death rates: The US compared with other high-income OECD countries, 2010. *American Journal of Medicine, 129*(3), 266–273.

Grossman, D. C., Stafford, H. A., Koepsell, T. D., Hill, R., Retzer, K. D., & Jones, W. (2012). Improving firearm

storage in Alaska native villages: A randomized trial of household gun cabinets. *American Journal of Public Health, 102*(Suppl 2), S291–S297.

Gun Violence Archive. (2020). *Mass shootings.* https://www.gunviolencearchive.org

Hankin, B., Abramson, L., Moffitt, T., Silva, P., McGee, R., & Angell, K. (1998). Development of depression from preadolescence to young adulthood: Emerging gender differences in a 10-year longitudinal study. *Journal of Abnormal Psychology, 107,* 128–140.

Hawes, A. M., Chancellor, K. E., Rogers, W. R., & Ledford, J. A. (2016). Fatal firearm injuries in Tennessee: A comparison study of Tennessee's two most populous counties 2009–2012. *Journal of Forensic Sciences, 61*(3), 666–670.

Hawton, K., & van Heeringen, K. (2009). Suicide. *Lancet, 33*(9672), 1372–1381.

Hiroeh, U., Appleby, L., Mortensen, P. B., & Dunn, G. (2001). Death by homicide, suicide, and other unnatural causes in people with mental illness: A population-based study. *Lancet, 358*(9299), 2110–2112.

Hoffmann, J. A., Farrell, C. A., Monuteaux, M. C., Fleegler, E. W., & Lee, L. K. (2020). Association of pediatric suicide with county-level poverty in the United States, 2007–2016. *JAMA Pediatrics, 174*(3), 287–294.

Humphreys, D. K., Gasparrini, A., & Wiebe, D. J. (2017). Evaluating the impact of Florida's "Stand Your Ground" self-defense law on homicide and suicide by firearm: An interrupted time series study. *JAMA Internal Medicine, 177*(1), 44–50.

Hyde, J., Mezulis, A., & Abramson, L. (2008). The ABCs of depression: Integrating affective, biological, and cognitive models to explain the emergence of the gender difference in depression. *Psychological Review, 115,* 291–313.

Jackman, G. A., Farah, M. M., Kellermann, A. L., & Simon, H. K. (2001). Seeing is believing: What do boys do when they find a real gun? *Pediatrics, 107*(6), 1247–1250.

Jacoby, S. F., Dong, B., Beard, J. H., Wiebe, D. J., & Morrison, C. N. (2018). The enduring impact of historical and structural racism on urban violence in Philadelphia. *Social Science & Medicine, 199,* 87–95.

Kalesan, B., Adhikarla, C., Pressley, J. C., Fagan, J. A., Xuan, Z., Siegel, M. B., & Galea, S. (2017). The hidden epidemic of firearm injury: Increasing firearm injury rates during 2001–2013. *American Journal of Epidemiology, 185*(7), 546–553.

Kalesan, B., Lagast, K., Villarreal, M., Pino, E., Fagan, J., & Galea, S. (2017). School shootings during 2013–2015 in the USA. *Injury Prevention, 23*(5), 321–327.

Kalesan, B., Vyliparambil, M. A., Bogue, E., Villarreal, M. D., Vasan, S., Fagan, J., DiMaggio, C. J., Stylianos, S., Galea, S., & Firearm Injury Research Group. (2016). Race and ethnicity, neighborhood poverty and pediatric firearm hospitalizations in the United States. *Annals of Epidemiology, 26*(1), 1–6.e1-2.

Karb, R. A., Subramanian, S. V., & Fleegler, E. W. (2016). County poverty concentration and disparities in unintentional injury deaths: A fourteen-year analysis of 1.6 million U.S. fatalities. *PLoS One, 11*(5), e0153516.

Kegler, S. R., Dahlberg, L. L., & Mercy, J. A. (2018, November 9). Firearm homicides and suicides in major metropolitan areas—United States, 2012–2013 and 2015–2016. *MMWR Morbidity and Mortality Weekly Report, 67*(44), 1233–1237.

Kivisto, A. J., Kivisto, K. L., Gurnell, E., Phalen, P., & Ray, B. (2020). Adolescent suicide, household firearm ownership, and the effects of child access prevention laws. *Journal of the American Academy of Child & Adolescent Psychiatry, S0890-8567*(20), 31882–31887.

Knopov, A., Sherman, R. J., Raifman, J. R., Larson, E., & Siegel, M. B. (2019). Household gun ownership and youth suicide rates at the state level, 2005–2015. *American Journal of Preventive Medicine, 56*(3), 335–342.

Kochanek, K., Murphy, S., Xu, J., & Arias, E. (2019). Deaths: Final data for 2017. *National Vital Statistics Reports, 68*(9), 1–77.

Lyneé Madeira, J. (2021). Firearm legislation and advocacy. In L. K. Lee & E. W. Fleegler (Eds.), *Pediatric firearm injuries and fatalities: The clinician's guide to polices and approaches to firearm harm prevention* (pp. 193–212). Springer International Publishing.

Lee, L. K., Fleegler, E. W., Farrell, C., Avakame, E., Srinivasan, S., Hemenway, D., & Miller, M. (2017). Firearm laws and firearm homicides: A systematic review. *JAMA Internal Medicine, 177*(1), 106–119.

Lee, L. K., & Mannix, R. (2018). Increasing fatality rates from preventable deaths in teenagers and young adults. *JAMA, 320*(6), 543–544.

Lee, L. K., Monteaux, M. C., Burghardt, L. C., Fleegler, E. W., Nigrovic, L. E., Meehan, W. P., Schutzman, S. A., & Mannix, R. (2015). Motor vehicle crash fatalities in states with primary versus secondary seat belt laws: A time-series analysis. *Annals of Internal Medicine, 163*(3), 184–190.

Lewinsohn, P., Rohde, P., Klein, D., & Seeley, J. (1999). Natural course of adolescent major depressive disorder: I. Continuity into young adulthood. *Journal of the American Academy of Child & Adolescent Psychiatry, 38*, 56–63.

Livingston, M. D., Rossheim, M. E., & Hall, K. S. (2019). A descriptive analysis of school and school shooter characteristics and the severity of school shootings in the United States, 1999–2018. *Journal of Adolescent Health, 64*, S797e9.

Mannix, R., Fleegler, E., Meehan, W. P., III, Schutzman, S. A., Hennelly, K., Nigrovic, L., & Lee, L. K. (2012). Booster seat laws and fatalities in children 4 to 7 years of age. *Pediatrics, 130*(6), 996–1002.

Mannix, R., Lee, L. K., & Fleegler, E. W. (2020, August 4). Coronavirus disease 2019 (COVID-19) and firearms in the United States: Will an epidemic of suicide follow? *Annals of Internal Medicine, 173*(3), 228–229.

Meehan, W. P., III, Lee, L. K., Fischer, C. M., & Mannix, R. C. (2013). Bicycle helmet laws are associated with a lower fatality rate from bicycle–motor vehicle collisions. *Journal of Pediatrics, 163*(3), 726–729.

Miller, M., Azrael, D., & Hemenway, D. (2004). The epidemiology of case fatality rates for suicide in the northeast. *Annals of Emergency Medicine, 43*(6), 723–730.

Miller, M., Barber, C., White, R. A., & Azrael, D. (2013). Firearms and suicide in the United States: Is risk independent of underlying suicidal behavior? *American Journal of Epidemiology, 178*(6), 946–955.

Monteaux, M. C., Azrael, D., & Miller, M. (2019). Association of increased safe household firearm storage with firearm suicide and unintentional death among US youths. *JAMA Pediatrics, 173*(7), 657–662.

Naureckas, S. M., Galanter, C., Naureckas, E. T., Donovan, M., & Christoffel, K. K. (1995). Children's and women's ability to fire handguns. *Archives of Pediatrics & Adolescent Medicine, 149*(12), 1318–1322.

Newman, K. S., Fox, C., Harding, D., Mehta, J., & Roth, W. (2008). *Rampage: The social roots of school shootings.* Basic Books.

Parker, K., Horowitz, J. M., Igielnik, R., Oliphant, J. B., & Brown, A. (2017). America's complex relationship with guns: An in-depth look at the attitudes and experiences of U.S. adults. *Pew Research Center.* https://www.pewsocial trends.org/2017/06/22/americas-complex-relationship-with-guns/

Pear, V. A, Castillo-Carniglia, A., Kagawa, R. M., Cerdá, M., & Wintemute, G. J. (2018). Firearm mortality in California, 2000–2015: The epidemiologic importance of within-state variation. *Annals of Epidemiology, 28*(5), 309–315.e2.

Rees, C. A., Lee, L. K., Fleegler, E. W., & Mannix, R. (2019). Mass school shootings in the United States: A novel root cause analysis using lay press reports. *Clinical Pediatrics, 58*(13), 1423–1428.

Riddell, C. A., Harper, S., Cerdá, M., & Kaufman, J. S. (2018). Comparison of rates of firearm and nonfirearm homicide and suicide in Black and White non-Hispanic men, by U.S. state. *Annals of Internal Medicine, 168*(10), 712–720.

Rowhani-Rahbar, A., Zatzick, D., Wang, J., Mills, B. M., Simonetti, J. A., Fan, M. D., Rivara, F. P. (2015). Firearm-related hospitalization and risk for subsequent violent injury, death, or crime perpetration: A cohort study. *Annals of Internal Medicine, 162*(7), 492–500.

Santaella-Tenorio, J., Cerdá, M., Villaveces, A., & Galea, S. (2016). What do we know about the association between firearm legislation and firearm-related injuries? *Epidemiologic Reviews, 38*(1), 140–157.

Schell, T. L., Peterson, S., Vegetabile, B. G., Scherling, A., Smart, R., & Morral, A. R. (2020). State-level estimates of household firearm ownership. *RAND Corporation.* https://www.rand.org/pubs/tools/TL354.html

Schmidt, C. J., Rupp, L., Pizarro, J. M., Lee, D. B., Branas, C. C., & Zimmerman, M. A. (2019). Risk and protective factors related to youth firearm violence: A scoping review and directions for future research. *Journal of Behavioral Medicine, 42*(4), 706–723.

Scott, J., Azrael, D., & Miller, M. (2018). Firearm storage in homes with children with self-harm risk factors. *Pediatrics, 141*(3), e20172600.

Siegel, M. (2020). Select a state to view the laws. *State Firearm Laws.* https://statefirearmlaws.org/

Siegel, M., Pahn, M., Xuan, Z., Fleegler, E., & Hemenway, D. (2019). The impact of state firearm laws on homicide and suicide deaths in the USA, 1991–2016: A panel study. *Journal of General Internal Medicine, 34*(10), 2021–2028.

Siegel, M., Pahn, M., Xuan, Z., Ross, C. S., Galea, S., Kalesan, B., Fleegler, E., & Goss, K. A. (2017). Firearm-related laws in all 50 US states, 1991–2016. *American Journal of Public Health, 107*(7), 1122–1129.

Siegel, M., Ross, C. S., & King, C., III. (2013). The relationship between gun ownership and firearm homicide rates in the United States, 1981–2010. *American Journal of Public Health, 103*(11), 2098–2105.

Siegel, M., Ross, C. S., & King, C., III. (2014). A new proxy measure for state-level gun ownership in studies of firearm injury prevention. *Injury Prevention, 20*(3), 204–207.

Siegel, M., Xuan, Z., Ross, C. S., Galea, S., Kalesan, B., Fleegler, E., & Goss, K. A. (2017). Easiness of legal access to concealed firearm permits and homicide rates in the United States. *American Journal of Public Health, 107*(12), 1923–1929.

Simonetti, J. A., Rowhani-Rahbar, A., & Rivara, F. P. (2017). The road ahead for personalized firearms. *JAMA Internal Medicine, 177*(1), 9–10.

Spitzer, S. A., Pear, V. A., McCort, C. D., & Wintemute, G. J. (2020). Incidence, distribution, and lethality of firearm injuries in California from 2005 to 2015. *JAMA Network Open, 3*(8), e2014736.

Statista. (2020). *Number of military fatalities in all major wars involving the United States from 1775 to 2020.* https://www.statista.com/statistics/1009819/total-us-military-fatalities-in-american-wars-1775-present

Stuart, H. (2003). Violence and mental illness: An overview. *World Psychiatry, 2*(2), 121–124.

Towers, S., Gomez-Lievano, A., Khan, M., Mubayi, A., & Castillo-Chavez, C. (2015). Contagion in mass killings and school shootings. *PLoS One, 10*(7), 1–12.

Tuan, W.-J., & Frey, J. J., III. (2017). Wisconsin firearm mortality, 2000–2014. *WMJ. 116*(4), 194–200.

Van Sparrentak, M., Chang, T., Miller, A. L., Nichols, L. P., & Sonneville, K. R. (2018). Youth opinions about guns and gun control in the United States. *JAMA Pediatrics, 172*(9), 884–886.

Vernick, J. S., O'Brien, M., Hepburn, L. M., Johnson, S. B., Webster, D. W., & Hargarten, S. W. (2003). Unintentional and undetermined firearm related deaths: A preventable death analysis for three safety devices. *Injury Prevention, 9*(4), 307–311.

Wallace, L. N. (2016). American preferences for "smart" guns versus traditional weapons: Results from a nationwide survey. *Preventive Medicine Reports, 4,* 11–16.

Walton, M. A., Epstein-Ngo, Q., Carter, P. M., Zimmerman, M. A., Blow, F. C., Buu, A., Goldstick, J., & Cunningham, R. M. (2017). Marijuana use trajectories among drug-using youth presenting to an urban emergency department: Violence and social influences. *Drug and Alcohol Dependence, 173,* 117–125.

# 12

# TOWARD THE INTEGRATION OF CHILD, YOUTH, AND FAMILY POLICY

## Applying Principles of Risk, Resilience, and Ecological Theory

**Paul Lanier, William J. Hall, Jeffrey M. Jenson, and Mark W. Fraser**

## RISK AND RESILIENCE WITHIN SYSTEMS OF OPPRESSION

This book has traced the origins and evolution of public policies that define major American service systems for children, youth, and families. Chapter authors have used the principles of risk and resilience to describe and assess policy responses to a range of child and adolescent problems and conditions. The concept of resilience brings us hope that, despite many challenges and adverse conditions, within all families is the natural potential to overcome and emerge stronger. However, although the potential for resilience exists in all families, the possibility for expressing this resilience is not equally granted to all families.

In Chapter 1, we introduced the intersectional anti-oppression framework in response to systems of injustice that exist in society. A key feature of oppressive systems is that some individuals are advantaged while others are disadvantaged. Currently, these differences in opportunity are on full display throughout the social and political events that have unfolded in recent years. We have seen clear examples of racism in policing while also witnessing the stark health disparities families of color have faced in the COVID-19 pandemic. By bringing systems of oppression into the open, perhaps we are in a better position to remove them at the roots. Then, we can tailor programs and policies to continually monitor and modify systems so oppressive forces do not reemerge.

Theory-driven research has a tremendous role to play in identifying systems of oppression, measuring how those systems confer risk on marginalized groups, and developing effective anti-oppressive policy and practice changes. However, we must reexamine existing theories, research paradigms, practices, and policies through an anti-oppressive framework. This is a challenging task and successful examples are limited.

A recent example of reexamining existing theory to inform research and policy is found in the culturally informed adverse childhood experiences framework (C-ACE; Bernard et al., 2020). Several chapters in this book referred to adverse childhood experiences (ACEs) research and the ongoing translation of findings demonstrating a strong association between childhood trauma and poor health outcomes. However, the original ACEs study was not conceptualized or designed to include racism as a potentially traumatic experience (Brown et al., 2009). The ACEs scale has been expanded to include a broader set of exposures that would be considered adverse experiences. Notably, the National Survey of Children's Health added racial and ethnic discrimination to its questionnaire (Bethell et al., 2017). With the inclusion of this question, studies now demonstrate the role that oppression can have on child development and the unique experience of Black and Hispanic/Latinx children compared to White children (Maguire-Jack et al., 2020). Bernard et al.'s C-ACE framework focuses specifically on integrating the experience of racial trauma on the mental health of Black youth. Future research will further test and refine this model to understand the contribution of historical and intergenerational racism on existing health disparities and the mechanisms through which health is impacted. By including an anti-oppression framework, the C-ACE model can be used to better identify and test specific strategies for assessment, intervention, and prevention efforts. As numerous public health efforts are rolled out to prevent and address ACEs, efforts to reduce racial disparities in mental health outcomes for Black youth would be strengthened by using the C-ACE framework relative to a generalized ACEs model. Similarly, efforts to understand risk and resilience in the ACEs framework should be reexamined and tailored for other groups that experience oppression.

As discussed in Chapter 1, families in the United States (U.S.) show increasing diversity in structure and composition. This diversity is surely a strength but presents challenges for policy systems that were largely developed with a singular vision of family in mind. An intersectional framework is required to fully capture how systems of oppression influence the well-being of diverse families. Although challenging, the effectiveness of a given policy or program reflects the extent to which it has been tailored and adapted to the individual needs, goals, and structure of each family. Conformity can no longer be the goal of social policy. The risks each family experiences are unique—as should be the protective response to fully unlock the potential for resilience each family possesses.

# POLICIES AND PROGRAMS ACROSS SERVICE SYSTEMS

Each chapter in this book began with a review of risk and protective factors that were relevant to problem behaviors or to conditions within particular policy domains, such as child welfare and mental health. Services in the areas of income maintenance, child welfare, developmental disabilities, education, health, juvenile justice, mental health, and substance use disorder treatment are usually developed vertically, with separate funding streams and administrative structures; however, you may have been struck by the similarity of risk and protective factors across substantive domains, despite the presence of long-standing systems silos. Prior reviews of risk and protection have also noted the overlap of risk and protective factors across problem domains (Fraser et al., 2004; Hawkins et al., 1992; Jenson & Bender, 2014; O'Connell et al., 2009). In its influential Connecting the Dots report, the Centers for Disease Control and Prevention (CDC) argued that the overlap of risk and protective factors signals a need to break down silos by promoting cross-system collaboration and coordination (Wilkins et al., 2014). The similarity of risk and protective factors is a clue both to the complexity of public responses to issues confronting children and families and to the potential for reform. In Chapter 1, we identified common risk and protective factors for child and adolescent problems at the individual, family, school, peer, community, and societal levels of influence. These characteristics and conditions are ubiquitous across all of the policy domains discussed in the book.

The presence of common risk and protective factors for different child and adolescent behaviors and conditions affords a special opportunity to think organically about creating policies that address the root causes of problem behaviors. For example, the authors in this volume have indicated that several common environmental factors, such as poverty and systemic racism, are associated with involvement in the juvenile justice system, poor educational outcomes, health and mental health disparities, and child maltreatment. It follows, then, that these risk factors should become the targets of coordinated and integrated policy and program responses in the juvenile justice, education, health care, and child welfare systems.

A parallel theme that emerged from each chapter concerned the lack of attention in policy development that has been afforded to the underlying correlates of child and adolescent outcomes. On balance, chapters described an incremental and reactive approach to the creation of policies that collect over time to form the basis for programs in public service systems for children, youth, and families. Policies tend to be the product of reform cycles that stem from changes in the nature and prevalence of social and health problems as well as changes in political cycles that apply different social constructions to concepts such as vulnerability. For example, the current COVID-19 pandemic has completely altered the delivery of health and mental health services. Physical distancing and stay-at-home policies forced children and adults to receive services from the home using telephone or video conferencing. A rapid shift to telehealth services required policy change to remove barriers that previously limited access to telehealth services. Specifically, the Centers for Medicare and Medicaid Services issued multiple reimbursement policy waivers to provide funding flexibility and parity (CDC, 2020) When incidence and prevalence rates for social and health problems increase dramatically, the attention of the public and policymakers is diverted to specific service systems or programs. When the prevalence of problems increases, policy reforms tend to be introduced at a fast pace but often without adequate consideration of unintended consequences or long-term effects. Adaptations that are made in reaction to crises run the risk of focusing too much on short-term outcomes and too little on outcomes that may be sustainable over the long haul.

This pattern of hurried, inadequately considered policy formulation is common. In Chapter 10, Wilson and colleagues noted that despite the clear need for reform in the field of juvenile justice, policymakers have been slow to reject the reactive policies of the tough-on-crime era. Similarly, Lanier, Feely, and Fraser (Chapter 5) identified fluctuations in mental health policy based on evolving beliefs about the appropriate role of institutional and community-based care for persons with serious mental illnesses. Further, the lack of support for community-based and trauma-informed mental health services leaves fewer opportunities for adaptive services that are challenging to deliver in institutional care settings. In addition, Johnson-Motoyama, Berrick, and Eastman (Chapter 3) began by describing the reactive U.S. child welfare system in contrast to more adaptive family support systems found in other countries. The authors describe wide variation in state policies and changes over time in federal policy that reflect shifts in social norms regarding child abuse and neglect and the balance of child protection with family rights. Examples of the cyclical and reformist nature of social policy for children and families are numerous.

Only the naive would not recognize the important contribution of social norms and public perceptions to public policy. After all, legislation is largely a result of the public's reaction to social conditions and problems. The discussion of the No Child Left Behind Act (Public Law [P.L.] 107-110) provided by Frey, Mandlawitz, Perry, Walker, and Mitchell in Chapter 4 illustrated the power of public perception in reshaping education. Public outcry for school reform and accountability in the past decade is reflected in many provisions of the act. Similar examples can be drawn from the evolution of public policies in the anti-poverty field (as discussed by Williams Shanks, Danziger, and Meehan in Chapter 2) and the developmental disabilities field (as discussed by McLean, Adams, and Bishop in Chapter 7).

The ongoing debates regarding health care policy clearly demonstrate the complexities inherent in balancing incremental change and public perception. Over a decade ago, the Patient Protection and Affordable Care Act (ACA; P.L. 11–148) passed through Congress following 18 months of deliberation. Congressional deliberations highlighted the tension between legislators who favored comprehensive reform and legislators who favored incremental change in health care policy. These same debates occur today in discussions over how best to expand health insurance coverage. Sentiment for comprehensive or incremental reform was also expressed in public actions taken by members of the medical profession, health insurance companies, and public interest groups. The ACA was the product of a long and contentious debate that led to a series of compromises among officials who held competing views on comprehensive and incremental change. Key provisions of the legislation are designed to make health care more affordable and accountable. The ACA bans insurance companies from discriminating against individuals with preexisting health conditions and provides a means for uninsured people to obtain health care. However, the effects of what many public officials perceive to be an ill-advised and radical change in health care policy will likely be debated—and adjudicated—for many years. In Chapter 6, Hall and colleagues discuss the effects of the ACA on health care policies and discuss adaptations needed in the context of the COVID-19 pandemic.

In Chapter 9, Finno-Velasquez and colleagues describe an immigration system that is constantly reacting to a heterogeneity of public perception regarding immigration. In contrast to other public policy areas in this book, the goal of federal policy (under the Trump administration) ignored resilience and child well-being in favor of a deterrence strategy that actively harmed children and families through practices such as parent–child separation at the border.

Sadly, the increase in gun violence affecting children in the U.S. demanded the inclusion of a chapter examining firearm policies. In Chapter 11, Rees and Fleegler provide a clear connection between the variation in social norms regarding firearm ownership and the variation in passage and enforcement of state firearm laws. Epidemiologic data on homicide and suicide deaths by state show a clear connection between norms, policies, and child deaths and injuries due to firearms. Even with evidence that such laws are effective at lower firearm mortality and morbidity rates, firearm policy is one distinct example of policy that has changed very little in the history of the U.S., despite clear need for reform.

Public policy should be based on the confluence of public concern and research knowledge. However, the urgency created by public perception and pressure sometimes precipitates changes that produce reforms with unintended and negative side effects. When pressured to respond to real or apparent changes in the nature of a child or adolescent problem behavior, officials frequently turn to convenient policy solutions that address symptoms but fail to address the underlying risk and protective factors associated with that problem (Jenson & Bender, 2014). The result of this process is ineffective, fragmented, and short-lived programs that sometimes do more harm than good. Arguably the greatest and most damaging effect is that such programs add to bureaucratic inertia, making systems more complicated, slower to respond with true reform, and less fertile for creating adaptations.

Few service systems for children, youth, and families have developed a deliberate or effective continuum of care. Nearly all chapter authors noted that primary care systems tend to offer a patchwork assortment of programs and services that are seldom delivered to children and families in a sequential or rational fashion. One exception might be the comprehensive strategy for the prevention, treatment, and control of juvenile delinquency, which was adopted by the juvenile justice system in the late 1990s. This strategy, developed and disseminated by the Office of Juvenile Justice and Delinquency Prevention (Howell, 2003; Zavlek, 2005), outlines a continuum of care and graduated sanctions (i.e., punishments related to the seriousness of offenses) that many states use as a framework for handling young offenders. The strategy emphasizes a continuum of service that matches the individual's needs (which are often identified through systematic risk assessment) and the individual's history of offending to appropriate interventions and sanctions. Recent studies indicate that a comprehensive approach to reducing recidivism among juvenile offenders is effective (e.g., Howell & Lipsey, 2012).

Finally, careful historical analysis reveals that untested and ineffective policies and programs are repeated over time. One example is the recurring use of media campaigns as a way to increase awareness about the dangers of substance use. Anthony, Jenson, and Howard note in Chapter 8 that this strategy had little effect on reducing substance use in the 1970s and early 1980s. However, recent public awareness of increasing drug use among adolescents has rekindled interest in media and information campaigns that alert young people and their parents to the dangers of alcohol and other illicit drug use. Federal policy in response to the opioid crisis currently prioritizes high-quality, evidence-based treatment and funding research to understand the best way to prevent and treat addiction. The design and development of policies related to opioid use may represent a shift to more adaptive and evidence-based policy making.

Perhaps the most salient point in each author's historical review of public policy is the absence of a uniform underlying framework to guide policy development. No common model or framework for policy development could be found across the ten policy domains reviewed by the authors. We believe that principles of risk and resilience—grounded in ecological theory—offer a useful framework for considering the conditions that affect children and that by applying a risk and protective factor perspective, we can better design social programs to address these conditions. Next, we offer some thoughts on how these principles might be used to develop policy for children, youth, and families.

# RISK AND RESILIENCE: AN ECOLOGICAL PERSPECTIVE FOR DEVELOPING CHILD, YOUTH, AND FAMILY POLICY

Rooted in ecological theory, principles of risk, protection, and resilience have been successfully applied to prevention and treatment with children and adolescents in varied settings. In particular, substance abuse and delinquency-prevention programs have been based on risk and protective factors occurring at levels of influence (e.g., environmental, interpersonal, and individual) that are compatible with ecological theory (Germain, 1991). However, the full utility of risk, protection, and ecological theory for policy development remains untapped.

Using a risk and protection–based approach to creating policies for children, youth, and families requires a step-by-step approach. These steps are outlined next and summarized in the developmental policy process shown in Figure 12.1.

## Step 1: Evaluate Risk and Protective Factors

Policymaking begins with developing an understanding of the risk and protective factors associated with a targeted child or adolescent outcome. Consistent with ecological theory, factors should be assessed or summarized at environmental, interpersonal, social, and individual levels. Chapter authors have reviewed risk and protective factors associated with each of the problem behaviors and conditions discussed in this book. Because common risk and protective factors have been identified for many social and health problems, it may not always be necessary for policymakers to conduct basic risk or protective factor assessments. In many fields, research studies already specify predominant risk and protective factors (e.g., Fraser, 2004; Hawkins, 2006; Herrenkohl et al., 2004; Jenson & Bender, 2014; Woolf, 2008). However, differences in local environmental conditions may necessitate new assessments in some circumstances. For example, an urban center may be concerned about the disproportionate nature of poverty or the needs of racial/ethnic groups in certain geographic areas. The ways in which risk and protective factors vary by region, gender, and culture are the subject of much current research. Although some risk and protective factors are common, risk factors also clearly vary from the tribal lands of the mountain and plains states to the urban centers of the East and West coasts. These differences complicate risk assessment and pose a major challenge for policymakers.

Thinking about policy from a risk and protection perspective offers two advantages. First, the perspective allows for the use of a common language across policy domains. This gives policymakers, advocates, practitioners, and researchers a uniform vocabulary to use in describing related behaviors, setting program objectives, and assessing program outcomes. Second, because concepts of risk and protection emerged from research in several related fields—child development, mental health, prevention science, social work, and public health in particular—we can build on diverse and cumulative scientific knowledge. This rapidly expanding knowledge base holds the potential—as demonstrated in many chapters of this book—to reform service systems across the country.

## Step 2: Assign Policy Responsibility in Ways That Promote Service Integration Across Systems

Policies based on empirical evidence about the risk and protective factors associated with child and youth problems should be developed and implemented across the policy arenas addressed in this book. Integrating key programs and services identified or implied by policies across and within systems of care should be a priority. Critical questions that should be considered in the policy development and integration processes include the following:

1.  Which service systems have primary responsibility for the programs and services defined or implied by the policy?

2.  Where does fiscal accountability lie for the programs and services defined or implied by the stated policy?

3.  Does the stated policy explicitly develop links between and within the major service systems for children, youth, and families?

4.  Do adequate implementation resources exist within or across the primary systems to achieve service integration?

5.  How can service systems integrate existing or new program resources, including staff, physical locations, training curricula, and evaluation tools and methods?

## Figure 12.1   A Developmental Process of Child, Youth, and Family Policy

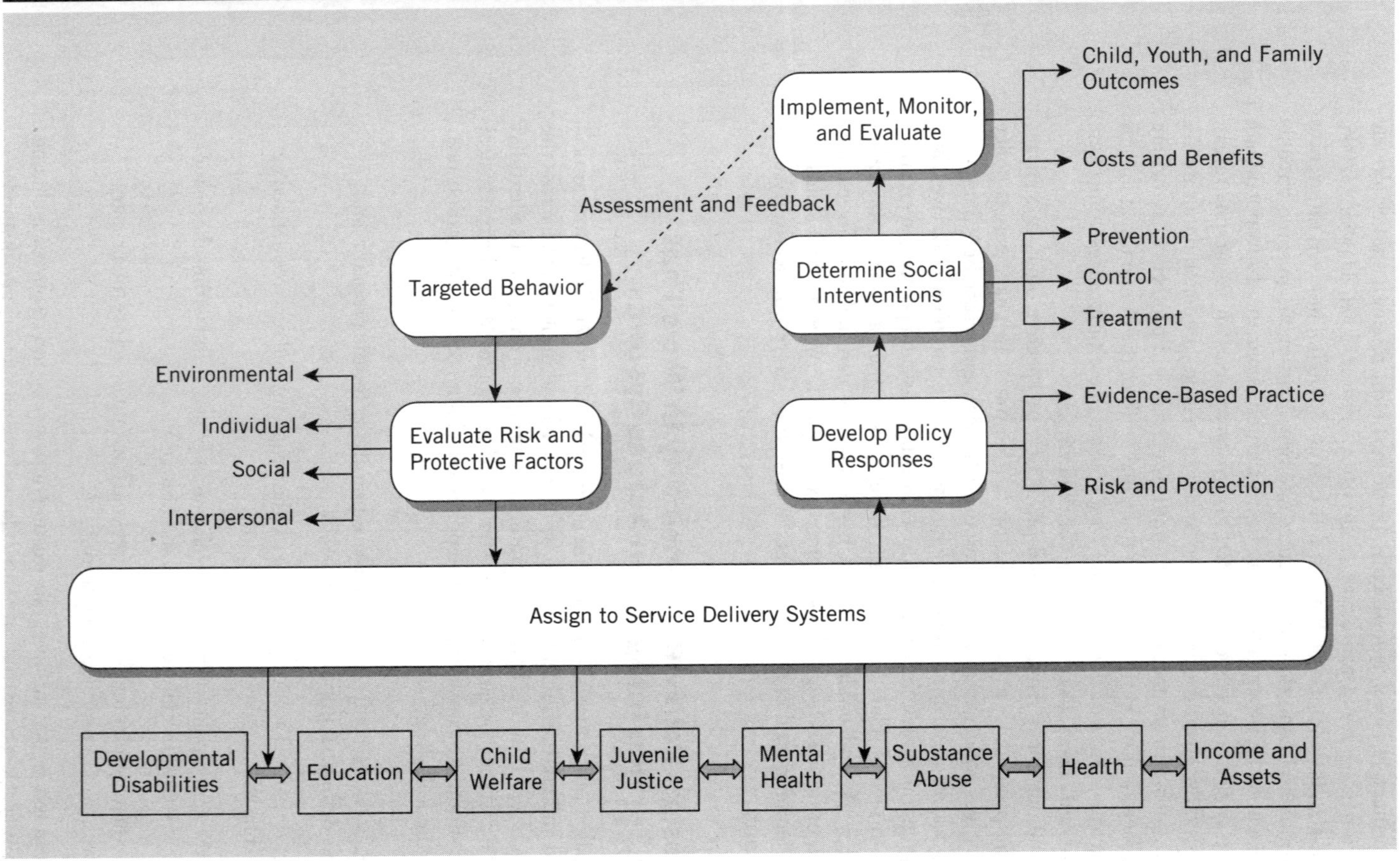

Targeted Behavior

Evaluate Risk and Protective Factors
- Environmental
- Individual
- Social
- Interpersonal

Assessment and Feedback

Implement, Monitor, and Evaluate
- Child, Youth, and Family Outcomes
- Costs and Benefits

Determine Social Interventions
- Prevention
- Control
- Treatment

Develop Policy Responses
- Evidence-Based Practice
- Risk and Protection

Assign to Service Delivery Systems

Developmental Disabilities — Education — Child Welfare — Juvenile Justice — Mental Health — Substance Abuse — Health — Income and Assets

Locating and integrating program components defined by social and health policies within and across service systems are challenging undertakings. Collaborative partnerships between executive leadership, administrators, practitioners, and researchers are necessary to achieve more fluid delivery and integration of policies aimed at children, youth, and families. Collaboration between service systems to prevent early and unwanted teen pregnancy illustrates policy and program efforts aimed at integration (see Box 12.1).[1]

A similar example illustrating the positive effects that system collaboration and integration can have on adolescent behavior is found in efforts to treat co-occurring substance abuse and mental health problems. Jenson and Potter (2003) tested an experimental intervention created to fill the mandate of legislation passed by the Colorado State Legislature. A legislative note mandated that the mental health and juvenile justice systems find innovative ways to treat co-occurring substance use and mental health problems among young offenders. The state systems responded by assessing risk and protective factors for adolescent substance abuse and mental health problems. An intervention was designed to place mental health case managers in juvenile justice facilities. Jenson and Potter conducted a longitudinal investigation of the program and found that the youth who received the intervention reported significant reductions in their levels of depression, anxiety, and substance use. This type of cross-system integration holds promise for reducing child and adolescent problem behaviors. Studies showing positive outcomes resulting from coordinated interventions involving systems from mental health, health, juvenile justice, and substance abuse domains illustrate the potential of social policies supporting programs that cross traditional boundaries (Finkelstein & Markoff, 2004; Graves et al., 2007; Kaufman et al., 2006). These findings are encouraging because they indicate that we are beginning to recognize the benefits of policies, programs, and services that use coordinated and collaborative efforts.

## The Value of Collaboration and Integration

### The Case of Early and Unwanted Teen Pregnancy

The birth rate among females 15–19 years (i.e., the teen birth rate) is currently the lowest in history, dropping more than half (58%) in the past decade (Pew Research Center, 2019) This positive and perhaps surprising trend is likely influenced by a host of factors but is partially attributed to improvements in the coordination of policies and programs between the nation's health care and educational systems. This collaborative effort included the following:

- The systematic dissemination of information by public health departments, government agencies, and schools aimed at educating and creating awareness among the public about the high rates of adolescent pregnancy in the U.S.

*(Continued)*

**BOX 12.1**

(Continued)

- The implementation of school-based prevention efforts aimed at delaying the onset of adolescents' sexual activity and educating students about the risks associated with unprotected sex.

- The creation of school-based health clinics to reach adolescents who might not have access to medical care and thus were likely to be at highest risk for early and unwanted pregnancy.

- The allocation of targeted federal, state, and local funds to establish community-based health clinics that educate young people at risk for early, unwanted pregnancy and offer treatment for young families.

The decline in teen pregnancy rates came at a time of increased collaboration between the nation's health care and educational systems. This successful collaboration demonstrated the potential of policy and program integration for reducing child and adolescent problems.

## Step 3: Use Evidence to Create Public Policy Responses

Empirical evidence gained from studies of risk and protective factors should be used to create child, youth, and family policies. Developing evidence-based policy, or at least evidence-informed policy, will require the dissemination of aggregate-level information about the etiology of child and adolescent problems to policymakers during the deliberation processes that lead to the creation of public policy. A critical step in dissemination is translating the empirical evidence in a manner that is immediately useable and practical for legislators and policy experts.

Recent developments in evidence-based practices (EBPs) offer an opportunity to advance the notion of creating policies for children and families from an empirical framework. In the 1990s, EBP evolved in the medical profession from a concept to a movement to a professional imperative aimed at helping physicians select effective treatments for their patients. Definitions and perceptions of what EBP is—and what it is not—vary widely. In what is arguably the most accepted definition of EBP, Sackett and colleagues (2000) stated that EBP is "the integration of best research evidence with clinical expertise and [client] values" (p. 1). This definition implies that EBP is a process characterized by specific steps and actions that require practitioners to locate, select, and implement the best available interventions for a targeted group or population.

An important parallel exists between the essential steps of EBP and the policymaking process illustrated in Figure 12.1. In both processes, the identification of risk and protective factors associated with specific problems lead to the design, selection, and testing of interventions. In an ideal setting, the best available interventions—meaning those with strong research evidence supporting their effectiveness—are then translated to broad-based social policies aimed at improving the lives of children and families.

Unfortunately, relatively few effective interventions manage to navigate the difficult path from implementation to policy. One recent exception is home visiting. Sparked in part by federal funding through the Maternal, Infant, and Early Childhood Home Visiting (MIECHV) program, a demand for evidence regarding home visiting has resulted in a large body of research on which to draw. The Home Visiting Evidence of Effectiveness review process included the launch of a website to allow decision makers to review and compare the results of curated research across numerous home visiting models (see https://homvee.acf.hhs.gov/). Examples of two evidence-based programs are the Nurse–Family Partnership (NFP) home visiting program (Olds et al., 1986) and Family Connects (Dodge & Goodman, 2019). Although the programs are similar in that they deliver services in the home (i.e., home visits), the models were developed with different populations in mind. The NFP program is targeted to guiding low-income mothers and their firstborn children toward successful futures through intensive services lasting from pregnancy to two years after the birth of a first child. In contrast, Family Connects is a universal program that offers supports to all families but focuses on a briefer period of time right after birth. The program then connects families with community resources and services. Controlled trials of both models have demonstrated positive effects on several maternal and child outcomes (Dodge et al., 2014; Olds et al., 2014). The successful translation of evidence from controlled intervention trials of the NFP and Family Connects to specific child and family policy (i.e., MIECHV) provides a template for other systems of care discussed in this book.

## Step 4: Determine the Course of Specific Individual and Social Interventions

To determine the course of individual and social interventions, policy officials should consider evidence that identifies evidence-based programs and services for children and adolescents. Policy creation that integrates principles of risk, resilience, and EBP requires a comprehensive review of empirical evidence about the efficacy of alternative intervention approaches. In essence, determining the appropriate course of social intervention begs the old question, "What works best for whom under what conditions?"

Several outlets have surfaced as sources for obtaining information about effective interventions for children and youth. In Chapter 1, we noted the work of the University of Colorado's Blueprints for Healthy Youth Development. The Blueprints initiative has identified a number of efficacious prevention programs that can be selected as the basis for a community or state's behavioral health prevention efforts (Blueprints for Healthy Youth Development, 2021). The Coalition for Evidence-Based Policy (2014) has compiled a compendium of early childhood, educational, and youth development programs that have been found effective in preventing violence and other childhood and adolescent problems. In addition, interdisciplinary groups such as the international Campbell and Cochrane Collaborations have provided public worldwide access to systematic reviews of the literature on treatment outcomes across a range of adolescent problems. These reviews offer a rich source of information for policy officials who are engaged in the process of recommending or selecting interventions for public systems of care (Campbell Collaboration Library, 2014; Cochrane Collaboration, 2014).

Decision makers are beginning to consider both program and cost-effectiveness when selecting interventions and creating policies for children and families. Historically, practitioners and policy officials have had little credible empirical evidence regarding the costs and benefits of social interventions to guide their decisions about which programs to select or to fund. Fortunately, this situation is changing through work conducted by numerous research teams, such as Aos and colleagues at the Washington State Institute for Public Policy (Aos et al., 2004; Lee et al., 2012). These researchers reviewed the benefits and costs of a wide range of prevention programs aimed at problems such as aggression, delinquency, school failure, and substance abuse. All of the programs included in their review had been previously tested in research using either an experimental design or a well-constructed quasi-experimental design. Findings from the study showed that some prevention programs yielded cost savings and effectively prevented or delayed the onset of problem behaviors. Equally important, Aos and associates produced tangible evidence in the form of a benefit-per-dollar cost figure for early childhood, prenatal and infant home visitation, youth development, mentoring, substance abuse, teen pregnancy, and juvenile offender programs. Benefits were greatest for juvenile offender programs. In these programs, the cost savings ranged from $1,900 to more than $31,000 per participant. Substantial benefits were also found among prenatal and infant home visitation programs, ranging from $6,200 to $17,200 in savings per individual youth. In addition, early childhood education programs and selected youth development programs were shown to produce significant benefits. The cost-saving figures generated by the Aos team point both to the importance of investing in effective programs and to the danger of funding ineffective programs. Policymakers and other decision makers are well advised to consider the findings and to implement the recommendations consistent with the growing evidence base. To make better use of the research literature on the effectiveness of interventions for children and adolescents (for a review, see Allen-Meares & Fraser, 2004) and to implement the kind of collaborative programs the authors have described in every chapter will require state and local officials to find ways of breaking down organizational barriers. In addition, policymakers will need to break through institutional isomorphism and exert leadership in overcoming the turf issues that have confounded previous reform efforts (e.g., the implementation of the Children's and Community Mental Health Services Improvement Act of 1992, which attempted to create systems of care within mental health). Unfortunately, many of the nation's educational systems, human services agencies, and state and community organizations fail to consider, select, or implement effective programs. There continues to be a significant gap between what we know to be effective in preventing and treating childhood and family problems and what programs are actually implemented; this gap must be narrowed (Fixsen et al., 2005). Policymakers should be encouraged to pay greater attention to the benefits gained by implementing proven and tested programs. Perceived barriers associated with replicating and implementing effective program strategies must be eliminated.

## Step 5: Implement, Monitor, and Evaluate Policies and Interventions

The development of collaborative systems of care will also require greater emphasis on monitoring and evaluating the interventions. The energy and enthusiasm associated with reforms must be converted into systemic procedures that monitor the implementation of new programs, provide feedback, and articulate consequences for failed or inconsistent implementation. This level of accountability implies using fidelity checks to ensure that interventions are being implemented as intended; conducting cost–benefit analyses to assess the economic consequences of programs and policies; and assessing child, youth, and parent outcomes. Monitoring and evaluation allow legislators and others to determine the outcomes of policies and programs; effective efforts can be refunded and ineffective approaches can be redesigned.

# A NEW KEY TO EFFECTIVE SOCIAL POLICY FOR CHILDREN AND FAMILIES: THE INTEGRATION OF INDIVIDUAL AND ECOLOGICAL RESILIENCE

Throughout the chapters of this book, we have studied the many ways social policy affects the lives of children and families. Further, we have seen how the inaction of policymakers leaves families to weather social and economic pressures and navigate complex, often disconnected systems. Improvements in key social and health indicators, such as reductions in the infant mortality rate and the more recent decline in youth violence, represent major successes in social policy over the past century. However, other critical indicators for children and families indicate that social policy has been less successful in many other areas. Rates of child poverty, for example, have not changed in 20 years and youth of color continue to experience unacceptable rates of school dropout. These social problems—and all the problems discussed in this book—are intrinsically tied to public policies and practices. While we must continue to implement effective policies that support all children, we must also confront complex problems such as systemic racism to begin narrowing racial disparities in poverty, infant mortality, and countless social and health indicators through targeted equity-based solutions. In the face of these challenges, what lessons can we learn from a century of policy experimentation and research on social and health problems?

Findings from studies of resilience in human development offer new evidence and emerging insights that may be useful in developing and implementing effective social policies for children and families. Recognizing that all people are social animals, how can we use the institution of government to advance concepts of resilience in the construction of social policy? First, if we think of democratic government as an extension of our social system, we should consider what types of policies best fit the lives of children and their families. Prior research has primarily explored resilience at the individual level. Investigators have asked questions such as, *What makes one child healthy and resilient to adversity when another similar child suffers? What happens to biological systems when developing children are forced to respond to stress with insufficient resources? Can individual interactions and interventions with children leverage natural brain plasticity to recover from severe trauma?* This focus on understanding individual-level resilience is important, particularly when considering the health outcomes associated with ACEs. At the same time, ecological systems theory reminds us that child development will always be influenced by factors at the family, community, and societal levels. Therefore, the question for future policy consideration becomes *How can we best construct social policies that improve the fit between the individual-level needs of children and their families and the broad continuum of services and programs aimed at promoting overall child and family well-being?*

One potential framework for better integrating individual-level resilience with a broader environmental context comes from the burgeoning field of ecology. In contrast to the social science focus on resilience in human social systems, the discipline of ecology examines resilience in the context of ecosystems that appear in nature. The recent focus on ecosystem resilience has gained widespread attention in the past decade due to the increasing risk to biological ecosystems from human impacts such as deforestation, climate change, and pollution. Similarly, in human ecosystems, the primary determinants of health also come from human-made systems and not innate biological differences. Social influences, including personal behavior and the social environment, are known to be at least as influential on population health as genes (McGinnis et al., 2002; Schroeder, 2007), and in parallel, biologists are now considering how human social systems influence natural ecology. The integration of individual-level and ecological resilience is key to creating effective social policies and programs for children and youth.

The ecologist C. S. Holling (1973) first defined ecological resilience as related to two concepts that may seem paradoxical: the resilience of ecosystems is both "stability" or "the maintenance of a predictable world" and "adaptation" or "systems that can absorb and accommodate future events in whatever unexpected form they may take" (p. 21). From this perspective, resilience occurs when a system adapts in order to maintain routine functioning. For example, we ask children and adults to change behaviors in order to function in social and educational settings. It is our contention that policy systems can and must also change to successfully achieve their purpose to promote child and family well-being.

Ecological theory focuses also on the interdependencies among different levels of ecology (Gunderson & Holling, 2002)—essentially, being able to see both the trees *and* the forest. In children's health, much of our focus is on promoting individual resilience or helping children face and deal with adversity. Food assistance programs certainly help families deal with basic needs. However, just as one species in a reef is dependent on the health of the entire reef ecosystem, we must also think about how the individual resilience of children and their families is influenced by the resilient nature of child and family policies and resultant systems of care.

Borrowing from ecological research, the concept of *panarchy* describes the interdependence of lower and higher levels of the ecology and the achievement of stability through change (Gunderson & Holling, 2002). Change in systems, whether a family system or desert ecosystem, is dynamic and is directly influenced by the adaptive cycles of other levels of the ecology. A family that brings an infant home for the first time experiences a dynamic cycle of disruption and adaptation. The success of that family in adapting is dependent on interactions with other systems, including extended family, neighbors, and the local community. Further, social policies such as paid family leave and access to health care will significantly affect the health and functioning of all members of a family with a newborn child. Although it is often hidden from families, the resilience of the policy system also has a direct effect on family functioning. Families suffer when health, education, and welfare systems are chaotic or in a constant state of disequilibrium. Systems that are resilient—meaning they are adaptable to changing conditions and circumstances—are able to learn from experience, achieve a steady state, and maintain their intended supportive structure and function. In many ways, our social policy systems are constantly on the defense, barely keeping up with the needs of families. Partly due to the political economy of small government and the stigma of government dependence, systems supported by public policies in the U.S. are disjointed across states and not robust against the winds of politics and social change, including the rise of populism and skepticism about scientific methods. The framework of panarchy suggests that the life cycle of a family is inherently connected to political and policy cycles. Understanding social policy requires a consideration of family–policy interdependence, and efforts to improve family well-being through policy must also consider historical cycles of sociopolitical change.

Recent research on child resilience has provided new insights into the potential return on investments made to support children and families. Much of research to date has focused on the negative effects of stress and adversity. Specifically, research on ACEs—noted frequently throughout this book—has identified a consistent pattern between exposure to adversity and negative health outcomes in children and adults. While we must continue to proactively prevent all ACEs in childhood, we are faced with the reality that 40% of all children under 18 years have experienced at least one ACE, according to the most recent National Survey of Children's Health (Child and Adolescent Health Measurement Initiative, 2020). So, while prevention is the top priority, existing systems must also be kept informed by the best science on the devastating effects of trauma on children and families.

Another solution to the nation's struggle to develop effective social policies may lie in recent research that has identified "hidden talents" or "stress-adapted skills" that often emerge in children when they are exposed to adverse experiences or environments (Ellis et al., 2020, p. 2). This research suggests that instead of conceptualizing children who grow up in stressful conditions as damaged or impaired, it is also possible that under the right conditions, these children are better adapted to respond to stress. We can assume that stress will inevitably be part of the human experience, so some children might be able to respond at a high level with the right scaffolding. Boyce (2019) explains this innate potential by describing children as either *orchids* or *dandelions*. Most children are like dandelions; they are generally resilient and can cope with most of the stress and adversity they face. On the other hand, some children are like orchids. Orchids show greater responsivity to stress and require more individual support to overcome adversity. The positive side of such adversity is that many children who have experienced high levels of stress go on to develop skills that can be identified, nurtured, and eventually used to benefit the individual. This emerging research is deeply rooted in evolutionary biology, and recent research demonstrates how children's genes, brains, and bodies respond to stress (risk) and adapt (resilience; see Ioannidis et al., 2020 for overview). In summary, we should not think about exposure to stress and adversity in childhood as deterministic or fatalistic. What is more important is how to uncover the potential strengths in all children in the wake of adversity. Given this emerging knowledge, it follows that adaptive social systems can best serve adaptive children and families. Our definitions of intelligence, our standards for behavior, our definitions of family, and our expectations for children and families must be flexible and adapt to new challenges.

## SUMMARY

In this book, we have suggested that this country needs a new framework for child, youth, and family policy. Specifically, we have argued that a risk and resilience model, grounded in principles of ecological theory and encircled by systems of oppression, offers potential for creating policies and programs that will lead to effective interventions for the problems that confront children and families in America.

The time is ripe for a new paradigm that will focus on the developmental processes—both risk and protective—that promote positive adaptation to the social and health problems that public policies are intended to address. Opinion polls assessing public willingness to fund early intervention and rehabilitation programs for children and youth have shown strong support for collaborative and community-based efforts (Baker et al., 2014; National Council on Crime and Delinquency, 2007).

Advances in strengths-based practice, assets-oriented programming, and positive youth development have emerged, and they complement the risk, protection, and resilience framework set forth in this volume (Catalano, 2007; Maton et al., 2004). Although more research is needed to better understand the interactive processes inherent in these approaches, the potential of the risk and resilience model for policy development should not be understated. Finally, recent trends in the acceptance of evidence-based practice have brought researchers and policy experts together in ways that were unseen in past years.

The principles of risk and resilience arose from research on developmental psychopathology and prevention science. Major advances have occurred in these fields in the articulation of the developmental trajectories of children who drop out of school, become delinquent, use illicit substances, experience serious emotional disorders, or have other poor developmental outcomes. At the same time, this knowledge has been used to design effective prevention programs, many of which have been described in the previous chapters. These programs attempt to reduce risk, strengthen protection, and alter developmental trajectories. Findings from these programs are promising (Dodge, 2009; Jenson & Bender, 2014).

In the glow of promise from these programs, we ask, *Is it adequate to construct policy on the basis of risk factors alone?* We think risk reduction alone is an insufficient goal for public policy, although achieving risk reduction would be a significant step forward. It is the hope incumbent in the concept of resilience—where children at high risk prevail over adversity through adaptation—that gives us pause. One driving force behind policy development must clearly be a moral imperative to reduce risk. However, from resilient children, we learn that risk reduction is defined, in part, by strategies that ameliorate or buffer adversities. In studying these protective processes, we often find that what protects children at risk also serves to promote positive developmental outcomes for all children (e.g., Fraser, 2004; Jenson et al., 2013).

From this perspective, public policy for children and youths should be guided by attempts toward reducing risk *while* promoting protection. For all children (including those at risk), public policy should promote competence in social and academic settings, confidence in interpersonal relationship, and self-efficacy in making life-course decisions. In addition, child policy should seek to foster connections to others who provide support and mentoring, the development of character or moral integrity regarding right and wrong behaviors, and feelings of caring or compassion for others who may be less fortunate (Catalano et al., 2002; Catalano

et al., 2004; Lerner et al., 2000; Lerner et al., 2005). Too often, policy development is influenced by changes in problem rates or by catalyzing events such as epidemics or disasters. Of course, it is important to respond when rates rise or events create great need. However, public policy for children and youth should be proactive rather than reactive. It should promote protective processes that nurture developmental outcomes for all children, especially those at great risk. In the sense of *Healthy People 2030* (U.S. Department of Health and Human Services, 2020), the intent of public policy for children, youth, and families should extend beyond the prevention of delinquency, substance use disorders, or other social and health problems. Rather, the intent of policy should express health-promoting societal goals related to positive developmental outcomes for all children and the creation of widely accessible means for achieving those outcomes. Although highly structured and focused programs may always be needed to help children who have special needs (e.g., children who are victimized by individual disadvantage or tragic events), public policy for children should be rooted in core commitments that strengthen families, improve schools, and reinvigorate neighborhoods.

Much remains to be done to solve the fragmented nature of child, youth, and family policy in the U.S. Individual service systems employ skilled practitioners, and each system can point to exemplary programs and innovative service delivery patterns. Despite those examples, child, youth, and family policies continue to suffer from the lack of an underlying and unifying framework that integrates services across problem domains and creates fully articulated systems of care. A risk and resilience perspective, coupled with ecological theory, holds promise as an organizing framework for future public policy efforts directed at the nation's young people. It is their future and our challenge.

# NOTE

1. Biglan, Brennan, Foster, and Holder (2004) used a similar format with a different example to demonstrate the importance of collaboration in developing strategies for working with high-risk youth.

# REFERENCES

Allen-Meares, P., & Fraser, M. W. (Eds.). (2004). *Intervention with children and adolescents: An interdisciplinary perspective*. Allyn & Bacon.

Aos, S., Lieb, R., Mayfield, J., Miller, M., & Pennucci, A. (2004). *Benefits and costs of prevention and early intervention programs for youth*. Washington State Institute for Public Policy.

Baker, T., Metcalfe, C. F., Berenblum, T., Aviv, G., & Gertz, M. (2014). Examining public preferences for the allocation of resources to rehabilitative versus punitive crime policies. *Criminal Justice Policy Review, 26*(5), 448–462. https://doi.org/10.1177%2F0887403414521462

Bernard, D. L., Calhoun, C. D., Banks, D. E., Halliday, C. A., Hughes-Halbert, C., & Danielson, C. K. (2020). Making the "C-ACE" for a culturally-informed adverse childhood experiences framework to understand the pervasive mental health impact of racism on Black youth. *Journal of Child & Adolescent Trauma*, 1–15. https://doi.org/10.1007/s40653-020-00319-9

Bethell, C. D., Carle, A., Hudziak, J., Gombojav, N., Powers, K., Wade, R., & Braveman, P. (2017). Methods to assess adverse childhood experiences of children and families: Toward approaches to promote child well-being in policy and practice. *Academic Pediatrics, 17*(7), S51–S69. https://doi.org/10.1016/j.acap.2017.04.161

Biglan, A., Brennan, P. A., Foster, S. L., & Holder, H. D. (2004). *Helping adolescents at risk. Prevention of multiple problems*. Guilford Press.

Blueprints for Healthy Youth Development (2021). *Providing a registry of experimentally proven programs*. https://www.blueprintsprograms.org/

Boyce, W. T. (2019). *The orchid and the dandelion: Why sensitive people struggle and how all can thrive*. Pan McMillan.

Brown, D. W., Anda, R. F., Tiemeier, H., Felitti, V. J., Edwards, V. J., Croft, J. B., & Giles, W. H. (2009). Adverse childhood experiences and the risk of premature mortality. *American Journal of Preventive Medicine, 37*(5), 389–396. https://doi.org/10.1016/j.amepre.2009.06.021

Campbell Collaboration Library. (2014). *The Campbell Collaboration Library of systematic reviews*. http://www.campbellcollaboration.org/library.php

Catalano, R. F. (2007). Prevention is a sound public and private investment. *Criminology and Public Policy, 6*(3), 377–398. http://doi.org/10.1111/j.1745-9133.2007.00443.x

Catalano, R. F., Berglund, M. L., Ryan, J. A. M., Lonczak, H. S., & Hawkins, J. D. (2004). Positive youth development in the United States: Research findings on evaluations of positive youth development programs. *Annals of the American Academy of Political and Social Science, 591*, 98–124. http://doi.org/10.1177/0002716203260102

Catalano, R. F., Hawkins, J. D., Berglund, L., Pollard, J. A., & Arthur, M. W. (2002). Prevention science and positive youth development: Competitive or cooperative frameworks? *Journal of Adolescent Health, 31*, 230–239. http://doi.org/10.1016/S1054–139X(02)00496–2

Centers for Disease Control and Prevention (CDC). (2020). *Using telehealth to expand access to essential health services during the COVID-19 pandemic*. https://www.cdc.gov/coronavirus/2019-ncov/hcp/telehealth.html

Child and Adolescent Health Measurement Initiative. (2020). *2018–2019 National Survey of Children's Health (NSCH) data query*. Data Resource Center for Child and Adolescent Health supported by the U.S. Department of Health and Human Services, Health Resources and Services

Coalition for Evidence-Based Policy. (2014). *What works in social policy? Findings from well-conducted randomized controlled trials*. http://evidencebasedprograms.org

Cochrane Collaboration. (2014). *Cochrane reviews*. http://www.cochrane.org/cochrane-reviews

Dodge, K. A. (2009). Community intervention and public policy in the prevention of antisocial behavior. *Journal of Child Psychology and Psychiatry*, *50*, 194–200. http://doi.org/10.1111/j.1469–7610.2008.01985.x

Dodge, K. A., & Goodman, W. B. (2019). Universal reach at birth: Family Connects. *The Future of Children*, *29*(1), 41–60.

Dodge, K. A., Goodman, W. B., Murphy, R. A., O'Donnell, K., Sato, J., & Guptill, S. (2014). Implementation and randomized controlled trial evaluation of universal postnatal nurse home visiting. *American Journal of Public Health*, *104*(S1), S136–S143. https://doi.org/10.2105/ajph.2013.301361

Ellis, B. J., Abrams, L. S., Masten, A. S., Sternberg, R. J., Tottenham, N., & Frankenhuis, W. E. (2020). Hidden talents in harsh environments. *Development and Psychopathology*, 1–19. https://doi.org/10.1017/S0954579420000887

Finkelstein, N., & Markoff, L. S. (2004). The Women Embracing Life and Living (WELL) project: Using the relational model to develop integrated systems of care for women with alcohol/drug use and mental health disorders with histories of violence. *Alcoholism Treatment Quarterly*, *22*, 63–80. http://doi.org/10.1300/J020v22n03_04

Fixsen, D. L., Naoom, S. F., Blasé, K. A., Friedman, R. M., & Wallace, F. (2005). *Implementation research: A synthesis of the literature* (FHMI Publication #231). University of South Florida, Louis de la Parre Florida Mental Health Institute, National Implementation Research Network.

Fraser, M. W. (Ed.). (2004). *Risk and resilience in childhood: An ecological perspective* (2nd ed.). NASW Press.

Fraser, M. W., Kirby, L. D., & Smokowski, P. R. (2004). Risk and resilience in childhood. In M. W. Fraser (Ed.), *Risk and resilience in childhood: An ecological perspective* (2nd ed., pp. 13–66). NASW Press.

Germain, C. B. (1991). *Human behavior in the social environment: An ecological view*. Columbia University Press.

Graves, K. N., Frabutt, J. M., & Shelton, T. L. (2007). Factors associated with mental health and juvenile justice involvement among children with severe emotional disturbance. *Youth Violence and Juvenile Justice*, *5*, 147–167. http://doi.org/10.1177/1541204006292870

Gunderson, L., & Holling, C. S. (Eds.). (2002). *Panarchy: Understanding transformations in human and natural systems*. Island Press.

Hawkins, J. D. (2006). Science, social work, prevention: Finding the intersections. *Social Work Research*, 137–152. http://doi.org/10.1093/swr/30.3.137

Hawkins, J. D., Catalano, R. F., & Miller, J. Y. (1992). Risk and protective factors for alcohol and other drug problems in adolescence and early adulthood: Implications for substance abuse prevention. *Psychological Bulletin*, *112*, 64–105. http://doi.org/10.1037/0033–2909.112.1.64

Herrenkohl, T. I., Chung, I. J., & Catalano, R. F. (2004). Review of research on predictors of youth violence and school-based and community-based prevention approaches. In P. Allen-Meares & M. W. Fraser (Eds.), *Intervention with children and adolescents: An interdisciplinary perspective* (pp. 449–476). Pearson Education.

Holling, C. S. (1973). Resilience and stability of ecological systems. *Annual Review of Ecology and Systematics*, *4*(1), 1–23. https://doi.org/10.1146/annurev.es.04.110173.000245

Howell, J. C. (2003). *Preventing and reducing juvenile delinquency: A comprehensive framework*. SAGE.

Howell, J. C., & Lipsey, M. W. (2012). Research-based guidelines for juvenile justice programs. *Justice Research and Policy*, *14*, 17–34. http://doi.org/10.3818/JRP.14.1.2012.17

Ioannidis, K., Askelund, A. D., Kievit, R., & Van Harmelen, A. (2020). The complex neurobiology of resilient functioning after child maltreatment. *BMC Medicine*, *18* (32), 1–16. https://doi.org/10.1186/s12916-020-1490-7

Jenson, J. M., Alter, C. F., Nicotera, N., Anthony, E. K., & Forrest-Bank, S. S. (2013). *Risk, resilience, and positive youth development: Developing effective community programs for high-risk youth. Lessons from the Denver Bridge Project*. Oxford University Press.

Jenson, J. M., & Bender, K. A. (2014). *Preventing child and adolescent behavior. Evidence-based strategies in schools, families, and communities*. Oxford University Press.

Jenson, J. M., & Potter, C. A. (2003). The effects of cross-system collaboration on mental health and substance abuse problems of detained youth. *Research on Social Work Practice*, *13*, 588–607. http://doi.org/10.1177/1049731503253405

Kaufman, J. S., Crusto, C. A., Quan, M., Ross, E., Friedman, S. R., O'Rielly, K., & Call, S. (2006). Utilizing program evaluation as a strategy to promote community change: Evaluation of a comprehensive, community-based, family violence initiative. *American Journal of Community*

Psychology, *38*, 191–200. http://doi.org/10.1007/s10464–006–9086–8

Lee, S., Aos, S., Drake, E., Pennucci, A., Miller, M., & Anderson, L. (2012). *Return on investment: Evidence-based options to improve statewide outcomes*. Washington State Institute for Public Policy.

Lerner, R. M., Almerigi, J. B., Theokas, C., & Lerner, J. V. (2005). Positive youth development: A view of the issues. *The Journal of Early Adolescence, 25*, 10–16. https://doi.org/10.1177/0272431604273211

Lerner, R. M., Fisher, C. B., & Weinberg, R. A. (2000). Toward a science for and of the people: Promoting civil society through the application of developmental science. *Child Development, 71*, 11–20. https://doi.org/10.1111/1467–8624.00113

Maguire-Jack, K., Lanier, P., & Lombardi, B. (2020). Investigating racial differences in clusters of adverse childhood experiences. *American Journal of Orthopsychiatry, 90*(1), 106–114. https://doi.org/10.1037/ort0000405

Maton, K. I., Schellenbach, C. J., Leadbeater, B. J., & Solarz, A. L. (2004). *Investing in children, youth, families, and communities. Strengths-based research and policy*. American Psychological Association. https://doi.org/10.1037/10660–000

McGinnis, J. M., Williams-Russo, P., & Knickman, J. R. (2002). The case for more active policy attention to health promotion. *Health Affairs, 21*(2), 78–93. https://doi.org/10.1377/hlthaff.21.2.78

National Council on Crime and Delinquency. (2007). *New NCCD poll shows public strongly favors youth rehabilitation and treatment*. http://www.nccd-crc.org/nccd/pubs/zogby PR0207.pdf

O'Connell, M. E., Boat, T., & Warner, K. E. (Eds.). (2009). *Preventing mental, emotional, and behavioral disorders among young people: Progress and possibilities*. National Research Council and Institute of Medicine. The National Academies Press.

Olds, D. L., Henderson, C. R., Tatelbaum, R., & Chamberlin, R. (1986). Improving the prenatal care and outcomes of pregnancy: A randomized trial of nurse home visitation, *Pediatrics, 77*, 16–28.

Olds, D. L., Kitzman, H., Knudtson, M. S., Anson, E., Smith, J. A., & Cole, R. (2014). Effect of home visiting by nurses on maternal and child mortality. Results of a 2-decade follow-up of a randomized clinical trial. *JAMA Pediatrics, 168*(9). https://doi.org/10.1001/jamapediatrics.2014.472

Pew Research Center. (2019). *Why is the teen birth rate falling?* https://www.pewresearch.org/fact-tank/2019/08/02/why-is-the-teen-birth-rate-falling/

Sackett, D. L., Straus, S. E., Richardson, W. S., Rosenberg, W., & Haynes, R. B. (2000). *Evidence-based medicine: How to practice and teach EBM* (2nd ed.). Churchill Livingstone.

Schroeder, S. A. (2007). We can do better—improving the health of the American people. *The New England Journal of Medicine, 357*, 1221–1228. https://doi.org/10.1056/NEJMsa073350

U.S. Department of Health and Human Services. (2020). *Healthy People 2030*. https://health.gov/healthypeople

Wilkins, N., Tsao, B., Hertz, M., Davis, R., & Klevens, J. (2014). *Connecting the dots: An overview of the links among multiple forms of violence*. National Center for Injury Prevention and Control, Centers for Disease Control and Prevention.

Woolf, S. H. (2008). The power of prevention and what it requires. *Journal of the American Medical Association, 299*, 2437–2439. http://doi.org/10.1001/jama.299.20.2437

Zavlek, S. (2005). *Promoting community-based facilities for violent juvenile offenders as part of a system of graduated sanctions* (NCJ 209326; Juvenile Justice Practice Series). U.S. Department of Justice, Office of Justice Programs, Office of Juvenile Justice and Delinquency Prevention.

# INDEX

Cerdá, 383, 386
CFSR process, 74–76
CFSRs (Child and Family Services Reviews), 74, 76
Chafee Foster Care Independence Program, 87
Chang, 93, 300–302, 325, 386
Chen, 26, 195, 219–20, 325, 327, 358
Chetty, 36–37, 54
Child & Adolescent Psychiatry, 94, 182, 184–86, 287, 383, 385
Child & Adolescent Trauma, 406
Child & Family Social Work, 91, 96
child abuse, 83, 88, 94–95, 97, 151, 361
   central, 67, 76
   national, 92
   preventing recurring, 77
   suspected, 66
Child Abuse & Neglect, 92, 94–97, 178, 358
Child Abuse Act, 67
child abuse and neglect, 9, 65–66, 68–69, 72–74, 80–82, 90–91, 93–94, 96–97, 147, 173, 183–85
child abuse prevention, 65, 82
Child Abuse Reauthorization Act, 65
Child Access Prevention Laws, 381
child and adolescent health, 182, 293, 406
child and adolescent psychiatry, 22, 183–84
Child and Family Services Improvement Act, 83
Child and Family Services Reviews (CFSRs), 74, 76
childcare, 5, 40, 43, 148, 240, 322
Child Care and Development Block Grant (CCDBG), 40, 49
childhood abuse, 92, 179, 326
childhood adversities, 24, 288–91, 294
   early, 297, 329
childhood disorders, 186
childhood obesity, 197–98, 217–18, 222–24, 226–27
childhood poverty, 46, 52, 234
   ameliorating, 27
childhood psychiatric disorders, 178
childhood schizophrenia, 142, 144, 146, 152
childhood trauma, 87, 181, 390
Child Mental Health Policy, 77, 139–85
child protection, 67–69, 80, 83, 91, 93, 97, 313, 392
child protection agencies, 65–68, 75–77, 81, 83
   public policy paradigm situates, 81
CHILD PROTECTIVE SERVICES, 66
Child Psychiatric Clinics, 179
Child Psychiatric Clinics of North America, 179

child psychiatry, 184
Child Psychology, 21, 97, 179–80, 183–84, 218–19, 257, 289, 360, 383, 407
child relationships, 6, 10, 33, 35, 74, 172, 203, 268, 329, 375
Children Act, 107, 247
Children and Youth Services Review, 24, 57, 60, 90–96, 325–26, 328
Children's Defense Fund, 2, 21, 147, 178, 181
Children's Health Insurance Program Reauthorization Act (CHIPRA), 190, 193
child safety, 64, 66, 68–69, 76, 82
   improving, 69
   public policy prioritizes, 75
child tax credit, 42, 45, 57–58
   expanded, 42
   monthly, 42
child traumatic stress, 179–80
Child Treatment Study, 140, 152
child victims, 65, 88, 185
child victims of sex trafficking, 65, 88
child visitation, 314
child welfare, 84–86, 89–91, 93, 95, 130–31, 160, 163, 167, 169–70, 172–73, 175, 177, 186, 326, 390
Child Welfare Act, 70, 85
child welfare agencies, 70–71, 88–89, 163
   mandated state, 88
Child Welfare Information Gateway, 65–67, 79, 84, 90
Child Welfare League, 84, 90–91
Child Welfare Policy, 63–97, 322
   federal, 72, 80
Child welfare practices, 84, 95
child welfare professionals, 65, 72, 85
Child welfare screening, 92, 320
child welfare services, 90, 93, 191, 321
   public, 326
child welfare system, 69–70, 73, 75, 77, 88, 94–95, 156–57, 160, 163, 173, 314, 316–17, 320–22, 326, 391–92
   modern, 334
   public, 326
Child Welfare Waiver Demonstration Program, 68–69
child welfare workers, 89, 328
CHIP (Children's Health Insurance Program), 162, 190, 193, 206, 209, 240, 248–51, 255, 279–80, 301–2, 304–5
CHIPRA (Children's Health Insurance Program Reauthorization Act), 190, 193
Chishti, 325

epidemic, 84, 205, 383, 385, 405

epidemiology, xii, 6, 141, 178, 218–19, 227, 363, 366, 383, 385–86

EPSDT (Early and Periodic Screening, Diagnostic, and Treatment), 170, 189, 191, 249, 280

ESEA (Elementary and Secondary Education Act), 107–11, 113–14, 116–21

ethnic disparities, 30, 43, 81, 95, 136, 256–57, 335, 341–42, 345, 357

facilities, 156, 160–61, 343
  correctional, 19, 335, 337, 354–55
  funded health care, 302
families, ix–xiii, 1–47, 49, 51–61, 63–64, 66–331, 333–34, 336–60, 363–64, 366–86, 389–95, 397–408
  blended, 4
  child's, 160
  eligible low-income at-risk, 43
  extended, 8, 10, 237, 403
  helping, 78
  higher-income, 237, 249
  high-income, 12
  improved, 234
  large, 147
  lower-income, 207
  low-income LPR, 305
  low socioeconomic, 245
  managing, 215
  middle-income, 250
  military, 212
  moderate-income, 118
  multigenerational, 4
  non-tribal, 84
  permanent, 70
  poor, 48
  professional, 129
  queer-headed, 4
  ravaged, 204
  recorded, 129
  refugee, 305, 321
  right, 173
  single-parent, 4, 214
  stark health disparities, 389
  track, 316
  tribal, 85
  vulnerable, 28, 139
  welfare recipient, 40
  witnessing, 347

  working-class, 129
  young, 398
Families First Coronavirus Relief Act, 308
Family First Prevention Services Act, 69, 84, 163, 172
Family Services Improvement Act, 83
FBI (Federal Bureau of Investigation), 274, 364, 384
FDA (Food and Drug Administration), 272, 281
Federal Bureau of Investigation (FBI), 274, 364, 384
federal policies, 40, 42, 67, 70, 77–80, 88–89, 117, 124, 172, 176, 392–94
  effective, 96
  new, 84
Federal School Safety Commission, 121–22
Federal Youth Correction Act, 334
Firearm Owners Protection Act (FOPA), 364, 377
Florida Mental Health Institute, 179–80
FOPA (Firearm Owners Protection Act), 364, 377
Foster Care Independence Act, 85
FPL (federal poverty level), 48, 154, 189–90, 192–93, 195, 249–50, 366
FQHCs (Federally Qualified Health Centers), 319, 330
Fraser & Terzian, 6, 8
Frontiers, 24, 180–81, 218

gay, 4, 22–23, 200, 220, 222, 225–26, 236, 257, 263, 354, 359–60
Gay & Lesbian Social Services, 289
GeMS (Gender Multispecialty Service), 215–16
Gender-Affirming Organizations, 215–16
gender identity, 7, 14, 19, 119, 121, 194, 208, 215, 354–55
Gender Multispecialty Service (GeMS), 215–16

Handicapped Children Act, 113, 161, 240–41
HCZ (Harlem Children's Zone), 52, 55, 57, 59
health care professionals, 66, 176, 221, 231
health care programs, 302
health insurance industry, 209–10
health insurance program, 212
  funded, 191
  government-sponsored, 209
health of immigrants, 329
health services, 174, 221, 302, 406
  addressed public mental, 169
  physical, 174
  psychological, 300
  receiving appropriate mental, 156
  receiving mental, 153

obesity and asthma in children, 224
obesity and asthma in US children, 217
OBRA, 161, 189, 191–92
obstacles for parents, 208
O'Connell, 10–11, 16, 19, 25, 391, 408
OECD (Organization for Economic Cooperation and Development), 122, 132, 135
OECD Education Working Papers, 132
Oesterle, 18, 23, 25
Office of Family Assistance, 59–60
Office of Justice Programs, 26, 292, 408
Office of Refugee Resettlement (ORR), 314–15
Office on Child Abuse and Neglect, 82
Ogden, 197, 221, 225
OJJDP (Office of Juvenile Justice and Delinquency Prevention), 25, 87, 95, 276, 285, 292–93, 335, 338, 349, 358, 360
Okpych, 79, 87, 91, 95
O'Malley, 218, 291
Omnibus Budget Reconciliation Act, 189, 191–92
ONDCP (Office of National Drug Control Policy), 271–77, 279, 285, 292–93
opioid use, 280–81, 394
Organization for Economic Cooperation and Development (OECD), 122, 132, 135
ORR (Office of Refugee Resettlement), 314–15
Orthopsychiatry, 25, 90–91, 178, 180, 183, 324, 329, 361, 408
Osofsky, 149, 153, 180, 183
out-of-home care, 68–72, 77–80, 84–85, 91, 94
out-of-home placements, 65, 69, 73, 90, 130, 141, 150, 169, 333, 341, 343–45
Owen, 218, 358
Oxford University Press, xiii, 21–24, 53–56, 58, 90, 93, 134, 224, 289–90, 347, 407
Oyserman, 148, 151, 183

Pacific Islander, 367, 370, 372–73
Pahn, 378, 386
Palgrave Macmillan, 54, 60–61
panarchy, 403, 407
pandemic, 1, 3, 22, 28–29, 31, 39–41, 44, 53–55, 153, 204, 307
Pandemic Unemployment Assistance (PUA), 307
Parental incarceration and child well-being, 359
parental rights, 97, 130
  relative's, 72
  terminate, 71
  terminating, 72, 316

parenthood
  early, 86
  single, 232
parenting, 8, 25, 56–57, 178, 181–83, 256, 347
  early, 86
  poor, 231
  positive, 78, 174
  responsive, 8
  supportive, 151
Parents Involved, 110, 116–17, 135
parents of children, 235, 238, 241, 246, 252, 254, 256–57, 313
parity, 174, 272–73, 391
  required, 281
Parker, 364, 386
Parolin, 45, 57
Parrott, 45, 57
Pastore, 214, 225
patchwork policies, 331
Patterson, 100–101, 135, 267, 291–92
PCMH, 211–12, 217
Pediatrics, 23–24, 55, 57, 90, 93, 95–96, 179–81, 217, 220–21, 223–25, 227, 255–59, 279–81, 287–88, 383–86
Pediatrics & Adolescent Medicine, 93, 134, 218, 225, 360, 383, 385
Pedroza, 325, 327, 329
peers, 8–9, 11, 13, 103–4, 143, 147–49, 152, 202–3, 235, 242, 374–75
  non-LGBTQ, 355
permanent residents, legal, 301, 311, 315
perpetrators, 374, 383
Perreira, 301, 325, 327, 329, 331
Perry Preschool Project, 173
persecution, 310, 314
personality change, 55
Peterson, 136, 386
petition, 308, 342, 344
petitioning, 342–43
Pew Research Center, 4, 21, 25, 327–28, 386, 397, 408
Phelan, 197, 225
physical activity, 3, 10, 15, 198, 213, 223–24
Physical distancing and stay-at-home policies, 391
Physician Leadership on National Drug Policy, 273–74, 279–80, 292
Pinto-Martin, 257
PISA (Programme for International Student Assessment), 122–23, 132, 134–35
Platt, 336, 360

public health approach to mental health, 172
Public health benefits, 21
public health crisis, 75
public health crisis of child maltreatment, 75
public health efforts, 390
public health emergencies, 187, 307
public health framework, 175, 262, 276–77
public health framework for prevention, 276
public health interventions, 15
Public Health Management Practice, 291
public health model, 171, 226, 286
public health organizations, 279, 281
Public Health Reports, 132, 178, 218, 221, 224, 329
public health social work, 23, 222
Public Health Social Work Intervention Approach, 15, 17
Public Health Social Work Section, 23, 222
public health workers, 188
Public High School Four-Year Adjusted Cohort Graduation Rates, 101
Public high school graduation rates, 135
public mental health efforts, earliest, 154
public policies, 19, 21, 58, 60, 78–79, 81, 139, 151, 287–88, 359, 361, 392–94, 398, 400–401, 403–8
public policies and practices, 401
public policy for children, 405
public policy for children and youths, 405
Public Report, 106–11
public schools, 2, 105–6, 110, 113, 116, 134, 160, 169, 176, 205, 239
    inadequate, 44
public school systems for African American, 105
public sectors of care, 281
public surveillance of harm to children, 65
public systems of care, 400
Puhl, 197, 225
punitive crime policies, 406
punitive policies, 295, 339
pupil expenditure, 246
Putnam-Hornstein, 80–81, 86, 92, 95, 97

Qualitative Health Research, 220
Quality in Health Care, 326
Quantifying disparities in urban firearm violence, 383
Quinn & Kinoshita, 307

race, 12, 14, 28–30, 32–33, 53–54, 59–60, 105–6, 112, 116–17, 246–47, 256, 310, 345, 357–59, 382–83
    potential caregiver's, 71
race discrimination system, 183

race/ethnicity, xii, 14, 34, 73, 101, 125, 194, 197, 364, 366–67, 369–73
racism, ix, 1, 12–13, 81, 150–51, 194, 233, 352–53, 356, 359, 389–90
    sustaining, 261
Rafferty, 214–16, 225
reauthorization of ESEA, 108–9, 111
Reauthorized funding for CHIP, 190
Rebuilding Communities and Making Connections programs, 52
receiving prenatal care, 213, 218
receiving preventive care, 192
receiving special education, 185
receiving TANF benefits, 305
reductions, 1–2, 51, 81, 94, 145, 269, 273, 277, 342, 344, 350–51
Rees, 374, 376, 382, 386, 393
referrals, 47, 66–68, 100, 141, 149, 172, 282, 343
    reform, 38, 46, 55, 116–17, 125, 304, 317, 336, 338, 391–93, 401
    child welfare services, 67
reform efforts
    educational, 114
    school-based, 126
refugees, 296, 303–4, 308, 310, 327, 329
rehabilitation, 19, 210, 273, 289–90, 333, 340
Reid, 125, 135, 178, 292
Reisner, 200, 215–16, 226
Reproductive Health Care, 213
Research on Social Work Practice, 21, 23, 97, 290, 293, 407
resegregation, 110, 116
Resilience and vulnerability, 24, 288–91, 294
Resnick, 183
resources, 6, 8, 11–12, 20–21, 44–45, 116, 118–19, 175, 215, 236–37, 279–80, 307, 309, 338, 349–50
    educational, 233, 237, 254
    limited parental, 44
    new program, 395
    poor, 27
reunification, 71, 78, 90–91, 94, 322
RI, 380–81
Rickwood, 10–11, 25
risk and protective factors, x–xi, 125, 200, 202, 223, 229, 239, 254, 262–64, 282, 285, 347–48, 390–91, 393–95, 397–98
risk and resilience, ix, xii, 97, 124–25, 132, 390
risk and resilience framework, 5, 124–25, 166
risk and resilience framework in education policy, 125
risk and resilience framework to individualize care, 166

substance use prevention services for children and families, 163
suburbs, 32
Sugai, 133, 135–36
sugar-sweetened beverages and childhood obesity, 197
suicidal ideation, 150, 185, 202–3, 222, 267, 371
suicidality, 87, 202–3, 219, 224
   adolescent firearm, 371
suicide, ix, xi, 146, 149–50, 202–3, 217–20, 222, 261, 263, 366, 369–71, 375, 378, 380, 383–86
   adolescent, 218, 385
   firearm-related, 366, 370–71, 378
   pediatric, 371, 384
Suicide Research, 223
suicide risk, 202, 213, 222, 371
suicide risk factors, 288
suicides in adolescents, 370, 383
Summerfelt, 178
Sun Belt states, 32
super predators, 339
supervision, 77, 88, 147–48, 286, 322, 343–44, 349–50
support immigrant children and families, 317
support immigrant families, 322
support intervention strategies, 269
supportive educational services for immigrant children and families, 306
Supportive School Discipline Initiative, 119
Supportive schools, 237
Support Services Act, 68–69
support state efforts, 118
support to private schools, 122
Supreme Court, 106, 110–13, 116, 122, 193–94, 241, 309, 313, 318, 334, 337–38, 341–42
Surgeon General, 141, 146–47, 171, 185, 277, 292
symptoms, 140–41, 143–44, 147, 158, 166, 180, 204, 232, 236, 256, 264
   children's autism spectrum disorder, 236
syphilis, 198–200
systematic dissemination of information by public health departments, 397
systematic review, 22–23, 25, 91, 134, 220–25, 228, 257, 326, 385
   rapid, 223–24
Systematic review of early risk factors for life-course-persistent, 347
Systematic review of kinship care, 97
system development, 166
Systemic approach for injury and violence prevention, 59

Systemic Factors Household, 34
system reforms, based child welfare, 68
System response, 286–87
systems impacting children, 321
systems of care, 156–58, 160, 162, 180, 184, 189, 191, 193, 280–81, 285, 395, 399–400, 403
   better US health, 220
   current federal health, 374
   supported health, 176
systems of care for children, 162, 189, 224, 281
systems of care for children and youth, 281
systems of care for CSHCN, 191
systems of care for youth, 183
Systems of Care Implementation Evaluations, 164
systems of oppression, xi, 12, 14, 19, 24, 389, 404
systems of prevention, 82
Szilagyi, 91

TANF (Temporary Assistance for Needy Families), 35, 37–39, 47, 49, 54, 60, 192, 251–52, 256, 304, 307
tax credits, 40, 43–44, 193, 305
Tax Policy Center, 40, 59
TAY, 85–87
Technical Assistance Partnership for Child and Family Mental Health, 184
telemental health for children and adolescents, 153
temporary assistance for needy families, 54, 192, 251–52, 256
Tennessee, 296, 365, 368, 384
Teplin, 293–94, 356, 361
Territorial AIDs Directors, 305, 328
Terzian, 22, 102, 134
Therapy and supplemental services, 250
Thomas, 10–11, 24–25, 219, 221, 257, 289
Thompson, 150, 183, 185
Thornberry, 338, 361
threats, 1–3, 11, 76, 297, 309, 316, 318, 350
Tiet, 150, 185
tough-on-crime era, 334–35, 339–40, 351, 392
Towers, 374, 386
TPS, 308, 311, 317
TPS designations, 311
Trafficked children and youth, 87
trafficking, 87–88, 92, 97, 304
   combat child, 97
training programs, 211
   implemented, 89
   public sector-sponsored, 56

# ABOUT THE EDITORS

**William J. Hall**, PhD, MSW, is an assistant professor in the School of Social Work at the University of North Carolina (UNC) at Chapel Hill. He has a BA in psychology and a MSW and PhD in social work, all from UNC. After his doctoral training, Dr. Hall completed a postdoctoral fellowship in mental health services research funded by the National Institute of Mental Health in a collaborative program between the Cecil G. Sheps Center for Health Services Research at UNC and the department of psychiatry and behavioral sciences at Duke University. Dr. Hall's primary research interest is understanding mental health disparities facing lesbian, gay, bisexual, transgender, or queer (LGBTQ) youth (i.e., depression, anxiety, and suicidality), including risk and protective factors as well as developing and evaluating interventions at multiple socio-ecological levels that address these problems. His intervention research has included cultural competency training with helping professionals, group counseling/psychotherapy, school-based interventions, and policy interventions. Dr. Hall has published dozens of peer-reviewed journal articles and scholarly book chapters on various topics, including school bullying, mental health, pediatric obesity prevention, health disparities, implicit attitudes, cultural competency of helping professionals, sexual health, LGBTQ issues, psychosocial interventions, and adolescent development. His research has been supported by the National Institutes of Health. He teaches courses in child and adolescent development, diversity and social oppression, social work with the LGBTQ community, and advanced research methods. His research and teaching have been informed by his 12 years of practice experience, which included policy advocacy as well as providing mental health, educational, and social services to children, youth, and families in a variety of nonprofit settings.

**Paul Lanier**, PhD, is the Wallace Kuralt Distinguished Associate Professor in the School of Social Work at the University of North Carolina at Chapel Hill. He is also the associate director for child and family well-being at the Jordan Institute for Families. His research focuses on developing, improving, and scaling up evidence-based strategies to improve well-being in early childhood. Dr. Lanier's work focuses on transforming child-serving systems, including child welfare, mental health, early education, and health care. He is a board member of the North Carolina Infant Mental Health Association and a Fellow with the Society for Social Work Research and the Doris Duke Fellowship for the Promotion of Child Well-Being. Dr. Lanier serves as an associate editor with the *Journal of Child and Family Studies* and the *Journal of Family Violence*.

**Jeffrey M. Jenson**, MSW, PhD, is the Philip and Eleanor Winn Endowed Professor Emeritus at the Graduate School of Social Work, University of Denver. His research focuses on the application of a public health approach to preventing child and adolescent health and behavior problems and on the evaluation of preventive interventions aimed at promoting healthy youth development. Dr. Jenson has published seven books and numerous articles and chapters on topics of child and adolescent development and prevention science. His books include *Preventing Child and Adolescent Problem Behavior: Evidence-Based Strategies in Schools, Families, and Communities* (2014) and *Social Policy for Children and Families: A Risk and Resilience Perspective* (2016), a recipient of the Best Edited Book Award from the Society for Research on Adolescence. Dr. Jenson is the former chair of the Coalition for the Promotion of Behavioral Health and a co-author of *Unleashing the Power of Prevention* (2015), a comprehensive framework aimed at helping communities and states implement tested and effective preventive interventions for behavioral health problems. He is the recipient of the Aaron Rosen Award from the Society for Social Work and Research and the Distinguished Scholar and University Lecturer Awards from the University of Denver. Dr. Jenson is a former editor-in-chief of the *Journal of the Society for Social Work and Research*. He is a former board member and treasurer of the Society for Prevention Research and a Fellow of the Society for Social Work and Research and the American Academy of Social Work and Social Welfare.

**Mark W. Fraser**, MSW, PhD, is Professor Emeritus at the School of Social Work, University of North Carolina, where he served as associate dean for research and held the Tate Distinguish Professorship until 2018. During his career, he won numerous awards for research and teaching, including the Aaron Rosen Award and the Distinguished Achievement Award from the Society for Social Work and Research. His work focused on risk and resilience in childhood, child and family interventions, and research methods. He published widely and, in addition to *Social Policy for Children and Families*, is the co-author or editor of eight books. These include *Families in Crisis* (1991), a study of intensive family preservation services, and *Evaluating Family-Based Services* (1995), a text on methods for family research. In *Risk and Resilience in Childhood* (2004), he and his colleagues described resilience-based perspectives for child maltreatment, substance abuse, and other social problems. In *Making Choices* (2000), Dr. Fraser and his co-authors developed a skills training program to help children build sustaining social relationships. In *The Context of Youth Violence* (2000), he explored violence from the perspective of resilience, risk, and protection, and in *Intervention with Children and Adolescents* (2003), he and his colleagues reviewed advances in intervention knowledge for social and health problems. In *Intervention Research: Developing Social Programs* (2009), he and his co-authors described a five-step approach to the design and development of social programs. His most recent book is *Propensity Score Analysis: Statistical Methods and Applications* (2014). Dr. Fraser served as the founding editor of the *Journal of the Society for Social Work and Research*. He is a Fellow Emeritus of the National Academies of Practice, the Society for Social Work and Research, and the American Academy of Social Work and Social Welfare.

**Meshan R. Adams** is a Master of Social Work student in the Sandra Rosenbaum School of Social Work and a LEND Trainee in the Waisman Center at the University of Wisconsin–Madison. He is interested in research that focuses on mitigating health disparities for people on the autism spectrum as well as other intellectual and developmental disabilities. He has five years of experience working with people with differing abilities as a respite worker and as a professional skill developer.

**Elizabeth K. Anthony**, MA, MSW, PhD, is an associate professor in the School of Social Work at Arizona State University. She earned her master's and doctoral degrees from the University of Denver and completed her postdoctoral fellowship at the University of California, Berkeley. Dr. Anthony's scholarship centers on the well-being of low-income children and adolescents. Her areas of expertise include resilience among children and adolescents exposed to environmental stressors, prevention of behavioral health concerns, measurement of well-being among children and adolescents, and innovative models to support families (such as peer parent models). Her recent scholarship challenges the false paradigms of individual youth resilience that perpetuate systemic racism. Dr. Anthony teaches doctoral and master's level research and clinical practice courses with adolescents.

**Jill Duerr Berrick**, MSW, PhD, serves as the Zellerbach Family Foundation Professor in the School of Social Welfare at University of California, Berkeley. Berrick's research focuses on the relationship of the state to vulnerable families, particularly those touched by the child welfare system. Her newest book, *The Impossible Imperative: Navigating the Competing Principles of Child Protection* (2017), examines child welfare professionals and the morally contentious and intellectually demanding choices they regularly face in their work with children and families.

**Lauren Bishop**, PhD, MSW, is an assistant professor in the Sandra Rosenbaum School of Social Work at the University of Wisconsin–Madison; she is an investigator at the Waisman Center and the Institute for Research on Poverty. Her National Institutes of Health–funded research focuses on empowering adults with developmental disabilities to live long, healthy, and self-determined lives in their communities. She is currently studying disparities in health and well-being in autistic adults as they age. Her social work practice experience includes roles as a school counselor and a social skills group leader for children, adolescents, and adults on the spectrum. Dr. Bishop is also broadly interested in identifying strategies to strengthen the social work workforce that assists individuals with developmental disabilities in the community.

**Marianna Corkill** is a graduate research assistant at the Center for Immigration and Child Welfare and a student pursuing a master's degree in social work from New Mexico State University in Las Cruces. After completing her Bachelor of Arts degree in global studies from the University of California, Santa Barbara, and a certificate in environmental studies from San Diego State University in 2012, she worked with Latino communities along the California–Mexico border. She taught environmental education to underserved and bilingual youth, connected low-income communities to municipal water and energy-saving programs, and advocated for affordable and sustainable public transportation. In 2016, she served as a Peace Corps volunteer in Panama. She worked for two years organizing environmental efforts in a 600-person sustenance farming town, followed by providing technical and cultural support to incoming volunteers. Upon returning to the United States, she began her MSW track as a Paul D. Coverdell Fellow.

**Sandra K. Danziger**, PhD, is a professor of social work (School of Social Work) and research professor of public policy (Gerald R. Ford School of Public Policy) at the University of Michigan. Her primary research interests and publications examine the effects of public anti-poverty and social service programs and policies on the well-being of disadvantaged families, particularly single mothers and their children. She is a co-investigator on the Michigan Recession and Recovery Study and was principal investigator on the Women's Employment Study that tracked the effects of the 1996 welfare reform. Professor Danziger was a 2009 Scholar-in-Residence at the Rockefeller Foundation Bellagio Center, Bellagio, Italy. She received the 2006 Society for Social Work Research Excellence in Research Award. She was a Visiting Scholar at the Russell Sage Foundation, New York, in 2002 to 2003, and, in 1994, was Visiting Research Scientist, Office of the Secretary, Assistant Secretary for Planning and Evaluation, U.S. Department of Health and Human Services, Washington, DC.

**Hayden C. Dawes**, MSW, LCSW, LCAS, is a PhD student at the University of North Carolina at Chapel Hill's School of Social Work, where his research aims to promote the mental health and social well-being of people of color and lesbian, gay, transgender, queer or questioning, intersex, and asexual or allied (LGBTQIA+) individuals by improving mental health services, systems, and policies. He is interested in advanced methods to intervene on providers' implicit and explicit biases. His practice experience includes hospital social work, mental health, work with United States veterans, and addiction treatment in addition to people involved in the legal system. In 2020, Mr. Dawes became a Robert Wood Johnson Foundation Health Policy Research Scholar.

**Ehren Dohler** is a doctoral student at the University of North Carolina at Chapel Hill's School of Social Work. His research focuses on affordable housing and homelessness and how housing can be a pathway to address poverty and inequality.

**Andrea Lane Eastman**, PhD, is a research assistant professor with the Children's Data Network at the University of Southern California Suzanne Dworak-Peck

School of Social Work. Her research uses linked, administrative data to document population-level racial and income disparities, evaluate program effectiveness, and answer policy-relevant questions concerning vulnerable youth in child protection and juvenile justice systems. Her scholarship is informed by previous experience at the California State Senate, where she served as a legislative aide and committee consultant on several initiatives surrounding vulnerable youth.

**Megan Feely**, PhD, MSCI, MSW, is an assistant professor in the University of Connecticut School of Social Work. Dr. Feely's work focuses on understanding child maltreatment to inform the primary and secondary prevention of maltreatment. She has a specific focus on understanding the role of community-based programs in reducing maltreatment and improving child well-being and on policies and programs that promote economic stability for families to prevent child maltreatment. She teaches courses on program planning, development, and evaluation as well as macro social work practice.

**Megan Finno-Velasquez**, PhD, LMSW, is an assistant professor and director of the Center on Immigration and Child Welfare in the School of Social Work at New Mexico State University in Albuquerque, New Mexico. Dr. Finno-Velasquez has spent the past 15 years working at the intersection of child welfare and immigration issues as a child welfare practitioner, administrator, and researcher. Her research centers around the impact of immigration policy on child welfare system experiences, culturally competent maltreatment prevention strategies, and improving child welfare service system response to the needs of immigrant families. In 2019, Dr. Finno-Velasquez was appointed director of immigration affairs for the New Mexico Children, Youth and Families Department, where she is building an immigration unit to improve policies and practices to support immigrant and refugee children along the Mexico border. Dr. Finno-Velasquez received her PhD from the University of Southern California's School of Social Work in 2015 and completed postdoctoral work with the Children's Data Network. She was a recipient of the Doris Duke Fellowships for the Promotion of Child Well-Being during her doctoral work. She completed her MSW from New Mexico Highlands University in 2007 and has a BS in psychology and Spanish from the University of Illinois at Urbana–Champaign.

**Eric W. Fleegler**, MD, MPH, is a pediatric emergency physician and health services researcher at Boston Children's Hospital and assistant professor of pediatrics and emergency medicine at Harvard Medical School. His clinical work includes attending in the emergency department as well as serving as director of the sedation service at Boston Children's Hospital. His research and innovation has focused on three major areas: (1) firearm injury research with a focus on epidemiology, risk factors, and the role of legislation in reducing firearm fatalities; (2) development and evaluation of tools to screen and refer families' health-related social needs, including HelpSteps, a web and mobile app that is the primary referral system for Massachusetts; and (3) disparities research looking at national-level health inequities by neighborhood poverty and hospital-level inequities in clinical care by race/ethnicity, primary language spoken, income, weight, and other factors. Dr. Fleegler is the co-director of the introduction to social medicine course at Harvard Medical School and regularly lectures around the country.

**Alexandria B. Forte**, MSW, is a doctoral student in the School of Social Work at the University of North Carolina at Chapel Hill. Alexandria's research interest includes food insecurity and its impact on mental health in BIPOC communities. Prior to entering doctoral school, Alexandria worked in schools creating programs to encourage healthy behaviors in youth, including understanding nutritional facts, the impact of food in the body, Centers for Disease Control and Prevention MyPlate guidelines, and making healthy choices.

**Mary E. Fraser**, DSW, has worked as a program and policy consultant to mental health departments in three states. Dr. Fraser wrote the Child and Adolescent Service System Program grant for the state of Utah in the early 1990s and served as that office's first director. She worked in the capacity of executive staff member to the North Carolina Legislative Oversight Committee on Mental Health Reform in 2000. Dr. Fraser's numerous publications focus on mental health policy and practice for children and families. She was previously a clinical adjunct professor in social work and psychiatry at the University of North Carolina at Chapel Hill.

**Andy J. Frey**, PhD, is a professor and director of the PhD program in the Kent School of Social Work at the University of Louisville. Dr. Frey's research interests and publications address the provision of school-based mental health and school social work services and prevention and intervention for young children with challenging behavior. Prior to his appointment at the University of Louisville, he was a school social worker and behavioral consultant in Douglas County, Colorado.

**Luke E. Hirst** is a MSW student in the School of Social Work at the University of North Carolina at Chapel Hill. After 14 years of experience working in the nonprofit sector and doing community organizing and advocacy, they plan to become a mental health therapist with a focus on serving people from marginalized communities.

**Matthew O. Howard**, PhD, died in 2018. He was the Frank A. Daniels Jr. Distinguished Professor of Human Services Policy Information in the School of Social Work at the University of North Carolina at Chapel Hill. Dr. Howard was a renowned expert in substance use disorders, particularly inhalant abuse, inert gas asphyxiation, and alcohol dependence among youths. Dr. Howard authored nearly 400 publications, including more than 300 peer-reviewed journal articles, book reviews, editorials, government reports, and abstracts. He was the recipient of three research grants from the National Institutes of Health aimed at understanding the natural history of inhalant abuse. Dr. Howard served as editor-in-chief of *Social Work Research* and the *Journal of Social Service Research* as well as North American editor of the *British Journal of Social*

*Work.* Dr. Howard was named a Fellow of the Society for Social Work and Research and a Fellow of the American Academy of Social Work and Social Welfare and received the University of North Carolina Excellence in Graduate Teaching Award in 2014.

**Michelle Johnson-Motoyama**, PhD, MSW, is an associate professor at the Ohio State University's (OSU) College of Social Work and faculty affiliate of the OSU Institute for Population Research. Her scholarship examines the role of social policies and programs in child maltreatment prevention and the reduction of racial and ethnic disparities in child and family well-being. Her research has been supported by the Centers for Disease Control and Prevention, the National Institutes of Health, the Robert Wood Johnson Foundation, Casey Family Programs, and other funders. She teaches graduate courses on prevention strategies, policy research methods, and intervention research methods. She is a leadership network member of the Social Work Grand Challenge to Build Healthy Relationships to End Violence. She holds BS and MSW degrees from the University of Illinois at Urbana–Champaign and a PhD in social welfare from the University of California, Berkeley.

**Anayeli Lopez**, PhD, MSW, is an assistant professor in the School of Social Work at New Mexico State University, in Las Cruces, New Mexico. Dr. Lopez received dual PhD degrees in social welfare from Boston College and ITESO–Jesuit University of Guadalajara in 2019. During her doctoral studies, she was the recipient of the Fellowship in International Social Welfare at Boston College–ITESO. Dr. Lopez practiced social work in Indiana, where she developed educational interventions, conducted outreach, and developed partnerships between local schools, community leaders, and Latino immigrant families to increase access to higher education among immigrant youth. Her current research focuses on the impact of immigration policies on the access to social services among immigrant families and children.

**Myrna R. Mandlawitz**, JD, is president of MRM Associates, LLC (a Washington, DC, lobbying firm) and has represented the School Social Work Association of America as its director of government relations since 1999. She is a specialist in legal and policy issues related to special education and children's mental health. Prior to establishing her own government relations practice, Ms. Mandlawitz served as government relations director for the National Association of State Directors of Special Education and spent 14 years as a classroom teacher in a large rural/suburban school district near Richmond, Virginia.

**Kiley J. McLean**, MSW, MSEd, is a PhD student in the Sandra Rosenbaum School of Social Work at the University of Wisconsin–Madison. She is also a Maternal and Child Health Wisconsin LEND (Leadership Education in Neurodevelopmental and Related Disabilities) advanced trainee. She is a part of a research team at the Waisman Center that aims to improve health equity for those with autism and other developmental disabilities. She teaches courses in social policy and disability. Her research and teaching are based in years of work with the disability community as a direct support professional, special education teacher, policy advocate, and, most recently, coach of a Wisconsin state championship Special Olympics team.

**Patrick J. Meehan**, PhD, MSW, is the program manager at the Center for Equitable Family and Community Well-Being at the University of Michigan School of Social Work. His research interests include children and families, poverty, and public institutions. He teaches courses on social welfare policy, diversity and oppression, and research methods. He received his MSW in 2011 from the University of Michigan and his PhD in social work and political science in 2019 from the University of Michigan.

**Brandon D. Mitchell**, MSW, is a doctoral student in the Kent School of Social Work at the University of Louisville. Brandon's research is focused on understanding and ameliorating disproportional rates in exclusionary discipline, the role orientation of the school social worker, and promoting pathways of educational equity.

**Danny Mora**, DMD, MS, is an adjunct assistant professor at the Adams School of Dentistry at the University of North Carolina (UNC) at Chapel Hill. He received his DMD, with honors, from the School of Dental Medicine in San Juan, Puerto Rico, and he has a MS in oral and maxillofacial pathology from UNC. Dr. Mora has 12 years of practice experience in general dentistry with military service members while serving in the U.S. Navy, in pediatric dentistry with underserved children and adolescents, and in supervising dental students serving members of the lesbian, gay, bisexual, transgender, or queer (LGBTQ+) community.

**Anna Parisi**, MSW, LCSW, LCAS, is a doctoral candidate in the School of Social Work at the University of North Carolina at Chapel Hill. Ms. Parisi's research focuses on the mental health and substance use service needs of system-impacted people, with a particular focus on women. Her research interests stem from her experience as a community mental health practitioner and are aimed at addressing the service gaps she witnessed during this work.

**Armon R. Perry**, PhD, MSW, is a professor at the University of Louisville's Kent School of Social Work. Dr. Perry teaches Introduction to Social Work and Social Work Practice with Families. Dr. Perry's research interests are fathers' involvement in the lives of their children and African American men's contributions to family functioning. In addition to his teaching and research, Dr. Perry has professional experience as a child protective services social worker and as a parent education curriculum facilitator.

**Jonathan Phillips**, MSW, is a doctoral student in the School of Social Work at the University of North Carolina at Chapel Hill. His dissertation is examining how community-level factors influence health care access and utilization among individuals with mental illness. As a research assistant, he is involved in the evaluation of an intervention that targets criminogenic risk factors among individuals with serious mental illness in prisons.

**Chris A. Rees**, MD, MPH, is a Fellow in Pediatric Emergency Medicine and Global Health at Boston Children's Hospital and Harvard Medical School. He provides clinical care for ill and injured children in the emergency department. Dr. Rees's primary scholarly focus is identifying and eliminating health care inequities, identifying risk factors for mortality among children in low- and middle-income countries, and improving diagnostics in resource-limited settings.

**Sophia Sepp**, LMSW, MPH, CHES, is the program manager at the Center on Immigration and Child Welfare (CICW) in the School of Social Work at New Mexico State University (NMSU). She is a graduate of the dual Master of Social Work and Master of Public Health program at NMSU. She received a Bachelor of Science in foreign service with a focus on international politics at Georgetown University in 2014. She has been learning, serving, and working in the borderlands at the intersection of immigration and child welfare issues for the past six years. Following her graduation from Georgetown, she moved to the border region (Las Cruces, New Mexico) to participate in a yearlong service program with Border Servant Corps (BSC), serving at a center that provides early childhood education and supportive services to young children and their families who are experiencing homelessness. Following her year of service, she became the program coordinator for the BSC yearlong fellowship program and also provided support to the BSC's border immersion and refugee hospitality programs, working closely with key agencies serving immigrants in the borderlands. Her experiences and passion for working with children and immigrant communities inspired her to pursue a career in social work and public health. During her MSW/MPH program, she completed field practicum experiences with the CICW and the New Mexico Children, Youth, and Families Department (NM CYFD), protective services division as a child welfare scholar. Upon graduation, she worked as an in-home services practitioner with NM CYFD, working directly with children and families to reduce the risk of future maltreatment. She now serves as the CICW's full-time program manager, coordinating and managing the Center's ongoing projects.

**Melissa Villodas** is a PhD student in the School of Social Work at the University of North Carolina at Chapel Hill (UNC–CH). Her research interests are on positive youth development and the impact of neighborhood characteristics on the mental health of youth living in socioeconomically disadvantaged communities. Melissa works as a research assistant with Dr. Amy Blank Wilson on a novel National Institute of Mental Health–funded R34 project evaluating an intervention for justice-involved individuals with serious mental illness and on a demonstration project developing a Tiny Homes Village for individuals living with mental illness. Before arriving at UNC–CH, Melissa worked as a clinical therapist for a treatment family foster care program in New York City and as the project director for the Youth and Young Adult Mental Health Research Group at New York University.

**Hill M. Walker**, PhD, is a professor of special education, co-director of the institute on violence and destructive behavior, and research director of the center on human development in the College of Education at the University of Oregon. He has a long-standing interest in behavioral assessment and in the development of effective intervention procedures for use in school settings with a range of behavior disorders. His research interests include social skills assessment, curriculum development and intervention, longitudinal studies of aggression and antisocial behavior, and the development of early screening procedures for detecting students who are at risk for social-behavioral adjustment problems and/or later school dropout.

**Amy Wilson**, PhD, MSW, is an associate professor and the Prudence F. and Peter J. Meehan Early Career Distinguished Scholar at the School of Social Work at the University of North Carolina at Chapel Hill. Amy is a social worker and mental health services researcher with expertise in both quantitative and qualitative research methods. She is a national expert in the development and testing of interventions for people with serious mental illness involved in the criminal justice system. She also uses her research expertise to work with both the juvenile justice and adult criminal justice systems to implement and evaluate the use of evidence-based practices.